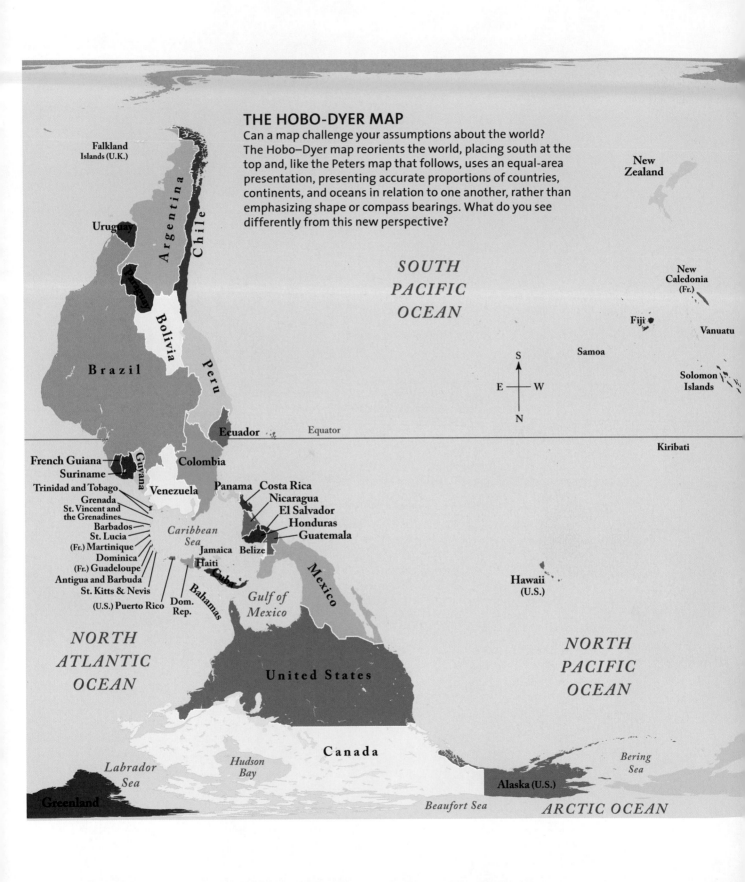

THE HOBO-DYER MAP

Can a map challenge your assumptions about the world?
The Hobo–Dyer map reorients the world, placing south at the
top and, like the Peters map that follows, uses an equal-area
presentation, presenting accurate proportions of countries,
continents, and oceans in relation to one another, rather than
emphasizing shape or compass bearings. What do you see
differently from this new perspective?

Falkland
Islands (U.K.)

New
Zealand

Argentina

Chile

Uruguay

Paraguay

Bolivia

Peru

Brazil

SOUTH
PACIFIC
OCEAN

New
Caledonia
(Fr.)

Fiji

Vanuatu

Samoa

S

E — W

N

Solomon
Islands

Ecuador

Equator

Kiribati

French Guiana
Suriname
Trinidad and Tobago
Grenada
St. Vincent and
the Grenadines
Barbados
St. Lucia
(Fr.) Martinique
Dominica
(Fr.) Guadeloupe
Antigua and Barbuda
St. Kitts & Nevis
(U.S.) Puerto Rico

Guyana

Colombia

Venezuela

Panama

Costa Rica
Nicaragua
El Salvador
Honduras
Guatemala

Caribbean
Sea

Jamaica

Belize

Haiti

Cuba

Dom.
Rep.

Bahamas

Gulf of
Mexico

Mexico

Hawaii
(U.S.)

NORTH
ATLANTIC
OCEAN

United States

NORTH
PACIFIC
OCEAN

Labrador
Sea

Hudson
Bay

Canada

Bering
Sea

Greenland

Beaufort Sea

Alaska (U.S.)

ARCTIC OCEAN

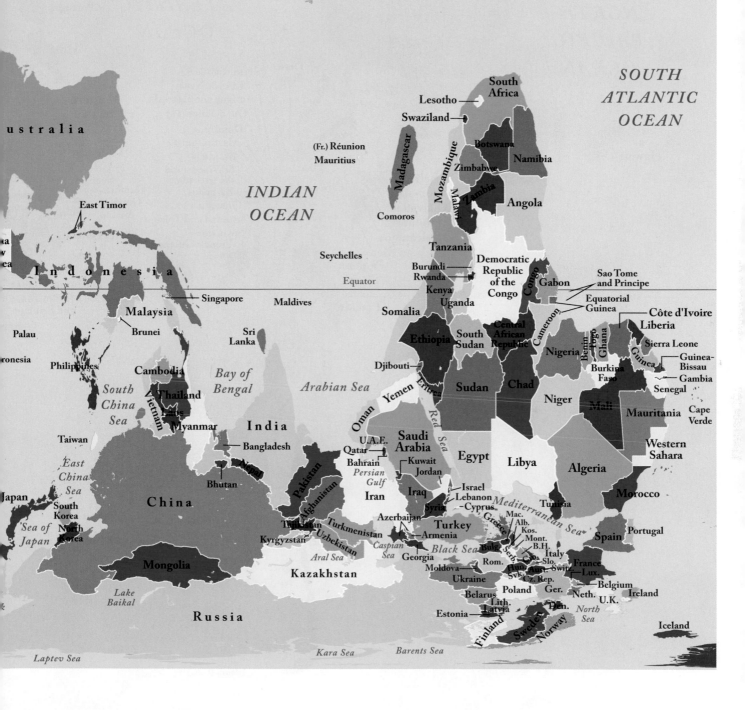

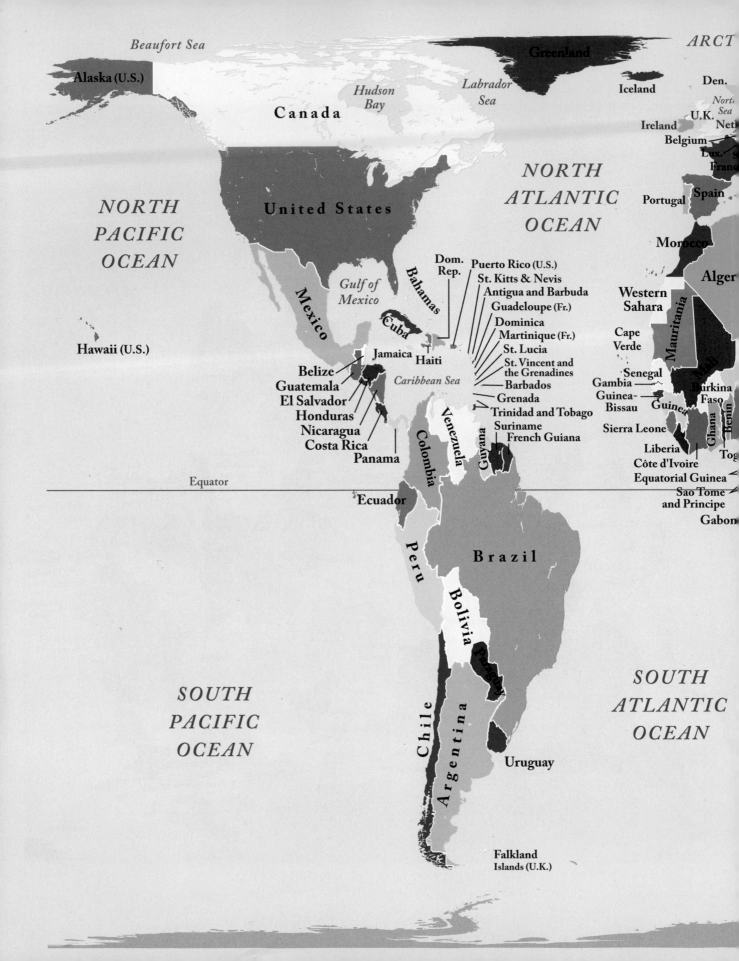

Beaufort Sea

Alaska (U.S.)

Greenland

ARCT

Labrador Sea

Iceland

Hudson Bay

Den.

Canada

North Sea

U.K.

Ireland

Neth

Belgium

Lux.

Franc

NORTH ATLANTIC OCEAN

Spain

Portugal

NORTH PACIFIC OCEAN

Morocco

United States

Western Sahara

Alger

Dom. Rep.

Puerto Rico (U.S.)

St. Kitts & Nevis

Cape Verde

Mauritania

Mali

Mexico

Gulf of Mexico

Bahamas

Antigua and Barbuda

Guadeloupe (Fr.)

Dominica

Cuba

Martinique (Fr.)

Senegal

Burkina Faso

St. Lucia

Hawaii (U.S.)

St. Vincent and the Grenadines

Gambia

Guinea

Jamaica

Haiti

Caribbean Sea

Barbados

Guinea-Bissau

Benin

Belize

Grenada

Sierra Leone

Ghana

Guatemala

Trinidad and Tobago

El Salvador

Suriname

Liberia

Tog

Honduras

Venezuela

Guyana

French Guiana

Côte d'Ivoire

Nicaragua

Equatorial Guinea

Costa Rica

Colombia

Sao Tome and Principe

Panama

Equator

Gabon

Ecuador

Peru

Brazil

Bolivia

Paraguay

SOUTH ATLANTIC OCEAN

SOUTH PACIFIC OCEAN

Chile

Argentina

Uruguay

Falkland Islands (U.K.)

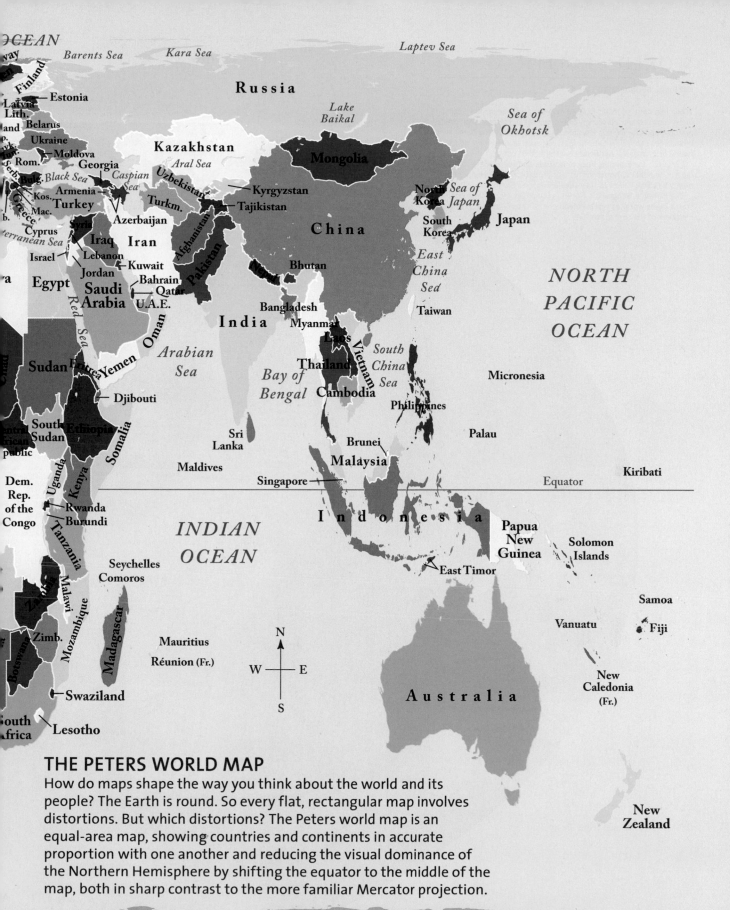

OCEAN

Barents Sea   Kara Sea   Laptev Sea

way
Finland
— Estonia   Russia
Latvia
Lith.   Lake
land   Baikal   Sea of
yk   Belarus   Okhotsk
Rom. — Ukraine   Kazakhstan   Mongolia
Serb. — Moldova   Aral Sea
Bulg. Georgia   Caspian Uzbekistan   North Sea of
Black Sea   Sea   Kyrgyzstan   Korea Japan   Japan
Greece Armenia   Turkm. — Tajikistan   South
Kos.   China   Korea
Mac. Turkey Azerbaijan   NORTH
b.   East
Cyprus   Iran   China   Taiwan   PACIFIC
terranean Sea Syria   Afghanistan Pakistan   Sea   OCEAN
Israel   Iraq Lebanon   Bhutan
a   Jordan — Kuwait   India Bangladesh
Egypt Saudi Bahrain   Myanmar
Arabia — Qatar   Oman   Laos
U.A.E.   Arabian   Thailand Vietnam South
Red Sea   Sea   Bay of   Cambodia China
Sudan Eritrea Yemen   Bengal   Sea
— Djibouti   Micronesia
South Ethiopia   Sri
Sudan   Somalia   Lanka   Brunei
entral   Maldives   Malaysia   Palau
rican   Singapore —   Equator   Kiribati
public Uganda Kenya
Dem. Rwanda   INDIAN   I n d o n e s i a   Papua
Rep. Burundi   New   Solomon
of the Tanzania   OCEAN   East Timor Guinea Islands
Congo
Seychelles
Comoros   Samoa
Zambia Malawi   Vanuatu   Fiji
Zimb. Mozambique Madagascar Mauritius   N
Botswana   Réunion (Fr.)   W   E   Australia New
Swaziland   S   Caledonia
outh Lesotho   (Fr.)
frica

THE PETERS WORLD MAP

How do maps shape the way you think about the world and its
people? The Earth is round. So every flat, rectangular map involves
distortions. But which distortions? The Peters world map is an
equal-area map, showing countries and continents in accurate
proportion with one another and reducing the visual dominance of
the Northern Hemisphere by shifting the equator to the middle of the   New
map, both in sharp contrast to the more familiar Mercator projection.   Zealand

A n t a r c t i c a

WORLD · POLITICAL

NATIONAL BOUNDARIES

While humanity's impact is quite evident, and even striking, on many remotely sensed scenes, sometimes, as in the case with most political boundaries, it is invisible. State, provincial, and national boundaries can follow natural features, such as mountain ridges, rivers, or coastlines. Artificial constructs that possess no physical reality—for example, lines of latitude and longitude—can also determine political borders. This world political map represents man's imaginary lines as they slice and divide Earth.

The National Geographic Society recognizes 192 independent states in the world as represented here. Of those nations, 185 are members of the United Nations.

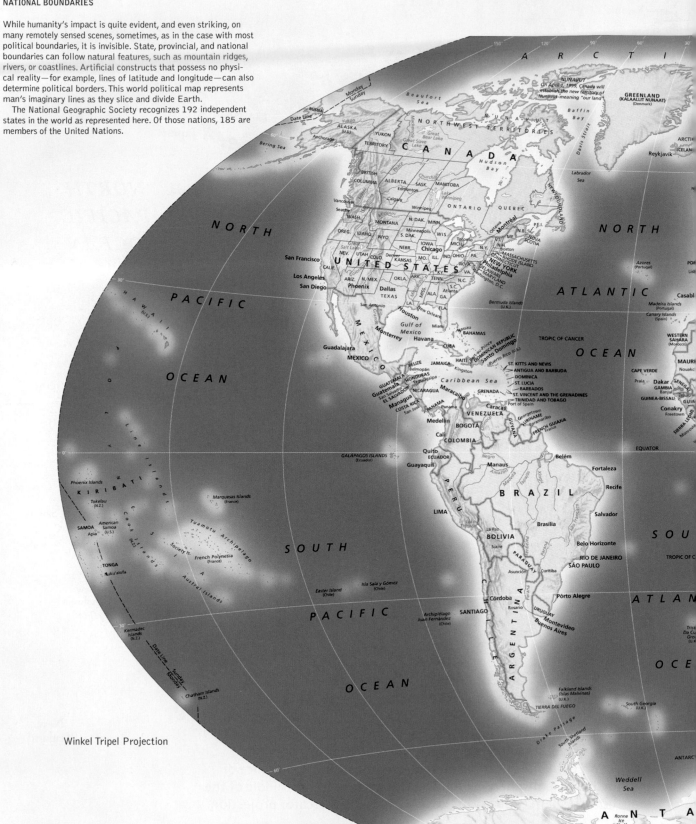

Winkel Tripel Projection

Cultural Anthropology

A TOOLKIT FOR A GLOBAL AGE

SECOND EDITION

KENNETH J. GUEST
BARUCH COLLEGE
THE CITY UNIVERSITY OF NEW YORK

W. W. NORTON & COMPANY

NEW YORK   LONDON

W. W. Norton & Company has been independent since its founding in 1923, when William Warder Norton and Mary D. Herter Norton first published lectures delivered at the People's Institute, the adult education division of New York City's Cooper Union. The firm soon expanded its program beyond the Institute, publishing books by celebrated academics from America and abroad. By mid-century, the two major pillars of Norton's publishing program—trade books and college texts—were firmly established. In the 1950s, the Norton family transferred control of the company to its employees, and today—with a staff of four hundred and a comparable number of trade, college, and professional titles published each year—W. W. Norton & Company stands as the largest and oldest publishing house owned wholly by its employees.

Editor: Peter Lesser
Project Editor: Caitlin Moran and Rachel Mayer
Assistant Editor: Samantha Held
Manuscript Editor: Jackie Estrada
Managing Editor, College: Marian Johnson
Managing Editor, College Digital Media: Kim Yi
Production Manager: Ashley Horna
Media Editor: Eileen Connell
Associate Media Editor: Mary Williams
Media Project Editor: Rachel Mayer
Media Editorial Assistant: Grace Tuttle
Marketing Manager, Cultural Anthropology: Julia Hall
Design Director: Hope Miller Goodell
Photo Editor: Trish Marx
Permissions Manager: Megan Schindel
Permissions Clearing: Elizabeth Trammell
Composition: Jouve North America
Manufacturing: TransContinental

Library of Congress Cataloging-in-Publication Data

Names: Guest, Kenneth J.
Title: Cultural anthropology : a toolkit for a global age / Kenneth J. Guest,
Baruch College, The City University of New York.
Description: Second edition. | New York, NY : W. W. Norton & Company, Inc., [2017] |
  Includes bibliographical references and index.
Identifiers: LCCN 2016024805 | ISBN 9780393265002 (pbk.)
Subjects: LCSH: Ethnology. | Applied anthropology. | Globalization.
  Classification: LCC GN316 G83 2016 | DDC 301—dc23 LC record available at
https://lccn.loc.gov/2016024805

ISBN: 978-0-393-26500-2

W. W. Norton & Company, Inc., 500 Fifth Avenue, New York, NY 10110-0017
wwnorton.com

W. W. Norton & Company Ltd., Castle House, 75/76 Wells Street, London W1T 3QT

1 2 3 4 5 6 7 8 9 0

About the Author

Kenneth J. Guest is Professor of Anthropology at Baruch College, CUNY, and author of *God in Chinatown: Religion and Survival in New York's Evolving Immigrant Community* (2003). His research focuses on immigration, religion, globalization, ethnicity, and entrepreneurialism.

Professor Guest's ethnographic research in China and the United States traces the immigration journey of recent Chinese immigrants from Fuzhou, southeast China, who, drawn by restaurant, garment shop, and construction jobs and facilitated by a vast human smuggling network, have revitalized New York's Chinatown. His writing explores the role of Fuzhounese religious communities in China and the United States; the religious revival sweeping coastal China; the Fuzhounese role in the rapidly expanding U.S. network of all-you-can-eat buffets and take-out restaurants; and the higher education experiences of the Fuzhounese second generation.

A native of Florida, Professor Guest studied Chinese at Beijing University and Middlebury College. He received his B.A. from Columbia University (East Asian Languages and Cultures), an M.A. from Union Theological Seminary (Religious Studies), and the M.A., M.Phil., and Ph.D. from The City University of New York Graduate Center (Anthropology).

Brief Contents

Contents

PART 1   Anthropology for the 21st Century

PART 2   Unmasking the Structures of Power

Chapter 7   Ethnicity and Nationalism   237

PART 3   Change in the Modern World

Preface

Anthropology may be the most important course you take in college. That may seem like a bold statement. But here's what I mean.

Cultural Anthropology: A Toolkit

The world in the twenty-first century is changing at a remarkable pace. We are experiencing an interaction with people, ideas, and systems that is intensifying at breathtaking speed. Communication technologies link people instantaneously across the globe. Economic activities challenge national boundaries. People are on the move within countries and between them. As a result, today we increasingly encounter the diversity of humanity, not on the other side of the world but in our schools, workplaces, neighborhoods, religious communities, and families. How will we develop the skills and strategies for engaging and navigating the complex, multicultural, global, and rapidly changing reality of the world around us?

Anthropology is the toolkit you are looking for. Cultural anthropology is the study of humans, particularly the many ways people around the world today and throughout human history have organized themselves to live together: to get along, to survive, to thrive, and to have meaningful lives. This second edition of *Cultural Anthropology: A Toolkit for a Global Age* will introduce you to the fascinating work of anthropologists and the research strategies and analytical perspectives that anthropologists have developed—our tools of the trade—that can help you better understand and engage today's world as you move through it.

I teach Introduction to Cultural Anthropology to hundreds of students every year at Baruch College, a senior college of The City University of New York. Baruch has an incredibly diverse student body, with immigrants from over a hundred countries, speaking dozens of languages and thinking about culture, race, gender, and family in as many different ways. Some of my students will become anthropology majors. More will become anthropology minors. But at Baruch, in fact, most students will become business majors.

This book emerges from my efforts to make anthropology relevant to all of my students as they navigate their everyday lives, think about the world as it is and as it is becoming, and consider tackling the crucial issues of our times. On a practical level, we all employ the skills of anthropology on a daily basis. Every time you walk into a room and try to figure out how to fit into a new group of people—in your classroom, in a student club, at the office, at a party, in your religious community, when your new love interest takes you home to meet the family—how in the world do you deduce what the rules are? Where you fit in? What you're supposed to do? What the power dynamics are? What you can contribute to the group? *Cultural Anthropology: A Toolkit for a Global Age* is designed to help you develop those skills—to think more deeply and analyze more carefully—and to prepare you to use them in diverse settings at home or around the world.

Why a New Textbook?

The world has changed dramatically in the past forty years and so has the field of anthropology. *Cultural Anthropology: A Toolkit for a Global Age* presents the theoretical, methodological, and pedagogical innovations that are transforming anthropology and highlights both historical and contemporary research that can provide students with insights about how anthropologists are approaching the crucial challenges and questions of our times.

Globalization

As the world is changing, so too are the people anthropologists study. Even the way anthropologists conduct research is changing. In the contemporary period of rapid globalization, the movement, connection, and interrelatedness that have always been a part of human reality have intensified and become more explicit, reminding us that our actions have consequences for the whole world, not just for our own lives and those of our families and friends. This book integrates globalization into every chapter, analyzing its effects throughout the text rather than in a series of boxes, icons, or the occasional extra chapter so commonly seen in contemporary textbooks. The introductory chapter, "Anthropology in a Global Age," establishes an analytical framework of globalization that is developed in every succeeding chapter—whether the topic is fieldwork, language, ethnicity, economics, kinship, or art—and gives students the tools to understand the impact of globalization on people's lives as they encounter it in ethnographic examples throughout the book.

Reframing the Culture Concept

The concept of culture has been central to anthropological analysis since the beginning of our field. But anthropologists have significantly reframed our thinking about culture over the past forty years. In the 1960s, Clifford Geertz synthesized anthropological thinking about culture as a system of meaning—shared norms, values, symbols, and categories. In the ensuing years, anthropologists have paid increasing attention to the relationship of power to culture, building on the work of Antonio Gramsci, Michel Foucault, and Eric Wolf to examine the ways cultural meanings are created, learned, taught, enforced, negotiated, and contested. *Cultural Anthropology: A Toolkit for a Global Age* integrates this holistic and complex concept of culture into every chapter, exploring both meaning and power in human culture. Chapter 6, for example, is entitled "Race and Racism," acknowledging that not only is race a social construction of ideas but also that ideas of race can be expressed and made real through cultural processes, institutions, and systems of power—racism—in ways that create patterns of stratification and inequality in U.S. culture and in cultures around the world.

Anthropology for the Twenty-First Century

Cultural Anthropology: A Toolkit for a Global Age reflects the field of anthropology as it is developing in the twenty-first century. While carefully covering the foundational work of early anthropologists, every chapter has been designed to introduce the cutting-edge research and theory that make anthropology relevant to today's world. Chapters on classic anthropological topics such as language, religion, kinship, and art incorporate contemporary research and help students understand why anthropological thinking matters in day-to-day life. A chapter on human origins presents the current scholarship in physical anthropology and creates opportunities for engaging the current U.S. evolution debates. Chapters on sexuality, the global economy, class and inequality, migration, and health, illness, and the body give students a sense of historical and contemporary research in the field and bring the presentation of anthropology fully into the twenty-first century.

Relevance

Cultural Anthropology responds to my students' request for relevance in a textbook. Each chapter opens with a recent event that raises central questions about the workings of human culture. Key questions throughout the chapter guide students through an introduction to the anthropological strategies and analytical frameworks that can enable them to think more deeply about the chapter-opening event and the underlying issues they may confront in their own lives. A student exercise in each chapter, "Your Turn: Fieldwork," provides students—either individually or in groups—with an opportunity to try out the ideas and strategies introduced in the chapter. "Thinking Like an Anthropologist" sections wrap up each chapter and challenge students to apply what they have learned.

Ethnography

Anthropologists conduct fascinating research about the lives of people all over the world. In many ways ethnography is at the heart of anthropology, reflecting our unique research strategies, our analytical methodologies, and our deep commitment to the project of cross-cultural understanding and engagement in our attempts to make the world a better place. But ethnographies often get lost in introductory textbooks. *Cultural Anthropology: A Toolkit for a Global Age* introduces over ninety separate ethnographic studies set in dozens of different countries, presenting both new research and classic studies in ways that are accessible to undergraduates so that the rich work of anthropologists comes alive over the course of the semester.

Biocultural Approach

Many popular narratives, including those associated with race, ethnicity, gender, sexuality, and kinship, suggest that who we are as humans—our human nature—is primarily shaped by our evolutionary past and determined by our genes and biology. *Cultural Anthropology* presents the latest thinking on human development as an ongoing biocultural process; biology, culture, and the environment are deeply intertwined in an ongoing interplay and interaction through which humans are continually evolving and changing, both on a species level and in our individual lifespans.

Anthropologists Engage the World

Whether anthropologists teach in a university or work as applied anthropologists, they use the practical tools and analytical insights of anthropology to actively engage crucial issues facing our world. In the "Anthropologists Engage the World" feature, this book introduces some of the field's leading personalities and practitioners discussing why they have chosen to be anthropologists, what tools they think anthropology brings to understanding and addressing global challenges, and why they think anthropology can help students understand how the world really works. This feature offers students insights into what it can mean to be an anthropologist and how the skills of anthropology can be invaluable for living in a global age.

WHAT'S NEW IN THE SECOND EDITION

Reflecting the dynamic nature of cultural anthropology, this new, second edition of *Cultural Anthropology: A Toolkit for a Global Age* includes revisions and updates to every chapter that introduce cutting edge developments in the discipline, new theoretical frameworks, and new ethnographies. New chapter openers, examples, and exercises continue the book's pedagogical approach to engage students in thinking like an anthropologist and provide them with an anthropological toolkit for analyzing and engaging the world around them.

All-new feature: The Social Life of Things

Attention to human artifacts—stuff, things—has a rich history in anthropology. Today an emerging anthropology of material culture is again deepening our attention to what our things can tell us about being human. This feature, drawn from contemporary ethnographies, is designed to give students the tools to conduct an anthropology of the stuff in their lives and highlights the stories of such familiar objects as blue jeans, Mardi Gras beads, undersea communication cables, U.S. census forms, unnecessarily gendered items, diamonds, landfills, and sushi, among other topics. This feature will broaden students' notions of culture beyond ideas and meanings to the material and concrete. And in the process they will better understand themselves and their interconnectedness—through stuff—with people all over the world.

New chapter opening stories on familiar topics and current events

Ferguson, the Flint water crisis, Syrian refugees, a Happy Meal, Bangladesh's Sundarban tidal forest, women Army Rangers, protesting sexual violence on campus, football concussions, Pope Francis and the television show *Transparent*: Ten new chapter openers challenge students to ask big questions and apply their anthropological toolkit to the real world challenges of today.

New Anthropologists Engage the World features

How are anthropologists applying their anthropological tools to real world problems? New features, based on first-hand interviews with the author, introduce students to Shannon Speed, Frans de Waal, JB Kwon, Gillian Tett, Jason De León, David Vine, David Simmons, and Dena Freeman.

Over twenty new ethnographies added throughout the text

Ethnographies are at the heart of anthropological inquiry. This edition introduces over twenty new ethnographies set in places including: Bolivia, Brazil, Chicago, Denmark and Sweden, Dubai, Egypt, Eritrea, India, Japan, Maine, Mexico and Washington State, the Middle East, New York, the North Atlantic, Senegal, Taiwan, and Tanzania.

New coverage of engaging, cutting-edge topics

- **The environment and climate change** Humans are reshaping the natural environment, leading scholars to rename the current geological period the Anthropocene. The book's focus on the environment begins in chapter one with a new section on the Anthropocene, an expanded section on sustainability in the Global Economy chapter, and ethnographies and explorations of current issues and events throughout the book, including: A Coca-Cola bottling factory in India; rising sea levels and Pacific Island nations; Native American language use and the environment; water crises in Flint, Michigan and Mumbai, India; environment and health disparities in Harlem; deforestation in Malaysia; climate activists in Bangladesh,

Paris, and U.S. college campuses; landfills in the U.S. Midwest; and water temples in Bali.

- **The anthropology of the body** Cross-cultural anthropological studies have challenged the notion of the body as isolated, natural, and universal and revealed a more complex picture of human bodies as products of specific environments, cultural experiences, and historical contexts. In addition to discussion of health and illness, the second edition adds new material on sickness.

- **Disabilities** Anthropology's increasing attention to the body has been accompanied by a recent expansion of work on issues of disability. Anthropologists have begun to bring their distinctive ethnographic methods to the task of understanding the embodied experiences of people with impairments and analyzing those experiences within broader forms of social inequality. New content has been added in chapters on Health, Illness, and the Body and Sexuality.

- **The anthropology of food** Always central to anthropological studies, food has received increased attention in recent years. The anthropology of food is explored throughout the book, including food production; food and colonialism; religious symbolism of food; water and inequality in Flint, Michigan and Mumbai India; soda bottling; the social life of a chocolate bar; the global trade in tuna; food and ethnic identity; migration of Chinese restaurant workers; and a new feature on the Happy Meal.

- **Anthropology's biocultural perspective** *Cultural Anthropology* presents the latest thinking on human evolution, development, and adaptation as an ongoing biocultural process in which biology, culture, and the environment are deeply intertwined in an ongoing interplay and interaction through which humans are continually evolving and changing, both on a species level and in our individual lifespans.

- **The anthropology of global financial markets** The 2008 fiscal crisis revealed how global financial markets, firms, and financial instruments like derivatives are reshaping the global economy. New content provides insight into the value that anthropological perspectives bring to analyzing these changes.

- **Visual anthropology and ethnographic film** Visual media has become an increasingly powerful tool of anthropological inquiry; this edition adds new content on visual anthropology, media worlds, ethnographic filmmaking, and indigenous media.

- **Primates** Primates provide key insights for understanding human origins and human nature. New content on primatologist Jane Goodall, primate tool-making, and the groundbreaking work of primatologist Frans de Waal has been added to the Human Origins chapter.

ADDITIONAL RESOURCES

Learn more at **wwnorton.com/instructors** and **digital.wwnorton.com/culturalanthro2**

The media package for *Cultural Anthropology: A Toolkit for a Global Age* provides additional pedagogical tools that inspire students to DO anthropology and apply it to their own lives. Instructors have everything they need to make traditional and online classes easier to manage: a DVD of clips that will enliven lectures and spark discussion; illustrated PowerPoints that include instructor-view lecture notes; and a fully customizable coursepack for Blackboard and other course-management systems. The coursepack includes optional access to InQuizitive, our new adaptive learning software.

For Students
NEW InQuizitive
Available at **digital.wwnorton.com/culturalanthro2**

This adaptive learning tool personalizes quiz questions in an engaging, game-like environment to help students master the learning goals outlined in each chapter of *Cultural Anthropology*. Used as a pre-lecture tool, InQuizitive helps students improve their reading comprehension and critical thinking skills so that they come to class better prepared to think like anthropologists.

Ebook
Available at **digital.wwnorton.com/culturalanthro2**

Cultural Anthropology is also available as an ebook. The Norton Ebook Reader provides students and instructors an enhanced reading experience at a fraction of the cost of a print textbook.

- **Easy to use.** The Norton Ebook Reader works on all computers and mobile devices and includes intuitive highlighting, note-taking, and bookmarking features that students who dog-ear their printed texts will love.

- **Enhances teaching and learning.** Note-sharing capability allows instructors to focus student reading by sharing notes with their classes, including embedded images and video. Reports on student and class-wide access and time on task allow instructors to monitor student reading and engagement.
- **Integrates with other learning tools.** The Norton Ebook Reader can also be integrated into your campus learning management system. When integration is enabled, every time students click on a link to the ebook from their campus LMS, they'll be redirected immediately to their text without having to sign in.
- **Saves your students money.** Norton ebooks are a fraction of the price of print textbooks. Learn more by contacting your local Norton representative. With a Norton ebook, your students automatically have access to InQuizitive, Norton's informative, adaptive quizzing environment, to ensure they get the most out of their reading and study.

For Instructors
Lecture PowerPoints
These visually dynamic lecture PowerPoint slides include a suggested classroom lecture outline in the notes field that will be particularly helpful to first-time teachers.

Art PowerPoints and JPEGs
All of the art from the book sized for classroom display.

Instructor Video
These documentary and ethnographic film clips are ideal for initiating classroom discussion and showing students how anthropology is relevant to their lives. The clips may also be streamed from the Coursepack. Each streamed clip is accompanied by questions that

can be used for short answer exercises or classroom discussion. Available in two formats:

- Streaming in the Coursepack
- Instructor DVD 978-0-393-93653-7

Coursepack

Chad T. Morris, Roanoke College and David Anderson, Radford University/Roanoke College

Cultural Anthropology's Coursepack offers a variety of assessment and review materials for instructors who use Blackboard and other learning management systems. In addition to chapter-based assignments, Test Banks and quizzes, and an optional ebook, this Coursepack includes interactive learning tools that will enliven hybrid, online, or traditional classes. Features include:

- A pre-test for each chapter
- Review and key term quizzes for each chapter
- "Thinking Like an Anthropologist" and "Your Turn: Fieldwork" exercises and activities
- Streaming film clips from the Instructor DVD, each supported by a quiz or exercise
- The Test Bank
- InQuizitive (Optional)

Test Bank

Lola D. Houston, University of Vermont.

The test bank for *Cultural Anthropology* is designed to help instructors prepare exams. Devised according to Bloom's taxonomy, the test bank includes 50-60 questions per chapter. In addition to Bloom's, each question is tagged with metadata that place it in the context of the chapter, as well as difficulty level, making it easy to construct tests that are meaningful and diagnostic.

NEW Interactive Instructor's Guide

Now in a newly redesigned and easier-to-navigate platform, the Interactive Instructor's Guide makes lecture development easy with an array of teaching resources that can be searched and browsed according to a number of criteria. Resources include chapter outlines and summaries; lecture ideas; discussion questions, recommended readings, videos, and websites; video exercises with streaming video; and activities with downloadable handouts. Instructors can subscribe to a mailing list to be notified of periodic updates and new content.

Acknowledgments

Writing a book of this scope is a humbling experience. I have been awed by the remarkable work of the anthropologists I have encountered, whether through written texts, films, or one-on-one conversations. And I have been inspired by the commitment of my fellow anthropologists to deep understanding of people and cultures, to the search for insights into how the world really works, and to engagement with the world and its people in ways that may help make the world a better place. I have learned a great deal, personally and professionally, on this journey. Along the way it has been my privilege to have the support and encouragement of a remarkable array of people.

First, I would like to thank all of the reviewers who shared comments on different stages of the manuscript and suggested ways to improve the book. I have adopted many of the recommendations that they made.

Augustine Agwuele, Texas State University

Hayder Al-Mohammad, University of Wisconsin, Madison
Tracy J. Andrews, Central Washington University
Iván Arenas, University of Illinois at Chicago
James D. Armstrong, College at Plattsburgh, State University of New York
Elizabeth Arnold, Grand Valley State University
Christine B. Avenarius, East Carolina University
Data Barata, California State University, Sacramento
Diane Baxter, University of Oregon
O. Hugo Benavides, Fordham University
Catherine Besteman, Colby College
Deborah A. Boehm, University of Nevada, Reno
Caroline B. Brettell, Southern Methodist University
Keri Brondo, University of Memphis
Susan Brownell, University of Missouri, St. Louis
Ronda Brulotte, University of New Mexico
Jan Brunson, University of Hawaii at Manoa
Pem Davidson Buck, Elizabethtown Community and Technical College
Andrew Buckser, State University of New York at Plattsburgh
Jerome Camal, University of Wisconsin, Madison
Jennifer Chase, University of North Texas
Leo Chavez, University of California, Irvine
Kun Chen, California State Polytechnic University, Pomona
Paula Clarke, Columbia College
Kimberley Coles, University of Redlands
Elizabeth E. Cooper, University of Alabama
Susan Bibler Coutin, University of California, Irvine
Sasha David, Los Angeles Harbor College
Joanna Davidson, Boston University
Dona Davis, University of South Dakota
Haley Duschinski, Ohio University
Terilee Edwards-Hewitt, Montgomery College
Susan Falls, Savannah College of Art and Design
Tessa Farmer, Whittier College
Carla Freeman, Emory University
Todd French, Depauw University
Jonathan Friedman, University of California, San Diego
John Fritz, Salt Lake Community College
Sue-Je Gage, Ithaca College
Ismael García Colón, College of Staten Island
Peter M. Gardner, University of Missouri
Daniel Goldstein, Rutgers University
Henri Gooren, Oakland University
Peter B. Gray, University of Nevada, Las Vegas

Thomas Gregor, Vanderbilt University
Hugh Gusterson, George Washington University
Joyce D. Hammond, Western Washington University
Melissa D. Hargrove, University of North Florida
Amy Harper, Central Oregon Community College
Tina Harris, University of Amsterdam
K. David Harrison, Swarthmore College
Angelique Haugerud, Rutgers University
Gilbert Herdt, San Francisco State University
Josiah Heyman, University of Texas at El Paso
Jude Higgins, Salt Lake Community College
Dorothy L. Hodgson, Rutgers University
Derek Honeyman, University of Arizona
Kendall House, Boise State University
Jayne Howell, California State University, Long Beach
Douglas William Hume, Northern Kentucky University
Arianne Ishaya, De Anza College
Alice James, Shippensburg University
Alana Jolley, Saddleback College
Jessica Jones-Coggins, Madison Area Technical College
Hannah Jopling, Fordham University
Ingrid Jordt, University of Wisconsin, Milwaukee
Peta Katz, University of North Carolina at Charlotte
Neal B. Keating, College at Brockport, State University of New York
Diane E. King, University of Kentucky
Ashley Kistler, Rollins College
Kathryn Kozaitis, Georgia State University
Don Kulick, Uppsala University
Clark Larsen, Ohio State University
David M. Lipset, University of Minnesota
Kathe Managan, Louisiana State University
Michael Mauer, College of the Canyons
Melanie Medeiros, State University of New York at Geneseo

Seth Messinger, University of Maryland, Baltimore County
Ryan Moore, Florida Atlantic University
Martin Muller, University of New Mexico
Rachel Newcomb, Rollins College
Jeremy Nienow, Inver Hills Community College
Craig Palmer, University of Missouri
Anastasia Panagakos, Cosumnes River College
Crystal Patil, University of Illinois at Chicago
Ramona Pérez, San Diego State University
Dana Pertermann, Blinn College
Holly Peters-Golden, University of Michigan
Mieka Brand Polanco, James Madison University
Erica Prussing, University of Iowa
James Quesada, San Francisco State University
Michelle Raisor, Blinn College
Rita Sakitt, Suffolk County Community College
Richard Sattler, University of Montana
Naomi Schiller, Brooklyn College
Scott Schnell, University of Iowa
Suzanne Simon, University of North Florida
Brian Spooner, University of Pennsylvania
Chelsea Starr, University of Phoenix
Erin E. Stiles, University of Nevada, Reno
Michelle Stokely, Indiana University Northwest
Noelle Sullivan, Northwestern University
Rania Sweis, University of Richmond
Patricia Tovar, John Jay College of Criminal Justice
Deana Weibel, Grand Valley State University
Chelsi West, University of Texas at Austin
Cassandra White, Georgia State University
Jennifer Wies, Eastern Kentucky University
Benjamin Wilreker, College of Southern Nevada
Scott Wilson, California State University, Long Beach
Jessica Winegar, Northwestern University
Paul C. Winther, Eastern Kentucky University

I would also like to thank the editors and staff at W. W. Norton who took a chance on this project to rethink the way anthropology is learned and taught. Julia Reidhead years ago encouraged me to keep my lecture notes in case I might write a textbook someday. Karl Bakeman guided me through the writing and production process of the first edition and has been integral to its continued success among my colleagues and students. The first edition's developmental editor Alice Vigliani pushed me to greater clarity of thinking and writing, and Jackie Estrada was an excellent copyeditor for this second edition. Trish Marx insightfully identified photo options that challenge the reader to think. Rachel Mayer, Caitlin Moran, and Ashley Horna masterfully stitched the many pieces of this project—words, photos, graphs, maps, captions, and more—into whole cloth, and managed to keep the countless pieces of the book moving through production. Norton's cultural anthropology marketing and sales team, Julia Hall, Natasha Zabohonski, Julie Sindel, Jonathan Mason, and Roy McClymont have advocated for the book with enthusiasm and boundless energy. Eileen Connell, Mary Williams, Grace Tuttle, and Alice Garrard put together all of the media resources that accompany the textbook. When it comes to creating new digital resources to help anthropologists teach in the classroom or teach online, I couldn't ask for a better team of people. Peter Lesser originally embraced the vision of this book, brought me into the Norton fold and, with assistant editor Samantha Held, has brought keen insight, an elegant sense of craftsmanship, enormous patience, and a generous collegiality to the creation of this second edition. Thanks to you all.

Heartfelt thanks to my many colleagues who have helped me think more deeply about anthropology, including members of the Sociology and Anthropology Department at Baruch College, especially Glenn Petersen, Robin Root, Carla Bellamy, Angie Beeman, Kyra Gaunt, Nancy Aries, Myrna Chase, and Shelley Watson, as well as Jane Schneider, Louise Lennihan, Ida Susser, Peter Kwong, Leith Mullings, Angelique Haugerud, Carol Greenhouse, Sally Merry, Hugh Gusterson, Daniel Goldstein, Sam Martinez, Alisse Waterston, Alessandro Angelini, Michael Blim, Jonathan Shannon, Christa Salamandra, Russell Sharman, Dana Davis, Jeff Maskovsky, Rudi Gaudio, Charlene Floyd, and Zoë Sheehan Saldana. Colleagues featured in "Anthropologists Engage the World" inspired me with their stories and their work. Members of the New York Academy of Sciences Anthropology Section helped me think more deeply about the relationship of culture and power. Leslie Aiello and the staff of the Wenner-Gren Foundation provided a vibrant venue to engage the cutting edges of anthropological research. The board of the American Ethnological Society allowed me to explore the theme of anthropologists engaging the world through their spring 2012 conference. My research assistants Andrew Hernann, Chris Grove, Suzanna Goldblatt, Lynn Horridge, Douaa Sheet and Chris Baum continually introduced me to the richness of contemporary scholarship and creative strategies for teaching and learning. Thanks also to a wonderful group of friends and family who have supported and encouraged me during this fascinating and challenging journey: K and Charlene, Douglas, Marybeth, Julia, Dayna, Asher, Sally and Steve, Marty and Linda, the guys at the Metro Diner—Nick, Marco and Antonio—the SPSA community, Shari, Vicki, Frances Helen, and especially Thomas Luke.

Finally, I would like to thank my students at Baruch College who every class ask to be introduced to an anthropology that is relevant to their daily lives, that tackles significant contemporary issues, and that provides them the tools of analysis and empowerment to live awake, conscious, and engaged. This book is dedicated to you and your potential to make the world a better place.

Perhaps the quintessential human task is to pass to the next generation the accumulated insights, understandings, and knowledge that will empower them to live life fully and meaningfully and to meet the challenges confronting humanity and the planet. I hope this book might contribute to that existential endeavor.

Cultural Anthropology
Second Edition

Anthropologists in the twenty-first century engage a world that is experiencing an unprecedented interaction of people, ideas, images, and things that continues to intensify. Communication technologies link people instantaneously across the globe. Economic activities challenge national boundaries. People are on the move between countries and within them. How can you use the tools of anthropology to engage this world on the move?

Indian village women protest the Coca-Cola company's exploitation of underground water supplies.

CHAPTER 1
Anthropology in a Global Age

Every morning the women of Plachimada, a rural area in southern India, begin a 5-kilometer (3-mile) trek in search of fresh water. The morning journey for water is a common task for many women across the world, for one-third of the planet's population lives with water scarcity. But such scarcity is new for the people of Plachimada, an area of typically rich agricultural harvests.

Local residents trace the changes to March 2000, when the Coca-Cola Company opened a bottling plant in the village. The plant is capable of producing 1.2 million bottles of Coke, Sprite, and Fanta every day. Nine liters of fresh water are needed to make one liter of Coke, so Plachimada's large underground aquifer was an attractive resource for the company. But according to local officials, when the company began to drill more wells and install high-powered pumps to extract groundwater for the factory, the local water table fell dramatically—from 45 meters (147.5 feet) below the surface to 150 meters (492 feet), far more than could be explained by periods of limited rainfall. Hundreds of local non–Coca-Cola wells ran dry, and harvests became much less productive. Local residents also claimed that Coca-Cola workers were dumping chemical wastes on land near the factory and that the runoff was polluting the groundwater. Local women organized protests and a sit-in at the factory gates.

With the assistance of local media and international human rights networks, the protestors' activism drew national and international attention. It even spurred solidarity actions, including support from university students in the United States, Canada, the United Kingdom, and Norway. As a result, the local village council withdrew the Coca-Cola factory's license. But the state government maintained its support. The case finally

MAP 1.1
Plachimada

reached the highest state court, which ruled that Coca-Cola must cease illegal extraction of groundwater in Plachimada. Coca-Cola closed the bottling plant in 2005. But similar battles over water use and pollution have erupted across India in the years since (Aiyer 2007; India Resource Center 2015; Shiva 2006).

For those of us who often enjoy a Coke with lunch or dinner—or breakfast—the story of the women of Plachimada offers a challenge to consider how our lives connect to theirs. It is a challenge to explore how a simple soft drink, made by a U.S. corporation with global operations, may link people halfway around the world in ways both simple and profound. This is also the challenge of anthropology today: to understand the rich diversity of human life and to see how our particular life experiences connect to those of others. By bringing these perspectives together, we can grasp more fully the totality and potential of human life.

At the same time, the world is changing before our eyes. Whether we call it a global village or a world without borders, we in the twenty-first century are experiencing a level of interaction among people, ideas, and systems that is intensifying at a breathtaking pace. Communication technologies link people instantaneously across the globe. Economic activities challenge national boundaries. People are on the move within countries and among them. Violence and terrorism disrupt lives. Humans have had remarkable success at feeding a growing world population, yet income inequality continues to increase—among nations and also within them. And increasing human diversity on our doorstep opens possibilities for both deeper understanding and greater misunderstanding. Clearly, the human community in the twenty-first century is being drawn further into a global web of interaction.

For today's college student, every day can be a cross-cultural experience. This may manifest itself in the most familiar places: the news you see on television, the music you listen to, the foods and beverages you consume, the women or men you date, the classmates you study with, the religious communities you attend. Today you can realistically imagine contacting any of our 7.2 billion co-inhabitants on the planet. You can read their posts on Facebook and watch their videos on YouTube. You can visit them. You wear clothes that they make. You make movies that they view. You can learn from them. You can affect their lives. How do you meet this challenge of deepening interaction and interdependence?

Anthropology provides a unique set of tools, including strategies and perspectives, for understanding our rapidly changing, globalizing world. Most of you are already budding cultural anthropologists without realizing it. Wherever you may live or go to school, you are probably experiencing a deepening encounter with the world's diversity. This phenomenon leads to broad questions such as: How do we approach human diversity in our universities, businesses, families, and religious communities? How do we understand the impact of global transformations on our lives?

In the twenty-first century, people are experiencing unprecedented levels of interaction, encounter, movement, and exchange. Here, traders gather at the port of Mopti, Mali, the region's most important commercial center at the confluence of the Niger and Bani rivers.

Whether our field is business or education, medicine or politics, we all need a skill set for analyzing and engaging a multicultural and increasingly interconnected world and workplace. *Cultural Anthropology: A Toolkit for a Global Age* introduces the anthropologist's tools of the trade to help you to better understand and engage the world as you move through it and, if you so choose, to apply those strategies to the challenges confronting us and our neighbors around the world. To begin our exploration of anthropology, we'll consider four key questions:

- What is anthropology?
- Through what lenses do anthropologists gain a comprehensive view of human cultures?
- What is globalization, and why is it important for anthropology?
- How is globalization transforming anthropology?

What Is Anthropology?

Anthropology is the study of the full scope of human diversity, past and present, and the application of that knowledge to help people of different backgrounds better understand one another. The word *anthropology* derives from the Greek words *anthropos* ("human") and *logos* ("thought," "reason," or "study"). The roots of anthropology lie in the eighteenth and nineteenth centuries, as Europeans' economic and colonial expansion increased that continent's contact with people worldwide.

anthropology: The study of the full scope of human diversity, past and present, and the application of that knowledge to help people of different backgrounds better understand one another.

Brief Background

Technological breakthroughs in transportation and communication during the eighteenth and nineteenth centuries—shipbuilding, the steam engine, railroads, the telegraph—rapidly transformed the long-distance movement of people, goods, and information, in terms of both speed and quantity. As colonization, communication, trade, and travel expanded, groups of merchants, missionaries, and government officials traveled the world and returned to Europe with reports and artifacts of what seemed to them to be "exotic" people and practices. More than ever before, Europeans encountered the incredible diversity of human cultures and appearances. *Who are these people?* they asked themselves. *Where did they come from? Why do they appear so different from us?*

From the field's inception in the mid-1800s, anthropologists have conducted research to answer specific questions confronting humanity. And they have applied their knowledge and insights to practical problems facing the world.

Franz Boas (1858–1942), one of the founders of American anthropology, became deeply involved in early-twentieth-century debates on immigration, serving for a term on a presidential commission examining U.S. immigration policies. In an era when many scholars and government officials considered the different people of Europe to be of distinct biological races, U.S. immigration policies privileged immigrants from northern and western Europe over those from southern and eastern Europe. Boas worked to undermine these racialized views of immigrants. He conducted studies that showed the wide variation of physical forms within groups of the same national origin, as well as the marked physical changes in the children and grandchildren of immigrants as they adapted to the environmental conditions in their new country (Baker 2004; Boas 1912).

Audrey Richards (1899–1984), studying the Bemba people in the 1930s in what is now Zambia, focused on issues of health and nutrition among women and children, bringing concerns for nutrition to the forefront of anthropology. Her ethnography, *Chisungu* (1956), featured a rigorous and detailed study of the coming-of-age rituals of young Bemba women and established new standards for the conduct of anthropological research. Richards's research is often credited with opening a pathway for the study of nutritional issues and women's and children's health in anthropology.

Today anthropologists apply their knowledge and research strategies to a wide range of social issues. For example, they study HIV/AIDS in Africa, immigrant farmworkers in the United States, ethnic conflict in the Dominican Republic, financial firms on Wall Street, street children in Brazil, and Muslim judicial courts in Egypt. Anthropologists trace the spread of disease, promote economic development in underdeveloped countries, conduct market research, and lead diversity-training programs in schools, corporations, and community organizations. Anthropologists also study our human origins, excavating and

analyzing the bones, artifacts, and DNA of our ancestors from millions of years ago to gain an understanding of who we are and where we've come from.

More than half of anthropologists today work in *applied anthropology*—that is, they work outside of academic settings to apply the strategies and insights of anthropology directly to current world problems (American Anthropological Association 2015). Even many of us who work full time in a college or university are deeply involved in public applied anthropology.

Anthropology's Unique Approach

Anthropology today retains its core commitment to understanding the richness of human diversity. Specifically, anthropology challenges us to move beyond **ethnocentrism**—the strong human tendency to believe that one's own culture or way of life is normal, natural, and superior to the beliefs and practices of others. Instead, as we will explore throughout this book, the anthropologist's toolkit of research strategies and analytical concepts enables us to appreciate, understand, and engage the diversity of human cultures in an increasingly

Anthropology's scope is global. Anthropologists' research spans issues as diverse as (*top left*) the needs of pregnant women in Guinea, West Africa; (*right*) the plight of Brazilian street children and (*bottom left*); the struggles of migrant farmworkers in central Florida.

ethnocentrism: The belief that one's own culture or way of life is normal and natural; using one's own culture to evaluate and judge the practices and ideals of others.

global age. To that end, anthropology has built upon the key concerns of early generations to develop a set of characteristics unique among the social sciences.

Anthropology Is Global in Scope Our work covers the whole world and is not constrained by geographic boundaries. Anthropology was once noted for the study of faraway, seemingly exotic villages in developing countries. But from the beginning, anthropologists have been studying not only in the islands of the South Pacific, in the rural villages of Africa, and among indigenous peoples in Australia and North America, but also among factory workers in Britain and France, among immigrants in New York, and in other communities in the industrializing world. Over the last thirty years, anthropology has turned significant attention to urban communities in industrialized nations. With the increase of studies in North America and Europe, it is fair to say that anthropologists now embrace the full scope of humanity—across geography and through time.

Anthropologists Start with People and Their Local Communities Although the whole world is our field, anthropologists are committed to understanding the local, everyday lives of the people we study. Our unique perspective focuses on the details and patterns of human life in the local community and then examines how particular cultures connect with the rest of humanity. Sociologists, economists, and political scientists primarily analyze broad trends, official organizations, and national policies, but anthropologists— particularly cultural anthropologists—adopt **ethnographic fieldwork** as their primary research strategy (see Chapter 3). They live with a community of people over an extended period to better understand their lives by "walking in their shoes."

Anthropologists have constantly worked to bring often-ignored voices into the global conversation. As a result, the field has a history of focusing on the cultures and struggles of non-Western and nonelite people. In recent years, some anthropologists have conducted research on elites—"studying up," as some have called it—by examining financial institutions, aid and development agencies, medical laboratories, and doctors (Gusterson 1997; Ho 2009; Nader 1972; Tett 2010). But the vast

ethnographic fieldwork: A primary research strategy in cultural anthropology typically involving living and interacting with a community of people over an extended period to better understand their lives.

Once noted for the study of seemingly far-away and "exotic" people and places, anthropologists today increasingly study the complex interaction of diverse communities in global cities like New York.

majority of our work has addressed the marginalized segments of society.

Anthropologists Study People and the Structures of Power Human communities are full of people, the institutions they have created for managing life in organized groups, and the systems of meaning they have built to make sense of it all. Anthropology maintains a commitment to studying both the people and the larger structures of power around them. These include families, governments, economic systems, educational institutions, militaries, the media, and religions, as well as ideas of race, ethnicity, gender, class, and sexuality.

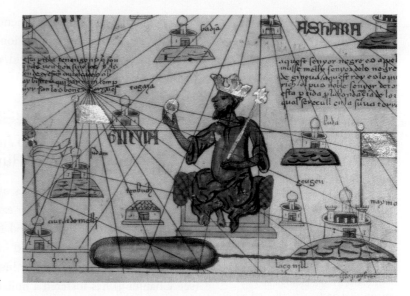

The King of Mali, West Africa, in 1375, is shown seated at the center of his vast kingdom—a key point along trade routes stretching across Africa and into the Middle East and beyond.

To comprehensively examine people's lives, anthropologists consider the structures that empower and constrain those people, both locally and globally. At the same time, anthropologists seek to understand the "agency" of local people—in other words, the central role of individuals and groups in determining their own lives, even in the face of overwhelming structures of power.

Anthropologists Believe That All Humans Are Connected Anthropologists believe that all humans share connections that are biological, cultural, economic, and ecological. Despite fanciful stories about the "discovery" of isolated, seemingly lost tribes of "stone age" people, anthropologists suggest that there are no truly isolated people in the world today and that there rarely, if ever, were any in the past. Clearly, some groups of people are less integrated than others into the global system under construction today. But none are completely isolated. And for some, their seeming isolation may be of recent historical origins. In fact, when we look more closely at the history of so-called primitive tribes in Africa and the Americas we find that many were complex state societies before colonialism and the slave trade led to their collapse.

Human history is the story of movement and interaction, not of isolation and disconnection. Although some anthropology textbooks show "tribal"-looking people in brightly colored, seemingly exotic clothing holding cell phones, which suggests the recent and rapid integration of isolated people into a high-tech, global world, anthropological research indicates that this imagined isolation never really existed. Yes, today's period of rapid globalization is intensifying the interactions among people and the flow of goods, technology, money, and ideas within and across national boundaries, but interaction and connection are not new phenomena. They have been central to human history. Our increasing connection today reminds us that our actions have consequences for the whole world, not just for our own lives and those of our families and friends.

Through What Lenses Do Anthropologists Gain a Comprehensive View of Human Cultures?

One of the unique characteristics of anthropology in the United States is that it has developed four "lenses" for examining humanity. Constituting the **four-field approach**, these interrelated fields are physical anthropology, archaeology, linguistic anthropology, and cultural anthropology. In Europe, the four fields are quite separate, but the history of anthropology in the United States (see Chapter 3) has fostered a holistic approach for examining the complexity of human origins and human culture, past and present.

Holism refers to anthropology's commitment to look at the whole picture of human life—culture, biology, history, and language—across space and time. The field's cross-cultural and comparative approach considers the life experiences of people in every part of the world, comparing and contrasting cultural beliefs and practices to understand human similarities and differences on a global scale. Anthropologists conduct research on the contemporary world and also look deep into human history.

Because we analyze both human culture and biology, anthropologists are in a unique position to offer insights into debates about the role of "nature" versus "nurture." How do biology, culture, and the environment interact to shape who we are as humans, individually and as groups? The four-field approach is key to implementing this holistic perspective within anthropology.

Physical Anthropology

Physical anthropology, sometimes called *biological anthropology,* is the study of humans from a biological perspective—in particular, how they have evolved over time and have adapted to their environments. Both the fossil record and genetic evidence suggest that the evolutionary line leading to modern humans split, between five and six million years ago, from the one leading to modern African

Paleoanthropologists trace the history of human evolution by reconstructing the human fossil record. Here, Ketut Wiradyana unearths a fossilized human skeleton buried in a cave in Indonesia's Aceh province.

apes. Modern humans thus share a common ancestor with other primates such as chimpanzees, apes, and monkeys. In fact, genetic studies reveal that humans share 97.7 percent of DNA with gorillas and 98.7 percent with chimpanzees. Through a complex evolutionary process that we are learning more about every day, *Homo sapiens* (the group of modern humans to which you and I belong) evolved in Africa fairly recently in the grand scheme of things—probably less than 200,000 years ago—and gradually spread across the planet (Larsen 2014).

Primatologist Jane Goodall studies chimpanzee behavior in an African nature preserve.

Physical anthropology has several areas of specialization. **Paleoanthropology** traces the history of human evolution by reconstructing the human fossil record. Thus, paleoanthropologists excavate the teeth, skulls, and other bones of our human ancestors and analyze them to track changes in human physical form over time. From these fossils they map changes in key categories such as overall body size, cranial capacity, hand structure, head shape, and pelvic position. Such changes reveal developments in walking, diet, intelligence, and capacity for cultural adaptation. Since the late 1970s, paleoanthropologists have also used molecular genetics to trace changes in human ancestors over time. The sequencing of DNA allows us to measure how closely humans are related to other primates and even to follow the movement of groups of people through the flow of genes. For instance, mitochondrial DNA (passed on from mother to daughter) indicates that modern *Homo sapiens* first appeared in Africa around 150,000 years ago and migrated out of Africa 100,000 years ago. This DNA evidence generally matches the findings of the archaeological record.

paleoanthropology: The study of the history of human evolution through the fossil record.

Primatology is another specialization within physical anthropology. Primatologists study living, nonhuman primates and primate fossils—including monkeys, apes, chimpanzees, and gorillas—to see what clues their biology, evolution, behavior, and social life might provide about our own, particularly our early human behavior. Careful observation of primates in their natural habitats and in captivity has offered significant insights into sexuality, parenting, male / female differences, cooperation, intergroup conflict, aggression, and problem solving.

primatology: The study of living nonhuman primates as well as primate fossils to better understand human evolution and early human behavior.

Physical anthropologists also study the diversity of human physical forms that have evolved over time. Humans come in all shapes and sizes. Our differences range from body size and facial shape to skin color, height, blood chemistry, and susceptibility to certain diseases. Physical anthropologists attribute general patterns of human physical variation to adaptation to different physical environments as humans spread from Africa across the other continents. Variations in skin color, for instance, can be traced to the need to adapt to different levels of ultraviolet light as humans migrated away from the equator (see Chapter 5).

However, studies of human biology show that the physical similarities among the world's people far outweigh the differences. In fact, there is more variation *within* what are assumed to be "groups" than *between* groups. This is clearly evident in terms of the thorny concept of race (see Chapter 6). A biologically distinct race would include people in a group who share a greater statistical frequency of genes and physical traits than people outside the group. Physical anthropologists find no evidence of distinct, fixed, biological races. Rather, there is only one human race. Attempts to identify distinct biological races are flawed and arbitrary, as no clear biological lines exist to define different races. Racial categories, which vary significantly from culture to culture, are loosely based on a few visible physical characteristics such as skin color, but they have no firm basis in genetics (Henze, and Moses 2007; Larsen 2014; Mukhopadhyay). We will return to this discussion of the biological and social dimensions of race in Chapters 5 and 6.

Archaeology

Archaeology involves the investigation of the human past by means of excavating and analyzing material remains (artifacts). The goal is not to recover buried treasure, but to understand past human life. Some archaeologists study the emergence of early states in places such as Egypt, India, China, and Mexico. They have unearthed grand sites such as the pyramids of Egypt and Mexico and the terra-cotta warriors guarding the tomb of China's Qin Dynasty emperor. Others focus on the histories of less spectacular sites that shed light on the everyday lives of people in local villages and households.

Archaeology is our only source of information about human societies before writing began (around 5,500 years ago). Because we are unable to travel back through time to observe human behavior, **prehistoric archaeology** seeks to reconstruct human behavior in the distant past (before written records) from artifacts that give significant clues about our ancestors' lives. Campsites, hunting grounds, buildings, burials, and especially garbage dumps are rich sources of material. There, archaeologists find tools, weapons, pottery, human and animal bones, jewelry, seeds, charcoal, ritual items, building foundations, and even coprolites (fossilized fecal matter). Through excavation and analysis of these material remains, archaeologists reconstruct family and work life. What animals did the people eat? What seeds did they plant? What tools and crafts did they make?

archaeology: The investigation of the human past by means of excavating and analyzing artifacts.

prehistoric archaeology: The reconstruction of human behavior in the distant past (before written records) through the examination of artifacts.

Coprolites reveal a great deal about the local diet. Burial sites provide significant data about how people treated their elders and their dead, what rituals they may have practiced, and their ideas about the afterlife. Archaeological evidence can suggest trade patterns, consumption habits, gender roles, and power stratification.

Unlike prehistoric archaeology, which looks at the time before writing, **historic archaeology** explores the more recent past and often combines the examination of physical remains and artifacts with that of written or oral records. Historic archaeologists excavate houses, stores, factories, sunken slave ships, even polar ice caps to better understand recent human history and the impact of humans on the environment. For example, recent excavations of former slave plantations in the southern United States, combined with historical records such as deeds, census forms, personal letters, and diaries, have provided rich insight into the lives of African slaves in the seventeenth and eighteenth centuries. Students in the North Atlantic Biocultural Organisation's international field school conduct excavations in Iceland that reveal not only historical information about the settling of the North Atlantic but also data on major changes in the contemporary global climate. Core samples from borings drilled through the glaciers reveal sediments deposited from the air over thousands of years as the glaciers formed; such samples allow archaeologists to track global warming and the impact of greenhouse gases on climate change.

Prehistoric garbage dumps provide rich sources of material for understanding the cultural practices of human ancestors. Today, "garbologists" also learn about contemporary culture by examining what people throw away, including in large trash landfills like the one pictured here. What might an anthropologist 200 years from now learn about your community by studying its garbage?

Linguistic Anthropology

Linguistic anthropology involves the study of human language in the past and the present. Languages are complex, vibrant, and constantly changing systems of symbols through which people communicate with one another. (Think about how hard it is to get your ideas across in your college papers, in text messages, or even in conversation with your parents.) Languages are very flexible and inventive. (Consider how English has adapted to the rise of the Internet to include such new words and concepts as *spam, instant messages, texting, Googling, Skyping, snapchat,* and *facetime.*) A language clearly reflects a people's ideas of and experiences with the world. But linguistic anthropologists suggest that language may also limit and constrain a people's views of the world. In other words, can we think clearly about something if we don't have an adequately sophisticated language?

historic archaeology: The exploration of the more recent past through an examination of physical remains and artifacts as well as written or oral records.

linguistic anthropology: The study of human language in the past and the present.

Language is perhaps the most distinctive feature of being human. It is the key to our ability to learn and share culture from generation to generation, to cooperate in groups, and to adapt to our environment. While some animals—including dolphins and whales, bees, and ravens—have a limited range of communication, human language is more complex, creative, and extensively used.

Linguistic anthropology includes three main areas of specialization. **Descriptive linguists** work to carefully describe spoken languages and preserve them as written languages. For example, some descriptive linguists spend years in rural areas helping local people construct a written language from their spoken language. **Historic linguists** study how language changes over time within a culture and as it moves across cultures. **Sociolinguists** study language in its social and cultural contexts. They examine how different speakers use language in different situations or with different people. They explore how language is affected by factors such as race, gender, age, class, or other relationships of power. Consider the so-called "N-word"—a very controversial word in the United States today. Sociolinguists would explore the word's usage in American English: Where did it come from? Who uses it, and in what situations? How does its meaning change according to the speaker and the context? When is it a term of racial hatred? When is it a term of camaraderie? We will explore these issues further in Chapter 4.

Cultural Anthropology

Cultural anthropology is the study of people's everyday lives and their communities—their behaviors, beliefs, and institutions. Cultural anthropologists explore all aspects of human culture, such as war and violence, love and sexuality, child rearing and death. They examine what people do and how they live, work, and play together. But they also search for patterns of meaning embedded within each culture, and they develop theories about how cultures work. Cultural anthropologists examine the ways in which local communities interact with global forces.

Ethnographic fieldwork is at the heart of cultural anthropology. Through **participant observation**—living and working with people on a daily basis, often for a year or more—the cultural anthropologist strives to see the world through the eyes of others. Intensive fieldwork has the power to educate the anthropologist by (1) making what may at first seem very unfamiliar into something that ultimately seems quite familiar, and (2) taking what has seemed very familiar and making it seem very strange. Through fieldwork, anthropologists look beyond the taken-for-granted, everyday experience of life to discover the complex systems of power and meaning that all people construct. These include the many systems we will cover throughout this book: gender, sexuality, race, ethnicity, religion, kinship, class, and economic and political systems.

descriptive linguists: Those who analyze languages and their component parts.

historic linguists: Those who study how language changes over time within a culture and how languages travel across cultures.

sociolinguists: Those who study language in its social and cultural contexts.

cultural anthropology: The study of people's communities, behaviors, beliefs, and institutions, including how people make meaning as they live, work, and play together.

participant observation: A key anthropological research strategy involving both participation in and observation of the daily life of the people being studied.

Cultural anthropologists analyze and compare ethnographic data across cultures in a process called **ethnology**. This process looks beyond specific local realities to see more general patterns of human behavior and to explore how local experiences intersect with global dynamics. Ultimately, through intensive ethnographic fieldwork and cross-cultural comparison, cultural anthropologists seek to help people better understand one another and the way the world works.

ethnology: The analysis and comparison of ethnographic data across cultures.

What Is Globalization, and Why Is It Important for Anthropology?

The term **globalization** refers to the worldwide intensification of interactions and increased movement of money, people, goods, and ideas within and across national borders. Growing integration of the global economy has driven the intense globalization of the past forty years. Corporations are relocating factories halfway around the world. People are crossing borders legally and illegally in search of work. Goods, services, and ideas are flowing along high-speed transportation and communication networks. People, organizations, and nations are being drawn into closer connection.

globalization: The worldwide intensification of interactions and increased movement of money, people, goods, and ideas within and across national borders.

Globalization is not an entirely new phenomenon. Intensification of global interaction occurred in earlier eras as breakthroughs in communication and transportation brought the world's people into closer contact. The present period of globalization, however, has reached a level of intensity previously unknown.

Although globalization is often portrayed in a positive light in the media and popular discourse, the realities are much more complicated. The new technologies associated with globalization may indeed allow more and more people to interact and communicate, but billions of other people are being left out of these advances. Moreover, along with the economic expansion and growth associated with globalization, there are equally significant global economic inequalities.

Syrian refugees land on the coast of Greece.

Globalization and Anthropology

Globalization and anthropology are intricately intertwined, both in history and in the contemporary world. As we have noted, the field of anthropology emerged in the mid-nineteenth century during a time of intense globalization. At that time, technological inventions in transportation and communication were consolidating a period of colonial encounter, the slave trade, and the emerging capitalist economic system and were enabling deeper interactions of people across cultures. Early anthropologists sought to organize the vast quantity of information being accumulated about people across the globe, though, unlike most contemporary anthropologists, who conduct research in the field, they did so primarily from the comfort of their own homes and meeting halls.

Today another era of even more intense globalization is transforming the lives of the people whom anthropologists study in every part of the world. And, as we will see throughout this book, it is also transforming the ways anthropologists conduct research and communicate their findings. To understand these sweeping changes, we must understand the key dynamics of globalization at play in the world today (Inda and Rosaldo 2002; Kearney 1995; Lewellen 2002; Trouillot 2003).

Globalization: Key Dynamics

Globalization today is characterized by several key dynamics: time-space compression, flexible accumulation, increasing migration, and uneven development, all of which are happening at in increasingly rapid pace. These dynamics are reshaping the ways humans adapt to the natural world, and the ways the natural world is adapting to us.

time-space compression: The rapid innovation of communication and transportation technologies associated with globalization that transforms the way people think about space (distances) and time.

Time-Space Compression According to the theory of **time-space compression**, the rapid innovation of communication and transportation technologies has transformed the way we think about space (distances) and time. Jet travel, supertankers, superhighways, high-speed railways, telephones, computers, the Internet, digital cameras, and cell phones have condensed time and space, changing our sense of how long it takes to do something and how far away someplace or someone is. The world is no longer as big as it used to be.

Consider these examples of a changing sense of time. Today we can fly from New York to Paris in eight hours or from Los Angeles to Hong Kong in twelve. A letter that once took ten days to send from Texas to Kenya can now be attached as a PDF and emailed with a few clicks of a mouse. We instant message, text message, Skype, videoconference, and FaceTime. These kinds of changes have transformed not only how long it takes us to do something, but also how quickly we expect other people to do things. For example, how much time do you have to respond to an email or a text message before someone thinks you are rude or irresponsible?

Flexible Accumulation A second characteristic of today's globalization, **flexible accumulation**, reflects the fact that advances in transportation and communication have enabled companies to move their production facilities and activities around the world in search of cheaper labor, lower taxes, and fewer environmental regulations—in other words, to be increasingly flexible about the way they accumulate profits (see Chapter 12). Companies in developed countries move their factories to export-processing zones in the developing world, a process called *offshoring*. Other corporations shift part of their work to employees in other parts of the world, a process called *outsourcing*. For example, General Motors used to make all of its automobiles in Flint, Michigan, but now the company has factories in Mexico, Brazil, China, and Thailand. Walmart, once known for its advertising campaign "Made in America," now has 7,000 factories in China.

Other examples span the globe as well: Phone and computer companies hire English-speaking operators and technicians in Bangalore, India, to answer customers' questions called in on 800 numbers. A company based in Sierre Leone, West Africa, processes traffic tickets issued in New York City. X-rays, CT scans, and MRIs taken in Colorado may be read and interpreted by doctors in Manila, the Philippines. Clearly, flexible accumulation allows corporations to maximize profits, while time-space compression enables the efficient management of global networks and distribution systems (Harvey 1990).

Increasing Migration A third characteristic of globalization is **increasing migration**, the accelerated movement of people both within countries and between countries. In fact, recent globalization has spurred the international migration of more than 232 million people, 46 million of them to the United States alone (see Chapter 13) (United Nations Department of Economic and Social Affairs, Population Division 2013). An estimated 700 million more are internal migrants within their own countries, usually moving from rural to urban areas in search of work. The Chinese government counts nearly 250 million internal migrants floating in China's cities, drawn by construction projects, service jobs, and export-oriented factories (Armstrong 2013; Liang, Li, Ma 2014).

In countries from Pakistan to Kenya to Peru, rural workers migrate to urban areas seeking to improve their lives and the lives of their families back home. This movement of people within and across national borders is stretching out human relationships and interactions across space and time. Immigrants send money home, call and email friends and family, and sometimes even travel back and forth. Migration is building connections between distant parts of the world, replacing face-to-face interactions with more remote

flexible accumulation: The increasingly flexible strategies that corporations use to accumulate profits in an era of globalization, enabled by innovative communication and transportation technologies.

increasing migration: The accelerated movement of people within and between countries.

encounters and potentially reducing the hold of the local environment over people's lives and imaginations.

Uneven Development Globalization is also characterized by **uneven development**. Although many people associate globalization with rapid economic development and progress, globalization has not brought equal benefits to the world's people. Some travel the globe for business or pleasure; others are limited to more local forms of transportation. Although 3.2 billion people now have Internet access, the distribution is uneven. 4 billion people in developing countries remain offline, representing two-thirds of their population. And only 9.5 percent of the 940 million people living in the least-developed countries have Internet access. Europe, North America, and Asia account for the vast majority of high-tech consumption, while areas of Africa are marginalized and excluded from the globalization process (International Telecommunication Union 2015). Such uneven development and uneven access to the benefits of globalization reflect the negative side of changes in the world today.

Although the global economy is creating extreme wealth, it is also creating extreme poverty. Excluding China (which has experienced rapid economic growth), global poverty has increased over the past twenty years. Fully 40 percent of the world's population live in poverty, defined as income of less than $2.00 per day. And nearly 1 billion people live in extreme poverty, surviving on less than $1.25 each day (United Nations 2015). Even in the United States, the wealthiest country in the world, some full-time workers who earn the minimum wage make so little money that they must rely on state welfare programs for food stamps and medical care for themselves and their children. In Chapter 12, we will explore the possibility that the rapid growth seen in globalization actually *depends on* uneven development—extracting the resources of some to fuel the success of others.

Globalization and the Environment

Of course, modern humans and our ancestors have been adapting to changes for millions of years. In fact, perhaps our most distinctive characteristic is our ability to adapt—to figure out how to survive and thrive in a world that is rapidly changing. Although change has been a constant, so has human adaptation, both biological and cultural.

Our species has successfully adapted genetically to changes in the natural environment over millions of years. We walk upright on two legs. We have binocular vision and see in color. We have opposable thumbs for grasping. Our bodies also adapt temporarily to changes in the environment on a daily basis. We sweat to keep cool in the heat, tan to block out the sun's ultraviolet rays, shiver to generate warmth in the cold, and breathe rapidly to take in more oxygen at high altitudes.

As our ancestors evolved and developed greater brain capacity, they invented cultural adaptations—tools, the controlled use of fire, and weapons—to navigate the natural environment. Today our use of culture to adapt to the world around us is incredibly sophisticated. In the United States, we like our air conditioners on a hot July afternoon and our radiators in the winter. Oxygen masks deploy for us in sky-high airplanes, and sunscreen protects us against sunburn and skin cancer. These are just a few familiar examples of adaptations our culture has made. Looking more broadly, the worldwide diversity of human culture itself is a testimony to human flexibility and adaptability to particular environments.

Shaping the Natural World To say that humans adapt to the natural world is only part of the story, for humans actively shape the natural world as well. Humans have planted, grazed, paved, excavated, and built on at least 40 percent of Earth's surface. Our activities have caused profound changes in the atmosphere, soil, and oceans. Human impact on the planet is so extensive that scholars in many disciplines have come to refer to the current historical period as the **Anthropocene**—a distinct era in which human activity is reshaping the planet in permanent ways. Whereas our ancestors struggled to adapt to the uncertainties of heat, cold, solar radiation, disease, natural disasters, famines, and droughts, today we confront changes and social forces that we ourselves have set in motion. These changes include climate change, water scarcity, overpopulation, extreme poverty, biological weapons, and nuclear missiles. These pose the greatest risks to human survival. As globalization intensifies, it escalates the human impact on the planet and on other humans, further accelerating the pace of change.

Human activity already threatens the world's ecological balance. We do not need to wait to see the effects. For instance, population growth and consumption patterns have placed incredible stress on Earth's water resources, both fresh water and saltwater. As the opening story of Plachimada, India, reveals, the struggle to gain access to the fresh water in lakes, rivers, and aquifers can be a source of conflict. Private companies are buying up rights to water in many countries, and bottled water sales have grown to a $50 billion global business.

Anthropocene: The current historical era in which human activity is reshaping the planet in permanent ways.

Actual stomach contents of a baby albatross on the remote north Pacific Midway Atoll, 2,000 miles from the nearest continent. Thousands die as their parents feed them lethal quantities of floating plastic trash that they mistake for food as they forage over the polluted Pacific Ocean. © Chris Jordan, courtesy of Kopeikin Gallery, Los Angeles.

THE SOCIAL LIFE OF THINGS
Finding the City in a Shoe

Our lives are entangled with things, what anthropologists refer to as "material culture." Yet the stuff of our daily lives can become almost invisible—so common that we take it for granted. If we pay attention, however, stuff talks. Things have a biography and tell a story that often reveals a great deal about who we are as humans, what we value, how our cultures work and, in a time of increasing globalization, how the world works. Let's consider, for instance, what a shoe can tell us about a city through the work of anthropologist Suzanne Scheld (2003).

1 Dakar, Senegal, a city of 2.4 million people on the coast of West Africa, is renowned for its vibrant, sprawling markets packed with a diverse and colorful array of locally made African print fabrics, footwear, and clothing sold alongside cheap Chinese knock-offs and second-hand clothing from abroad.

2 In Dakar, fashion is important, and dressing to impress is central to Senegalese social life. Wearing the right clothes and shoes projects an image of success, privilege, upward mobility, and cosmopolitanism—global awareness and even the experience of global travel and connections.

3 A curious craze for imported Sebago shoes emerged in Dakar fashion culture in the 1990s and 2000s. Sebago's boat shoe became a fashion standard and status symbol, avidly consumed by a broad cross section of the population despite the country's weak economy and the imported shoe's high price.

④ Key to the Sebago fashion craze are thousands of Senegalese who have moved abroad to seek education and work. Today 20,000 Senegalese, like the restaurant server and patron at right, live in New York City working in low-skilled jobs while building an extensive network of institutions to serve fellow immigrants.

 ⑤ The Sebago Corporation started making pennyloafers for the U.S. market in the 1940s, and in the 1960s the brand took off globally. In the 1990s Sebago relocated its French (and West African) distribution center to New York to facilitate direct coordination with African traders. Sebago had no retail stores in Dakar, nor any advertising. Instead, the rising demand in Dakar for Sebago shoes encouraged an informal network of young Senegalese "suitcase traders" who would carry 100–200 pairs of Sebago shoes at a time. Their direct knowledge of Dakar fashion trends informed their selection of Sebago products, which in turn shaped the Dakar fashion market. Sebago shoes, and those who wore them, became associated with transnational migrant Senegalese who symbolized possibility, privilege, mobility, and cosmopolitanism.

Movement of Sebago shoes along informal transnational networks of small-scale traders and their rise in the fashion scene in Dakar illuminate the complex global flows of things, people, ideas, and money characteristic of globalization today. Time and space are compressed, migration increases, and the very boundaries of the city blur, making Dakar and New York feel like nearly continuous social spaces. Globalization transforms anthropological research and the communities we study. All this told through the story of a shoe.

- In recent years anthropologists have been developing an anthropology of stuff—or what we call "material culture." After reviewing this feature, can you begin to see how exploring the social life of a shoe can help you better understand the character of a city in today's global age?
- Can you apply this idea to another object with which you are familiar? Try the Your Turn exercise on page 28 to see what tracing the social life of a can of Coke might tell you about globalization.

Holly Barker
Globalization and Climate Change in the Marshall Islands

"While islands may be distant in our psyches we need to remember that our planet is also a remote island in the universe and its future, like that of the Marshall Islands, is ultimately one and the same." (Barker 2008)

Anthropologist Holly Barker focuses her work on the Marshall Islands, a group of coral atolls spread over a seventy-square-mile area in the northern Pacific Ocean. Although Pacific islands may conjure images of warm water, white sandy beaches, and blissful vacation escapes, Barker's work focuses on much less idyllic matters, such as the impact of twelve years of atmospheric nuclear testing conducted by the United States in the Marshalls after World War II and the current impact of climate change on the islands' people. Though some in developed nations may debate the effects of climate change, small island nations around the world are on the front lines of climate change today.

Barker first arrived in the Marshall Islands in 1988 as a volunteer with the U.S. Peace Corps to teach English on a remote island of fisherfolk and subsistence farmers. After 400 years of colonization by various countries, the Marshall Islands had finally achieved independence from the United States two years earlier.

Upon returning to the United States, Barker worked for Rhode Island Senator Claiborne Pell in Washington, D.C., but nobody on Capitol Hill had time to hear about the Marshall Islands. "So one day I just called up the Marshall Islands embassy and encouraged them to make an appointment with the senator. But they had never had any luck with that and simply replied, 'Why don't you come and work for us?' So I did—for seventeen years. It was a phenomenal experience. My role as the anthropologist was to show the Marshallese government leaders how the U.S. government works and then get out of the way and let them speak for themselves. They certainly know what to say and what they want to ask for. That's not the role of an outsider. My role was to help them make connections and be effective in the U.S. cultural context."

When Barker began her graduate studies in anthropology, she was still employed by the embassy. "I was learning all the ideas of anthropology and applying them immediately to my job, thinking about anthropological theories and then connecting them back to the Marshall Islands. I wasn't just studying academic ideas in isolation. I was coming to work every day and putting them to use. That brought anthropology alive for me. I remember learning about the concept of structural violence, looking at how institutions do harm to people. There I was in D.C. looking at the political system's failure to recognize health-care needs of the Marshallese and trying to push the U.S. political institutions to change policies that were leaving people dying without access to health care. Then I began to see concepts like structural violence with shocking clarity."

Today the Marshall Islands confront the rising impact of climate change: "For the older generation of the Marshallese, the life-defining issue was certainly

Anthropologist Holly Barker

nuclear testing. They're a culture and nation with amazing resilience, to constantly work through those kinds of issues and still have their culture intact. But for the next generation or two removed from the testing, their life-threatening issue is climate change. On the islands there's no buffer. The effects are profound. The current generation will see the tombs of ancestors fall into the sea and watch their inheritance be swept away by the encroaching waters. They can see the change. It's rapid. Globalization makes everything seem to happen faster. But the wholesale relocation of communities is something we're not prepared for yet. That's the challenge I think with globalization. We're used to seeing rural people slowly shifting to urban environments, new uses of technology, or gradual cultural changes. But with climate change on islands, we're talking about rapidly making environmental refugees of gigantic proportions.

"We don't have the luxury to only think about our own lives anymore. Our atmospheres are connected. Our seas are connected. Everything is. Today we need to step back and see the Earth through a wider lens. The same holds for the islands. We imagine the islands as these little beautiful paradises that exist in tourist brochures without the human beings that populate these places. We think of them as oases, retreats that await us anytime we want happiness. But we don't think of them as places that we take our own irresponsibilities to. That would mean thinking about the islands and their history as test sites for our nuclear bombs and their experience of climate change—places colonial powers take activities that they don't want in their own nations. Despite the fact that small island nations are responsible for only three-hundredths of 1 percent of the global carbon emissions from burning fossil fuels that drive global warming, they are the ones confronting the most devastating impacts of climate change so far. If we can't deal with the Marshallese, who are U.S. allies and formerly colonized by the United States—if we can't take care of people with whom we have a unique history and entangled close relationships, how will we deal with the multitude elsewhere? So it calls for us to do a better job. To be clearer about how we are all connected."

Barker teaches the Introduction to Cultural Anthropology course at the University of Washington and tries to get across this basic idea to her students: "We need you! We as a society cannot afford for you not to become engaged. Each generation gets passed the inheritance, the legacy, to carry on human beings into the next generation. To be adequately equipped for that, you have to be able to see the potential of human beings around you. You have to be able to communicate across boundaries. I feel that in every generation we are compelled to get the next generation ready to deal with the challenges that are undoubtedly coming their way. Anthropology is a discipline that provides the skills and theories but also the hope, the sense of our human potential, and the possibilities of doing better. Anthropology is about being the best human beings we can be. Sometimes we screw up and screw up massively. But we have the potential to do better. Anthropology asks that of us and gives us the tools to make it possible."

> *Anthropology is about being the best human beings we can be. Sometimes we screw up and screw up massively. But we have the potential to do better. Anthropology asks that of us and gives us the tools to make it possible.*

The seemingly vast oceans are also experiencing significant distress. The oil spill created by the British Petroleum Deepwater Horizon disaster in 2010 poured 210 million gallons of crude oil into the Gulf of Mexico over the course of two months. In the middle of the Pacific Ocean sits a floating island of plastic the size of Texas, caught in an intersection of ocean currents. The plastic originates mainly from consumers in Asia and North America. Pollution from garbage, sewage, and agricultural fertilizer runoff, combined with overfishing and spills from offshore oil drilling, may kill off edible sea life completely by 2048 (Worm et al. 2006). These sobering realities are characteristic of today's global age and the impacts of increasing globalization.

Humans and Climate Change Human activity is also producing rapid **climate change**. Driven by the increase of greenhouse gases in the atmosphere, largely from the burning of fossil fuels, global warming is already reshaping the physical world and threatening to radically change much of modern human civilization. Scientists predict a rise in average global temperatures of between 2.5 and 10 degrees Fahrenheit by 2100 (National Aeronautics and Space Administration 2015). Changing weather patterns have already begun to alter agricultural patterns and crop yields. Global warming has spurred rapid melting of polar ice and glaciers, well before most scientists had predicted, and the pace is increasing.

Melting glaciers mean rising sea levels. Given the current speed of melting, a one- to four-foot sea-level rise by 2100 is entirely possible (National Aeronautics and Space Administration 2015). Half of the world's population lives within fifty miles of the coast, so the implications are enormous—especially in low-lying delta regions. Bangladesh, home to more than 150 million people, will be largely underwater. Miami—parts of which already flood during heavy rain storms—will have an ocean on both sides. Should all the glacier ice on Greenland melt, sea levels would rise an estimated twenty-three feet.

How will the planet cope with the growth of the human population from 7.2 billion in 2015 to more than 9 billion in 2050? Our ancestors have successfully adapted to the natural world around us for millions of years, but human activity and technological innovation now threaten to overwhelm the natural world beyond its ability to adapt to us.

How Is Globalization Transforming Anthropology?

The field of anthropology has changed significantly in the past thirty years as the world has been transformed by globalization. Just as the local cultures and communities we study are changing in response to these forces, our focus and strategies must also change.

climate change: Changes to Earth's climate, including global warming produced primarily by increasing concentrations of greenhouse gases created by the burning of fossil fuels.

Changing Communities

Globalization is changing the communities we study. Today vulnerable people and cultures are encountering powerful economic forces that are reshaping family, gender roles, ethnicity, sexuality, love, and work patterns. Debates over the effects of globalization on local cultures and communities are intense. Critics of globalization warn of the dangers of homogenization and the loss of traditional local cultures as products marketed by global companies flood into local communities. (Many of these brands originate in Western countries, including Coca-Cola, Microsoft, McDonald's, Levi's, Disney, Walmart, CNN, and Hollywood.) Yet globalization's proponents note the new exposure to diversity that is now available to people worldwide, opening possibilities for personal choice that were previously unimaginable. As with the case of Plachimada, India—and as we will see throughout this book—although global forces are increasingly affecting local communities, local communities are also actively working to reshape encounters with globalization to their own benefit: fighting detrimental changes, negotiating better terms of engagement, and embracing new opportunities.

Changing Research Strategies

Anthropologists are also changing research strategies to reflect the transformations affecting the communities we study (see Chapter 3). Today it is impossible to study a local community without considering the global forces that affect it. Thus, anthropologists are engaging in more multi-sited ethnographies, comparing communities linked, for instance, by migration, production, or communication. My own research is a case in point.

Multi-sited Ethnography: China and New York When I began my fieldwork in New York City's Chinatown in 1997, I anticipated conducting a year-long study of Chinese immigrant religious communities—Christian, Buddhist, and Daoist—and their role in the lives of new immigrants. I soon realized, however, that I did not understand why tens of thousands of immigrants from Fuzhou, China, were taking such great risks—some hiring human smugglers at enormous cost—to come and work in low-paying jobs in restaurants, garment shops, construction trades, and nail salons. To figure out why so many were leaving China, one summer I followed their immigrant journey back home.

MAP 1.3
Fuzhou/New York

I boarded a plane from New York to Hong Kong and on to Fuzhou, the capital of Fujian Province on China's southeast coast. From Fuzhou, I took a local bus to a small town at the end of the line. A ferry carried me across a river to a three-wheeled motor taxi that transported me across dirt roads to the main square of a rural fishing village at the foot of a small mountain. I began to hike up the slope and finally caught a ride on a motorcycle to my destination.

YOUR TURN: FIELDWORK

Making a Can of Coke Unfamiliar

Throughout this book we will be exploring how anthropology's holistic, cross-cultural, and comparative approach can help us think more deeply about other people and cultures and live more consciously in our global world. As humans we take for granted many things about our lives and how the world works, whether it is our notions of race or the cheap cost of a bar of chocolate or a can of Coke. But anthropologists often describe how doing fieldwork can make the familiar strange and the strange familiar.

Take a can of Coke, for instance. After rereading the opening story of the Coca-Cola factory in Plachimada, India, go buy a can of Coke and put it on your desk. Can you make this most familiar cultural object unfamiliar? What would an anthropologist want to know about that can of Coke? What can you learn about yourself, your culture, or globalization in general from that can of Coke? How does the social life of a can of Coke intersect with the lives of people in each stage of its production, distribution, and consumption? Spend 30 to 40 minutes researching the following questions on the Internet.

- What's in it? Where did the ingredients come from?
- Who made it? What is their life like?
- What is the impact of Coke on the local community where it is produced? Where it is consumed?
- What is the relationship of the people in Plachimada to a can of Coke? Do they drink it? Do they work in the factory that makes it? How much do they earn? How much has the Coca-Cola factory changed their lives? Has it affected people in the community differently based on age, gender, or class?
- What do you pay for a twelve-ounce can? What are the real social costs of producing a can of Coke—in terms of water, power systems, sewage treatment, pollution, garbage disposal, and roads for transportation? Who pays for them?
- What is the environmental impact of making a can of Coke, considering what it takes to grow and process ingredients such as high-fructose corn syrup and the quantity of water required to produce the finished product?

By exploring the complex social life of a can of Coke, you are applying a set of analytical tools that may help you look more carefully and consciously at other familiar elements of culture.

What can you learn about yourself, your culture, or globalization in general from a can of Coke?

Rural Fuzhou villagers worship at a Chinese temple constructed with funds sent home by community members working in the United States.

Back in New York, I had met the master of a temple, an immigrant from Fuzhou who was raising money from other immigrant workers to rebuild their temple in China. He had invited me to visit their hometown and participate in a temple festival. Now, finally arriving at the temple after a transcontinental journey, I was greeted by hundreds of pilgrims from neighboring towns and villages. "What are you doing here?" one asked. When I told them that I was an anthropologist from the United States, that I had met some of their fellow villagers in New York, and that I had come to learn about their village, they began to laugh. "Go back to New York!" they said. "Most of our village is there already, not here in this little place." Then we all laughed together, acknowledging the irony of my traveling to China when they wanted to go to New York—but also marveling at the remarkable connection built across the 10,000 miles between this little village and one of the most urban metropolises in the world.

Over the years I have made many trips back to the villages around Fuzhou. My research experiences have brought alive the ways in which globalization is transforming the world and the practice of anthropology. Today 70 percent of the village population resides in the United States, but the villagers live out time-space compression as they continue to build strong ties between New York and China. They travel back and forth. They build temples, roads, and schools back home. They transfer money by wire. They call, text, Skype, and post videos online. They send children back to China to be raised by grandparents in the village. Parents in New York watch their children play in the village using webcams and the Internet.

Back home, local factories built by global corporations produce toys for Disney and McDonald's and Mardi Gras beads for the city of New Orleans. The local jobs provide employment alternatives, but they have not replaced migration out of China as the best option for improving local lives.

These changes are happening incredibly rapidly, transforming people's lives and communities on opposite sides of the world. But globalization brings uneven benefits that break down along lines of ethnicity, gender, age, language, legal status, kinship, and class. These disparities give rise to issues that we will

TOOLKIT

Thinking Like an Anthropologist: Living in a Global Age

As you begin your exploration of anthropology, the women of Plachimada discussed in the chapter opening may provide you with a powerful image to keep in mind and challenge you to think more anthropologically about the world and its people. *Cultural Anthropology: A Toolkit for a Global Age* is designed to help you explore the richness of human diversity, uncover your conscious and subconscious ideas of how the world works (or should work), and develop some strategies for living, working, and learning in an environment where diversity is a part of daily life.

Solving the challenges that face the human race in your lifetime will require greater engagement, interaction, and cooperation—not more isolation and ignorance. The future of the planet requires everyone to develop the skills of an anthropologist if our species is to thrive and, perhaps, even to survive. These skills include cross-cultural knowledge and sensitivity; perceptiveness of other people; understanding of systems of meaning and

systems of power; and consciousness of one's own culture, assumptions, beliefs, and power. By the end of this book, you will have many of the skills needed to think carefully about these questions.

- What is anthropology?
- Through what lenses do anthropologists gain a comprehensive view of human cultures?
- What is globalization, and why is it important for anthropology?
- How is globalization transforming anthropology?

You also will discover that the study of anthropology helps you rethink many of your assumptions about the world and how it works. For the magic of anthropology lies in unmasking the underlying structures of life, in spurring the analytical imagination, and in providing the skills to be alert, aware, sensitive, and successful in a rapidly changing—and often confusing—multicultural and global world.

address in depth throughout this book. Such changes mean that I as an anthropologist have to adjust my own fieldwork to span my subjects' entire reality, a reality that now encompasses a village in China, the metropolis of New York City, and many people and places in between (Guest 2003, 2011). And as you will discover throughout this book, other anthropologists are likewise adapting their strategies to meet the challenges of globalization. Learning to think like an anthropologist will enable you to better navigate our increasingly interconnected world.

Key Terms

anthropology (p. 7)

ethnocentrism (p. 9)

ethnographic fieldwork (p. 10)

four-field approach (p. 12)

holism (p. 12)

physical anthropology (p. 12)

paleoanthropology (p. 13)

primatology (p. 13)

archaeology (p. 14)

prehistoric archaeology (p. 14)

historic archaeology (p. 15)

linguistic anthropology (p. 15)

descriptive linguists (p. 16)

historic linguists (p. 16)

sociolinguists (p. 16)

cultural anthropology (p. 16)

participant observation (p. 16)

ethnology (p. 17)

globalization (p. 17)

time-space compression (p. 18)

flexible accumulation (p. 19)

increasing migration (p. 19)

uneven development (p. 20)

Anthropocene (p. 21)

climate change (p. 26)

For Further Exploration

Do the Math. 2012. 350.org. Documentary film about global climate change. http://act.350.org/signup/math-movie

Guest, Kenneth J. 2003. *God in Chinatown: Religion and Survival in New York's Evolving Immigrant Community.* New York: NYU Press.

United Nations. "Millennium Development Goals: End Poverty 2015." www.un.org/millenniumgoals/poverty.shtml

U.S. Census Bureau. "U.S. and World Population Clocks." www.census.gov/main/www/popclock.html

What can you learn about culture from a McDonald's Happy Meal?

CHAPTER 2
Culture

What can you learn about culture—particularly American culture—from a McDonald's Happy Meal? The Happy Meal is perhaps the most iconic menu item for the world's largest chain of hamburger fast-food restaurants, serving 68 million customers in 119 countries. What can we learn by looking a little more carefully?

Opening up the bright red box with the broad yellow smile, you find a paper-wrapped hamburger and a miniature side of French Fries. A choice of yogurt or apple slices, juice or soda, and a toy for a boy or a girl complete the menu. The packaging is covered with games and advertisements. All this for just over $3.00. Clearly, many people like their food fast, cheap, processed, predictable, and entertaining—high in saturated fat, sugar, and salt followed by a chaser of sugary, carbonated, and caffeinated soda.

Each element of the Happy Meal has its own elaborate journey. Imagine its point of origin, the hands it has passed through, the aspects of economic and political systems it intersects, its place on the table and in our mouths, and its steps to a final resting spot. By the time it reaches our table the Happy Meal has been shaped by ideas of the American diet, government regulation, industrial agricultural production, the environment, social movements, health concerns, labor practices, consumer leverage, gender norms, and connections to workers and consumers across the globe.

For instance, the U.S. Department of Agriculture regulates what can go into a hamburger. The tiny box of fries and apple slices are a response to consumer pressure for healthier food. The amount of water required to produce 10 pounds of beef is equivalent to that used by the average American family in a year. Expanding cattle ranching destroys climate-cooling rainforests in Central and South America. Young women in Chinese sweatshop factories make the toys. The costs of producing a Happy Meal far exceed its sale price. And McDonald's' gender assumptions determine which toy your child receives.

Turning an anthropological eye to food opens a window on the complex thing we call culture: the intricate patterns of ideas and behaviors humans create to live together in groups. Although we may consider eating as "doing what comes naturally," as an instinctive impulse, eating varies widely across cultures. What you eat, how you eat, and even who you eat with are shaped by culture, including ideas about religion, gender, race, ethnic identity, immigration, class, and age.

Eating is an intensely intimate cultural practice with complicated social meanings. Consider the role of food in your own family gatherings, romantic encounters, celebratory events, and religious rituals—the elaborate rules and deep significances.

Food is also closely linked to power. Who eats and who doesn't? In a time of unprecedented abundance, still 11 percent of the population does not have enough to eat on any given day, 663 million people lack access to safe drinking water, and 30 percent of the world's children are undernourished (World Health Organization 2015). The study of food can illuminate the deep fault lines and often entrenched patterns of stratification and inequality within and between cultures.

As anthropologists, we can begin to see that a Happy Meal is not simply a happy meal. It is deeply embedded in processes central to American cultural life, and in this increasingly globalized world, to processes that affect every person on our planet (Anderson 2005; Counihan and Van Esterik, 2013; Robbins 2013; Watson and Caldwell, 2004).

In this chapter, we will apply an anthropologist's viewpoint to culture and consider its crucial role in shaping how we behave and what we think. In particular, we will consider:

- What is culture?
- How has the culture concept developed in anthropology?
- How are culture and power related?
- How much of who you are is shaped by biology, and how much by culture?
- How is culture created?
- How is globalization transforming culture?

By the end of the chapter you should have a clear sense of how anthropologists think about culture and use culture to analyze human life. By exploring this seemingly familiar concept, you can become conscious of the many unconscious patterns of belief and action that you accept as normal and natural. You can also begin to see how such patterns shape your everyday choices and even your basic

conceptions of what is real and what isn't. By examining the rich diversity and complexity of human cultural expressions, you may also begin to grasp more fully the potential and possibilities for your own life.

All humans must eat. But what we eat, how we eat, and who we eat with are shaped by local cultures. (*Top left*) a street market in Bangkok; Thailand; (*right*) an interfaith Passover Seder with Muslims and Jews in Guba, Azerbaijan; (*bottom left*) planning a business startup in London.

What Is Culture?

When people hear the word *culture*, they often think about the material goods or artistic forms produced by distinct groups of people—Chinese food, Middle Eastern music, Indian clothing, Greek architecture, African dances. Sometimes people assume that culture means elite art forms such as those displayed in museums, operas, or ballets. But for anthropologists, culture is much more: It encompasses people's entire way of life.

Culture is a system of knowledge, beliefs, patterns of behavior, artifacts, and institutions that are created, learned, shared, and contested by a group of people. Culture is our manual for understanding and interacting with the people and the world around us. It includes shared norms, values, symbols, mental maps of reality, and material objects as well as structures of power—including the media, education, religion, and politics—in which our understanding of the world is shaped, reinforced, and negotiated. A cultural group may be large or small, and it may have within it significant diversity of region,

culture: A system of knowledge, beliefs, patterns of behavior, artifacts, and institutions that are created, learned, shared, and contested by a group of people.

religion, race, gender, sexuality, class, generation, and ethnic identity. It may not be accepted by everyone, even those living in a particular place or time. But ultimately, the culture that we learn has the potential to shape our ideas of what is normal and natural, what we can say and do, and even what we can think.

Culture Is Learned and Taught

Humans do not genetically inherit culture. We learn culture throughout our lives from the people and cultural institutions that surround us. Anthropologists call the process of learning culture **enculturation**. Some aspects of culture we learn through formal instruction: English classes in school, religious instruction, visits to the doctor, history lessons, dance classes. Other processes of enculturation are informal and even unconscious as we absorb culture from family, friends, and the media. All humans are equally capable of learning culture and of learning any culture they are exposed to.

The process of social learning, passing cultural information within populations and across generations, is not unique to humans. Many animals learn social behavior from their immediate group: Wolves learn hunting strategies from the wolf pack. Whales learn to produce and distinguish the unique calls of their pod. Among monkeys and apes, our closest biological relatives, learned behaviors are even more common. Chimpanzees have been observed teaching their young to create rudimentary tools, stripping bark from a twig that they then insert into an anthill to extract a tasty and nutritious treat. But the human capacity to learn culture is unparalleled.

Culture is taught as well as learned. Humans establish cultural institutions as mechanisms for enculturating their members. Schools, medical and legal systems, media, and religious institutions promote the ideas and concepts that are considered central to the culture. Rules, regulations, laws, teachers, doctors, religious leaders, police officers, and sometimes militaries promote and enforce what is considered appropriate behavior and thinking.

Culture Is Shared Yet Contested

No individual has his or her own culture. Culture is a shared experience developed as a result of living as a member of a group. Through enculturation, humans learn how to communicate and establish patterns of behavior that allow life in community, often in close proximity and sometimes with limited resources. Cultures may be shared by groups, large and small. For example, anthropologists may speak of Indian culture (1 billion people), of U.S. culture (300 million people) or of the culture of the Yanomami tribe (several thousand people) living in the Amazonian rainforest. There may be smaller cultures within larger cultures. For instance, your college classroom has a culture, one that you must learn in order to succeed academically. A classroom culture includes shared

enculturation: The process of learning culture.

understandings of what to wear, how to sit, when to arrive or leave, how to communicate with classmates and the instructor, and how to challenge authority, as well as formal and informal processes of enculturation.

Although culture is shared by members of groups, it is also constantly contested, negotiated, and changing. Culture is never static. Just as cultural institutions serve as structures for promoting enculturation, they also serve as arenas for challenging, debating, and changing core cultural beliefs and behaviors. Intense debates erupt over school curriculums, medical practices, media content, religious practices, and government policies as members of a culture engage in sometimes dramatic confrontations about their collective purpose and direction.

How is culture learned and taught? Here, kindergartners learn Mandarin Chinese at the New York Chinese School.

Culture Is Symbolic and Material

Through enculturation, over time the members of a culture develop a shared body of cultural knowledge and patterns of behavior. Though anthropologists no longer think of culture as a completely separate, unique possession of a specific group of people, most argue that a common cultural core exists, at least among the dominant segments of the culture. Norms, values, symbols, and mental maps of reality are four elements that an anthropologist may consider in attempting to understand the complex workings of a culture. These are not universal; they vary from culture to culture. Even within a culture not everyone shares equally in that cultural knowledge, nor does everyone agree completely on it. But the elements of a culture powerfully frame what its participants can say, what they can do, and even what they think is possible and impossible, real or unreal.

Norms **Norms** are ideas or rules about how people should behave in particular situations or toward certain other people—what is considered "normal" and appropriate behavior. Norms may include what to wear on certain occasions such as weddings, funerals, work, and school; what you can say in polite company; how younger people should treat older people; and who you can date or, as the opening anecdote demonstrated, what you can eat when. Many norms are assumed, not written down. We learn them over time—consciously and unconsciously—and incorporate them into our patterns of daily living. Other norms are formalized in writing and made publicly available, such as a country's

norms: Ideas or rules about how people should behave in particular situations or toward certain other people.

laws, a system of medical or business ethics, or the code of academic integrity in your college or university. Norms may vary for segments of the population, imposing different expectations on men and women, for instance, or children and adults. Cultural norms may be widely accepted, but they also may be debated, challenged, and changed, particularly when norms enforced by a dominant group disadvantage or oppress a minority within the population.

Consider the question of whom you can marry. You may consider the decision to be a matter of personal choice, but in many cultures the decision is not left to the whims of young people. The results are too important. Often it is two families who arrange the marriage, not two individuals, although these patterns are under pressure from the globalization of Western cultural practices.

Cultures have clear norms, based on ideas of age, kinship, sexuality, race, religion, class, and legal status, that specify what is normal and what is not. Let's consider some extreme cases. In Nazi Germany, the Nuremburg Laws passed in 1935 banned marriage or sexual relations between German Jews and persons with German or related blood. From 1949 to 1985, South Africa's apartheid government, dominated by white lawmakers, declared marriage and sex between whites and "coloreds" (people of mixed race), Asians, and blacks to be a crime under the Prohibition of Mixed Marriages Act and the Immorality Act. In the history of the United States, as many as forty states passed anti-miscegenation laws—that is, laws barring interracial marriage and sex. Such laws targeted marriages between whites and nonwhites—primarily blacks, but also Asians and Native Americans. Only in 1967 did the U.S. Supreme Court unanimously rule (in *Loving v. Virginia*) that these laws were unconstitutional, thereby striking down statutes still on the books in sixteen states (all the former slave states plus Oklahoma).

Cultural norms may discourage *exogamy* (marriage outside one's "group") and encourage *endogamy* (marriage within one's "group"). Think about your own family. Who could you bring home to your parents? Could you cross boundaries of race, ethnicity, nationality, religion, class, or gender? Although U.S. culture has very few formal rules about whom one can marry—with some exclusions around age, sexuality, and certain kinship relations—cultural norms still powerfully inform and enforce our behavior.

Most people, though not all, accept and follow a culture's norms. If they choose to challenge the norms, other members of the culture have means for enforcing its standards, whether through

Jeanne Lowe sits beside a family portrait in her Hercules, California home, as she recalls how in 1948 she couldn't marry Bill Lowe, the man she loved, because the state banned interracial marriages.

shunning, institutionalized punishment such as fines or imprisonment, or, in more extreme cases, violence and threats of violence.

Values Cultures promote and cultivate a core set of **values**—fundamental beliefs about what is important, what makes a good life, and what is true, right, and beautiful. Values reflect shared ultimate standards that should guide people's behavior, as well as goals that people feel are important for themselves, their families, and their community. What would you identify as the core values of U.S. culture? Individualism? Independence? Care for the most vulnerable? Freedom of speech, press, and religion? Equal access to social mobility?

As with all elements of culture, cultural values are not fixed. They can be debated and contested. And they may have varying degrees of influence. For example, if you pick up a newspaper in any country you will find a deep debate about cultural values. Perhaps the debate focuses on modesty versus public displays of affection in India, economic growth versus environmental pollution in China, or land settlement versus peace in the Middle East. In the United States, while the value of privacy is held dear, so is the value of security. The proper balance of the two is constantly being contested and debated. Under what conditions should the U.S. government be able to breach your privacy by eavesdropping on telephone calls and emails, or unlocking your iPhone, in order to ensure your safety?

Ultimately, values are not simply platitudes about people's ideals about the good life. Values are powerful cultural tools for clarifying cultural goals and motivating people to action. When enshrined in law, values can become powerful political and economic tools. Values can be so potent that some people are willing to kill or die for them.

Symbols Cultures include complex systems of symbols and symbolic actions—in realms such as language, art, religion, politics, and economics—that convey meaning to other participants. In essence, a **symbol** is something that stands for something else. For example, language enables humans to communicate abstract ideas through the symbols of written and spoken words, as well as unspoken sounds and gestures (see Chapter 4). People shake hands, wave, whistle, nod, smile, give two thumbs up, give thumbs down, give someone the middle finger. These symbols are not universal, but within their particular cultural context they convey certain meanings.

Much symbolic communication is nonverbal, action-based, and unconscious. Religions include powerful systems of symbols that represent deeper meanings to their adherents. Consider mandalas, the Koran, the Torah, the Christian cross, holy water, statues of the Buddha—all carry greater meanings and value than the physical material they are constructed of. National flags, which are mere pieces of colored cloth, are symbols that stir deep political

values: Fundamental beliefs about what is important, what makes a good life, and what is true, right, and beautiful.

symbol: Anything that represents something else.

Money is symbolic, and only, 10 percent of the world's money exists in tangible form. Here traders move money electronically at Euronext stock exchange in Amsterdam, the Netherlands.

emotions. Even money is simply a symbolic representation of value guaranteed by the sponsoring government. It has no value, except in its symbolism. Estimates suggest that only about 10 percent of money today exists in physical form. The rest moves electronically through banks, stock markets, and credit accounts (Graeber 2011). Symbols change in meaning over time and from culture to culture. Not understanding another culture's collective understandings—sets of symbolic actions—can lead to embarrassing misunderstandings and cross-cultural miscues.

Mental Maps of Reality Along with norms, values, and symbols, another key component of culture is **mental maps of reality**. These are "maps" that humans construct of what kinds of people and what kinds of things exist. Because the world presents overwhelming quantities of data to our senses, our brains create shortcuts—maps—to navigate our experience and organize all the data that come our way. A roadmap condenses a large world into a manageable format (one that you can hold in your hands or view on your portable GPS system) and helps us navigate the territory. Likewise, our mental maps organize the world into categories that help us sort out our experiences and what they mean. We do not want all the details all the time. We could not handle them anyway. From our general mental maps we can then dig deeper as required.

Our mental maps are shaped through enculturation, but they are not fixed. Like other elements of culture, they can be challenged and redrawn. Today, globalization continues to put pressure on mental maps of reality as people on the planet are drawn into closer contact with the world's diversity. We will examine these transformations throughout this book, especially in chapters on language, race, ethnicity, gender, sexuality, and kinship.

mental maps of reality: Cultural classifications of what kinds of people and things exist, and the assignment of meaning to those classifications.

Mental maps have two important functions. *First, mental maps classify reality*. Starting in the eighteenth century, European naturalists such as Carolus Linnaeus (1707–1778) began creating systems of classification for the natural world. These systems included five kingdoms subdivided into phylum, class, order, family, genus, and species. Through observation (this was before genetics), these naturalists sought to organize a logical framework to divide the world into kinds of things and kinds of people. In a similar way, our cultures' mental maps seek to classify reality—though often a culture's mental maps are drawn from the distinct vantage point of those in power.

A culture creates a concept such as time. Then we arbitrarily divide it into millennia, centuries, decades, years, seasons, months, weeks, hours, morning, afternoon, evening, minutes, seconds. Categories of time are assumed to be scientific, universal, and "natural." But mostly they are cultural constructs. The current Gregorian calendar, which is used in much of the world, was introduced in 1582 by the Catholic Church, but its adoption occurred gradually; it was accepted in the United States in 1756, replacing the earlier Julian calendar, and in China in 1949. Until 1949 and still today, much of China relies on a lunar calendar in which months and days align with the waxing and waning of the moon. New Year's Day shifts each year. So do Chinese holidays and festivals. Even in the Gregorian calendar, the length of the year is modified to fit into a neat mental map of reality. A year (how long it takes Earth to orbit the sun) is approximately 365.2425 days long, so every four years the Gregorian calendar must add a day, creating a leap year of 366 days rather than 365.

Now check your watch. Even the question of what time it is depends on accepting a global system of time zones centered at the Greenwich meridian in England. But countries regularly modify the system according to their needs. The mainland United States has four time zones. China, approximately the same physical size, uses only one time zone. Russia has eleven. There is a time change of three and a half hours when you cross the border between China and Afghanistan. As these examples demonstrate, categories that seem completely fixed and "natural" are in reality flexible and variable, showing the potential role of culture in defining our fundamental notions of reality.

Mental maps of reality become problematic when people treat cultural notions of difference as being scientifically or biologically "natural." Race is a key example. As we will see in Chapter 6, the notion of race is assumed in popular culture and conversation to have a biological basis. There is, however, no scientific basis for this assumption. The particular racial categories in any given culture do not correlate directly to any biological differences. Although most people in the United States would name whites, blacks, Hispanics, Asians, and perhaps Native Americans as distinct races, no genetic line marks clear differences among these categories. The classifications are created

What does it mean to be a child laborer in your culture? (*Left*) a boy in Dhaka, Bangladesh, makes balloons for export; (*Right*) a girl in Nangarhar province, Afghanistan, works at a brick-making factory.

by our culture and are specific to our culture. Other cultures draw different mental maps of the reality of human physical variation. The Japanese use different racial categories than the United States. Brazilians have more than 500 racial classifications.

Second, mental maps assign meaning to what has been classified. Not only do people in a culture develop mental maps of things and people, they also place values and meanings on those maps. For example, we divide the life span into categories—infants, children, adolescents, teenagers, young adults, adults, and seniors, for example—but then we give different values to different ages. Some carry more respect, more protection, and more rights, privileges, and responsibilities. In the United States, these categories determine at what age you can marry, have sex, drink alcohol, drive, vote, go to war, stand trial, retire, or collect Social Security and Medicare benefits.

In considering the earlier discussion of time, we can see how these classifications gain value and meaning. U.S. culture puts a premium on time, discourages idle leisure, and encourages people to work hard and stay busy. "Time is money!" we often hear, and so it should not be wasted. Assuming that our mental maps of reality are natural can cause us to disregard the cultural values of others. For instance, we may see as lazy those whose cultures value a midday nap. This effect of our mental maps is important for anthropologists to understand (Wolf-Meyer 2012).

Ethnocentrism, Cultural Relativism, and Human Rights
Anthropology challenges the strong human tendency toward ethnocentrism, the belief that one's own culture or way of life is normal, natural, or even superior, and the tendency to use one's own culture to evaluate and judge the cultural

ideas and practices of others. With intensifying globalization, the world's people are increasingly confronting the diversity of global cultures. Multicultural encounters happen closer and closer to home. Anthropology seeks to broaden our worldview, to enable people to see their own culture as one expression within the context of global cultural diversity, and to recognize that what may seem unusual or unnatural from one cultural perspective may be normal and commonplace from another.

For generations, anthropologists have adopted an approach to cross-cultural research known as **cultural relativism** to counteract the effects of ethnocentrism on our work. Cultural relativism calls for the suspension of judgment while attempting to understand a group's beliefs and practices within their own cultural context. Anthropologists begin with the assumption that shared norms, values, beliefs, and practices make sense to the participants in a culture. The anthropologist's task is first to understand a culture's internal logic and system of meaning. Thus, anthropologists seek to objectively, accurately, and sensitively represent the diversity of human life and culture.

Anthropologists may at times struggle with situations in which the cultural practices they are studying do not match their own ideas of fairness and justice. The commitment to a research strategy of cultural relativism does not, however, require anthropologists to ignore their own sense of right and wrong, disregard international standards of human rights, or defend the cultural practices of a particular group. In fact, anthropologists frequently raise challenging questions on matters of human rights. Are there international human rights standards that should be available to all humans regardless of their particular culture or religion? What is a particular culture's ability to meet the basic human needs of its people, or of certain segments of a population that may be marginalized—needs for food, shelter, health, education, safety, and equal treatment under the law?

The American Anthropological Association's (AAA) Declaration on Anthropology and Human Rights draws heavily on international principles as articulated in three United Nations documents: the Universal Declaration of Human Rights, the International Covenant on Civil and Political Rights, and the International Covenant on Social, Economic, and Cultural Rights. Reflecting a commitment to cross-cultural research, the AAA's statement also warns against an overreliance on the abstract legal uniformity of Western traditions. Ultimately, each anthropologist must choose how to apply international standards of human rights to cultural practices considered in his or her research.

To fully grasp the anthropological understanding of culture, we will examine the historical development of the culture concept before turning our attention to more recent notions of culture as a system of meaning and as a system of power.

cultural relativism: Understanding a group's beliefs and practices within their own cultural context, without making judgments.

British anthropologist Edward Burnett Tylor.

How Has the Culture Concept Developed in Anthropology?

The concept of culture has been central to anthropology ever since the English anthropologist Edward Burnett Tylor (1832–1917) crafted his definition in the opening paragraph of his book *Primitive Culture* in 1871: "Culture or Civilization, taken in its wide ethnographic sense, is that complex whole which includes knowledge, belief, art, morals, law, custom and any other capabilities and habits acquired by man as a member of society."

Tylor understood culture to be a unified and complex system of ideas and behavior learned over time, passed down from generation to generation, and shared by members of a particular group. Over the past century and a half, culture has become more than a definition; it is now a key theoretical framework for anthropologists attempting to understand humans and their interactions.

Early Evolutionary Frameworks

Edward Burnett Tylor and James Frazer (1854–1941) of England and Lewis Henry Morgan (1818–1881) of the United States were among the leading early anthropologists who sought to professionalize a field long dominated by wealthy collectors of artifacts. They sought to organize the vast quantities of data about the diversity of cultures worldwide that were being accumulated through colonial and missionary enterprises during the nineteenth century. These anthropologists were influenced by Charles Darwin's theory of biological evolution (see Chapter 5), which maintains that the diversity of biological species resulted from gradual change over time in response to environmental pressures. Thus, they suggested that the vast diversity of cultures represented different stages in the evolution of human culture.

Early anthropologists suggested that all cultures would naturally evolve through the same sequence of stages, a concept known as **unilineal cultural evolution**. They set about plotting the world's cultures along a continuum from most simple to most complex, using the terms *savage*, *barbarian*, and *civilized*. Western cultures were, perhaps too predictably, considered the most evolved or civilized. By arranging all of the world cultures along this continuum, the early anthropologists believed that they could trace the path of human cultural evolution, understand where some cultures had come from, and predict where other cultures were headed.

While Tylor and others developed the theory of unilineal cultural evolution at least in part to combat the prevalent racist belief that many non-Europeans were of a different species, the theory has itself been criticized as racist for ranking different cultural expressions in a hierarchy with European culture, considered the ideal, at the apex (Stocking 1968). Franz Boas, the founder of American anthropology, and Bronislaw Malinowski, a Polish anthropologist who spent most of his life teaching in England, represent two main schools of anthropology that moved beyond the evolutionary framework for viewing cultural differences.

unilineal cultural evolution: The theory proposed by nineteenth-century anthropologists that all cultures naturally evolve through the same sequence of stages from simple to complex.

American Historical Particularism

Franz Boas (1858–1942) conducted fieldwork among the Kwakiutl indigenous people of the Pacific Northwest of the United States and Canada before becoming a professor of anthropology at Columbia University in New York and a curator of the American Museum of Natural History. Boas rejected unilineal cultural evolution, its generalizations, and its comparative method. Instead he advocated for an approach called **historical particularism**. He claimed that cultures arise from different causes, not uniform processes. According to Boas, anthropologists could not rely on an evolutionary formula to explain differences among cultures but must study the particular history of each culture to see how it developed. Evolutionists such as Tylor, Frazer, and Morgan argued that similarities among cultures emerged through independent invention as different cultures independently arrived at similar solutions to similar problems. Boas, in contrast, while not ruling out some independent invention, turned to the idea of *diffusion*—the borrowing of cultural traits and patterns from other cultures—to explain apparent similarities.

historical particularism: The idea, attributed to Franz Boas, that cultures develop in specific ways because of their unique histories.

Boas's belief in the powerful role of culture in shaping human life exhibited itself in his early twentieth-century studies of immigrants. His research with the children of immigrants from Europe revealed the remarkable effects of culture and environment on their physical forms, challenging the role of biology as a tool for discrimination. As a Jewish immigrant himself, Boas was particularly sensitive to the dangers of racial stereotyping, and his work throughout his career served to challenge white supremacy, the inferior ranking of non-European people, and other expressions of racism.

Boas's students Ruth Benedict (1887–1948) and Margaret Mead (1901–1979) continued his emphasis on the powerful role of culture in shaping human life and the need to explore the unique development of each culture. Benedict's popular studies, *Patterns of Culture* (1934) and *The Chrysanthemum and the Sword* (1946), explored the ways in which cultural traits and entire cultures are uniquely patterned and integrated. Mead conducted research in Samoa, Bali, and Papua New Guinea and became perhaps the most famous anthropologist of the twentieth century, promoting her findings and the unique tools of anthropology to the general American public.

American anthropologist Ruth Benedict.

Mead turned her attention particularly to enculturation and its powerful effects on cultural patterns and personality types. In her book *Coming of Age in Samoa* (1928), she explored the seeming sexual freedom and experimentation of Samoan young people and compared it with the repressed sexuality of young people in the United States, suggesting the important role of enculturation in shaping behavior—even behavior that is imagined to have powerful biological origins. Mead's controversial research and findings over her career challenged biological assumptions about gender, demonstrating cross-cultural variations in expressions of what it meant to be male or female, and contributing to heated debates about the roles of women and men in U.S. culture in the twentieth century.

British Structural Functionalism

Between the 1920s and 1960s, in a rejection of unilineal cultural evolution, many British social anthropologists viewed anthropology more as a science and field-work more as a science experiment that could focus on the specific details of a local **society**. These anthropologists viewed human societies as living organisms, and through fieldwork they sought to analyze each part of the "body." Each part of society—including the kinship, religious, political, and economic structures—fit together and had its unique function within the larger structure. Like a living organism, a society worked to maintain an internal balance, or equilibrium, that kept the system working. Under this conceptual framework, called **structural functionalism**, British social anthropologists employed a synchronic approach to control their science experiments—analyzing contemporary societies at a fixed point in time without regard to historical context. By isolating as many variables as possible, especially by excluding history and outside influences such as neighboring groups or larger national or global dynamics, these anthropologists sought to focus narrowly on the culture at hand.

Early practitioners of this approach included Bronislaw Malinowski (1884–1942), who used an early form of functionalism in his ethnography of the Trobriand Islands, *Argonauts of the Western Pacific* (1922), discussed in more detail in Chapter 3; and E. E. Evans-Pritchard (1902–1973) in his classic ethnography of the Sudan, *The Nuer* (1940), which we will consider further in Chapters 3 and 10. Later, British anthropologists, including Max Gluckman (1911–1975) in his work on rituals of rebellion, and Victor Turner (1920–1983) in his work on religious symbols and rituals, critiqued earlier structural functionalists for ignoring the dynamics of conflict, tension, and change within the societies they studied. Their intervention marked a significant turn in the study of society and culture by British anthropologists.

Culture and Meaning

One predominant view within anthropology in recent decades sees culture primarily as a set of ideas or knowledge shared by a group of people that provides a common body of information about how to behave, why to behave that way, and what that behavior means. The anthropologist Clifford Geertz (1926–2006), a key figure in this **interpretivist approach**, urged anthropologists to explore culture primarily as a symbolic system in which even simple, seemingly straightforward actions can convey deep meanings.

In a classic example, Geertz (1973c) examines the difference between a wink and a twitch of the eye. Both involve the same movement of the eye muscles, but the wink carries a meaning, which can change depending on the context in

society: The focus of early British anthropological research whose structure and function could be isolated and studied scientifically.

structural functionalism: A conceptual framework positing that each element of society serves a particular function to keep the entire system in equilibrium.

MAP 2.1
Trobriand Islands

interpretivist approach: A conceptual framework that sees culture primarily as a symbolic system of deep meaning.

MAP 2.2
Bali

thick description: A research strategy that combines detailed description of cultural activity with an analysis of the layers of deep cultural meaning in which those activities are embedded.

which it occurs. A wink can imply flirting, including a friend in a secret, or slyly signaling agreement. Deciphering the meaning requires a complex, collective (shared) understanding of unspoken communication in a specific cultural context. Collective understandings of symbols and symbolic actions enable people to interact with one another in subtle yet complex ways without constantly stopping to explain themselves.

Geertz's essay "Deep Play: Notes on the Balinese Cockfight" (1973a) describes in intricate detail a cockfight—a common activity even today in local communities across Bali, a small island in the South Pacific. Geertz describes the elaborate breeding, raising, and training of the roosters; the scene of bedlam at the fight; the careful selection of the birds; the rituals of the knife man, who provides the razors for the birds' feet; the fight itself; the raucous betting before and during the fight; and the aftermath, with the cutting up of the losing cock and the dividing of its parts among participants in the fight.

Geertz argues that such careful description of cultural activity is an essential part of understanding Balinese culture. But it is not enough. He claims that we must engage in **thick description**, looking beneath the surface activities to see the layers of deep cultural meaning in which those activities are embedded. The cockfight is not simply a cockfight. It also represents generations of competition among the village families for prestige, power, and resources within the community. It symbolizes the negotiation of those families' prestige status and standing within the larger groups. For Geertz, all activities of the cockfight reflect these deeper webs of meaning, and their analysis requires extensive description that uncovers those deeper meanings. Indeed, according to Geertz, every cultural action is more than the action itself; it is also a symbol of deeper meaning. (Even the seemingly simple act of eating, as described in the chapter opener, carries a deeper cultural meaning.)

Geertz's culture concept has provided a key theoretical framework for much of the anthropological research in following decades. But, as we will see in the following section, it has also been criticized for not adequately considering the relations of power within a culture and the contested processes by which cultural meanings—norms, values, symbols, mental maps of reality—are established.

How Are Culture and Power Related?

For many years, anthropologists focused primarily on culture as a system of ideas, as represented in the section you have just read. But more recent scholarship has pushed anthropology to consider the deep interconnections between culture and power in more sophisticated ways (Foucault 1977; Gramsci 1971; Wolf 1982), and the chapters of this book take this challenge seriously.

Power is often described as the ability or potential to bring about change through action or influence, either one's own or that of a group or institution. This may include the ability to influence through force or the threat of force. Power is embedded in many kinds of social relations, from interpersonal relations, to institutions, to structural frameworks of whole societies. In effect, power is everywhere and individuals participate in systems of power in complex ways. Throughout this book we will work to unmask the dynamics of power embedded in culture, including systems of power such as race and racism, ethnicity and nationalism, gender, human sexuality, economics, and family.

The anthropologist Eric Wolf (1923–1999) urged anthropologists to see power as an aspect of all human relationships. Consider the relationships in your own life: teacher/student, parent/child, employer/employee, landlord/tenant, lender/borrower, boyfriend/girlfriend. Wolf (1990, 1999) argued that all such human relationships have a power dynamic. Though cultures are often assumed to be composed of groups of similar people who uniformly share norms and values, in reality people in a given culture are usually diverse and their relationships are complicated.

Power in a culture reflects **stratification**—uneven distribution of resources and privileges—among participants that often persists over generations. Some people are drawn into the center of the culture. Others are ignored, marginalized, or even annihilated. Power may be stratified along lines of gender, racial or ethnic group, class, age, family, religion, sexuality, or legal status. These structures of power organize relationships among people and create a framework through which access to cultural resources is distributed. As a result, some people are able to participate more fully in the culture than others. This balance of power is not fixed; it fluctuates over time. By examining the way access to the resources,

power: The ability or potential to bring about change through action or influence.

stratification: The uneven distribution of resources and privileges among participants in a group or culture.

privileges, and opportunities of a culture are shared unevenly and unequally, we can begin to use culture as a conceptual guide to power and its workings.

Power and Cultural Institutions

One key to understanding the relationship between culture and power is to recognize that a culture is more than a set of ideas or patterns of behavior shared among a collection of individuals. A culture also includes the powerful institutions that these people create to promote and maintain their core values. Ethnographic research must consider a wide range of institutions that play central roles in the enculturation process. For example, schools teach a shared history, language, patterns of social interaction, notions of health, and scientific ideas of what exists in the world and how the world works. Religious institutions promote moral and ethical codes of behavior. The various media convey images of what is considered normal, natural, and valued. Other prominent cultural institutions that reflect and shape core norms and values include the family, medicine, government, courts, police, and the military.

A young Muslim woman with two French flags pulled over her head covering marches in Paris against a French ban on religious symbols, including head coverings, in public schools.

These cultural institutions are also locations where people can debate and contest cultural norms and values. In 2003, an intense debate erupted in France about Muslim girls wearing headscarves to public schools. Although few girls actually wore headscarves, the controversy took on particular intensity in the aftermath of the events of September 11, 2001, the invasions of Afghanistan and Iraq, and terrorist incidents in Europe. For many non-Muslim people in France, the wearing of head coverings represented a grave danger to French society, particularly its commitment to equality for women, its history of ethnic assimilation, and its tradition of the separation of church and state. Passage of a law banning the headscarf from public schools was intended as a signal (to people both inside and outside France) of the country's commitment to these principles. But many Muslim girls believed that wearing the head scarf also expressed a commitment to French values—the country's commitment to religious freedom and liberty.

Despite legal challenges, strikes by students, and street demonstrations in opposition to the law, in 2004 the French government banned any clothing in public schools that indicates particular religious beliefs. Although the language of the law was broadly stated to include all religions, everyone understood that the headscarves of Muslim girls were the target. France's public schools had become the venue for debating, contesting, and enforcing key French cultural norms and values (Bowen 2006). As we will see, cultural institutions such as schools are not only places where norms are enforced, but also places where powerful ideas of what is normal and natural are shaped.

Hegemony

The Italian political philosopher Antonio Gramsci (1891–1937) described two aspects of power. *Material power,* the first component, includes political, economic, or military power. It exerts itself through coercion or brute force. The second aspect of power involves the ability to create consent and agreement within a population, a condition that Gramsci (1971) called **hegemony**.

Gramsci recognized the tremendous power of culture—particularly the cultural institutions of media, schools, and religion—to shape, often unconsciously, what people think is normal, natural, and possible, and thereby directly influence the scope of human action and interaction. Cultures, which develop slowly over time, include a shared belief system of what is right and what is wrong, and what is normal and appropriate. In this hegemony of ideas, some thoughts and actions become unthinkable, and group members develop a set of "beliefs" about what is normal and appropriate that come to be seen as natural "truths." The French sociologist Michel Foucault (1926–1984), in *Discipline and Punish* (1977), described this hegemonic aspect of power as the ability to make people discipline their own behavior so that they believe and act in certain "normal" ways—often against their own interests, even without a tangible threat of punishment for misbehavior.

Jean and John Comaroff describe the workings of hegemony in their study of colonialism in South Africa, particularly in the interaction between indigenous Tswana-speaking people and British missionaries between 1820 and 1920. Whereas

hegemony: The ability of a dominant group to create consent and agreement within a population without the use or threat of force.

Presbyterians at their main rural mission station in Tembuland, South Africa.

British colonialists used force to establish military and economic control over South Africa, British missionaries sought to convert Africans to Christianity by convincing them of the supremacy of an alternative set of worldviews. Missionary churches and schools introduced Christian ideas embedded in European images and messages about numerous cultural practices, including education, language, notions of ritual, rainmaking, time, clothing, and architecture, as well as relationships of gender, kinship, and property. The Comaroffs show how, instead of through military conquest, missionaries attempted to change these indigenous people by redefining how they thought about their everyday lives. Though the Tswana often contested the missionaries' worldviews, this new hegemony gradually influenced fundamental notions of what was normal, thinkable, doable, and sayable in South Africa for generations that followed (Comaroff and Comaroff 1991).

MAP 2.3
South Africa

Earlier in this chapter we discussed anti-miscegenation laws in the history of the United States. These laws drew upon cultural beliefs in "natural" biological differences among races and the seemingly unnatural, deviant practice of intermarriage. Despite the elimination of these formal laws, a certain hegemony of thought remains: Many in U.S. culture still see interracial marriage as unthinkable and undoable. As evidence, consider current intermarriage rates in the United States (Figure 2.1). According to the U.S. Census Bureau (2010), there were 5,303,000 interracial married couples in 2010, only 8.78 percent of all marriages in the U.S.

Clearly, although U.S. culture has very few formal rules about whom one can marry, cultural norms combined with long-term geographic and institutional patterns of segregation still powerfully inform and enforce our behavior.

FIGURE 2.1 U.S. Interracial Marriage Patterns, 2010

INTERRACIAL MARRIAGES

Interracial couples
8.78%

Same-race couples
91.22%

White–Hispanic	3.32% (2,005,000)
White–Asian	1.24% (748,000)
Black–White	0.83% (504,000)
Black–Hispanic	0.21% (129,000)
Black–Asian	0.08% (48,000)
More than one/some other race	3.10% (1,869,000)

SOURCE: *U.S. Census Bureau. 2010. "America's Families and Living Arrangements: 2010," Table FG3. www.census.gov/hhes/families/files/cps2010/tabFG4-all.xls.*

As this example shows, views against interracial marriage do not require legal sanction to remain dominant, hegemonic norms.

Human Agency

Although hegemony can be very powerful, it does not completely dominate people's thinking. Individuals and groups have the power to contest cultural norms, values, mental maps of reality, symbols, institutions, and structures of power—a potential known as **agency**. Cultural beliefs and practices are not timeless; they change and can be changed. Cultures are not biologically determined; they are created over time by particular groups of people. By examining human agency, we see how culture serves as a realm in which battles over power take place—where people debate, negotiate, contest, and enforce what is considered normal, what people can say, do, and even think.

Although a dominant group may have greater access to power, resources, rights, or privileges, the systems of power they create are never absolute, and their dominance is never complete. Individuals and groups with less power or no power may contest the dominant power relationships and structures, whether through political, economic, religious, or military means. At times these forms of resistance are visible, public, and well organized, including negotiations, protests, strikes, or rebellions. At other times the resistance may be more subtle, discreet, and diffuse.

For example, James Scott's book *Weapons of the Weak: Everyday Forms of Peasant Resistance* (1985) identifies strategies that people in very weak positions use to express their agency and to resist the dominant group. Scott focuses on a village in northwestern Malaysia that has undergone rapid economic transformation as a result of technological changes in the local rice-growing process. The introduction of large-scale irrigation, double cropping, and harvesting machines has made the harvest more plentiful but has also thrown many landless farmers out of work. The changes have benefited the village elite (mostly Chinese) and hurt the poor (mostly Malay). In light of these stark inequalities, Scott asks why the poor farmers who are the majority do not revolt and overturn the social and economic order that makes them poor and keeps them poor. Scott suggests that the poor farmers understand the potential risks of resistance and the dangerous consequences for themselves and their families that could result from a conflict with the rich and powerful minority. So they often avoid obvious, public displays of resistance and choose subtler, nonconfrontational forms of resistance, including foot-dragging, slowdowns, theft, sabotage, trickery, arson, and false compliance with regulations.

Some scholars question whether these are really forms of resistance because they are not aimed at, and do not necessarily achieve, change. But Scott argues that not all resistance is revolutionary and that many acts of everyday resistance can bring change over time. Through these processes of contestation, the norms and values, mental maps of reality, symbols, organizations, and institutions that

agency: The potential power of individuals and groups to contest cultural norms, values, mental maps of reality, symbols, institutions, and structures of power.

MAP 2.4
Malaysia

appear to be timeless and accepted are actually undergoing constant change and renegotiation as people express their human agency even in the face of overwhelming displays of power.

How Much of Who You Are Is Shaped by Biology, and How Much by Culture?

Biology is important. We live in our bodies, after all. We feel, smell, taste, hear, and see the world around us through our bodies. We communicate with and through our bodies. And, yes, we have certain biological drives that are essential for survival. All humans must eat, drink, and sleep. But current research in physical and cultural anthropology shows that no matter how strong our biological needs or our hormones, odors, and appetites might be, culture and the environment in which we live exert powerful influences on what we think, on how we behave, on the shape and functions of our individual bodies, and even on how humans have evolved over time.

Nature and Nurture

Popular American discourse often assigns biology—and usually genes—the primary role in determining who we are. Anthropological research, however, consistently reveals the powerful role culture and environment play in shaping our lives and bodies. Human genetic codes are 99.9 percent identical, so if behavior were entirely driven by our genes, we should expect to find very similar—even universal—behavioral responses to biological influences. Instead we find remarkable physical and behavioral variety across cultures. Even the most basic human activities, such as eating, drinking, and sleeping, are carried out in remarkably distinct ways. All humans must do these things. But shared biological needs do not ensure shared cultural patterns.

Of course, food and liquid enter the body through the mouth and get digested in the stomach and intestines. But what goes in and how it goes in are other stories. Perhaps you find dog or snake or pony to be inedible, although these are delicacies in other cultures. Many Chinese dislike cheese, a staple of North American and European diets. Even how and where you eat and drink, or how many times a day, varies from culture to culture. You may use forks, knives, spoons, chopsticks, or hands. You may eat once a day, three times a day, or—like many Americans—six times a day (breakfast, "coffee break," lunch, afternoon snack, dinner, midnight snack). You may prefer caviar or a Happy Meal.

Everyone sleeps each day, but some people sleep six hours a night, others eight. Americans nap, Argentinians take a siesta, and Chinese *xiu-xi*. Many college students average six hours of sleep a night during the week and ten on the weekend. Whom you sleep with also varies by culture, with variations including husbands and wives, parents and children, siblings, mothers and children, grandparents and grandchildren. All these patterns vary by culture, and even within a culture they may vary by age, gender, and class.

Assessing Evolutionary Perspectives

Despite the cross-cultural evidence of human behavioral variation, many popular debates continue to claim that basic patterns of human behavior, intellectual capacity, and psychological tendencies are determined by biology, from warfare and sexuality to the shortage of women in math and science careers. Today for instance, popular psychology commonly suggests that the problems men have with women (and vice versa) can be traced to evolutionary differences. One popular relationship self-help book, which has sold over 50 million copies, even suggests that *Men Are from Mars and Women Are from Venus* (Gray 1993). The title implies that men and women are so fundamentally different that they might as well be different species from different planets.

These popular notions draw heavily on the work of evolutionary psychologists (see Buss 1991, 1999; Tooby and Cosmides 1992) who believe that fundamental aspects of who we are, how we think and behave, and how we organize our societies are directly related to how we evolved over millions of years and are hardwired in our DNA. They argue that (1) patterns of survival, which developed when humans were primarily hunters and gatherers, selected for different physical and mental abilities among men and women, and (2) these abilities became fixed in our DNA and continue to evidence themselves in patterns of life today and, in fact, drive much of human behavior (Pinker 2002). So, the argument goes, as hunters, men developed better spatial skills and higher levels of aggression. Women, the gatherers, stayed closer to home and became more nurturing and empathetic. These evolutionary processes, it is suggested, explain gender differences today.

Most anthropologists have been highly critical of evolutionary psychological approaches for significantly overstating the importance of a genetic inheritance fixed in deep evolutionary time and for underestimating the role of culture and the environment in shaping human physical and behavioral diversity (McKinnon and Silverman 2005). Anthropological studies of hunter-gatherer societies have shown that the division of roles imagined by evolutionary psychologists was never so distinct (Fedigan 1986; Stange 1997). Men also gathered, women also hunted, and there were many other shared social tasks as well. Although contemporary genetic discoveries are opening new realms of understanding about human biology, we are not close to linking certain genes or groups of genes with particular behaviors or characteristics. At best, we can imagine these connections based on contemporary patterns of behavior. But it often appears just as likely that contemporary and culturally specific—largely Euro-American—notions of human nature are being projected back onto a mythological version of human prehistory.

Epigenetics and the Human Genome

The most recent scientific research reveals the ways culture and the environment can directly affect our bodies and the workings of our DNA. The Human Genome Project, launched in 1990, completed mapping the human genome in 2003. Hailed for its potential to uncover the mysteries of human variation, more than a decade later many questions remain about how exactly genes contribute to physical variation. While genetic studies have emphasized the analysis of the gene sequence with which one is born, an emerging field of **epigenetics** has begun to explore ways in which the environment into which one is born can directly affect the expression of genes during one's lifetime. In particular, epigenetics examines variations caused not by changes in the actual DNA sequence but by environmental factors that switch genes on and off and affect how cells read genes. The epigenetic marks may change in response to many of the processes anthropologists frequently study—nutrition, stress, disease, social inequality, and migration. A genetic disposition for aggression or violence must be "turned on" to lead to violent behavior. Living in a happy home decreases that likelihood. Poverty, a dysfunctional family life, and abuse all increase these chances. Epigenetic marks can be inherited across generations, facilitating intergenerational transmission of environmental information that may shape the direction of evolutionary change within the species (Fuentes 2013; Thayer and Non 2015; Wade and Ferree 2015).

epigenetics: An area of study in the field of genetics exploring ways environmental factors directly affect the expression of genes in ways that may be inherited between generations.

The Human Microbiome

Even our notions of discrete, distinct, and autonomous biological bodies are proving to be cultural stories rather than scientific fact. The human body contains approximately 100 trillion cells. About 90 percent are independent microorganisms that live within our bodies and form what has come to be known as the **human microbiome**. This microbiome weighs about as much as the human brain, includes a vast array of microorganisms and their genes, and plays a key role in many bodily functions, including human digestion, vitamin production, drug metabolism, and immunity. Humans and our microbes are functionally a large, interdependent, symbiotic community that works as a unit and has direct effects on human health and disease, such as allergies, asthma, chemotherapy effectiveness, heart disease, and weight loss. Until now, studies of human evolution have focused on the 10 percent of our cells and 0.7 percent of our genes that we typically call human. But with deeper awareness of our microbiome, future research may illuminate how the other 90 percent of our cells and 99.3 percent of the genes in our microbiome have evolved over time. Certainly industrialization, globalization, and modern sanitation have significantly changed our relationship to our environment and to our microbiome (Palsson 2013; Warinner and Lewis 2015).

human microbiome: The complete collection of microorganisms in the human body's ecosystem.

From Human Beings to Human Becomings

While genes clearly play an important role in human evolution and individual human development, the emerging science of epigenetics reveals that our genes are highly susceptible to environmental factors. And research into the human microbiome shows that our bodies do not function in isolation as discrete biological units as our popular cultural narratives would lead us to believe. Contemporary anthropological research calls for a much more complex view of human evolution and individual development over a lifetime that incorporates multiple architects of the human physical form and behavior. An emerging synthesis looks at genes as part of a developmental history in which biology and culture are deeply intertwined and entangled in a dynamic and ongoing biocultural process of change (Fuentes 2013). Some scholars (see Ingold and Palsson 2013) suggest that these new formulations should lead us to think of ourselves not as human beings—shaped long ago by a completed evolutionary process—but as human *becomings* who are continually evolving and adapting, both on the species level and within the individual lifespan.

Connecting Culture and Behavior

While direct links between specific genes and behavior have proven difficult to identify, we have much clearer indications of the ways cultural patterns and beliefs shape human behavior. Culture is learned from the people around us. It is not written into our DNA. Instead we are born with the ability to learn any culture that we might be born into or move into. We have the ability to learn any language and master any set of beliefs, practices, norms, or values. This may seem obvious, but it is a crucial principle to understand as we examine the many cultural patterns in our own experience that we regard as normal, even natural. Such cultural practices are not universal to all humans. Rather, they are uniquely created in each culture. Recognition of this fact allows us to question the biological basis for most if not all of human behavior and to consider how learned patterns of belief and practice have been created and how they might be changed. Later in this book, in the chapters on race, ethnicity, gender, family, and human sexuality, we will explore the intersections of biology and culture in further detail.

As popular as it may be to think that nature has driven our development as humans, even our long evolutionary process has been deeply influenced by culture. Ultimately, it is culture that has made us human, enabling us to evolve physically and in our patterns of relationship with others. When we examine human origins in Chapter 5, we will begin to see, for example, that with the development of simple stone tools as early as 2.5 million years ago, culture allowed our ancestors to adapt to the world around them. Stone tools (in particular, hand axes and choppers) enabled our ancestors to butcher meat more quickly and efficiently, thereby providing higher quantities of protein for the developing brain and influencing the direction of our physical adaptation. In cases such as these, the power of culture to direct and modify biological instincts is indisputable. Over time, cultural adaptations—from the control of fire, to the development of language, to the invention of condoms and birth control pills—have replaced genetic adaptations as the primary way humans adapt to and manipulate their physical and social environments.

How Is Culture Created?

Culture does not emerge out of the blue. It is created over time, shaped by people and the institutions they establish in relationship to the environment around them. Culture is not fixed. It is invented, changed, contested, and negotiated. Nor is it bounded. It moves and flows across regions and between people. Just as we have examined the relationship between culture and power, we can analyze the processes through which culture is created by considering the origins of a consumer culture as part of twentieth-century capitalism.

Culture and economics are closely linked. The German political philosopher Max Weber (1864–1920), in his book *The Protestant Ethic and the Spirit of Capitalism* (1905), linked the emergence of capitalism in Europe directly to the cultural ideas of Protestant Christianity that developed in the seventeenth century. Weber suggests that although the material conditions for the emergence of capitalism were present in other cultures, those cultures lacked the necessary

William Ury
Negotiating Anthropologically

Anthropologist William Ury specializes as a mediator and negotiation advisor in conflicts from workplace disputes to labor strikes to ethnic wars in the Middle East, the Balkans, and the former Soviet Union. More recently, he has been involved in helping to end a civil war in Indonesia and helping to prevent one in Venezuela. An author of numerous books, including *Getting to Yes* (Fisher, Ury, and Patton 2012) and *The Power of a Positive No* (Ury 2007), Ury was the co-founder of Harvard University's Program on Negotiation and is currently a Distinguished Senior Fellow of the Harvard Negotiation Project.

In his work of conflict resolution, Ury sees a deep connection between anthropology and mediation and negotiation: "At the heart of anthropology is the ability to put yourself in the shoes of someone whose culture on the surface seems quite different from your own. That is the essential competence of mediation as well. Mediators need the ability to put themselves in the shoes of both parties, or all parties, to try to understand how they see the world and what their interests and needs are. We need to try to understand "the other" from within their frame of reference, and then try to understand the rules of the game as they see them."

Central to Ury's conflict-resolution strategy is the concept of the third side. Although many conflicts involve two opposing sides, Ury works to resolve conflicts by mobilizing the surrounding community—the third side—around the conflict. The third side plays a constructive role in the negotiations by reminding the arguing parties what is really at stake, thus helping to restore a sense of perspective to an often emotionally charged situation.

"Yes, we're capable of violence. We're also capable of cooperating and resolving our differences. Each of us has the ability to exert peer pressure and use the power of community to prevent conflicts, to resolve conflicts that arise, and to contain those conflicts that might escalate.

"That to me is the essential challenge today in this world: How do we mobilize a third side powerful enough to become a container for the conflicts that exist in today's world? How do we transform those conflicts from destructive forms such as violence to constructive forms such as cooperation? But the third side is not new. It is actually an articulation of patterns that humans have developed over our evolutionary trajectory to survive, function, and thrive—patterns that our cultures have forgotten or moved away from. We're having to rediscover the third side. That's what's interesting. We're having to reinvent what is actually our most ancient of human heritages for dealing with conflict. The challenge before us is to translate the third side into forms that work in today's system.

"I've had the privilege over the last thirty-five years of having a front-seat view of a revolution taking place around the planet—a revolution in the way that human beings make decisions. I think of it as the negotiation revolution. A generation or two ago, the principal method for making decisions in most areas in life was pretty much top-down. The people on the top of the pyramid gave the orders, and

Anthropologist William Ury

the people on the bottom followed them. But there's been a process, a trend, that goes back several centuries in some cases, but is most evident in the past thirty years, toward a flattening of those pyramids of power into organizational forms that resemble networks. As this happens, decision-making changes gradually from vertical to horizontal, from top-down orders to joint problem-solving. Today, in order to get something done, we are more and more reliant on people over whom we exercise no direct control. This is increasingly true in politics in democracies, in work, and at home. So, effectively, what we're doing is negotiating all the time—restoring negotiation as one of the preeminent forms of making decisions. And because there's often no clear authority that enforces what to do, it means we need to turn to the third side, with the use of mediation and community councils, for example, to help resolve issues that can't be resolved by both sides alone.

"Amazingly, this heritage comes from our hunter-gatherer ancestors. Hunting and gathering was the dominant form of human subsistence for 99 percent of our history. Today this way of life is disappearing from the face of the planet. I find it fascinating that we are experiencing at just this time a phenomenon I like to think of as 'the great recurrence.' There's a way in which many of the older patterns and organizational forms, particularly of cooperation, are reemerging in a new way. Acknowledging the huge difference in conditions today, there are some striking similarities between the world we are now entering and the world that our hunter-gatherer ancestors faced. Today you see humans roaming around the globe again, increasingly nomadic, and also being dependent upon resources that aren't concentrated as land and crops are. Today our principal resource appears to be information, which is also scattered and requires a lot of cooperation to produce. The basic organizational form that increasingly seems to work in today's information society is more horizontal and less hierarchical. In this time of horizontal relationships, we need to reinvent the third side, which is our oldest human heritage for transforming conflict."

In thinking about the significance of anthropology, Ury offers this insight: "In a macro sense, right now we are living in an era in which, for the first time in the human story, thanks to the communications revolution, thanks to the Internet, thanks to other processes of globalization, all the human tribes on the planet are in touch with each other. Thousands of language groups—call them tribes if you like—are all in touch. Future anthropologists may look back one day and call it the era of the 'human family reunion.' Like many family reunions, this one is not all peace and light. There are a lot of injustices and resentments. So the question is: How are we going to get along? How are we going to understand each other? Anthropology is a key discipline to understand what's going on at this macro level.

"Then at a micro level, because the classroom is becoming more and more multicultural, students are going to see evidence of the human family reunion right there in the classroom. How do you understand 'the other'? How do you understand other cultures, other ways of seeing the world? This ability to understand the other is actually critical to success at work, whether you work in the nonprofit sector, in business, or in government. It's the essential perspective you need to be able to negotiate for what you want and need, because you're likely going to be dealing with people who come from very different backgrounds. The ability to understand others and to negotiate in this diverse world depends crucially on the basic competencies that you learn in anthropology."

> *The ability to understand others and to negotiate in this diverse world depends crucially on the basic competencies that you learn in anthropology.*

values to allow capitalism to take hold. In contrast, thrift, modesty, moderation, frugality, and self-denial—values Weber considered central to the "Protestant ethic"—led to a very particular relationship to the accumulation of capital that enabled early capitalism to flourish in the West. As capitalism has grown and shifted over the centuries into its present global form, so has the culture that supports and shapes it.

Manufacturing the Desire to Consume

Twentieth- and early twenty-first-century global capitalism is deeply tied to a culture of consumerism that has emerged with the support and promotion of corporations, governments, and financial institutions. The culture of consumerism includes norms, values, beliefs, practices, and institutions that have become commonplace and accepted as normal and that cultivate the desire to acquire consumer goods to enhance one's lifestyle (McCracken 1991, 2005).

Advertising, marketing, and financial services industries work to transform the cultural values of frugality, modesty, and self-denial of the old Protestant ethic into patterns of spending and consumption associated with acquiring the material goods of a middle-class lifestyle. The culture of consumerism promotes spending and consumption even when people don't have money. Today, through global marketing and media advertising campaigns, increased trade, and rising migration, the desire for this lifestyle is being promoted around the world. Over the last few decades, following economic and political reforms in India, China, Russia, and the Middle East, hundreds of millions more people are now seeking that middle-class lifestyle seen on television and advertised on the Internet. This trend is placing incredible stress on the planet's natural resources and environment.

In many parts of the world, consumerism has become more than an economic activity. It is a way of life, a way of looking at the world—a culture. In fact, many key cultural rituals now focus on consumption. In the United States, holidays such as Valentine's Day, Mother's Day, and Father's Day all promote the purchase of gifts, as do birthdays, weddings, and anniversaries. Christmas, which in early U.S. history featured public drinking, lewd behavior, and aggressive begging, by the nineteenth century was being transformed into a family-centered ritual of gift giving by parents to children. Moreover, the invented character of Santa Claus was promoted as the mythical mediator of gift exchange and the symbol of Christmas consumer marketing (Nissenbaum 1996).

What stirs your desire to consume? Shopping on Black Friday at Macy's flagship location in New York. Black Friday, the day after Thanksgiving, marks the start of the U. S. holiday shopping season.

College Students and Consumer Culture

College students are not immune to efforts to create a consumer culture. In fact, you are deeply immersed in it. With your classmates, try this collective project. Ask yourself what you need to have in order to feel like an average college student. Think about all the things you own. List your electronics (computer, cell phone, iPod, television, sound system) and your school supplies (books, notebooks, pens, calculator, backpack). Go through your closets and dressers and list your clothing. Don't forget your clothes for different seasons and special occasions, as well as accessories (bags, hats, belts, and shoes) and grooming items and cosmetics. Include your mode of transportation, household furnishings, appliances, and so on. Once you have created your own list or a collective list with your classmates, continue your analysis with a few questions: Did you find differences based on gender, age, race, or ethnic identity? Where were things made, and what does that suggest to you about globalization? What did all of these things cost? Now ask yourself whether each of these are things that you *need* or things that you *want*. For all of those items you identify as things you want more than you absolutely need, ask yourself how the desire to acquire them—to consume them—was aroused and cultivated. Take into account our discussion about how culture is created, and consider how those insights can be applied to this exercise.

Advertising

The advertising industry is key in arousing our desires for goods and services. Consider that children in the United States watch up to 40,000 television commercials a year (Vitelli 2013). In addition, they are bombarded with advertising on the Internet, cell phones, mp3 players, video games, and YouTube videos. Many children's television programs are themselves thinly disguised advertisements for products featuring their characters, from lunch boxes to clothing to action figures. Advertising appears before and during movies in the theater, at sporting events, in department stores and shopping malls, on billboards, and in store windows. Your favorite websites and social media are covered with advertisements. So are your clothes. Even your classroom is full of advertisements that you most likely do not notice: all the labels and tags on computers, pens, notebooks, backpacks, food packaging, and soda cans.

Advertising is a powerful tool of enculturation, teaching us how to be "successful" in consumer culture, how to be cool and normal. Commercials promise that clothes, perfume, deodorant, haircuts, and expensive gifts will bring us love. Having our teeth straightened and whitened will help us network. A large, expensive car and proper insurance will protect our families and make us responsible and mature men and women. Magazines, television shows, and films promote stars we are encouraged to emulate. If only we could dress like them and imitate their lifestyles, then we would be more desirable. The culture of consumerism tells us that having these things will bring us better friends, better sex, stronger families, higher-paying jobs, fancier houses, faster cars, sharper picture definition, and truer sound quality. Do you find yourself believing this is true?

Financial Services and Credit Cards

The financial services industry makes sure that once our desires are aroused, we have access to money to make our dreams a reality—at a small price. With the advent of computers and the deregulation of banking in the 1970s, credit cards burst on the scene, transforming the financial environment. Banks, chain stores, and financial services corporations carry out intensive marketing to promote their cards. In 2015, the average American carried 2.24 credit cards, and U.S. credit card debt was $712 billion, an average of $15,355 per household (DiGangi 2016; El Issa 2015).

College students are a key target of the credit industry, which promotes credit cards on campus and through the mail regardless of students' ability to repay. Credit cards grease the wheels of consumer culture. To pay them off, we need to intensify our participation: Work harder. Make more money. Then we can shop more. Underlying these shifts is the fundamental drive of contemporary capitalism for perpetual growth. People need to buy, make, invest, and profit more and more each year if the economy is to keep growing. And so contemporary capitalism invests heavily to arouse our desire and promote the expansion of the culture of consumerism.

As credit card limits maxed out in the 1990s, banks and mortgage companies encouraged homeowners to refinance their homes, taking out second mortgages to pay for day-to-day expenses and speculating that housing prices would remain high and continue to increase. Unfortunately, in the latter part of the 2000s housing prices collapsed, homeowners owed more in mortgages than the remaining value of their homes, loan payments were missed, and banks and financial service companies placed millions of homes into foreclosure. These outcomes are indicative of the pitfalls of the twentieth- and early twenty-first centuries' emphasis on a capitalistic consumer culture.

How Is Globalization Transforming Culture?

Cultures have never been made up of completely isolated or bounded groups of people located in a particular place. As we discussed in Chapter 1, anthropologists resist the myths of isolated and "primitive" groups who have lived on their own without contact. Encounter, interaction, movement, and exchange have been much more fundamental aspects of humanity. Cultures have always been influenced by the flow of people, ideas, and goods, whether through migration, trade, or invasion. Today's flows of globalization are intensifying the exchange and diffusion of people, ideas, and goods, creating more interaction and engagement among cultures. Let's consider three key interrelated effects of globalization on local cultures: homogenization, the global flows of culture through migration, and increased cosmopolitanism.

The Global and Local in Tension: Homogenizing or Diversifying

The development of global corporations, products, and markets has led some anthropologists and cultural activists to warn of a homogenized, global culture dominated by McDonald's, Levi's, Coca-Cola, CNN, Hollywood, and U.S. cultural values. Will the spread of this culture—fueled by goods, images, and ideas from Western cultures—create a homogenizing process that will diminish the diversity of the world's cultures as foreign influences inundate local practices, products, and ways of thinking?

Let's consider McDonald's. Launched in the 1940s in San Bernardino, California, today McDonald's operates in 119 countries. And though McDonald's is a global brand, as the company has expanded it has adapted its menu in response to local tastes and culinary traditions, local laws, and religious beliefs. In Egypt, where McDonald's has over seventy locations, the menu includes McFalafel Sandwiches. In Morocco and other parts of the Middle East, the McArabia, a grilled chicken sandwich, is served on flatbread. McDonald's serves a teriyaki McBurger in Japan, McSpaghetti in the Philippines, and certified halal food in Malaysia. It has kosher stores in Israel, McCurrywurst hot sausages in Germany, and the McBurrito in Mexico. Clearly local cultures need not be homogenized by global encounters but may instead transform global practices and commodities to reflect their local character.

A McDonald's restaurant in downtown Manila, capital of the Philippines, advertises the McDo Rice Burger, a local product added to McDonald's standard global menu.

To many people in developing countries, the elements of global culture symbolically represent the opportunity for economic advancement and participation in the idealized middle-class lifestyle of consumption associated with these consumer products. In *Golden Arches East: McDonald's in East Asia* (1998), James Watson suggests that East Asians in Tokyo, Japan; Seoul, Korea; Hong Kong; Beijing, China; and Taipei, Taiwan, go to McDonald's not so much for the food but to participate in what they view as a middle-class activity. By eating out and eating Western

THE SOCIAL LIFE OF THINGS
Blue Jeans: Global Production and Local Culture

Americans love their blue jeans. The pants are comfortable yet tough, intimate yet anonymous. They shape to fit the contours of our bodies. You can dress them up or dress them down. Blue jeans are also a global fashion phenomenon. On average, people worldwide own 2.6 pairs and wear them 3.5 days a week. On any given day the majority of people in the world may be wearing blue jeans (Miller and Woodward 2011). How do anthropologists make sense of the global love of this seemingly ordinary pair of trousers?

1 A simple pair of jeans passes through many hands in a global production process. Designed and commissioned by global corporations, jeans are made in 60 to 70 countries by 30–40 million workers, primarily young women laboring in sweatshop conditions in developing countries in what amounts to a global assembly line. Cotton may come from Turkey, thread from North Carolina, and woven fabric from Italy before being sewn in Cambodia, and then dyed, chemically washed, and distressed in factories in Mexico.

2 How do marketing and advertisements manufacture the desire for blue jeans? How do advertisements project desired values of modernity, cosmopolitanism, and individualism onto a simple pair of pants?

3 Though produced globally, jeans can reveal local expressions of identity. In the favelas of Rio de Janeiro, Brazil, stretch jeans worn in the heat, sweat, and dancing of funk balls emerge through the movement and music as an expression of the erotic. In Germany young men of Turkish, Middle Eastern, and other immigrant backgrounds, primarily from working-class, low-income families, choose jeans to resist their marginalization in the dominant culture.

Anthropologists are interested not just in cultural norms, values, symbols, and mental maps of reality; they are also interested in people's stuff, what we call material culture. The social life of these garments reveals the stories of the people who make, move, sell, wear, give, borrow, and discard them. And the way these things move through the world reveals the unexpected ways people are interconnected and intertwined in today's global age.

- Why do you think blue jeans have become so popular on a global scale?
- How many pairs do you own? How many days a week do you wear them? What do your jeans say about you?
- Look in your closet. What stories do your clothes tell?

fast food, they hope to align themselves with the Western middle-class norms and values to which they aspire (Yan 2004).

Migration and the Global Flows of Culture

The movement of people in large numbers within and across national boundaries associated with contemporary globalization reveals that cultures are not necessarily bound to a particular geographic location. People migrate with their cultural beliefs and practices. They incorporate the cultural practices of their homelands into their new communities. They build links to their homelands through which culture continues to be exchanged.

Robert Smith's book *Mexican New York* (2006) reveals one example of the deep transnational connections—links across national borders—that have become increasingly common in today's globalizing world. Direct flights physically link immigrants living in the suburbs of New York City to their hometowns in Mexico in five hours. Telephone calls, emails, and videoconferences connect families and communities. The Mexican town of Tihuateca relies heavily on money sent back from villagers in New York City to build roads, water systems, and schools. Community leaders travel between countries to strengthen relationships, promote projects, and raise funds. In Boston, meanwhile, immigrants from India, Pakistan, Ireland, and Brazil maintain intense connections with their home communities, particularly through transnational religious practices. And a charismatic preacher from Brazil can lead thousands of Brazilians gathered in a Boston auditorium in worship by satellite hookup (Levitt 2007). These stories and many others reveal how global flows of people are transforming local cultures in both the sending and the receiving countries (see also Chapter 13).

Increasing Cosmopolitanism

A third significant effect of globalization on culture is that the increasing flow of people, ideas, and products has allowed worldwide access to cultural patterns that are new, innovative, and stimulating. Local cultures are exposed to a greater range of cultural ideas and products—such as agricultural strategies and medicines, to name just two. Globalization means that communities in the most remote parts of the world increasingly participate in experiences that bridge and link cultural practices, norms, and values across great distances, leading to what some scholars have called a new cosmopolitanism.

Cosmopolitanism is a very broad, sometimes global, outlook, rather than a limited, local one—an outlook that combines both universality and difference (Appiah 2006). The term is usually used to describe sophisticated urban professionals who travel and feel at home in different parts of the world. But anthropologist Lila Abu-Lughod's study *Dramas of Nationhood: The Politics of Television in Egypt* (2005) explores the emergence of cosmopolitanism even among Egypt's rural poor. Her book explores the role of television dramas—much like American soap operas, but more in tune with political and social issues—in creating ideas of a national culture, even among rural Egyptians, and crafting the identity of the new Egyptian citizen.

Abu-Lughod's ethnography of television pushes us to move beyond notions of single cultures sharing a set of ideas and meanings distinct from other cultures in an era of mass media, migration, and globalization. Television, she argues, "is an extraordinary technology for breaking the boundaries and intensifying and multiplying encounters among life-worlds, sensibilities and ideas" (2005, 45). By the 1990s, there were 6 million television sets in Egypt, and more than 90 percent of the population had access. In this reality, television provides material—produced somewhere else—that is consumed locally; it is inserted into, mixed up with, and interpreted by local knowledge and systems of meaning. As Abu-Lughod writes:

> Thinking about Zaynab [Abu-Lughod's key informant] watching Egyptian dramatic serials and films, interviews with criminals, broadcasts of Parliament in session, American soap operas, imported nature programs that take her to the Caribbean or the Serengeti Plain, and advertisements for candy, ceramic toilets, chicken stock cubes and Coca-Cola leads me to begin thinking about her and others in this village not as members of some kind of

MAP 2.5
Egypt

In a globalizing age, local cultures are increasingly exposed to a vast array of people, ideas, and products. Here, a montage of images from a day on Egyptian television, with channels from Egypt and across the Middle East, includes comedy and music from Lebanon, old Egyptian films, American entertainment, and news and religious discussion programs.

unified Egyptian or Upper Egyptian peasant culture—one in which it is improper for women over thirty to marry or older women to be out and about going to school—but in terms of the cosmopolitanism they might represent. (2005, 46)

Even though poverty prevents the people in Abu-Lughod's study from fully participating in the consumer culture of commodities promoted by television programming and commercials, they are not untouched by these features of cosmopolitanism.

TOOLKIT

Thinking Like an Anthropologist: Unpacking a Happy Meal

Every day, culture is all around us. It informs our thoughts and actions; guides us through complex interactions in our families, schools, jobs, and other personal relationships; and even shapes the way we perceive reality. Thinking like an anthropologist can help you to better understand yourself and those around you, and to analyze your own culture and other cultures you encounter in this globalizing world.

In thinking about the Happy Meal and the anthropology of food discussed in the chapter opener, consider the questions we have raised about culture:

- What is culture?
- How has the culture concept developed in anthropology?
- How are culture and power related?
- How much of who you are is shaped by biology, and how much by culture?
- How is culture created?
- How is globalization transforming culture?

Perhaps you have worked in a food-related industry at some point in your life—as a waiter, cook, cleaner, cashier, or delivery person. Drawing on your own experience, how can the key questions of this chapter help you think more deeply about the journey of a Happy Meal from production through distribution, consumption, and disposal? You have participated in cultural food practices at home: shopping, preparing, eating, discussing, disposing of, and perhaps even growing your food. When you think carefully about the experience, how would you begin to explain the complex interactions that go into your food and the cultural practices surrounding it? How is food tied into your culture? How are food and power related? How are biology and culture both shaping your experience with food? How was your food culture created? And how is your experience with food being transformed by globalization?

After putting these questions into anthropological perspective, take a moment to think again about the Happy Meal. Perhaps the last time you ate at McDonald's you did not think particularly deeply about the complex social life of the food that you were eating. But now that you are thinking like an anthropologist, you can.

Key Terms
culture (p. 35)
enculturation (p. 36)
norms (p. 37)
values (p. 39)
symbol (p. 39)
mental maps of reality (p. 40)

The influences of globalization ensure that even in rural Egyptian peasant culture, the knowledge of other worlds comes not only from television but also from foreign friends, tourists, visiting scholars/anthropologists, relatives migrating to find work in cities, imported movies and electronics, and even teachers trained by the Egyptian state and their approved textbooks. This is just one example of the powerful effects of the intersection of culture and globalization. No matter where you look in the twenty-first century, you are sure to find some elements of this intersection.

For Further Exploration

American Anthropological Association. "Declaration on Anthropology and Human Rights." www.aaanet .org/about/Policies/statements/Declaration-on -Anthropology-and-Human-Rights.cfm

Counihan, Carole, and Penny Van Esterik, eds. 2013. *Food and Culture: A Reader,* 3rd ed. New York: Taylor and Francis.

Guess Who's Coming to Dinner. 1967. Directed by Stanley Kramer. Sony Pictures. Classic film starring Sidney Poitier, Spencer Tracy, and Katharine Hepburn that addresses interracial marriage. U.S. anti-miscegenation laws were struck down by the U.S. Supreme Court during the year of the film's release.

Hopkins, Nancy. 1999. "A Study on the Status of Women Faculty in Science at MIT." *MIT Faculty Newsletter 11* (4): 1–15. http://web.mit.edu/fnl/women/fnl114x.pdf

The Nuer. 1971. By Robert Gardner and Hilary Harris for the Film Study Center at Harvard University. Documentary film about the lives of the Sudanese Nuer group.

Ury, William. 2002. *Must We Fight? From the Battlefield to the Schoolyard—A New Perspective on Violent Conflict and Its Prevention.* San Francisco, CA: Jossey-Bass.

Ury, William. 2010. "The Walk from 'No' to 'Yes.'" www .ted.com/talks/william_ury.html. TED Conference talk by anthropologist William Ury about creative cross-cultural strategies for conflict resolution.

Mother and child in a Rio de
Janeiro favela, Brazil.

CHAPTER 3
Fieldwork and Ethnography

I have seen death without weeping,
The destiny of the Northeast is death,
Cattle they kill,
To the people they do
Something worse

—Anonymous Brazilian singer (1965)

Over many years, Nancy Scheper-Hughes, now a professor of cultural anthropology at the University of California, Berkeley, invested herself in trying to understand the lives of the women and children of one particular shantytown in Brazil. Her research resulted in numerous articles and an award-winning ethnography, *Death without Weeping: The Violence of Everyday Life in Brazil* (1992). Scheper-Hughes's efforts reflect the deep commitment of anthropologists to *ethnographic fieldwork*—a research strategy for understanding the world through intense interaction with a local community of people over an extended period. Take a few moments to read this excerpt drawn from her fieldwork experience:

> "Why do the church bells ring so often?" I asked Nailza de Arruda soon after I moved into a corner of her tiny mud-walled hut near the top of the shantytown called the Alto do Cruzeiro (Crucifix Hill). I was then a Peace Corps volunteer and community development/health worker. It was the dry and blazing hot summer of 1965, the months following the military coup in Brazil, and save for the rusty, clanging bells of N. S. das Dores church, an eerie quiet had settled

over the market town that I call Bom Jesus da Mata. Beneath the quiet, however, there was chaos and panic. "It's nothing," replied Nailza, "just another little angel gone to heaven."

Nailza had sent more than her share of little angels to heaven, and sometimes at night I could hear her engaged in a muffled but passionate discourse with one of them, two-year-old Joana. Joana's photograph, taken as she lay propped up in her tiny cardboard coffin, her eyes open, hung on a wall next to one of Nailza and Ze Antonio taken on the day they eloped.

Nailza could barely remember the other infants and babies who came and went in close succession. Most had died unnamed and were hastily baptized in their coffins. Few lived more than a month or two. Only Joana, properly baptized in church at the close of her first year and placed under the protection of a powerful saint, Joan of Arc, had been expected to live. And Nailza had dangerously allowed herself to love the little girl.

In addressing the dead child, Nailza's voice would range from tearful imploring to angry recrimination: "Why did you leave me? Was your patron saint so greedy that she could not allow me one child on this earth?" Ze Antonio advised me to ignore Nailza's odd behavior which he understood as a kind of madness that, like the birth and death of children, came and went. Indeed the premature birth of a stillborn son some months later "cured" Nailza of her "inappropriate" grief, and the day came when she removed Joana's photo and carefully packed it away.

More than fifteen years elapsed before I returned to the Alto do Cruzeiro, and it was anthropology that provided the vehicle of my return. Since 1982 I have returned several times in order to pursue a problem that first attracted my attention in the 1960s. My involvement with the people of the Alto do Cruzeiro now spans a quarter of a century and three generations of parenting in a community where mothers and daughters are often simultaneously pregnant.

The Alto do Cruzeiro is one of three shantytowns surrounding the large market town of Bom Jesus in the sugar plantation zone of Pernambuco in Northeast Brazil, one of the many zones of neglect that have emerged in the shadow of the now tarnished economic miracle of Brazil. For the women and children of the Alto do Cruzeiro the only miracle is that some of them have managed to stay alive at all. . . .

My research agenda never wavered. The questions I addressed first crystallized during a veritable "die-off" of Alto babies during

MAP 3.1
Brazil

a severe drought in 1965. The food and water shortages and the political and economic chaos occasioned by the military coup were reflected in the handwritten entries of births and deaths in the dusty, yellowed pages of the ledger books kept at the public registry office in Bom Jesus. More than 350 babies died in the Alto during 1965 alone—this from a shantytown population of little more than 5,000. But that wasn't what surprised me. There were reasons enough for the deaths in the miserable conditions of shantytown life. What puzzled me was the seeming indifference of Alto women to the death of their infants and their willingness to attribute to their own tiny offspring an aversion to life that made their death seem wholly natural, indeed all but anticipated.

Although I found that it was possible, and hardly difficult, to rescue infants and toddlers from death by diarrhea and dehydration with a simple sugar, salt, and water solution (even bottled Coca-Cola worked fine), it was more difficult to enlist a mother herself in the rescue of a child she perceived as ill-fated for life or better off dead, or to convince her to take back into her threatened and besieged home a baby she had already come to think of as an angel rather than as a son or daughter.

I learned that the high expectancy of death, and the ability to face child death with stoicism and equanimity, produced patterns of nurturing that differentiated between those infants thought of as thrivers and survivors and those thought of as born already "wanting to die." The survivors were nurtured, while stigmatized, doomed infants were left to die, as mothers say, *a mingua*, "of neglect." Mothers stepped back and allowed nature to take its course. This pattern, which I call mortal selective neglect, is called passive infanticide by anthropologist Marvin Harris. The Alto situation, although culturally specific in the form that it takes, is not unique to Third World shantytown communities and may have its correlates in our own impoverished urban communities in some cases of "failure to thrive" infants. . . .

Part of learning how to mother in the Alto do Cruzeiro is learning when to let go of a child who shows that it "wants" to die or that it has no "knack" or no "taste" for life. Another part is learning when it is safe to let oneself love a child. Frequent child death remains a powerful shaper of maternal thinking and practice. In the absence of firm expectation that a child will survive, mother love as we conceptualize it (whether in popular terms or in the psychobiological notion of maternal bonding) is attenuated

Burial of an infant in the Alto do Cruzeiro favela in northeast Brazil. How did anthropologist Nancy Scheper-Hughes make sense of the "death without weeping" that she found in this poor community?

and delayed with consequences for infant survival. In an environment already precarious to young life, the emotional detachment of mothers toward some of their babies contributes even further to the spiral of high mortality—high fertility in a kind of macabre lock-step dance of death. . . .

What, then, can be said of these women? What emotions, what sentiments motivate them? How are they able to do what, in fact, must be done? What does mother love mean in this inhospitable context? Are grief, mourning, and melancholia present, although deeply repressed? If so, where shall we look for them? And if not, how are we to understand the moral visions and moral sensibilities that guide their actions?

I have been criticized more than once for presenting an unflattering portrait of poor Brazilian women, women who are, after all, themselves the victims of severe social and institutional neglect. I have described these women as allowing some of their children to die, as if this were an unnatural and inhuman action rather than, as I would assert, the way any one of us might act, reasonably and rationally, under similarly desperate conditions. Perhaps I have not emphasized enough the real pathogens in this environment of high risk: poverty, deprivation, sexism, chronic hunger, and economic exploitation. If mother love is, as many psychologists and some feminists believe, a seemingly natural and universal maternal script, what does it mean to women for whom scarcity, loss, sickness, and deprivation have made that love frantic and robbed them of their grief, seeming to turn hearts to stone? . . .

Life in the Alto do Cruzeiro resembles nothing so much as a battlefield or an emergency room in an overcrowded inner-city public hospital. Consequently, mortality is guided by a kind of "life-boat ethics," the morality of triage. The seemingly studied indifference toward the suffering of some of their infants, conveyed in such sayings as "little critters have no feelings," is understandable in light of these women's obligation to carry on with their reproductive and nurturing lives.

In their slowness to anthropomorphize and personalize their infants, everything is mobilized so as to prevent maternal overattachment and, therefore, grief at death. The bereaved mother is told not to cry, that her tears will dampen the wings of her little angel so that she cannot fly up to her heavenly home. Grief at the death of an angel is not only inappropriate, it is a symptom of madness and of a profound lack of faith. (Scheper-Hughes 1989, 8ff)

What did you learn about fieldwork by reading this story? Nancy Scheper-Hughes, a middle-class woman from the United States, traveled to one of the poorest places in the world, learned the language, lived in the community, built relationships of trust, accompanied local people through the births and deaths of their children, and searched for meaning in the midst of the pain. As you might imagine from the reading, the fieldwork experience can become more than a strategy for understanding human culture. Fieldwork has the potential to radically transform the anthropologist. Can you imagine making the same commitment Scheper-Hughes did?

The term *fieldwork* implies going out to "the field" to do extensive research. Although in the history of anthropology this may have meant going a long way from home, as Scheper-Hughes did, contemporary anthropologists also study human culture and activities in their own countries and local contexts. By exploring the practice of fieldwork, you will gain a deeper understanding of how anthropologists go about their work. In particular, in this chapter we will consider:

- What is unique about ethnographic fieldwork, and why do anthropologists conduct this kind of research?
- How did the idea of fieldwork develop?
- How do anthropologists get started conducting fieldwork?
- How do anthropologists write ethnography?
- What moral and ethical concerns guide anthropologists in their research and writing?
- How are fieldwork strategies changing in response to globalization?

By the end of the chapter you will see both how professional anthropologists employ fieldwork strategies and how fieldwork can provide a valuable toolkit for gathering information to make decisions in your own life. Fieldwork skills and strategies can help you navigate the many unfamiliar or cross-cultural experiences you will encounter at work or school, in your neighborhood, or in your family. And hopefully you will see how key fieldwork strategies can help you become a more engaged and responsible citizen of the world.

What Is Unique about Ethnographic Fieldwork, and Why Do Anthropologists Conduct This Kind of Research?

Ethnographic fieldwork is the unique set of practices that anthropologists—particularly cultural anthropologists—have developed to put people first as we analyze how human societies work. Chemists conduct experiments in

ethnographic fieldwork: A primary research strategy in cultural anthropology typically involving living and interacting with a community of people over an extended period to better understand their lives.

laboratories. Economists analyze financial trends. Demographers crunch census data. Historians pore over records and library archives. Sociologists, economists, and political scientists analyze trends, quantifiable data, official organizations, and national policies. But anthropologists start with people and their local communities. Even though the whole world is our field, our unique perspective first focuses on the details and patterns of human life in the local setting.

Fieldwork Begins with People

Through fieldwork, we try to understand people's everyday lives, to see what they do and to understand why. By living with others over an extended period, we seek to understand their experience through their eyes. We participate in their activities, take careful notes, conduct interviews, take photographs, and record music. We make maps of communities, both of the physical environment and of family and social relationships. Although careful observation of the details of daily life is the first step, through intensive fieldwork anthropologists look beyond the taken-for-granted, everyday experience of life to discover the complex systems of power and meaning that people construct to shape their existence. These include the many systems discussed throughout this book: gender, sexuality, race, ethnicity, religion, kinship, and economic and political systems. As we extend our analysis as anthropologists, we try to see how local lives compare to others and fit into larger human patterns and global contexts.

Fieldwork Shapes the Anthropologist

Fieldwork experience is considered an essential part of an anthropologist's training. It is the activity through which we learn the basic tools of our trade, earn credibility as effective observers of culture, and establish our reputation as full members of the discipline. Through the process, we learn the basic research strategies of our discipline and hone those skills: careful listening and observation, engagement with strangers, cross-cultural interaction, and deep analysis of human interactions and systems of power and inequality. Through fieldwork we learn empathy for those around us, develop a more global consciousness, and uncover our own ethnocentrism. Indeed, fieldwork is a rite of passage, an initiation into our discipline, and a common bond among anthropologists who have been through the experience.

Fieldwork transforms us. In fact, it is quite common for anthropologists entering the field to experience culture shock—a sense of disorientation caused by the overwhelmingly new and unfamiliar people and experiences encountered every day. Over time, the disorientation may fade as the unfamiliar becomes familiar. But then, many anthropologists feel culture shock again when returning home, where their new perspective causes previously familiar people and customs to seem very strange.

The Nacirema In a now-famous article, "Body Ritual among the Nacirema" (1956), anthropologist Horace Miner helps readers understand the dichotomy between familiar and strange that anthropologists face when studying other cultures. Miner's article examines the cultural beliefs and practices of a group in North America that has developed elaborate and unique practices focusing on care of the human body. He labels this group the "Nacirema."

Miner hypothesizes that underlying the extensive rituals he has documented lies a belief that the human body is essentially ugly, is constantly endangered by forces of disease and decay, and must be treated with great care. Thus, the Nacirema have established extensive daily rituals and ceremonies, rigorously taught to their children, to avoid these dangers. For example, Miner describes the typical household shrine—the primary venue for Nacirema body rituals:

> While each family has at least one shrine, the rituals associated with it are not family ceremonies but are private and secret. . . . The focal point of the shrine is a box or chest which is built into the wall. In this chest are kept the many charms and magical potions without which no native believes he could live. . . . Beneath the charm-box is a small font. Each day every member of the family, in succession, enters the shrine room, bows his head before the charm-box, mingles different sorts of holy water in the font, and proceeds with a brief rite of ablution. (Miner 1956, 503–4)

A healing specialist conducts an elaborate ceremony, the facial treatment, a key body ritual among the Nacirema.

In addition, the Nacirema regularly visit medicine men and "holy-mouth men." These individuals are specialists who provide ritual advice and magical potions.

> The Nacirema have an almost pathological horror of and fascination with the mouth, the condition of which is believed to have a supernatural influence on all social relationships. Were it not for the rituals of the mouth, they believe that their teeth would fall out, their gums bleed, their jaws shrink, their friends desert them and their lovers reject them. The daily body ritual performed by everyone includes a mouth-rite. It was reported to me that the ritual consists of inserting a small bundle of hog hairs into the mouth, along with certain magical powders, and then moving the bundle in a highly formalized series of gestures. (504)

Do these exotic rituals of a seemingly distant tribe sound completely strange to you, or are they vaguely familiar? Miner's descriptions of the Nacirema are intended to make the strange seem familiar and the familiar strange. "Nacirema" is actually "American" spelled backward. Miner's passages describe the typical American bathroom and personal hygiene habits: "Holy water" pours into the sink. The "charm-box" is a medicine cabinet. The Nacirema medicine men are doctors, and the "holy-mouth men" are dentists. The "mouth-rite" is toothbrushing.

Development of the anthropological perspective through fieldwork, in which we investigate the beliefs and practices of other cultures, enables us to perceive our own cultural activities in a new light. Even the most familiar aspects of our lives may then appear exotic, bizarre, or strange when viewed through the lens of anthropology. Through this cross-cultural training, anthropology offers the opportunity to unlock our ability to imagine, see, and analyze the incredible diversity of human cultures. It also enables us to avoid the tendencies of ethnocentrism, in which we often view our own cultural practices as "normal" and against which we are inclined to judge the cultural beliefs and practices of others.

Fieldwork as Social Science and as Art

Fieldwork is simultaneously a social scientific method and an art form. It is a strategy for gathering data about the human condition, particularly through the life experiences of local people in local situations. Fieldwork is an experiment for testing hypotheses and building theories about the diversity of human behavior and the interaction of people with systems of power—a scientific method for examining how the social world really works. As such, anthropologists have developed techniques such as participant observation, field notes, interviews, kinship and social network analysis, life histories, and mapping—all of which we will discuss in this chapter.

But fieldwork is also an art. Its success depends on the anthropologist's more intuitive ability to negotiate complex interactions, usually in an unfamiliar cultural environment, to build relationships of trust, to make sense of patterns of behavior, to be conscious of one's own biases and particular vantage point. Ethnographic fieldwork depends on the ability of an outsider—the anthropologist—to develop close personal relationships over time in a local community and to understand the everyday experiences of often-unfamiliar people. It requires the anthropologist to risk being changed in the process—the risk of mutual transformation. Successful ethnographic fieldwork also depends on the anthropologist's ability to tell the subjects' stories to an audience that has no knowledge of them and in ways that accurately reflect the subjects' lives and shed light on the general human condition. This is also an art.

Fieldwork Informs Daily Life

Anthropologist Brackette Williams suggests that fieldwork can even be a kind of "homework"—a strategy for gathering information that will help the anthropologist make informed decisions in order to act morally and to weigh in advance the likely consequences of her or his actions. Williams studied homelessness and begging in New York City and Tucson, Arizona, over a period of several years. She began with some very practical questions about whether to give money to homeless people begging on the subway she took to work in New York City every day.

In her article "The Public I/Eye: Conducting Fieldwork to Do Homework on Homelessness and Begging in Two U.S. Cities," she writes:

> My goal in the investigation was not to write an ethnography of homelessness, begging, charity, work, and their interconnections but simply to try to understand whether or to whom I might or ought to give charity. As I do in making decisions about what I take to be politically proper conduct in most social interaction, I tried to become as conscious as possible of the character and process of the acts that constitute the social interaction. Like everyone else, I was daily confronted with a multitude of decision points at which I had to figure out why I did one thing and not another. (Williams 1995, 25)

MAP 3.2
Tucson/New York

Williams began with careful observation of all the people involved, including homeless individuals and all the others on the subway. She continued with informal and formal interviews, careful note taking, and background reading. In the process she began to identify a clear set of stories and begging styles and to examine the complicated set of responses made by people on the subway who were being asked for money.

Williams suggests that this approach to her daily dilemma was not only an interesting use of her ethnographic fieldwork skills and training but also "socially required homework" for anyone who confronts complex problems in daily life, whether with family, friends, school, work, or politics. Can you imagine using this strategy to explore a problem, puzzle, or question in your life?

Early anthropologists encountered a world of people already in motion. The 1375 Catalan Atlas shows the world as it was then known. It depicts the location of continents and islands as well as information on ancient and medieval tales, regional politics, astronomy, and astrology.

How Did the Idea of Fieldwork Develop?

Early Accounts of Encounters with Others

Descriptive accounts of other cultures existed long before anthropologists came on the scene. For centuries, explorers, missionaries, traders, government bureaucrats, and travelers recorded descriptions of the people they encountered. For example, nearly 2,500 years ago, the Greek historian Herodotus wrote about his travels in Egypt, Persia, and the area now known as Ukraine. In the thirteenth century, the Venetian explorer Marco Polo chronicled his travels from Italy across the silk route to China. And the Chinese admiral Zheng He reported on his extended voyages to India, the Middle East, and East Africa in the fifteenth century, seventy years before Columbus arrived in the Americas. These are just a few of the many early accounts of encounters with other peoples across the globe.

Nineteenth-Century Anthropology and the Colonial Encounter

The roots of anthropology and of fieldwork lie in the intense globalization of the late nineteenth century. At that time, the increased international movement of Europeans—particularly merchants, colonial administrators, and missionaries—generated a broad array of data that stimulated scientists and philosophers of the day to make sense of the emerging picture of humanity's incredible diversity (Stocking 1983). They asked questions like these: Who are these other people? Why are their foods, clothing, architecture, rituals, family structures, and political and economic systems so different from ours and from one another's? Are they related to us biologically? If so, how?

Fieldwork was not a common practice at the beginning of our discipline. In fact, many early anthropologists, such as Edward Burnett Tylor (1832–1917), are now considered "armchair anthropologists" because they did not conduct their own research; instead they worked at home in their armchairs analyzing the reports of others. One early exception was Louis Henry Morgan (1818–1881), who conducted fieldwork among Native Americans in the United States. As we discussed in Chapter 2, Tylor and Morgan were leading figures in attempts to organize the data that was accumulating, to catalogue human diversity, and to make sense of the many questions it stimulated. These men applied the theory of unilineal cultural evolution—the idea that all cultures would naturally evolve through the same sequence of stages from simple to complex and that the diversity of human cultural expressions represented different stages in the evolution of human culture, which could be classified in comparison to one another.

American anthropologist Franz Boas in Inuit clothing during fieldwork in the Pacific Northwest of North America, 1883.

The Professionalization of Social Scientific Data Gathering and Analysis

Succeeding generations of anthropologists in Europe and North America rejected unilineal cultural evolution as being too Eurocentric, too ethnocentric, too hierarchical, and lacking adequate data to support its grand claims. Anthropologists in the early twentieth century developed more-sophisticated research methods—particularly ethnographic fieldwork—to professionalize social scientific data gathering.

Franz Boas: Fieldwork and the Four-Field Approach In the United States, Franz Boas (1858–1942) and his students focused on developing a four-field approach to anthropological research, which included gathering cultural, linguistic, archaeological, and biological data. Boas's early work among the indigenous Kwakiutl people of the Pacific Northwest of the United States and Canada firmly grounded him in the fieldwork process, as he learned about others' culture through extensive participation in their daily lives, religious rituals, and economic activities. After settling in New York City in the early twentieth century as a professor of anthropology at Columbia University and curator of the American Museum of Natural History, Boas (and his students) embarked on a massive project to document Native American cultures being devastated by the westward expansion of European settlers across the continent.

Often called **salvage ethnography**, Boas's approach involved the rapid gathering of all available material, including historical artifacts, photographs, recordings of spoken languages, songs, and detailed information about cultural beliefs and practices—from religious rituals to family patterns, from gender roles to political structures. With limited time and financial resources, these ethnographers often met with a small number of elderly informants and focused on conducting oral interviews rather than observing actual behavior. Despite the limitations of this emerging fieldwork, these early projects built upon Boas's commitment to historical particularism when investigating local cultures (see Chapter 2) and defined a continuing characteristic of American anthropology: a combined focus on culture, biology, artifacts, and language that today we call the four-field approach (see Chapter 1).

Another key contribution of Boas and his students was a commitment to the development of cultural relativism as a basic fieldwork perspective: to see each culture on its own merits; to understand it first from the inside, according to its own logic and structure. This rejection of ethnocentrism became a cornerstone of anthropology for generations to come (Stocking 1989).

Bronislaw Malinowski: The Father of Fieldwork Across the Pacific Ocean, Bronislaw Malinowski (1884–1942), considered by many to be the "father of fieldwork," went even further than Boas in developing cultural anthropology's research methods. Malinowski, a Polish citizen who later became a leading

salvage ethnography: Fieldwork strategy developed by Franz Boas to collect cultural, material, linguistic, and biological information about Native American populations being devastated by the westward expansion of European settlers.

British anthropologist Bronislaw Malinowski at a bachelor's house in Kasanai, Trobriand Islands, ca. 1915–18.

British anthropologist E. E. Evans-Pritchard seated among Nuer men and boys in southern Sudan, ca. 1930.

participant observation: A key anthropological research strategy involving both participation in and observation of the daily life of the people being studied.

MAP 3.3
The Nuer Region of East Africa

figure in British anthropology, found himself stuck for a year on the Trobriand Islands as a result of World War I. His classic ethnography, *Argonauts of the Western Pacific* (1922), has become most famous for its examination of the Kula ring, an elaborate system of exchange. The ring involved thousands of individuals across many islands, some of whom traveled hundreds of miles by canoe to exchange Kula valuables (in particular, shell necklaces and armbands).

Argonauts also set new standards for fieldwork. In the opening chapter, Malinowski proposes a set of guidelines for conducting fieldwork based on his own experience. He urges fellow anthropologists to stay for a long period in their field sites, learn the local language, get off the veranda (that is, leave the safety of their front porch to mingle with the local people), engage in participant observation, and explore the "mundane imponderabilia"—the seemingly commonplace, everyday items and activities of local life. Using these strategies enabled Malinowski to analyze the complex dynamics of the Kula ring, both its system of economic exchange and its social networking.

Although some of these suggestions may seem obvious to us nearly a century later, Malinowski's formulation of a comprehensive strategy for understanding local culture was groundbreaking and has withstood the test of time. Of particular importance has been his conceptualization of **participant observation** as the cornerstone of fieldwork. For anthropologists, it is not enough to observe from a distance. We must learn about people by participating in their daily activities, walking in their shoes, seeing through their eyes. Participant observation gives depth to our observations and helps guard against mistaken assumptions based on observation from a distance (Kuper 1983).

E. E. Evans-Pritchard and British Social Anthropology Between the 1920s and 1960s, many British social anthropologists viewed anthropology more as a science designed to discover the component elements and patterns of society (see Chapter 2). Fieldwork was their key methodology for conducting their scientific experiments. Adopting a *synchronic approach*, they sought to control their experiments by limiting consideration of the larger historical and social context in order to isolate as many variables as possible.

E. E. Evans-Pritchard (1902–1973), one of the leading figures during this period, wrote a classic ethnography in this style. In *The Nuer* (1940), based on his research with a Sudanese "tribe" over eleven months between 1930 and 1936,

Evans-Pritchard systematically documents the group's social structure—political, economic, and kinship—capturing the intricate details of community life. But later anthropologists have criticized his failure to consider the historical context and larger social world. Indeed, the Nuer in Evans-Pritchard's study lived under British occupation in the Sudan, and many Nuer participated in resistance to British occupation despite an intensive British pacification campaign against the Sudanese during the time of Evans-Pritchard's research. Later anthropologists have questioned how he could have omitted such important details and ignored his status as a British subject when it had such potential for undermining his research success.

American anthropologist Margaret Mead with a mother and child in the Admiralty Islands, South Pacific, 1953.

Margaret Mead: Fieldwork and Public Anthropology Margaret Mead conducted pioneering fieldwork in the 1920s, famously examining teen sexuality in *Coming of Age in Samoa* (1928) and, later, the wide diversity of gender roles in three separate groups in Papua New Guinea (1935). Perhaps most significant, however, Mead mobilized her fieldwork findings to engage in crucial scholarly and public debates at home in the United States. At a time when many in the United States argued that gender roles were biologically determined, Mead's fieldwork testified to the fact that U.S. cultural norms were not found cross-culturally but were culturally specific. Mead's unique blending of fieldwork and dynamic writing provided her with the authority and opportunity to engage a broad public audience and made her a powerful figure in the roiling cultural debates of her generation.

MAP 3.4
Samoa

The People of Puerto Rico: **A Turn to the Global** During the 1950s a team of anthropologists headed by Julian Steward, and including Sydney Mintz and Eric Wolf, engaged in a collaborative fieldwork project at multiple sites on the island of Puerto Rico. Steward's resulting ethnography, *The People of Puerto Rico* (1956), marked the beginning of a significant anthropological turn away from studies of seemingly isolated, small-scale, nonindustrial societies toward studies that examined the integration of local communities into a modern world system. In particular, the new focus explored the impact of colonialism and the spread of capitalism on local people. Mintz, in *Sweetness and Power* (1985), later expanded his fieldwork interests in Puerto Rican sugar production to consider the intersections of local histories and local production of sugar with global flows of colonialism and capitalism. Wolf, in *Europe and the People Without History* (1982), continued a lifetime commitment to reassert forgotten local histories—or the stories of people ignored by history—into the story of the modern world economic system.

Annette Weiner: Feminism and Reflexivity In the 1980s, anthropologist Annette Weiner retraced Malinowski's footsteps to conduct a new study of the Trobriand Islands sixty years later. Weiner quickly noticed aspects of Trobriand culture that had not surfaced in Malinowski's writings. In particular, she took careful note of the substantial role women played in the island economy. Whereas Malinowski had focused attention on the elaborate male-dominated system of economic exchange among islands, Weiner found that women had equally important economic roles and equally valuable accumulations of wealth.

In the course of her fieldwork, Weiner came to believe that Malinowski's conclusions were not necessarily wrong but were incomplete. By the time of Weiner's study (1988), anthropologists were carefully considering the need for **reflexivity** in conducting fieldwork—that is, a critical self-examination of the role of the anthropologist and an awareness that who one is affects what one finds out. Malinowski's age and gender influenced what he saw and what others were comfortable telling him. By the 1980s, feminist anthropologists such as Weiner and Kathleen Gough (1971), who revisited Evans-Pritchard's work with the Nuer, were pushing anthropologists to be more critically aware of how their own position in relationship to those they studied affected their scope of vision.

reflexivity: A critical self-examination of the role the anthropologist plays and an awareness that one's identity affects one's fieldwork and theoretical analyses.

Barbara Myerhoff: A Turn to Home Barbara Myerhoff's first book, *Peyote Hunt* (1974), traces the pilgrimage of the Huichol Indians across the Sierra Madre of Mexico as they retell, reclaim, and reinvigorate their religious myths, rituals, and symbols. In her second book, *Number Our Days* (1978), Myerhoff turns her attention closer to home. Her fieldwork focuses on the struggles of older Jewish immigrants in a Southern California community and the Aliyah Senior Citizens' Center through which they create and remember ritual life and community as a means of keeping control of their daily activities and faculties as they age. Their words pour off the pages of her book

Anthropologist Barbara Myerhoff with two members of the Aliyah Senior Citizens' Center in Southern California, the focus of her book *Number Our Days*.

as she allows them to tell their life stories. Myerhoff becomes a character in her own book, tracing her interactions and engagements with the members of the center and reflecting poignantly on the process of self-reflection and transformation that she experiences as a younger Jewish woman studying a community of older Jews.

Number Our Days marks a turn in anthropology from the study of the "other" to the study of the self—what Victor Turner calls in his foreword to Myerhoff's book "being thrice-born." The first birth is in our own culture. The second birth immerses the anthropologist in the depths of another culture through fieldwork. Finally, the return home is like a third birth as the anthropologist rediscovers his or her own culture, now strange and unfamiliar in a global context.

Engaged Anthropology

Over the past thirty years, an increasing number of anthropologists, including Nancy Scheper-Hughes, whose work bookends this chapter, have identified their work as **engaged anthropology**. Engaged anthropologists intentionally seek to apply the research strategies and analytical perspectives of the discipline to address the concrete challenges facing local communities and the world at large. In this regard, engaged anthropology challenges the assumptions that anthropology, as a science, should focus on producing objective, unbiased, neutral accounts of human behavior and that anthropologists should work as disengaged observers while conducting research. Engaged anthropologists argue that in a world of conflict and inequality, social scientists must develop an active, politically committed and morally engaged practice. Engaged anthropology, then, is characterized by a commitment not only to revealing and critiquing but also to confronting systems of power and inequality. Design, implementation, and analysis of research involve close collaboration with colleagues and co-researchers in the community. Advocacy and activism with local communities on matters of mutual concern are central tenets of engaged anthropology (Scheper-Hughes 1995; Speed 2006).

As we have seen in the work of Boas and Mead, for example, this form of engagement is not new to anthropology. The field has had a strong strain of engagement since its inception. As early as 1870, John W. Powell, the first director of the U.S. Bureau of Ethnology and Geologic Survey, testified before Congress about the genocide of Native Americans following the westward expansion and construction of the railroads. African American anthropologist, novelist, journalist, playwright, and activist Zora Neale Hurston (1891–1960) vividly illuminated the culture and folklore of the early twentieth-century African American diaspora (1935, 1938; McClaurin 2007). Beatrice Medicine

engaged anthropology: Applying the research strategies and analytical perspectives of anthropology to address concrete challenges facing local communities and the world at large.

Shannon Speed
Exploring an Activist, Engaged Anthropology

Shannon Speed is a professor of anthropology and director of Native American and Indigenous Studies at the University of Texas at Austin who has conducted fieldwork in southern Mexico and the United States. Reflecting on her journey into anthropology, she credits the importance of fieldwork—and particularly an engaged, activist fieldwork—for helping her link her personal and political commitments to her scholarship and her work abroad to work at home in the United States.

"I grew up as a Native American in the U.S. so I had an acute sense of the deeply egregious history of government behavior toward the native inhabitants of this land and then more broadly of the behavior of the state toward the indigenous populations of other countries—questions of imperialism and human rights.

"I was drawn to cultural anthropology because it gave me the ability to look at what was happening to real people in the real world. I was drawn to ethnographic field methods as a way of approaching a topic by going out and living with and learning from the perspectives of the people I would be writing about, rather than seeking archival data. So field methods were important for me, as were the kinds of analytical approaches and understanding the not-always-obvious cultural and social dynamics that were shaping the forces of power and oppression."

During graduate school, Speed, a Chickasaw tribal citizen, set out to study the role of mixed-heritage identity among Native Americans and what that meant for the Chickasaw Nation in particular. But a different opportunity quickly presented itself. In January 1994 a group of indigenous people in the southern Mexican state of Chiapas occupied several cities in a dramatic uprising to demand that the Mexican government return their ancestral lands and protect their human rights. Moved by the creative and courageous struggles of indigenous people in those areas for indigenous rights, indigenous identity, social justice, and women's rights, Speed soon shifted her research to this Zapatista movement in Chiapas.

There, Speed conducted what she calls engaged activist anthropology—a commitment to working with the local people in their struggles, as part of the fieldwork process. During her more than five years of fieldwork, Speed worked for two human rights organizations and engaged directly in human rights monitoring and advocacy in collaboration with the communities affected. "There are lots of reasons to engage in activist research," Speed says. "In Chiapas the conflict was so intense that there was a clear sense from people that you are with us or against us. Who are you? Why should we trust you? You couldn't just walk in there and start doing fieldwork. If you did, you wouldn't get very far. You really needed to live there, be involved and be engaged in the issues in order to develop the relationships to understand anything. Otherwise nobody would trust you."

Anthropologist Shannon Speed

"Most anthropologists do participant observation, living there and engaging in their day-to-day activities. But an activist engagement takes on an additional level of intensity because you have shared political goals. And you develop a dual accountability. As anthropologists we certainly have a level of accountability to our field. But with an activist anthropology you're making a commitment to be accountable also to the local people about your representations and interpretations. I think that ultimately makes for a better anthropology on an ethical basis. And it can also provide and produce new wisdom and knowledge. That kind of long-term approach in anthropology was very helpful to my work in Chiapas."

Establishing rapport with people during fieldwork can be a complex process under any circumstance, but building relationships of trust in Chiapas proved particularly challenging, as many indigenous people were wary of anthropology's reputation, both in Mexico and globally, of working in tandem with European colonialism. "Anthropology can be a bad word for indigenous people. And that was definitely the case in Chiapas. There is this history of anthropologists creating representations of indigenous people that are not good for them. Because of the current conflict, people were distrustful of everyone generally. But they were particularly distrustful of anthropologists."

Long-term fieldwork can be a mutually transformative experience, shaping the lives of both the anthropologist and those being studied. Speed notes the many ways in which her work with indigenous people in Chiapas reshaped her teaching, research, and activism back home. Since her return, she has helped develop a Native American and Indigenous Studies Program at the University of Texas at Austin and has become increasingly active in helping to shape the work of a number of Native American councils and conferences.

Recently, she has become deeply involved in monitoring human rights of Mexican and Central American immigrants held in U.S. detention centers in Austin, visiting indigenous women and advocating for them.

Speed's advocacy on behalf of detained immigrant women has included writing extensively about their stories, including numerous newspaper editorials questioning both the living conditions of the family detention centers and the morality of imprisoning women and children who are fleeing violence at home.

In reflecting on ways anthropology can be transformative for undergraduates, Speed reflects, "Cultural anthropology, more than any other course, is going to allow you to stand outside of your cultural blinders and see the world in a different way. Potentially to understand yourself for the first time as part of the human family, instead of just as a member of one of the many subsets that sees itself in opposition to all of the other subsets. Once you take off your cultural blinders, you can begin to see that your way of thinking isn't the only way to think about the world. That has the potential to transform everything in the way you view yourself in relation to the world around you."

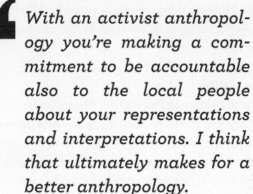

With an activist anthropology you're making a commitment to be accountable also to the local people about your representations and interpretations. I think that ultimately makes for a better anthropology.

(1924–2005), Native American anthropologist, long advocated for the rights of women, children, Native Americans, and gay, lesbian, and transgender people. In recent decades, this focus on engagement, advocacy, and activism has taken an increasingly central role in anthropologists' research strategies (Low and Merry 2010).

How Do Anthropologists Get Started Conducting Fieldwork?

Today cultural anthropologists call on a set of techniques designed to assess the complexity of human interactions and social organizations. You probably use some variation of these techniques as you go about daily life and make decisions for yourself and others. For a moment, imagine yourself doing fieldwork with Nancy Scheper-Hughes in the Brazilian shantytown of Alto do Cruzeiro. How would you prepare yourself? What strategies would you use? How would you analyze your data? What equipment would you need to conduct your research?

Preparation

anthropologist's toolkit: The tools needed to conduct fieldwork, including information, perspectives, strategies and even equipment.

Prior to beginning fieldwork, anthropologists go through an intense process of preparation, carefully assembling an **anthropologist's toolkit**: all the information, perspectives, strategies, and even equipment that may be needed. We start by reading everything we can find about our research site and the particular issues we will be examining. This *literature review* provides a crucial background for the experiences to come. Following Malinowski's recommendation, anthropologists also learn the language of their field site. The ability to speak the local language eliminates the need to work through interpreters and allows us to participate in the community's everyday activities and conversations, which richly reflect local culture.

Before going to the field, anthropologists search out possible contacts: other scholars who have worked there, community leaders, government officials, perhaps even a host family. A specific research question or problem is defined and a research design created. Grant applications are submitted to seek financial support for the research. Permission to conduct the study is sought ahead of time from the local community and, where necessary, from appropriate government agencies. Protocols are developed to protect those who will be the focus of research. Anthropologists attend to many of these logistical matters following a preliminary visit to the intended field site before fully engaging the fieldwork process.

Finally, we assemble all the equipment needed to conduct our research. What tools would Nancy Scheper-Hughes have needed to conduct her research on a daily basis in Brazil? Today this aspect of your anthropologist's toolkit—most likely a backpack—might include a notebook, pens, camera, voice recorder, maps, cell phone, batteries and chargers, dictionary, watch, and identification.

If you look back at the excerpt from Scheper-Hughes's work on pages 71–74, you can see evidence of some of the preparation strategies discussed here. Here's how she developed her research question:

> The questions I addressed first crystallized during a veritable "die-off" of Alto babies during a severe drought in 1965. . . . But that wasn't what surprised me. . . . What puzzled me was the seeming indifference of Alto women to the death of their infants and their willingness to attribute to their own tiny offspring an aversion to life that made their death seem wholly natural.

Here she refers to work done in terms of a literature review:

> Mothers stepped back and allowed nature to take its course. This pattern, which I call mortal selective neglect, is called passive infanticide by anthropologist Marvin Harris. The Alto situation . . . is not unique to Third World shantytown communities and may have its correlates in our own impoverished urban communities in some cases of "failure to thrive" infants.

Strategies

Once in the field, anthropologists apply a variety of research strategies for gathering quantitative and qualitative data. **Quantitative data** include statistical information about a community—data that can be measured and compared, including details of population demographics and economic activity. **Qualitative data** include information that cannot be counted but may be even more significant for understanding the dynamics of a community. Qualitative data consist of personal stories and interviews, life histories, and general observations about daily life drawn from participant observation. Qualitative data enable the ethnographer to connect the dots and answer the questions of why people behave in certain ways or organize their lives in particular patterns.

Central to a cultural anthropologist's research is participant observation. By participating in our subjects' daily activities, we experience their lives from the perspective of an insider. Through participant observation over time, we establish *rapport*—relationships of trust and familiarity with members of the community we study. The deepening of that rapport through intense engagement

quantitative data: Statistical information about a community that can be measured and compared.

qualitative data: Descriptive data drawn from nonstatistical sources, including personal stories, interviews, life histories, and participant observation.

key informant: A community member who advises the anthropologist on community issues, provides feedback, and warns against cultural miscues. Also called *cultural consultant.*

life history: A form of interview that traces the biography of a person over time, examining changes in the person's life and illuminating the interlocking network of relationships in the community.

survey: An information-gathering tool for quantitative data analysis.

kinship analysis: A fieldwork strategy of examining interlocking relationships of power built on marriage and family ties.

social network analysis: A method for examining relationships in a community, often conducted by identifying whom people turn to in times of need.

field notes: The anthropologist's written observations and reflections on places, practices, events, and interviews.

enables the anthropologist to move from being an outsider toward being an insider. Over time in a community, anthropologists seek out people who will be our advisors, teachers, and guides—sometimes called **key informants** or cultural consultants. Key informants may suggest issues to explore, introduce community members to interview, provide feedback on research insights, and warn against cultural miscues. (Again, quoting from Scheper-Hughes: "Ze Antonio advised me to ignore Nailza's odd behavior, which he understood as a kind of madness that, like the birth and death of children, came and went.")

Another key research method is the *interview*. Anthropologists are constantly conducting interviews while in the field. Some interviews are very informal, essentially involving a form of data gathering through everyday conversation. Other interviews are highly structured, closely following a set of questions. Semi-structured interviews use those questions as a framework but leave room for the interviewee to guide the conversation. One particular form of interview, a **life history**, traces the life story of a key informant as a means of understanding change over time in that person's life and illuminating the interlocking network of relationships in the community. Life histories provide insights into the frameworks of meaning that individuals build around their life experiences. **Surveys** can also be developed and administered to gather quantitative data and reach a broader sample of participants around key issues, but rarely do they substitute for participant observation and face-to-face interviews as the anthropologist's primary strategy for data collection.

Anthropologists also map human relations. **Kinship analysis** enables us to explore the interlocking relationships of power built on family and marriage (see Chapter 10). In more urban areas where family networks are diffuse, a **social network analysis** may prove illuminating. One of the simplest ways to analyze a social network is to identify who people turn to in times of need.

Central to our data-gathering strategy, anthropologists write detailed **field notes** of our observations and reflections. These field notes take various forms. Some are elaborate descriptions of people, places, events, sounds, and smells. Others are reflections on patterns and themes that emerge, questions to be asked, and issues to be pursued. Some field notes are personal reflections on the experience of doing fieldwork—how it feels physically and emotionally to be engaged in the process. Although the rigorous recording of field notes may sometimes seem tedious, the collection of data over time allows the anthropologist to revisit details of earlier experiences, to compare information and impressions over time, and to analyze changes, trends, patterns, and themes.

Sophisticated computer programs can assist in the organization and categorization of data about people, places, and institutions. But in the final analysis, the ability to recognize key themes and patterns relies on the instincts and insights of the ethnographer. Dedication to rigorous recording of field notes supports the process of thick description as defined by Clifford Geertz (see Chapter 2), in which detailed description affords deeper insights into the underlying meaning of words and actions.

Mapping

Often one of the first steps an anthropologist takes upon entering a new community is to map the surroundings. **Mapping** takes many forms and produces many different products. While walking the streets of the field site, the ethnographer develops a spatial awareness of where people live, work, worship, play, and eat, and of the space through which they move. After all, human culture exists in real physical space. And culture shapes the way space is constructed and used. Likewise, physical surroundings influence human culture, shaping the boundaries of behavior and imagination. Careful observation and description, recorded in maps and field notes, provide the material for deeper analysis of these community dynamics.

mapping: The analysis of the physical and/or geographic space where fieldwork is being conducted.

Student-made maps of blocks along East Broadway, a street on Manhattan's Lower East Side that serves as both a gateway into the country and the economic hub for Chinese immigrants seeking a foothold in the United States today.

Mapping a Block

Develop your ethnographic skills of observation and description by drawing a map of a block or public space in your community and writing a narrative description of what you find.

Select an interesting location for your mapping project. You may choose to map a block defined as an area bounded on four sides by streets; as both sides of a single street (include the corners); or as the four corners of an intersection. Alternatively, you may choose to map an outdoor public space such as a park or campus quadrangle, or an indoor space such as a shopping mall or your college's student center. In these cases, focus on what is inside the space or inside the building's four walls.

Bring your anthropologist's toolkit, and spend time in your chosen location. Take careful notes. Pay attention to details. Draw a map of what you see. For an outdoor space, note streets, buildings, businesses, residences, schools, hospitals, and infrastructure such as streetlights, sewers, telephone and electric lines, and satellite dishes, as well as transportation and pedestrian traffic. For an indoor space, note rooms, offices, businesses, hallways, entry and exit locations, public and private areas, lighting, sounds, and smells. Also note the people—their activities, movements, characteristics gender, age, and race. Notice who or what is absent that you might have expected to find. Not all information presents itself immediately, so be patient. Consider taking photos or shooting video of your location as part of your data gathering and to supplement your hand-drawn map. Consider asking people to tell you about the space you are mapping from their perspective. To observe changes in your location, visit more than once. Vary the time of day or the day of the week. Write a description of the block, comparing the findings of your multiple visits.

If time permits, continue your mapping project by examining census data for your location. You can access U.S. census data at http://projects.nytimes.com/census/2010/explorer. Also consider searching local archives and databases to collect historical information about how your chosen location has changed over time.

When presenting your mapping project, consider supplementing your hand-drawn map and narrative description with photos, Google Earth images, film clips, and statistical data. Compare and analyze your maps with classmates. If you are working in a team, consider posting your research as a blog or wiki to promote collaboration, integrate multiple media sources, and enhance your presentation.

---

built environment: The intentionally designed features of human settlement, including buildings, transportation and public service infrastructure, and public spaces.

Urban ethnographers describe the power of the **built environment** to shape human life. Most humans live in a built environment, not one made up solely or primarily of nature. By focusing on the built environment—what we have built around us—scholars can analyze the intentional development of human settlements, neighborhoods, towns, and cities. Growth of the built environment is rarely random. Rather, it is guided by political and economic choices that determine funding for roads, public transportation, parks, schools, lighting, sewers, water systems, electrical grids, hospitals, police and fire stations, and other public services and infrastructure. Local governments establish and enforce tax and zoning regulations to control the construction of buildings and approved uses. Mapping the components of this built environment may shed light on key dynamics of power and influence in a community.

Anthropologists turn to quantitative data to map who is present in a community, including characteristics such as age, gender, family type, and employment status. This demographic data may be available through the local or national census, or the anthropologist may choose to gather the data directly by surveying the community if the sample size is manageable. To map historical change over time in an area and discern its causes, anthropologists also turn to archives, newspaper databases, minutes and records of local organizations, historical photos, and personal descriptions, in addition to census data.

Mapping today may be aided by online tools such as satellite imagery, geographic information system (GIS) devices and data, online archives, and electronic databases. All can be extremely helpful in establishing location, orientation, and, in the case of photo archives, changes over time. On their own, however, these tools do not provide the deep immersion sought by anthropologists conducting fieldwork. Instead anthropologists place primary emphasis on careful, firsthand observation and documentation of physical space as a valuable strategy for understanding the day-to-day dynamics of cultural life.

Mapping may produce a tremendous variety of products. Hand-drawn maps reveal the intricate character of the built environment and force the ethnographer toward a deeper consciousness of details. Photos present a visual map seen through the camera's lens, a map that may be extremely valuable when writing up an ethnographic report and in leaving a visual record of a particular place viewed at a particular time. Film captures moving images and sounds that may make the fieldwork site come alive for those who are unable to experience it firsthand. Blogs and wikis present opportunities to work collaboratively and publicly in the mapping process, creating open-source documents that can be regularly updated, enhanced, and engaged with by members of a research team or by members of the community under study.

Skills and Perspectives

Successful fieldwork requires a unique set of skills and perspectives that are hard to teach in the classroom. Ethnographers must begin with open-mindedness about the people and places they study. We must be wary of any prejudices we might have formed before our arrival, and we must be reluctant to judge once we are in the field. Boas's notion of cultural relativism is an essential starting point: Can we see the world through the eyes of those we are studying? Can we understand their systems of meaning and internal logic? The tradition of anthropology suggests that cultural relativism must be the starting point if we are to accurately hear and retell the stories of others.

A successful ethnographer must also be a skilled listener. We spend a lot of time in conversation, but much of that time involves listening, not talking. The ability to ask good questions and listen carefully to the responses is essential. A skilled listener hears both what is said and what is not said—something we refer to as zeros. **Zeros** are the elements of a story or a picture that are not told or seen—key details omitted from the conversation or key people absent from the room. Zeros offer insights into issues and topics that may be too sensitive to discuss or display publicly.

A good ethnographer must be patient, flexible, and open to the unexpected. Sometimes sitting still in one place is the best research strategy because it offers opportunities to observe and experience unplanned events and unexpected people. For instance, I have a favorite tea shop in one Chinese village where I like to sit and wait to see what happens. The overscheduled fieldworker can easily miss the "mundane imponderabilia" that constitute the richness of everyday life.

At times the most important, illuminating conversations and interviews are not planned ahead of time. On a research trip to China, for example, I had hoped to better understand the Catholic Church in the area where I was doing fieldwork. I visited a number of parishes but realized that I really needed an interview with the bishop—the head of all Catholic churches in the region. Unable to arrange one through official channels, I was about to leave China but made one last visit to a large rural church. As I climbed the hill from the town to the church, I met an old man sitting on the steps reading a book. I greeted him, and as we began to talk his outer cloak fell back to reveal a large cross hanging around his neck. "Are you by any chance the bishop?" I asked. "Yes, my son," he answered. "How may I help you?"

Patience and a commitment to conduct research over an extended period allow the ethnographic experience to come to us on its own terms, not on the schedule we assign to it. This is one of the significant differences between anthropology and journalism. It is also a hard lesson to learn and a hard skill to develop.

A final perspective essential for a successful ethnographer is openness to the possibility of **mutual transformation** in the fieldwork process. This is risky business because it exposes the personal component of anthropological research. It is clear that by participating in fieldwork, anthropologists alter—in ways large and small—the character of the community being studied. But if you ask them about their fieldwork experience, they will acknowledge that in the process they themselves become transformed on a very personal level—their self-understanding, their empathy for others, their worldviews. The practice of participant observation over time entails building deep relationships with people from another culture and directly engages the ethnographer in the life of the community.

Nancy Scheper-Hughes could not have returned unchanged by her research experience. The people of Alto do Cruzeiro would not let her simply observe their lives; they made her work with them to organize a neighborhood

zeros: Elements of a story or a picture that are not told or seen and yet offer key insights into issues that might be too sensitive to discuss or display publicly.

mutual transformation: The potential for both the anthropologist and the members of the community being studied to be transformed by the interactions of fieldwork.

organization to address community problems. Indeed, the potential for the fieldworker to affect the local community is very great. So is the potential for the people being studied to transform the fieldworker.

Analysis

As the fieldwork experience proceeds, anthropologists regularly reflect on and analyze the trends, issues, themes, and patterns that emerge from their carefully collected data. One framework for analysis that we will examine in this book is power: Who has it? How do they get it and keep it? Who uses it, and why? Where is the money, and who controls it? The anthropologist Eric Wolf thought of culture as a mechanism for facilitating relationships of power—among families, between genders, and among religions, classes, and political entities (1999). Good ethnographers constantly assess the relations of power in the communities they study.

Ethnographers also submit their local data and analysis to cross-cultural comparisons. We endeavor to begin from an **emic** perspective—that is, understanding the local community on its own terms. But the anthropological commitment to understanding human diversity and the complexity of human cultures also requires taking an **etic** perspective—viewing the local community from the anthropologist's perspective as an outsider. This provides a foundation for comparison with other relevant case studies. The overarching process of comparison and assessment, called **ethnology**, uses the wealth of anthropological studies to compare the activities, trends, and patterns of power across cultures. The process enables us to better see what is unique in a particular context and how it contributes to identifying larger patterns of cultural beliefs and practices. Perhaps the largest effort to facilitate worldwide comparative studies is the Human Relations Area Files at Yale University (http://hraf.yale.edu/), which has been building a database of ethnographic material since 1949 to encourage cross-cultural analysis.

emic: An approach to gathering data that investigates how local people think and how they understand the world.

etic: Description of local behavior and beliefs from the anthropologist's perspective in ways that can be compared across cultures.

ethnology: The analysis and comparison of ethnographic data across cultures.

How Do Anthropologists Write Ethnography?

After gathering data through fieldwork, anthropologists must decide how to tell the stories of the people they study. Although ethnographic films are a vibrant part of our field, most anthropologists make their contributions through ethnographic writing—either articles or books. The art of ethnographic writing has been a particularly hot topic within anthropology for the past twenty-five years, and both style and content have changed dramatically since Malinowski and Evans-Pritchard published their books in the early twentieth century.

Ethnography has changed as anthropology has changed. More women and people of color are writing, bringing their unique perspectives into the anthropological discourse. More people from non-Western countries are writing, challenging the position of Western writers as unquestioned authorities on other cultures. And with better communication systems, people are reading what we write about them, even when we write it halfway around the world. This has had a profound effect on the conversations between author and subject and on the ethnographer's final product.

It is unavoidable that what we write will in some way provide only a limited view of the lives of those we study. The process of collecting, organizing, and analyzing our data presumes not only that we present facts but also that we choose which facts to present, which people to highlight, and which stories to tell. As authors, we have the power to interpret the people and their experiences to our audience. This is an awesome and sometimes overwhelming responsibility, which often leaves the ethnographer at a loss for how to proceed. In researching my book *God in Chinatown*, for instance, I conducted more than one hundred interviews, each lasting one hour or more. The process of selecting certain stories and specific quotations was arduous.

Polyvocality

Changes in ethnographic fieldwork and writing over recent decades have sought to make the process more participatory and transparent. Today most ethnographic projects involve people from the community in the research process and include their voices more directly in the written product. Nancy Scheper-Hughes, for example, strives to include both her own voice and those of the people of Alto do Cruziero in her writing. In this chapter's opening excerpt, through direct quotes we hear the bereaved mother Nailza trying to make sense of the death of her daughter Joana ("Why did you leave me? Was your patron saint so greedy that she could not allow me one child on this earth?").

Polyvocality—the use of many voices in ethnographic writing—allows the reader to hear directly from the people in the study and, by bringing their stories to life, makes them more vibrant and available to the reader. Anthropologists also increase polyvocality in their research by inviting key informants to help design the research, including interview and survey questions. Others may be invited to read sections of the manuscript as it is being drafted. In contemporary ethnographic writing, the author's voice also comes out more clearly as ethnographies have moved from the style of Evans-Pritchard (1940) toward that of Geertz (1973a)—from being a scientific report toward being thick description and an interpretation of what is observed.

Reflexivity

In this chapter's opening story, Nancy Scheper-Hughes's feelings about her experiences come through in the text, making the ethnographer herself

polyvocality: The practice of using many different voices in ethnographic writing and research question development, allowing the reader to hear more directly from the people in the study.

come alive as well. This practice of reflexivity—self-reflection on the experience of doing fieldwork—has become more prevalent in written ethnographies. Contemporary writers make an effort to reveal their own position in relationship to their study so that readers can assess what biases, strengths, or handicaps the author may have. The ethnographer's age, gender, race/ethnicity, nationality, sexuality, and religious background may have a direct impact on the ease with which he or she establishes rapport or gains access to the research community and on the successful analysis of his or her findings. A careful ethnographer must address these issues in the research design and implementation and may choose to reflect on them in the written report.

Tone and Style

Anthropologists today write for a wide variety of audiences, and the tone and style of our writing shift accordingly. We write for students, both undergraduate and graduate, in the hopes of inspiring an interest in a particular topic or in fieldwork itself. We write for colleagues or other specialists in the field with whom we engage in debates and discussions. A recent emphasis on creating a public anthropology, one that more directly explores contemporary issues and problems, has led some anthropologists to write for the general public and even for government agencies and nongovernmental organizations that might address problems in the community by using the information presented in the anthropologists' reports.

We also write for the people we study. In today's world of global communications, the people we are writing about often read our work, even across barriers of language and geography. People expect to see their lives accurately portrayed and their community's concerns appropriately expressed. Balancing the expectations and needs of these at times contradictory audiences makes the ethnographer's task quite complicated.

Ethnographic Authority

Ultimately, the ethnographer must wrestle with the question of ethnographic authority: What right does he or she have to present certain material, make certain claims, and draw certain conclusions? That authority is not automatically given, so writers make efforts, often early on in the ethnography, to establish their credentials and identify the grounds on which readers should trust them and the decisions they made during fieldwork and writing. These attempts to establish ethnographic authority include discussions of the length of time engaged in the study, language skills, special training and preparation, research design and implementation, and the quality of the relationship with subjects in the study. The quality and persuasiveness of the writing can also be significant in establishing the ethnographer's credibility. The inclusion of direct quotes can confirm the author's conclusions, provide more direct access to the fieldworker's data, and enable the reader to better assess the author's conclusions.

Experiments in Ethnographic Writing

Ethnographic writing can take many literary forms. (e.g., Crapanzano 1980; Stoller and Olkes 1987; Behar 1996, 2003).Contemporary ethnographers explore the full range. James Clifford suggests that in the ever-changing world of those being studied, an anthropologist can really only know some of the truth. Ethnographic writing should reflect this self-acknowledged limit on the experience of reality. Once acknowledged and presented in this way, the "cultural" text— a ritual, an institution, a life history—can come alive, set free from the ethnographer's limited gaze to become "a speaking object, who sees as well as is seen, who evades, argues, probes back" (Clifford and Marcus 1986, 14)

In *A Thrice Told Tale* (1992), Margery Wolf presents three perspectives on one set of events that occurred during her fieldwork in Taiwan in the 1960s. In a village where Wolf was studying, a young mother began to act very strangely, at times suicidal. The villagers could not agree on what ailed her. Some said that a god possessed her, others that she was becoming a shaman. A number of villagers felt she had a terrible mental illness that required medication, physical restraint, or institutionalization. The most skeptical said that her husband was manipulating her, attempting to get money and sympathy from neighbors and fellow villagers. Eventually, the woman was sent away from the village to live with her mother. But this did not end the debate for many of the villagers.

Drawing on her field notes of the time, Wolf created three different texts. First, she presents a fictional short story written soon after the events occurred. Second, she presents her actual field notes as a kind of text—raw and unedited, available for the reader to analyze and assess. Finally, thirty years later, Wolf produced an anthropological article published in *American Ethnologist*, one of the field's leading academic journals. By presenting these three texts side by side, three different representations of the same event, Wolf explored the many uses of field notes and the experimental ethnography they can inform.

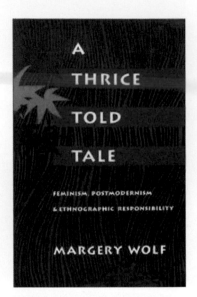

In *A Thrice Told Tale*, anthropologist Margery Wolf tells the story of a woman in a Taiwanese village from three distinct perspectives, revealing the multiple ways that the same events can be represented, even by the same anthropologist.

MAP 3.5
Taiwan

What Moral and Ethical Concerns Guide Anthropologists in Their Research and Writing?

Anthropologists often face moral and ethical dilemmas while conducting fieldwork. These dilemmas require us to make choices that may affect the quality of our research and the people we study. Indeed, the moral and ethical implications of anthropological research and writing are of deep concern within the discipline and have been particularly hot topics at various times in its history. As a result, the American Anthropological Association (AAA) has developed an extensive set of ethical guidelines, which you can view at www.aaanet.org.

Do No Harm

At the core of our ethics code is the mandate to do no harm. Even though as anthropologists we seek to contribute to general human knowledge, and perhaps shed light on a specific cultural, economic, or political problem, we must not do so at the expense of the people we study. In fact, this issue spurred the creation of the AAA's code of ethics. The organization's website presents a great variety of advice about the anthropologist's responsibility to the people being studied.

Several key examples in the history of anthropology demonstrate the importance of the "Do no harm" mandate. In the 1960s and 1970s, anthropologists came under heavy criticism for their role in colonialism, particularly for intentionally and unintentionally providing information on local cultures to colonial administrators and military agents. After World War II, anthropology as a discipline was criticized for aiding the European colonial encounter, assisting colonial administrators by providing detailed descriptions and analysis of local populations, many of which were actively engaged in struggles against colonial rule. Anthropology was criticized for helping to create an image of colonial subjects as unable to govern themselves and in need of Western guidance and rule (Asad 1973). During the Vietnam War in the 1960s, some anthropologists were criticized for collaborating with the U.S. military occupation and counterinsurgency efforts. In the 1970s, the AAA experienced internal political turmoil as it addressed accusations of covert research conducted

The relationship of anthropology to colonialism and war has been complicated. During the Vietnam War, for instance, some anthropologists were criticized for collaborating with the U.S. military occupation and counterinsurgency efforts. *(left)* An American soldier in rural Vietnam, 1967. Recently, the controversy continued as the U.S. military's Human Terrain Systems program (2007–2014) recruited anthropologists *(right)* to help troops understand local culture and make better decisions in the field.

in Southeast Asia by anthropologists (Petersen 2015; Price 2004; Wakin 1992; Wolf and Jorgensen 1970).

More recently, the ethical practices of two American researchers, anthropologist Napolean Chagnon and geneticist/physician James Neel, who worked among Brazil's indigenous Yanomami people (Chagnon 1968) in the 1960s and following, have come under question. In his book *Darkness in El Dorado* (2000), journalist Patrick Tierney claimed, among other things, that Chagnon and Neel compromised their subjects' health to see how unprotected indigenous populations would respond to the introduction of infectious disease. Later investigations did not support Tierney's most serious charges, and the original findings of the AAA against Chagnon and Neel were rescinded. The controversy, however, stimulated a significant debate within anthropology about the code of ethics expected of all members.

Recently the U.S. military has actively recruited anthropologists for service as cross-cultural experts in Iraq and Afghanistan, renewing impassioned debates within the discipline about the proper role of anthropologists in military and covert operations. Through the Human Terrain Systems program, between 2007 and 2014 the U.S. military recruited, trained, and deployed anthropologists to be embedded with combat units and to advise military commanders on building local community relationships. Though this program has ended, a similarly controversial project, the Minerva Initiative of the U.S. Department of Defense that funds social science research of benefit to U.S. military planning and operations, has raised concerns among anthropologists (Gusterson 2008). The role of anthropologists in military-sponsored "nation building" projects has been supported by some (McFate 2005) but criticized by many others, who have warned of the "weaponizing of anthropology"—turning anthropological research strategies and knowledge into a tool of war (Price 2011).

Obtain Informed Consent

One of the key principles for protecting research subjects involves obtaining **informed consent**. It is imperative that those whom we study agree to participate in the project. To do so, they must understand clearly what the project involves and the fact that they have the right to refuse to participate. After all, anthropological research is not undercover investigation using covert means and deception. The anthropologist's hallmark research strategy is participant observation, which requires establishing rapport—that is, building relationships of trust over time. To develop rapport, the subjects of our studies must be clearly informed about the goals and scope of our projects and must willingly consent to being a part of them.

U.S. federal regulations protect human subjects involved in any research, and proposals to conduct research on humans, including anthropological research,

informed consent: A key strategy for protecting those being studied by ensuring that they are fully informed of the goals of the project and have clearly indicated their consent to participate.

must be reviewed by the sponsoring organization. Such regulations were originally designed to cover medical research, but anthropologists—whether students or professionals—now participate in these institutional reviews before conducting research.

Ensure Anonymity

Anthropologists take precautions to ensure the privacy and safety of the people they study by providing anonymity in research notes and in publications. We frequently change the names and disguise the identities of individuals or, at times, whole communities. For example, Nancy Scheper-Hughes disguises the identities of people and places in Brazil to protect the community and individuals she worked with (for example, "the market town that I call Bom Jesus da Mata"). **Anonymity** provides protection for the people in our studies who may be quite vulnerable and whose lives we describe in intimate detail. This consideration becomes particularly important and sometimes controversial in situations in which research involves illegal activities—for instance, Claire Sterk's ethnography about prostitution (2000) or Philippe Bourgois's work with drug dealers in New York City (2003).

anonymity: Protecting the identities of the people involved in a study by changing or omitting their names or other identifying characteristics.

How Are Fieldwork Strategies Changing in Response to Globalization?

The increased movement of people, information, money, and goods associated with globalization has transformed ethnographic fieldwork in terms of both its process and its content.

Changes in Process

Changes in communication and transportation have altered the ongoing relationship between the anthropologist and the community being studied. Global communication allows the fieldworker and the community to maintain contact long after the anthropologist has left the field, facilitating a flow of data, discussions, and interpretation that in the past would have been very difficult to continue. The expansion of global transportation networks further increases the opportunities for personal interactions between an anthropologist and someone from the researched community outside the original research setting.

Changes in Content

Globalization has also deeply affected fieldwork content. No longer can an anthropologist study a local community in isolation from global processes. As even the most remote areas are affected by intensifying globalization—whether

THE SOCIAL LIFE OF THINGS
Mardi Gras Beads

Many anthropologists today are experimenting with ethnographic filmmaking to present their field-work research. The medium is proving especially effective in capturing the impact of globalization on local communities and the movement of people, things, and ideas. David Redmon and Ashley Sabin trace the global journey of Mardi Gras beads in their multi-sited ethnographic film *Mardi Gras: Made in China.*

The first Mardi Gras revelers paraded through the streets of New Orleans in 1857, celebrating Fat Tuesday, a day of parties, drinking, and general excess immediately preceding the Christian season of fasting before Easter. Today Mardi Gras attracts tens of thousands of tourists, to see its marching bands, parades, and floats.

Colorful plastic beads, medallions, and other inexpensive jewelry circulate throughout the Mardi Gras celebration. Beads are sold in shops, thrown ostentatiously from floats, worn draped around the necks of revelers, and exchanged between friends and strangers. Since the late 1970s revelers have exchanged beads for displays of nudity. Particularly men offer beads to entice women to bare their breasts, adding to the raucous and bawdy celebrations.

3 But where do these beads come from? Redmon and Sabin trace their production to a factory on China's southeast coast where workers, 90 percent of whom are women, live year-round toiling six or seven days a week, sometimes as much as 16 hours a day, to make toys, clothes, and trinkets for Western buyers like Disney, McDonalds, and Walmart. Factory conditions are grim. Workers operate dangerous machinery and inhale toxic fumes. Work and social life are tightly disciplined by supervisors who limit trips to the bathroom and prohibit romantic liaisons, even those after work hours.

4 Redmon and Sabin involve both the Mardi Gras revelers and Chinese factory workers as collaborators in telling their stories through a multimedia "cultural exchange", bringing the effects of globalization into focus. In New Orleans, they show startled revelers video footage of beads being made by young girls in the Chinese factory. Then, returning to China, they reveal to the workers pictures of how their beads are used in the United States. "Tell them not to do that!" says one young woman, embarrassed by the Mardi Gras scenes. "They are only little beads. They're not worth it!"

- Redmon and Sabin's fieldwork and ethnographic film shed light on the personal effects of globalization. Having considered the social life of Mardi Gras beads, is there something in your daily life that you would like to trace back to its origins?
- What story do you think your chosen object would tell?
- Given the opportunity, what do you think the producers and consumers of this object might say to one another?

through media, tourism, investment, migration, or global warming—ethnographers are increasingly integrating the local with the global in their studies. In some cases, particularly in studies of migration, ethnographic fieldwork is now multi-sited, encompassing research in two or more locations to more fully represent the scope of the issue under study.

Nancy Scheper-Hughes's career reflects many recent changes in ethnographic fieldwork. Her earliest research, introduced in the chapter opener, focused on local life in the Brazilian shantytown Alto do Cruzeiro. She has carefully monitored changes in the community in the ensuing years, including dramatic recent improvements in infant mortality rates stemming from Brazilian economic growth combined with direct government promotion of local health care services (Scheper-Hughes 2013), and she is reporting these changes in a revised and updated version of her classic ethnography, *Death Without Weeping*.

Scheper-Hughes's other recent work places Alto do Cruzeiro in the middle of an illicit global trade in harvested human organs (Scheper-Hughes 2002). While she continues to explore the richness of local life in Brazil, she has expanded her scope to examine how the experiences of the poor in one community are mirrored in the lives of poor people in many other countries and are linked by a gruesome global trade driven by demand from the world's economic elite.

> For many years I have been documenting the violence of everyday life—the many small wars and invisible genocides—resulting from the structural violence of poverty and the increasing public hostility to the bodies, minds, children, and reproductive capacities of the urban poor. Here I will be addressing an uncanny dimension of the usual story of race and class hatred to which we have become so accustomed. This is the covert violence occurring in the context of a new and thriving global trade in human organs and other body parts for transplant surgery.
>
> Descend with me for a few moments into that murky realm of the surreal and the magical, into the maelstrom of bizarre stories, fantastic allegations and a hideous class of rumors that circulate in the world's shantytowns and squatter camps, where this collaborative research project had its origins. The rumors were of kidnapping, mutilation, and dismemberment—removal of blood and organs—for commercial sale. I want to convey to you the terror and panic that these rumors induce in the nervous and hungry residents of urban shantytowns, tent cities, squatter camps, and other "informal settlements" in the Third World.

I first heard the rumor in the shantytowns of Northeast Brazil in the mid-1980s, when I was completing research for my book, *Death Without Weeping*, on maternal thinking and practice in the context of extremely high infant and child mortality. The rumors told of the abduction and mutilation of poor children who were eyed greedily as fodder for an international traffic in organs for wealthy transplant patients in the first world. Residents of the ramshackle hillside favela of Alto do Cruzeiro, the primary site of my research, reported multiple sightings of large blue and yellow combi-vans [the so-called "gypsy taxis" used by the poor the world over] driven by American or Japanese "agents" said to be scouring poor neighborhoods in search of stray youngsters, loose kids and street children, kids that presumably no one would miss. The children would be grabbed and shoved into the van. Later their discarded and eviscerated bodies—minus certain organs—heart, lungs, liver, kidneys, and eyes—would turn up on roadsides, between rows of sugarcane, or in hospital dumpsters. "They are looking for donor organs. You may think this is just nonsense," said my friend and research assistant, "Little Irente" in 1987. "*But we have seen things with our own eyes in the hospitals and the morgues and we know better.*" . . .

Soon after I began writing articles that interpreted the Brazilian organ-stealing rumors in terms of the normal, accepted, everyday violence practiced against the bodies of the poor and the marginal in public medical clinics, in hospitals, and in police mortuaries, where their ills and afflictions were often treated with scorn, neglect, and general disrespect, I began to hear other variants of the organ-theft stories from anthropologists working in Argentina, Colombia, Peru, Guatemala, Honduras, Mexico, India and Korea. Though most of the stories came from Central and South America, organ-theft rumors were also surfacing in Poland and Russia, where it was reported that poor children's organs were being sold to rich Arabs for transplant surgery. Luise White recorded blood-sucking / blood-stealing vampire stories from East and Central Africa, and South African anthropologist Isak Niehaus recorded blood- and organ-stealing rumors in the Transvaal collected during fieldwork in 1990–93. The African variants told of "firemen" or paramedics driving red combi-vans looking to capture unsuspecting people to drug and to kill in order to drain their blood or remove their organs and other body parts—genitals and eyes in particular—for

A middleman and two young Filipino men with scars; each of the two men has sold a kidney as part of the global trade in human organs.

magical medicine (*muti*) or for more traditional medical purposes. The Italian variants identified a black ambulance as the kidnap vehicle.

The rumors had powerful effects, resulting in a precipitous decline in voluntary organ donation in some countries, including Brazil and Argentina. What does it mean when a lot of people around the world begin to tell variants of the same bizarre and unlikely story? How does an anthropologist go about interpreting the uncanny and the social imaginary of poor, third-world peoples?

To the anthropologist . . . working closely with the urban poor, the rumors spoke to the ontological insecurity of people "to whom almost anything could be done." They reflected everyday threats to bodily security, urban violence, police terror, social anarchy, theft, loss and fragmentation. Many of the poor imagined, with some reason as it turns out, that autopsies were performed to harvest usable tissues and body parts from those whose bodies had reverted to the state: "Little people like ourselves are worth more dead than alive." At the very least the rumors were "like the scriptures" metaphorically true, operating by means of symbolic substitution. The rumors express the existential and ontological insecurities of poor people living on the margins of the postcolonial global economies where their labor, their bodies, and their reproductive capacities are treated as spare parts to be bought, bartered, or stolen. Underlying the rumors was a real concern with a growing commodification of the body and of body parts in these global economic exchanges. (Scheper-Hughes 2002, 33–36)

As an engaged medical anthropologist, Scheper-Hughes has spent countless hours investigating the extensive illegal international trade in smuggled human organs. Contemporary globalization, especially the time-space compression of transportation and communication, enables trafficking networks to spread across national boundaries and around the world. These same cornerstones of globalization have allowed Scheper-Hughes and her organization, Organs Watch, based at the University of California, to develop an extensive global network of anthropologists, human rights activists, transplant surgeons, journalists, and government agencies that have collaborated to address issues of human organ trafficking in India, Pakistan, Israel, South Africa, Turkey, Moldova, Brazil, the Philippines, and the United States.

As a member of two World Health Organization panels on transplant trafficking and transplant safety, Scheper-Hughes has seen firsthand the global search for kidneys: the often-poor kidney sellers; the kidney hunters who track them down; and the kidney buyers willing to cross borders, break laws, and pay as much as $150,000 in advance to the organ brokers for a chance at a new kidney and a new life. In 2009 the U.S. Federal Bureau of Investigation arrested a Brooklyn rabbi who had been arranging kidney sales, highlighting the deep integration of illegal international organ trafficking into developed-country markets where, for example, over 100,000 Americans linger on a kidney waiting list, struggling through dialysis to stay alive, and where the wait times for a donor in some parts of the country are as long as nine years.

The trajectory of Scheper-Hughes's career from fieldwork in a small favela in Brazil to fieldwork in international organ-trafficking networks reflects many of the transformations shaping anthropological fieldwork over the last forty years. No local community can be viewed as isolated. Anthropologists must consider each local fieldwork site in light of the myriad ways in which local dynamics link to the world beyond. Today fieldwork includes attention to global flows, networks, and processes as anthropologists trace patterns across national and cultural boundaries while keeping one foot grounded in the lives of people in local communities.

TOOLKIT

Thinking Like an Anthropologist: Applying Aspects of Fieldwork to Your Own Life

You don't have to go to Brazil to use the skills of an anthropologist. Maybe you will be inspired by this book—or by a language you study, a professor whose class you take, or a new friend you meet—to explore a culture in another part of the world. Or maybe you will apply these skills nearer to home. In Chapter 1 you were asked to begin seeing yourself as a budding anthropologist, one who is already working hard to understand the complicated, globalizing world and how you fit into it. Fieldwork skills are the key to navigating what lies ahead of you.

As you think back to the fieldwork of Nancy Scheper-Hughes, remember the questions we asked at the beginning of the chapter:

- What is unique about ethnographic fieldwork, and why do anthropologists conduct this kind of research?
- How did the idea of fieldwork develop?
- How do anthropologists get started conducting fieldwork?
- How do anthropologists write ethnography?
- What moral and ethical concerns guide anthropologists in their research and writing?
- How are fieldwork strategies changing in response to globalization?

Consider how the concepts we have discussed can be applied not only by a professional anthropologist but also by each one of us in our daily lives.

You already use many of the strategies, skills, and perspectives of ethnographic fieldwork to navigate your daily journey through life. Whether in your family, your workplace, or your school, you have to understand the people with whom you interact. You participate and observe, establish rapport, listen, interview, gather life histories, and map out family and social networks. If you keep a journal or diary, you have already started taking field notes about the people and cultural patterns around you. You are constantly assessing who has power, how they got it, and how they use it. While you may already use many of these tools, the goal of this chapter has been to show the rigor with which they can be applied if you take fieldwork seriously and to enable you to apply them in a more systematic and self-conscious way in your daily life.

Key Terms

ethnographic fieldwork (p. 75)
salvage ethnography (p. 81)
participant observation (p. 82)
reflexivity (p. 84)
engaged anthropology (p. 85)
anthropologist's toolkit (p. 88)
quantitative data (p. 89)
qualitative data (p. 89)
key informant (p. 90)
life history (p. 90)
survey (p. 90)
kinship analysis (p. 90)
social network analysis (p. 90)
field notes (p. 90)
mapping (p. 91)
built environment (p. 92)
zeros (p. 94)
mutual transformation (p. 94)
emic (p. 95)

etic (p. 95)

ethnology (p. 95)

polyvocality (p. 96)

informed consent (p. 100)

anonymity (p. 101)

For Further Exploration

Borofsky, Robert. 2005. *Yanomami: The Fierce Controversy and What We Can Learn from It.* Berkeley: University of California Press. Examines the ethical dilemmas of the Yanomami controversy as scholars debate the issues and students decide where they stand. Book royalties support improved Yanomami health care.

Dan Rather Reports: Kidney Pirates. Jan. 12, 2010. http://blip.tv/hdnet-news-and-documentaries/dan-rather-reports-kidney-pirates-5455011. Documentary about the global trade in human organs, featuring Nancy Scheper-Hughes.

Evans-Pritchard, Edward E. 1963. "Some Reminiscences and Reflections on Fieldwork." In *Witchcraft, Oracles and Magic among the Azande*, 239–54. Oxford, UK: Clarendon Press. Personal reflections on fieldwork.

Malinowski, Bronislaw. (1922) 2002. "Introduction: The Subject, Method and Scope of This Enquiry." In *Argonauts of the Western Pacific*, 1–25. Reprint, London: Routledge. Personal reflections on fieldwork.

Mardi Gras: Made in China. 2005. Directed by David Redmon. Carnivalesque Films. Ethnographic film showing factory in China making Mardi Gras beads and their use in the New Orleans festival.

Mead, Margaret. 1972. *Blackberry Winter; My Earlier Years.* New York: Morrow. Personal reflections on fieldwork.

Rabinow, Paul, and Robert Neelly Bellah. 1977. *Reflections on Fieldwork in Morocco.* Berkeley: University of California Press. Personal reflections on fieldwork.

Redmon, David, 2014. *Beads, Bodies and Trash: Public Sex, Global Labor and the Disposability of Mardi Gras.* Routledge Press.

Scheper-Hughes, Nancy. 1989. "Death Without Weeping: Has Poverty Ravaged Mother Love in the Shantytowns of Brazil?" *Natural History* 98 (10): 8–16. Read the full article that was excerpted at the beginning of this chapter.

Scheper-Hughes, Nancy. 2013. "No More Angel Babies on the Alto do Cruzeiro: A Dispatch from Brazil's Revolution in Child Survival." *Natural History.* www.naturalhistorymag.com/features/282558/no-more-angel-babies-on-the-alto-do-cruzeiro. Report on dramatic recent improvements in child survival in the area of Scheper-Hughes's original fieldwork.

U.S. Census Data by zip code. http://projects.nytimes.com/census/2010/explorer. Explore the demographics of your community by accessing U.S. Census data available through this *New York Times* website.

Wolf, Margery. 1992. *A Thrice Told Tale.* Stanford, CA: Stanford University Press. One anthropologist's experiment with ethnographic writing, presenting one story from a Taiwanese village in three different ways.

Could language use have marked you with "a reasonable suspicion of being undocumented" under a 2010 Arizona law?

CHAPTER 4
Language

Everything you and I have worked for is being wiped out before our eyes. Our borders, our language, and our culture are under siege.

—*Michael Savage, American author, radio talk show host and activist, 2003*

In April 2010, the state of Arizona passed a law mandating police to arrest anyone who gives a reasonable suspicion of being an undocumented immigrant. If that person cannot prove his or her legal status, he or she must be detained immediately. The law treats a very contentious issue. Arizona lawmakers argue that the law responds to the federal government's failure to monitor borders and protect U.S. citizens from foreigners who they fear will take their jobs and endanger their neighborhoods. The statement quoted above echoes this sentiment, revealing the way many people closely link increasing language diversity to social upheaval. Civil rights activists, however, ask how police will determine "a reasonable suspicion of being undocumented." They fear that law enforcement officers will rely on how the person looks (skin color), dresses, or speaks. Will someone who speaks Spanish or who speaks English with a Spanish accent be more likely to be arrested and detained? Is language an effective screen for legal status or citizenship?

Debates about language have been raging in the United States over the past twenty years. Thirty-one states have passed English-only laws limiting classroom instruction, driver's license exams, road signs, and even health warnings to one language. The U.S. House of Representatives has passed legislation several times declaring English to be the national language of the United States, although these bills have never been signed into law. The United States, historically, has been a country of many languages: Spanish, French, Dutch, German, Italian, Chinese, not to mention hundreds of Native American languages and hundreds of others spoken by contemporary immigrants. Spanish has been spoken in what is now the U.S. South and Southwest since the 1500s, when the Spanish conquistadors Francisco Vázquez de Coronado and Hernando Cortéz explored and colonized the area on behalf of the Spanish Crown. How has language come to be such a hot-button issue in the United States today?

Nearly seven thousand languages are currently in use in the world. Through linguistic anthropology, one of the four fields of anthropology, we explore not only the details of a language's vocabulary and grammar but also the role of language in people's lives—both as individuals and as communities. Languages are not abstract concepts with ideal forms perfectly displayed in a dictionary or a textbook. Languages are dynamic and alive. Communication is a social act. Words are part of actions. We call a friend, text a classmate, tell a story, say a prayer, ask a favor. Human language uses an infinite number of forms to communicate a vast array of information. We communicate through poetry, prose, gestures, signs, touch, text messaging—even anthropology textbooks. Not only can we communicate content in great detail, but we also have the wondrous capacity to share the content of our imaginations, our anger, fear, joy, and the deepest longings of our souls.

Humans are born with the ability to learn language—not a particular language, but whatever one they are exposed to as they grow up. Exactly what we learn and the context in which we learn it vary widely. Languages change and grow, constantly adapting to the needs and circumstances of the people who speak them. Although the number of languages shrinks every year under the pressures of globalization, the remarkable diversity of human language reflects humans' dramatically different ways of perceiving, thinking about, and engaging with the world. Because languages are deeply embedded in culture—languages *are* culture—they also become arenas where norms and values are created, enforced, and contested, where group identity is negotiated, and where systems of power and status are taught and challenged.

In this chapter we will consider how anthropologists study human language and communication. In particular, we will ask:

- What is language and where does it come from?
- How does language shape our ways of thinking?
- How do systems of power intersect with language and communication?
- What are the effects of globalization on language?
- How is the digital age changing the way people communicate?

By the end of the chapter you will have a better understanding of how language works, have the conceptual tools to analyze the role of language in your personal life and within your language community, and comprehend the forces that will shape language and communication in our increasingly global future.

What Is Language and Where Does It Come From?

Language is a system of communication that uses symbols—such as words, sounds, and gestures—organized according to certain rules, to convey any kind of information. All animals communicate in some fashion, often relying on a *call system* of sounds and gestures that are prompted by environmental stimuli. Ants share information through chemical trails and pheromones; bees dance to communicate distance and direction to flower petals and nectar. Dogs growl or bark to express hostility or warning. And a border collie named Betsy, featured on the cover of *National Geographic* magazine, could recognize more than 340 distinct words and commands (Morrell 2008). Dolphins produce complicated vocal signals—clicks, whistles, squeaks, trills. Whales have been found to "sing"—to create a vocalization that appears to have a unique tune or accent for each clan or pod of whales.

Although these are all examples of communication—providing information by a sender to a receiver—they are not symbolic language as humans use it. In comparison, human language is a complex system that involves the combination of many small, meaningful elements into larger syllables, words, and sentences following certain rules but with infinite variations. Human language involves sounds and gestures along with myriad symbols that have deep historical and cultural meaning. It is remarkably flexible and creative, rapidly adapting to changes in human life and the environment.

The Origins of Human Language

In searching for the evolutionary origins of human language, anthropologists, particularly primatologists, have investigated language use and communication among our nearest primate relatives—chimpanzees, orangutans, and other great apes—with some surprising results. In their natural habitats, primates produce an astonishing array of vocalizations to communicate information about food, sex, and potential predators. These calls are passed along genetically through the generations. Nonhuman primates lack the physical apparatus to create human sounds and human speech. Specifically, their ability to manipulate their vocal cords, tongue, and lips is far more limited than that of humans. But do they have the mental capacity to create human language? Scholars have conducted a set of landmark studies to explore this question of nonhuman primate language capabilities.

language: A system of communication organized by rules that uses symbols such as words, sounds, and gestures to convey information.

All animals communicate in some fashion. A border collie named Betsy could recognize more than 340 distinct words and commands.

Do nonhuman primates have the capacity to create human language? Koko, a gorilla, with Francine Patterson, learned over 400 signs in sign language.

A chimpanzee named Viki, raised by researchers as a member of a family in the 1950s, was systematically taught human speech but was only able to master four words: *mama, papa, up,* and *cup* (Hayes 1951). But what if Viki's inability to speak arose from her limited physical capacity rather than her cognitive ability? Later studies explored this possibility by teaching primates American Sign Language rather than spoken English. Because chimps, gorillas, orangutans, and other primates use their hands extensively to express themselves, the theory was that sign language might more accurately reflect their cognitive capacity for language.

A number of primates have been taught, trained, and observed over the last half century in primate research facilities in the United States. A chimpanzee named Washoe, who died in 2007 at age forty-two, was the first to use sign language, mastering more than 130 different signs (Gardner, Gardner, and Van Cantfort 1989). Koko, a gorilla, learned more than 400 signs (Patterson 1978). Chantek, an orangutan born at a primate research center in Georgia in 1977, was raised much like a human child from nine months of age by anthropologist Lyn Miles at the University of Tennessee at Chattanooga. Now living at Zoo Atlanta in a special habitat, Chantek has mastered several hundred signs and can also understand some spoken English. Reports on the language development of Washoe, Koko, and Chantek suggest that they have the ability to move beyond rote memorization of certain signs and indicate a more humanlike capacity to lie, swear, tell jokes, invent new words by combining signs, and even try to teach language to others (Fouts 1997; Miles 1993).

Scholars disagree about the final implications of research on nonhuman primate language capacity. Some have suggested that although this capacity is not as complex as human language, these nonhuman primates can develop language skills at the level of a two- or three-year-old human child (Miles 1993). Others argue that their behavior is mostly imitative—imitating their caregivers rather than using language creatively (Sebeok and Umiker-Sebeok 1980; Terrace et al. 1979). Certainly chimpanzees, gorillas, and orangutans can master rudimentary language signs and can even, at times, exhibit key aspects of human language skills. Their language use reflects *productivity*, meaning that they can use known words to invent new word combinations. Their language can also exhibit *displacement*—that is, the ability to use words to refer to objects not immediately present or events happening in the past or future. But, fundamentally, these primates do not use language in the human sense. In their natural habitats, they do not create and use basic language elements. They cannot achieve the extremely complex human language system that is perhaps the most distinct aspect of human culture and that enables us to store and pass on to succeeding generations huge quantities of information not embedded in our genes.

If our most immediate primate relatives do not approach the physical or mental language capacity of humans, then how did human language capacity evolve? Recent genetic information and archaeological evidence provide strong clues. Let's consider the genetic information first. Around 1990, a family in Britain (now known only as KE to protect their privacy) was discovered to have a rare mutation of the *FOXP2* gene. The same variant of *FOXP2* is found in chimpanzees. More than half of the members of the KE family inherited severe speech problems that made them unintelligible even to their own relatives (Trivedi 2001). Not only were affected family members unable to physically form words because of a limited ability to make fine lip and tongue movements, but cognitive differences also led them to have difficulty in recognizing and using grammar. As children, these family members were taught to use certain hand gestures to compensate. Genetic analysis indicates that the presence of the particular *FOXP2* gene variant may be crucial for activating and inactivating key human speech capacities, an evolutionary development that appears to be essential to human speech. Such analysis also traces the emergence of human language to within the past 150,000 years.

Archaeological evidence provides further clues to the origins of human language. Fossilized brain casts from archaic *Homo sapiens* known as Neandertals (who lived from about 130,000 to about 30,000 years ago) and even earlier *Homo* species reveal the neurological and anatomical features necessary for speech. Our early human ancestors' capacity to cooperate in hunting and tool making also suggests that some language ability may have existed over 2 million years ago, before the evolution of *Homo sapiens*. Cultural evidence supporting extensive language use by modern humans appears around 50,000 years ago, including art, tool making, and other technologies that required language to facilitate their transmission from generation to generation. Language as it has developed among modern humans would have enhanced the capacity for group cooperation and the transmission of cultural knowledge; in this way, it conferred a significant advantage in adapting to less hospitable natural environments and increasing the potential for survival.

Descriptive Linguistics

Language is a system of symbols. It is a system of otherwise meaningless sounds, marks (writing), and gestures that are made meaningful by a group of people through the collective history and tradition of their culture. Think of the English word *pig*. Say it out loud. Now create a mental image of a pig. Why do those three letters and that particular sound represent a pig? They don't look like a pig or sound like any of the noises that a pig makes. But when you say the word, an image is transferred from your brain into sound, which travels

descriptive linguistics: The study of the sounds, symbols, and gestures of a language, and their combination into forms that communicate meaning.

phonemes: The smallest units of sound that can make a difference in meaning.

phonology: The study of what sounds exist and which ones are important in a particular language.

morphemes: The smallest units of sound that carry meaning on their own.

morphology: The study of patterns and rules of how sounds combine to make morphemes.

syntax: The specific patterns and rules for combining morphemes to construct phrases and sentences.

grammar: The combined set of observations about the rules governing the formation of morphemes and syntax that guide language use.

through the air into another person's ears and to that person's brain, where an image appears that is similar to yours—if not precisely the same. **Descriptive linguistics** is the study of the construction of those sounds, their meanings, and their combination into forms that communicate meaning. Linguistic anthropologists focus on describing language as it is used and not on prescribing how people should use it.

Through descriptive linguistics, anthropologists work to describe the elements and rules of a particular language. Imagine that you went to conduct linguistic research in a village in the mountains of the Philippines where the residents had no writing system for their local language. Your task might be to learn that oral language and to create a system for representing it in writing, perhaps using the International Phonic Alphabet. Where would you begin? After identifying a person or a few people from the village who would be your teachers, perhaps you would work your way from the most simple aspects of the language to the most complex. A language has a limited number of **phonemes**—the smallest units of sound that can make a difference in meaning. For instance, the English letters *b* and *p* sound very similar, but they make a significant difference in meaning. If you failed to carefully distinguish the different phoneme use in the village where you were working, you might mistakenly switch one for the other in a word followed by the sound *ig* when describing your host's home. In that case, you would end up with *pig* instead of *big*. The study of what sounds exist and which ones are important in a particular language is called **phonology**.

Extending your linguistic analysis, you would know that **morphemes** are the smallest units of sound that carry meaning on their own. (Phonemes, in contrast, have no meaning of their own.) So, for instance, the morphemes *cow* and *horse* can convey meaning without needing additional sounds. The study of the patterns and rules of how sounds combine to make morphemes is called **morphology**. In human languages, we combine morphemes to form phrases and sentences, relying on specific patterns and rules called **syntax**. So, following Standard American English syntax, we would place a possessive pronoun before the noun, not afterward. We would say or write *my pig*, not *pig my*—although the latter pattern might be linguistically appropriate in another language. **Grammar** encompasses the combined set of observations about the rules governing the formation of morphemes and syntax that guide language use.

Nonverbal Communication: Kinesics and Paralanguage

To fully describe and understand another language, the linguist must master more than its spoken and written elements. Human language is accompanied by and embedded in a gesture–call system made up of nonverbal elements that

also convey significant amounts of information. These elements include body movements, noises, tone of voice, touch, and proxemics—cultural understandings about the use of space. **Kinesics**, the study of the relationship between body movements and communication, explores all the facial expressions, gestures, and postures that convey messages with or without words. For example, nods, handshakes, bows, and arms folded tightly across the chest all communicate information, although their meanings are not universal; they vary from culture to culture. The thumbs-up and the "okay" hand signals used in North America are considered rude gestures in certain other cultures. North Americans point with their fingers, but Filipinos point with their lips. Have you ever had the experience of making a motion or gesture that someone else misunderstood? If so, what was the cultural context?

Sign language, while involving elaborate and meaningful movements, is not simply a part of the gesture–call system described here. Rather it is considered to be a language itself, expressed visually rather than aurally.

Human language is also accompanied by **paralanguage**—an extensive set of noises (such as laughs, cries, sighs, yells) and tones of voice that convey significant information about the speaker. Paralanguage indicates whether the speaker is (for example) happy, sad, angry, tired, scared, disgusted, or enthusiastic. Try saying the sentence "The exam is on Thursday" using each of these tones of voice. The effect on communication is really quite stunning.

As much as 90 percent of emotional information is communicated through body movements and paralanguage. No wonder that email and text messaging have developed an extensive set of "emoticons" and "emojis"—symbols that indicate the emotional content intended by the sender. Emails and text

Humans have been communicating in writing for thousands of years. (*left*) Ancient Egyptian stele with hieroglyphs, ca. twenty-seventh to twenty-fifth century BCE (*right*) Rune stone on Adelso Island near Stockholm, Sweden, eleventh century CE.

kinesics: The study of the relationship between body movements and communication.

paralanguage: An extensive set of noises (such as laughs, cries, sighs, and yells) and tones of voice that convey significant information about the speaker.

:-)	=	Smile
:-(	=	Frown
;-)	=	Wink
:-P	=	Tongue Out
:-D	=	Laughing
:-[	=	Embarrassed
:-\	=	Undecided
=-O	=	Surprise
:-*	=	Kiss
>:o	=	Yell
8-)	=	Cool
:-$	=	Money Mouth
:-!	=	Foot in mouth
O:-)	=	Innocent
:'(	=	Cry
:-X	=	Lips are Sealed

Did you ever wonder why emoticons developed in emails and text messages?

Sapir-Whorf hypothesis: The idea that different languages create different ways of thinking.

messaging are beneficial developments in that they allow rapid response over distances great and small in our globalizing world, and they are increasingly used in the business world and personal life. But because they are devoid of the kinesics and paralanguage that play such key roles in face-to-face human communication, they significantly increase the potential for misunderstandings. Do you trust email or text messaging to communicate your most intimate thoughts? Can you remember an instance when they failed to adequately convey your meaning?

How Does Language Shape Our Ways of Thinking?

The power of language to shape human thought and culture has been a hot topic in linguistic anthropology for many generations. Linguistic anthropologists have considered questions such as: Is there an underlying, genetically structured grammar to all languages? Do languages evolve in response to local environments? Do vocabularies and classifications of reality embedded in a language affect the way its speakers think and see the world? In this section we will look at research on the relationships among language, thought, and culture, as well as a culturally specific phenomenon known as *focal vocabulary*.

Language, Thought, and Culture

In the nineteenth and twentieth centuries, a number of linguists, including Ferdinand de Saussure and Claude Levi-Strauss, proposed theories of language that assumed an underlying structure to all the world's languages. In the 1950s Noam Chomsky, a linguist and philosopher, suggested that the human brain is hardwired with a basic framework for organizing language that creates a universal grammar—a similar structure in all languages (1957). In Chomsky's view, all humans share a similar language ability and ways of thinking. He felt that this proposition explains our ability to learn other languages and to translate fluidly from one language to another.

The work of Edward Sapir and his student Benjamin Lee Whorf—later given the name **Sapir-Whorf hypothesis**—took a different direction, suggesting that different languages create different ways of thinking (Sapir and Swadesh 1946). Their hypothesis proposed that languages establish certain mental categories, or classifications of reality, almost like a grammar for organizing the worldview that shapes peoples' ways of perceiving the world. Whorf's linguistic research with the Hopi, a Native American group in the southwestern United States, suggested that the Hopi language differs from English both in vocabulary and in basic grammatical categories that are key to conceptualizing how the world works. For instance, rather than using separate verb tenses expressing past, present, and future, the Hopi language combines past and present into one. Whorf suggested that this pattern reflects a different conceptualization of time and a unique worldview in which past and present reflect lived reality whereas the future is hypothetical or potential (Carroll 1956).

"Shakespeare in the Bush": A Tiv Interpretation of *Hamlet* Laura Bohannan explores the challenges that different vocabulary and conceptualizations of the world pose for translation between languages and cultures. She relates her discoveries in her article "Shakespeare in the Bush: An American Anthropologist Set Out to Study the Tiv of West Africa and Was Taught the True Meaning of *Hamlet*" (1966). While Bohannan was conducting fieldwork in a small village in Nigeria, Tiv elders asked her to tell them a story from her own culture. She attempted to explain *Hamlet*, one of the classic stories of English literature, but time and again was unable to translate directly from English to Tiv. Words such as *chief* and *leader* hold distinctly different meanings and roles in the two cultures; they do not translate to people with a different cultural worldview. The "dead" in Hamlet do not translate because the Tiv have no concept of ghosts. Instead, they imagined Shakespeare's characters as beset by witchcraft.

MAP 4.1
Nigeria

As Bohannan attempted to use Tiv words to tell Shakespeare's story, the original meanings of the English words became blurred, and the standard message of *Hamlet* was lost in translation. Bohannan's insights as related in "Shakespeare in the Bush" reveal both the power of our environment to shape our language and the power of our language to shape the way we see the world.

"Wisdom Sits in Places": The Western Apache Worldview Keith Basso's beautifully written ethnography *Wisdom Sits in Places* (1996) explores the connections among language, thought, and culture for the Western Apache. His exploration focuses on the unique names that these people give to places in the surrounding natural landscape and the stories and cultural values that they connect to those places.

Over thirty years of living and working on the Fort Apache Reservation of Arizona, Basso mapped the Apache names and stories for 296 locations spread over forty-five square miles. Each place on the landscape had become part of Apache folklore and a key touchstone in instilling the community's values. Through the use of place names in storytelling, these places—with their deep sense of meaning—had become detached from the physical landscape and integrated into the people's daily thought and behavior. Places in the landscape were intimately linked to stories of the Apache ancestors' struggles and wisdom, and then were reinterpreted for the living generation.

MAP 4.2
Fort Apache Reservation

Basso recalls watching stories being shot like arrows at people in conversations, usually by elders telling a story to make a point. Consider the following

The North Fork of the White River flows through a canyon on the Fort Apache Indian Reservation, Whiteriver, Arizona. Western Apache speakers link natural landscape features, like these, to popular folktales so that mention of the place evokes key cultural values.

example. A teenage girl, recently returned from a boarding school in Utah, attended a coming-of-age ritual for another girl in the community. Despite the well-known tradition that participants wear their hair down as a sign of respect for the ritual and its sponsors, this young girl wore her hair up in pink curlers. Although people were uniformly unhappy with her behavior, no one spoke to her about it. Several weeks later, the girl attended a birthday party given by her grandmother for a grandson. After dinner, as the company gathered in conversation, Basso recalls how the grandmother began to tell the well-known historical tale of the "forgetful Apache policeman who behaved too much like a white man"—a story associated with a particular place in the local landscape named Men Stand Above Here and There. When the story was finished, the granddaughter quietly stood up and walked back to her home. When Basso asked the grandmother what had happened, she replied, "I shot her with an arrow" (Basso 1996, 56–57).

Two years later, Basso met the young woman again and asked if she remembered the evening at her grandmother's home. "I think maybe my grandmother was getting after me, but then I think maybe not, maybe she's working on somebody else. Then I think back on that dance and I know it's me for sure. I sure don't like how she's talking about me, so I quit looking like that. I threw those curlers away." As Basso and the girl passed near the rock outcropping called Men Stand Above Here and There—the place associated with the grandmother's story—the girl said, "I know that place. It stalks me every day."

This young woman had been the target of an Apache historical tale told by her grandmother and reinforced by a physical landmark she knew well. The landmark would always remind her—and other tribal members—of the tension between retaining traditional Apache values and adopting aspects of white culture. In this way, Basso's ethnography illustrates the deep connection among stories, the individual, and the landscape; among language, thought, and culture.

The Role of Focal Vocabulary

Contemporary studies in linguistic anthropology suggest that although the vocabulary and grammar of the language we learn may influence the way we see the world, language does not control or restrict our thinking. Languages are dynamic. They change and adapt as the natural and cultural worlds shift. Humans creatively invent new words and concepts to describe and discuss the changing world as they experience it. Evidence of this adaptability can be found in a language's **lexicon**—all the words for names, ideas, and events that make up a language's dictionary.

Of particular interest to linguistic anthropologists is a language's **focal vocabulary**—that is, words and terminology that develop with particular sophistication to describe the unique cultural realities experienced by a group of people. Thus the Bolivian Aymar Indians have two hundred names for potatoes, reflecting the potato's role as a major source of food in their diet. The Nuer of Sudan, studied by E. E. Evans-Pritchard (1940), relied on cattle in their economy, political system, and kinship structures; thus, they developed more than 400 words to distinguish different types of cattle. In today's globalizing world, a focal vocabulary has emerged to describe and engage in digital communication. Words such as *mouse, modem, download*, and *attachment*—even *email, texting*, and *tweet*—are very recent creations designed to facilitate communication among those working in the digital communication age.

Even the human description of the color spectrum varies across and within cultures, seemingly according to need. Anthropologist Robin Lakoff (2004) examined how color terms in American English have expanded over the last fifty years, being promoted by the fashion and cosmetics industries. An extensive color vocabulary is not uniform among Americans; it varies primarily by gender. Women are far more likely than men, for instance, to be able to distinguish between salmon and peach, teal and turquoise, or cranberry and dusky orange. A similar gender-based focal vocabulary exists in American sports language. Men are far more likely than women to use the common basketball terms such as *back door, box out, zone, dish, reverse layup, in the bonus, in the paint, isolation play, from downtown!*, or *and one!* This highly specialized set of terms and distinctions allows complex communication about complicated human activity but is applicable in extremely limited scenarios.

Clearly, language, including vocabulary, provides categories for recognizing and organizing the world; but language also reflects reality. Language is not rigidly structured or controlling. It is remarkably flexible and fluid, responding to changes in the surrounding culture and enabling us to describe and analyze our world with remarkable specificity.

How Do Systems of Power Intersect with Language and Communication?

Language comes alive when people communicate with one another. But languages are deeply embedded in the patterns of particular cultures. What people actually say and how they say it are intricately connected to the cultural context,

lexicon: All the words for names, ideas, and events that make up a language's dictionary.

focal vocabulary: The words and terminology that develop with particular sophistication to describe the unique cultural realities experienced by a group of people.

sociolinguistics: The study of the ways culture shapes language and language shapes culture, particularly the intersection of language with cultural categories and systems of power such as age, race, ethnicity, sexuality, gender, and class.

to the speakers' social position, and to the larger systems of power within which the language operates. Linguistic anthropologists, especially sociolinguists, study these connections. **Sociolinguistics**, which we will consider in this section, is the study of the ways in which culture shapes language and language shapes culture, particularly the intersection of language with cultural categories and systems of power such as age, race, ethnicity, sexuality, gender, and class (Wardhaugh 2009).

The "N-Word"

Words can be very powerful. They can hurt. They can heal. Some do so more than others. Words are also symbols. They can carry profound meanings based on the history of their use in a culture. As we explore the intersection of language and culture, particularly the intersection of language and systems of power, a consideration of the history and contemporary usage of the "N-word" provides rich insights. In U.S. culture, the "N-word" carries such powerful connotations that many people are reluctant to say it out loud or put it in print. Television stations censor it from their broadcasts. Politicians shy away from controversy over its usage. It is so powerful that most people only refer to it as the "N-word."

Nigger has been used as a derogatory term for African Americans throughout much of U.S. history—as a symbol of white power, slavery, and the threat of violence. In the twentieth century, the use of the "N-word" in public discourse was replaced successively by the use of *Negro, colored, black*, and *African American*. In 1962, the U.S. federal government legally changed the offending name on all public properties under its control, replacing it with *Negro* (Severson 2011). The "N-word," however, has not disappeared. It continues to hold tremendous symbolic power as its use invokes the history of racism, inequality, and the threat to make those dangers real in the present.

Despite its sordid history, use of the "N-word" has been revived among African American youth and in hip-hop and rap music. As a result, a debate has raged even within the African American community about its appropriateness. Many older African Americans reject its use because of its long-standing association with U.S. systems of race and racism. In contrast, younger generations often articulate their desire to appropriate the term for their own generation and rob it of its historical power.

My students remind me that some young people today quite commonly use the "N-word" to express friendship and camaraderie, not anger and hostility. At the same time, they recognize distinct rules about this usage—rules that factor in race, gender, age, and status and that attempt to mitigate against the former role of the "N-word" in this country's systems of race and racism. These young people carefully say "nigga," dropping the hard "r" ending, perhaps

taking a slight edge off the word's powerful meaning. They only use it among friends. White people rarely address a person of color with the greeting. Boys never call girls "nigga." Girls rarely use it among themselves. Young people never use it in reference to older people. And students never use it in addressing a professor.

Think about how you feel when you hear the "N-word" spoken aloud. Is your reaction affected by your race, gender, age, or status, or by those of the speaker? Do you feel comfortable using the "N-word" in daily speech? If so, where, when, and with whom? If not, what is the source of your discomfort? Is it ever appropriate for a white person to use it in the U.S. cultural context? Sociolinguists study language in this way. They examine the use of language in its specific contexts and the way language shapes and is shaped by other dynamics of power.

Language and Gender

Ethnic and racial dynamics are not the only sources of tension in communication. Have you ever walked away from a conversation with someone of the opposite sex and thought to yourself, that person has no idea what I'm talking about! You are not alone. Bookstores are full of titles that promise to help you figure it out: *Men Are from Mars, Women Are from Venus* (Gray 2004); *The 5 Love Languages: The Secret to Love That Lasts* (Chapman 2010); *You Just Don't Understand: Women and Men in Conversation* (Tannen 2001). Clearly, women and men are developing different patterns of language use. How and why?

Did you ever wonder why men and women struggle to communicate with each other? Are their brains wired differently for language, or have they grown up in different social worlds learning different communication skills?

There is no hard evidence that the brains of men and women are wired differently, leading to gender differences in language and other behavior. But linguistic anthropologists have examined the powerful role of culture in shaping language. In this instance, language and gender are intricately intertwined in personal and public conversations, among groups of men or groups of women, and in mixed-sex talk. In particular, linguists use two main theoretical frameworks for analyzing these patterns. The frameworks are sometimes known as the *difference model* and the *dominance model*.

Linguistic anthropologist Deborah Tannen's popular book *You Just Don't Understand: Women and Men in Conversation* (2001) is built on the difference model. Tannen suggests that conversations between men and women are basically a form of cross-cultural communication. Between the ages of five and fifteen, boys and girls grow up in different linguistic worlds. At the time when most children are developing and perfecting their communication skills, boys and girls are operating in largely segregated gender groups. Girls mostly hang out in small groups, indoors in more intimate conversations. Boys tend to play in larger groups, often outdoors, and compete with one another for group status, often through verbal jokes, stories, and challenges. These patterns, according to Tannen, are reinforced in later years through socializing, sports, and work. No wonder that boys and girls have a difficult time communicating with each other when they finally begin to look for relationships. It is as if they have grown up in two different cultures, two different worlds.

But is miscommunication always rooted in misunderstanding? Or are there real, underlying conflicts between the genders that lead to the miscommunication (Cameron 2007)? Other linguistic anthropologists, working from the dominance model, examine how the cultures of communication learned by boys and girls intertwine with gender dynamics throughout the larger culture: at home, school, work, and play, and even through religion. According to these scholars, if gender stratification and hierarchy are prevalent in the larger culture (see Chapter 8), and if men are generally in positions of superiority, then language will reflect men's dominance and may play a key role in enabling it (Lakoff 2004; West 1998).

Research on mixed-sex communication over the past thirty years consistently shows that many men adopt linguistic strategies that allow them to establish and maintain dominance in conversation and in social interaction. Men are more likely to use dominant speech acts such as commands, explanations, contradictions, criticisms, challenges, and accusations. Women are more likely to ask, request, agree, support, accommodate, accept, and apologize. Men are more likely to interrupt other speakers to insert their ideas or concerns, express doubts, or offer advice.

Despite stereotypes to the contrary, men also tend to dominate conversations through the amount of talking they do. Men claim more "air time" than women in meetings, seminars, boardrooms, and classrooms—especially in public forums where they see some possibility of maintaining or increasing their power and status. Working from the dominance model of mixed-sex communication, many linguistic anthropologists suggest that language and gender, as reflected in male and female communication patterns, are intricately connected to patterns of stratification in the culture at large (Holmes 1998).

Does "No" Really Mean "No"? Don Kulick's (2003) study of the use of the word *no* in sexual relations considers how words can take on different meanings depending on the gender of the speaker and the listener. What does "no" mean when a woman says it to a man who desires sex? In court cases involving rape or sexual harassment, men regularly state that they have misunderstood a woman's refusal of their sexual advances. They often blame the victim for not being clear enough with her "no." How can this miscommunication be possible? After all, "no" means "no." Or does it?

According to Kulick's findings, some men apparently think a woman's "no" actually means "yes" or "keep trying." Kulick suggests that men don't hear the actual word but instead hear what they think the word is supposed to mean. Specifically, his study suggests that men in a patriarchal (male-dominated) culture may not even hear a woman's "no" because it does not make sense within their cultural expectations of what a woman is supposed to say. Because U.S. culture casts women as sexual objects, "no" does not meet the cultural expectations of what a woman is or how a woman should behave. Within U.S. cultural formations of gender roles and sexuality, women are imagined to say "no," to resist, when they actually mean "yes." Is it possible that based on their gender, the men and women in your class might even react differently to hearing the results of this study?

The power of culture to shape the meaning of language can have implications for men as well. Men in U.S. culture are expected to say "yes" to women's sexual initiatives, never "no." With a "no" the man risks undermining his masculine identity, perhaps raising questions about his sexuality. A simple and straightforward linguistic expression—*No!*—struggles for clarity in the murky cultural context of gender relationships and power (MacKinnon 1993). As U.S. colleges and universities struggle to address widespread incidents of sexual harassment and abuse and seek to empower students to communicate more directly and successfully about their intentions and desires, attention to the intersections of language, gender, and power become increasingly important.

Language and Dialect

Politics and power can play key roles in how we evaluate a system of communication. For instance, how do we distinguish between a language and a dialect? Is it purely on a linguistic basis? A language is commonly described as a complete system of communication, while a **dialect** is considered a nonstandard variation of a language. Naming something a dialect generally places it in a subordinate relationship to the language. However, from a linguistic anthropologist's perspective, the distinction is not always simple. Human languages vary widely in spoken and written form and in accent, pronunciation, vocabulary, and grammar. Yet, from a linguistic perspective, all languages serve as effective communication tools for the people who speak them.

The categorization and evaluation of certain ways of speaking as a dialect and others as a language can frequently be traced to the exertion of power—political power of the nation, the state, the media, and even the stratification among racial and ethnic groups. Yiddish linguist Max Weinreich reputedly once said that a language is a dialect with an army and a navy. In other words, the elevated status associated with a language derives not from its superior linguistic form or communication capacity, but from its ability to establish—perhaps impose through force, if necessary—a particular form as the norm by which to judge other ways of speaking. A particular language variation or way of speaking may be elevated in a culture as the **prestige language**, associated with wealth, success, education, and power.

French sociologist Pierre Bourdieu proposes that language skills serve as a type of cultural capital—a resource or asset available to language users that can be converted into financial capital, such as wages and benefits. Mastery over it brings a set of resources that enable the individual to be more successful. Bourdieu notes that linguistic standards are established and reinforced by

dialect: A nonstandard variation of a language.

prestige language: A particular language variation or way of speaking that is associated with wealth, success, education, and power.

Language and Gender in the Classroom

The classroom is one of the most important places in which we learn social roles, including gender roles. We learn not only from the materials we read but also, and perhaps more important, from the people and the institution around us. Talk is a key component of education. We learn through talking, thinking out loud, exploring new ideas with a group of people, and making ideas our own.

But studies have consistently shown that boys dominate classroom conversations. Myra Sadker and David Sadker (1985) surveyed one hundred classrooms and found that boys spoke three times as much as girls and called out answers eight times as often. A study in East Midlands, northeast England (Swann 2007), used video recordings of teachers and students to document both verbal and nonverbal patterns of behavior. There, boys contributed more often and used more words than girls. But the differences were not uniform by gender. Some of the boys were quieter than some of the girls. And classroom conditions affected the action. Boys spoke more when open classroom discussion allowed them to just jump in. When teachers called on students by name, girls had a slight advantage. In another classroom, if the teacher called on students in response to raised hands, boys again were favored; the videotapes showed that they raised their hands more quickly and decisively.

Swann suggests that the unequal participation of boys and girls must be viewed in light of a wide variety of linguistic and nonlinguistic features that combine to create an environment where boys feel more comfortable and secure to actively participate in classroom talk. For instance, she notes that students in the classroom do not act alone; rather, they engage with a teacher who mediates and controls the dynamics, who calls on students directly, and whose body language, positioning, and gaze informally promote certain communication patterns. The classroom reflects larger cultural patterns

Can you see ways in which gender affects language use in your classrooms?

according to which it may seem normal for men to talk more, leading to complicity by boys, girls, and the adults who teach them.

Can you see the dynamics of gender and language at work in your own life? This week, conduct an analysis of gender and language in the classroom. As you attend classes, take careful notes about who speaks. Are they male or female? How long do they speak? Try to be more specific and count the number of words they use. What tendencies do you notice in the speech acts of men and women and the way they present themselves through language? Also, consider that classrooms are mediated and controlled by an instructor. What is the instructor's role in encouraging or discouraging communication by men and women in the classroom, either through words or through body language? How often does he or she call on men and women? Does the instructor's body language or gaze affect participation? Does the instructor's own gender influence the way he or she interacts with members of the class? Analyze your observations to develop a hypothesis about language and gender in the classroom.

a culture's educational institutions, government, media, and religious organizations. They may be taught in schools, used in national media broadcasts such as radio and television, or selected as a sign of competence in business hiring practices. Other language variations are then judged against the norm of the prestige language, and their speakers—often said to be speaking a dialect—are associated with inferior positions within the culture (Bourdieu 1982, 1984).

Language Variation in the United States

As the chapter-opening story illustrates, the United States is home to people speaking nearly 400 languages, including 169 distinct Native American languages whose origins predate European conquest (U.S. Census Bureau 2011b). Some 41 million people speak Spanish as their first language, and another 11 million are bilingual (Instituto Cervantes 2015). The 38 million immigrants in the U.S. bring unprecedented language diversity—though, as we will discuss in Chapter 13, 90 percent of the children of immigrants learn to speak English proficiently (Pew Research Center 2013).

Although globally the English language varies widely in pronunciation, vocabulary, and grammar, in the United States—through national television, radio, and the educational system—the midwestern accent and grammatical usage have become the prestige language variation. This is sometimes called Standard Spoken American English (SSAE), or simply Standard American English (SAE), against which all other variations are judged. As we explored in this chapter's opening story, judgments about language can have consequences well beyond the realm of communication. We turn first to consider issues of class and race as they intersect with Standard American English.

Language and Class Stratification Speakers of a language are viewed not only as individuals but also as members of a speech community that exists within a complicated and often stratified culture. Language, along with occupation, education, and socioeconomic status, is often used as an indicator of social class. Language variation in the United States that does not conform to the national prestige norm often has a negative implication: it is seen to indicate that the speaker is uneducated or low class, even though these speech variations are standard within their speech community and not linguistically flawed. This evaluation may have concrete effects on the life chances of speakers.

In examining the intersection of language and class, William Labov (1972b) conducted a study of the variation in pronunciation of the letter *r* in words like *car, floor, card*, and *fourth* in New York City. The pronunciation of *r* varies widely across the United States and has changed over the country's history, including both *r* and *r*-less usage. Areas around Boston and the South originally adopted and continue to retain *r*-less pronunciation modeled after British prestige speech patterns. After an early period of pronouncing the *r*, residents

of New York City in the nineteenth century began to go *r*-less. But by the late twentieth century, the *r* was returning to prestige-speak.

Labov surveyed sales clerks in three Manhattan department stores with different clientele: Saks on 50th Street and Fifth Avenue, the most prestigious; Macy's on 34th Street and Herald Square; and Klein's at Union Square and 14th Street, the least prestigious. Labov found that sales clerks' use of *r* increased both with the prestige of the store and within each store according to the escalation of prices on each floor. His study closely linked the increased pronunciation of *r* with increased prestige. Employers, perhaps subconsciously associating *r*-less pronunciation with the lower classes, used speech patterns to evaluate potential sales clerks, matched workers' language to the relative prestige of their stores, and assigned sales tasks according to the employees' perceived class, thereby directly affecting employee wages.

Code Switching in Academia In cultures with distinct language variations, dialects, and accents, individuals may become skilled at **code switching**—that is, switching back and forth between one variation and another according to cultural context. Code switching takes many forms, as speakers may switch from language to language and from linguistic style to style.

Educational systems tend to resist acknowledging speech variations as equally effective, instead choosing to promote a prestigious version as inherently better. (For instance, think about the linguistic standards your instructor used to grade your last English paper.) In educational environments, as a result, students, teachers, and administrators all learn to switch frequently from informal to formal styles of speaking and writing as required. Talking with friends in the hallway may assume a very different form than responding to a professor's query in class. Writing a text message or a post on Facebook elicits a

Language is often used as an indicator of social class. Do you think employers at the H&M casual clothing store (*left*) or at Hugo Boss (*right*), a luxury men's clothing store, hire sales clerks whose language use reflects the relative prestige of their stores?

code switching: Switching back and forth between one linguistic variant and another depending on the cultural context.

distinctly different writing style compared with polishing a research paper for a class assignment.

I recently received the following email from a student who appears to have struggled to understand when to switch codes:

> Hi, how r u? this is xxxx from ur class which is on monday n wednesday @ 9:30. i just wanted to ask u that about the book critique. I know what i as suppose to do in terms of writing about the book however i am lost n not sure wht i should do abt the articles and how u want us to relate it to our paper. I mean am i suppose to write abt the book n then relate it to da article n den offer my own opinion on it? plz let me know how i should b doing dis or if this is how i should be doing it. . . . . . Thank you

While this use of language may serve perfectly well in a text or email with a friend or peer, the failure to code switch in a communication with a professor runs the risk of sending the wrong signals. What evaluations might a professor make of a communication like this one written by a student in text-speak?

African American English: "Spoken Soul" Linguistic anthropologists and other scholars of language have extensively studied one particular form of English that is spoken by millions of African Americans in the United States. At times, this variation has been referred to as Black English, Black English Vernacular, African American Vernacular English, or African American English (AAE). The language habits of African Americans in the U.S. are not homogenous but vary according to region, gender, social class, and age, and not all African Americans speak AAE. Even among those who do, there are significant differences.

TABLE 4.1 Contrasts between Standard American English and African American English

Standard English	Standard English Contraction	African American English Vernacular
You are ready	You're ready	You ready
He is ready	He's ready	He ready
We are ready	We're ready	We ready
They are ready	They're ready	They ready

SOURCE: William Labov. 1972a. *Language in the Inner City: Studies in the Black English Vernacular.* Philadelphia: University of Pennsylvania Press.

African American English is perhaps the most stigmatized variation of Standard American English, mistakenly criticized as broken or flawed English and associated with urban African American youth. But from a linguistic perspective, AAE is a complete, consistent, and logical variation of the English language with a unique history and a distinct and coherent pronunciation, vocabulary, and grammar. Studies by Labov (1972a) and other scholars have carefully demonstrated that African American English is not an ungrammatical jumble but a sophisticated linguistic system with clear rules and patterns (Table 4.1).

Here, the Oakland, California, Task Force on the Education of African American Students presents a resolution on Ebonics in public education, on January 12, 1997.

Scholars disagree about the exact origins of AAE. Some trace its vocabulary and grammar to the West African linguistic roots of enslaved people who were brought forcibly to work in the American colonies. Others trace its heritage to nonstandard English used by poor English immigrants who interacted with African slave workers in the plantation system of the American South. The creole languages—blends between the indigenous language and the colonial language—found in Jamaica, Trinidad, Barbados, and Guyana that developed during and after the slave trade may also have been potential sources for the unique forms that AAE has taken (Green 2002; Rickford and Rickford 2000).

Despite its stigmatization within certain parts of American society and the intense cultural pressure to assimilate to Standard American English, AAE not only has survived and developed but has become a symbol of identity and solidarity for many within the African American community. Rickford and Rickford (2000) document how this "Spoken Soul"—spoken by African Americans of all ages across the United States and closely associated with African American identity and culture—comes alive in the African American community. Indeed, it is vibrant in homes, schools, streets, and churches and on the airwaves. It is representative of a culture, history, and worldview that are distinct from white culture and ways of speaking.

The linguistic status of African American English entered prominently into the U.S. national debate in 1996. At that time, the Oakland Unified School District in California recommended recognizing it, under the name Ebonics—from *ebony* ("black") + *phonics* ("sounds")—as a distinct language and supporting student speakers of AAE as if they were learning Standard American English as a second language in school. In response, critics from across the country warned that the "teaching of Ebonics" in U.S. public schools would undermine the use of Standard American English, which they considered central to U.S. national identity, unity, and progress.

Under pressure, the Oakland school district revised its plan, but the controversy effectively obscured their efforts to address a local problem with national implications—the struggles of African American children to succeed in school. Today, resistance to recognizing African American English continues, creating negative stereotypes that undermine efforts to understand the unique linguistic character of AAE and the struggles that young AAE speakers may have in educational settings dominated by Standard American English. In fact, the debate about English language diversity and the place of Standard American English in U.S. culture continues through efforts at the local, state, and national levels (Ahearn 2012).

Mock Spanish Despite efforts by linguistic anthropologists to educate the public that all languages are linguistically equal, as we have seen in this chapter's opening story, language is often used as an indicator of social position and status. The hierarchical relationship between Spanish and English in the United States offers insights into the process of creating and maintaining hierarchies of power—including hierarchies of race—that stigmatize and marginalize speakers of nonprestige languages.

Bonnie Urciuoli's (1996) study of bilingual Puerto Ricans in New York City found that speakers experience language in two distinct spheres. In an inner sphere of communication with family, friends, and neighbors, both English and Spanish are used freely. Linguistic boundaries are blurred as speakers create fluent and elaborate patterns of communication drawing from both languages. In contrast, in the outer sphere, speakers encounter strangers and gatekeepers: government officials, schoolteachers, hospital staff, and employers. In the outer sphere, bilinguals experience powerful expectations that English and Spanish will be kept separate. Linguistic boundaries are expected to remain sharp and language use neatly ordered. Even the Spanish accents of fluent English-speaking Puerto Ricans are met with resistance and marked as signs of racial difference and otherness. The shift between inner and outer spheres creates intense stress for speakers who are fluently bilingual in the inner sphere but confront intolerance for mixing and "disorder" in the outer sphere. Puerto Rican use of English is frequently found wanting in the outer sphere when compared with the dominant expectations of monolinguistic orderliness.

Jane Hill (2008) suggests that an opposite dynamic exists for whites who use Spanish in the United States. Whereas Puerto Ricans are disciplined at the boundary of English and Spanish, whites are allowed to cross the boundary without repercussions. Whites use heavily accented Spanish, broken Spanish grammar, and colloquial Spanish terms, mixing English and Spanish without

criticism. The language mixture includes terms such as *macho*, *adios*, *hasta la vista*, and *cojones* in a kind of Mock Spanish that makes fun of Spanish speakers while enhancing the status of English speakers as cosmopolitan, authentic, or humorous. Written use of Spanish by whites on street signs, public health announcements, T-shirts, and greeting cards is often ungrammatical. Elements of Spanish and English morphology are mixed, adding the suffix *-o* and modifiers such as *mucho* or *el* to create terms such as *el-cheap-o* or *mucho-trouble-o*.

Hill says these practices are allowed and sometimes celebrated because language use in the United States occurs in a "white public space." In this space, white language use is considered normal, objective, and standard, unnoticed and almost invisible even when mixing Spanish and English; in contrast, language used by Spanish speakers is visibly marginalized. Hill warns that the use of Mock Spanish and the marginalization of Spanish speakers within the white public sphere borders on a "racist discourse" that elevates whiteness and English while denigrating other ethnic groups and Spanish-speaking populations. Such a discourse, warns Hill, creates opportunities for racist political campaigns and moral panics about the future of the nation.

As the examples discussed above indicate, language and power intersect in many arenas. Socioeconomic class, educational environments, and racial/ethnic group status are just some of these. In addition, the histories of languages themselves can reflect the effects of systems of power. The study of historical linguistics, discussed next, explores how languages evolve in relation to factors such as geography, migration, and political control.

Historical Linguistics

Historical linguistics is the study of the development of language over time, including its changes and variations. By analyzing vocabulary and linguistic patterns, historical linguists trace the connections between languages and identify their origins. For example, through comparative analysis of vocabulary, syntax, and grammar, we know that Spanish and French historically developed from their parent language, Latin. English, German, Dutch, and Scandinavian languages evolved from an earlier proto-Germanic language. Both Latin and proto-Germanic branched out from an even earlier language called Proto-Indo-European; it was spoken more than 6,000 years ago and also gave birth to the languages spoken today in Greece, India, Iran, and Eastern Europe (Mallory and Adams 2006; McWhorter 2001).

Over thousands of years of adaptation, growth, and change, human language developed more along the lines of a **language continuum** rather than into distinct languages. In a language continuum, people who live near one another speak in a way that is mutually intelligible. The farther one travels, the more the language varies, but it tends to be at least partially mutually intelligible to those living nearby—if not 100 percent, then substantially. Although disrupted to some extent over centuries by migration and the strengthening of nation-states, language continuums still exist in many parts of the world. For instance, a strong language continuum has existed between Italy and France. If you were to walk from village to village beginning at the southern tip of Italy, travel northward, and then head northwest into France, you would find that people at either end of the journey would not be able to communicate with one another—their languages would be mutually unintelligible. But along the journey, the local residents of each village you pass through would be able to understand their neighbors in the nearby villages. Changes would be evident from location to location, but communication would be mutually intelligible.

Today we are taught to think that all people in France speak French and that those in Italy speak Italian. This is a definition of language based more on power—the establishment of a national border—than linguistics. In this case, the border between languages is established not by mutual intelligibility but by politics. It is just as likely, because of the language continuum, that when crossing the border from Italy to France, you would find that the people in the villages on either side of the border can understand one another. Of course, the people on the French side may be considered to be speaking a "dialect" of French, whereas "standard French" (based on the French spoken in Paris) is promoted through the government, the schools, and the national media. In effect, "standard French" has an army and a navy. The local language spoken in the village on the French/Italian border does not. This language continuum has been disrupted in recent years by the efforts of the French government to

---

historical linguistics: The study of the development of language over time, including its changes and variations.

language continuum: The idea that variation in languages appears gradually over distance so that groups of people who live near one another speak in a way that is mutually intelligible.

impose a standard dialect across the country. But new laws passed by the European Union have guaranteed that national governments recognize minority languages within their borders and have given new standing to local languages.

An extensive language continuum exists in China as well. Though written Chinese is essentially the same throughout the country, there are thousands of local variations of spoken Chinese, most of which are mutually unintelligible. For example, speakers of Mandarin, Cantonese, Shanghainese, Fuzhounese, and Sichuanese cannot understand one another. Linguistically none is considered superior or inferior to another, but they do vary in prestige. Mandarin is the most widely spoken Chinese language variation. Called *Putonghua* ("the common language") or *Guoyu* ("the national language"), Mandarin is based on the local version of Chinese spoken in and around the national capital, Beijing. For centuries, imperial administrators who governed areas across China on behalf of the emperor in Beijing adopted Mandarin, so it became the norm associated with China's economic and political elite. After the Chinese civil war in 1949, the new government established *Putonghua* as the national standard for all media broadcasts as well as for instruction in all schools. As a result, regardless of the local variations of the Chinese language, today everyone learns *Putonghua* as a second language. But this is a political decision, not a statement of its linguistic superiority.

Clearly, languages evolve as human groups use them, adapt them, or surrender them to more prevalent forms. The current age of globalization will provide even more opportunities for languages to meet and either mix or remain largely unchanged. This means that the field of historical linguistics will continue to trace dynamic aspects of language variation and change well into the future.

What Are the Effects of Globalization on Language?

The movement of people throughout human history has played a role in the way that languages change and develop. As people move, elements of vocabulary and grammar are loaned to and imposed on populations that come into contact. Languages are full of loanwords that have been adopted from others. The encounter of linguistic communities occurs with increasing rapidity in the contemporary era of globalization. Still, approximately 7,000 languages resound around the world today (Figure 4.1). A few have hundreds of millions of speakers. Most have a few thousand. However, globalization is consolidating language use among a small group of languages while threatening the extinction of thousands of others (Table 4.2).

Diminishing Language Diversity

The current pattern of increasing global interconnection threatens to diminish language diversity worldwide. In an earlier era of globalization, colonialism spread English, Spanish, Portuguese, French, Dutch, German, and Russian beyond Europe to people around the globe. Because these former colonial languages provide points of access to the current global economic and political system, many of them continue to expand today. In addition, increasing migration to urban centers often leads speakers of less widely used languages to assimilate and adopt the more widely used language. The more prominent languages—including the former colonial languages and other regional or national languages—dominate global media, including television, radio, print, and digital media. Through this dominance they are crowding out the less widely used languages and their speakers.

As a result of these dynamics, today the eight most prominent languages are spoken by more than 40 percent of the world's population. The top 84 languages account for 80 percent of humanity. The 4,000 least widely used languages, in total, account for only 0.12 percent of the world's language users (Lewis 2016). English has a unique position in the world at the moment, with as many as two billion speakers. Many of these are nonnative speakers who learn English as a second language because of its central role in universities, medicine, computing, entertainment, and intergovernmental relationships. English is currently a prestige language that provides effective access to international economic activity and political engagement.

Hastening Language Loss

Linguistic anthropologists warn that as many as half of the 7,000 languages in the world today could be lost by the end of the twenty-first century. In 2016,

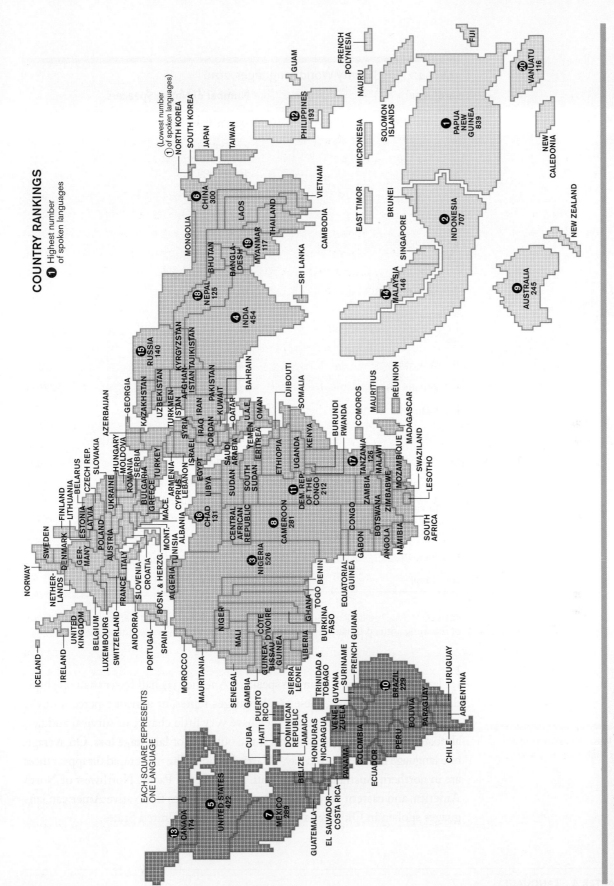

COUNTRY RANKINGS

1 Highest number of spoken languages

1 (Lowest number of spoken languages)

EACH SQUARE REPRESENTS ONE LANGUAGE

1 PAPUA NEW GUINEA 839
2 INDONESIA 707
3 NIGERIA 526
4 INDIA 454
5 UNITED STATES 422
6 CHINA 300
7 MEXICO 289
8 CAMEROON 281
9 AUSTRALIA 245
10 BRAZIL 229
11 DEM. REP. OF THE CONGO 212
12 PHILIPPINES 193
13 CANADA 174
14 MALAYSIA 146
15 RUSSIA 140
16 CHAD 131
17 TANZANIA 126
18 NEPAL 125
19 MYANMAR 117
20 VANUATU 116

FIGURE 4.1 World Languages by Country, 2015

The languages of the world are spread across countries in ways that may surprise you. Take a moment to identify the twenty countries with the most language diversity and the country with the least language diversity.

SOURCE: M. Paul Lewis, Gary F. Simons, and Charles D. Fennig (eds.). 2015. *Ethnologue: Languages of the World,* 18th ed. Dallas, TX: SIL International. Online version: www.ethnologue.com

TABLE 4.2 Top Twenty World Languages, 2016

Language	Number of Native Speakers
1. Chinese	1,302 million
2. Spanish	427 million
3. English	339 million
4. Arabic	267 million
5. Hindi	260 million
6. Portuguese	202 million
7. Bengali	189 million
8. Russian	171 million
9. Japanese	128 million
10. Lahnda	117 million
11. Javanese	84.3 million
12. Korean	77.3 million
13. German	76.9 million
14. French	75.9 million
15. Telugu	74.2 million
16. Marathi	71.8 million
17. Turkish	71.4 million
18. Urdu	68.6 million
19. Vietnamese	68.0 million
20. Tamil	67.8 million

SOURCE: M. Paul Lewis, Gary F. Simons, and Charles D. Fennig (eds.). 2016. *Ethnologue: Languages of the World*, 19th ed. Dallas, TX: SIL International. Online version: www.ethnologue.com

language loss: The extinction of languages that have very few speakers.

132 languages had fewer than ten speakers. Another 337 had fewer than one hundred speakers. Together, these 469 languages represent almost 7 percent of the world's languages (Lewis 2016). They have very little chance of survival and face almost certain language death. This is the outcome of **language loss**. On average, one language is lost every ten days (Harrison 2007). The most rapid disappearances are in northern Australia, central South America, the Pacific Northwest of North America, and eastern Siberia; this group also includes the Native American languages spoken in Oklahoma and the southwestern United States.

Languages develop over time to enable human groups to adapt to a particular environment and to share information that is essential to their local culture. When a language is lost, when it is crowded out by more widely used languages, we lose all of the bodies of information and local knowledge that had been developed—perhaps over thousands of years—by that community. Within a language is embedded rich knowledge about plants, animals, and medicines. Within a language is embedded a particular group's unique way of knowing the world and thinking and talking about human experience.

Language Revitalization Most languages have never been written down. Does this surprise you? If you are a speaker of one of the more prominent languages, such as English, perhaps it does. As many of the less widely used languages face extinction, some groups are undertaking efforts to preserve them in written form.

Documenting a local language may involve years of work in a detailed and painstaking process that draws on all the basic skills of fieldwork and descriptive linguistics. One of the most extensive efforts to create written records of small languages is the work of a group called the Summer Institute of Linguistics (SIL), which together with its partner, the Wycliffe Bible Translators, trains missionaries in linguistic and anthropological methods and sends them to the field, often to remote areas, to live with a community and create a written language in order to translate the Christian Bible into the local language.

Some linguistic anthropologists consider SIL's work to be controversial. They are concerned that the Christian nature of the project means that certain aspects of local culture—including indigenous religious beliefs, ritual language, songs, and art connected to local religion—are at risk of being ignored and extinguished. Other scholars acknowledge the significant data that would be lost if SIL translators were not doing the detailed work of documenting hundreds of local languages that are threatened with extinction in small communities worldwide. Despite this controversy, SIL has succeeded in producing a widely used compendium of all the world's languages called *Ethnologue*. Although it started with only forty entries in 1951 as a language guide for Christian missionaries, in 2016 *Ethnologue*'s nineteenth edition catalogued 7,097 languages (Lewis 2016).

Preserving Endangered Languages Information technology is beginning to transform the ways in which linguistic anthropologists document and preserve endangered languages, creating new opportunities for revitalization. Consider the Native American Lakota language. Its approximately 25,000 speakers live primarily in tribal areas scattered across North and South Dakota, as well as in cities, towns, and rural areas throughout the United States. Their tribally owned lands are in some of the poorest U.S. counties. Few children learn Lakota today,

Globalization threatens the loss of many smaller local languages, and with them their local knowledge and ways of understanding the world. (*left*) A Seri herbalist carries home lavender from the desert. The Seri are an indigenous people in Mexico. (*right*) Ramona Dick is an elder in the Washoe tribe, which is based in Nevada and California. As a child, she refused to be sent to a school where students were required to speak only English.

threatening the language with eventual extinction. So the Lakota have placed a high priority on preserving their language and culture and increasing Lakota language use among young people. Linguists have been working to document the Lakota language by collecting and preserving language samples, cultural knowledge, and artifacts. Some have even done intensive immersion in the Lakota language. But limited resources, combined with the geographic dispersion of Lakota speakers, have inhibited these efforts.

In 2009, a small local company, LiveAndTell, built an online digital platform for Lakota language preservation and instruction. Using participatory social media technology similar to that of YouTube and Flickr, LiveAndTell created opportunities for Lakota speakers to collaborate, create, and share digital artifacts. Families wrote family stories and posted photos, audio recordings, videos, and online annotations. School research projects were uploaded to community sites. In these ways, the dispersed Lakota language community has created an online archive of the living language. For instance, one contributor posted a picture of a car and then tagged each part—steering wheel, mirror, tire, and so on—with the Lakota name and an audio file of its pronunciation. Entries like these provide detailed linguistic information that is not available in standard dictionaries and may never come to light in formal oral interviews with professional linguists (Arobba et al. 2010).

As the Lakota example shows, innovative use of information technology has the potential to transform the study of endangered languages. For a discussion of additional efforts to preserve small languages, see "Anthropologists Engage the World," pages 142–143.

How Is the Digital Age Changing the Way People Communicate?

Human communication has experienced periods of rapid and dramatic transformation. The invention of the printing press, along with the printing of the Gutenberg Bible in Germany in the 1400s, transformed human communication through the mass production of books, newspapers, and pamphlets. These printed materials facilitated the widespread exchange of ideas and information across vast distances. Today the transformation of communication proceeds at a spectacular pace and on a global scale. Technological developments in communication are collapsing our basic notions of time and space and driving today's globalization process.

In their book *Born Digital*, John Palfrey and Urs Gasser (2008) discuss the emergence of what they call **digital natives**, a generation of people—including many of you reading this book—born after 1980 who have been raised in the digital age and have spent their entire lives thinking digitally. Think about your own communication equipment. It fits comfortably in your hands: laptops, smartphones, tablets, digital video cameras, and e-readers. High-speed cable and wireless Internet enable you to travel swiftly and easily in a digital world of texts, tweets, posts, Snapchats, file sharing, Googling, Skype, Instagram, and YouTube. You use social networking sites like Facebook to enhance interactions with "friends." You navigate around websites, wikis, blogs, and online gaming. All of this is new in the last thirty years, most of it in the last twenty.

Palfrey and Gasser refer to a slightly older generation as *digital immigrants*. Members of this generation (including the author of this book) use the technology and platforms of the digital age but have had to learn them as if immigrating into a new culture or learning a second language. Digital technology is never as comfortable and easy for us as it is for digital natives.

Clearly, the digital age is transforming the way a huge segment of the world's population communicates, studies, gathers information, gets their news, writes, and works. Across the globe, businesses, politicians, religious groups, social service agencies, human rights groups, factory workers, other laborers, and students are exploring new ways of communicating, publicizing their work, and building networks of support.

Digital Activism

The digital age—especially the development of mobile phones, the Internet, search engines, Facebook, YouTube, and Twitter—has transformed political

digital natives: A generation of people born after 1980 who have been raised in the digital age.

David Harrison
The Language Extinction Crisis

David Harrison became interested in endangered and little-documented languages almost by accident. "I was in a summer language program in Lithuania. We visited a small town, Trakai, and our guide told us that a minority people called the Karaim lived in this town. And I just happened to have my little tape recorder with me.

"So I went off and I knocked on a few doors and asked around. And I found a gentleman named Mykolas Firkovičius who turned out to be the spiritual leader of the Karaim community. He sat down with me for an interview and explained that their language was going extinct, that there were only a couple hundred speakers left. They were all elderly, and the younger generation had switched over to speaking Lithuanian and Russian, the more dominant languages. So I was completely fascinated by this idea that languages could go extinct."

As a field researcher, Harrison focused his investigations on Turkic languages in central Asia, including Tuvan, Tsengel Tuvan, Tofa, Ös (Middle Chulym), and Monchak. More recently he has studied languages of northeast India, as well as Siletz Dee-ni in Oregon and Kallawaya in Bolivia. His ethnographic research examines indigenous knowledge, folklore, oral epics, conceptual systems, and naming practices.

"My research focus and my specialty involves thinking about language extinction not only as a very personal, lived experience in the lives of people, but also as a global trend that has social and real-life consequences for all of us. So, I've devoted the last decade or more to traveling around the world, taking the pulse of some of the world's smallest languages, and meeting with the last speakers of these languages.

"We are in the middle of a language extinction crisis. It can be a bit depressing because languages don't voluntarily go extinct. Languages go extinct because of politi-

cal and social oppression and coercion, and in some cases even genocide, where the policies of nation-states force the language assimilation of a whole people. As horrible as that sounds, that was historically the practice and the policy of the U.S. government as well as the Canadian government. Many modern nation-states have engaged in this project, to forcibly unite indigenous peoples. We're still living in the aftermath of genocide-inflicted assimilation. Talk to any person in the Native American community involved in language, especially the elders, and you will hear horror stories about being sent off to boarding schools where they were punished for speaking their languages, made to feel ashamed of doing it."

On his visits to indigenous communities, Harrison finds that people are responding to the disappearance of their languages. Youth especially are developing ways to use cultural activism and new technologies to revitalize endangered languages. "I don't want to paint it only as a grim scenario. There's also a very exciting, global grassroots movement to sustain small languages. I encounter a younger generation that I like to refer to as 'language

Linguistic anthropologist David Harrison

warriors'—people who have made a strategic choice to not let their language go extinct. They're doing very exciting things, like performing hip-hop in the language, or text messaging in the language, using social media in their language. They're doing creative things with it. They're telling their stories. They're making films, creating Facebook pages."

Globalization has both negative and positive impacts on language diversity, says Harrison. "Globalization allows a small number of very large languages to spread and dominate and impose themselves. And so you can think of this as creating the conditions under which smaller languages are forced into extinction. On the other hand, I see that through social media and community collaboration, small languages can achieve a global voice, reaching many times more people than their number of speakers."

Why does the diversity of languages matter to everyone, including those of us who speak globalized languages like English? Harrison believes that each language frames our conception of the world differently, a notion called *linguistic relativity*. Languages employ metaphors in different ways, for example. "If you are helplessly in love with someone in Tuvan, you say, 'My liver aches.' Because to them, the liver is the seat of emotion. Now, we know that's not true, of course. The brain is the seat of emotion, but that doesn't stop us from using the heart as the seat of emotion in American culture. So, two very different cultural choices about where we think emotion resides. But a metaphor is very powerful when it's used by your culture."

Language shapes our idea of time, as well. "In English, we think of the future of being in front of us, being in front of us physically, being in front of us in space. We say things like, 'I'm looking forward to next week,' or 'Christmas is coming up soon.' And we think of the past as being behind us. But in Tuva, they reverse the space-time mapping. They talk about the future as being behind them, unseen, invisible, as if it were sneaking up from behind. And the past is what's out in front of you because you can see it. So, when you find a very different metaphor, or a different way of seeing the world in another language, it forces you to circle back and realize that your own cultural assumptions are not about the world per se, but rather just one of many ways to frame and understand the world. And I think this is one of the virtues of anthropology, to question your own cultural views and values, and realize that they are just that. They are relative."

> **"** *As soon as you study another language, even a little tiny bit, . . . you stop being a prisoner of your own cultural point of view.* **"**

Harrison was raised monolingual, but he stresses the deep importance of learning other languages. "As soon as you study another language, even a little tiny bit, you immediately begin to see how differently it views the world, in terms of everything from numbers, to the names we give our relatives, to concepts like love. You stop being a prisoner of your own cultural point of view. You're suddenly able to leverage these very different understandings of the world. That expands your ability to think, as well as to solve problems. No culture has a monopoly on human genius. We never know where the next great idea is going to come from. Different languages and cultures produce different patterns of thinking and different ways of solving problems. So, linguistic diversity is intellectual diversity; it's the foundation for intellectual diversity, and that's the foundation for how we're going to survive on this planet."

activism. In fact, a growing phenomenon of today's global age is digital activism, as evidenced by the events of the 2011 Arab Spring throughout North Africa; political movements in Iran, Syria, and Myanmar; and the Occupy Wall Street protests in the United States and beyond (see Chapter 14).

At least 700 million of China's 1.3 billion people participate in the digital age thanks to massive investments by the Chinese government to keep cell phone and Internet service costs low. This infrastructure now provides the framework for China's digital activists, including tens of thousands of migrant workers who are organizing for their rights in a country that has adamantly resisted independent labor unions and popular democracy movements (Barboza and Bradsher 2010; Yang 2009). As China's experience illustrates, even governments that devote extensive resources to monitoring and censoring digital communication struggle to keep up with highly decentralized sources of information available in the digital age and made possible by the very technologies required for economic modernization.

During the spring and summer of 2010, a wave of worker strikes hit foreign companies operating in China. Over the previous twenty years, abundant and inexpensive Chinese labor, low taxes, and lax environmental laws had drawn companies to relocate their production sites to China. But in recent years thousands of isolated strikes and uprisings have spread across the vast nation to protest environmental degradation, local government corruption, and oppressive working conditions. The successful strikes in 2010 against Honda and other foreign companies drew particular attention because of the strikers' extensive use of digital technology to mobilize workers, coordinate strikes among factory workers in different parts of the country, standardize wage demands, and communicate their situation to the Chinese public and the international press. Striking women workers shot photos and video of violence by factory security guards and uploaded them to Chinese sites such as Youku.com and 56.com. Text messages kept fellow workers apprised of quick changes in strategy.

As we will examine further in Chapter 14, students, democracy advocates, human rights organizations, and other digital activists in countries from South Korea to Burma, Ukraine, and Iran have utilized cell phones, digital cameras, Internet cafés, Twitter, and Facebook to amplify ideas, coordinate activities, broadcast developments, and ask for donations. Activities such as these are unique to the digital age and will surely continue as individuals and groups use social media and other electronic networks to communicate their shared experiences and objectives.

The Digital Divide

Despite the rapid expansion of digital communication over the last several decades, a vast digital divide separates the world into digital haves and have-nots. Though 95 percent of the world's population now has access to a cell phone, the digital divide today is marked by vast discrepancies to access and connectivity. This division reflects the tendency of globalization to increase uneven development (see Chapter 1).

Participation in the digital age requires computers, cell phones, Internet access, education systems that emphasize critical thinking, and even more fundamentally, electricity—a commodity that is not available to many people in the world on a consistent basis. A laptop that is so common in U.S. colleges and universities, for instance, costs more than many of the world's people earn in a year. Additionally, the quality of connectivity—smartphones versus basic mobile phones, narrow or broadband Internet—limits the quality of access. Are users experiences limited to access only? Or can they also retrieve data, interact with others and innovate? Access to these technological and connectivity resources is stratified on a global level, often along lines of gender, race, class, and nationality. Of the world's 7.2 billion people in the 2014, only 40 percent were using the Internet, though that number dropped to only 32 percent in developing countries and rose to 78 percent in more economically developed countries. The uneven development is reflected regionally as well. 75 percent of Europeans and 65 percent of those in the Americas used the Internet compared to 41 percent in the Middle East, 32 percent in Asia/Pacific, and only 19 percent in Africa. Even in a country such as China, where national investments have narrowed the digital divide to the extent that 700 million people now have access to cell phones and the Internet, 600 million Chinese still find themselves shut out of the digital age.

THE SOCIAL LIFE OF THINGS
Undersea Cable Networks and Global Communication

Would it surprise you to find out that 99 percent of all digital connections linking people between continents flow through undersea fiber optic cables, not satellites (which are slower and more expensive)? Web searches, emails, phone calls, text messages, YouTube videos, and Netflix films circulate globally through an unseen undersea communication infrastructure connecting hundreds of millions of users (Starosielski 2015).

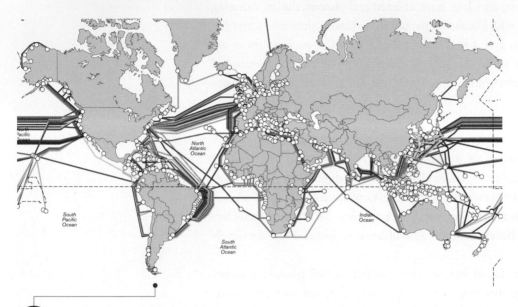

1 223 international fiber optic cable systems follow undersea routes to move data signals at the speed of light across the ocean floor. In addition they shape our knowledge of the ocean, linking ocean observatories, facilitating deep sea mineral exploration, and enabling militaries to acoustically monitor marine activity. These cables wind through remote, rural, and aquatic environments, where they are vulnerable to fishing nets, icebergs, oil drilling, atmospheric currents, anchors, hurricanes, tectonic shifts, volcanic activity, local populations, and sabotage.

2 Places where undersea cables emerge from the deep ocean—through coastal waters, across beaches, and into local communities—have become points of conflict with fisherman, boaters, environmental advocates, and local developers. Cable landing points also reveal the politics, economics, and inequalities of communication infrastructures: 45 cables connect to the U.S. mainland; most countries have fewer than 5; and the African continent was only connected in the past twenty years.

3 Cable stations on land link national and international cable systems and are sites for monitoring and maintaining cables. To avoid attention, the stations tend to be inaccessible and nondescript industrial buildings surrounded by surveillance cameras and barbed wire. Cable stations have also become sites of conflict as local residents resist displacement and challenge cable companies over territory, obstruct network development, and even force diversion of cables to alternative routes.

While our image of digital networks usually revolves around cities, undersea cables stretch our imaginations to the out-of-the-way places that shape global communication today. These fragile and unseen cable connections create the avenues for circulation of information, but if they were severed or interrupted, the Internet and much of global communications would effectively split into separate continental clusters.

- Next time you pick up a hand-held digital device—a laptop, cell phone, online gaming console—can you imagine the grounded pathways your digital communication may take?
- Why do you think there are differences in the number of cable landing points in each country? Are there characteristics beyond population size that might account for these differences?

Thinking Like an Anthropologist: Language, Immigration, and U.S. Culture

As you encounter the complexities of language in daily life—communicating with a boyfriend or girlfriend, collaborating with classmates from other places, studying abroad, working with people in multinational corporations, debating immigration policy, or understanding gender in classroom dynamics—thinking like an anthropologist can help you better understand your own experiences and those of others. First, take a moment to review the questions we asked at the beginning of this chapter:

- What is language and where does it come from?
- How does language shape our ways of thinking?
- How do systems of power intersect with language and communication?
- What are the effects of globalization on language?
- How is the digital age changing the way people communicate?

In our opening story, we considered how language has entered the immigration debates in Arizona. Now that you have been studying anthropology—and in this chapter, linguistic anthropology—how would you analyze the underlying issues at play in this debate? Why has language become such a hot-button issue in U.S. politics? How is English intertwined with notions of American identity, class, and belonging? As we will see in Chapter 13, the long-held model of incorporating new immigrants into U.S. culture—the melting pot that blends everyone's diversity into one big stew—now competes with a salad bowl metaphor in which immigrants don't blend in completely but contribute their unique diversity to a multicultural salad. This new model has encountered resistance, particularly from people who fear a fragmentation of U.S. culture.

Language use has become symbolic of these larger debates. Studies consistently show that the children of immigrants grow up speaking English as their first language, not the language of their parents' country of origin (Portes, Fernandez-Kelly, and Haller 2009). Yet the debate over language instruction in education continues. Along with Arizona's restrictive immigration laws, the Arizona Department of Education has seen a 180 degree turn in its policies for bilingual education programs. Facing a teacher shortage in the 1990s, Arizona recruited thousands of bilingual teachers to lead bilingual classes for the tens of thousands of students who may have grown up speaking Spanish at home. Many of the new teachers were recruited from Latin America, and their first language was Spanish. Then, in 2000, Arizona voters passed a referendum mandating that instruction of nonnative English speakers be in English only. In 2010 the state adopted further policy changes including new fluency standards for teachers, focusing on pronunciation and writing. Teachers who were unable to meet the new standards were removed from the classrooms of nonnative English speakers (Jordan 2010).

The Arizona education debates reveal the way that language functions as more than a system of symbols that enable people to communicate. Language is also a key cultural arena in which norms are established, values are promoted, and relationships of power are negotiated.

Key Terms

For Further Exploration

Ahearn, Laura. 2012. *Living Language: An Introduction to Linguistic Anthropology.* Malden, MA: Wiley-Blackwell.

Basso, Keith. 1996. *Wisdom Sits in Places: Landscape and Language among the Western Apache.* Albuquerque: University of New Mexico Press.

Berkman Center for Internet & Society at Harvard University. http://cyber.law.harvard.edu. Website dedicated to exploring the development of cyberspace, particularly related to legal issues and censorship. Hosts online lectures and discussions.

The Linguists. 2008. Produced and directed by Seth Kramer, Daniel A. Miller, and Jeremy Newberger. Ironbound Films. www.thelinguists.com. A documentary film following the work of David Harrison and Greg Anderson as they track and record dying languages around the world.

National Geographic. Disappearing Languages. www .languagehotspots.org. An interactive website on languages nearing extinction.

N-Word: Divided We Stand. 2007. Produced by Helena Echegoyen. A Post Consumer Media Production, distributed by MediaLink Entertainment. A video exploring the history and current usage of the "N-word" in American culture.

Tannen, Deborah. 2001. *You Just Don't Understand: Women and Men in Conversation,* 2nd ed. New York: Ballantine Books.

Wesch, Michael. 2008. *An Anthropological Introduction to YouTube.* www.youtube.com /watch?v=TPAO-IZ4_hU&feature=channel.

Wesch, Michael. 2007. *A Vision of Students Today.* www .youtube.com/watch?v=dGCJ46vyR9o&feature= channel.

Who are we? Where did we come from? What can we learn from our human ancestors? Here a young woman looks through a replica of a Neandertal skull in the Neanderthal Museum in Krapina, Croatia, site of many Neandertal fossil finds since 1899.

CHAPTER 5
Human Origins

Who are we? Where do we come from? What does it really mean to be human? Theologians, philosophers, and historians in every culture have asked these questions. Each of us individually, at one time or another, has also likely wondered about the meaning of life. This chapter examines the unique perspectives of physical anthropologists on the origins of the human species, and it explores amazing discoveries that are opening windows onto our past and, perhaps, our future. Let's begin with a few stories about discoveries relating to these topics.

- In 1923, scientists began to unearth hundreds of fossils in caves overlooking a river valley at Zhoukoudian, outside Beijing (then called Peking), China. The fossils of what came to be known as Peking Man, dating to approximately 780,000–400,000 years before the present (yBP), were found along with fossils from more than fifty other individuals, some 17,000 stone artifacts, and clear evidence that these human ancestors had controlled fire and used it to cook and keep warm. Peking Man—who walked upright and stood 57 to 70 inches tall—had the same physical characteristics as fossils of *Homo erectus* found earlier in Africa and Indonesia. Such similarities revealed the early and unexpected spread of this species as far as East Asia.

- In 1924, Australian anthropologist Raymond Dart, working in South Africa, received a box of curious rocks and fossils from a local quarry in the nearby town of Taung. Intrigued by one in particular, he spent months painstakingly chipping away at the fossilized rock until the encased fossil emerged—a child's skull. What came to be known as Dart's Taung child—about age four when it died—was the first fossil evidence of a group of prehuman ancestors, Australopithecines.

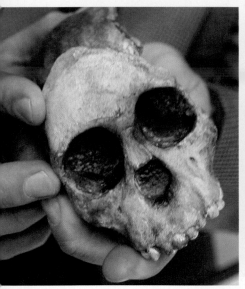 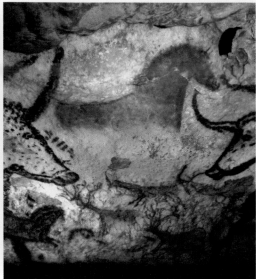 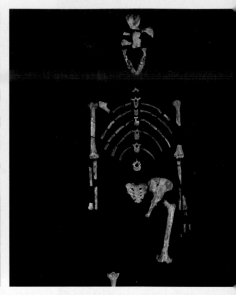

These individuals were smaller in stature than modern humans and lived in Africa between 4 million and 1 million years ago (mya).

- In 1940, four teenagers hiking with their dog in southwestern France stumbled upon a complex of caves filled with more than 2,000 spectacular wall paintings and carvings. Lascaux Cave's depictions of large animals, humans, and abstract forms dating to 16,000 yBP revealed the complex artistry and symbolism fashioned by so-called modern humans, who were still hunting and gathering as their main means of survival.

- In 1960, at age twenty-six, British primatologist Jane Goodall traveled to Tanzania, Africa, to begin the first-ever study of chimpanzees in the wild. Living among the chimpanzees in Gombe, a remote area along the shores of Lake Tanganyika, Goodall observed and recorded their behavior in unprecedented detail. Contrary to popular assumptions at the time about chimpanzees, she found them to be highly intelligent and to have close social bonds between mothers and offspring as well as between siblings. Goodall was the first to document tool use by nonhuman primates, as she observed chimpanzees using sticks to fish termites out of termite nests and crumpling leaves to serve as sponges for collecting water. Ultimately Goodall's research over 50 years has revealed the deep continuities between humans and other primates—physically, socially, and cognitively—and transformed our notions of human nature in the process.

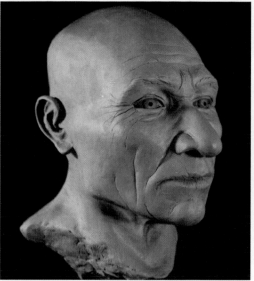

Amazing discoveries are opening windows onto our past and, perhaps, our future. (*left to right*) Replica of the skull of the Taung child, an Australopithecine found in South Africa. Wall paintings, Lascaux Cave, southwestern France. Lucy, an Australopithecine, East Africa's Rift Valley. Laetoli footprints, Tanzania, left by two human ancestors 3.6 million years ago. Reconstruction of Kennewick Man, Washington State.

- One November morning in 1974, northeast of the Olduvai Gorge in an arid region of Hadar, Ethiopia, archaeologist Donald Johanson and his graduate student, Tom Gray, turned their Land Rover aside on a hunch. On the slope of a gully that their team had examined unsuccessfully on previous occasions, Johanson spied a protruding arm bone and near it the back of a skull, a piece of a femur, and many more pieces of a skeleton exposed by recent wind and rain. Eventually more than 40 percent of a 3.2-million-year-old *Australopithecus afarensis* was excavated. "Lucy"—who was 44 inches tall, weighed approximately 65 pounds, and looked like a chimpanzee but walked erect like modern humans—was named as the team celebrated while listening to the Beatles' song "Lucy in the Sky with Diamonds."

- In 1976, in nearby Laetoli, Tanzania, two paleoanthropologists in a group headed by Mary Leakey were playfully tossing elephant dung at one another. When one stumbled to the ground, the loose soil parted to reveal a trail of footprints fossilized just below the surface. Apparently 3.6 million years before, as rain fell on ground recently covered by ash from a volcanic explosion, two human ancestors, one tall and one small, had hiked together across the plain. Their footsteps, preserved in the ash when it dried like cement (along with the imprints of many other animals present in the area at the time), provide evidence of exactly how early our ancestors were walking in ways hardly different from our own.

- In 1996, two young men headed out to see a hydroplane boat race on the Columbia River near Kennewick in Washington State. While wading along the riverbank, they stumbled upon a skull and other bones. Eager to make the race on time, they hid their discovery in nearby bushes. Returning later, they put the skull in a bucket and carried it back to their truck before eventually handing it to a passing off-duty police officer. Eventually a full skeleton was recovered from the riverbank and shallows. What has come to be known as Kennewick Man dates to 9,200 yBP, making it one of the earliest descendants of the first immigrants to the Americas and an ancestor of today's Native Americans. Additional evidence from the site has offered insights into the culture and lifestyle of humans nearly 10,000 years ago, including clear indications that members of the forty-six-year-old man's group had buried him themselves.

- In 2010 biologist Svante Pääbo and a team from the Department of Genetics at the Max Planck Institute for Evolutionary Anthropology in Germany announced they had successfully extracted and sequenced the complete DNA of a Neandertal fossil found in Croatia, dating to between 38,000 and 44,000 years ago. In 2012 they extracted DNA from a finger bone and molar found in Denisova Cave in southern Siberia belonging to a hominin that lived about

Biologist Svante Pääbo analyzes DNA extracted from fossils to better understand our recent human origins.

50,000 years ago but that was genetically distinct from Neandertals and modern humans—suggesting that multiple distinct groups may have been living at the same time in Eurasia—a scene more complex than previously thought. Pääbo's work on the *FOXP2* gene—sometimes known as "the speech and language gene" (see Chapter 4)—shows that Neandertal and modern humans share an identical version and so may have shared similar language capabilities.

These stories represent just a few of the thousands of discoveries that illuminate our human origins. This chapter considers what we know about where we have come from, how we know it, and what we may be able to learn about where our species is heading. In particular, the chapter considers the following questions:

- Where do humans fit in the story of life on Earth?
- How do scientists learn about prehistoric life?
- How does the theory of evolution explain the diversity of life?
- How does evolution work?
- What do we know about our human ancestors?
- What has made modern humans so successful at survival?
- Where did variations in human skin color come from?
- Are we still evolving?

By the end of the chapter you will have caught a glimpse of the story of human evolution over time, our unparalleled ability to combine biology and culture to survive and thrive, and the deep connection of humans with all life around us.

Where Do Humans Fit in the Story of Life on Earth?

The story of humans makes a very short chapter in the overall narrative of Earth's natural history and of the universe as a whole. The story of fully modern humans, those *Homo sapiens* anatomically like those of us living today, is even more limited. How do we begin to see ourselves in this larger story, when today we often regard history as only that which has been recorded since the invention of writing, while everything else is relegated to prehistory? Archaeologists and physical anthropologists offer us some insights.

Deep Time

To understand where humans have come from, we need a sense of the natural history of our planet and universe. Scholars call this **deep time** (Gould 1987). The universe is calculated to be 14 billion years old and planet Earth only 4.5 billion. Life on Earth emerged 3.5 billion years ago in the form of single-celled

deep time: A framework for considering the span of human history within the much larger age of the universe and planet Earth.

organisms; more complicated multicelled organisms appeared a billion years later. The dinosaurs lived between 230 and 65 mya. Primates—a group that now includes humans, chimpanzees, monkeys, gorillas, bonobos, orangutans, lemurs, tarsiers, and others—emerged between 65 and 55 mya. Contemporary humans and great apes, including orangutans, gorillas, and chimpanzees, shared a common ancestor as recently as between 15 and 12 mya. The ancestors of modern orangutans branched off from the common line at this point. Then, between 7 and 6 mya, our ancestors branched off from the line that eventually led to chimpanzees.

How can you conceptualize this deep time? Perhaps you might start with your own family—your direct ancestors. Many of us have met our grandparents. A few may have met a great-grandparent. But beyond two or three generations, our recollections get fuzzy. Can you imagine ten generations back to the founding of the United States in 1776? Or twenty-five generations back to the sailing of Christopher Columbus in 1492? How about five hundred generations back to the first use of agriculture by humans 10,000 years ago? Now can you imagine eight thousand generations back to the first modern human who looked like us about 170,000 years ago? You still haven't begun to scratch the surface of deep time. To understand the process through which life on Earth has emerged and evolved requires stretching your imagination even farther.

We calculate 60 seconds in every minute; 3,600 seconds in an hour; 86,400 in a day; 604,800 in a week; and 31,536,000 in a year. If we start counting seconds, and if we say that every second equals one year, then we would reach back to the origins of the first modern humans in just over two days of counting. To reach the time when dinosaurs became extinct (65 mya), we would have to count continuously each second for 2 years. To reach 1 billion seconds, we would have to count for 31 years and 8 months, night and day. To mark 4.5 billion years in seconds—the beginning of planet Earth—would require counting for more than 139 years nonstop, night and day, every second. From this perspective, the modern human chapter in the story of Earth's natural history is indeed remarkably brief. Humans do not take up much space on the deep time calendar.

How Do Scientists Learn about Prehistoric Life?

Scientists have gathered an immense amount of physical evidence over the past 200 years about the life of modern humans, our immediate human ancestors, and all living beings on Earth. Living organisms provide a vivid record of how evolution has worked, but we only see the lineages that have survived. Far more have not. Yet thousands of fossil finds and recent genetic research tell a fascinating story of the many species that came before us and led to life on Earth as we currently know it.

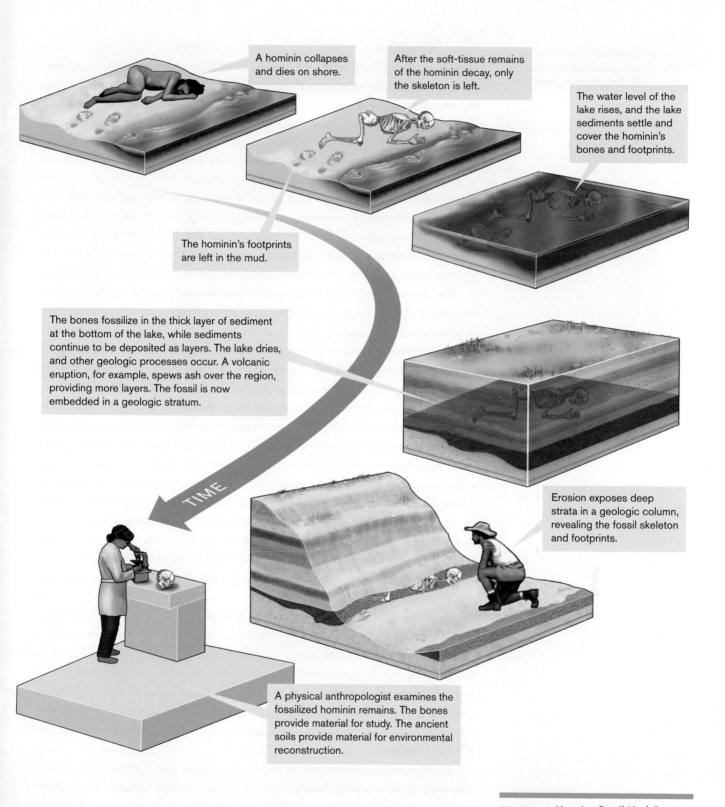

A hominin collapses and dies on shore.

After the soft-tissue remains of the hominin decay, only the skeleton is left.

The water level of the lake rises, and the lake sediments settle and cover the hominin's bones and footprints.

The hominin's footprints are left in the mud.

The bones fossilize in the thick layer of sediment at the bottom of the lake, while sediments continue to be deposited as layers. The lake dries, and other geologic processes occur. A volcanic eruption, for example, spews ash over the region, providing more layers. The fossil is now embedded in a geologic stratum.

TIME

Erosion exposes deep strata in a geologic column, revealing the fossil skeleton and footprints.

A physical anthropologist examines the fossilized hominin remains. The bones provide material for study. The ancient soils provide material for environmental reconstruction.

FIGURE 5.1 How Is a Fossil Made?

fossils: The remains of an organism that have been preserved by a natural chemical process that turns them partially or wholly into rock.

Fossil Evidence

Fossils are the remains of organisms that have been preserved through a natural chemical process that turns them partially or wholly into rock (Figure 5.1). A fossil may also be an impression of those remains left behind, imprinted and preserved in surrounding sediment; these "trace fossils" can include impressions of hair, skin, or other soft tissues, or even leaves, seeds, and feathers. Fossils are like memories of life on Earth in the past. They recall for us moments in our history that have been set aside but not forgotten.

Fossils provide the only direct physical evidence of our past and how various species, including our own, have changed over time. Fossils are not only evidence of past physical forms of living beings but also, as with the incredible Laetoli footprints already described, evidence of their behavior. As we collect fossils, we use them to reconstruct our past and our evolution through time.

The human fossil record is far from complete, despite the rapidly increasing rate of discoveries in recent years. One difficulty in completing the picture is that very few organisms end up as fossils. In fact, it takes rather unique circumstances to create and preserve a fossil. Today, bones and teeth represent 99 percent of the fossil record. Why? Largely because of their density and hardness. Teeth are the hardest part of the human body. Bones, particularly skulls and leg bones, are dense and large. The larger and harder the physical remains, the better their chance of becoming fossilized because they take longer to decay. Soft tissues such as skin or internal organs decay too rapidly to be fossilized, so discoveries of that type are rare. Furthermore, to become a fossil, a leg bone or a skull must be protected from scavengers. It must be buried in certain kinds of sediment—oxygen-free, with limited bacterial activity that would promote decomposition, and of the right chemical composition to facilitate its transformation partially or wholly into rock. Moreover, not all areas and periods experience the kind of geologic activity best suited for creating and preserving fossils. Given these challenges, fossilization is an extremely rare event.

Another difficulty in reconstructing the human past is that not all periods of time or species of living organism are equally represented in the fossil record. To become a part of our story, not only do physical remains need to be fossilized, but they must be found thousands and millions of years later. For instance, there are many fossils of early human ancestors in eastern and southern Africa, such as the Taung child or Lucy. But in all likelihood this is not the whole story. Our ancestors may have lived over a much greater expanse of the African continent.

Until recently, the fossil record had not confirmed this. But then came a 2001 discovery in the southern Sahara desert (in Chad, Central Africa): *Sahelanthropus tchadensis*, dating to between 7 and 6 mya, provided the long-sought evidence of a wide-ranging prehuman habitat (Brunet et al. 2002). The discovery, found with animal fossils in the same site—bones and teeth of horses, elephants, crocodiles, fish, rodents, and other primates—showed that this *Sahelanthropus* lived near a lake in a forested area. Such bits of information offer additional insight into the lifestyles and behavior of an ancestor who (counting years in seconds) lived 81 days ago on our clock of deep time.

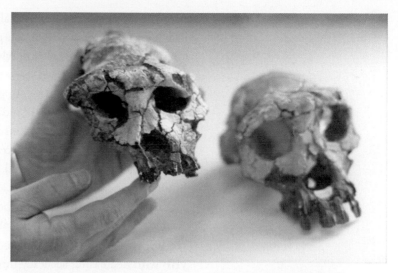

Sahelanthropus tchadensis, an early human ancestor that lived between 7 and 6 million years ago in what is now Chad, Central Africa.

Our contemporary ability to explore and excavate has been restricted in certain areas. Geologic activity such as volcanic eruptions, earthquakes, and plate shifts (steady but slow movement of the tectonic plates underlying Earth's crust) has transformed the face of the planet over millions of years. So have global warming and cooling cycles. Thus, what may have been open savannah grassland may now be dense forest, making it almost impossible to explore. Areas where geologic activity has exposed lower layers are easier to investigate. In East Africa, for instance, the greatest number of discoveries have been in dry, arid regions where geologic activity has exposed the deep strata of sediment and where wind, rain, and natural erosion continue to expose fossils just beneath the surface. Limestone caves have preserved the largest number of fossils in southern Africa. In Europe, many finds have come from public works projects involving road construction and building excavation.

Finding fossils also requires painstaking efforts by paleoanthropologists—scientists who study the fossil remains of our human ancestors. Their work involves extensive searches, intensive time commitments, meticulous research, and a fair amount of luck. Moreover, they must handle recovered fossils with extreme care. To excavate the remains, paleoanthropologists use small brushes and tools as delicate as the ones your dentist might employ. All items are mapped, numbered, and photographed. Careful record is made of the sediment in which each fossil is found and any fossilized plant or animal remains that may be with it. This recordkeeping serves not only to establish the context in which the organism lived but also to assist in establishing the time frame during which it lived.

Absolute and Relative Dating

There are two primary means for dating fossils and placing them in chronological relationship to the vast record of natural history and human evolution. We date the fossil itself, a process called *absolute dating*. We also date the context in which the fossil was found, a process called *relative dating*. Relative dating entails comparing the fossil to what is found nearby, including plants, animals, or cultural artifacts such as stone tools whose dates have been previously established. Most often, relative dating relies on *stratigraphy*—a process that determines the ages of the layers of sediment above and below the fossil. This process reflects the geologic assumptions that what is deeper is older and that layers of sediment have built up over succeeding millennia.

Absolute dating of the fossil itself draws on various assessment tools. Two important chemical assessments are radiocarbon (carbon-14) dating for organic material and radiopotassium (potassium-40) dating for nonorganic matter. *Radiocarbon dating* tracks the half-life of carbon as it decays in organic matter. It is most accurate in assessing the age of matter dating to less than 50,000 yBP with decreasing accuracy through 75,000 yBP. Radiocarbon dating can be used directly on bones and teeth to establish their age within this timeframe.

Radiopotassium dating does not measure the organic material in a fossil, but rather measures the amount of argon in volcanic rock and ash found on or around a fossil. This dating process is based on the fact that the heat of volcanic eruptions eliminates all argon from ash and rock. The only argon in volcanic rock and ash found today has been created since the eruption by the decay of potassium, which produces new argon at a steady rate. Measuring the new argon enables us to calculate when materials erupted from a volcano and so provides a reliable date for any fossil found in such material. Because volcanic eruptions spread a layer of ash over vast distances, this method has proven extremely valuable in determining the age of many fossil finds (Larsen 2014).

Of course, even these "absolute" dating techniques do not provide a precise year, month, or day of origin. However, they do yield a reliable date range that enables us to see where fossils fit in the vast record of natural history and to further understand the major events in the story of evolution.

DNA Analysis

Over the past thirty years, breakthroughs in our understanding of DNA have provided another tool for dating key events in the evolution of species. **DNA** (deoxyribonucleic acid) provides the genetic code for an organism, essentially giving it a "blueprint" for development and growth. Because DNA mutates (changes spontaneously or in response to the environment) at a steady rate, the number of mutations can serve to date an organism's evolutionary history. This type of analysis is called *paleogenetics*.

Genetic studies of mitochondrial DNA—passed down from generation to generation through our mothers—on people worldwide indicate that all living modern humans have a matrilineal "most common ancestor." This ancestor lived in Africa approximately 170,000 years ago—that is, eight thousand generations

DNA: Deoxyribonucleic acid; the feature of a cell that provides the genetic code for an organism.

A paleogeneticist extracts DNA from a sample of fossilized Neandertal bone.

back from the present (Cann, Stoneking, and Wilson 1987). Mitochondrial DNA comparisons reveal more variation in Africa, evidence of an older population there, and less variation the farther away from Africa one goes. These observations support earlier theories based on the fossil record that we are all from Africa originally. DNA studies indicate that modern humans migrated out of Africa less than 100,000 years ago, first populating the Middle East, then the southern coast of Asia and the Pacific, followed by another expansion into Europe, Northern Asia and eventually the Americas (Boyd and Silk 2015; Li et al. 2008).

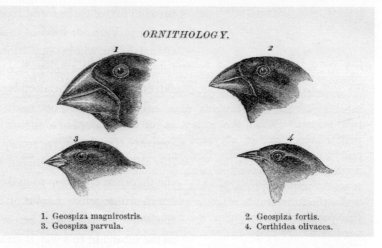

ORNITHOLOGY.

1. Geospiza magnirostris.
3. Geospiza parvula.
2. Geospiza fortis.
4. Certhidea olivacea.

Charles Darwin's sketches of finches with beaks adapted to different diets, observed in the Galapagos Islands, spurred his thinking about natural selection.

New technology is also enabling physical anthropologists to extract DNA from the bones and teeth of ancient fossils. The recovered genetic material reveals a great deal about ancient human populations, including the diseases they were exposed to, their population movements, and distinctions among groups. For example, by comparing similarities between DNA in living Native Americans and their ancestors' fossil remains, scientists have discovered that Native Americans' genetic structure is quite old and thus most likely derives from a single, common group of founding ancestors. DNA patterns among some northeast Asians suggest that this founding group migrated from northeast Asia to the Americas, either by boat or across the land bridge exposed during the recent ice age. According to calculations of DNA mutation rates, the migration likely took place around 15,000 yBP, corresponding roughly to the archaeological record (Forster et al. 1996).

How Does the Theory of Evolution Explain the Diversity of Life?

Physical anthropologists consider the **theory of evolution** to be the key to understanding the diversity of life on Earth today and how it relates to life in the past. The theory states that biological adaptation to changes in the natural environment occurs over generations. The fundamental concept of evolution is that all living species share a common ancestry from which they have descended. The more closely two organisms are related biologically, the more recent their common ancestor.

Biological differences between species and within species—called *variation*—come from random genetic changes in individual organisms that have allowed

theory of evolution: The theory that biological adaptations in organisms occur in response to changes in the natural environment and develop in populations over generations.

them to better survive and reproduce when shifts in the natural environment or competition for food or mates have made life more difficult. Evolutionary change in the whole population does not occur at once, but over many generations. Sometimes it takes place gradually and sometimes in fits and starts, as the success of the new variation leads to higher rates of survival and reproduction.

By *theory* we do not mean a guess or an untested assumption. Rather, we mean an overarching idea that links and makes sense of many pieces of factual evidence. Theories serve to explain the relationship between facts and to predict the outcome of observed natural processes. Physical anthropologists use the theory of evolution to make sense of how all the fossil finds and DNA discoveries fit together. Evolution explains the relationship of current living things to those that have come before and predicts how biological change will occur in the future. In this way, it creates a scientific framework for the history of life on Earth. Theories can be tested. In fact, the theory of evolution through natural selection has been tested extensively over the nearly 160 years since the English naturalist Charles Darwin (1809–1882) first articulated it in his book *On the Origin of Species by Means of Natural Selection, or the Preservation of Favoured Races in the Struggle for Life* (1859).

Evolution versus Creationism

Evolution is not a controversial subject among scientists. Evolution is a reality upon which biology, genetics, chemistry, epidemiology, and many other sciences are predicated. Evolution is, however, a controversial topic in U.S. culture. For more than a hundred years it has stirred courtroom battles, school board fights, election campaigns, and theological debates.

In 2013, an opinion poll conducted by the Pew Forum on Religion in Public Life found the U.S. population to be divided on the origins of life. Among respondents, 33 percent stated that they believe humans and other living organisms have existed in their present form since the beginning of time; 60 percent believed that life has evolved over time; and 7 percent did not know. Among those who believe life has evolved over time, 24 percent said that a supreme being has guided evolution, 32 percent said that evolution has occurred through natural processes such as natural selection (see later discussion), and 4 percent did not know how life has evolved.

Opposition to evolution most often rests on the literal interpretation of biblical texts and the related religious conviction that God created Earth and all the creatures on it. In this view, humans are a special creation, not the result of random adaptations to changes in the natural environment. Young Earth **creationism**, which is popular among many evangelical Protestant Christians, argues that God created Earth between 6,000 and 10,000 years ago, based on calculations of the genealogy of biblical ancestors. Young Earth creationists attribute fossil finds to the extinctions that occurred during the worldwide flood

creationism: A belief that God created Earth and all living creatures in their present form as recently as 6,000 years ago.

described in the biblical book of Genesis, when not all creatures were saved on Noah's ark. Other proponents of creationism accept that Earth is 4.5 billion years old, but they argue that God—not the process of evolution—created the separate species (Rosenhouse 2012; Scott 2009).

A recent version of creationism, called **intelligent design**, proposes an evidence-based rather than religious-based argument to undermine theories of evolution through natural selection. Proponents suggest that life is too complex to be random. Consider the human eye, they argue. How could its complex inner workings have evolved through natural selection? This complexity, according to intelligent design supporters, requires the involvement of an intelligent designer. Though the identity of the intelligent designer is not specified, the promotion of intelligent design theory by particular Christian groups and related think tanks leaves the impression that the designer is the Christian God (Scott 2009).

As we can see in the Pew poll, a firm belief in God's active role in individual lives and human history is common for many Americans, regardless of political persuasion—whether conservative or progressive, left, right, or middle. Religious belief and acceptance of the reality of evolution are not mutually exclusive. In fact, many national religious organizations have taken positions supporting evolution and opposing the teaching of creationism in the science curriculum of public schools. The Catholic Church since 1950 has held evolution to be compatible with Christian teachings, and in the United States the following churches have made similar statements: the United Methodist Church, the Presbyterian Church, the Episcopal Church, the United Church of Christ, and the Central Council of American Rabbis (Lieberman and Kirk 1996). Moreover, surveys of scientists find that most of them are people of faith.

Schools have often been the arena for cultural battles over evolution. Here, evangelist T. T. Martin's books against the theory of evolution are sold in Dayton, Tennessee, 1925, scene of the Scopes trial. Clarence Darrow (*left*), a lawyer for the American Civil Liberties Union, defended John Scopes, a biology teacher, in his test of Tennessee's law banning the teaching of evolution. William Jennings Bryan (*right*), testified for the prosecution as a Bible expert.

intelligent design: An updated version of creationism that claims to propose an evidence-based argument to contradict the theory of evolution.

In the Pew poll, even half of the general population who accepted the notion of evolution also indicated that they believe God intervenes in history and creates through evolution.

Battles over the Teaching of Evolution

In the United States, cultural battles over evolution and religion have often taken place in the educational arena. These conflicts reflect some people's strong religious convictions that it is not appropriate for schools to teach a theory of human origins that contradicts their beliefs.

In 1925, high school teacher John Scopes was fined $100 under Tennessee's Butler Act for teaching evolution. The now-famous Scopes Trial became a lightning rod for the battle between science and religion, drawing attention nationwide. After trial and appeal, Tennessee's supreme court upheld the Butler Act but threw out Scopes's fine on a technicality. In 1968, the U.S. Supreme Court overturned state laws banning the teaching of evolution, citing the Constitution's clause against establishing a state religion. The bans, the Court found, were driven by religious beliefs. (Tennessee had repealed the Butler Act in 1967.)

Battles over the teaching of evolution continue. In a landmark 2005 U.S. federal court case, *Tammy Kitzmiller v. Dover Area School District*, eleven parents of children in the Dover, Pennsylvania, school district brought suit to challenge the district's requirement that high school science teachers include intelligent design as an alternative to evolution as an "explanation of the origin of life." After a three-month court battle, including expert witnesses on evolution and intelligent design, the judge (a self-described conservative Republican) ruled that intelligent design had no basis in science and should not be taught in a public high school science curriculum. What was your own high school experience in this regard? If you attended school outside the United States, did you learn anything about evolution, creationism, or other explanations for the origins of human life?

Cultural battles over the origins of human life continue unabated in the United States and are unlikely to subside anytime soon. The scientific community, however, remains unified on the central role of the theory of evolution in explaining both the origins of humanity and the natural processes of change and adaptation in all living organisms.

How Does Evolution Work?

Evolution is happening around us all the time. Modern medicine, biology, chemistry, genetics, and even pest control rely on the principles of evolution. For example, the widespread appearance of drug-resistant bacteria is directly related to their successful evolution in the face of antibiotics. And scientists' inability to develop a cure for HIV/AIDS reflects one particular virus's ability to evolve rapidly. Even the survival of cockroaches despite increasingly stronger pesticides is a testimony to ongoing evolutionary success.

Evolution is harder to study in humans because of the relatively long time between generations, as well as people's general reluctance to be studied. But the unified study of evolution that brings together biology, taxonomy, genetics, morphology, comparative anatomy, paleontology, and physical anthropology provides clear evidence of evolution in our human past and the continuing activity of evolutionary forces in the human present. Four key evolutionary forces are natural selection, mutation, gene flow, and genetic drift.

Two peppered moths. One, primarily black, is well camouflaged against the tree's moss and lichen. The other, white with black spots, stands exposed. Which do you think is more vulnerable to predators? Which is more likely to survive to reproduce the species?

Natural Selection

Natural selection is often directly associated with Darwin's theory of evolution and the catchphrase "survival of the fittest." **Natural selection** occurs when individuals within a population have certain characteristics that provide an advantage that enables them to survive and reproduce at a higher rate than others in the population. This reproductive success shows their "fitness" to survive in a particular environment. If they survive and reproduce more successfully, their unique genetic advantage has been "selected" by the natural environment and will become increasingly prevalent in the population.

natural selection: The evolutionary process by which some organisms, with features that enable them to adapt to the environment, preferentially survive and reproduce, thereby increasing the frequency of those features in the population.

The peppered moth, *Biston betularia*, provides an example of natural selection in the animal world. Until the mid-1800s the peppered moth population in Great Britain was primarily white with black specks. This coloration provided important camouflage in the light-colored moss and lichen growing on tree trunks and was an effective protection against the moths' primary predators—birds. However, from the late nineteenth century to the mid-twentieth century, the peppered moth population's coloration gradually shifted so that 90 percent of the moths were black, not white. How did this happen?

During the Industrial Revolution, pollution—particularly from coal-burning factories—blanketed surrounding trees with a layer of black soot, covering the lichen and changing the peppered moths' natural environment. The mainly white moths were now much more visible and vulnerable to predators, but the few moths born black were likely to avoid detection, survive, and reproduce. The coloration of the population gradually shifted to primarily black through the process of natural selection. When environmental protections implemented in the late twentieth century reduced pollution and soot levels, trees returned to their earlier lighter coloration. When we consider the powerful process of natural selection in evolution, perhaps it is not surprising that in response, white peppered moths again increased in the population, rising from 10 percent in 1983 to more than 90 percent in the late 1990s (Larsen 2014).

Sickle-cell anemia provides an example of natural selection at work in the human population. Sickle-cell anemia is a genetically inherited blood disease with no known cure. The disease gives red blood cells a sickle shape, not a round shape, thus limiting their ability to carry oxygen through narrow capillaries and resulting in anemia and death. In general, the sickle-cell gene does not provide an advantage for survival and reproduction. Thus, we might expect the sickle-cell gene to be selected out in the evolutionary process. Surprisingly, though, in the mid-twentieth century medical research in certain African countries—mainly along the equator—found that 20 to 30 percent of the populations carried the sickle-cell gene. If sickle-cell anemia is generally associated with such high rates of disease, why would these populations carry it at such unusually high rates?

Researchers, including Anthony Allison (2004) working in Kenya and Frank B. Livingstone (1958) working in West Africa, uncovered a fascinating connection. They found that high rates of the sickle-cell gene appeared in areas with widespread incidence of malaria, a deadly parasitic infection spread by mosquitoes. Furthermore, they found that groups in regions of endemic malaria had higher survival rates for malaria infection if they carried the sickle-cell gene. Apparently the gene, although not advantageous in areas without malaria, actually provided a selective advantage in areas with widespread malaria. People with the sickle-cell gene were more likely to survive and reproduce in this environment than those without it. As a result, the rate of sickle-cell anemia increased in the population, in response to the process of natural selection.

The geographic distribution of sickle-cell anemia extends beyond Africa, occurring also in the Mediterranean region, parts of the Arabian peninsula, and parts of Southeast Asia. In these areas it provides human populations with protection against the widespread risk of malaria infection.

Mutation

Research in molecular biology during the twentieth century produced significant discoveries that shed light on the role of mutation as another crucial evolutionary force. We now know that DNA provides the genetic code for an organism's cells, giving them a blueprint for development and growth. As a result, the organism is said to develop according to its particular genotype—that is, the hereditary factors that provide a framework for the organism's physical form. DNA almost always replicates itself exactly, but sometimes an error or collection of errors spontaneously occurs in the copying process. If uncorrected by enzymes that monitor the DNA, a mutation results. A **mutation** is a deviation from the standard DNA code.

Mutations may occur spontaneously in the copying process, or they may result from environmental agents called mutagens (which are usually of human origin). A **mutagen** is any agent that increases the frequency or extent of mutation. Mutagens increasingly are being identified in the human environment and include X-rays and toxic chemicals. Although rare, considering the large number of DNA copies made in a lifetime, spontaneous mutations do occur; in humans, one new potentially significant mutation occurs in every other person born (Larsen 2014).

The impact of mutations is highly variable and depends on the location of the mutation within an individual's DNA sequence and chromosomes. Most mutations are harmless and have no impact on an individual's health, well-being, or survival, although the most extreme mutations may result in debilitating conditions such as Down syndrome or Klinefelter syndrome. On a population level, mutations make no difference unless they provide an advantage for survival and reproduction that can be extended to the group. In the process of evolution, mutations are particularly notable because they are the only source of new genetic material in a population.

Gene Flow

Today human populations are not small and isolated, but large and interconnected. They interact and interbreed relatively freely. In fact, as globalization and access to international travel accelerate, this pattern introduces ample opportunity for another evolutionary force to show its impact—gene flow.

Gene flow is the swapping of genetic material within a population and among diverse populations. As genes travel from one population to another in a species, they increase the diversity of the gene pool in a particular population and decrease the genetic diversity between groups. Gene flow explains the deep genetic similarities within the human population (which is 99.9 percent identical genetically) and the deep interconnections of the human gene pool.

Genes flow as people migrate. For instance, Christopher Columbus's voyage to the Americas marked the beginning of an extensive gene flow from Europe to the Americas. Marriage patterns and kinship structures within populations also play a role in facilitating or restricting gene flow. Some groups are highly endogamous (they marry primarily within their group). As a result, they experience very limited gene flow with other groups and have limited genetic diversity within their group. Other marriage patterns of exogamy (marrying outside the group) promote gene flow among populations related by marriage. Gene flow among and between populations continues to increase today as time-space compression and global migration are increasing the levels of interaction and interbreeding, not only with nearby but also with distant populations.

mutation: A deviation from the standard DNA code.

mutagen: Any agent that increases the frequency or extent of mutations.

gene flow: The movement of genetic material within a population and among diverse populations.

Genetic Drift

Genetic drift, the fourth force of evolution, is the random, unpredictable changes in gene frequencies in a population from one generation to the next. Genetic drift is more rapid in smaller, more isolated populations as a small number of changes can have a statistically more significant influence. When multiplied over generations, this drift within the gene pool can quickly compound, causing isolated populations to become genetically distinct.

Founder effect is one example of genetic drift. When a small part of a population—perhaps several hundred members with some unique genetic and perhaps phenotypical characteristics—breaks off from the larger group, migrates to a new location, and begins to reproduce separately from the original population, it effectively "founds," or establishes, a new and distinct group. Its new and distinct gene variations are reinforced over generations and reshape the expanding population. Scholars often cite founder effect to explain the origins of Native Americans and, in particular, their distinctive genetic characteristics. Some genetic evidence suggests that a small group of Asians with unique phenotypical characteristics broke off and migrated into the Americas likely about 15,000 yBP and perhaps earlier. There they began to reproduce separately from the larger Asian population, founding a new population that eventually settled throughout the Americas (Larsen 2014).

Perhaps you can imagine the four forces of evolution at work (admittedly in an oversimplified example) on the student body in your college. Start with your current classroom, which may represent a gene pool of 20 to 300 students. Imagine that your class formed a distinct, isolated reproductive group. Over several generations of swapping genetic material among your classmates and their offspring, the genetic makeup of the individuals would become more similar, representing the effects of gene flow. Of course, spontaneous mutations would continue to occur to add diversity to the population; but unless the natural environment changed dramatically and selected some particular mutation for enhanced survival, these mutations would have little or no effect on the population.

Now imagine that after several generations some of your classmates or their offspring were to migrate across the hall to a nearby class of similarly isolated students and swap some genetic material. This would be another example of gene migration. It would increase the genetic diversity within the two classrooms and decrease the diversity that may have emerged between the two populations in your college species. Then imagine further that several students get angry for some reason, break away from the others, and establish their own population in another unoccupied classroom, swapping genetic material exclusively among themselves over generations and producing offspring. There, in this smaller, isolated population, random, unpredictable changes in the gene frequency—perhaps the emergence of more redheads than in the original population—would have a statistically more significant chance of influencing the evolutionary trajectory of the new group. This would be an example of genetic drift and founder effect. The four forces of evolution are useful in considering the story of our human ancestors, to which we now turn.

What Do We Know about Our Human Ancestors?

Human evolution took a dramatic turn between 6 and 7 mya. At that time, the ancestral line leading to modern humans split from the line leading to today's chimpanzees. Seven million years is a fleeting moment in deep time and in the evolution of living organisms on the planet. But in these seven million years the key characteristics of being human have emerged. They include bipedalism (walking on two feet instead of four), expanded brain capacity and complex mental functions, creation and use of tools and other forms of culture (including language), and global migration.

The Awash River Valley: "Where It All Began"

The fossil and DNA evidence of human evolution over the past six to seven million years continues to emerge from sites and artifacts worldwide. Recent discoveries shed even more light on the movement of our human ancestors toward the physical form, mental capacity, and cultural capabilities of modern *Homo sapiens*. One site in particular, the Middle Awash River Valley in northeastern Ethiopia, has provided many of the most remarkable finds of the past twenty-five years.

Ethiopians call the area of the Middle Awash River Valley the place "where it all began." The arid territory, populated by herders, their cows, and small villages of simple mud and brick homes, rests on the fault line of three tectonic plates that are slowly pulling apart at a rate of one centimeter per year. Regular earthquakes, flooding, and geologic shifts of Earth's crust have created a landscape of ridges and ravines with geologic strata exposed to wind and water erosion—perfect for revealing fossils to paleoanthropologists. The Middle Awash site has become one of the richest troves of discoveries in the world, not only in the number of finds but also in the representation of almost every major grouping of human ancestor over the last six million years. This remarkable record of many species in one location enables scholars to identify patterns of continuity and change that fill in the historical record of evolutionary change in our immediate human ancestors (White et al. 2009).

Paleoanthropologists group our immediate ancestors into five primary categories. Pre-Australopithecines, an intermediate form between apes and humans, lived between 7 and 4 mya. Australopithecines, including the Taung Child and

MAP 5.1
Middle Awash River Valley

(*left*) The Awash River Valley, north-eastern Ethiopia, and its landscape of ridges and ravines, has provided many of the most remarkable fossil finds of the past 25 years. (*right*) Fossil hunters in the Awash River Valley excavate a lower jaw of *Ardipithecus ramidus*, 4.4 million years old.

species: A group of related organisms that can interbreed and produce fertile, viable offspring.

bipedalism: The ability to habitually walk on two legs; one of the key distinguishing characteristics of humans and our immediate ancestors.

Lucy discussed earlier, lived between 4 and 1 mya. The genus *Homo* emerged from the Australopithecines: first with the species *Homo habilis* between 2.5 and 1.8 mya; then with the species *Homo erectus* between 1.8 million and 300,000 yBP; and finally with the species *Homo sapiens*. Early archaic *Homo sapiens* emerged as early as 350,000 yBP, and fully modern *Homo sapiens* with modern people's anatomical characteristics emerged as early as 200,000 yBP (Larsen 2014). By **species** we refer to a group of related organisms that can interbreed and produce fertile, viable offspring. Discoveries in the Middle Awash area have provided insights into almost all of these species.

Pre-*Australopithecus*

Two species of pre-*Australopithecus*, the 5.8 mya *Ardipithecus kadabba* and the 4.4 mya *Ardipithecus ramidus*, were discovered in the Middle Awash region in the 1990s. These species provided the first evidence of a transitional figure between the primate line and australopithecines and later humans. The 2001 find of another pre-australopithecine in Chad—*Sahelanthropus tchadensis*, dating to between 7 and 6 mya—confirmed the hypothesis that our pre-australopithecine ancestors lived over a broad expanse of Africa (Brunet et al. 2002).

Together, the *Ardipithecus* and *Sahelanthropus* fossils—including a partial skeleton, skull, bones, and teeth—showed two key signs of the evolutionary transition toward humans. Despite being extraordinarily primitive and about one meter tall, all showed signs of **bipedalism** (walking on two feet rather than all four limbs) and a clear change in dental patterns toward smaller and non-projecting canine teeth adapted for chewing (rather than shredding, which is characteristic of earlier ancestral primates) (Larsen 2014). The discovery of fossilized seed and wood in the surrounding sediment, along with the teeth and bones of forest-dwelling monkeys, suggests that these early ancestors lived in wooded settings. The shapes of particular foot bones, the femur, and the pelvis suggest that these individuals spent a great deal of time on the ground, but still some time in the trees.

The shift to bipedalism is one of the key distinguishing characteristics of humans and our immediate ancestors. It is usually attributed to the evolutionary advantages of moving from trees to the ground as the pre-Australopithecines adapted to a cooling environment that had less forest and more savannah grassland. Bipedalism offered numerous benefits. It provided a significant advantage over walking on all four limbs when gathering and carrying food, and it allowed our ancestors to see greater distances over open spaces, reach food higher up on trees and bushes, stay cooler with less body mass exposed to direct sunlight, carry infants more efficiently, and move quickly over long, open distances. Imagine all the activities made possible today—millions of years later—by the shift to bipedalism, especially the use of modern technology from automobiles to laptop computers to cell phones!

The new evidence from the Awash River Valley and other sites that pre-*Australopithecus* lived in wooded environments along the lake edge rather than primarily on the savannah seems to establish a slightly different environment for the evolution of bipedalism. But it does not contradict the narrative completely. Scholars' understanding of this geologic and environmental period is still in formation. We may find that the pre-Australopithecines' habitat of intermittent woodlands, open grasslands, and lakes was also conducive to the evolutionary shift to bipedalism (White et al. 2009).

Australopithecus

The genus *Australopithecus*, dating from 4 to 1 mya, is the second major grouping of human ancestors after the split seven million years ago. Researchers have collected hundreds of fossils from at least seven species of australopithecines, including the following: *Australopithecus (A.) anamensis* (4 mya), *A. afarensis* (3.6 to 3 mya, including Lucy), *A. africanus* (3 to 2 mya), *A. robustus*, *A. aethiopicus*, *A. boisei*, and *A. garhi*. Rather than a direct line of descent from one species to the next, the australopithecine lineage looks more like the branches of a tree (Figure 5.2). Some australopithecine species appear to have ended, either dying out or assimilating into other groups. A few, such as *A. afarensis* and *A. garhi*, are clearly part of the lineage that eventually led to modern humans. Scholars are still sorting out where some others fit in.

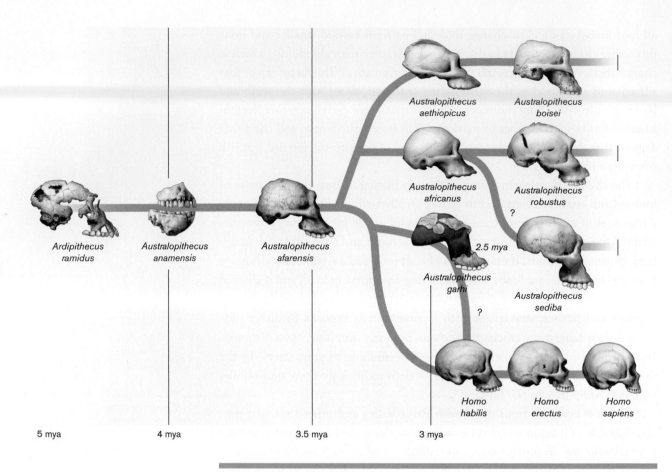

| 5 mya | 4 mya | 3.5 mya | 3 mya |

FIGURE 5.2 Hominin Lineages

The evolutionary relationships among the various *Australopithecus* species suggest two main lineages: one leading eventually to modern *Homo sapiens* and the other leading to a number of other australopithecine species.

A. garhi, found at the Middle Awash River Valley site in 1999, dates to around 2.5 mya and is most likely the immediate ancestor of the *Homo* genus to which we belong. *A. garhi* is considered the first human ancestor to have made and used stone tools. Although no tools were found at its excavation site, recovered animal bones show cut marks where stone tools were used to remove flesh from the bone. At a contemporary site on the nearby Gona River, stone tools have been recovered. These **Oldowan tools**, named by Mary and Louis Leakey after the Olduvai Gorge where the style was first discovered, include a variety of stones shaped into chopping and cutting edges by striking one stone surface against another to break flakes away from a core.

Evidence of bone tools used for digging has also been found. All indications are that by 2.5 mya our Australopithecine ancestors were creating tools and using these early cultural forms to manipulate and adapt to the natural world around them. They may have made and used tools before this period;

Oldowan tools: Stone tools shaped for chopping and cutting found in the Olduvai Gorge and associated with *Australopithecus garhi*.

but if the tools were constructed of wood, grass, or other soft material, they would have been less likely to be preserved.

Australopithecines became extinct by 1 mya. The reasons for their disappearance are unclear. Paleoanthropologists have noted, however, that over a period of three million years, the Australopithecines' brain size and body size remained consistent. Eventually the evolutionary advantages that earlier made them more successful than the pre-Australopithecines may not have been sufficient to adjust to new environmental changes or competition for resources with *Homo habilis* or *Homo erectus* (Larsen 2014).

By 2.5 mya, our ancestors were making tools to manipulate and shape the natural world around them. These Oldowan stone tools, dating to around 1.85 mya, were shaped by striking one stone surface against another and were used for chopping and cutting.

Homo habilis

When *Homo habilis* emerged around 2.5 mya and then *Homo erectus* around 1.8 mya, both were for a time contemporary with australopithecines. However, with these two new groups our ancestors experienced a dramatic increase in intelligence and the use of material culture. And this increase accelerated with the appearance of *Homo sapiens* between 500,000 yBP and 350,000 yBP.

Homo habilis lived in southern and eastern Africa, showing roughly the same geographic distribution as the Australopithecines. Distinguishing characteristics of *Homo habilis* compared to Australopithecines include increased cranial capacity, presumably greater mental capacity, and increased use of tools. Stone tools are more common at *Homo habilis* sites. At a key moment in human evolutionary history, it appears that the introduction of culture—in this case, stone tools—may have had a powerful effect on biological evolution. Better tools allowed more efficient processing of meat and so higher energy intake. Increased energy intake in turn supported an increase in cranial capacity, brain size, and—most likely—mental functions.

Although *Homo habilis* differed from australopithecines in intelligence and tool use, the two groups, contemporaries for a time, were quite similar in other areas. Excavations in Tanzania's Olduvai Gorge in 1980 uncovered a partial skeleton of a *Homo habilis*—an individual only 3.5 feet tall, about the same size as an australopithecine. Like australopithecines, the *Homo habilis* skeleton also had short legs relative to its arms. This observation suggests that although fully bipedal, *Homo habilis* did not share the efficient walking stride of later *Homo erectus* and *Homo sapiens*. This factor may have contributed to the later *Homo erectus* being the first of these immediate ancestors to migrate out of Africa (Johanson et al. 1987).

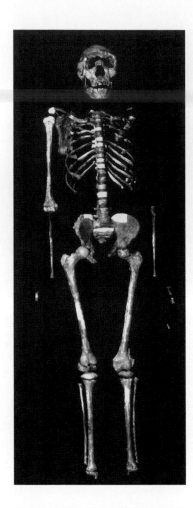

An 80-percent-complete skeleton of an eleven-year-old boy *Homo erectus*, sometimes called Turkana Boy, Nariokotome, Kenya.

Acheulian stone tools: Stone tools associated with *Homo erectus*, including specialized hand axes for cutting, pounding, and scraping.

Homo erectus

Homo erectus lived between 1.8 mya and 300,000 yBP, overlapping with australopithecines, *Homo habilis*, and even our own species, *Homo sapiens*. Fossils of *Homo erectus* have been found in Africa, Asia, and Europe. The earliest and most spectacular fossil is an 80 percent complete skeleton of an eleven-year-old boy found in 1984 on the shore of Lake Turkana in Nariokotome, Kenya. Nariokotome Boy, sometimes called Turkana Boy, looked much more like modern humans than *Homo habilis*, standing 66 inches tall. His shorter arms and longer legs indicate a fully modern stride that shows fully developed bipedalism and adaptation to life on the ground, not in the trees. *Homo erectus* was significantly larger than *Australopithecus* and 35 percent larger than *Homo habilis*, including a significantly larger cranial capacity (McHenry and Coffing 2000).

Homo erectus was the first of our direct ancestors to migrate out of Africa. Indeed, migration is a pattern of movement that has come to characterize human life. Fossil evidence indicates that *Homo erectus* rapidly spread eastward, arriving in the area of modern-day Georgia (in southwest Asia) as early as 1.7 mya, and in the area of modern-day Indonesia between 1.8 and 1.6 mya. *Homo erectus* increasingly turned to cultural innovations to build adaptive strategies as they moved out of Africa. Remnants of game found at *Homo erectus* sites, including bones of hippos, baboons, and elephants, indicate enhanced use of tools for throwing and thrusting (such as spears) as well as chopping, cutting, and scraping. The **Acheulian stone tools** associated with *Homo erectus*, including specialized hand axes for cutting, pounding, and scraping, are more varied and performed many more tasks than the tools of the Australopithecines or *Homo habilis*.

Hunting game would have required complex social structures as groups cooperated to track and kill large, fast, or dangerous animals. Although scholars are not sure exactly when speech developed among our human ancestors, the more complex social interactions required for big-game hunting indicate that some rudimentary capacity to communicate may have been present. Speech developed certainly within the past two million years, although perhaps quite late in that period.

There are various claims for the early use of fire. Researchers have discovered burned animal bones and plant remains in Wonderwerk Cave in South Africa, along with Acheulian tools that indicate *Homo erectus* made and used fire for cooking by 1 mya. The *Homo erectus* site at Zhoukoudian outside Beijing, China, dated to between 780,000 and 400,000 yBP, reveals burned remnants of bones, stone tools, plants, charcoal, and ash that suggest *Homo erectus* individuals in this location also made use of fire. For *Homo erectus*, the cultural development of controlled use of fire provided light, warmth, and the ability to cook food, making it easier to chew, digest, and process nutrients (Larsen 2014; Shapiro 1974).

Homo erectus successfully colonized Africa, Asia, and finally Europe, with sites in Spain and Italy dating between 800,000 and 400,000 yBP. Their migration relied on the unique ability to use biology and culture—including hunting, migration, tools, fire, and forms of communication—to adapt to and control their surroundings, even extreme environments of hot and cold (Anton and Swisher 2004). The increasing role of culture in turn continued to influence biology. Increased tool use for food processing and preparation, from cutting to cooking, led to a reduction in the size of teeth, jaws, and face, eventually drawing the physical proportions of these ancestors closer to our own (Anton 2003). Brain size and complex mental activities increased, supported by greater energy intake.

Homo sapiens

Homo sapiens, dating from between 500,000 yBP and 350,000 yBP to the present, constitute the fifth major group in our evolutionary chain. They include both archaic *Homo sapiens*, who lived between 350,000 and 28,000 yBP, and modern *Homo sapiens*, who appeared as early as 200,000 yBP in Africa and eventually replaced archaic *Homo sapiens*.

Archaic *Homo sapiens*, including one late variety prevalent in Europe—**Neandertals**—have often been depicted as slow, unintelligent, and inarticulate cave dwellers who were far removed physically and mentally from modern humans. But these views are inaccurate. The brains of Neandertals had achieved modern size. These individuals were physically active and able to survive and settle in the most extreme of natural environments. They made elaborate tools. They hunted big game with sophistication and success, revealing strength, intelligence, culture, and social organization. Neandertals buried their dead. Carefully laid out skeletons have been recovered from burial pits, showing a distinct level of care and intention between the living and the dead. Neandertal anatomy would have enabled them to speak.

Neandertal: A late variety of archaic *Homo sapien* prevalent in Europe.

Like those of *Homo erectus*, archaic *Homo sapiens* fossils can be found in Africa, Asia, and Europe. Excavations throughout these regions have uncovered quite a few nearly complete skeletons and accompanying artifacts. Neandertals provide some of the most well known and most studied fossils of our human ancestors (Trinkaus and Shipman 1994).

Modern *Homo sapiens* emerged in Africa as early as 200,000 yBP. One of the earliest modern *Homo sapiens* finds, discovered in the Middle Awash River Valley, dates to 160,000 yBP. Its physical characteristics suggest a body and a mental capacity much like our own. By 100,000 yBP, modern *Homo sapiens* were migrating out of Africa into Asia and Europe. The exact reasons for their migration may never be known but likely include effects of climate change on the natural habitat, stress on food resources because of increasing population, and competition for scarce resources (Larsen 2014).

YOUR TURN: FIELDWORK

Human Origins in the Museum

After reading this chapter, visit your local natural history museum. You may find one on campus or in the nearest town, or you may need to travel some distance. Museums are designed to teach the public about art and history through personal interactions with artifacts and displays. At the museum, take some time to walk through displays, focusing on the exhibits that teach about human origins. How are the exhibits presented? How is human behavior portrayed in any dioramas of family life, food preparation and cooking, hunting, and use of tools and technology? How do they compare to the presentation of material in this textbook? Do the exhibits help you think about human evolution from a new angle? Compare your findings with your classmates. Would you suggest any changes to strengthen the displays?

Consider interviewing other museum visitors about their experience of the human origins displays. What did they learn from their visit? What most surprised them? Did any part of the display make them uncomfortable or contradict something that they had previously thought? Compare your findings with classmates.

If you are unable to visit a museum in person, spend time investigating the online exhibit of the American Museum of Natural History's Hall of Human Origins (www.amnh.org/exhibitions/permanent-exhibitions/human-origins-and-cultural-halls/anne-and-bernard-spitzer-hall-of-human-origins/) or the Smithsonian Institution's human origins website (http://humanorigins.si.edu). These are extensive sites with rich text and excellent photos and graphics.

"out of Africa" theory: The theory that modern *Homo sapiens* evolved first in Africa, migrated outward, and eventually replaced the archaic *Homo sapiens*. Also called *replacement theory*.

Fossil records show at least a four-thousand-year period, between 32,000 and 28,000 yBP, when archaic and modern *Homo sapiens* coexisted in Europe. By the time modern *Homo sapiens* first encountered Neandertals, the Neandertal culture would have been technically and behaviorally quite advanced. DNA and fossil records suggest that archaic *Homo sapiens* migrated out of Africa first. Modern *Homo sapiens* who also evolved in Africa, migrated outward and eventually replaced the archaic *Homo sapiens* (Larsen 2014). In this **"out of Africa"** (or **replacement**) **theory**, archaic *Homo sapiens* may have lost a resource war to their more modern successors. But genetic studies reveal that in parts of the world Neandertals also interbred and gradually assimilated into the modern human population, contributing a small portion of their DNA to the modern *Homo sapiens* gene pool—our very own (Boyd and Silk 2015; Stringer and McKie 1998).

Archaeological evidence shows that many modern *Homo sapiens* advances in behavior and culture occurred first in Africa—not in Europe, as scholars had earlier thought. The first ornamentation of shell beads was widespread in the area of modern-day Congo, Central Africa, by 80,000 yBP. The first evidence of fishing was also found in Congo, dating to 75,000 yBP. Painting, abstract art, and the use of symbolism also appear to have originated in Africa (see Chapter 17), although the stunning imagery of artwork found in French and

Spanish caves has garnered much of the media and scientific attention (Powell, Shennan, and Thomas 2009).

By 40,000 yBP, intrepid modern *Homo sapiens* immigrants had settled in Australia and the Pacific Islands. In a cooling climate, water was drawn toward the polar caps, with the effect of lowering sea levels, exposing more land and creating more avenues for human migration.

Until recently, all human remains discovered in East Asia dating to 40,000 yBP or later appeared to be fully modern *Homo sapiens*. Recent research, however, challenges the impression of successive, discreet steps in human evolution in this region and globally. Fossil remains from Denisova Cave in north-central Asia suggest that the species of human ancestor living there around 40,000 yBP was genetically distinct from Neandertals but was not *Homo sapiens*. What appears to be a new species may instead possibly be an isolated *Homo sapiens* descendant of *Homo erectus*, complicating the picture of human evolution in the region (Krause et al. 2010).

Emerging evidence continues to debunk stereotypes of Neandertals as far removed physically and mentally from modern humans. For instance, the careful burial of this Neandertal, discovered at La Chapelle-aux-Saints, France, reveals a distinct level of intentionality between the living and the dead.

In 2003, the skeletal remains of a very short, primitive species were discovered on the island of Flores in Indonesia and quickly dubbed "the Hobbit" in the popular press. The skeleton, dated to 18,000 yBP, revealed a very tiny brain similar in size to the brains of earlier Australopithecines and only a quarter of the size of a living human's brain. Primitive wrist bones appear to be like those found in apes. Some scholars have argued that, especially with no evidence of ancestors, the find may simply be a modern human suffering from a genetic abnormality such as microcephaly. Most scholars, however, suggest this skeleton may be evidence of a group of primitive humans (named *Homo floresiensis* by Peter Brown and colleagues [2004]) that became isolated in early human evolution. The primitive wrist bones and general characteristics of the fossil have led many to think that this may be a new species that originated in Africa well before *Homo sapiens*.

With these two finds, the picture of our human ancestors as late as 30,000 yBP becomes unexpectedly complicated (Larsen 2014). In addition, continuing work on Neandertal DNA confirms their presence in multiple sites globally, though by 30,000 yBP they appear to have been barely holding on in the

Frans de Waal
Seeing Human Nature in Our Primate Relatives

Primatologist Frans de Waal, professor in the Department of Psychology at Emory University and director of the Living Links Center for the Advanced Study of Ape and Human Evolution, is one of the world's leading scholars in the exploration of the behavioral and cognitive connections between apes and humans. His research has explored primate social behavior, conflict resolution, cooperation, empathy, inequality aversion, and food sharing as well as primate cognition.

"I'm interested generally in the continuity between humans and other species. I do not see humans as separate from the animal kingdom. I see them as part of it. In that regard, the primates are special because they are the ones that provide the bridge between humans and other animal species. The DNA tells us we are very closely related. In fact I would say we are actually all part of one genus though for historical reasons we have a separate genus for ourselves."

De Waal urges us to recognize the fuzziness of the distinctions within our extended primate family—genetic, anatomical, social, and cognitive. "In social behavior all of the distinctions we have made over time—that we are the only moral beings, the only cultural beings, the only beings with empathy, the only beings with a social organization— all of those things have fallen apart over the last fifty years because studies have shown that all of these things can be found in other primates. The only distinction that I think has probably held up is human language.

"I think in every way we are all animals—even on the cultural side, which is the way we usually contrast ourselves with other animals. But we have done lots of studies on culture in chimpanzees and other primates and whales and dolphins and all sorts of animals. An animal that is raised in isolation will not survive because it doesn't have the knowledge to survive. Animals need to have a context in which they learn what to do and what not to do; what kind of predators to avoid; what kinds of food to eat. Today we can begin to look at animals as cultural beings. They acquire a lot of knowledge from their interactions with others."

De Waal's work challenges popular stereotypes of apes as primarily and naturally aggressive, selfish, competitive, and territorial. Instead, by exploring how they live in groups, de Waal's findings expose highly developed patterns of cooperation, conflict resolution, expressions of empathy, and concern for fairness. Of particular significance has been de Waal's study of bonobos in Africa (see Chapter 14).

"We are used to comparing humans with chimpanzees. We have been doing this for 100 years. Chimpanzees are our nearest relatives. But the bonobo is equally as close to us as the chimpanzee. The bonobo was discovered much later and there are fewer of them. As a result people don't know as much about bonobos as they do about chimps. Anatomically bonobos are more like humans than chimpanzees are. They have longer legs than chimpanzees. So when they stand upright, which they do very often, they look almost exactly like [our ancestor] *Ardipithecus*.

Primatologist Frans de Waal.

"Chimpanzees are very popular with scientists who explain human evolution by looking at humans as conquerors and aggressors. In that context, if you look at human males as aggressive, territorial, and dominance oriented, and that is what made us successful, then the chimpanzee is the ideal and the bonobo seems like a strange animal.

"But bonobos are very interesting in this regard. They are a female-dominated society. They are much less belligerent and aggressive than chimpanzees. But the only reason female bonobos dominate the males is because they have a lot of alliances going on. They are not physically bigger and stronger than males. So they do it mostly through cooperation. They also resolve conflict sexually."

> *I think in every way we are all animals—even on the cultural side.*

De Waal sees empathy and concern for fairness as key to primates' evolutionary success, enabling them to live and work together in groups.

"It used to be that people thought that empathy—meaning you could be in touch with the feelings of somebody else—that this was a uniquely human phenomenon, that the good things we have are human and the bad things we have are animal.

"But today there are many studies of empathy in animals. We study how chimpanzees and bonobos respond to someone's distress, when someone loses a fight or falls out of a tree or is scared by a snake. How do they respond to them? They go over to them and embrace them and kiss them and try to calm them down. We call this consolation behavior.

"We also look at the sense of fairness. In one study (http://www.youtube.com/watch?v=meiU6TxysCg) two capuchin monkeys are given a simple task. If you reward both of them with cucumber for the task, they are perfectly fine. If you give them both grapes for the task, they are both perfectly fine. But if you give one of them grapes and the other cucumber—and grapes are ten times better than cucumber—then the one who gets cucumber becomes incredibly upset.

"In capuchin monkeys the one who gets the cucumber will refuse the task and sometimes refuse the food. But chimpanzees go even further than this. With chimpanzees we've had situations in which the one who gets the grape will refuse the grape unless the other one also gets a grape.

"With chimpanzees we see an even more complete sense of fairness, very similar to the one that is found in humans, in which they try to equalize outcomes even if that is not in their own favor. We think the human sense of fairness and the primate sense of fairness is related to high levels of cooperation."

"Cooperation is a very old theme in animal behavior. You find it in ants and bees, in dolphins and elephants and primates. And this cooperation is very highly developed. They exchange favors. They have to trust each other. They have empathic impulses, at least the mammals do. They help each other."

De Waal argues that primate research can shed light on the natural instincts in humans—what is programmed into our DNA. "Basically my argument is that in all of these domains both the positive side of behavior like altruism and the negative side like competition, exist. The sad thing is that 'nature' is often used to justify things. So if we say it is natural, this means that there is nothing you can do about it. If warfare is natural, then you cannot avoid having warfare going on. If people say being selfish is natural, then people buy into that right away. The word 'natural' has great power." Arguing for a more complex view of both ape and human nature, de Waal says, "I would argue that being kind, cooperative, and trusting is also natural."

Homo floresiensis (left), dubbed "the Hobbit," compared to the cranium of a modern human (right). Discovered in Indonesia, Homo floresiensis dates to 18,000 yBP.

Iberian peninsula of western Europe before their ultimate demise (Krause et al. 2007). Modern humans, originating in Africa, were spreading everywhere by 30,000 yBP. Taken together, these four species present an emerging picture of dynamic human evolution that reveals surprising diversity in our immediate past, really just a blink of an eye before the present in the scope of deep time (Larsen 2014).

By around 15,000 yBP, a founding population of modern *Homo sapiens* had left northeastern Asia and traveled perhaps by boat or across the newly exposed Bering land bridge between Siberia and Alaska. Subsequently they populated North and South America and completed our species' colonization of the entire planet (Steele and Powell 1993).

What Has Made Modern Humans So Successful at Survival?

One of the key characteristics of humans is our ability to adapt to a changing world. Human adaptation takes four primary forms: genetic adaptation through evolution; developmental adaptation during the individual life cycle; acclimatization to immediate environmental changes; and cultural adaptation using tools to moderate or control the effects of the natural environment. Together, these four types of adaptation provide humans with a remarkable set of tools to survive, thrive, and pass our genetic inheritance on to future generations.

Genetic Adaptation

genetic adaptation: Changes in genetics that occur at a population level as a result of natural selection.

Genetic adaptation occurs at the population level as a result of natural selection. We have already discussed human genetic adaptations to malaria through the sickle-cell mutation. Later in the chapter we will examine human genetic adaptation to ultraviolet (UV) light. In examining genetic adaptation, anthropologists focus not on changes to an individual's genotype but on cumulative changes that occur as a population evolves over many generations. Genetic adaptations are inherited from one generation to another, and they are not reversible in an individual's lifetime.

Developmental Adaptation

developmental adaptation: The way in which human growth and development can be influenced by factors other than genetics, such as nutrition, disease, and stress.

Although DNA provides a blueprint for an individual's growth, one's actual development is strongly influenced by the environment and the events one experiences. **Developmental adaptations** begin in the womb and continue through the human growth cycle, influenced by nutrition, disease, and other environmental factors. Height, for instance, is influenced not only by DNA but also by the quality and quantity of food eaten and the diseases experienced. Did you have enough calories, calcium, and vitamins during your growth spurts?

Were you immunized against polio, measles, mumps, and rubella? If so, you were able to maximize the growth potential in your DNA blueprint.

Research has confirmed that nutrition and stress during prenatal development have a dramatic impact on our physical and mental abilities. Inadequate nutrition or a mother's smoking, drinking, or drug intake can create powerful stresses on the fetus. David Barker's *fetal origins hypothesis*, now commonly referred to as the developmental origins of health and disease, suggests that individuals who experienced these stresses in the womb or during the first two years of childhood tend to be smaller, more prone to disease, and likely to have shorter lives than those who did not. Prenatal and early postnatal adaptations may help in the survival of the fetus and infant by shaping an appropriate trajectory of growth in response to environmental cures. But that developmental trajectory may result in adverse health effects when a mismatch with the predicted long-term environment occurs. Barker, a nutrition scientist, studied 16,000 people in Hertfordshire, England, and found a direct correlation between low birth weight and death from coronary disease. Specifically, individuals born weighing less than 5.5 pounds were twice as likely to die of coronary heart disease at some point over their lifetime than individuals weighing 7.5 pounds or more at birth (Barker 1998).

Another study of developmental adaptation has focused on children who grow up at high altitudes in the highlands of South America. These individuals develop larger lung capacity, an adaptation that enables them to process more oxygen in a low-oxygen environment. This developmental adaptation is permanent and does not reverse if the individuals move to a lower altitude later in life. But like all developmental adaptations, the development of larger lungs affects only the individual's body; it does not affect the underlying genetic code in the individual's DNA and so is not passed on to the next generation. What is inherited is the ability to make this developmental adaptation in the next generation, if necessary (Beall 2001, 2006).

The Aymara people, who dwell in the Andes region of highland Bolivia, develop larger lung capacity as a result of living at such a high altitude. This allows them to process more oxygen in a low-oxygen environment, an example of developmental adaptation.

Acclimatization

Beginning in the womb and continuing through old age, humans also experience temporary physiological adaptations, sometimes called **acclimatization**. These occur every day as our bodies make temporary adjustments to changes in the environment. When your body is hot, it perspires to cool down. When the weather is cold outside, you may start to shiver—an attempt to stay warm

acclimatization: The process of the body temporarily adjusting to changes in the environment.

A member of the Denver Broncos football team receives oxygen to combat the effects of the high altitude in Denver, Colorado, an example of cultural adaptation to the natural environment.

cultural adaptation: A complex innovation, such as fans, furnaces, and lights, that allows humans to cope with their environment.

by moving. When it is dark outside, your pupils dilate to allow in more natural light; in bright sun, they narrow to protect your eyes. If you travel to high altitudes where the air has less oxygen, your heart rate speeds up and your breathing becomes shallower to extract more oxygen from the air. All of these are temporary, usually short-term, adaptations to changes in the immediate environment.

Cultural Adaptation

Humans' innovative, complex, and widespread **cultural adaptations** to the natural environment set us apart from other animal species. When it is cold outside, we light a fire, put on a coat, build a shelter, or turn up the furnace. When it is hot outside, we turn on the fan or the air conditioner. When it is dark, we turn on the lights; when it is too bright, we pull down the shades. When professional basketball and football teams travel to play games in high-altitude cities such as Denver, they keep an oxygen tank next to the bench to make it easier for the players to breathe. Airplanes are equipped with oxygen masks to help passengers deal with the low oxygen levels at high altitudes in the event of a "sudden drop in cabin pressure" during the flight.

Cultural adaptations have even affected our biological evolution. The cultural invention of stone tools as early as 2.5 mya enabled our human ancestors to butcher and process meat more efficiently and provided the increased energy intake needed for the development of larger brains. Today, culture is the primary way we adapt to the natural environment.

Where Did Variations in Human Skin Color Come From?

Skin color comes in infinite variations, and it, too, reflects adaptation to the environment through natural selection. Physical anthropologists suggest that such variations are a direct result of genetic adaptations to varying levels of UV light (Jablonski and Chaplin 2000). Where UV light is strongest—for instance, near the equator or at higher altitudes—skin color is darkest. Where UV light is weakest—closer to the poles—skin color is lightest. But how do these variations actually happen?

The Role of Ultraviolet Light

Jablonski and Chaplin (2000) argue that variation in skin color is the result of a genetic balancing act between getting too much UV light and too little. Too much UV light can destroy folic acid in the body, a vitamin that is essential to healthy fetal development. In fact, extremely low levels of folic acid can lead to birth defects. (Although too much UV light can also lead to skin cancers, these develop later in life and do not affect reproduction and evolution of the species.)

Too little UV light can also be a problem since it is essential to the process of synthesizing vitamin D, which in turn is necessary for absorbing calcium. We need calcium to build and preserve strong bones. A lack of vitamin D may lead to bone-softening diseases such as rickets in children and osteomalacia in adults. The latter is particularly devastating for women whose weakened pelvic bones may be unable to support the stress of giving birth. The nutrients needed for the body to synthesize vitamin D are also found in a few fatty fish such as salmon, tuna, mackerel, sardines, and catfish—foods not commonly associated with the early human diet. UV light is the primary and most readily available source of the vitamin (Jablonski 2006).

Melanin and Melanocytes

Melanin, the pigment that gives our skin color, is produced by melanocytes in the skin. All humans have a similar number of these pigment-producing cells, but not all of them are genetically programmed to create the same amount. Melanin is a natural sunscreen. Because we know that our ancestors all originated in Africa, which is close to the equator, we can assume that they had more active melanocytes, more melanin, and darker skin as an adaptation to a high UV light environment.

melanin: The pigment that gives human skin its color.

When humans began to migrate out of Africa, away from the equator and into areas with less UV light, the role of melanin-rich dark skin as a powerful sunscreen likely became less positive, as it blocked too much of the UV light needed to synthesize vitamin D. American physiologist William Loomis (1967) suggests that because of these conditions, as groups of humans migrated out of Africa away from the equator, natural mutations that created lighter skin color would have been more successful and helped those individuals survive and reproduce more effectively. Gradually, over hundreds or thousands of generations and many miles of migration, changes in the natural environment interacted with variations in skin color to select the color variation most effective for survival. As levels of UV light change gradually with increasing distance from the equator, so did skin color shift gradually as the human population migrated, adapting genetically to changes in the natural environment. Individuals with appropriate levels of melanin to absorb the UV light in a region would be more likely to survive and reproduce, gradually expanding their representation in the population's gene pool. The maps in Figure 5.3 show the corresponding clinal variations (reflecting gradual change over space and time) of UV light and skin color.

Skin color varies so gradually that there are no clear boundaries between one population and another, nor color groupings that distinguish one population from another. Nevertheless, imaginations of distinct populations—sometimes called races—identifiable by skin color or other physical features

THE SOCIAL LIFE OF THINGS
Chimpanzee Tools and What It Means to Be Human

What can we learn about human origins from looking at our living primate relatives? Is there really the huge distance between us that is imagined in popular culture? Recent findings about primates' use of tools challenge many of our preconceptions.

1 When primatologist Jane Goodall launched her field study of chimpanzees in the forest along Tanzania's Lake Tanganyika in the 1960s, she observed chimpanzees making and using tools. Her findings surprised the scientific community because to that point, the use of material culture—things—was considered to be exclusive to humans and key to what makes humans unique.

2 Goodall observed adult chimpanzees "fishing" for termites (which are highly nutritious). In an elaborate process, a chimpanzee chooses a branch or twig thin enough to pass through holes of a termite nest. After removing all extra branches and leaves, the chimpanzee pokes the twig into a termite hill, withdraws it, and eats the termites that cling to the twig.

3 Goodall also observed chimpanzees create a kind of sponge by crumpling up leaves and dipping them into crooks of trees to soak up rain water, then squeezing the water into their mouths.

 Primatologist Jill Pruetz observed chimpanzees making spearlike objects—trimmed pointed twigs—to thrust into the hollows of trees and kill strepsirhines (sometimes called bushbabies), the first observed case of nonhuman primates using tools to hunt other mammals.

 In Tai Forest in Africa's Ivory Coast, chimpanzees have been observed cracking hard-shelled nuts by using a stone as a hammer and a second heavy, flat stone or protruding root as an anvil. Adult chimpanzees have also been observed teaching this technique to their young, revealing chimpanzees' capacity for social learning—passing cultural information from one generation to the next.

Tool use by chimpanzees and other nonhuman primates reveals they are extraordinarily intelligent, learn quickly, think abstractly, have strong visual abilities and are social learners—able to pass information along to others. These discoveries narrow the perceived chasm between humans and our closest relatives and blur what once were thought to be sharp dividing lines between us in material culture, or the making and use of things.

- What stereotypes about non-human primates do you have that are challenged by the photos and content in this feature?
- Knowing that humans and chimpanzees had a common ancestor as recently as 6–7 million years ago, can you now begin to imagine our ancestors' earliest tool use and cultural activities?

have been prominent in cultures worldwide with powerful effect. In Chapter 6 we explore the implications of these ideas for the cultural construction of race and racism.

Physiological and Cultural Adaptations to Ultraviolet Light

Humans adapt to UV light in other ways, both physical and cultural. Tanning, for instance, is an adaptation of our bodies to UV light; but it is a temporary acclimatization, not a permanent change. Tanning does not affect the genes and is not passed along through the gene pool to the next generation. If I were to move from New York to Miami, my "white" skin's melanocytes would become more active, making more pigmentation—a tan—for protection. But even if I lived in Miami for thirty years, working and playing every day in the sun, my tan would never become permanent. If I later moved back to New York, my tan would gradually fade and my melanin production and skin color would return to their pre-Miami white. Modern-day human cultural adaptations to UV light include sunscreen, hats, sunglasses, long-sleeve shirts, and umbrellas to protect lighter-colored skin from damage.

Another cultural adaptation to UV light is announced on the front of every milk carton: "vitamin D fortified." Why is vitamin D added to milk? In the early twentieth century, the rise of industrial jobs in northern U.S. cities combined with increased mechanization of agriculture in the South to spur a vast migration of African Americans from southern farms to northern factories. Cases of rickets and osteomalacia became rampant in African American populations that were no longer exposed to enough UV light in northern states. With the discovery of dietary vitamin D, a public health campaign led the U.S. government to initiate a program of fortifying milk and milk-based infant formulas in the 1930s. This cultural response to low levels of UV light led to a near disappearance of rickets in the United States by the 1960s. However, rickets has reemerged as a health concern in recent years as cultural practices have limited people's exposure to sunlight without regard to the dangers of vitamin D deficiency (Rajakumar and Thomas 2005).

Are We Still Evolving?

Today, living organisms—including humans—continue to adapt to changes in the natural environment. Indeed, evolution is happening all around us. Bacteria are evolving in response to antibiotics. Hospitals in the United States are reporting an alarming rise in drug-resistant infections, and health-care workers worldwide are finding strains of tuberculosis that are resistant to many common antibiotic treatments. Insects are evolving in response to pesticides, with the emergence of DDT-resistant mosquitoes ending twentieth-century hopes of eliminating

FIGURE 5.3 Skin Color Variation

(a) Clinal distribution of ultraviolet (UV) light intensity, with highest intensity near the equator and lowest near the poles. (b) Clinal distribution of skin color, closely tracking the intensity of ultraviolet light.

(a)

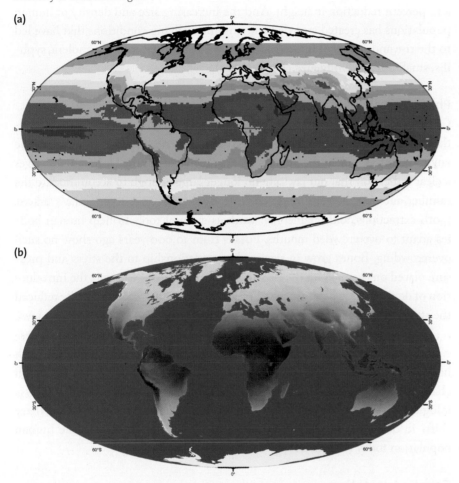

(b)

SOURCE: Modified from Nina G. Jablonski. 2006. *Skin: A Natural History*. Berkeley: University of California Press. Images by George Chaplin.

malaria. Studies of fish are revealing the emergence of smaller bodies and faster reproduction to compensate for overfishing. Clearly, species are continuing to adapt as their diversity and mutations interact with changes in the natural environment that alter the conditions for survival and reproduction (Larsen 2014).

Humans, too, continue to adapt and evolve. We have clear evidence, for instance, of the significant biological changes shaped by the rise of agriculture beginning 10,000 years ago. While the turn to agriculture—farming and herding—has created the conditions for rapid growth of the human population and has long been considered an improvement in the human condition, the subsequent changes have also brought significant negative health effects for the human body. For instance, increased workload has changed bone shape, strength, and density, leading to increasing osteoarthritis in the spine, hands, hips and knees and to an increase in injuries. The invention of more complex tools and technologies reduced human reliance on physical strength and led to a 10 percent reduction in height. And the increasing size and density of human populations has created crowded and unsanitary living conditions that have led to the rise and spread of infectious diseases like measles, mumps, cholera, syphilis, small pox, and influenza (Larsen 2014).

Physiological Adaptation

Changes in the human face and dentition over the last 10,000 years provide further evidence of how the human form continues to be shaped in response to the environment. A look at the mouths of most teenagers in the United States gives a clear indication that our jaws are no longer large enough to accommodate the number and size of teeth inherited from our recent ancestors. Today's braces, tooth extractions, and retainers all work as cultural tools to help human bodies adapt to overcrowded mouths. Fossils from 10,000 years ago show no such overcrowding. Bones grow in size in direct relationship to the stress and pressure placed on them. With the rise of agriculture 10,000 years ago, the introduction of domesticated plants such as grains into the human diet gradually reduced the stresses on the human jaw and the stimulation needed to produce large jaws.

Tooth size, however, is not susceptible to the same environmental pressures. Reduction in jaw size without a change in the size and number of teeth has led to a lot of overcrowded mouths in the twenty-first century. Although changes in jaw size and face shape may relate more directly to individuals' physiological adaptation to diet rather than genetic changes in the population, these shifts in dentition do reveal evolution and adaptation at work in the human population today (Larsen 2014).

Genetic Adaptation

Current genetic evolution in the human species is harder to see. The long human life cycle and our general reluctance to be subjects of laboratory experiments make the task of observing change over time difficult. The conditions for evolution, however, are very clearly present. Spontaneous mutations continue to occur in every species, including humans. And the natural environment of human life—of all life—is changing dramatically. Global warming is altering weather patterns and causing sea levels to rise. Ozone depletion is allowing more exposure to solar radiation. Pollution is adding carcinogenic mutagens to the air, water, and soil. The environment, a key element in shaping genetic adaptations, is undergoing significant changes. Environmental conditions exist today that could put pressure on the human physical form and create an environment suitable to genetic adaptation.

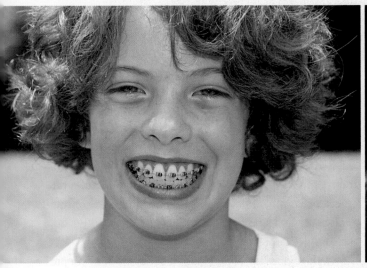
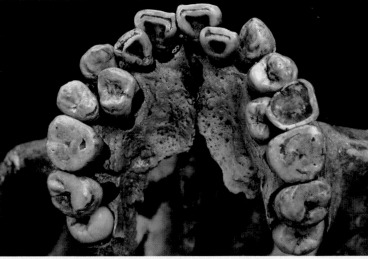

As the environment changes, it will affect the biology and evolution of all living organisms. Other animal species—from corals to birds to polar bears to orangutans—are already facing massive extinctions. As the world changes around us, our generation and future generations will change as well. There are good reasons to believe that current trends in energy consumption, population growth, and economic globalization will continue. As a result, we can expect intense and perhaps cataclysmic pressures on the human species that will force us to adapt. What specific form those adaptations might take we cannot predict.

Cultural Adaptation

Culture is now the primary tool that humans use to adapt to changes in the environment. As humans face increasing levels of UV light, our first adaptive line of defense is to use sunscreens, sun-protective clothing, and sunglasses. As sea levels rise or warming waters stimulate stronger hurricanes and tropical storms, we build seawalls and levees to protect our homes and communities. As diseases such as tuberculosis, malaria, and HIV/AIDS mutate and develop more virulent strains, humans turn to more intense pharmaceutical research and expensive antivirals, pesticides, and antibiotics. But will these cultural adaptations be enough to protect us as a species if the changes to the natural environment are extreme?

Perhaps just as important, who will have access to these cultural tools? When drought caused by changes in climate patterns disrupts clean water supplies, not everyone will have the resources to dig deeper wells, build water filtration plants, or construct aqueducts to move water across parched lands. When hurricanes increase in strength or frequency, not everyone will have seawalls and levees high enough or strong enough to guarantee protection. Not all humans will have an equal chance at survival.

(*left*) Straightening teeth has become so common that in the United States orthodontics is a multibillion-dollar industry. (*right*) Crowding of the teeth appears in some archaeological skeletal remains, but it became common only after humans adopted agriculture around 10,000 years ago.

TOOLKIT

Thinking Like an Anthropologist: Looking Ahead, Looking Behind

Where did we come from? Where are we going? What does it mean to be human? Throughout this chapter we have explored our human origins and pondered these questions, as well as the others listed below. The chapter's opening stories provide windows into the evidence that physical anthropologists are uncovering about the human story in the perspective of deep time.

- Where do humans fit in the story of life on Earth?
- How do scientists learn about prehistoric life?
- How does the theory of evolution explain the diversity of life?
- How does evolution work?
- What do we know about our human ancestors?
- What has made modern humans so successful at survival?
- Where did variations in human skin color come from?
- Are we still evolving?

Everything we do today is contingent on the evolutionary developments discussed in this chapter, including opposable thumbs, bipedalism, and an enlarged brain. Which one of our Australopithecine ancestors could have imagined humans today walking and texting? Or speaking into cell phones and communicating with others on the opposite side of the world? Or the elaborate forms of symbolic and abstract art, media, and language that our brains have enabled us to create? Today we integrate these evolutionary developments into the most contemporary context, and they have repercussions that we ourselves have difficulty imagining.

Where does the explosion of technology fit in our process of adaptation? Will this change our notion of what it means to be human? How will digital technology influence our cognitive development? What is the cumulative impact of television, videos, cell phones, the computer, and the Internet? Is it possible to imagine that the way we have evolved may actually limit our capacity to see the world and understand it? As we have discussed, the human chapter in the story of life on Earth is just a few brief pages in the encyclopedic narrative of deep time. But the pace of change in contemporary human culture is extraordinarily rapid, and we must carefully consider the developments of the present, seen in the context of our evolutionary past, to catch a glimpse of where we are going.

Key Terms

deep time (p. 155)

fossils (p. 158)

DNA (p. 160)

theory of evolution (p. 161)

creationism (p. 162)

intelligent design (p. 163)

natural selection (p. 165)

mutation (p. 167)

mutagen (p. 167)

gene flow (p. 167)

genetic drift (p. 168)

species (p. 170)

bipedalism (p. 170)

Oldowan tools (p. 172)

Acheulian stone tools (p. 174)

Neandertal (p. 175)

"out of Africa" (replacement) theory (p. 176)

genetic adaptation (p. 180)

developmental adaptation (p. 180)

acclimatization (p. 181)

cultural adaptation (p. 182)

melanin (p. 183)

For Further Exploration

Cave of Forgotten Dreams. 2010. Directed by Werner Herzog. IFC Films. Documentary film explores the art in Chauvet Cave in southern France.

De Waal, Frans, 2013. *The Bonobo and the Atheist: In Search of Humanism among the Primates.* New York: W.W. Norton.

De Waal, Frans, 2016. *Are We Smart Enough to Know How Smart Animals Are?* New York: W.W. Norton.

Frans de Waal: Moral Behavior in Animals. Ted Talk. https://www.youtube.com/watch?v=GcJxRqTs5nk

Jablonski, Nina G. 2006. *Skin: A Natural History.* Berkeley: University of California Press.

The Jane Goodall Institute. http://www.janegoodall.org

National Center for Science Education. www.ncse.com. Resources to further explore the processes of evolution and the debates between evolution and creationism.

Pew Forum on Religion & Public Life. www.pewforum.org. This website explores American attitudes toward religion and politics.

What lies beneath the surface of any beautiful scene? The project of anthropology includes unmasking the structures of power—the deep complexities of how humans organize themselves in groups. In Part 2 we will explore structures of race, ethnicity, gender, sexuality, kinship, and class in order to help you develop the analytical tools to see more deeply, navigate more carefully, and engage more fully the world around you. Here, women smoke a hookah at a coffee shop in Cairo, Egypt.

How do we make sense of the continuing inequality in the United States that breaks so clearly along lines of race? Here, police in military gear arrest a demonstrator during protests in Ferguson, Missouri, in August 2014.

CHAPTER 6
Race and Racism

On the afternoon of August 9, 2014, twenty-eight-year-old white police officer Darren Wilson shot and killed unarmed eighteen-year-old African American Michael Brown after a 90-second encounter on a street in Ferguson, Missouri. Over the following weeks, growing crowds of demonstrators organized in Ferguson to express their outrage over Michael Brown's shooting and long-simmering grievances of discriminatory treatment at the hands of the Ferguson Police Department and courts. As demonstrations intensified, the police rapidly escalated their response. A nightly curfew was declared. Police in riot gear with gas masks, shields, and batons—backed up by helicopters, floodlights, and armored vehicles with snipers perched atop—fired tear gas, concussion grenades and rubber bullets to control and disperse crowds. Much of the nation and the world watched in disbelief.

In November of 2014, a local grand jury, after hearing the evidence, chose to not indict Officer Wilson, accepting his statement that he feared for his safety and declaring that he had acted in self-defense. Demonstrations erupted again. In March 2015, after a six-month investigation, the U.S. Department of Justice cleared Officer Wilson of any civil rights violations in the shooting of Michael Brown.

But a second DOJ report on the Ferguson Police Department offered deeper insights into the roots of the racial tension running through the Ferguson uprising (U.S. Department of Justice 2015). The DOJ investigation found that in a town of 21,200 residents, of whom 67 percent were African American, during the previous two years African Americans comprised 85 percent of all traffic stops, 90 percent of all tickets, 93 percent of arrests, and 95 percent of citations for jaywalking or disturbing the peace, violations that hinge significantly on police discretion. When whites were charged for similar discretionary offenses, Ferguson courts dismissed the charges 68 percent more often. Ferguson police used force almost exclusively against blacks and were twice as likely to search a black motorist as a white motorist after a traffic stop even though white motorists were more likely to have drugs or other contraband. The DOJ report unambiguously concluded that the Ferguson Police Department routinely violated the constitutional rights of the town's African American residents. Its findings of racial profiling, discrimination, use of excessive force and patterns of unlawful conduct confirmed the long-standing complaints of Ferguson residents that, in the most fundamental ways, the criminal justice system worked differently for whites and blacks.

The tragic death of Michael Brown, the events in Ferguson, the torrent of deadly encounters between police and African Americans, and the growth of the Black Lives Matter movement have again pushed race and racism directly into the U.S. national spotlight. Race and racism are incredibly difficult topics of conversation in U.S. culture, whether we are in a classroom, a courtroom, a religious setting, the halls of Congress, the streets of Ferguson, Missouri, or our own local communities. How do we create opportunities to explore ideas of race and the way those ideas shape our lives and culture? In a country that likes to think of itself as color-blind, how do we as anthropologists make sense of the continuing inequality in income, wealth, education, access to health care, police enforcement, and incarceration rates that breaks so clearly along color lines (Shanklin 1998)?

Anthropologists view race as a framework of categories created to divide the human population. Western Europeans originally developed this framework as part of their global expansion beginning in the 1400s (Sanjek 1994). As they encountered, mapped, and colonized people in Africa, Asia, the Pacific, and the Americas, Europeans placed them into an "international hierarchy of races, colors, religions and cultures" (Trouillot 1994, 146). The exact labels and expressions have varied over time and place as colonial powers engaged with local cultures and confronted local resistance. But the underlying project—to stratify people into groups based on assumptions of natural differences in intelligence, attractiveness, capacity for civilization, and fundamental worth in relation to people of European descent—has been remarkably consistent (Mullings 2005a).

As we will explore in this chapter, today anthropologists find no scientific basis for classifications of race. Genetically there is only one race—the human race, with all its apparent diversity. Yet despite consistent efforts over the last century by anthropologists and others to counter the inaccurate belief that races are biologically real, race has remained a powerful framework through which many people see human diversity and through which those in power organize the distribution of privileges and resources. Race—which is scientifically not real—has become culturally real in the pervasive racism found in many parts of the globe, including the United States.

Over the past 500 years, race as a way of organizing the world has been put to destructive use, wreaking an enormous toll on both its victims and its proponents. Race and racism have justified the conquest, enslavement, forced transportation, and economic and political domination of some humans by others. Today race and racism have become so integral to patterns of human relations in many parts of the world that inherited racial categories may seem to be natural, and the inequality built on racism may seem to represent "real" differences among "real" races.

In this chapter we will critique arguments for the existence of discrete biological human groups called "races." We will consider the roots of race and racism in the European colonial past and their expression in various places today. We will examine the construction of race in the United States over the past 400 years and the way race and racism continue to shape U.S. culture. In particular, we will consider the following questions:

- Do biologically separate races exist?
- How is race constructed around the world?
- How is race constructed in the United States?
- What is racism?

We will examine **race** as a flawed system of classification, created, and re-created over time, that uses certain physical characteristics (such as skin color, hair texture, eye shape, and eye color) to divide the human population into a few supposedly discrete biological groups and attribute to them unique combinations of physical ability, mental capacity, personality traits, cultural patterns, and capacity for civilization. Drawing on anthropological research, we will see, however, that racial categories have no biological basis. We might even say that races, as a biological concept, do not exist. The danger in this statement about biological race is that it may lead us to the mistaken conclusion that race does not exist. On the contrary, race has very real consequences.

Race is a deeply influential system of thinking that affects people and institutions. Over time, imagined categories of race have shaped our cultural institutions—schools, places of worship, media, political parties, economic practices—and have organized the allocation of wealth, power, and privilege at all levels of society. Race has served to create and justify patterns of power and inequality within cultures worldwide, and many people have learned to see those patterns as normal and reasonable. So in this chapter we will also examine **racism**: individuals' thoughts and actions, as well as institutional patterns and policies, that create or reproduce unequal access to power, privilege, resources, and opportunities based on imagined differences among groups (Omi and Winant 1994).

race: A flawed system of classification, with no biological basis, that uses certain physical characteristics to divide the human population into supposedly discrete groups.

racism: Individuals' thoughts and actions and institutional patterns and policies that create or reproduce unequal access to power, privilege, resources, and opportunities based on imagined differences among groups.

By the end of the chapter you will have the anthropological tools to understand not only the flaws in arguments for biologically discrete races but also the history and current expressions of race and racism globally and in the United States. You will be prepared to apply those tools, if you so choose, to engage in efforts against racism on your college campus, in your community, and throughout the world.

Do Biologically Separate Races Exist?

Many of us were enculturated to believe that "race" refers to distinct physical characteristics that mark individuals as clearly belonging in one group and not in another. However, anthropologists see race very differently. Contemporary studies of human genetics reveal no biologically distinct human groups. We can state this with certainty despite centuries of scientific effort to prove the existence of distinct biological races, and despite widespread popular belief that different races exist. In fact, humans are almost identical, sharing more than 99.9 percent of our DNA. The small differences that do exist are not distributed in any way that would correspond with popular or scientific notions of separate races. Race is not fixed in nature but, as we will explore later in this chapter, is created, perpetuated, and changed by people through individual and collective action.

First, however, let's explore some of the science behind race.

Fuzzy Boundaries in a Well-Integrated Gene Pool

Some physical anthropologists have compared modern humans to a little village that has grown very quickly. Throughout the short 200,000-year history of modern humans, we have basically been functioning as one enormous, interconnected gene pool, swapping genetic material back and forth (by interbreeding) quite freely within the village. Over the years, our family trees have intersected again and again.

If you trace your own family back for thirty generations—parents to grandparents to great-grandparents, and so on—you will find that in less than a thousand years you have accumulated one billion relatives. So it is not hard to imagine the myriad and unpredictable exchanges of genetic material among that large a group. Now extend your family tree back 100,000 years—the time it has taken for a few small groups of humans to migrate out of Africa and populate the entire planet. It is easy to imagine the billions of times this growing population has exchanged genetic material. Such deep integration of the human gene pool means that no clear and absolute genetic lines can be drawn to separate people into distinct, biologically discrete, "racial" populations.

As a result of this gene flow, human variation changes gradually over geographic space in a continuum (what physical anthropologists refer to as a *cline*), not by abrupt shifts or clearly marked groups. Even skin color, perhaps most frequently imagined to demarcate separate races, in fact varies so gradually over geographic space that there are no clear boundaries between one population and another, nor color groupings that distinguish one population from another.

What can you know about a person's genetic makeup based on her (or his) outward appearance? Variations of skin color or other visible characteristics often associated with race are shaped by less than 0.1 percent of our genetic code. Contrary to certain stereotypes, they do not predict anything else about a person's genetic makeup, physical or mental capabilities, culture, or personality.

If you flew from western Africa to Russia, you would notice distinct variations in physical human form between the population where you boarded the plane and the population where you disembarked. But if you walked from western Africa to Russia, there would never be a point along the way where you would be able to stop and say that the people on one side of the road are of one race and the people on the other side are of a different race.

Perhaps more surprising, a person from western Africa who starts walking east may have more in common genetically with someone at the end of her trek in Russia than she does with a neighbor at home. This seems hard to imagine because we have been enculturated to believe that a very small number of traits—including skin color, hair texture, and eye color and shape—can serve to categorize people into distinct groups and predict larger genetic patterns. This is a flawed assumption. The human gene pool continues to be highly integrated. Genetic variations such as skin color, expressed in an individual's external appearance, are only 0.1 percent of that person's genetic code; they do not predict anything else about his or her genetic makeup. People in a particular region of the world whose ancestors inhabited that area for an extended period may have some increased probability of genetic similarity because of the greater probability of swapping genetic material with those geographically closer. But group boundaries are fuzzy and porous. People move and genes flow. Ultimately, group genetic probabilities cannot predict any one individual's genetic makeup.

The Wild Goose Chase: Linking Phenotype to Genotype

In considering human physical diversity, physical anthropologists distinguish between genotype and phenotype. **Genotype** refers to the inherited genetic factors that provide a framework for an organism's physical form; these factors constitute the total genetic endowment that the organism, in turn, can pass down to its descendants. In contrast, **phenotype** refers to the way genes are expressed in an organism's physical form (both visible and invisible) as a result of the interaction of genotype with environmental factors, such as nutrition, disease, and stress.

The widespread belief that certain phenotypes such as skin color are linked to physical and mental capabilities, personality types, or cultural patterns is incorrect but deeply ingrained and difficult to reimagine.

As individuals, we may make snap judgments based on phenotypical traits that we erroneously assume indicate a person's "race"; with a quick glance we may think we know something significant about that individual. On the basis of phenotype alone, we may consider someone to be smarter, faster, stronger, safe or dangerous, better at business, better at math, a better dancer or singer, more prone to alcoholism, more artistic, more susceptible to certain diseases, a

genotype: The inherited genetic factors that provide the framework for an organism's physical form.

phenotype: The way genes are expressed in an organism's physical form as a result of genotype interaction with environmental factors.

better lover. You might call this the "White Men Can't Jump" or "Asians Are Better at Math" way of thinking about race and genes. We assume that we can know something significant about a person's genetic makeup just by looking at her phenotype. But can we really tell anything about someone from the way he or she looks?

A relatively small number of genes control the traits frequently used today to distinguish one "race" from another—skin color, eye shape, or hair texture. As a result, in the short history of modern humans these genes have been able to change rapidly in response to the environment. For example, as humans moved out of Africa and across the globe into a wide variety of physical environments, traits such as skin color, shaped by a relatively small cluster of genes, were more susceptible to environmental pressures and adapted more quickly. In contrast, traits such as intelligence, athletic or artistic ability, and social skills appear to be shaped by complex combinations of thousands or tens of thousands of genes, so they have been much less susceptible to environmental pressures. Adaptations in skin color were not accompanied by adaptations in, say, intelligence, musical ability, or physical ability. It is important to note that genetic research consistently shows that the genes that influence skin color, eye shape, or hair texture are not linked to any other genes and cannot predict anything about the rest of a person's underlying genotype (Mukhopadhyay, Henze, and Moses 2007).

Jonathan Marks, a leading physical anthropologist, compares the problem of sorting people into races with the problem children might have in sorting blocks into categories. Imagine that you start with a pile of blocks and ask a group of children to sort them into "large" and "small." They might agree on some—the largest and the smallest. But others in between might be harder to classify. "The fact that the blocks can be sorted into the categories given, however, does not imply that there are two kinds of blocks in the universe, large and small—and that the child has uncovered a transcendent pattern in the sizing of the blocks. It simply means that if categories are given, they can be imposed upon the blocks" (Marks 1995, 159).

What if you asked the children to sort instead by color or to distinguish among wooden, metal, and plastic blocks? What about blocks with smooth sides or grooved sides? The children could sort the blocks into any of these categories. But if you didn't link the multiple characteristics of the blocks—all the red blocks wooden, or all the plastic blocks grooved—the children would end up with a completely different arrangement of blocks depending on whatever categories they arbitrarily decided to sort for.

The same is true for humans and the concept of race. If you give people a limited range of categories for skin color groups, they will be able to place many people into these categories. Some individuals who lie in the boundaries

Looks can be deceiving. Which group is more genetically diverse?

may be more difficult to categorize. But would this exercise uncover some deep, intrinsic pattern about humans? No, because traits like skin color are not linked to any other particular set of genes and cannot serve to predict anything else about the underlying genotype.

Why Not Construct Race on the Basis of Earwax?

From a genetic viewpoint, the use of skin color as the primary variable in constructing a person's "race" appears to be quite arbitrary. A number of other genes or gene combinations create phenotypic differences that could serve the same purpose. Why not choose eye color, hairiness (amount and location), earlobe shape, fingerprints, nose shape, tongue rolling, tooth shape and size, double-jointed fingers, height, or weight? Another possibility could be earwax.

There are two primary types of earwax (Jurmain and Nelson 1994). One is dry, gray, and crumbly. The other is wet, yellow, and sticky. Fully 90 percent of Europeans and only 4 percent of people in northern China have the second variety. Imagine dividing up your classmates into races based on one of these earwax characteristics, rather than skin color. How would you configure the group? Do you think that one subgroup/race would have any natural advantages over the others?

Can you imagine hierarchical systems of race that affect distribution of power and resources and that are based on differences in earwax? What if students in your college were guaranteed individual tutoring by the instructor if they had wet earwax? What if students were required to sit in the back of the room, where it is harder to hear the lecture, if they had dry earwax? Surely, such distinctions will strike you as absurd. Why not, then, regard distinctions made on the basis of skin color as equally absurd?

Would you be surprised to learn that there is more genetic difference between two penguins than between two humans? Penguins appear identical to the human eye and are found in a small range of habitats (unlike humans, who range over the entire globe). But penguins have been around a lot longer than modern humans, so they have had more time to evolve and develop greater genetic variation within their species. Does knowing this fact challenge you to be more skeptical of assumed links between outward appearances and underlying genotype?

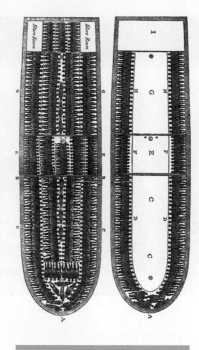

Diagram of a slave ship from the Atlantic slave trade.

How Is Race Constructed around the World?

Racial categories are human constructs; they are not found in nature. Yet they have become so deeply internalized that they feel natural and provide one of the most powerful frameworks through which we experience the world (Mukhopadhyay, Henze, and Moses 2007). Anthropologists examine race and racism on a global scale and thus from different angles, identifying their similarities and variations and, in the process, revealing the ways those concepts have evolved and might be changed through individual and collective action.

Race and the Legacy of Colonialism

Contemporary global expressions of race and racism are deeply rooted in the systems of classification that western Europeans created as they expanded their colonial empires into Africa, Asia, the Pacific, and the Americas beginning in the 1400s. **Colonialism** became the centerpiece of European global economic activity, combining economic, military, and political control of people and places to fuel Europe's economic expansion and enhance the European position in the emerging global economy (see Chapter 12). The classification of people based on phenotype, particularly skin color, became the key framework for creating a hierarchy of races—with Europeans at the top—that linked people's looks with assumptions about their intelligence, physical abilities, capacity for culture, and basic worth. Eventually this framework served to justify colonial conquests, the transatlantic slave trade, and the eradication of much of the indigenous population of the Americas (Gregory and Sanjek 1994).

colonialism: The practice by which a nation-state extends political, economic, and military power beyond its own borders over an extended period of time to secure access to raw materials, cheap labor, and markets in other countries or regions.

Taking a global perspective, anthropologists often refer to "racisms" in the plural, reflecting the varieties of ways race has been constructed among people in different places. Locally, racisms and systems of racial classification are complex frameworks built out of the encounter of colonialism with local cultural patterns, global migration, and specific movements of resistance. While racializing systems around the world may all have their roots in European colonialism, they manifest themselves differently in different places and at different times.

Racial frameworks and systems of racism have changed significantly over the last century. After World War II, colonial-era racist political and legal structures shifted as national liberation movements struggled to end occupations by foreign powers. In addition, in this postcolonial period, anti-racist liberation movements challenged long-term patterns of race and racial discrimination. Notably, the anti-apartheid movement in South Africa resisted dominant white rule, eventually reversing decades of legal structural discrimination and violence. The civil rights movement challenged more than 300 years of race-based inequality in the United States. Today globalization has brought about new experiences of race and racism (as we will see in the case studies that follow).

Indeed, in today's global world, flexible accumulation produces new relationships between corporations and workers; the migration of workers within countries and across national borders yields new racial formations; and time-space compression enhances communication tools that can be employed to resist old hierarchies while also perpetuating old racial frameworks on a global scale. Racisms today, though rooted in similar historic realities, are shifting as they intersect with other systems of power, whether those are ethnicity, gender, sexuality, kinship, or class (Mullings 2005a). The exact expression of these constructs varies from culture to culture and place to place, depending on why races were originally invented and how they have been used to establish and maintain hierarchies of power.

Race, Skin Color, and Class in the Dominican Republic When Christopher Columbus landed on the island of Hispaniola (now comprising the Dominican Republic and Haiti) in 1492, he launched the complicated story of race,

colonization, and globalization for the people who would inherit the land over the next five hundred years. Within fifty years of Columbus's arrival, perhaps hundreds of thousands of the indigenous inhabitants had been killed through brutal forced labor, new diseases introduced from Europe, and suicide. The Spanish imported the first African slaves in 1520 to work the sugar plantations that were feeding Europeans' growing sugar addiction (Mintz 1985). Subsequently, the French took possession of the western third of the island and continued the slaving practice until they were overthrown by a slave rebellion in the Haitian Revolution of 1804 (Trouillot 1994). The island's residents established an independent nation of former African slaves—the first in the world—and changed the dynamic of the growing global economy and slave trade (see Chapter 12).

MAP 6.1
Haiti / Dominican Republic

On the eastern two-thirds of the island, Dominican nationalists declared independence from Spain in 1821 and moved to shape a distinct national identity in opposition to Haiti. They emphasized the connection to their former colonial ruler, Spain, not to Africa, and they integrated into the economic system dominated by Europe and the United States, where racial thinking was stratified around whiteness. Dominicans' early identification as Hispanics, not as blacks, is a dynamic that still pervades the population's racial thinking today.

The Dominican Republic is an active participant in the current global economic system. Sugar, coffee, cacao, and tobacco production for export still play a significant role in the national economy. More recently, tourism, export-processing factories, and money sent home from Dominican migrants have expanded Dominican integration into the global economy, an integration that reaches to the island's most rural levels. Race, with a significant overlay of class, has become a powerful framework for organizing difference and creating stratification in the Dominican Republic. In a small country of 10 million people where linguistic (Spanish) and religious (Catholic) differences are limited, skin color serves as the key signifier—although higher-class status can "lighten" Dominicans, a dynamic we will also explore next in the case of Brazil. Unlike the United States, where conceptions of race are usually limited to four or five skin-color classifications, Dominicans use a wide range of variable and often inconsistent color terms, including *coffee, chocolate, cinnamon, wheat, indio, rosy, faded, blond, fair, dark*, and *ashen*.

None of the Dominican racial identifiers denote "black." A cornerstone of this framework is the rejection of African ancestry and of blackness more generally. Haitians, who are generally darker skinned than many Dominicans, mostly speak Creole, not Spanish, and they practice Catholicism intertwined with African religious beliefs. These factors combine to mark Haitians as racially "other" in the Dominican Republic. The republic's agriculture, tourism, and construction trades draw a steady stream of Haitian migrants across the border, both legally and illegally. Haitian migrants do back-breaking labor for meager wages and endure constant discrimination by Dominicans. Anti-Haitian sentiment is widespread, and false stereotypes repeated in popular conversation and in the press warn of the "Haitian threat" to the economy and national stability (Gregory 2006; Howard 2001; Martinez 1996; Simmons 2011). Most recently, in 2013 the top Dominican court ruled that children born of undocumented foreigners—85 percent of whom are Haitian—would be stripped of their citizenship. And in 2015 the government of the Dominican Republic began a process of registering the estimated 500,000 undocumented residents and deporting those found to be without citizenship.

However, in a sign of how complicated the constructs of race and racism are, anti-black and anti-Haitian sentiments are not uniform across the Dominican Republic. In both urban and rural settings, individual encounters within a local community context often overcome the stereotypes. Samuel Martinez points out that "even as a numerically sizable minority of Dominicans voice blatantly racist sentiments, it is common for people of lower-income groups to identify themselves and their loved ones as 'black' in song and folklore" (2003, 89). Deborah Pacini-Hernandez (1995) has documented the song-dance genre *bachata* that is prevalent in poor urban neighborhoods and rural work sites. *Bachata* commonly uses *negro, prieto*, and *morena*, terms for black or dark men and women, to refer to the singers, their lovers, and their audience. These uses reflect a more sympathetic engagement with blackness and race at the local level, among the rural and urban working classes who have dark skin and lower social status.

The work of Martinez and Pacini-Hernandez challenges us to acknowledge the complexity of analyzing race in the Dominican Republic. In fact, their work underscores the importance of examining local expressions of race and racism and the ways in which communities continue to reimagine the racial categories imposed by colonial powers, contemporary Western media, and powerful local elites.

Class, Gender, and Hundreds of Races in Brazil Brazil provides another location to explore the cultural construction of race and the application of ideas of race to the creation of stratification. The United States and Brazil are today the two largest multiracial countries in the Western Hemisphere, although they have traveled two very different paths in framing racial identities and hierarchies. By the time Brazil outlawed slavery in 1888, the country had the largest African population in the New World. This situation reflected the grim fact that during and after Brazil's time as a colony of Portugal (1500–1815), 40 percent of all Africans in the Atlantic slave trade were brought to Brazil to work on Portuguese plantations and mines. Brazil was the last country in the Americas to outlaw slavery—a full generation after the U.S. Emancipation Proclamation in 1863.

Today Brazilians describe the human physical diversity called "race" in great detail. Although Brazil's system of racial classification is color-coded, its color terminology is far more expansive, encompassing hundreds of categories (Freyre 1933; Harris 1964, 1970). Terms include *alva* (pure white), *alva-escuro* (off-white), *alva-rosada* (pinkish white), *branca* (white), *clara* (light), *branca morena* (darkish white), *branca suja* (dirty white), *café* (coffee colored), *café com leite* (coffee with milk), *canela* (cinnamon), *preta* (black), and *pretinha* (lighter black) (Fluehr-Lobban 2006). Race categories follow along a nuanced continuum of appearance rather than a few rigid categories such as those used in the United States.

Brazil's population of Europeans, Africans, and indigenous people has had a long history of interracial mixing. The Portuguese colonial government promoted assimilation and did not bar **miscegenation**—that is, interracial marriage. As a result, many single Portuguese men who settled in Brazil chose to intermarry. Nor has Brazil applied the rule of hypodescent—the "one drop of blood" rule—that in the United States meant that having even one black

Bachata music portrays the complex understanding of race in the Dominican Republic.

MAP 6.2
Brazil

miscegenation: A demeaning historical term for interracial marriage.

ancestor out of many could mark an individual as black (see "The Rule of Hypodescent" later in this chapter). As a result, a Brazilian family may include children who are categorized as various shades of white, brown, and black.

Race in Brazil is not solely a function of skin color. In fact, race intersects closely with class—including land ownership, wealth, and education—in determining social status. Because of the power of class, a Brazilian's racial position can be modified by his or her level of affluence. Affluence can shift a Brazilian's racial identity in spite of skin color and other supposedly "racial" markers (Walker 2002).

Some scholars refer to Brazil as a "racial democracy" and extol the nation as an exceptional example of racial harmony (Freyre 1933; Harris 1964; and Kottak 2006). Brazil's government abolished the use of racial categories in the 1930s and constitutionally banned racism in 1951. The complex and fluid color classifications—and the absence of political and legal mechanisms to establish and enforce a clear color line between black and white—are seen as a sign of tolerance. In addition, the incorporation of key African cultural practices (including carnival, samba, Candomblé religious practices, capoeira, and specific cuisine) as symbols of the Brazilian nation is often cited as supporting evidence for the racial democracy thesis (Downey 2005).

Other scholars have noted that despite the appearance of racial democracy, inequality exists in almost every area of Brazilian life and is directly linked to color. Darker-skinned Brazilians face higher levels of exclusion and injustice, including a systemic correlation between color and economics. Most of the poor are Afro-Brazilians. Most of the rich are white. Racial democracy may instead be simply a myth that serves as a cornerstone of Brazil's national denial of the existence of racism (Harrison 2002b; Roth-Gordon 2016; Smith 2016).

In *Laughter Out of Place* (2003), anthropologist Donna Goldstein writes about poor working women from the bleak favela (shantytown), ironically named Felicidade Eterna ("eternal happiness"), who support their families as domestic workers in the homes of middle-class Brazilian families in the affluent sections of Rio de Janeiro. Gloria, poor and dark skinned, raising fourteen children, including nine of her own, works as a domestic servant, shopping, cooking, and cleaning. She earns five dollars a day—just enough to feed herself and her family. The pay is off the books, so she has no legal labor protections, no insurance, and no pension. Goldstein links the contemporary culture of domestic work, particularly the employer–domestic servant relationships, to the historic institution of slavery in Brazil. Middle-class families enjoy a kind of learned helplessness similar to that of the slave owner—allowing their workers to do the dirty, manual chores. The employer–domestic servant relationship, like the owner–slave relationship, is characterized by domination, strict rules, and social separation.

How do Brazil's marginalized and oppressed people make sense of their lives—lives overburdened with poverty, violence, and work at the bottom of a global hierarchy of race, class, and gender, yet lives that also display dignity and resilience? Goldstein explores the role of laughter and humor as means to cope with persistent brutality. She particularly notes a humor that recognizes life's absurdities and ironies and provides perspective to a sense of injustice. She recalls, for instance, the awkwardness of "laughter out of place," as domestic workers and employers laugh at different times and for different reasons when they watch the local soap operas that dramatize middle-class Brazilian life. The distinctive life experiences of worker and employer create vastly different viewing experiences, casting the televised dramas and traumas of the Brazilian middle class in sharp contrast to the survival needs of the domestic workers living in the favela—a contrast so absurd as to evoke laughter out of place.

Race, Gender, and Globalization in Malaysia The development of the idea of race in Malaysia, mixed with notions of ethnicity and religion, reveals how "race" is not a fixed category. A hierarchy of race was originally introduced into Malaysia (originally called Malaya) by Dutch, Portuguese, and British colonialists, and it continues to change in today's postcolonial era in response to the globalization of media, finance, labor, and diseases (including HIV/AIDS), which cross national boundaries.

When Portuguese and Dutch colonial powers led western Europe's expansion into Malaysia in the sixteenth and early seventeenth centuries, social relations in the country were primarily organized around land. Geography, local cultural practices, and economic strategies were the main differences among people, not assumptions about biology, phenotype, or the idea of race. The local land-oriented groups initially resisted colonial attempts to exploit Malaysia's mineral resources. Beginning in 1786, however, overwhelming British military power and persistent colonial administration began a three-hundred-year process that dismantled Malaysian social patterns and replaced them with a European-style, race-based structure with three distinct categories: Indian, Chinese, and Malay.

Differing treatment of the three groups reinforced the race-based system. British colonial authorities recruited immigrant laborers from India to work on coffee, sugar, and rubber plantations, and they brought in Chinese laborers to mine tin. They also trained some Indians for mid-level, colonial civil service jobs and encouraged Chinese immigrant entrepreneurs in the main port cities

MAP 6.3
Malaysia

to establish the urban small-business core of the national economy. The British left the majority, largely rural, and uneducated Malay population working in the rice paddies, although a few local Malay elite were co-opted into the colonial administration.

Even though the country's economic activities have shifted over the centuries, particularly after Malaysian independence in 1957, the racial categories that the British established are still in use today. They are no longer legally enforced, but the patterns of economic and political interaction organized along racial lines continue. Deep dissatisfaction over the constructed racial identities, and particularly the vast economic inequities that operate along racial lines, have led to social unrest and political struggle, including massive rioting in 1969. Again in 2005, Malays, who constitute 50 percent of the population, took to the streets to protest what they considered to be an unequal distribution of wealth among the main social groups in the country, which also include Chinese (23 percent), Indians (7 percent), and the indigenous Orang Asli.

In an attempt to minimize racial disparities, Malaysia opened its doors in the 1970s to the forces of globalization by establishing one of the first export-processing zones in Southeast Asia. These low-tax, low-wage zones attracted multinational corporations in search of cheap labor to supply products for a global assembly line, especially in the electronics industry. Over the past forty years, factories in Malaysia's export-processing zones have attracted hundreds of thousands of young migrant women workers, popularly known as Minah Karan (Ong 1987).

Minah Karan have reframed the racial order that British colonial administrators established centuries ago. Although export-processing zones were established as geographically bounded areas where manufacturing could take place, they have also served as places where many different people interact with a frequency and diversity not seen before in Malaysia. As a result, factories, and the export-processing zones in general, have become places of multiracial encounters in a nation with clear racial boundaries. As factories have drawn workers from across Malaysia and from neighboring countries, unusual and countercultural "mixing" has been taking place. In this context, mixing may simply mean enjoying social interactions or may also refer to sexual relations among individuals of different social groups. Malay, Chinese, Indian, and other immigrant women mix on the factory floor. Rural, young, and unmarried women workers interact with male, married, Chinese and Indian managers and engineers.

The name Minah Karan suggests the complicated interaction of ideas of race with ideas of gender, foreignness, sexuality, modernity, moral deterioration, and sexually transmitted diseases such as HIV/AIDS. Women factory

workers, many of them teenagers, have broken the gender–racial boundaries of Malaysian culture by working in the multiracial, multigendered, foreign-owned factories. *Minah*, a common Malay woman's name, reflects the mass migration of rural workers to the factories. However, *Karan* carries two meanings. The first ("electric current") situates these women in the electronics factories. But the second meaning implies sexual electricity. These young women—predominantly rural, unmarried, and Malay—have driven the expansion of electronics-exporting factories, a key factor in the growth of the national, regional, and global economies. Their work has provided financial resources for their rural families back home during times of agricultural distress, and by giving these women access to wages it has transformed gender relationships at many levels.

Though imagined as "electric" by some, this racial mixing appears to others as morally questionable. By working away from their villages, earning their own income as young women, laboring on night shifts, and generally operating outside the disciplinary oversight of family members and community elders, these women have been stigmatized as undisciplined, "loose," and "easy." Early on, observers considered their mixing with men and people of other classes,

The racial framework established by British colonialists, while no longer legally enforced, still shapes Malaysian culture today. (*clockwise from left*) A young Malay woman assembles electronic components in a Malaysian export-processing factory; Malaysian Chinese entrepreneurs open a coffee shop; a diverse group of students crossing the street in Penang, Malaysia.

kinship networks, and social groups as risky, even dangerous, behavior that might lead to moral contamination, impurity, and disease.

Anthropologist Robin Root has conducted research on HIV/AIDS inside the electronics factories. In particular, she has examined the intersection of globalization, Malaysian ideas of race and sexuality, and the real and imagined risks of disease for the women factory workers. Indeed the risks for HIV/AIDS are elevated in the export-processing zones. But Root finds that many Malaysians exercise a moral imagination in which they assume these risks are elevated because of the racial and sexual mixing. In the process, these imaginations have served to reinforce the colonial era three-race hierarchy and resisted change brought by globalization, including the possibility of change in racial and gender boundaries, by discouraging women from working in these factories and by stigmatizing those who do so (Root 2006).

How Is Race Constructed in the United States?

Race is perhaps the most significant means used to mark difference in U.S. culture. References to it can be found on census forms, school applications, and birth certificates, as well as in the media and casual conversation. Race is also a key framework that shapes the allocation of power, privilege, rewards, and status, and it infuses all of our political, economic, religious, recreational, educational, and cultural institutions (Smedley 1993). Yet it is one of the least discussed topics in U.S. culture and one of most difficult to explore, even in anthropology. How do we begin to engage this difficult dialogue?

At the beginning of every semester I ask my students to start the process by naming the different races. This seems like an easy task at first. Then students begin to struggle with the categories that U.S. culture has handed them. We quickly see that ideas of race are complicated by geography, language, skin color, and even religion. "Who is Asian?" I ask. "Are Filipinos Asian? Or are they Pacific Islanders? Are the people who live in the eastern two-thirds of Russia Asians? After all, they do live on the continent of Asia. Are Pakistanis Asian?"

"They were before Pakistan was partitioned from India. Now they're Middle Easterners," says a student.

"Middle Eastern is not one of the racial categories usually on the list," I reply. "And by the way, can race shift along political lines?"

"Middle Easterners are white," says another student.

"But what countries are in the Middle East?" asks another. "Professor, my mom is from China and my dad is from Bolivia. What race am I?"

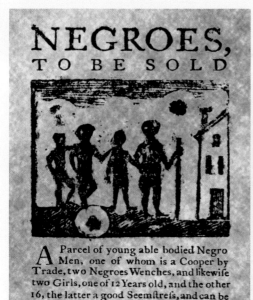

(*left*) An advertisement for a slave auction, June 23, 1768. (*right*) A slave family picking cotton in the fields near Savannah, Georgia, ca. 1860s.

How can anthropology help make sense of race as you experience it in the classroom, your workplace, your family, and today's rapidly globalizing world? Because race is not biologically fixed, we must instead examine the process through which race has been—and still is being—constructed in the United States.

History of U.S. Racial Categories: Constructing Whiteness

The U.S. racial system developed at the intersection of slavery and the European conquest of indigenous people of the North American continent. From its origins, American colonial life was built on the importation of indentured workers from Europe and enslaved people from Africa, along with the expropriation of land from Native Americans. Intensive agricultural work, particularly in the U.S. South, required a reliable and plentiful labor supply. Native Americans suffered quick and brutal extermination in other parts of the Americas through forced labor, violence, and disease, but they largely resisted forced labor in the North American colonies. European indentured laborers were in short supply. So imported enslaved Africans became the preferred workforce. Over 300 years, millions were forcibly transported to the Americas through the transatlantic slave trade.

The economics of slavery benefited all the American colonies. In Dutch New Amsterdam (now New York City), people of African descent made up 25 percent of the population as early as 1640. New York served as a hub for the slave trade. Slave ships delivered Africans for resale across the colonies as well

THE SOCIAL LIFE OF THINGS
Race and the U.S. Census

The U.S. Census, taken every ten years since 1790, provides a fascinating window into the changing conception of "race." The census form provides clear indications that race has been and still is an evolving human construction. The changing race categories do not reflect a change in human genotype or phenotype, but in how the government describes and organizes the diversity of people within its borders.

1 The 1850 census had three categories: White, Black, and Mulatto. Mulatto referred to people of mixed race. Respondents did not identify their own race; instead, census workers assigned them to a racial category based on their appearance.

The Name of every Person whose usual place of abode on the first day of June, 1850, was in this family.	Age.	Sex.	Color, (White, black, or mulatto.)	Profession, Occupation, or Trade of each Male Person over 15 years of age.	Value of Real Estate owned.	PLACE OF BIRTH. Naming the State, Territory, or Country.	Married within the year.	Attended School within the year.	Persons over 20 y'rs of age who cannot read & write.
3	4	5	6	7	8	9	10	11	12
George Watson	5	M				Ills			
Hester M Watson	4	F				"			
Daniel Watson	2	M				"			

2 The 1870 census expanded to five categories to incorporate new immigrants from China and to count the Native American population: White, Black, Mulatto, Chinese, and Indian (Native American).

The name of every person whose place of abode on the first day of June, 1870, was in this family.	Age at last birth-day. If under 1 year, give months in fractions, thus, ¹⁄₁₂	Sex.—Males (M.), Females (F.)	Color.—White (W.), Black (B.), Mulatto (M.), Chinese (C.), Indian (I.)
3	4	5	6

3 By 1940, the census form had eight categories, eliminating the option for mixed race and adding more categories from Asia, including Hindu, a religion: White, Negro, Indian, Chinese, Japanese, Filipino, Hindu, and Korean.

8. Is Person 1 of Hispanic, Latino, or Spanish origin?
- ☐ No, not of Hispanic, Latino, or Spanish origin
- ☐ Yes, Mexican, Mexican Am., Chicano
- ☐ Yes, Puerto Rican
- ☐ Yes, Cuban
- ☐ Yes, another Hispanic, Latino, or Spanish origin — *Print origin, for example, Argentinean, Colombian, Dominican, Nicaraguan, Salvadoran, Spaniard, and so on.*

_____

9. What is Person 1's race? *Mark* ☒ *one or more boxes.*
- ☐ White
- ☐ Black, African Am., or Negro
- ☐ American Indian or Alaska Native — *Print name of enrolled or principal tribe.*

_____

- ☐ Asian Indian   ☐ Japanese   ☐ Native Hawaiian
- ☐ Chinese   ☐ Korean   ☐ Guamanian or Chamorro
- ☐ Filipino   ☐ Vietnamese   ☐ Samoan
- ☐ Other Asian — *Print race, for example, Hmong, Laotian, Thai, Pakistani, Cambodian, and so on.*   ☐ Other Pacific Islander — *Print race, for example, Fijian, Tongan, and so on.*

_____

- ☐ Some other race — *Print race.*

_____

4 The 2010 census form included fourteen separate "race" boxes. Respondents could check one, many, or all of them. Racial categories under debate provide a glimpse at the nation's changing future. For instance, increased immigration from Latin America, Asia, the Pacific Islands, and the Middle East has complicated both the census form and discussions about race in the United States.

The position of Hispanics is also in flux. Beginning with the 2000 census, "Hispanic/Latino/Spanish" was separated from the race question and placed in its own separate question. In effect, this became a separate ethnic identity, which the census form now suggests is the only U. S. ethnic group that could be of any race.

The census and its race categories are more than descriptions of the American population. Census data is used to draw congressional districts, enforce civil rights laws, and allocate billions of dollars in federal aid. So, adjustments to the census form have very real political and economic consequences. Discussions about the 2020 census form are already underway within the U.S. government.

- Do you think the Hispanic category should be returned to the race question? Why or why not?
- Do you think Middle Eastern should be its own racial category? Why or why not? How do you think imaginations of a separate Middle Eastern race have been shaped by events over the past fifteen years?

as to plantations in Latin America and the Caribbean. Cargo ships brought the products of slave labor—cotton, sugarcane, tobacco—to New York on their way back to Europe. Throughout the American South, Africans were enslaved to work on agricultural plantations. In fact, plantation owners often sought out those Africans who had specialized agricultural knowledge. In *Deep Roots: Rice Farmers in West Africa and the African Diaspora* (2008), Edda Fields-Black uses linguistic, archaeological, and historical evidence to demonstrate how tidal rice-growing technology developed among the Baga and Nalu of coastal Guinea in West Africa and how this technology spread to the rice industry in South Carolina and Georgia (see also Carney 2002).

The unique slave system that emerged relied not only on the legal right of landholders to enslave but also on the widespread acceptance of **white supremacy**—the belief that nonwhites were biologically different, intellectually inferior, and not fully human in a spiritual sense. Reflecting these ideas, the U.S. Census from 1790 to 1860 counted slaves as only three-fifths of a person. Only in 1868 did the Fourteenth Amendment to the U.S. Constitution put an end to this practice. Subsequently, the 1870 census was the first to count all people as whole people.

The term *white* was itself a construction, first appearing in a public document in reference to a separate race only in 1691 in Virginia. Colonial laws created and rigidly regulated **whiteness**, establishing sharp boundaries of who was white and who was not. Intermarriage was outlawed—a practice that the U.S. Supreme Court did not overturn until 1967. Mixing was punished by the loss of white status.

Anthropologist Pem Buck's *Worked to the Bone* (2001) documents the ways in which white privilege was invented in early 1700s Virginia to prevent rebellion among poor landless whites who were beginning to join with enslaved African workers against the European economic elite. Elites introduced a set of privileges reserved for whites—the right to own a gun, livestock, and land; the right to obtain freedom at the end of indenture; the right to discipline blacks; and eventually the right to vote. These legal privileges were designed to ensure the cooperation of poor working whites and white indentured servants, who together constituted a majority of the early colonial populations, and to drive a wedge between the European and African laborers who had much in common.

Efforts to eliminate slavery spread rapidly but unevenly after the American Revolution (1775–83), culminating in the Civil War (1861–65) and President Abraham Lincoln's 1863 Emancipation Proclamation. Yet long-established patterns of unequal treatment and entrenched ideas of white racial superiority persisted, providing the foundation for continuing inequality, discrimination, and white dominance. **Jim Crow** segregation laws throughout the South legally enforced the boundaries between whites and blacks in housing, education,

white supremacy: The belief that whites are biologically different from and superior to people of other races.

whiteness: A culturally constructed concept originating in 1691 Virginia designed to establish clear boundaries of who is white and who is not, a process central to the formation of U.S. racial stratification.

Jim Crow: Laws implemented after the U.S. Civil War to legally enforce segregation, particularly in the South, after the end of slavery.

voting rights, property ownership, and access to public services such as transportation, bathrooms, and water fountains. Vigilante white-supremacist groups such as the Ku Klux Klan, founded in 1866, emerged to enforce through violence and terror what they considered to be the natural racial order. Especially in the South, lynchings became a widespread means to intimidate blacks, enforce segregation, and ensure behavior that whites considered normal and appropriate. Between 1870 and the 1940s, untold thousands of African American men and women were tortured and brutally murdered (Brundage 1993).

The Rule of Hypodescent

Imposition of the rule of hypodescent has been key to drawing and maintaining boundaries between the races since the days of slavery, when one single drop of "black blood"—that is, one African ancestor—constituted blackness. *Hypo* literally means "lower." Through **hypodescent** the race of children of mixed marriages is assigned to the lower or subordinate category of the two parents—or, in many cases, the subordinate category of any one of many ancestors.

Hypodescent rules were enshrined in the laws of many U.S. states and backed by the U.S. Supreme Court. Consider the 1982 court case of Susie Phipps. Born looking "white," Phipps grew up assuming she was white. But when she requested a copy of her birth certificate in 1977, she found herself listed as "colored." A 1970 Louisiana law mandated that a person be designated black if his or her ancestry was even one-thirty-second black—referring to any one of the thirty-two most recent ancestors. Phipps lost a court challenge to this categorization because the state produced evidence that she was three-thirty-seconds black—more than enough to satisfy the 1970 legal standard. Both the Louisiana Supreme Court and the U.S. Supreme Court refused to review the lower court's ruling and allowed the decision to stand (Fluehr-Lobban 2006; Jaynes 1982). Phipps's case reveals the process through which U.S. categories of race have been created and the tortured legal logic employed to assign individuals to particular racial categories. Also on full display are (1) the central role of the state in establishing and maintaining boundaries between the races it has constructed, and (2) the powerful influence of the legacies of slavery and past discrimination on the present (Omi and Winant 1994).

hypodescent: Sometimes called the "one drop of blood rule"; the assignment of children of racially "mixed" unions to the subordinate group.

A segregated summer social event—an annual barbecue—on an Alabama plantation, ca. 1935.

Although hypodescent is no longer enforced in law, it is still widely practiced in U.S. culture. A prominent contemporary example would be U.S. president Barack Obama. His mother was a white woman from Kansas (she was also an anthropologist). His father was a black man from Kenya in East Africa. They met as students in Hawaii, where Obama was born. Though 50 percent of his genes came from his father and 50 percent from his mother, the concept of hypodescent still shapes the way some people regard Obama's race.

Race and Immigration

For four centuries, the boundaries of whiteness in the United States have been carefully guarded, and a group's admission to that category has been rare and difficult. When the nation encountered diverse immigration from Asia and eastern and southern Europe beginning in the nineteenth century, debate raged about where the newcomers fit: Were the Chinese white? Were the Irish, Germans, Greeks, Italians, eastern Europeans, Jews, and Catholics really white, or were they biologically distinct from earlier immigrants from England, France, and the Nordic countries? Where would people from Mexico, Central America, and South America be placed in the U.S. racial framework?

The struggle to guard the boundaries of whiteness in order to protect the power and privileges reserved for whites has been particularly intense at certain times, generating passionate debate and sparking a sentiment of **nativism**— that is, the desire to favor native inhabitants over new immigrants. Nativists in the nineteenth century fought particularly hard to preserve the so-called racial purity of the nation's Anglo-Saxon origins. Riots, violence, discrimination, and anti-immigrant sentiment were commonplace.

Chinese and Irish Immigrants: What Race? Chinese immigrants first arrived in large numbers in the 1850s to work in California's gold mines, on its farms, and in railroad construction. Because they constituted the first group of Asians to come to this country, other residents struggled to place them in the U.S. racial hierarchy. European immigrant laborers saw the Chinese as competitors for jobs and branded them the Yellow Peril—a "race" that could not be trusted. Federal and state governments treated the Chinese immigrants ambivalently at best and often with great hostility.

nativism: The favoring of certain long-term inhabitants, namely whites, over new immigrants.

Where did new Chinese immigrants fit in the U.S. racial hierarchy? Miners, including four Chinese, in California, ca. 1852.

Consider the 1854 California court case *People v. Hall*. In a lower court case leading up to this one, a Chinese man had provided eyewitness testimony to a murder committed by a white man, George W. Hall. Hall was convicted on the basis of this testimony. However, upon appeal, the California Supreme Court overturned Hall's conviction, claiming that the eyewitness had no standing in the court. The justices pronounced that the Chinese were "a race of people whom nature has marked as inferior, and who are incapable of progress or intellectual development beyond a certain point, as their history has shown; differing in language, opinions, color, and physical conformation, between whom and ourselves nature has placed an impassable difference" (Gross 2010). Thus, the Chinese were not white in the eyes of the law. Like African Americans of the time, they had no legal standing in the courts. Their eyewitness testimony was inadmissible.

Today most people consider Irish, Italians, Greeks, and eastern Europeans to be white, but none of these groups were received as white when they first came to the United States. They initially faced discrimination, prejudice, and exclusion because they were not Anglo-Saxon Protestants. When the Irish immigrants arrived in the 1840s and 1850s, they were poor, rural, Catholic, landless, and fleeing intense poverty and disease as a result of the Irish potato famine. Thus, they were seen as an inferior race (Ignatiev 1995). Similarly, the 23 million eastern and southern European immigrants who arrived in the United States between 1880 and 1920 (mostly Italians and eastern European Jews) were generally considered to be members of separate, inferior races—not white. Scientists, politicians, preachers, and the press warned against destroying the unity and purity of the United States by allowing their immigration. In 1924, the anti-immigrant National Origin Act closed the doors to the large waves of immigrant workers who had been arriving in the United States in the nineteenth and early twentieth centuries. Over the next four decades, the legislation barred all but a few who were not of northern or western European origins (Binder and Reimers 1995; Foner 2000). The act remained in effect until 1965.

Confronted with increasing immigration and diversity, the U.S. legal and political systems struggled for consistent definitions of who was white and who was not. Consider the 1923 U.S. Supreme Court case in which Bhagat Singh Thind, an upper-class Sikh immigrant from India, applied for U.S. citizenship. Despite the 1790 U.S. law limiting the right to naturalization (that is, becoming a citizen) to

A 1903 cartoon from the magazine *Judge* illustrates anti-immigrant sentiment at the turn of the twentieth century. A tide of newcomers—Riff Raff Immigration—representing the criminal element of other countries washes up on American shores, to the displeasure of Uncle Sam, presenting a "danger" to American ideas and institutions.

whites, Thind argued that as a part of the original "Aryan" or Caucasian race, he was white. Even though the justices agreed with his claim of Aryan or Caucasian ancestry, the Court found that Thind was not white as used in "common speech, to be interpreted in accordance with the understanding of the common man" (Lopez 2006, 66). Popular anti-immigrant and nativist sentiment had overcome even the pseudoscience of race prevalent at the time.

How exactly did the Irish, the Italians, and the eastern European Jews become "white"? Their increasing numbers, their intermarriage with members of other white groups, and their upward class mobility created conditions for inclusion in the white category. Karen Brodkin's book *How the Jews Became White Folks* (1998) offers additional insights into the whitening process of immigrants after World War II. At that time, the U.S. economy was emerging virtually unscathed from the war's destruction, unlike its competitors in Europe and Japan. And rapid growth in the U.S. economy was supporting an unparalleled expansion of the nation's middle class. Brodkin suggests that an extensive government program to reintegrate soldiers after the war paved the road to upward mobility for many U.S. citizens.

Indeed, the GI Bill of Rights provided a wide array of programs to 16 million soldiers, who were primarily white and male. The benefits included preferential hiring, financial support during the job search, small-business loans, subsidized home mortgages, and educational benefits that included college tuition and living expenses. Newly trained and educated veterans quickly filled the needs of the growing U.S. economy for professionals, technicians, and managers—jobs that offered opportunities for upward mobility and, thus, racial mobility. These educational opportunities, the dramatic rise in home ownership, and the expansion of new corporate jobs dramatically enlarged the U.S. middle class. The simultaneous elevation of living standards and financial assets of both native whites and new European immigrants softened earlier boundaries of whiteness and allowed the status of many immigrants to shift from racially nonwhite to ethnic white.

Middle Easterners Racial categories continue to be created and contested in the United States today. Where, for example, do people from the Middle East fit? Are Saudis, Iranians, Afghanis, Kurds, Syrians, Turks, and Egyptians "white," African American, or Asian? The shifting characterization of people from the Middle East—especially after the terrorist attacks of September 11, 2001, and the ensuing "war on terror"—reveals newly contested terrain in the race debate and demonstrates how conceptions of race in the United States are constantly changing.

In a study of fourth graders in Brooklyn, New York, after the September 11 attacks, Maria Kromidas (2004) explores the way nine-year-old children engage issues of race, religion, and region to create racial categories, assign certain people (both children and adults) to them, and enforce those boundaries through language, humor, and social interaction.

Using the common U.S. Census categories, the school that Kromidas studied could be described as 28 percent black, 1 percent white, 46 percent Hispanic, and 25 percent Asian. But these four categories do not reveal the diversity of the school and its neighborhood—a diversity that makes the students' formulations of race all the more complicated. Although the students and the surrounding community are predominantly African American and second- and third-generation Latino, a significant part of the population is composed of new immigrants from Nigeria, Bangladesh, Guyana, Jamaica, and the Dominican Republic.

In light of the events of September 11, students in the elementary school seem preoccupied with the potential danger from a perceived enemy—one they see racially as "brown, foreign, strange, and Muslim" (Kromidas 2004, 29). Though the children do not consider their Muslim classmates to be "evil" or "terrorists," they do take note of these classmates' identities as never before. Kromidas ("MK" in the dialogues below) notes in particular the equation of enemies with Indians, Pakistanis, or Afghanis, and eventually all Arabic ("Araback") people. Here we see a racial construction, a lumping together of unrelated people based on a general phenotype—in this case, skin color.

Consider the following small-group student discussions:

EXAMPLE 1

SHERI:	We were talking about who started it first, and if they kill a lot of white people. . . . I mean a lot of people we got to go to war right then.
MK:	Who are they?
SHERI:	The Indians.
MK:	The Indians?
SHERI:	I don't know—that's what I call them.
JONATHAN:	The Pakistans!
MK:	The Pakistans?
SODIQ:	The Afghanistans!
MK:	The Afghanistans?
JOSEPH:	The terrorists.

Later that afternoon:

EXAMPLE 2

SHERI:	I feel sorry for the Afghanistan people.
SUSANNA:	Why do you feel sorry after what they did?
SHERI:	Because they gonna die!
	(*Most of the class breaks up with laughter.*)

LATISHA:	(*standing up*) I feel happy!
	(*laughter*)
LATISHA:	No, no, no . . . because they want to kill our people, they're going to die too. They want to have a party when we die, so we should celebrate! [*referring to news clips of street celebrations in the Middle East after September 11*]
ANUPA:	If they die, it will be better for us.
MK:	Who are they?
ANUPA:	The Araback people.
MARISELA:	The Afghanistans have always hated the Americans. I know because I always watch the news. (Kromidas 2004, 18–19)

These conversations yield some interesting observations. First, the students have taken on images presented in the media and from the conversations of adults around them; second, the students manipulate those images to create patterns of exclusion in their own context. Through their conversations, language groups, social interactions, and friendship networks, the students seek to clarify boundaries and to include and exclude newcomers according to what they see as racial characteristics. In the racial maps of the United States, South-Asian Americans and Arab Americans do not have a clear place. Kromidas suggests that in the classroom, as in U.S. culture at large, the fourth graders of New York City are creating a new racial category and placing people in it. The category is generally defined as not white, not black, but brown; foreign, strange, Muslim, and possibly enemy.

Before September 11, "Middle Eastern" was not considered a separate race in the United States. Officially, the government's Office of Management and Budget includes people of Middle Eastern descent as whites, along with people of European and North African descent. But the **racialization** (that is, giving a racial character) of Middle Easterners in U.S. culture after September 11 suggests a movement away from whiteness as reflected in Kromidas's study of fourth graders in Brooklyn.

racialization: The process of categorizing, differentiating, and attributing a particular racial character to a person or group of people.

What Is Racism?

Having considered the ways concepts of race are constructed in the United States and globally, we now turn to consider the ways ideas of race are used to construct and maintain systems of power that we call racism. Racism draws on the culturally constructed categories of race to rank people as superior or inferior and to differentially allocate access to power, privilege, resources, and opportunities.

Types of Racism

Racism has multiple aspects that include individual and institutional components as well as the set of ideas—the ideology—that acts like glue to hold them together.

Individual Racism **Individual racism** is expressed through prejudiced beliefs and discriminatory actions. Being prejudiced involves making negative assumptions about a person's abilities or intentions based on the person's perceived race. Discriminating involves taking negative actions toward a person on the basis of his or her perceived race. Individual racism may be expressed through a lack of respect or through suspicion, scapegoating, and violence ranging from police brutality to hate crimes (Jones 2000). Individual, personally mediated acts of racism may be intentional or unintentional. They may be acts of commission (things that are done) or acts of omission (things that are left undone).

Individual racism can also be expressed through microaggressions. **Microaggressions** refer to common, everyday verbal or behavioral indignities and slights that communicate hostile, derogatory, and negative messages about someone's race, gender, sexual orientation, or religion. Racial microaggressions in the U.S. context include subtle slights, snubs, or insults directed toward people of color often by well-intentioned whites who are unaware that they have transgressed against someone: moving a handbag, checking a wallet, locking a car door, changing seats, commenting "You speak English well," or asking "Where do you come from?" These actions and comments may communicate that someone is considered prone to criminality, not to be trusted, is different, or is considered a stranger. Underlying these acts is a hidden cultural curriculum through which people have been taught certain biases associated with race, gender, sexual orientation, or religion which are then acted out intentionally or unintentionally. Research has shown that microaggressions create intense psychological dilemmas and that the cumulative and constant experience of microaggressions over a lifetime can lead to depression, frustration, and rage (Sue 2010, 2015).

Institutional Racism Racism is more than individual prejudiced beliefs or discriminatory acts. Racism also includes **institutional racism**, sometimes called *structural racism*—patterns by which racial inequality is structured through key cultural institutions, policies, and systems. These include education, health, housing, employment, the legal system (legislatures, courts, and prison systems), law enforcement, and the media. Institutional racism originates in historical events and legal sanctions. But, even when outlawed, it can persist through contemporary patterns of institutional behavior that perpetuate the historical injustices (Cazenave 2011; Feagin and Feagin 2011; Jones 2000; Neubeck and Cazenave 2001).

individual racism: Personal prejudiced beliefs and discriminatory actions based on race.

microaggressions: Common, everyday verbal or behavioral indignities and slights that communicate hostile, derogatory, and negative messages about someone's race, gender, sexual orientation or religion.

institutional racism: Patterns by which racial inequality is structured through key cultural institutions, policies, and systems.

In the United States, stratification along racial lines is a legacy of discrete historical events that include slavery, Jim Crow legal segregation, expropriation of indigenous lands, and immigration restrictions. Through these legal forms of institutional racism, the political, economic, and educational systems were organized to privilege whiteness. Today, despite the elimination of legal racial discrimination and segregation, patterns of inequality still break along color lines as a result of continuing individual and institutional racism. Such racism is evident in employment rates, income and wealth differentials, home ownership, residential patterns, criminal sentencing patterns, incarceration rates, application of the death penalty, infant mortality, access to health care, life expectancy, investments in public education, college enrollments, and access to the vote (Alexander 2012).

For example, the U.S. educational system has been a site for intense contestation over race and racism. In 1896—three decades after the end of slavery—the Supreme Court ruled in *Plessy v. Ferguson* that state-sponsored segregation, including in public schools, was constitutional as long as the separate facilities for separate races were equal. Across the South, individual white school administrators often refused, on overtly racist grounds, to allow children of color—black, Hispanic, Asian American—entrance to school buildings. But these individual actions alone did not constitute the total system of racism at work. They were systematically supported and enforced by government institutions: local boards of education, legislators, local police with guns and dogs, and court systems—including the U.S. Supreme Court.

Only in 1954 did the Supreme Court reverse itself in the case of *Brown v. Board of Education*, declaring unanimously that state laws establishing separate public schools for black and white students were unconstitutional and that separate educational facilities were inherently unequal. At the time, seventeen states, primarily across the South, required racial segregation. Sixteen prohibited it. Even after the Supreme Court ruling banning segregated schools, the federal government was forced to intervene in states like Mississippi and Arkansas, sending national guard troops to escort students to classes in order to end racist practices and protect student safety.

Contemporary racial disparities in school funding reveal how historical patterns of institutional racism can continue long after discrimination has been declared illegal (Miller and Epstein 2011). In 2003, the New York Court of Appeals, the state's highest court, found a long-standing disparity in state funding of public schools in New York City and suburban areas. New York City public schools, with high proportions of students of color, received an average of $10,469 per student, whereas schools in more affluent, predominantly white New York suburbs received $13,760 per student. The courts ordered New York State to increase its annual education budget by up to $5.6 billion to cover the costs of redressing this inequality while also providing $9.2 billion for capital improvement of New York City school buildings. The State of New York has yet to fully comply with these requirements.

Racial Ideology Racism relies on a third component—a set of popular ideas about race, or a **racial ideology**—that allows the discriminatory behaviors of individuals and institutions to seem reasonable, rational, and normal. Ideas about the superiority of one race over another—shaped and reinforced in the school system, religious institutions, government, and the media—caused people in the United States to believe that slavery was natural, that the European settlers had a God-given right to "civilize" and "tame" the American West, and that segregated schools were a reasonable approach to providing public education. As these ideas became ingrained in day-to-day relationships and institutional patterns of behavior, they ultimately provided the ideological glue that held racial stratification in place.

A racially segregated classroom in Monroe Elementary School, Topeka, Kansas, March 1953. Students Linda Brown (*front right*) and her sister Terry Lynn (*far left, second row back*), along with their parents, initiated the landmark civil rights lawsuit *Brown v. Board of Education*.

racial ideology: A set of popular ideas about race that allows the discriminatory behaviors of individuals and institutions to seem reasonable, rational, and normal.

Today, social scientists note that contemporary racial ideologies are much more subtle, often drawing on core U.S. values of individualism, social mobility, meritocracy, and color blindness to make their case. So, for instance, in his book *Racism without Racists* (2010), sociologist Eduardo Bonilla-Silva critiques the contemporary calls in U.S. culture for color blindness—the elimination of race as a consideration in a wide range of institutional processes from college admissions to the reporting of arrests by police. The ideology of color blindness suggests that the best way to end discrimination in the post–civil rights era is to treat individuals as equally as possible without regard to race. Bonilla-Silva warns that while the desire to transcend race by adopting a stance of color blindness appears reasonable and fair, the approach ignores the uneven playing field created by centuries of legal racism in areas such as wealth, property ownership, education, health, and employment. A color-blind ideology, Bonilla-Silva suggests, may actually perpetuate racial inequality by obscuring the historical effects of racism, the continuing legacy of racial discrimination, and the entrenched patterns of institutional behavior that undergird racism today.

In a country like the United States, which prides itself on being a meritocracy (a system that views people as a product of their own efforts and in which equal opportunity is available to all), the continuing existence of racism and skin-color privilege in the twenty-first century is difficult for many people to acknowledge. When the dominant culture celebrates the ideals of individualism and equal access to social mobility, it is ironic that for many people, success depends not only on hard work, intelligence, and creativity but also on the often unrecognized and unearned assets—cultural, political, and economic—that have accrued over hundreds of years of discrimination and unequal opportunity based on race.

Resisting Racism

Along with the history of individual and institutional racism, it is important to also acknowledge the long tradition of work against racism that continues today. Anthropologist Steven Gregory's ethnography *Black Corona* (1998) tells the story of the organized political resistance by a predominantly African American community in Corona, Queens, in New York City, when confronted by attitudes and policy expressions of racial discrimination. The African American community in Corona dates back to the 1820s, and it expanded under an influx of middle-class residents from Harlem in the first half of the twentieth century. By the 1970s, however, Corona, like many other urban U.S. communities, began to feel the devastating impact of globalization, particularly flexible accumulation, as New York City's economy deindustrialized. At this time, the city's economy moved from an industrial and manufacturing base to one driven by finance, information, and services (Baker 1995; Harvey 1990). As New York lost thousands of manufacturing jobs and billions of dollars in tax revenue and federal funds, residents of Corona struggled during the transition.

In the face of drastic government cutbacks to basic community services such as housing, education, and public safety, residents of Corona's LeFrak City—a public housing complex containing 6,000 rental apartments—mobilized to demand sustained public investment in the maintenance and security of the property from their landlord, the City of New York. Confronting stereotypes of the apartment complex as a site of crime, welfare dependency, and family disorganization, African American parents in LeFrak City founded Concerned Community Adults (CCA), a community-based civic association, to engage in neighborhood improvement projects and strengthen relationships with the city's politicians and agencies. The CCA's Youth Forum organized neighborhood young people for social activities and leadership formation; together with the CCA, it worked to improve relations with the local police, who regularly harassed youth in the area. Through community-based action, LeFrak City residents worked with churches, community groups, and informal associations to establish their position as political actors, assert control over the neighborhood's physical condition, and insist on self-definition rather than accept the stereotypes held by surrounding communities and city leaders.

In the early 1990s, the Port Authority of New York and New Jersey—which controls the area's airports, bridges, and port facilities—announced plans to build

MAP 6.4
Queens, New York

an elevated light rail train between Manhattan's central business district and LaGuardia Airport that would cut directly through the heart of Corona's African American community. Residents had had extensive negative experiences battling the city over earlier plans to expand LaGuardia, which abuts Corona, that involved the loss of waterfront properties to the construction of runways, highway access, and exposure to the pollution of adjacent Flushing Bay. In its new plan, the Port Authority, representing the City of New York, argued that the city needed improved public transportation between Manhattan and LaGuardia to compete in the global economy and in the burgeoning global financial services industry. The elevated rail line through Corona, the argument went, would be good for the city's economy.

Corona residents warned that construction of this major infrastructure project through their community would not have any local benefit but instead would generate severe environmental consequences, lower the quality of life in the neighborhood, and divide and isolate portions of the community. They demanded that the rail line be built underground on property already owned by New York City between Corona and the airport that had been carved out to build the Grand Central Parkway years earlier. Local residents formed neighborhood committees and alliances with existing civic organizations, community groups, and churches. They engaged the city's public planning process and established alternative political forums outside the government's control to press for their case. They also created multicultural alliances with concerned groups in neighboring communities. Eventually the Port Authority abandoned the planned elevated train.

Gregory's ethnographic study of Corona's African American community reveals the power of local communities of color to mobilize and engage in political activism. It also demonstrates how such groups can contest the stereotypes of urban black communities and the practices of racial discrimination and exclusion, whether those involve housing, policing, or the environmental and community impacts of public infrastructure projects.

For a look at efforts to combat racism in a different context, see "Anthropologists Engage the World," on pages 228–229.

The history of race in the United States includes a strong tradition of resistance to individual and institutional racism. Here, demonstrators protest against unfair lending practices and mortgage foreclosures.

JB Kwon
Anti-Racism Work During and After Ferguson

When students are spending their nights protesting on the streets of Ferguson, Missouri, sleeping for a few hours and then coming to class, what's a professor to do? JB Kwon, an anthropology professor at nearby Webster University, decided it was time to join them.

"When events in Ferguson happened I remember thinking to myself, these are my students. These are not strangers. Many of them lived in Ferguson or a surrounding municipality where they have many of the same conditions as Ferguson. They were angry and hurt and scared. So it was important for me to be there for them, to seek them out, to talk to them, to go to protests. Just to begin to talk with them about their experiences and what was going on.

"A lot of my students were actively involved in the protests. They were getting attacked by police. They were

Anthropologist JB Kwon

running. They were occupying the freeway. But they were courageous enough to stand up for what they wanted and needed. At least they knew they had a faculty person who would be there and support them.

"Then in my classes they began to talk about policing, segregation, education policies, incarceration. Providing analytical frameworks to help them think about their place in St. Louis became very exciting."

JB Kwon has spent much of his academic life studying social movements, with particular attention to issues of race and class. For his Ph.D. dissertation research he travelled to South Korea to study a protest movement of laid off automobile factory workers.

"My father had worked in a small factory in Korea. And when we immigrated to Wisconsin in 1977 he worked in a machine shop before starting up his own small business. In high school and the first couple of years in college I worked in his factory. It was the first time I really understood and experienced what my father was going through. I think for immigrant children there can be a sense of shame about poverty and, in Wisconsin where we had very few Asians, about racial difference. So that tension and conflict was always there. Going to Korea gave me a chance to explore these issues of race and class. And to meet other Korean men who worked in factories as a way of better understanding my parents.

"I spent a lot of time in Korea going to protests, trying to understand protests, how they work, what they did for people. What keeps three or four hundred men together for two years? Labor struggles and political struggles do not always end as you want. This struggle did not. Some did return to their jobs but not in the way they wanted to, with the prestige and benefits that they had before."

After moving to Webster in St. Louis, Kwon began researching the local history of racial dynamics and building his courses around the exploration of race, ethnicity, and class in the city. "When I went to St. Louis I didn't know what the situation was. But in many ways my students have taught me. They were learning something that I needed to learn about. One important thing they said was, don't call it 'Ferguson'. This is not 'Ferguson'. It's my home. My neighborhood. It happened in Ferguson. But it's not all of Ferguson. There's something very complex about that. They were trying to say it's not as simple as you think. There's a history of stigmatizing north St. Louis as a place of danger. But it's not that kind of place. We have family there, went to school there, our friends are there. We need to make more of it than that.

"What happened in Ferguson and surrounding communities made visible a history of structural violence and institutional racism. St. Louis is highly segregated. And there is this long history of policies that led to segregation and the formation of these municipalities that used zoning and real estate practices to keep certain populations out. Then you see the gradual movement from the city to North city to North County—white flight—with African Americans moving in behind."

Kwon has been working to translate his classroom research and teaching into community conversations about race, class, and structural forms of violence by leading workshops and training sessions with key leaders in St. Louis.

"A lot of people get caught up in the immediate violence that they see every day, like the police violence. But I try to help them think that police violence is reflective of larger forms of violence. Working with leaders in the community, companies, schools—I try to push them to look at institutional racism. How did it happen? How did we get here? And now that you're in a situation to make decisions, can you begin to recognize how your institution either undermines or perpetuates this inequality? I want to look

> **"** *What happened in Ferguson made visible a history of structural violence and institutional racism.* **"**

at how racism happens without an individual perpetrator. How do institutions function as a part of structural racism? If you can then decide to change your institutions then you can make a difference. The question is, are you going to make decisions that lead to racial equity?

"I hope that I'm making some kind of difference. It's also a great opportunity for me to meet some of the stakeholders in the city and some of the people who are committed to making the city a better place. There are a lot of great people doing a lot of amazing work. Small-scale work. Not-for-profit work. Conversations. People are doing things. People are involved. That's been the biggest reward. The more I do these things the more I meet those kinds of people. And I think St. Louis is not what I thought. There is a lot more going on."

Kwon advises students that anti-racism work should start with the basics. "Go out and talk with people. Listen to people. You have to meet people where they are. If you expect people to be where you are you just come out frustrated. You have to think about where they are and think about how you can meet them. Then you can really be involved in the conversation."

While Kwon encourages students to get involved in issues they are passionate about, he also reminds students of the practical aspects to this kind of engagement. "What you're learning in terms of organizing, communication, written and oral interpersonal communication, public speaking, managing social relationships, planning, these are what an employer is looking for. Organizing, getting out and meeting people—this is not peripheral to your education but essential. It's at the heart of what you're doing. You're applying critical thinking and all the skills you're learning in an anthropology class. It's a really sought after commodity and vital skills that will help you with your future."

Race, Racism, and Whiteness

Popular conversations about race and racism tend to focus on the experiences of people of color. Whiteness is typically ignored, perhaps taken for granted. But analyzing race in the United States requires a careful look at whiteness. Anthropologists refer to "white" as an unmarked category—one with tremendous power, but one that typically defies analysis and is rarely discussed. Recent scholarship has been moving whiteness into the mainstream debates about race in the United States (Hargrove 2009; Harrison 1998, 2002a; Hartigan 1999; Marable 2002; Mullings 2005a; Roediger 1992).

Although the events of the U.S. civil rights movement occurred well before most of today's college students were born, the media images of police blocking African Americans from attending white schools, riding in the front of the bus, sitting at department store lunch counters, or drinking from "whites-only" water fountains remain etched in our collective cultural memory. Although the overt signs declaring access for "whites only" have been outlawed and removed, many patterns of interpersonal and institutional behavior have resisted change (McIntosh 1989).

"White Privilege" In her article "White Privilege: Unpacking the Invisible Knapsack" (1989), anthropologist Peggy McIntosh writes of "an invisible package of unearned assets" that are a legacy of generations of racial discrimination. Through these assets, whites have become the beneficiaries of cultural norms, values, mental maps of reality, and institutions. Unearned advantages and unearned power are conferred systematically and differentially on one group over others, whether those benefits lie in health, education, housing, employment, banking and mortgages, or the criminal justice system.

McIntosh articulates an extensive list of these privileges, ranging from the mundane to the profound. They include (1) going shopping without being followed or harassed by store security; (2) using checks, credit cards, or cash and counting on skin color to not work against the appearance of financial responsibility; (3) seeing people of your "race" widely represented in the news, social media, and educational curricula; (4) swearing, dressing in second-hand clothes, or not answering letters or emails without having people attribute these choices to bad morals, poverty, or the illiteracy of your "race"; (5) feeling confident that you have not been singled out by race when a police officer pulls you over or an airport security guard decides to conduct a full-body scan; (6) criticizing the government and its policies without being considered an outsider.

As we have discussed in this chapter, since the early European settlement of North America, the boundaries of whiteness have been carefully constructed and guarded. Today the skin-color privileges associated with whiteness still pass

Initiating a Classroom Conversation about Race

Race and racism can be incredibly difficult topics of conversation in U.S. culture. How can the toolkit of anthropology help build relationships of rapport and trust that lead to deeper mutual understanding and opportunities for collective action?

Addressing issues of race and racism requires first opening up an honest conversation. In the classroom or in another setting on campus—perhaps your dorm, student organization, or religious group—write down your personal reflections and recollections about race and racism as provoked by the questions below. Then form discussion groups of four to five people. Make sure the groups are racially inclusive, if possible. Read and discuss what you have written, giving everyone a chance to participate, before exploring your conversation further.

1. What is your first recollection of race? of racism?
2. How would you describe the cultural environment in which you were raised: racially homogeneous? multiracial-multicultural? something else? What was the mix between home/community and school?
3. What patterns of race relations do you recall from high school? How much healthy social interaction was there across racial lines? What about interracial dating?
4. What patterns of race relations do you find on your college campus? Have you encountered race and racism on campus?
5. Complete this sentence: *The most important thing that our country needs to do NOW about race is* _____.
6. What obstacles do you encounter in discussing and addressing race and racism?

Now consider ways that the concepts of race and racism introduced in this chapter might help you understand the stories and experiences that emerge in these conversations.

Source: Adapted from Fluehr-Lobban 2006.

down from generation to generation. They are simply harder to see. Acknowledging this fact enables us to analyze the functioning and effects of race and racism as a complete system.

As McIntosh writes, "For me white privilege has turned out to be an elusive and fugitive subject. The pressure to avoid it is great, for in facing it I must give up the myth of meritocracy. If these things are true, this is not such a free country, one's life is not what one makes it; many doors open for certain people through no virtues of their own" (1989, 12). Moving forward, McIntosh urges students to distinguish between (1) the positive advantages that we wish everyone could have and that we can all work to spread, and (2) the negative types of advantages that, unless challenged and corrected, will always reinforce current racial hierarchies.

Intersections of Race and Class It is important to note the powerful intersection of race and class. **Intersectionality** provides a framework for analyzing the many factors—especially class and gender—that determine how race is lived and how all three systems of power and stratification build on and shape one another. In *Living with Racism: The Black Middle-Class Experience* (1994), sociologist Joe Feagin and psychologist Melvin Sikes write about middle-class African Americans who, despite their class status, continue to face racial discrimination. In Chapter 11 on class and inequality, anthropologist Leith Mullings reflects on a similar dynamic in New York City's Harlem community. Though reflecting a privileged class status in comparison to other African Americans, the class advantages of middle-class African Americans are still limited by racial disadvantage. Because race and class intersect so deeply, improved class status cannot be assumed to bring a decrease in the experience of racial discrimination.

Whiteness is also stratified along deep, intersecting lines of class and region, gender and sexuality so that not all people of European descent benefit equally from the system of white privilege. In a study of a town she calls Shellcracker Haven, southwest of Gainesville, Florida, anthropologist Jane Gibson (1996) explored the process through which a community of poor whites has been systematically cut off from their local means of making a living. By imposing restrictions on fishing, gaming, and trapping as well as on agricultural activities—all of which benefit large-scale businesses—the Florida state government and its agencies have gradually prevented Shellcracker Haven's residents from making a living on the land or nearby water.

Gibson argues that these policies of disenfranchisement have been rationalized by stereotypes that state authorities promote. Such stereotypes portray the local people as "white trash," "swamp trash," and "crackers"; as dirty, skinny, shoeless, toothless, illiterate, and unintelligent. The stereotypes deflect attention from the skewed distribution of wealth and power and the uneven investments in roads, education, and health care that result from state policies. Poor whites are a subordinated group, distinct from successful middle- and upper-class whites in the state.

Gibson's study reveals that whiteness is not monolithic. Indeed, people who place themselves in this racial group experience a wide range of life chances. Poor whites in the United States comprise a mix of 29.9 million people, both urban and rural, who do not necessarily reflect the advantages of whiteness (U.S. Census Bureau 2013b). The worst stereotypes portray poor whites as backward, inbred, lazy, illiterate, and uncultured. Epithets such as "redneck," "hillbilly," and "white trash" distance these whites from the middle-class social norms and economic success stereotypically associated with their whiteness

MAP 6.5
Florida

(Hartigan 2005). Although the historical development, regional particularities, and current circumstances vary among groups of poor whites, their poverty and social ostracism mark an extreme end of the U.S. class spectrum. In the current age of globalization, economic restructuring and global competition are further undermining the white privilege for many poor and working-class whites as manufacturing jobs leave the United States.

In this chapter we have begun our work as budding anthropologists to unmask the structures of power, starting with race and racism. We have seen how flawed ideas of "race" serve as a rationale for very real systems of power built around racial stratification both in the United States and around the world. As globalization, particularly global migration, brings cultural systems of meaning and stratification into closer contact, your ability to analyze and engage dynamics of race and racism will prove to be increasingly important. In the following chapters we will consider other systems of power—including ethnicity, gender, sexuality, kinship, and class—and their points of mutual intersection with race.

Anthropologists of race in the United States have studied the often "unmarked" category of whiteness. The privileges of whiteness in the United States are not experienced uniformly but rather are stratified along deep lines of class, region, gender, and sexuality.

Thinking Like an Anthropologist: Shifting Our Perspectives on Race and Racism

As you encounter race and racism in your life—on campus, in the classroom, at the workplace, in the news, or in your family—thinking like an anthropologist can help you to better understand these experiences. As you untangle this knotty problem, remember to think about the big questions we addressed in this chapter:

- Do biologically separate races exist?
- How is race constructed around the world?
- How is race constructed in the United States?
- What is racism?

After reading this chapter, you should be better equipped to engage the challenges of race and racism. As you think back on the chapter-opening story about the events in Ferguson, Missouri, how would you apply the ideas of this chapter to assist your analysis and inform your responses?

Race and racism continue to be powerful dynamics in American culture. Following Michael Brown's death in Ferguson, violent encounters between police and African Americans have continued to draw significant attention across the country. Eric Garner was choked to death during an arrest on Staten Island, NY, for selling loose cigarettes. Twelve-year-old Tamir Rice of Cleveland was shot to death in the playground near his home when officers on the scene for just a few seconds mistook his toy gun for a weapon. John Crawford III was killed in an Ohio Walmart after he picked up a BB gun from the shelf. The death of Freddie Gray in police custody sparked weeks of unrest in Baltimore. Alton Sterling, arrested for selling CDs on the sidewalk, was shot while pinned to the ground by police in Baton Rouge, Louisiana. Philando Castile was killed by an officer during a traffic stop outside St. Paul, Minnesota.

At the same time, the events of Ferguson have spurred efforts to address ongoing patterns of racism. The Black Lives Matter social movement launched rallies, marches, die-ins, and disruptions of political candidates, using social media and direct action to bring attention to the deaths of African Americans in encounters with law enforcement, racial profiling, and racial inequality in the U.S. criminal justice system (Bonilla and Rosa 2015). Under intense pressure after the massacre of nine people in the historic African Methodist Episcopal Church in downtown Charleston, the South Carolina legislature voted to remove the Confederate battle flag flying over the Statehouse, 150 years after the end of the Civil War. Students at Missouri University staged demonstrations—supported by the school's football players who threatened to boycott their upcoming games—to demand school administrators address a series of racist incidents on campus.

How can an anthropological approach to the study of race and racism help us analyze and confront these and similar acts of violence? How can we learn a language about race and racism that will allow us to talk and work together across lines of race, gender, sexuality, class, and political perspective to confront the continuing American legacy of racism? As we have seen throughout this chapter, the anthropological study of race examines not only the social construction of race and the establishment of systems of racism but also takes seriously movements against racism that emerge from communities of color and their allies. How can you begin to engage these crucial issues of our time and to apply these anthropological concepts to your life today?

Key Terms

race (p. 197)

racism (p. 197)

genotype (p. 200)

phenotype (p. 200)

colonialism (p. 203)

miscegenation (p. 207)

white supremacy (p. 216)

whiteness (p. 216)

Jim Crow (p. 216)

hypodescent (p. 217)

nativism (p. 218)

racialization (p. 222)

individual racism (p. 223)

microaggressions (p. 223)

institutional racism (p. 223)

racial ideology (p. 225)

intersectionality (p. 232)

For Further Exploration

Alexander, Michelle. 2012. *The New Jim Crow: Mass Incarceration in the Age of Colorblindness* (rev. ed.) New York: The New Press.

American Anthropological Association. 1997. "Response to OMB Directive 15: Race and Ethnic Standards for Federal Statistics and Administrative Reporting." September. www.aaanet.org/gvt/ombdraft.htm. Response to revision of race categories in the 2000 U.S. Census form.

American Anthropological Association. 1998. "Statement on 'Race.'" May 17. www.aaanet.org/stmts/racepp.htm.

American Anthropological Association. 2015. *Race: Are We So Different?* www.understandingrace.org/home .html. Visit the AAA's online exhibit exploring an anthropological approach to race.

American Experience. 1986. *Eyes on the Prize: America's Civil Rights Movement 1954–1985.* Blackside. See the "Fighting Back (1957–1962)" segment on Southern school desegregation.

Bonilla, Yarimar, and Jonathan Rosa. 2015. "#Ferguson: Digital Protest, Hashtag Ethnography, and the Racial Politics of Social Media in the United States." *American Ethnologist* 42(1):4–17.

Duke, David Hughes, and John Duke. 2012. *From Silence to Recognition.* Documentary with interviews of Jewish students who faced discrimination by Emory University's School of Dentistry from 1948 to 1961.

Jones, Camara Phyllis. 2000. "Levels of Racism: A Theoretic Framework and a Gardener's Tale." *American Journal of Public Health* 90 (8): 1212–15.

Race: The Power of an Illusion. 2003. California Newsreel. View the three-part television series on DVD, then visit the related PBS website at www.pbs.org/race/ for further discussions, exercises, and resources.

Rothstein, Richard. 2014. *The Making of Ferguson: Public Policies at the Root of Its Troubles.* Washington, DC: Economic Policy Institute. www.epi.org/files/2014 /making-of-ferguson-final.pdf

Sue, Derald Wing. 2015. *Race Talk and the Conspiracy of Silence: Understanding and Facilitating Difficult Dialogues on Race.* Hoboken, NJ: Wiley.

U.S. Department of Justice. Civil Rights Division. 2015. "Investigation of the Ferguson Police Department." March 4. www.justice.gov/sites/default/files/opa /press-releases/attachments/2015/03/04/ferguson _police_department_report.pdf.

What can soccer teach us about ethnicity and nationalism? Here Germany's Jerome Boateng (*left*) challenges for the ball against his half-brother, Ghana's Kevin-Prince Boateng, during a 2010 World Cup soccer match in Johannesburg, South Africa.

CHAPTER 7
Ethnicity and Nationalism

When the World Cup soccer tournament opened in June 2010 in South Africa, teams from thirty-two nations carried the hopes and dreams of their supporters into the competition. Soccer stadiums filled up with fans painted in national colors, draped in national flags, and singing national songs and anthems. Other fans tuned in to television and radio broadcasts around the world, exulting and suffering along with the fates of their national teams. Over three years, 205 teams had battled through 848 matches to reach South Africa—the most extensive global tournament in history. At the time of the World Cup final, more than 700 million people gathered worldwide in pubs, restaurants, and crowded town squares to watch Spain play the Netherlands. What can we learn about ethnicity and nationalism from the World Cup?

Jerome Boateng and Kevin-Prince Boateng, two half-brothers born in Germany to a Ghanaian father and German mothers, both played in the World Cup—but for different national teams. Jerome played for Germany, the country of his birth. Kevin-Prince played for the Ghanaian national team, representing the country of his father's birth. What makes someone a member of a certain nation? The simple answer, it seems, should be birth. But in today's age of globalization, nationality is not so simple. The rules of FIFA, the world soccer federation, state that to play for a national team, a player must either be born in that country or have a parent or grandparent from that country. A player can also establish a new nationality by living in a new country for five years. But once a choice of nationality is made, it is irrevocable. As the son of an immigrant from Ghana, but born in Germany, Kevin-Prince could choose his nationality. In the World Cup, we see the complications of identity for children of immigrants and the changing rules of nationality on the international stage.

But what exactly is a nation? When Germany knocked England out of the World Cup, commentators in the United Kingdom lamented the death of the "90-minute nation" (Younge 2010). What did this mean? First, consider that England no longer exists as a separate nation. It is now part of the United Kingdom—along with Scotland, Wales, and Northern Ireland. In fact, the disappearance of England within the United Kingdom is a sore point for many of English descent. Their rival ethnic groups have gained political recognition in recent years. Scotland has a parliament; Wales and Northern Ireland have national assemblies. But politically, England has been subsumed into the United Kingdom.

The soccer pitch is one of the few places where English ethnic identity and nationalism can still be expressed. The game was born in England. In consideration of this, FIFA allows the English to continue fielding a World Cup team even without a nation. When the England team takes the field, English ethnicity and nationalism reemerge. The flag of England's patron saint, St. George, flies high over the prime minister's residence, temporarily replacing the Union Jack. Period costumes emerge on the streets of London. Traditional English songs resound in pubs. Through sports, the nation exists as long as England is playing. But at the end of a 90-minute game, the "90-minute nation" returns to its place within the United Kingdom.

Let's consider another example. Midway through the World Cup, the French national team imploded as the world and the French nation watched. The whole team went on strike, refusing to practice before a crucial match that resulted in a humiliating early exit from the tournament. What had happened? During the competition, a vitriolic rant by one of the team's stars, laced with ethnic comments, set off intense conflicts within the diverse French team—whose racial and ethnic composition reflects the country's colonial past and recent immigration. Indeed, immigration, nationality, and race had been red-hot topics in France long before the 2015 terrorist attacks in Paris. With a long colonial past in Africa and Asia and significant recent immigration from these former colonies, France seethes with conflict over who is really French. Riots have erupted in immigrant neighborhoods (Newman 2015). The national government banned Muslim women from wearing the veil in public. And in response to terror threats, the French government wrestles with how to balance security and privacy concerns of its citizens. Thus one must ask: What does it mean to be "French"? What are the standards for assessing this claim of ethnic and national identity? The difficult French national debates over ethnicity and nationalism were clearly on display and under negotiation at the 2010 World Cup.

The World Cup is more than a series of soccer matches. As anthropologists, we know that sports are more than just a game. Yes, games happen in real time with dirt and sweat, tactics and strategies, wins and losses and ties. But games are also symbolic, both for the players and for their fans. Victory and defeat, disappointment and heroism are wrapped up in a drama larger than life. Sports are a venue for the creation and negotiation of personal and national identity. They are sites of moral education about sportsmanship, leadership, the value of compromise, how to cope with victory and defeat, how to perform masculinity or femininity, and how to work together with diverse people (Mac-Clancy 1996). Wrapped up in an international competition like the World Cup are emotionally fraught matters: national identity and citizenship, the national and ethnic imaginations of people worldwide, the history of colonialism and independence, old rivalries, national pride, the expression of national character, and the negotiation of a people's place on the modern world stage. Moreover, the spectacle of the World Cup illustrates how the promotion of nationalism by the media, corporations, and national leaders has direct benefits for viewership, profit, and political power.

In this chapter we will explore ethnicity and nationalism from an anthropological perspective. In particular, we will ask three key questions:

- What does "ethnicity" mean to anthropologists?
- How and why is ethnicity created, mobilized, and contested?
- What is the relationship of ethnicity to the nation?

After reading this chapter you will have the tools to understand and analyze the role of ethnicity and nationalism in your own life and in communities and countries worldwide.

What Does "Ethnicity" Mean to Anthropologists?

We hear the word *ethnicity* all the time. The press reports on "long-held ethnic conflicts" that shatter the peace in Rwanda, Iraq, India, and the former Yugoslavia. We check boxes on college applications and U.S. census forms to identify our ethnicity or race. We shop in the "ethnic foods" aisle of our super-sized grocery store to find refried beans, soy sauce, pita, and wasabi. Our use of *ethnicity* is not particularly consistent or terribly clear. In recent years in the United States, *ethnicity* has been increasingly substituted for *race* when describing group differences. *Ethnic* is often paired with *minority*, a term signifying a smaller group that differs from the dominant, majority culture in language, food, dress, immigrant history, national origin, or religion. But this usage ignores the ethnic identity of the majority. The same lack of clarity is true for our use of the terms *nation, nationalism*, and *nation-state*, all of which often blur together and at times seem indistinguishable from *ethnicity*.

Ethnicity as Identity

Over a lifetime, humans develop complex identities that connect to many people in many ways. We build a sense of relationship, belonging, and shared identity through connections to family, religion, hometown, language, shared history, citizenship, sports, age, gender, sexuality, education, and profession. These powerful identities influence what we eat, who we date, where we work, how we live, and even how we die. **Ethnicity** is one of the most powerful identities that humans develop: it is a sense of connection to a group of people who we believe share a common history, culture, and (sometimes) ancestry and who are distinct from others outside the group (Ericksen 2010; Jenkins 1996). Ethnicity can be seen as a more expansive version of kinship—the culturally specific creation of relatives—only including a much larger group and extending further in space and time. As we will see in this chapter, the construction of ethnicity, like kinship, is quite complicated, moving well beyond easy equation with biological ancestry. In this chapter we will explore the ways ethnicity may be perceived, felt, and imagined by a group as well as the ways it may be imposed on a group by others.

With the intensification of globalization and the increasing flows of people, goods, and ideas across borders, one might anticipate that the power of ethnicity to frame people's actions and to influence world events would diminish. Instead, ethnicity seems to be flourishing—rising in prominence in both

ethnicity: A sense of historical, cultural, and sometimes ancestral connection to a group of people who are imagined to be distinct from those outside the group.

local and global affairs. Why is it so powerful? When threatened or challenged, people often turn to local alliances for support, safety, and protection. Ethnicity is one of the strongest sources of solidarity available.

As the effects of globalization intersect with systems of power at the local level, many people turn to ethnic networks and expressions of ethnic identity to protect their local way of life in the face of intense pressures of homogenization. As we will consider later in this chapter, ethnicity can also serve political purposes on the national and local levels as political elites and other ethno-entrepreneurs may impose or enforce ethnic distinctions or use calls for ethnic solidarity to mobilize support against perceived enemies inside and outside the nation-state. Rather than diminishing in the face of globalization, ethnicity emerges even more powerfully in specific situations of conflict, tension, and opportunity.

In what ways do stories, paintings, and even Thanksgiving turkey floats help create an American ethnic identity? (*left*) A 1914 depiction of the first Thanksgiving at Plymouth, Massachusetts. (*right*) The Tom Turkey float moves through Times Square during the Macy's Thanksgiving Day Parade, in New York City.

Creating Ethnic Identity

Anthropologists see ethnicity as a cultural construction, not as a natural formation based on biology or inherent human nature. Fredrik Barth (1969) describes ethnicity as the "social organization of cultural difference"; in other words, people construct a sense of ethnicity as they organize themselves in relation to others whom they perceive as either culturally similar or culturally different. Ethnic identity starts with what people believe about themselves and how others see them. Identity formation begins early and continues throughout our lives. People learn, practice, and teach ethnicity. Anthropologists who study it seek to understand how it is created and reinforced, how boundaries are constructed, how group identity is shaped, and how differences with others are mobilized and perpetuated (Jenkins 2008). Who do you consider to be in your ethnic group? Who belongs to a different group?

Native American scholar and activist Vine Deloria Jr., whose book *Custer Died for Your Sins: An Indian Manifesto,* challenges popular versions of the American origin myth.

Ethnic identity is taught and reinforced in a number of ways. One key method is the creation and telling of **origin myths**. By myth, we do not mean falsehood but rather a story with meaning. In the United States, the "American" origin myth includes stories of historical events—such as the landing of the *Mayflower*, the first Thanksgiving, the Boston Tea Party, the American Revolution, the Civil War, the settling of the West—that are retold to emphasize a shared destiny as well as shared values of freedom, exploration, individualism, and multiculturalism. The American origin myth of the first Thanksgiving is ritually enacted each year with a national holiday. Schoolchildren produce dramas and artwork based on textbook stories. Families gather to feast, usually eating certain traditional foods. Nationally televised parades and sporting events add to the ritual's celebratory character. However, origin myths—like all elements of culture—are continuously promoted, revised, and negotiated. For example, recent years have seen more open discussion of the brutal conquest of Native Americans (Deloria 1969) and, in books such as Howard Zinn's *A People's History of the United States* (2005), more challenges to classic textbook representations of the American origin myth.

People create and promote certain **ethnic boundary markers** in an attempt to signify who is in the group and who is not. These may include a collective name; shared cultural practices such as food, clothing, and architecture; a belief in common history and ancestors; association with a particular territory; a shared language or religion; and an imagination of shared physical characteristics. But ethnic boundaries are usually not clearly fixed and defined. Our social worlds rarely have distinct groups with clear boundaries. Not everyone imagined to be inside the group is the same; not everyone imagined to be outside the group is noticeably different. No group is completely homogeneous. Boundaries between groups can be quite porous. People move between groups through marriage, migration, and adoption. Identity, including ethnic identity, can be fluid and flexible, reflecting shifting alliances and strength over time and according to need. Groups may vanish in situations of war or violence. New ethnic groups may come into existence when part of an existing group splits off or two groups form a new one (Ericksen 2010).

Because ethnicity is not biologically fixed, self-identification with a particular ethnic group can change according to one's social location. This occurs through a process called **situational negotiation of identity**. For example, Kevin-Prince Boateng in our chapter-opening story could have chosen to be German, German-Ghanaian, Ghanaian, African, Afro-European, or perhaps even a member of his father's local ethnic group in Ghana. At points during his life he may choose to identify himself with any of these, depending on the situation. Have you ever had the experience of identifying with a different aspect of your identity as you moved between groups or locations? As another example, the following section explores how immigrants from India to the United States undergo changing ethnic perspectives as they become Indian Americans.

Constructing Indian Identity in the United States The immigration experience profoundly affects ethnicity and ethnic identification. New immigrants reshape their home-country ethnic identification to build alliances and solidarity in their new host country. In her book *From the Ganges to the Hudson* (1995), anthropologist Johanna Lessinger explores the process by which a new Indian ethnic identity is created and publicly demonstrated through consumption, public festivals, and Indian immigrant media. Indian immigrants arrive in New York from all corners of their homeland, speaking different languages, following diverse cultural practices and religions, and reflecting class and caste stratifications. In India, a country of more than 1.2 billion people, these individuals would identify themselves as representing different ethnicities shaped by geography, language, food, and cultural practices. But after arriving in New York as immigrants from India, they all begin the process of becoming Indian American.

The India Day Parade in New York City helps to construct an Indian-American identity in the United States.

New York City's Little India, a bustling shopping district in Jackson Heights, Queens, has become the symbolic center of Indian immigrant life and a key to the construction of Indian ethnic identity in the United States. Vibrant with the sights, sounds, and smells of India, the streets are lined with Indian grocery and spice shops, Indian restaurants, clothing and jewelry stores, travel agencies, music and video distributors, and electronics stores. Indian immigrants come from all parts of New York City and the metropolitan region to walk the streets of Little India and shop, eat, and take in the many symbols of "home."

Here Indian immigrants have created a wide-ranging ethnic infrastructure that supports and promotes the construction of a unified Indian ethnic identity in their new homeland. The infrastructure includes ethnic associations, religious temples, cultural societies, newspapers, television programming, and major public festivals. One of the largest festivals is the India Day Parade held in late August to mark India's nationhood and independence from British colonialism. Like the dozens of ethnic parade celebrations in New York each year, Indian immigrant community organizations, business owners, and hometown associations sponsor marching bands, singers, dancers, banners, and a vast array of colorful floats. Holding a public festival like the

MAP 7.1
New York/India

India Day Parade is a powerful way to stake a claim to a place in the multiethnic mosaic that is New York—to send a clear signal to all New Yorkers, including the political establishment, that Indians are here, are organized, and want to be taken seriously.

Ethnic boundaries are often fluid, messy, and contested. For example, exactly who is Indian American? For over fifteen years, until 2010, the South Asian Lesbian and Gay Alliance (SALGA) requested permission to march in the India Day Parade, only to be denied by parade organizers. Members of SALGA held demonstrations each year along the parade route, holding signs that read "We are also Indians!" Despite the parade organizers' desire to build a broad-based Indian American identity and coalition, they were willing to declare SALGA not Indian enough to participate in the event. In this situation, sexuality became a more powerful boundary marker than country of origin. The rift over the India Day Parade became a very public and symbolic representation of the contestation of ethnic boundary markers—a struggle that reveals deep disagreements among Indian immigrants and many of their children—and the debate involved in defining who is Indian in the United States.

How and Why Is Ethnicity Created, Mobilized, and Contested?

For many of the world's people, ethnicity is not a pressing matter in daily life. But it can be activated when power relationships undergo negotiation in a community or a nation. Then people call on shared ideas of ethnicity to rally others to participate in their causes, whether those causes involve ensuring self-protection, building alliances, constructing economic networks, or establishing a country. Ethnicity can also be activated by charismatic entrepreneurs of ethnicity who seek support from co-ethnics in their fight for political, economic, or military power against real or perceived enemies. The sections that follow illustrate how ethnicity can be harnessed for either harmful or beneficial outcomes.

Ethnicity as a Source of Conflict

Anthropologists explore the complex ways culture can be invented, transformed into ethnicity, and mobilized in situations of ethnic conflict (Eller 1999). The anthropological study of ethnic conflict requires an open-mindedness to new ideas of how ethnicity is formed and how it works—ideas that may be at odds with our everyday usage of the terms *ethnicity* and *ethnic groups*. Rogers Brubaker, in his book *Ethnicity without Groups* (2004), warns against "groupism" when studying ethnicity. Anthropologists may anticipate that we will work with clearly defined groups having fixed boundaries and homogenous membership who will act in a unified fashion. But this is not what we find on the ground as we explore ethnicity on the local level. Ethnicity is much more complicated, involving people with many perspectives, disagreements, and at times competing loyalties. The strong bonds of ethnicity that we associate with ethnic groups may wax and wane.

Why do the power and intensity of ethnicity harden and crystallize at certain times into ethnic conflict? As in the cases of Rwanda and the former Yugoslavia that follow, Brubaker encourages paying attention to ethnic group–making projects. Such projects occur when **identity entrepreneurs**—political, military, and religious leaders—promote a worldview through the lens of ethnicity. They use war, propaganda, and state power to mobilize people against those whom they perceive as a danger. Ethnicity may not actually be the problem. Rather, the struggle for wealth and power uses the convenient narrative of ethnic difference to galvanize a population to collective action. Once the wedge of ethnic difference has been driven into a population and used to achieve power, it can be self-perpetuating and extremely difficult to break. In these instances, ethnic conflict may intensify into violent acts, including **genocide**—the deliberate and systematic destruction of an ethnic or religious group (Eller 1999; Ericksen 2010; Scheper-Hughes and Bourgois 2004).

Identity entrepreneurs: Political, military, or religious leaders who promote a worldview through the lens of ethnicity and use war, propaganda, and state power to mobilize people against those whom they perceive as a danger.

genocide: The deliberate and systematic destruction of an ethnic or religious group.

Mobilizing Ethnic Differences in Rwanda In 1994, the East African country of Rwanda was shattered by a horrific genocide involving two main groups, Hutu and Tutsi. Over a few months, as many as one million Tutsi and an unknown number of moderate Hutus died in a slaughter perpetrated by extremist Hutu death squads. In a country of only seven million people before the genocide, where Hutu made up 85 percent of the population and Tutsi 15 percent, how did this tragic genocide occur? How did Tutsi and Hutu, who have lived together in the region for generations and centuries, come to perceive such clear differences between them and choose to act on those differences in such violent ways?

Before German and Belgian colonial rule in the early twentieth century, Hutu and Tutsi were distinguished mainly by occupation and social status. Hutu were primarily farmers; Tutsi were cattle owners. The two groups share a common language and religious affiliations. Intermarriage has been quite common. Children of mixed marriages inherited their fathers' identity. Although Tutsi were later stereotyped as taller and thinner than Hutu, it is not possible to distinguish between members of the two groups by looks alone.

In a common colonial practice used in countries worldwide, colonial governments chose one native group to serve as educated and privileged intermediaries between the local population and the colonial administration. The Belgian

MAP 7.2
Rwanda

colonial government (1919–62) elevated Tutsi to the most influential positions in Rwandan society, to the exclusion of Hutu leaders. In an attempt to rationalize its prejudicial behavior, in the 1920s the Belgian colonial government hired scientists to measure Hutu and Tutsi anatomy—including skull size—so as to physically differentiate between the two groups. These flawed studies, based on the pseudoscience of eugenics that developed in Europe and the United States, declared that Tutsi were taller, bigger brained, and lighter skinned—closer in physical form to Europeans and thus "naturally" suited to the role assigned to them by the Belgian colonial government.

To maintain and enforce this segregation, in 1933 the Belgian colonial government established a national identity card that included the category "ethnicity." Even after independence in 1962, Rwandan officials continued to use the identity card, forcing all citizens to be labeled as Hutu, Tutsi, Twa (a small minority population), or naturalized (born outside Rwanda). The cards were discontinued only in 1996 after the genocide.

Many Hutu resented the Belgians' decision to elevate Tutsi to power in the colonial government. Periodic protests in the early years of colonial occupation were followed by a major uprising against Tutsi elites in 1956. In 1959, the Hutu seized power and forced many Tutsi into exile in neighboring countries. At independence in 1962, the Hutu consolidated full power and implemented repressive policies toward the Tutsi. A full-blown civil war erupted in 1990. Subsequently, a 1993 United Nations–backed cease-fire collapsed when the plane of the Rwandan president, a Hutu, was shot down in April 1994.

What followed was an extensive genocide campaign by Hutu extremists who blamed Tutsi for the death of their president. Rwandan radio broadcast instructions to kill all Tutsi, including spouses and family members, as well as any Hutu moderates who were unwilling to cooperate. Hutu civilian death squads implemented the "Hutu Power" genocide program, a deliberate and seemingly long-planned extermination of Tutsi. Tutsi and moderate Hutu were killed largely by hand with machetes and clubs after local officials gathered them up into schools and churches. Hutu death squads used the Rwandan identity cards to identify Tutsi victims for extermination.

What role did ethnicity play in the Rwandan genocide? Western press and government reports referred to the extermination as "tribal violence," the result of "ancient ethnic hatreds" and a failed nation-state. However, we can see how colonial European policies constructed and enforced notions of difference between Hutu and Tutsi—including notions of physical and mental difference—that were not deep-rooted historical patterns but that nonetheless later served to rationalize genocide (Mamdani 2002). Indeed, the twentieth-century history of Rwanda reveals the ways in which local ethnic relationships can be broken down and reconstituted in long-lasting ways by a foreign superpower that uses ethnicity as a

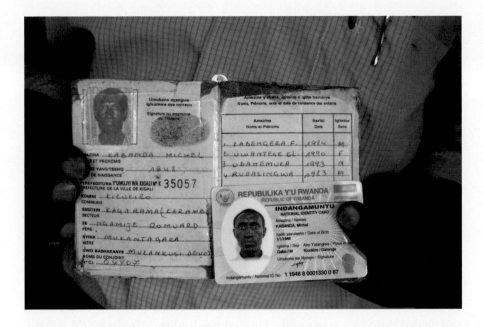

Rwandan identity cards listing each citizen's ethnic identity were discontinued only in 1996 after the genocide of as many as one million Tutsi.

weapon to divide and rule and how those new patterns of ethnicity can be mobilized to fuel a struggle for economic, political, and military power (Eller 1999).

Remaking Identity: Hutu Refugees in Tanzania In neighboring Burundi, where Tutsi outnumber Hutu, a series of massacres in the 1970s led to the exodus of many Hutu refugees to Tanzania. Anthropologist Liisa Malkki's ethnography *Purity and Exile: Violence, Memory and National Cosmology among Hutu Refugees in Tanzania* (1995) focuses on the lives of Hutu refugees in a remote resettlement camp and their experiences of atrocity, displacement, and exile. Through a year of fieldwork, Malkki collected dozens of life histories, which she calls mythico-histories—stories through which refugees worked to remake sense of their past, present and future.

Through these mythico-histories Hutu refugees reimagined their conceptions of community, history, and ethnic identity often in stark contrast to both Tutsi accounts of the conflict and Western accounts of the colonial history in Rwanda and Burundi. Hutus instead told of how their essential nature had emerged through the experience of atrocity and exile. Rather than victims and outcasts, their stories told of a distinct Hutu people with a long history as Burundians while the Tutsi were foreign usurpers. In their narrative, the trials of dispossession and dislocation prepared their "nation in exile" for a restoration to Burundi. To reinforce this sense of Hutu identity, refugees held to certain purity practices while in exile—discouraging intermarriage, preserving their language, and acquiring official recognition as refugees rather than blending into the surrounding Tanzanian community.

MAP 7.3
Tanzania

By recounting the Hutu refugee mythico-histories, Malkki sheds light on the dilemmas of displaced people in a world that assumes the nation-state is the natural frame for viewing ethnicity and ethnic identity. In the process, she captures the creative strategies displaced people deploy to sustain themselves and imagine a better future. When considering the intersections of ethnicity, ethnic conflict, and the nation-state, Malkki urges us to move beyond easy explanations of contemporary conflicts as inevitable or natural outcomes of ancient tribal hatreds. Instead, Malkki's work pushes us to see the complex histories and processes of identity making that are often obscured by labels like "refugee" and "ethnic conflict" (Haugerud 1998; Malkki 1995; Roseberry 1997).

Orchestrating Ethnic Conflict in the Former Yugoslavia The disintegration of the former Yugoslavia in the late 1980s and early 1990s led to a devastating civil war that harnessed ethnicity as a powerful weapon of conflict and hatred. The war began in 1992 among Catholic Croats, Orthodox Christian Serbs, and Bosnian Muslims as national political leaders scrambled for control over land and power. The region is one of the most ethnically diverse in the world, and the area's national boundaries have shifted constantly over the past 150 years. But in direct contrast to journalistic accounts of the 1992–1995 war, which traced its origins to ancient ethnic hatreds that condemned the country's people to an endless cycle of violence, Norwegian anthropologist Tone Bringa has offered a different perspective. In her ethnography *Being Muslim the Bosnian Way* (1995), she declares, "The war was not created by those villagers. . . . The war has been orchestrated from places where the people I lived and worked among were not represented and where their voices were not heard" (5).

Beginning in 1987, Bringa conducted fieldwork in a diverse, Muslim-Catholic village in central Bosnia. She carefully describes the integrated social structures of daily village life—including the role of women, religion, and the family—and pays particular attention to the way Muslims practiced their faith. Bringa did not find a village populated with people who had always hated one another. They spoke the same language, went to school together, traded in the same local market, and shared village life as friends and neighbors. Bringa pointedly notes that despite the usual tensions any small community would face, these people of different faiths had lived together peacefully for 500 years.

Significant change occurred in the community during the short time of Bringa's fieldwork. When she began her research, local Muslims based their identity on differences in religious practices from those of their Catholic neighbors. The emphasis was on practices such as scheduling of worship, prayer, and holiday celebrations, not on religious beliefs and convictions. However, these perceptions of self and others changed as war broke out and state leaders imposed new ethnic and cultural policies. Gradually, local Muslims were forced

MAP 7.4
Bosnia

to identify less with their local community and more with the religious beliefs of other Bosnian Muslims, and they had to turn to the outside Muslim world as a source of solidarity and support.

When Bringa returned to the village in the spring of 1993—revealed in riveting scenes from her documentary film *Bosnia: We Are All Neighbors* (1993)—to her horror she found that almost every Muslim home had been destroyed by Croat forces, with assistance from local Croat men of the village. All 400 Muslims in the village (two-thirds of its population) had fled, been killed, or been placed in concentration camps. **Ethnic cleansing**— efforts of one ethnic or religious group to remove or destroy another group in a particular geographic area—had shattered the dynamic and peaceful fabric of village life that

Bosnian Muslim women comfort one another near coffins of family members, victims of "ethnic cleansing," exhumed from a nearby mass grave.

ethnic cleansing: Efforts by representatives of one ethnic or religious group to remove or destroy another group in a particular geographic area.

Bringa recalled from only a few years earlier. As she writes in the preface to her book, "My anthropological training had not prepared me to deal with the very rapid and total disintegration of the community. . . . [T]his war has made sense neither to the anthropologist nor to the people who taught her about their way of life" (Bringa 1995, xviii). Her second documentary, *Returning Home: Revival of a Bosnian Village* (Bringa and Loizos 2002), examines the return of some of the Muslim refugees and the attempt to reconstruct the village life that was destroyed during the civil war. In Bringa's account of Bosnian village life we can see the vulnerability of local ethnic identities to manipulation by outside political and military forces (Coles 2007; Eller 1999).

Ethnicity as a Source of Opportunity

Ethnicity is not only mobilized to rally support in times of conflict. Ethnicity can also be mobilized to create opportunities, including engagement in everyday economics. Today ethnicity is being packaged and produced for a multibillion-dollar market: food, clothing, music, fashion, and cultural artifacts. People eat at ethnic restaurants, buy ethnic music, and decorate their homes and offices with ethnic furnishings. Perhaps you have some "ethnic" items in your dorm room or at home. John and Jean Comaroff, in their book *Ethnicity, Inc.* (2009), examine how the purposeful creation of ethnicity facilitates big business. The Comaroffs pay particular attention to the way ethnically defined populations are branding themselves and becoming ethno-corporations in

How can ethnic groups become ethno-corporations? Here, exterior and interior shots of the Pequot Foxwoods Resort, in Connecticut.

order to capitalize on their ethnicity. Ethno–theme parks, cultural villages, and ecotourism all promote the ethnic experience to attract investors and customers (Chio 2014; Nelson 1999). These are just a few pieces of the "Ethnicity, Inc." puzzle. (In contrast, for an example of a majority group's marketing of minority theme parks, see the group of images on the following page.)

Native Americans and the Ethno-Corporation The marketing of ethnicity is not uncommon globally, as marginalized indigenous groups seek to capitalize on their identity to attract investors and customers. Native Americans in the United States in recent years have established corporate entities to manage tribal land and invest tribal resources for the profit of their members, or "shareholders." Casinos have become big business, and the rise of casino capitalism has driven increasing opportunities for Native American groups to strategically expand from "tribe" to "ethno-corporation." Sovereignty agreements signed long ago with the U.S. government allow the expansion of the gaming industry on native land. Outside venture capital is readily available to underwrite these new opportunities (Darian-Smith 2004).

The Comaroffs (2009) note the effects of ethno-corporations on Native American life and culture. Clearly, Native American ethnicity and culture are being cultivated and marketed to promote economic projects, both in the gaming industry and beyond.

Ethno-enterprises in turn cultivate ethnicity. The massive Pequot Foxwoods Resort in Mashantucket, Connecticut, for instance, not only runs a lucrative casino but also supports the Mashantucket Pequot Museum and Research Center, complete with a library, archives, linguistic collections of the Pequot Indians' "traditional culture," and space for conferences and workshops

Each year, half a million tourists visit the Dai Minority Park in China's southwestern Yunnan Province. This is one of many ethno-parks owned and operated by members of China's Han majority (96 percent of the population), who market the nation's fifty-five ethnic minorities to a primarily middle-class Han clientele (Chio 2014). Here, tourists can live in Dai-style houses, eat ethnic meals, and participate in reenactments of ritual celebrations such as the water festival, pictured here, originally an annual three-day festival but now performed every day for the entertainment of visitors. How might ethno–theme parks benefit the Chinese government's goal of national unity? How do you think they affect the local communities?

on Native American topics. The Comaroffs note that as these ethnically defined groups increasingly become engaged in profit seeking and are more successful as corporations, the question of membership becomes more controversial and requires careful regulation. Genetics, birthright, and ideas of ethnicity based on "blood"—which historically have been privileged by the U.S. government when determining tribal affiliation—take on greater power than cultural ideas of ethnicity based on notions of belonging.

MAP 7.5
South Africa

Bafokeng, Inc., in South Africa For another look at ethnicity being mobilized for economic benefits, the story of one group in South Africa is remarkable for its corporate success. The Bafokeng, a Tswana nation in South Africa's North West province, trace their history in the area to the twelfth century. Between 1840 and the mid-1860s, their land was taken by white colonial settlers. Thereafter the Bafokeng, who could not own land under the new regime, went to work as laborers on the farms that had once been theirs; later they toiled in diamond mines to the south. Ultimately, though, to recover their land, the Bafokeng decided to try to buy it back. Pooling portions of their wage labor under the auspices of the Tswana king, and with a white German missionary serving as their proxy, the Bafokeng began a long-term strategy to repurchase their farms. Eventually, they reacquired thirty-three farms by the early twentieth century. To protect their land rights, the natives registered these farms under the name of the Royal Bafokeng Nation, Inc.—a private, corporate owner—not in the names of individuals.

Tensions rose dramatically when, in 1924, surveyors discovered that the Merensky Reef geologic formation that lay directly under Bafokeng land was the world's largest source of platinum metals and held significant deposits of chromite and graphite as well. Battles with the state and corporations over mining rights continued until the 1960s, when a deal was reached with a private company to provide the Bafokeng with royalties on all minerals extracted from their land. Once again, the Bafokeng placed their revenues into a communal trust.

Over time, the Royal Bafokeng Nation (RBN) has become a wealthy $3.4 billion corporate conglomerate with an extensive web of investments and holdings—including mining and construction companies, investment companies, and even a premier soccer team—in South Africa and beyond. At home, it has invested heavily in jobs programs by establishing mid-size companies such as Bafokeng Civil Works, Bafokeng Brick and Tile, Bafokeng Chrome, Bafokeng Bakery, and a Bafokeng shopping center. The RBN has also invested in infrastructure such as roads, bridges, reservoirs, electricity, schools, and health clinics, and it has established a fund for Bafokeng individuals who are pursuing professional training or higher education. The ethnic group has become an ethno-enterprise—built, branded, packaged, and advertised on the Bafokeng ethnic name and identity.

Many scholars, politicians, and economists expected the RBN to wither away in the face of globalization, modernity, and the homogenizing influence of the capitalist economy. However, the RBN ethno-corporation provides a remarkable example of the ways in which ethnicity can be mobilized by stakeholders in identity-based businesses to create alternative strategies for survival and success in the global marketplace.

Despite their corporate success, all is not well within the Bafokeng nation itself. Questions regularly arise about who benefits from this version of "Ethnicity, Inc." Individual Bafokeng do not own shares in RBN, Inc. Its money is not distributed among members but is reinvested in the corporation. Despite investments in job programs, infrastructure, and education in the homeland, recent studies show that the Bafokeng have a 39 percent unemployment rate, 95 percent use pit latrines for toilets, and less than 13 percent have electricity. With extreme poverty rates, some observers refer to the Bafokeng as "a rich nation of poor people" (Comaroff and Comaroff 2009, 109). How would you assess the effectiveness of this mobilization of ethnicity by the Bafokeng?

Assimilation versus Multiculturalism: Ethnic Interaction in the United States

The United States has an extremely complicated history of dealing with people of different geographic origins, religions, skin colors, and ethnic backgrounds. The relationship of "ethnic" and "American" (as applied to the United States) remains controversial today. From the outset, immigration from various regions in Europe, the enslavement and forced migration of Africans, and the conquest of Native American peoples made the United States one of the most ethnically diverse countries in the world. But these diverse groups and additional waves of immigrants over the past 200 years have experienced extremely different paths to incorporation into U.S. culture. In fact, these paths have often followed color lines that divide people of lighter and darker complexions.

Scholars have often used the **melting pot** metaphor to describe the standard path into U.S. culture. In the melting pot, minorities adopt the patterns and norms of the dominant culture and eventually cease to exist as separate groups—a process scholars call **assimilation**. Eventually all cooked in the same pot, diverse groups become assimilated into one big stew. According to this metaphor, tens of millions of European immigrants from dozens of countries with myriad languages, cultures, and religious practices have been transformed into ethnic whites through marriage, work, education, and the use of English.

But in reality the melting pot has never been completely successful in the United States, even for people of European descent. The creation of whiteness, as we saw in Chapter 6, was often contentious and difficult, marked by intense rivalries and violence. Nathan Glazer and Daniel Patrick Moynihan's landmark study *Beyond the Melting Pot* (1970) found a failure to reach complete assimilation among European immigrants and their descendants as late as the third generation. And many scholars suggest that the melting pot metaphor never meaningfully represented the experiences of Native Americans and people of African descent.

melting pot: A metaphor used to describe the process of immigrant assimilation into U.S. dominant culture.

assimilation: The process through which minorities accept the patterns and norms of the dominant culture and cease to exist as separate groups.

The incredibly diverse flows of immigration to the United States since 1965 have made earlier familiar categories increasingly inadequate to capture the rapidly shifting ethnic character of the nation's population today. For many Africans, Native Americans, Latinos, and Asian immigrants, the United States has been resistant to their assimilation into the dominant culture, regardless of their educational level or socioeconomic status. Yet, as discussed in Chapters 6 and 13 (on race and migration, respectively), immigrants and their children are creating new ethnic identities and new ways of becoming American. Today a multiculturalist narrative competes with the melting pot metaphor to represent the role of ethnicity in U.S. culture. **Multiculturalism** refers to the process through which new immigrants and their children enculturate into the dominant national culture and yet retain an ethnic culture. In multiculturalism, both identities may be held at the same time.

Tensions over which model will be dominant in the U.S. ethnicity story—assimilation or multiculturalism—are constantly rising to the surface. For example, attempts to establish English as the official language of towns, states, and even the U.S. federal government can be seen as (1) an effort to mandate language assimilation into the melting pot, and (2) a reassertion of the dominant culture's centrality against the rising trend toward multiculturalism (Rumbaut and Portes 2001).

What Is the Relationship of Ethnicity to the Nation?

Almost all people today imagine themselves as part of a nation-state. But this has not always been the case. **States**—regional structures of political, economic, and military rule—have existed for thousands of years, beginning in the regions now known as modern-day Iraq, China, and India. But the nation-state is a relatively new development. The term signifies more than a geographic territory with borders enforced by a central government. **Nation-state** assumes a distinct political entity whose population shares a sense of culture, ancestry, and destiny as a people. **Citizenship** refers to legal membership in a nation-state. Though the term **nation** once was used to describe a group of people who shared a place of origin, today the word *nation* is often used interchangeably with *nation-state*. **Nationalism** emerges when a sense of ethnic community combines with a desire to create and maintain a nation-state in a location where that sense of common destiny can be lived out (Gellner 1983; Hearn 2006; Wolf 2001).

Imagined Communities and Invented Traditions

Across the world over the past 200 years, people have shifted their primary associations and identifications from family, village, town, and city to an

multiculturalism: A pattern of ethnic relations in which new immigrants and their children enculturate into the dominant national culture and yet retain an ethnic culture.

state: An autonomous regional structure of political, economic, and military rule with a central government authorized to make laws and use force to maintain order and defend its territory.

nation-state: A political entity, located within a geographic territory with enforced borders, where the population shares a sense of culture, ancestry, and destiny as a people.

citizenship: Legal membership in a nation-state.

nation: A term once used to describe a group of people who shared a place of origin; now used interchangeably with *nation-state*.

nationalism: The desire of an ethnic community to create and/or maintain a nation-state.

almost universal identification with a nation or the desire to create a nation. Yet despite our contemporary assumptions that identification with an ethnic group or a nation has deep history, anthropological research reveals that most ethnic groups and nations are recent historical creations, our connection to people within these groups are recently imagined, and our shared traditions are recently invented.

Political Scientist Benedict Anderson (1983) conceived of the nation as an **imagined community**. He called it "imagined" because almost all of the people within it have never met and most likely will never meet. They may be separated by sharp divisions of class, politics, or religion and yet imagine themselves to have a common heritage and collective responsibility to one another and their nation. This sense of membership in an imagined national community can be strong enough to lead people into battle to protect their shared interests.

Anderson traces the imagined communities in Europe to the development of print communication in the capitalist economies that emerged in the eighteenth and nineteenth centuries. As people shared communication and information through newspapers and books published in a common language, Anderson suggests, they began to define themselves—to imagine themselves— as part of the same nation, the same community. Anderson's conception of imagined communities has become an essential analytical tool for thinking about nations and nationalisms.

Historians Eric Hobsbawm and Terence Ranger (1983), suggest that nations are not ancient configurations but instead are recent constructions with invented traditions. Nations may evoke a sense of deep history and inspire a broad sense of unity, but they are, in fact, relatively new. For example, we imagine the French nation-state to have a deep and unitary history, but prior to the 1800s the French were a scattered collection of urban and rural people who spoke different languages, celebrated different holidays and festivals, practiced different religions, and held primary loyalty not to the French state but to their city, town, village, or extended family. It was two national infrastructure projects, launched in the early 1800s, that ultimately played key roles in inventing a French nation.

What did these infrastructure projects involve? First, a new education system was introduced on a national scale. Its textbooks promoted a shared sense of French history, and perhaps most important, all

imagined community: The invented sense of connection and shared traditions that underlies identification with a particular ethnic group or nation whose members likely will never all meet.

MAP 7.6
France

French classroom, 1829. What role can education play in creating a sense of common nationality?

schools used the Paris dialect of French as the medium of instruction. This created a standard national language—a lingua franca—that facilitated communication among the population. Second, the construction of an extensive network of roads and railways integrated rural areas into a national market economy. This new transportation infrastructure promoted the rapid flow of goods between agricultural and industrial sectors and allowed the regular movement of workers between countryside and city, thereby providing a national labor pool for France's growing economy. These national infrastructure projects proved crucial to transforming the diverse people living within the territorial boundaries of what is now modern-day France into a French people with a common sense of identity, history, language, and tradition (Weber 1976).

Globalization and Transnational Citizenship in Eritrea Today, globalization is reshaping the ways nation-states operate and are experienced within and beyond their borders. For example, Victoria Bernal's ethnography *Nation as Network* (2014) explores the recent history of Eritrea, a small multi-ethnic nation in the Horn of Africa, and the ways Eritrean out-migration in recent decades has combined with new media technologies to transform notions of the nation-state and citizenship. While these concepts have typically been rooted directly in national territory, Bernal's study suggests that in a rapidly globalizing world, they increasingly span and transgress national boundaries.

War and violence have been constant factors for Eritreans in recent decades, from the country's struggle for independence to ensuing border wars with neighboring states. The country's citizens have faced increasing militarization and repression by the Eritrean state, which the United Nations Human Rights Council (2015) criticized for arbitrary arrests, detentions, torture, extrajudicial executions, forced labor and sexual abuse. Freedom of speech, press, assembly, and association are limited, and all citizens are required to participate in an indefinite period of national service.

Over this time, tens of thousands of Eritreans have chosen to move abroad in search of economic opportunities and political stability. Scattered over many countries and continents, they have formed what immigration scholars call a **diaspora**—an extensive network of Eritreans living outside their ancestral homeland yet maintaining emotional and material ties to home—through which they continue to participate passionately in Eritrean politics and economic life. They send money to family members back home. They make investments. And through a dynamic network of websites, blogs, and other social media, they connect with one another, debate Eritrean politics, mobilize actions and campaigns, and communicate their political views to the Eritrean state and a wider audience of nongovernmental organizations and human rights groups. Eritrean political and economic elites actively cultivate the diaspora's

MAP 7.7
Eritrea

diaspora: A group of people living outside their ancestral homeland yet maintaining emotional and material ties to home.

YOUR TURN: FIELDWORK

Seeing the Business of Ethnicity

Anthropologists examine the many ways ethnicities and ethnic identities can be invented, performed, and changed over time and according to one's social location. Now it's your turn.

Let's consider the ways ethnicities may be constructed and put to work in an everyday setting. Plan a fieldwork visit to a restaurant that you consider to be identified with a particular ethnicity. Drawing on your skills of participant observation, take careful fieldnotes of the ways you see ethnicity being constructed and performed, either consciously or unconsciously.

At this restaurant, what makes you feel you are having an authentic "ethnic" experience? Consider the food and beverages. Are there unique ingredients, styles of preparation, smells, colors, condiments, or desserts? Is the food presented in a special manner, with distinct platters, utensils, plates, glasses? Consider the restaurant staff. What is unique about their national origins, language use, clothing, mannerisms, or style of self-presentation? Consider the décor. What do you notice about the architecture, signage, restaurant name, interior décor, placemats, pictures, colors, lighting, music, plants?

To dig deeper and to begin to analyze your observations, request an interview with the owner or manager— someone who can provide an overview of the business. Start by asking the following:

- What makes your restaurant unique in terms of ethnicity or ethnic identity?
- How is this restaurant the same or different from ones in your place of origin?
- Do you think your displays of ethnicity help (or hurt) your restaurant's sales?
- If the restaurant were more like those "back home," would that help or hurt sales? Why?
- Where do you find or purchase your markers of ethnic identity: food, decorations, staff?
- Do you share an ethnic identity with the people who provide your supplies, equipment, and personnel?

Ask if it would be appropriate to take pictures of elements that particularly perform or represent ethnic identity.

Compare your fieldnotes and findings with a classmate. Discuss the similar and different ways ethnicity was put to work, consciously or unconsciously, in your fieldsite.

---

involvement and rely on their financial contributions to support Eritrea's welfare and warfare.

Bernal documents the ways the activities of the Ethiopian diaspora create new opportunities to experiment with political expression, including dissent and other activities that would not be safe in Eritrea itself. New communication technologies enable Eritreans in diaspora to participate in a kind of "infopolitics" in which the management of information becomes a central aspect of power relations between the state and its citizens. Their online presence creates an alternative public sphere in which to challenge Eritrea's authoritarian government, question the narratives of the country's mainstream media, and more generally undermine practices of secrecy and censorship. In the process, this transnational network of Eritreans in diaspora participates in robust ways in the building of Eritrea as a nation—both in the struggle over Eritrean economic and political priorities and in the making and remaking of the conceptual boundaries of the Eritrean state, Eritrean citizenship, and Eritrean identity (Bernal 2014; Ivana 2015).

Anti-Colonialism and Nationalism

At times, efforts to imagine a national identity among a diverse group of people gain strength through the need—perceived or real—to join together against the threat of a common enemy. The outsiders—"others" who do not belong to the group—may be stereotyped along lines of religion, race, language, ethnicity, or political beliefs. War is the most dramatic strategy for evoking nationalism and mobilizing a population for the project of nation building.

Through their colonial conquests over more than 400 years, the emerging nation-states of Europe, and later Japan in Asia, redrew the political borders of much of the world to suit their own economic and political interests. In the search for raw materials, cheap labor, and markets for their expanding economies, they mapped out territorial boundaries without regard to local ethnic, political, economic, or religious realities (see Chapter 12 on the global economy). In the process, colonial activity disrupted long-established and complex local and regional social, economic, and political relationships. Colonialism had a particularly negative impact on indigenous people around the world who faced forced labor, relocations, forced assimilation, violence and genocide (Maybury-Lewis 2002).

The destruction of European and Japanese economies during World War II (1939–45) weakened the colonial powers' ability to control their colonies. As a result, national independence movements that had been gaining strength in colonies throughout Asia, Africa, the Middle East, Latin America, and the Caribbean before World War II and had developed military capabilities and guerrilla fighting tactics during the war were strongly positioned to turn their efforts toward liberating their countries from the colonial occupiers. The anti-colonialist efforts led to a rise of nationalism in former colonies as disparate populations banded together to reassert local control (Cesaire 1955; Fanon 1961).

The Challenges of Developing a Sense of Nationhood

Of the nearly two hundred nation-states in the world today, fewer than one-third existed in their current form 40 years ago. Dozens of states were created after World War II as nationalist movements won independence from colonial powers in Asia, the Middle East, and Africa. Dozens more were created in Central Asia and Eastern Europe following the collapse of the former

Soviet Union and the breakdown of previously socialist states in the 1990s. Only a handful of the nation-states that exist today date back to the nineteenth century, and almost none have existed for more than 200 years, certainly not in their present form. As a result, by the end of the colonial era few of the newly formed countries had homogeneous populations. Most now encompassed multiple ethnicities and identities within state borders that previously had not existed. Such disparities caused thorny problems for nationalist movements and for the nation-states that formed after independence (Robbins 2013). The following case studies from Zimbabwe, Iraq, and Argentina explore the challenges experienced by emerging nations in the postcolonial period and will expand your understanding of the intersection of nation, nationalism, nation building, and the modern nation-state. Can you identify in these examples the key concepts introduced in this chapter?

MAP 7.8
Zimbabwe

Guerrillas, Spirit Mediums, and Nationalism in Zimbabwe Zimbabwe was the last African colony to become independent (in 1980). In *Guns and Rain: Guerrillas and Spirit Mediums in Zimbabwe* (1985), anthropologist David Lan examines the role of local religious beliefs and practices of ordinary people in the nationalist movement for liberation. In the rural Shona region of northern Zimbabwe bordering Mozambique, during the precolonial period social life was organized around chiefs and chiefdoms. Local leaders were most often the direct descendants of a line of chiefs and kings, but their authority rested on their ability to bring rain to the farming communities under their protection and jurisdiction. This authority was traditionally legitimized through a public ritual led by the local spirit medium—a religious specialist who could communicate directly with the spirits of the ancestors. While in a trance, the spirit medium would be possessed by *Mhondoro*, the spirits of dead Shona kings and chiefs. Through the medium, these royal ancestors would confer their blessing and legitimacy on the new chief.

Enos Pondai, a spirit medium, was imprisoned by the colonial government of Rhodesia (now Zimbabwe) for resisting government authority and assisting guerrilla fighters during the nation's war of independence.

But during nearly 100 years under British colonialism, the British administration usurped the role of selecting local chiefs. As a result, the chiefs, who no longer had the conferred support of the ancestors, lost much of their authority in the eyes of the local population. Spirit mediums, ignored and marginalized from the colonial political process, yet with their own claims to authority through their ability to communicate with *Mhondoro*, often became points of resistance to colonial rule. When the struggle for independence began in the 1970s, guerrilla fighters opposing the British needed the support of the local population, especially the rural farming population that made up most of the country. Lan tells of the strategic alliance formed in the north between guerrilla fighters—many of whom were not Shona—and local spirit mediums to provide legitimacy, support, and protection to their struggle.

Through the alliance, spirit mediums drew on their deep history and connections in local communities to give legitimacy to the guerrillas fighting against the British colonial occupation. Using elaborate rituals, the spirit mediums—possessed by *Mhondoro*—allowed the spirits of dead Shona kings and chiefs to recognize the guerrillas as incarnations of royal warriors of the past and as legitimate leaders in the current liberation struggle. In the process, the spirit mediums placed combatants under the direct protection of the ancestors and thereby legitimized their cause in the eyes of the local communities. For a time, the power of the anti-colonial guerrilla fighters who brought guns supplanted that of the local chiefs who brought rain.

Anthropologist Lan records detailed interviews with fighters who vividly recounted how their ancestors protected and guided them to safety and victory. After liberation, the ancestors were celebrated by the common people in the streets and by the new national leaders as well. Banners and pictures of the ancestors hung in public places, and they were effectively installed as protectors of the new Zimbabwe. The liberation struggle had brought renewed, deep connections between tradition and modernity, past and present, ancestors and the living. The reinvented ethnic traditions merged with nationalist movements to promote and sustain Zimbabwe's anti-colonialist struggles.

Are There Any Iraqis in Iraq? Since the U.S. invasion and occupation of Iraq in 2003, news reports have featured stories of ethnic violence among Sunni, Shia, and Kurds—violence that the media portrays as the true obstacle to democracy and peace. The front pages of newspapers and the leads on evening news tell stories of seemingly endless and senseless suicide bombings, roadside explosives, armed militias, kidnappings, assassinations, and warfare. Elections are held, but the elected officials, torn by intense ethnic, religious, and political differences, are unable to form a functioning government. In the same way that the Western press typically reports what it describes as ethnic conflicts around the world—whether in Rwanda, Sudan, Sri Lanka, India, or the former Yugoslavia—deep and long-standing ethnic and religious cleavages in Iraq are blamed for an environment in which civil war and government collapse are almost inevitable. The same narrative has been used to explain Iraq's inability to protect its borders and defend its citizens against the invading forces of ISIL (the Islamic State in Iraq and the Levant—sometimes called ISIS), which, beginning in 2014, occupied the key western Iraqi cities of Fallujah, Mosul, Tikrit, and other territories.

Why, after so many years of nation building with U.S. economic and military support, have the Iraqi people been unable to form a strong government and military and stop the violence? Aren't there any Iraqis in Iraq—people who would put the country first, ahead of other ethnic or religious differences?

MAP 7.9
Iraq

As anthropologists, we are extremely interested in the formation of ethnicity, the way it is organized for political purposes, and the transformation of local identification with a particular ethnic group into a spirit of nationalism that seeks to create a nation-state as its full expression. Let's dig deeper into the complexities of ethnicity, religion, nationalism, and politics in Iraq.

Iraq does not have an ancient history as a nation. Although cities such as Baghdad have an ancient history in the region of Mesopotamia, sometimes called the "cradle of civilization," the country of Iraq did not exist before World War I. Even then, Iraq was not formed through local initiative. A secret treaty between France and Great Britain (the Sykes-Picot Agreement), signed during World War I, carved up their opponent, the Ottoman Empire, to form many of the countries we find in the Middle East today. The two European powers, with Russia's consent, drew national borders—including those of present-day Iraq—to meet their needs for economic access, trade routes, and political control. The powers mapped out these borders with little regard for the history, politics, religions, and ethnic makeup of the local populations.

With a mandate from the new League of Nations in 1920, the British established a monarchical government in the new state of Iraq and recruited and empowered leaders from the minority Sunni population to run the government. Members of the Shia and Kurd populations, excluded from leadership roles in the government, actively fought for independence from British colonial occupation. Britain subsequently granted full independence to Iraq in 1932 (with the exception of another brief military occupation during World War II), but the Sunni minority retained control of the government until the fall of Saddam Hussein in 2003.

After the U.S. military occupied Iraq in 2003, the people of Iraq inherited a collapsed state structure and confronted the prospects of "nation building" in a country under foreign occupation that had experienced decades of state-sponsored violence. Yet media representations of Iraq consistently traced its problems to the roots of ethnic conflict. Social scientists from many fields question these simple storylines that portray deep ethnic and religious hatreds as the cause of Iraq's current difficulties (Ericksen 2010). Ethnicity, they warn, should never be seen that simply or monolithically. A more careful examination may find that (1) ethnic and religious lines are not drawn so clearly, and (2) other identities based on factors such as region, family, and class—even international relations—may also play key roles in the unfolding of events. With a weak state unable to provide security to its population, people turn to other strategies for mobilizing support, safety, and the means for achieving a livelihood (Eller 1999).

Haley Duschinski
Ethnicity and Nationalism in the India-Pakistan Borderland

For more than fifteen years, anthropologist Haley Duschinski has been conducting research on the ongoing conflict in Kashmir Valley, the homeland of the Kashmiri ethnic community. Located high in the Himalayas on the disputed border between India and Pakistan, Kashmir has become the most densely militarized zone in the world. More than 500,000 Indian security forces patrol the towns and villages, stationed in sandbag bunkers and sprawling camps as a massive popular uprising of Kashmiris resists Indian rule. In recent years, summer uprisings have led to frequent strikes, street protests, funeral processions, stone pelting, curfews, and tear gassing. And the use of lethal force by Indian security personnel against civilians—including human rights abuses, extrajudicial killing, disappearance, rape, and torture—has become commonplace. As Duschinski notes, "The militarization of Kashmiri society is absolutely pervasive—both in terms of the constant presence of the troops, and also in the way in which their presence has shaped all aspects of life."

Duschinski's long-term research in Kashmir has closely followed the shifting strategies of an independence movement to draw on notions of shared ethnic Kashmiri identity to mobilize for self-determination against the rule of the Indian state.

"Young people are at the forefront of the movement today, driving it forward. Their ethnic identity—what it means for them to be Kashmiri—is largely defined by their shared experience of struggling against oppression, their shared experience of having to fight for the right to determine their own political futures. And they are developing different creative forms to articulate their demands and to express the complex realities of what it means to live life under occupation."

Their creative resistance strategies include everything from stone pelting at security forces, to protest demonstrations, mock trials and tribunals, documentation proj-

ects, and all kinds of artistic expressions. The movement now includes Kashmir's first rapper, MC Kash; its first novelist to reach a wide Western audience, Mirza Waheed; and its first graphic novelist, Malik Sajad.

In the last few years Kashmir activists have sought to engage an international audience, hoping to build international support for their movement. "Kashmiris largely reject the legitimacy of the Indian state in their homeland. Under the emergency laws, the state has been carrying out violence against them, but they have no legal redress within the formal legal system. The question is, How should people seek redress? Their only alternative has been to make legal appeals to the very state that has been responsible for carrying out the violations in the first place. And they do—they fight these human rights cases in the courts. I track these legal battles as part of my fieldwork. But they also recognize that the international community is another potential audience for their complaints

Anthropologist Haley Duschinski during fieldwork in Srinagar, Kashmir Valley.

and one that might be able to apply moral pressure on the Indian state to respond, not only to the legal claims but also to the political claims about the future of the region.

"India and Pakistan have pursued various forms of dialogue regarding the Kashmir conflict over the decades, but Kashmiris have had a hard time making the case that they should have a seat at that table, that their voices should be heard. Anthropology, by its nature, foregrounds and privileges the needs, priorities, and concerns of local people. This has real-world relevance in conflict situations, where people's local perspectives are often overlooked or seen as secondary to larger national security or geopolitical concerns."

What drew Duschinski, a native of a small town in South Carolina, to become interested in Kashmir? "The local economy of my hometown was completely dominated by a major nuclear weapons production site built in the 1950s and active throughout the Cold War. In high school, I became politically active in opposition to it. It was part of my life from a young age, which meant that I grew up always thinking about the state capacity for mass violence, how our national security program shapes people's lives, my responsibilities as a U.S. citizen to my own country and to the rest of the world.

"I've always struggled to make sense of state violence in my own society, including direct violence of warfare as well as indirect violence of institutionalized racism, discrimination, and inequality that are structured into our democratic system. This led me, in college, to develop an interest in India—which is, after all, the world's largest democracy. Learning about political processes in India, especially patterns of state oppression and local community forms of resistance, helps me understand similar dynamics in my own society more clearly."

Duschinski relates the practice of anthropology to developing what the cultural critic Edward Said has called "wakefulness": "For me, this wakefulness comes from a fundamental commitment to the project of ethnography, which is grounded in participant observation. It comes through training yourself to live on the threshold between insider and outsider status so that you're fully participating in the world around you, but you're always constantly observing it, analyzing it, and critiquing it. You have to train your mind to see the world that way. You have to train your body to inhabit that space. Participant observation is not just a tool that we use during fieldwork. It becomes part of your way of being in the world.

"Wakefulness is about living in that state of constant awareness—and not just passively being there, but owning it, wanting to see the world against the grain, and being willing to describe what you see. This carries certain risks because it often means analyzing and interpreting situations in ways that run counter to dominant ideologies and the status quo. There's a revolutionary potential embedded in the heart of anthropology. And I think this is why many Kashmiri students appreciate the project of anthropology. Their homeland is a contested border territory, and they've grown up seeing the world from the margins, from the peripheries. The way they see the world does not fit neatly into nationalist narratives or dominant discourses. Instead, it fundamentally challenges them. Anthropology legitimizes that alternative standpoint, privileges it, calls for it. Anthropology trains you to inhabit that space and live your life there—awake."

> *Wakefulness is about living in that state of constant awareness—and not just passively being there, but owning it, wanting to see the world against the grain, and being willing to describe what you see.*

MAP 7.10
Argentina

Sports and National Identity in Argentina As discussed in the chapter opener, sports are more than just a game. Sports are a venue for creating and negotiating personal and national identity, imagining one's community, and inventing traditions (MacClancy 1996). In *Masculinities: Football, Polo and the Tango in Argentina* (1999), anthropologist Eduardo Archetti suggests that football (called soccer in the United States)—and, to a lesser extent, polo and the tango—has been key to the making of the Argentine national identity.

Argentina began as a country of immigrants. Between 1870 and 1914—at the same time that the United States experienced massive waves of immigration—six million European immigrants, rich and poor, arrived in Argentina. Most came from Italy and Spain, but together the newcomers represented dozens of European ethnic groups and nationalities all looking for a fresh start on the other side of the Atlantic Ocean. Thus, Argentina's rural and urban areas became places of intense ethnic and cultural mixing. Buenos Aires, the capital city, was completely transformed. What had been a pre-modern city on the edges of the world economy became a global, cosmopolitan center full of cultural connections and dislocations where Argentina intersected with the world. Imagining a national community with a sense of cohesion, connection, and identity out of this ethnic and cultural diversity would not be easy. Soccer would play a key role in the transformation. Archetti suggests that as Argentinians reinvented soccer, they invented themselves.

British immigrants had brought soccer to Argentina in the nineteenth century. The sport became so popular that by the 1920s, Argentina had established itself as a world soccer leader. In a few decades, soccer had been transformed from a foreign import to a national obsession, played with a unique style and passion.

Today football is the national sport, a passion that cuts across boundaries of class, region, race, and ethnic status. The soccer exploits of Argentina's local and national teams are told and retold in living rooms, at bars, and at pickup games, and they are frequent topics in the press and popular novels. When the national team competes in tournaments abroad, or when players travel to perform for club teams elsewhere in the world, football becomes not only a forum for establishing a national identity but also a symbolic arena for representing Argentina and its citizens on the world stage.

When asked, Argentinians say that the most successful players—like Diego Maradona or Lionel Messi—and teams are those that faithfully mirror the authentic national style. This particular brand they trace to the *potrero*—the empty and uneven lots of confined outdoor spaces where neighborhood boys play after school without teachers or coaches. There one controls the ball by creative dribbling. In this unique social and spatial context, Argentina's boys

develop the style of soccer that is unique to their country—a style not of efficiency, practicality, results, force, and goals, but of creativity, imagination, spontaneity, improvisation, inventiveness, and freedom. This style—the creation of beauty, joy, elegance, and the unexpected, the creation of the beautiful game—has become a symbolic expression of the national capabilities and potential of the Argentinian people.

As globalization creates flows of people, ideas, goods, and images across borders and builds linkages among local communities worldwide, we might anticipate that ethnicity and nationalism—which are associated with local and national identities—would have less capacity to shape people's lives and influence the way people make decisions. Instead, in many parts of the world we see an intensification of ethnic and national identities and related conflicts. Understanding the processes through which ethnicity and nationalism are imagined and mobilized and their traditions are invented, often over relatively short periods, can provide a set of tools for analyzing the role of ethnicity in our world today.

THE SOCIAL LIFE OF THINGS
Architecture and Dubai's New Ethnic and National Identity

Over the past twenty-five years, Dubai, the largest city in the United Arab Emirates (UAE), located on the edge of the desert at the gate of the Persian Gulf, has grown from a small-scale trading port to a glittering city at the center of the global economy. Its distinctive skyscrapers, sprawling shopping malls, office parks, and cultural sites represent a dramatic (and state-sponsored) refashioning of Dubai's identity as a city and of the Dubayyan people's ethnic identity (Kanna 2011).

1 As recently as 1967, Dubai had only 59,000 inhabitants living along the Dubai Creek, divided along ethnic and tribal lines into Arabs, Persians, and others from India, Sudan, Iraq, Lebanon, Egypt, and Palestine. Increased demand for UAE oil supported increased infrastructure spending in Dubai by the ruling Maktoum family and smoothed over existing ethnic divisions.

2 Architecturally eye-catching buildings designed by the world's star architects have been at the heart of Dubai's twenty-year effort to fashion a new identity as a global city: cosmopolitan, connected, modern, unified, and happy—a new Mecca of business, culture, and the arts. Today Dubai boasts the world's tallest building, tallest hotel, biggest shopping mall, and largest artificial islands. New office towers and commercial parks attract global financial corporate headquarters.

Dubai has also refashioned itself as a tourist destination with art galleries, cultural events, amusements, and unparalleled shopping experiences in its dizzying array of fantastical indoor shopping malls. The Mall of the Emirates, for instance, one of the largest in the world, includes five indoor ski slopes on an 85-meter high mountain and a chance to play with penguins. Dubai expects 20 million tourists annually by 2020.

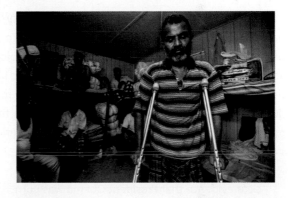

Dubai's identity makeover has a complicated story of ethnicity underneath. Dubai's new skyline has been built by tens of thousands of migrant foreign workers from places such as India, Pakistan, and Bangladesh. These people have limited legal rights and live in vast labor camps on the outskirts of the city. The precarious status of these exploited workers has reopened long-ignored ethnic tensions that the state has struggled to address.

What does it mean to be a Dubayyan today? Architecture and new urban spaces have become key elements in reimagining Dubai as a cosmopolitan, global city that transcends history, class, ethnicity, and culture. But building the new Dubai has required a complex mix of people, particularly low-wage, foreign workers who have reopened the past and complicated the future.

- Think of your local town or city. What images and identity does its built environment project?
- Have distinctive architectural elements been introduced to refashion the identity of the area and its people? How? By whom? And why?

TOOLKIT

Thinking Like an Anthropologist: Who Is an American?
In the opening story of the World Cup—one of the most global of all sporting events—and in the ethnographic examples throughout the chapter, we have seen how ethnic identity and nationalism continue to be imagined, built, nurtured, taught, learned, promoted, negotiated, and contested. And we have explored an anthropological perspective on three questions that connect the concepts of ethnicity and nationalism:

- What does "ethnicity" mean to anthropologists?
- How and why is ethnicity created, mobilized, and contested?
- What is the relationship of ethnicity to the nation?

Few of us are aware of the role of ethnicity and nationalism in our lives or how our culture works to promote them. As you learn to think like an anthropologist yourself, can you begin to see the process of ethnic identity construction at work in your own life and in the major debates of the culture that surrounds you? Consider these recent debates about who is and who is not an American:

- Despite an official birth certificate and other clear evidence that President Obama was born in the state of Hawaii on August 4, 1961, more than 20 percent of Americans surveyed in a September 2015 poll by CNN/ORG claim that he is not a U.S. citizen, and 29 percent believe President Obama is a Muslim, despite repeated professions of his Christian faith (CNN/ORC International 2015). How is that possible?
- Some leading politicians want to change the Fourteenth Amendment of the U.S. Constitution. The amendment was passed after the Civil War to protect African Americans by ensuring that anyone born in the United States is granted full rights of citizenship. "Anchor babies," children born in the United States to Hispanic parents who are undocumented immigrants, are the target of these recent suggested changes to the Constitution. Some people fear that these babies are being "dropped as an anchor" so their parents can become citizens when their child attains the age of twenty-one. Do you think the U.S. Constitution should be amended to address this issue? Or is this debate simply a substitute for a larger struggle over who belongs to U.S. culture and who does not? How should a child's nationality and citizenship be defined?
- In 2015–2016 leading presidential candidates evoked notions of ethnicity, nationalism and citizenship to rally voters, suggesting that Muslims should be required to register with the federal government; that 10–15 million undocumented immigrants living in the U.S., including children who accompanied them and who have grown up in the U.S., should be deported; that Muslim mosques should be placed under surveillance; and that the U.S. should only accept Syrian refugees if they are Christian. What role do ethno-political entrepreneurs play in attempts to define immigrants and Muslims in particular as ethnic outsiders in the United States?

After reading this chapter, you should be better prepared with the anthropological tools to understand the ways ethnicity and nationalism work in your life and in your imagined communities—whether they are built around family, religion, hometown, ethnic group, or nation-state.

Key Terms

ethnicity (p. 240)

origin myth (p. 242)

ethnic boundary marker (p. 242)

situational negotiation of identity (p. 242)

identity entrepreneurs (p. 245)

genocide (p. 245)

ethnic cleansing (p. 249)

melting pot (p. 253)

assimilation (p. 253)

multiculturalism (p. 254)

state (p. 254)

nation-state (p. 254)

citizenship (p. 254)

nation (p. 254)

nationalism (p. 254)

imagined community (p. 255)

diaspora (p. 256)

For Further Exploration

Bringa, Tone. 1993. *Bosnia: We Are All Neighbors*. Granada Television. Film of a Bosnian village studied by anthropologist Bringa before and after ethnic cleansing in 1993.

Bringa, Tone, and Peter Loizos. 2002. *Returning Home: Revival of a Bosnian Village*. Sage Film & Video (Sarajevo). Returning refugees attempt to restore community in their Bosnian village.

Chio, Jenny T. 2013. *Peasant Family Happiness*. Berkeley Media, LLC. Documentary depicting the everyday experience of "doing tourism" in two rural ethnic tourism villages in contemporary China. 70 minutes.

Cultural Survival, www.culturalsurvival.org. Organization started by anthropologists that advocates for indigenous people's rights and supports indigenous communities' self-determination, cultures, and political resilience.

Deloria, Vine, Jr. 1969. *Custer Died for Your Sins: An Indian Manifesto*. New York: Macmillan. A collection of essays exploring Native American life in the United States.

Gandhi. 1982. Goldcrest Films. Biographical film that portrays anti-colonial efforts to build a united India; the devastating strife between Hindus and Muslims; and the partition of India, Pakistan, and later Bangladesh.

Gourevitch, Philip. 1999. *We Wish to Inform You That Tomorrow We Will Be Killed with Our Families: Stories from Rwanda*. New York: Macmillan Picador.

Hotel Rwanda. 2005. Lions Gate Entertainment and United Artists. Movie about the dramatic rescue of Rwandans during the 1994 genocide.

Mississippi Masala. 1991. Set in Mississippi, the film depicts the challenges of romance between African Americans and Indian Americans.

The Namesake. 2006. Mirabai Films and UTV Motion Pictures. Film based on the Jhumpa Lahiri novel of the same name depicts the struggles of two first-generation immigrants from India to the U.S. and their children.

United Nations. 1948. "Convention on the Prevention and Punishment of the Crime of Genocide." December 9. www.un.org/millennium/law/iv-1.htm.

United Nations. 2008. "Declaration on the Rights of Indigenous People." http://www.un.org/esa/socdev/unpfii/documents/DRIPS_en.pdf.

Zinn, Howard. 2005. *A People's History of the United States: 1492–Present* (rev. ed.). New York: Harper. A fresh look at American history and its origin myths.

Why are women underrepresented in the U.S. military? Here, Captain Kristen Griest, center, trains at the Army Ranger School, an elite U.S. military program for special operations forces.

CHAPTER 8
Gender

On Friday, August 21, 2015, Captain Kristen Griest and First Lieutenant Shaye Haver became the first women to complete the United States Army's elite Ranger School at Fort Benning, Georgia. Both had previously graduated from the prestigious United States Military Academy at West Point, after which Griest deployed to Afghanistan in the military police and Haver served as an Apache attack helicopter pilot based at Fort Carson in Colorado. The Ranger's grueling 62-day leadership course tests soldiers' physical and mental ability to overcome fatigue, hunger, and stress while leading small-unit combat operations in adverse situations. Of the 19 women and 381 men who began the training, only 2 women and 94 men finished.

Though awarded the coveted black-and-gold Ranger tab, neither Griest nor Haver was eligible to join the elite 75th Ranger Regiment. U.S. military rules still barred women from direct combat roles, including service in the infantry, armored divisions, and special operations units like the Army Rangers.

Rather than highlighting an isolated incident, Griest and Haver's story illuminates deep tensions at the intersection of gender and power in the U.S. military and other U.S. cultural institutions. Fifteen percent of 1.4 million active-duty U.S. military personnel are women, and the number continues to increase. (Globally, women comprise a significant portion of the military in many countries, including Israel (33 percent), China (25 percent), France (15 percent), South Africa (26 percent) and Eritrea (30 percent)). The U.S. military has a reputation for leadership in creating integrated forces, including the integration of African Americans after World War II and more recently the inclusion of gay men and lesbians in 2011.

Issues of gender, however—including the appropriate role of women in combat, the scarcity of women in senior leadership, the high incidence of sexual assaults and the question of whether young women, like their male counterparts, should be required to register for the draft—still roil its ranks.

On December 3, 2015, three months after Griest and Haver graduated, Defense Secretary Ash Carter announced that all military positions, including combat positions, would be open to women. They would be allowed to drive tanks, fire mortars, lead infantry soldiers into combat, and engage in special operations. But what had really changed about women and men that brought about this policy shift?

Questions of gender—that is, the characteristics associated with being a woman or man in a particular culture and the ways those characteristics intersect with dynamics of power—are central to the practice of anthropology. Since the pioneering work of Margaret Mead challenged U.S. cultural assumptions about human sexuality and gender roles (see Chapter 3), anthropologists, especially feminist anthropologists, have been at the forefront of attempts to use the tools and analysis of anthropology to analyze the role of gender in crucial contemporary debates, social movements, and political struggles. Over the last forty years, **gender studies**—research into understanding who we are as men and women—has become one of the most significant subfields of anthropology. Indeed, anthropologists consider the ways in which gender is constructed to be a central element in every aspect of human culture, including sexuality, health, family, religion, economics, politics, sports, and individual identity formation.

As we have seen throughout this book, people create diverse cultures with fluid categories to define complex aspects of the human experience. The same holds true for gender. Even biological sex is far more fluid and complex than people are taught. As we will see later in this chapter, nature creates diversity, not rigid categories. As globalization transforms gender roles and gender relations on both the local level and a global scale, anthropologists play an essential role in mapping the changing gender terrain of the modern world. In this chapter we will explore these issues in more detail:

- Are men and women born or made?
- Are there more than two sexes?
- How do anthropologists explore the relationship between gender and power?
- How is globalization transforming gender roles and stratification?

By the end of this chapter you will be better prepared to understand the roles that sex and gender play in the culture around you, including in the classroom, in the family, in the workplace, in places of worship, and at the ballot box.

gender studies: Research into masculinity and femininity as flexible, complex, and historically and culturally constructed categories.

You will also be able to apply anthropological insights into gender issues as they emerge in your own life—insights that will serve you well as boyfriend or girlfriend, spouse, parent, student, teacher, worker, manager, and community leader in our increasingly global world.

Are Men and Women Born or Made?

"That's just the way guys are," some women sigh when a man says or does some stereotypical "man" thing. "Women!" a man may exclaim, hands in the air, as if all the other guys in the room know exactly what he means. But what *do* they mean? Is there some essential male or female nature that differentially shapes the personalities, emotions, patterns of personal relationships, career choices, leadership styles, and economic and political engagements of women and men?

Distinguishing between Sex and Gender

Much of what we stereotypically consider to be "natural" male or female behavior— driven by biology—might turn out, upon more careful inspection, to be imposed by cultural expectations of how men and women should behave. To help explore the relationship between the biological and cultural aspects of being men and women, anthropologists distinguish between sex and gender. **Sex**, from an anthropological viewpoint, refers to the observable physical differences between male and female human beings, especially the biological differences related to human reproduction. **Gender** is composed of the expectations of thought and behavior that each culture assigns to people of different sexes.

Historically, biological science has tended to create distinct mental maps of reality for male and female anatomy. Three primary factors have generally been considered in determining biological sex: (1) genitalia, (2) gonads (testes and ovaries, which produce different hormones), and (3) chromosome patterns (women have two X chromosomes; men have one X and one Y). Within this context, human males and females are said to display **sexual dimorphism**— that is, they differ physically in primary sexual characteristics as well as in secondary sexual characteristics such as breast size, hair distribution, and pitch of voice. Men and women on average also differ in weight, height, and strength. An average man is heavier, taller, and stronger than an average woman. Women on average have more long-term physical endurance and live longer.

But sexual dimorphism among humans is far from absolute. In fact, human male and female bodies are much more similar than different. In comparison to other animal species, human sexual dimorphism, particularly with regard to body size and voice timbre, is relatively modest (Fedigan 1982). On average, human males (U.S. average, 190 pounds) weigh about 15 percent more than

sex: The observable physical differences between male and female, especially biological differences related to human reproduction.

gender: The expectations of thought and behavior that each culture assigns to people of different sexes.

sexual dimorphism: The phenotypic differences between males and females of the same species.

Gender roles, even those stereotypically associated with male strength and aggression, are in flux across the globe. Here, U.S. Marines Sergeant Savanna E. Malendoski patrols in Helmand Province, southern Afghanistan.

females (U.S. average, 163 pounds) (Ogden et al. 2004). In comparison, male gorillas on average are double the size of female gorillas (Cawthon Lang 2005). Many biological characteristics associated with human sexual dimorphism fall along a continuum—a range—in which men and women overlap significantly. Not all men are taller than all women, though many are. Not all women live longer than all men, though most do. And as we will see later in this chapter, even primary characteristics of biological sex do not always fit into the two assumed categories of male and female.

In popular conversations, emphasis is often placed on the role of biology in shaping gender identities and behaviors. Research consistently reveals, however, that biology and culture closely intertwine. Culture, for instance, constantly shapes and reshapes our bodies throughout our lives, whether through nutrition, exercise, stress, exposure to disease, or social stimulation. Our bodies are designed to respond to our environments and life experiences. Our DNA, for instance, can be turned on and off by environmental factors. Our brains are constantly reshaped by the stimuli they receive. Even our hormone production is closely tied to the experiences we have with others. Testosterone levels rise and fall in response to what is going on around us. Studies have even shown that if fathers are actively involved with the children, their bodies respond in ways to help them be good dads (Kuzawa et al. 2009; Muller et al. 2009; Wade and Ferree 2015).

Cross-cultural anthropological research challenges the assumed links between biology and behavior. Knowing a person's biological sex does not enable us to predict what roles that person will play in a given culture. In some cultures, people with two X chromosomes do most of the cooking, farming, public speaking, and ritual activity; in others, people with one X and one Y chromosome fill those roles. Alternatively, the tasks may be done by both but stratified by power and prestige. In many Western cultures, for instance, both XX and XY cook. But women tend to cook in the home, while men predominate as restaurant chefs. Clearly, this is not a biologically driven division of labor. What could be the cultural reasons?

Even roles stereotypically associated with male strength and aggression do not fit an assumed binary gender division. Women do heavy labor—like the women of Plachimada in this book's opening chapter who rise early to carry water drums miles from the well to their homes. In addition, the predominance of men in violence and warfare is shifting as militaries in many parts of the world rely on women soldiers to fly remote-controlled predator drones, launch missiles, and engage in firefights on the front lines of battle. Because biology cannot predict the roles that men and women play in a given culture, anthropologists consider how gender is constructed culture by culture, and they explore the implications of those constructions for the men and women in each context.

The Cultural Construction of Gender

Humans are born with biological sex, but we learn to be women and men. From the moment of birth we begin to learn culture, including how to walk, talk, eat, dress, think, practice religion, raise children, respond to violence, and express our emotions like a man or a woman (Mauss 1979). We learn what kinds of behavior are perceived as masculine or feminine. Thus, anthropologists refer to the **cultural construction of gender**.

Family, friends, the media, doctors, educational institutions, religious communities, sports, and law all enculturate us with a sense of gender that becomes normative and seems natural. For example, parents "do gender" with their children. They assign them boy or girl names; dress them in appropriately gendered clothing, colors, and jewelry; and give them the "right" haircuts. Parents even speak to their children in gendered tones of voice. As we see gender being performed all around us, we learn to perform it in our turn. In these ways gender is taught, learned, performed, and policed.

Over a lifetime, gender becomes a powerful, and mostly invisible, framework that shapes the way we see ourselves and others (Bern 1981, 1983). Our relationships with others become an elaborate gendered dance of playing, dating, mating, parenting, and loving that reinforces our learned ideas of **masculinity** and **femininity** and establishes differing roles and expectations. Gender is also a potent cultural system through which we organize our collective lives, not necessarily on the basis of merit or skill but on the constructed categories of what it means to be a man or a woman (Bonvillain 2007; Brettell and Sargent 2009 Lorber 1994; Rubin 1975).

The following sections describe several ethnographic studies that explore the cultural construction of gender.

cultural construction of gender: The ways humans learn to behave as a man or woman and to recognize behaviors as masculine or feminine within their cultural context.

masculinity: The ideas and practices associated with manhood.

femininity: The ideas and practices associated with womanhood.

Teaching Gender in the United States: Boys, Girls, and Youth Sports

Sports is a key cultural arena in which individuals learn gender roles. A study of young boys and girls playing co-ed T-ball provides insights into how gender in the United States is subtly and not-so-subtly taught, learned, and enforced through youth sports (Landers and Fine 1996). T-ball is the precursor to baseball in

Nature or Nurture?

Try this exercise, which aims to challenge your assumptions about how biology and culture—sometimes called nature and nurture—interact to shape us as men and women.

Write down the first things that come to mind in response to this question: If you woke up tomorrow and you were a different gender, how would your life be different? Think about it. Start from the minute you wake up. Trace your morning routine, what you would wear, what you would eat, what you would do in the bathroom, what you would experience at school or the office, what would happen after work. Would suddenly being a different gender change what you could normally do or say, or where you could go? Would people respond to you differently? Which differences would be determined by the change in your biology, and which ones by cultural expectations of what it means to be a particular gender?

Women, if you woke up tomorrow and found that you were a man, how would your day be different?

which kids hit a ball off a stationary, upright plastic stick (a tee) rather than a ball thrown from a pitcher.

Landers and Fine found that T-ball coaches established a hierarchy of opportunity, training, and encouragement that favored boys over girls. Boys consistently received more playing time than girls, played positions (such as shortstop or first base) that provided more opportunities to touch the ball and develop their skills, and had more opportunities to practice hitting the ball at the plate. Boys frequently received coaching advice, while girls' mistakes went uncorrected. Parents and other players supported this hierarchy of training and opportunity and, along with the coaches, offered less or more encouragement along gender lines. For example, boys received more words of praise for their successes. These hierarchies were apparent not only between boys and girls, but within gendered groups as well. Among the boys, praise and opportunity were unequally distributed: Those who were already stronger, faster, better coordinated, or more advanced in baseball skills were favored over those who were

How is gender taught and learned through youth sports like this T-ball game?

not as advanced. Moving beyond the T-ball experience, the researchers noted that ideal forms of masculinity and manliness are taught, learned, and enforced on the baseball field as well, promoting aggressiveness, assertiveness, competitiveness, physical strength and skill, and a drive to succeed and win (Landers and Fine 1996).

Did you ever participate in youth sports, either in the United States or in another country? If so, what was your experience like? Did your parents sign you up for certain sports—basketball, soccer, lacrosse, football, wrestling, ice hockey, dance, gymnastics, figure skating, cheerleading? If so, what role might their ideas of gender have played in their choice? Landers and Fine's study suggests that attributes stereotypically associated with boys such as athleticism, assertiveness, aggression, strength, and competitiveness are actively constructed along gender lines through a wide variety of youth sports. In considering their study, can you see the ramifications of such gender training on individuals' attitudes and behaviors as they become adults with responsible roles in family, work, and politics?

While recognizing the physical differences between men and women—modest as they are when considering the diversity of the whole human population—how do we factor in the role of culture in something like sports and athleticism? Gender enculturation in sports and physical play begins early and happens in varied settings. I remember taking my toddler son to the playground and watching as other parents encouraged their little boys to run, climb, and jump while urging their little girls to play nicely in the sandbox. Starting in everyday settings like this, perhaps we can begin to imagine the cumulative effects of parental expectations, peer pressure, and media images on girls' motivation to engage in intense physical activity and competition (or boy's willingness to express emotions, play with dolls, or take care of younger siblings). As a result, sports may reflect less about real physical differences in speed, endurance, and strength and more about how a given culture constructs and maintains gender and sex norms. Perhaps becoming a world-class athlete depends more on opportunity, encouragement, coaching, nutrition, training facilities, and wealth than on being a man or a woman.

Today, as training and opportunities increase, women are closing the performance gap with men in many sports. The gap between male and female marathon winners, for instance, has rapidly closed to less than 10 minutes, and women are improving their times faster than men. But the persistence of inequality throughout sports culture precludes an accurate comparison between women and men athletes at the current time (Wade and Ferree 2015).

Constructing Masculinity in a U.S. High School Since the 1970s, gender studies have focused primarily on women. Recent studies, however, have begun to explore the gender construction of male identity as well as the broader construction of masculinity. The ethnography described here touches on several key aspects of this complex process.

C. J. Pascoe's ethnography *Dude, You're a Fag* (2007) explores the construction of gender—and particularly masculinity—in a suburban, working-class, racially diverse high school in north-central California. Calling someone a fag, what Pascoe calls "fag discourse," occurred almost exclusively among white male students in a daily banter of teasing, bullying, and harassment. Basing her conclusions on interviews with students, Pascoe found that calling someone a fag was not about whether someone was or was not gay; instead, it was directed at guys who danced like girls, cared about their clothing, seemed too emotional, or did something incompetent. In other words, white male students directed the epithet at other males who were not considered sufficiently masculine. Gay guys were tolerated as long as they were not effeminate, as long as they could throw a football around. Among the teenagers in Pascoe's study, fag discourse became a powerful tool for enforcing the boundaries of masculinity—a disciplinary mechanism for making sure "boys are boys" through the fear of abuse or violence.

Moreover, Pascoe points out that masculinity is not always associated with men. Girls can act masculine as well. She describes a group of "masculine" girls who play on the girls' basketball team and "perform masculinity" by the way they dress, display their sexuality, and dominate public spaces around the school. Jessie, a lesbian, is also president of the student council and homecoming queen. Her popularity appears to be related to her performance of masculinity. In these contexts, masculinity and dominance are linked to women's bodies, not to men's. Pascoe thus points out the ways in which both guys and

Cartoon Commercials and the Construction of Gender

I want you to watch cartoons this weekend! Actually, I want you to watch the commercials in between the cartoons. These are directed at children who wake up early on Saturday mornings and plug in to the television for a few hours until their parents get up.

Children watch an average of 40,000 commercials a year on television (American Academy of Pediatrics 2006). This is a staggeringly high number, even though the Children's Television Act of 1990 limits commercials to 10.5 minutes per hour on the weekend and 12.5 minutes per hour on weekdays. (It jumps to 16 minutes per hour during prime time.) So kids watch a lot of commercials. What do they learn about gender on Saturday mornings?

When you view a commercial during this exercise, try to categorize it by target audience: boy or girl. You won't have a hard time with most. Pay attention to the gendering messages: colors, products, tone of voice of the models and voiceovers. On a recent Saturday morning I was amazed by how many commercials targeting girls were produced in pink, purple, and powder blue colors for toys ranging from bunnies to babies. Girls were encouraged to take care of small, cuddly, needy pets and babies, feed them, change their diapers, wipe their tears. Hovering mothers encouraged their efforts. The commercials for boys, in contrast, were produced in dark green, blue, and black. Loud voices, outdoor activities, motion, action, and adventure served to promote toy trucks, balls, guns,

What lessons do children learn about gender as they watch 40,000 commercials a year?

missiles, and warrior figures. What do you see when you watch? Make a list, and compare it with those of your classmates. Discuss how the media promote different constructions of gender.

girls can perform masculinity and girls can adopt masculinity to gain status (Bridges 2007; Calderwood 2008; Wilkins 2008).

Think for a moment about how you establish and guard your own gender identity—masculine or feminine. Do your experiences have any similarities to those of the teenagers in Pascoe's study (either the aggressors or the targets)? Have your actions and experiences changed as you moved from high school to

THE SOCIAL LIFE OF THINGS
Unnecessarily Gendered Products

You've seen them. Pink and blue toothbrushes, razors, and deodorant sticks. Kids' clothes for princesses and kings. Coke cans emblazoned with "bro" and "grillmaster" next to Diet Coke cans that read "sweetie" and "mom." Pink nurse toy kits and blue doctor kits. Different soap fragrances. Separately colored crayon boxes for boys and girls. Accessories for Barbie and Ken. Chocolates for Mother's Day and ties and socks for Father's Day. Unnecessarily gendered products.

Women and men live surprisingly similar lives in the United States today. We grow up together, go to school together, and work in the same places. Why then are so many of the things we buy so distinctly, and unnecessarily, gendered—given masculine or feminine characteristics? What is the impact of these gendered products on how we think, what we do, and even how much money we have (Consumer Reports 2010; Wade 2015)?

1 Unnecessarily gendered products split us into two groups. They reinforce cultural ideas that men and women are distinct, even when we're not. They suggest that gender is central to how we think about ourselves and organize our lives, even when it isn't.

2 Pointlessly gendered products reinforce stereotypes. Gendered clothes, cosmetics, exercise machines, hair, bodies, speech, and movement pressure us to conform. They marginalize those of us who don't follow the gender norms, and they ignore the more fluid reality of gender performance that does not fit the stereotypes.

③ Unnecessarily gendered products help shape the gender ideology—the set of ideas—that makes gender inequality seem reasonable and rational. They explicitly tell us that women and men play different and unequal roles, that women should be subordinate to men and dependent upon them. Girls should be nurses and boys doctors (who makes more money and has more status?). Girls should be princesses and boys kings (who is in charge?).

④ Gendered packaging, descriptions, and product names promote masculine and feminine versions of the same item—shaving cream, body wash, pain reliever, antiperspirant, haircuts, shirts, shoes, bathing suits—often with higher prices for women for no apparent reason.

Gender is the culturally constructed set of ideas about how women and men should behave, think, and feel. Examining unnecessarily gendered items offers insights into the processes by which gender is constructed in U.S. culture, how gender roles are shaped, how gender ideology is created, and how gender inequality is made to seem reasonable and rational.

- Next time you go to the pharmacy, compare gendered versions of similar products. Compare for ingredients, size, and price. Try transgressing the gendered labeling and packaging to buy a product promoted for a different gender. How do you feel at the checkout counter? Why?
- Can you begin to see how something as simple as unnecessarily gendered products can negatively affect your life choices and chances?

college? Have you ever purposely adopted "masculine" or "feminine" attributes to fit in or gain status?

The Performance of Gender

Recently, anthropologists have moved from focusing on gender roles toward examining **gender performance**. Gender roles can mistakenly be seen as reflecting stable, fixed identities that fall in one of two opposite extremes—male or female. But anthropologists increasingly see gender as a continuum of behaviors that range between masculine and feminine. Rather than being something fixed in the psyche, gender is an identity that is expressed through action (Butler 1990).

My students, when identifying stereotypical masculine and feminine characteristics, often create something similar to the following list:

- *Masculine*: aggressive, physical, tough, competitive, sports oriented, testosterone driven, strong, unemotional
- *Feminine*: gentle, kind, loving, nurturing, smart, persuasive, talkative, enticing, emotional

But we know that both women and men can display any of these characteristics. And any individual may display various characteristics at different times depending on the setting. A man may perform his masculinity—his gender—differently when watching football with his buddies than while out on a date.

Indeed, people regularly make choices—conscious and unconscious—about how they will express their gender identity, for whom, and in what context. This is why we say that gender is performed. A man may drive a truck to make a living but also gently change his baby's diapers and take her in a stroller to play in the park. A woman may enjoy sewing dresses for her daughters but also dominate boardroom discussions as CEO of a company.

The recent explosion of Viagra use presents a dramatic example of the shifting of gender performance. Think about what it means to be a man in U.S. culture. Can an individual be a sexual, masculine man without an erection? Viagra was originally marketed to older men with erectile dysfunction. Lately, though, the target audience has shifted to include a younger generation of men perhaps dealing with performance anxiety in the face of sexually empowered women. Certainly, the marketing of Viagra fuels the culture's masculinity myth of the "real man" who is always ready for sex. But Viagra also ties ideas of men's sexual and social worth to an erect penis (Loe 2004).

Machismo in Mexico The construction of masculinity does not necessarily yield a rigid result, as the following study reveals. In *The Meanings of Macho*

A lot of guys have occasional erection problems.

I chose not to accept mine and asked about VIAGRA.

VIAGRA
(sildenafil citrate) tablets
Love life again.

What does this Viagra advertisement suggest about what it means to be a man in U.S. culture?

What does it mean to be macho? A couple and their baby on a stroll in Mexico City.

MAP 8.1
Mexico City

(2007), Matthew Gutmann examines what it means to be a man, *ser hombre*, for the men and women of a small neighborhood in Mexico City. Common understandings of *machismo* as the concept has spread around the world feature stereotypes of self-centered, sexist, toughguys. When macho is applied to men in Latin America, especially working-class Mexican men, these stereotypes can also include insinuations of violence, drug use, infidelity, and gambling. However, Gutmann's research in a working-class community reveals a complex male world of fathers, husbands, friends, and lovers that does not fit the common stereotypes.

For the men whom Gutmann studied, machismo and masculinity constitute a shifting landscape. What it means to be a man (or a woman) in the community can depend on the particular man or woman or the particular circumstance. One of Gutmann's key informants, the elderly Don Timo, rails against effeminate men but has himself crossed stereotypical gender boundaries by actively helping to raise his children. Two other informants, Tono and Gabriel, who are tough young men, argue about a father's proper role in buying children's Christmas presents. These examples illustrate the fluidity of male identity in the population that Gutmann studied.

Ultimately, Guttmann discovered such complex male identities that he found it impossible to use any simple formula to describe a typical Mexican man, a Mexican urban working-class man, or a macho Mexican. Instead he found the men in the community he studied to be working out their roles together with women, debating and deciding about household chores, child rearing, sex, the use of money, work outside the home, and the use of alcohol

(Limon 1997; Parker 1999). How do these processes take place in your own family?

Viewing gender as performance enables us to broaden our thinking beyond easy dichotomies and universal characteristics of "man" and "woman." Of course, stretching the norms of gender performance can pose challenges, because the audience involved may not always accept or tolerate the shifting gender roles. For example, a woman performing unorthodox gender identity may have difficulty being identified with her own gender group. Kath Weston (1991) shows how certain jobs, such as automobile repair, include expectations of masculine gender performance, such as carrying a large tool case, expressing physical strength, and taking risks. The gender performance of women auto mechanics challenges common gender assumptions and may make it hard for other people to view them in the same group as women who choose more typically feminine-gendered employment.

Are men and women born or made? Anthropological research suggests that rather than looking for some essential male or female nature rooted in biology that shapes everything from personality to economic activity, a more fruitful exploration must consider both the ways biology and culture shape one another and the ways in which ideas of gender are constructed and performed in response to each culture's gender norms and expectations. In so doing, gender can be seen less as a naturally limiting framework and more as a set of fluid constructs that can be changed over time. By taking this approach, we can more easily see that stratification based on gender is not fixed and natural; rather, it emerges as a result of decisions to arrange access to power, privilege, and resources in particular ways.

Are There More Than Two Sexes?

As our earlier discussion of sexual dimorphism indicated, primary characteristics of biological sex do not always fit neatly into the two assumed categories of male and female. Moreover, even when we can identify a person's biological sex, we cannot predict what roles that person will play in a given culture. The sections that follow make these points abundantly clear.

Case Study: Caster Semenya—Female Athletes and Gender Stereotypes
Caster Semenya (b. 1991) grew up in Masehlong, a rural South African village of subsistence farmers living in small brick houses and mud huts with little running water or electricity. In August 2009, at age eighteen, Semenya surprised the world by winning the gold medal in the 800-meter race at the track and field world championship sponsored by the International Association of

MAP 8.2
South Africa

Athletics Federations (IAAF) in Berlin, Germany. Within days, however, she was stripped of her medal and prize money. She was barred from international competition and plunged into a worldwide controversy and media frenzy.

What happened? Spurred by rumors promoted by sports blogs in South Africa, the Australian track and field association—whose runners Semenya defeated in Germany—filed charges that she was not a woman. These questions were not new. Despite her birth certificate showing the designation "female," as well as Semenya growing up as a girl and identifying herself as a woman, her powerful physique, vocal quality, and running prowess had frequently elicited questions from her competitors. According to her coach, Semenya sometimes addressed these challenges through a joint trip to the women's room with a member of the opposing team. But the IAAF investigation became an international incident. The IAAF subjected Semenya to a series of "gender tests" in which a panel of supposed experts—including a gynecologist, an endocrinologist, and, surprisingly, a psychologist—attempted to determine her sex and her qualifications to run against other women in international competition. But how would they decide if she was a woman?

How would you decide?

Nearly a year later, the IAAF cleared Semenya to compete in international events against women. Her gold medal and prize money were returned to her. The South African government had long since authorized her to compete in

South Africa. The IAAF, however, refused to release the results of its inquiry, citing privacy issues. An unverified report of her gender test that was leaked to the press suggested that Semenya might have a common sex variation—specifically, female external genitalia matched with internal testes. Or perhaps she has a chromosomal variation. Like millions of others, Semenya might be intersex, meaning that biologically she does not fit neatly into the category of male or female (Zirin and Wolf 2010).

Caster Semenya's experience raises important anthropological questions. These include not only how we ultimately distinguish between biological sexes (man and woman) but also how we understand gender—that is, what it means to be a man or a woman in a particular culture. Perhaps the uproar around Caster Semenya tells us even more about our cultural ideas of what men and women are supposed to be like—that is, it underscores the cultural construction of gender.

A Theory of Five Sexes

Biologist Anne Fausto-Sterling (1993) has proposed a theory that sheds light on the issue of fluidity versus rigidity in conceptualizing categories of biological sex and how they relate to gender identity. In her article "The Five Sexes: Why Male and Female Are Not Enough," Fausto-Sterling describes the middle ground between these two absolute categories. This middle ground encompasses a diversity of physical expressions along the continuum between male and female that once were labeled "hermaphrodite" and now are described as **intersex**.

A review of medical data from 1955 to 2000 suggests that "approximately 1.7% of all live births do not conform to [the] ideal of absolute sex chromosome, gonadal, genital and hormonal dimorphism" (Blackless et al. 2000, 151). Using these statistics, we may estimate that millions of people are born with some combination of male and female genitalia, gonads, and chromosomes. Some have a balance of female and male sexual characteristics—for instance, one testis and one ovary. Others have female genitalia but testes rather than ovaries. Still others have male genitalia with ovaries rather than testes.

Most Western societies ignore the existence of middle sexes. More commonly, they legally require a determination between male and female at birth. Furthermore, since the 1960s, Western medicine has taken the extreme steps of attempting to "manage" intersexuality through surgery and hormonal treatments. According to the 2000 American Academy of Pediatrics policy statement on intersex surgery, "the birth of a child with ambiguous genitalia constitutes a social emergency" (American Academy of Pediatrics 2000, 138). Medical procedures—most performed before a child comes of age and can

intersex: The state of being born with a combination of male and female genitalia, gonads, and/or chromosomes.

decide for him- or herself—aim to return intersex infants to the cultural norm for heterosexual males and females, although about 90 percent of the surgeries make ambiguous male anatomy into female. Decisions are often based on the size of the penis: The smaller the phallus, the more likely the surgery will reassign the person as female. These interventions represent what French social scientist Michel Foucault ([1976] 1990) has referred to as *biopower*—the power of the state to regulate the body—in this case through control of biological sex characteristics to meet a cultural need for clear distinctions between the sexes.

These medical interventions have faced increasing criticism both within the medical profession and among advocacy and support groups such as the Intersex Society of North America (www.isna.org), the AIS-DSD support group (www.aisdsd.org) and InterACT: Advocates for Intersex Youth (http://interact advocates.org). Such groups have worked to educate the public and the medical community about the experiences of intersex people, particularly about their right to control decisions about their sexual and gender identities. In 2006, *Pediatrics*, the journal of the American Academy of Pediatrics, published new guidelines that urge practicing greater patient-centered care, avoiding "elective" surgery until the person is old enough to make his or her own decision, and eliminating misleading and outdated language (such as *hermaphrodite*) that distracts from treating the whole person.

The presence of middle sexes suggests that we must reconceptualize one of our most rigid mental maps of reality—the one separating male and female. In the process, perhaps we will recognize that just as gender is culturally constructed, even our ideas of human biology have been culturally constructed as well. Acknowledgment of a diversity of physical expressions along the continuum between male and female may, in turn, allow for a less dualistic and more holistic approach to understanding the complex relationship between biology and gender (Davis 2015).

Alternate Sexes, Alternate Genders

Cross-cultural studies show that not every culture fixes sexuality and gender in two distinct categories. Many cultures allow room for diversity. For example, even though India's dominant system for mapping sex and gender strongly emphasizes two opposite but complementary roles (male and female), Indian culture also recognizes many alternative constructions. Hindu religion acknowledges these variations in myth, art, and ritual. Hindu myths feature androgynous and intersex figures, and Hindu art depicts a blending of sexes and genders, including males with wombs, breasts, or pregnant bellies. In terms of Hindu ritual, the following discussion explores the role of one alternative group, known as *hijras*, in expressing gender diversity in India.

Hindu religious myth, art, and ritual acknowledge alternative gender constructions like this depiction of Ardhanari, an androgynous deity composed of Shiva and his consort Shakti.

transgender: A gender identity or performance that does not fit with cultural norms related to one's assigned sex at birth.

The Role of *Hijras* in Hindu Ritual *Hijras* are religious followers of the Hindu Mother Goddess, Bahuchara Mata, who is often depicted and described as transgender. (The term **transgender** refers to individuals whose gender identities or performances do not fit with cultural norms related to their assigned sex at birth.) Most *hijras* are born as men, though some may be intersex. In *Neither Man nor Woman: The Hijras of India* (1998) and subsequent writing, Serena Nanda has analyzed these individuals and their role in demonstrating gender diversity.

Through ritual initiation and, for some, extensive ritual surgery to remove penis and testicles (an operation now outlawed in India), *hijras* become an alternative sex and gender. Culturally they are viewed as neither man nor woman, although they tend to adopt many characteristics of the woman's role. They dress, walk, and talk like women and may have sex with men. Because of their transgression of cultural and religious boundaries, they are at once both feared and revered. Many live in *hijra* religious communities on the margins of Hindu society. *Hijras* often face extreme discrimination in employment, housing, health, and education. Many support themselves through begging, ritual performances, and sex work. Violence against them is not uncommon, particularly against *hijra* sex workers.

At the same time, *hijras* are revered as auspicious and powerful ritual figures. They perform at weddings and at birth celebrations—particularly at the birth of a son. Not only do they bless the child and family, they also entertain the celebrants and guests with burlesque and sexually suggestive songs, dance, and comedy. Their life in the middle ground between strong cultural norms of male and female contributes to their ritual power (Nanda 1998). These insights underscore the potential for more complex understandings of sex and gender that move beyond assumptions of two discrete categories of male and female, masculine and feminine.

Two-Spirits in Native North American Cultures According to accounts written over the past one hundred years, many Native North American cultures have had traditions of gender diversity. Such traditions have allowed a gender alternative described in the older anthropological literature as *berdache* and now more commonly referred to as Two-Spirits (Roscoe 1991; Williams 1992). Some of these transgender men and women adopted roles and behaviors of the opposite gender. In certain cases, people considered them to have both feminine and masculine spirits. Often they were considered to have supernatural powers and thus held special privileges in the community.

In recent years the term *berdache*, introduced by French colonialists, has fallen into disrepute among scholars and activists. Since 1990 the term *Two-Spirits*, a direct borrowing from the Ojibwa language, has risen in popular and

scholarly usage after being proposed by participants in the Third Native American/First Nations Gay and Lesbian Conference in Winnepeg, Canada. No common term exists across Native cultures for alternative gender patterns, nor are the historical or contemporary practices indicated by these terms by any means uniform. Instead, many different terms have served to represent local expressions of alternative gender and sexuality among Native Americans—for example, *winkte* (Sioux), *kwido* (Tewa), and *nadleeh* (Navajo) (Jacobs 1997).

Current studies of sex and gender diversity in contemporary Native American communities attempt to de-romanticize the accounts offered by earlier anthropologists, historians, and other social scientists of a tolerant Native American life for those who were not heterosexual. These idealized views do not match the experiences of many gay, lesbian, transgender, transsexual, or Two-Spirit Native Americans today who have experienced homophobia rather than acceptance both within and beyond their Native American communities (Jacobs 1997).

Steven Barrios (*left*), a leader of Montana's Two Spirit Society, works to eliminate homophobia among Native Americans. Caitlyn Jenner (*right*), a transgender woman, was a public figure for four decades as Bruce Jenner, Olympic decathlon champion and reality show personality. Her public transition from male-identified to female-identified has brought increased visibility to the often difficult and violent experiences of transgender women and men and other gender noncomforming people in the United States.

How Do Anthropologists Explore the Relationship between Gender and Power?

Although gender may often be regarded as affecting individuals on a personal basis—for instance, how you negotiate relationships with people you date, study with, or work for—anthropologists also explore how gender structures relationships of power that have far-reaching effects. Understanding these processes becomes increasingly important as individuals and cultures experience heightened interaction in today's global age (Mascia-Lees 2009).

In September 2015, the United Nations announced the establishment of its fifteen-year Sustainable Development Goals, including its Goal 5: Achieve Gender Equality and Empower all Women and Girls. Within this goal the signatory nations committed to:

- End all forms of discrimination against women and girls.
- Eliminate violence against all women and girls, including trafficking and sexual and other types of exploitation.
- Eliminate child, early, and forced marriage and female genital mutilation.
- Recognize and value unpaid care and domestic work.
- Ensure equal opportunities for women's leadership at all levels of public decision making.
- Ensure universal access to sexual and reproductive health and reproductive rights.
- Undertake reforms to give women equal rights to economic resources.
- Enhance the use of information and communications technology to empower women.
- Adopt and strengthen policies and legislation for gender equality and empowerment of all women and girls.

A quick look at some statistics reveals the current contours of women's struggles worldwide: Sixty percent of the world's poorest people are women and girls. Over half of all children unable to attend school are girls. The chance of dying because of pregnancy in sub-Saharan Africa is 1 in 196, but in the developed world it is only 1 in 6,250. Young women ages fifteen to twenty-five are being infected with HIV/AIDS three times faster than men in the same age group. Women are disproportionally affected by environmental degradation. And less than 22 percent of the world's parliamentarians are women (United Nations Development Programme 2015). It is not hard to conclude from these facts that gender plays a key role in power relationships on many levels and in many arenas. For a look at one anthropologist's efforts to address women's rights to safe sex and family planning in sub-Sarahan Africa, see the Anthropologists Engage the World feature on Ida Susser (292–293).

Revisiting Early Research on Male Dominance

As gender studies emerged in anthropology in the 1970s, one of the first targets of research was the apparent universality of male dominance across cultures. In searching for an explanation for what appeared to be women's universally low status, anthropologist Sherri Ortner (1974) proposed the existence of a pervasive, symbolic association of women with nature and men with culture (which was more highly valued). Ortner argued that the biological functions of reproduction, breast-feeding, and child rearing associated women with nature and placed them at a consistent disadvantage in negotiating relationships of power.

At the same time, Michelle Rosaldo (1974) saw the gender roles of men and women across cultures as being split between public and private spheres. Women, constrained by their role in reproduction, were confined to the private, or domestic, sphere—including the home, family, and childbearing. Men tended to dominate the public sphere—politics, economic exchange, and religious ritual. Because wealth and social status accrued to activities in the public sphere, men gained and maintained more power, privilege, and prestige than women did. Some scholars speculated that these patterns were rooted in the human evolutionary past—a proposition we will challenge later in this chapter. Others suggested that they might derive from men's superior physical strength (see also Chodorow 1974).

As scholars looked more carefully at women's lives in particular cultures, however, the picture became even more complicated. Previous assumptions about universal male dominance, including the gendered division of labor and uniformly separate spheres of activity and power, were revealed to be historically inaccurate, overly simplistic in their reading of contemporary cultures, and prone to overlook the specific contexts of stratification and inequality (Leacock 1981). This was true not only for women's lives but for men's as well, where wealth, power, and prestige were stratified both within and between gender groups (Quinn 1977; Rosaldo 1980).

Feminist scholars also began to revisit earlier anthropological research. Perhaps not surprisingly, these scholars discovered the significant role of women in cultures that earlier anthropologists had reported to be uniformly dominated by men. In one important reconsideration of a classic anthropological text, Annette Weiner (1976) revisited Bronislaw Malinowski's research on the Trobriand Islands, an archipelago of coral atolls just east of Papua New Guinea in the South Pacific. Malinowski (1922) had carefully detailed the Trobriand economic system, which included a local exchange of yams and the now famous (in anthropology) Kula Ring, an elaborate exchange of cowry shell necklaces and armbands made as men circulated around the chain of islands. Later anthropological literature drew extensively on Malinowski's ethnographic descriptions of the Trobriand economy and related theories of exchange.

When Weiner reexamined the economic practices of the Trobriand Islands in the 1970s with an eye to the role of gender in shaping economic activity, she found that Malinowski's research was incomplete. In *Women of Value, Men of Renown: New Perspectives in Trobriand Exchange* (1976), Weiner describes the much more complex and significant roles of Trobriand Island women in

MAP 8.3
Trobriand Islands

Ida Susser
Advancing Gender Equality and Health Outcomes

In the age of HIV/AIDS, how can women assert their right to safe sex and family planning? This is the central question of Ida Susser's most recent work in sub-Saharan Africa. Susser is an engaged scholar working alongside communities on matters of gender, health, equality, and well-being. This work requires not only a diverse set of knowledge and skills but also a commitment to building close partnerships with those whom she studies.

From a young age, Susser became aware of social differences. "I was always interested in anthropology because of my background. I was born in South Africa under apartheid, and my parents were forced to leave for political reasons when I was age six. So I lived the life of an exiled immigrant from when I was very little."

As a child in northern England, Susser learned about working-class history. "I think I approached my new neighborhood like an ethnographic experience, including when I went to visit people in their homes.

"At age twelve, my parents took me to India, and I remember vividly the misery and poverty. Then we moved to the United States when I was fifteen. It was terrible having to deal with the social cliques of my American high school!"

Susser attributes her interest in anthropology to these childhood experiences, because they provided a way to understand social difference and inequality.

When Susser enrolled as an undergraduate at Barnard College in New York City in the late 1960s, the world was undergoing massive political upheaval, and college campuses were centers of activism and protest. Later, as a graduate student at Columbia University, "I was involved in the feminist movement, so I knew I wanted to study women's matters. At the time, Richard Nixon was talking about the Silent Majority. Who were the silent working class? Are they silent? What do they say when they're not silent? It was clear to me that the issue of gender was con-nected to labor, women's work. So first I went to the factory. Then I went to the neighborhood to understand how women organized their lives outside the factory."

Susser's research became the core of her first book, *Norman Street* ([1982] 2012), a classic ethnography of urban life in Brooklyn amid enormous social change. "I picked a white working-class population because the popular image was that they were patriarchal, against abortion, against welfare, against state funding. I wanted to understand where that idea of the white working class came from. This research happened at the time of the fiscal crisis in New York. It was huge. It was as big an event as 9/11.

Anthropologist Ida Susser

It was *the* transforming event. All kinds of services were being cut: food stamps, housing, fire engines, libraries. How could I do this work and not take that into account? So my research focused on how families fight back, how they struggle and address their problems."

Susser's engaged approach to anthropology seeks to help change the world she studies. "When I came to Brooklyn, I made it my job to support women in welfare and in organizing demonstrations, to support people raising funds, to stand up for people at City Hall. I never thought of myself as a fly on the wall. Anthropology teaches us that you learn about people by participating in their lives."

Susser advises: "The task of the researcher is to document a problem and then place the issues within a broader theoretical framework. As a citizen of the world and a public intellectual, you see a problem and document. You use your disciplinary training to think through how social movements work and how they can achieve social transformation. How do you understand that on the ground? Then analyze the processes that may or may not have led to significant social changes!

"Of course, I do not believe in limiting the research to the grassroots local level. The analysis of the broader political situation requires interviews at City Hall and with corporate leaders as well as with the members of the working-class community."

In post-apartheid South Africa around 1992, Susser became interested in the gender dynamics of community-based programs for HIV prevention. She found that no one was studying the relations of men and women in terms of HIV/AIDS. "We had a training program called Social Con-

texts of AIDS in 1996 in Namibia with Richard Lee and faculty at the University of Namibia, funded through a Fogarty Grant from Columbia University. We trained people to do fieldwork, to understand AIDS in context, to understand prevention, to address the question of stigma. We would observe and discuss how these issues are being addressed in Africa, what policies are in place. We worked with nursing faculty, pastors, and army personnel, and now they are running the show, doing their own research."

More recently, Susser helped to found Athena, a global network of individuals and organizations working to address the links among gender equity, human rights, and HIV/AIDS. Key to this work has been the development and distribution of a microbicide developed to protect women from contracting HIV. "Why is a microbicide so important for the gendered treatment of HIV/AIDS? The gel kills the virus but not the sperm, so women can still have children. People can still create families. One of the biggest disasters of AIDS is that it destroys the family, it destroys human relations." It is this careful analysis of the relationship of culture to health and particularly the gendered treatment of HIV/AIDS that Susser is helping to innovate.

As an engaged anthropologist, Susser uses her skills and training to bridge the gulf between the scientific community and local communities affected by HIV/AIDS. She works to analyze the social and political contexts in which people can bring about effective social change. And she works to ensure that new health and reproductive technologies fit with the desires and goals of local women and that young women have control over their reproductive lives and health.

> *I never thought of myself as a fly on the wall. Anthropology teaches us that you learn about people by participating in their lives.*

In contrast to Malinowski's earlier study (1922), why did feminist anthropologist Annette Weiner's research (1976) find Trobriand Island women engaged in significant economic activity, including the elaborate exchange of banana leaf bundles and banana fiber skirts (*left*), as well as participation in the yam harvest festival (*right*)?

economic exchange, kinship, and ritual life. Women engaged in an elaborate economic activity involving the exchange of bundles of banana leaves and banana fiber skirts as gifts made by women for other women in commemoration of individuals who had died. These exchanges were closely interconnected with the yam exchanges that Malinowski had described, but his failure to see the significance of the women's activity engendered an inaccurate view of them as inconsequential to Trobriand economic life.

The emerging anthropological scholarship of gender in the 1970s provided new tools for Weiner to overcome gender blindness and, instead, see the fullness of Trobriand culture. She wrote:

> Any study that does not include the role of women—as seen by women—as part of the way the society is structured remains only a partial study of that society. Whether women are publicly valued or privately secluded, whether they control politics, a range of economic commodities, or merely magic spells, they function within that society, not as objects, but as individuals with some measure of control. (Weiner 1976, 228)

Weiner's example and admonition resonate throughout anthropology today. Attention to the processes and implications of the construction of gender has become standard for all ethnographic research. Today analysis of gender is not isolated to studies of women but occurs throughout the discipline in studies of both women and men. Furthermore, contemporary anthropological research acknowledges that gender cannot be viewed on its own but must be examined as it intersects with dynamics of race, class, and sexuality (Di Leonardo 1991; Moore 2011; Mullings 2005b; Sacks 1989; Stoler 2010). This textbook reflects such an integration, including a full chapter on gender while incorporating attention to gender in all other chapters as well.

Gender Stereotypes, Gender Ideology, and Gender Stratification

The emphasis in gender studies on the cultural construction of gender challenges anthropologists to explore the dynamics of specific cultures to understand what processes serve to construct gender in each society. Today anthropologists are asking questions like these: What are the processes that create **gender stratification**—an unequal distribution of power in which gender shapes who has access to a group's resources, opportunities, rights, and privileges? What are the gender stereotypes and gender ideologies that support a gendered system of power (Brodkin 2007)?

Gender stereotypes are widely held and powerful, preconceived notions about the attributes of, differences between, and proper roles for women and men in a culture. Men, for instance, may be stereotyped as more aggressive, whereas women might be seen as more nurturing. These stereotypes create important assumptions about what men and women might expect from one another. **Gender ideology** is a set of cultural ideas—usually stereotypical—about men's and women's essential character, capabilities, and value that consciously or unconsciously promote and justify gender stratification. Gender stereotypes and ideologies vary from culture to culture, though their effects may appear similar when viewed through a global lens.

We now consider two examples of the ways in which gender ideologies have influenced thinking in U.S. culture.

The Egg and the Sperm Emily Martin (1991) has explored the ways in which cultural ideas about gender—that is, gender ideologies—have influenced the way biologists have understood, described, and taught about human reproduction. In particular, Martin discusses what she calls the fairy tale of the egg and the sperm. By examining the most widely used college biology textbooks at the time of her research, Martin found that the distinct roles of eggs and sperm were described in stereotypical ways, even if those descriptions did not match up with more recent scientific findings. The sperm was frequently described as the more active of the two:

> Take the egg and sperm. It is remarkable how "femininely" the egg behaves and how "masculinely" the sperm. The egg is seen as

gender stratification: An unequal distribution of power in which gender shapes who has access to a group's resources, opportunities, rights, and privileges.

gender stereotypes: Widely held preconceived notions about the attributes of, differences between, and proper roles for men and women in a culture.

gender ideology: A set of cultural ideas, usually stereotypical, about the essential character of different genders that functions to promote and justify gender stratification.

large and passive. It does not move or journey, but passively "is transported," "is swept," or even "drifts" along the fallopian tube. In utter contrast, sperm are small, "streamlined," and invariably active. They "deliver" their genes to the egg, "activate the developmental program of the egg," and have a "velocity" that is often remarked upon. Their tails are "strong" and efficiently powered. Together with the forces of ejaculation, they can "propel the semen into the deepest recesses of the vagina." For this they need "energy," "fuel," so that with a "whiplashlike motion and strong lurches" they can "burrow through the egg coat" and "penetrate" it. (Martin 1991, 489)

As this excerpt illustrates, the textbooks that Martin studied described the aggressive sperm as being propelled by strongly beating tails searching for the egg in competition with fellow ejaculates attacking and penetrating the protective barriers of the egg to fertilize the passive, waiting, receiving egg.

Yet Martin cites biology research that reveals a very different dynamic. The tail of the sperm actually beats quite weakly and does not propel the sperm forward. Instead the tail serves only to move the head from side to side enough to keep it from getting stuck on all surfaces except the egg. When the egg and the sperm do connect, the sperm is not the assertive aggressor. Rather, adhesive molecules on both create a chemical bond that keeps them attached. Then the sperm and egg work in tandem. The sperm secretes a dissolving fluid that allows it to move toward the egg's nucleus. At the same time, the egg draws the sperm in and actually moves its own nucleus to meet the sperm and better enable fertilization. Thus, rather than displaying active and passive roles, the egg and the sperm appear to be mutually active partners in an egalitarian relationship.

According to Martin, writing in the early 1990s, images of the egg and sperm found in popular and scientific writing have been commonly based on cultural stereotypes of male and female. Moreover, the scientific language of biology has promoted these gender stereotypes. Men are considered more active, vigorous, adventurous, and important than women, who are seen as passive, receptive, nurturing, and less valuable and significant. Martin warns that by reading stereotypical feminine and masculine behavior into our accounts of eggs and sperm, we enshrine these gender roles in nature—we make them seem natural. In turn, when this narrative becomes a common description of nature, it reinforces culturally constructed gender patterns, roles, and hierarchies. It is possible to express the effect of such a process of misinformation in this (mistaken) way: "Of course those characteristics of men and women are natural and normal—they show up at the very beginning with the behavior of the sperm and the egg!"

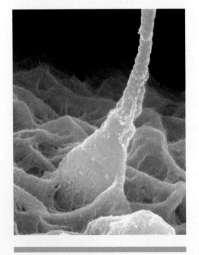

Are the stories you have been told about the meeting of the sperm (blue) and egg drawn from biological research or cultural gender stereotypes?

Martin also warns of the social risks of attributing human personalities to eggs and sperm—for instance, describing them like a human couple engaged in deliberate human activity to make a baby. U.S. culture continues to debate when "life" begins—at fertilization, at viability, or at birth. Describing the egg and sperm as engaged in intentional action—a key criterion for personhood—risks opening the door to more scrutiny of pregnant women and restriction of their health choices, from amniocentesis to abortion to fetal surgeries.

Man the Hunter, Woman the Gatherer Another familiar story that lies at the heart of U.S. gender ideologies is the tale of Man the Hunter, Woman the Gatherer. This fiction is frequently invoked to explain contemporary differences in gender roles by referencing the effects of human evolution. In our deep past, the story goes, human males—being larger and stronger than females—hunted to sustain themselves, their sexual partners, and their offspring (Lee and Devore 1968). Hunting required aggression, inventiveness, dominant behavior, male bonding, mobility, time away from the home, and less time with offspring—all patterns that we imagine have become hardwired into the human brain or imprinted on the human DNA. The ancient pleasure of killing animals supposedly shaped the human male psyche for aggression and violence and continues to drive men today. Women, in contrast, were gatherers (Dahlberg 1981). They collected fruits, seeds, and nuts and were more sedentary, home oriented, child centered, nurturing, cooperative, talkative, and passive.

This story, closely associated today with the field of evolutionary psychology, underlies much contemporary thinking about the origins and "naturalness" of gender relations. Contemporary gender roles, division of labor, and stratification of power, resources, rights, and privileges are assumed to have emerged directly from physical or mental differences that developed during human evolution. So, for instance, because early human males were hunters two million years ago, today modern human men prefer to go off to work, compete in the marketplace, and leave child rearing and housecleaning to the women. Quite simple, really—or is it?

Despite the popularity of this scenario in explaining contemporary male and female behavior, anthropological evidence does not support it. Yes, food foraging—hunting, scavenging, and gathering—was our ancestors' primary survival strategy for millions of years before the introduction of agriculture 10,000 years ago. Hundreds of thousands of people still live in societies where food foraging is a significant means of making a living. But no contemporary foraging societies or nonhuman primate groups display the division of labor described in the Man the Hunter, Woman the Gatherer story. In known foraging societies, women are not sedentary or passive members of the group (Stange 1997).

Though men appear to have done 70 percent of the hunting, it is not even clear that hunting was the foundational activity of early human groups. In fact, human patterns of group interaction more likely developed through the gathering and sharing of plant and seed resources. Archaeological evidence reveals that early hominid teeth were adapted to an omnivorous diet—most likely of plants, seeds, and meat, depending on what food was available in a particular season or area. Hunting would have contributed to this foundation when available, rather than the reverse. Meat may have been a part of the diet, but there is no conclusive evidence that our earliest human ancestors hunted prey themselves. Just as likely, they scavenged meat left behind by other predators (Fedigan 1986).

Anthropologists find no evidence to prove the existence of historical patterns of male dominance, including the protection of dependent women and children. Instead contemporary food-foraging cultures and the archaeological record on gender roles reveal a highly flexible division of labor that enabled human groups to quickly adapt to changing conditions. In fact, a flexibility of roles rather than a clear division of labor may more properly define the key characteristic of male-female relationships over human evolutionary history. Based on the evidence currently available, Man the Hunter, Woman the Gatherer—much like Martin's description of the fairy tale of the egg and the sperm—appears to be a modern-day cultural myth about gender projected back onto human evolutionary history that serves to imbue contemporary gender patterns with an appearance of inevitability and "naturalness" (Fedigan 1986).

Ancient petroglyphs (rock carvings) discovered in the mountains north of the Saudi Arabian city of Hael appear to depict a hunting party. Were they men, as the hunter-gatherer stereotype would suggest?

Despite the archaeological, physical, and cultural evidence that anthropologists have accumulated to debunk the Man the Hunter, Woman the Gatherer myth, it is still a daunting task to shake free of the popular idea in U.S. culture that men and women have some essential—and essentially different—nature that was shaped in our deep past. The stereotypical "boys will be boys" and "that's just a girl thing" approach to gender differences has become a powerful gender ideology, deeply ingrained in the day-to-day conversations, expectations, relationships, work patterns, pay packages, promotions, and political activities of contemporary life.

Perhaps it is simpler to believe that our genetic blueprint predetermines who we are as men and women. Perhaps this belief in the inevitability of gendered cultural patterns makes us feel better about the gender inequality structured into our cultural practices and institutions. Why try to change what is "inevitable and natural"? But if these cultural ways of thinking about gender mask the essential changeability of gender, then the burden lies more heavily on the individual, the community, and the body politic to challenge patterns of power, privilege, and prestige drawn along gender lines.

Enforcing Gender Roles and Hierarchies through Violence

Normative gender roles, identities, ideologies, and hierarchies are constructed and enforced through family attitudes, peer pressure, and institutional practices in education, media, religion, and the state. But they are also policed through gender violence. The term **gender violence** denotes forms of violence shaped by the gender identities of the people involved.

Globally, gender violence takes many forms. It includes verbal abuse, stalking, harassment, and any form of psychological or physical threat that evokes the fear of violence. Gender violence also includes rape, sex trafficking, dowry death, female infanticide, female genital cutting, and the battering and abuse of intimate partners and family members. (The latter is known in the United States as domestic violence.) In recent years, international attention has turned to gender violence during wartime, particularly sexual violence and the use of rape as a weapon of war. This form of brutality has been used against both women and men (Cahn 2004; Copelon 1995).

Whether occurring on college campuses or in the midst of war, gender violence reveals a destructive interplay between gender and other systems of power, including sexuality, race, ethnicity, and class.

Domestic Violence Domestic violence—sometimes referred to as intimate partner violence—is a widespread problem in U.S. culture. By this we refer to physical, sexual, or psychological harm by a current or former partner or spouse. Statistics reveal that one in three women in the United States will be

gender violence: Forms of violence shaped by the gender identities of the people involved.

abused by an intimate partner in her lifetime. Seventy-six percent of all domestic violence victims are women. Women are most often victimized by someone they know, not by a stranger. Women between the ages of twenty and twenty-four are at the greatest risk of nonfatal intimate partner violence. Intimate partner violence affects people of all ages, races, and classes, including both heterosexual and same-sex partners. (See the National Coalition Against Domestic Violence at www.ncadv.org, and the Domestic Violence Resource Center at www.dvrc-or.org.)

Violence or the threat of violence serves to maintain control over others in a systematic pattern of dominance. Rather than a primordial instinctive action, domestic violence is deeply rooted in cultural patterns of violence that are passed down from generation to generation. Witnessing violence against one's parents is the strongest risk factor in transmitting violent behavior from one generation to another. Studies show that boys who witness domestic violence are twice as likely to abuse their own partners or children as boys who do not witness such activity (Straus and Gelles 1990).

Gender Violence on Campus Gender violence can occur in many contexts. For example, colleges and universities in the United States are not immune to the problems that arise at the intersection of gender, sexuality, and power. A study published by the U.S. Department of Justice reported that "young women at college face a greater risk of rape and other types of sexual assault than women in the general population or in a comparable age group" (Fisher, Cullen, and Turner 2000). In the college study, 90 percent of rapes were committed by someone the victim knew, usually a boyfriend, former boyfriend, coworker, classmate, friend, or acquaintance—a far higher percentage than in the general population. Although unwanted sexual contact and sexual threats may occur at bars, nightclubs, or work, almost all rapes and attempted rapes happen on campus. Almost 60 percent occurred in the victim's residence, 31 percent in other campus living quarters, and 10 percent in fraternities.

The film *Boys Don't Cry* (1999) portrayed the real-life story of Brandon Teena, a transgender man who was beaten, raped, and murdered by his male acquaintances when they discovered that he had female genitalia.

structural gender violence: Gendered societal patterns of unequal access to wealth, power, and basic resources such as food, shelter, and health care that differentially affect women in particular.

Violence against Gay Men and Lesbians Many gay men, lesbians, and bisexual and transgender individuals are targets of homophobia and violence. These types of gender violence, both verbal and physical, may serve as a form of discipline that asserts heterosexual gender norms on those who do not conform (recall the discussion of "fag discourse" earlier in this chapter). Transgender people—those whose gender identities or performance do not fit with cultural norms related to their assigned sex at birth—are particularly vulnerable (Currah, Juang, and Minter 2006).

Structural Gender Violence In addition to interpersonal forms, anthropologists examine **structural gender violence**. This includes inequalities of wealth, power, privilege, and access to cultural resources that are stratified by gender. Poverty, hunger, and poor health affect victims' lives in violent and painful ways. The impact is often stratified along gender lines. These structural forms of gendered violence are largely invisible, rarely discussed, and too often dismissed as almost normal or inevitable (Merry 2008).

Challenging Gender Ideologies and Stratification

Women challenge and resist gender stereotypes, ideologies, inequalities, and violence directly and indirectly through creative local strategies, often building movements from the bottom up. Although lacking the global media attention or global solidarity afforded to international social movements, these local initiatives begin with women's culture-specific experiences (Abu-Lughod 2000). The following example provides a dramatic illustration of women challenging gender ideology, stratification, and violence.

Mothers of "The Disappeared" in El Salvador Between 1977 and 1992, the Central American country of El Salvador was torn by a brutal civil war. Threatened by calls for economic equality and political openness, the government unleashed military and military-related death squads in a campaign of violence and terror that targeted students, peasants, union leaders, and anyone else critical of its policies. All who expressed opposition to government policies were labeled subversive and subject to reprisal.

MAP 8.4
El Salvador

Over the course of the civil war the military assassinated, imprisoned, tortured, raped, and "disappeared" tens of thousands of El Salvadorans. One in every one hundred was murdered or disappeared. The late 1970s were marked by particularly brutal campaigns. Every morning, residents of the capital city awoke to the sight of dead bodies—visibly tortured—left lying in the streets or dumped on the outskirts of town by the death squads. Many were disappeared—that is, detained and never seen again.

The grassroots women's organization CO-MADRES (The Committee of Mothers and Relatives of Political Prisoners, Disappeared, and Assassinated of El Salvador) emerged against this backdrop. The committee was one of a number of "motherist" groups across Central America in which the mothers of victims mobilized for human rights and against violence. Originally founded in 1977 by nine mothers, CO-MADRES quickly grew to include teachers, workers, students, lawyers, housewives, and shopkeepers—still mostly mothers, but with a few fathers as well. CO-MADRES became one of the first groups in El Salvador to challenge the brutal actions of the government and the military.

Initially, the women of CO-MADRES focused on demanding information from government, military, and paramilitary groups about family members who had been incarcerated, assassinated, or disappeared. The women occupied government buildings, demonstrated in public parks and plazas, and held hunger strikes to exert pressure on the state. Searching for their missing relatives, they demanded access to prisons and prisoner lists, uncovered clandestine cemeteries, and formed alliances with international human rights groups to publicize the El Salvadoran government's atrocities.

As they became better organized, the women of CO-MADRES began to participate in movements for greater democratization, particularly demanding the inclusion of women at all levels of El Salvador's political decision-making bodies. Eventually, along with other feminist movements emerging globally, CO-MADRES began to address concerns about the prevalence of gender-based violence and rape and the absence of sex education and sexual autonomy for women in El Salvador.

CO-MADRES continued to work throughout the period of the El Salvadoran civil war despite attacks on the organization and its leaders by the government and its allies. CO-MADRES offices were bombed on multiple occasions. A majority of active CO-MADRES members and all of its leaders were detained, tortured, and raped: forty-eight were detained, five assassinated, and three disappeared. In El Salvador, rape became a common experience for the women activists of CO-MADRES and for urban and rural Salvadoran women, whether they participated in a social movement or not.

CO-MADRES activist Alicia Panameno de Garcia, in an interview with anthropologist Lynn Stephen, shared how rape had become a widely used weapon of state-sponsored torture and how psychologically difficult it was to talk about it openly, even with other women victims:

ALICIA: Rape was one of those things we didn't really think about. We weren't really prepared for it happening to us. We didn't think that the military would systematically be using these practices. So the first few women were detained and they were raped and because we are taught that women are supposed to be pure, they didn't talk about that. They didn't say, "They did this to me."

L.S: They didn't talk about it?

ALICIA: Yes. But little by little we discovered it. The women started talking about it. They had to because it had consequences for their health. They needed medical assistance and when we would give people medical aid we started discovering that every one of the women had been raped. (Stephen 1995, 818)

Over time, the CO-MADRES members found that detained men were also being raped as part of their torture. The men were even more reluctant to talk about it than the women.

Eventually, CO-MADRES created a space for women to publicly discuss their experiences, to bring the sexual brutality of the military out into the open, and to talk about their fears—particularly that their husbands would abandon them. Working with other human rights organizations, the group began a process to hold the state accountable for these violations and call into question discriminatory legal codes that provided no rights to rape victims.

The story of CO-MADRES is just one example of the determined, creative, and often risk-filled efforts that women undertake across the globe to address gendered expressions of inequality, stratification, and violence. In an evolving response to their experiences in the midst of El Salvador's civil war, the women of CO-MADRES created a social movement that integrated traditional cultural expressions of femininity—ideas of motherhood, child rearing, and sacrifice for one's children—with direct confrontation of military death squads and government authorities as they demanded equality for women and sought to protect their families and their communities (Martin 1999; Molyneux 1999; Stephen 1995).

How Is Globalization Transforming Gender Roles and Stratification?

Beginning in the 1980s, anthropologists turned their attention to the impact of globalization on women and gender dynamics in local economies. Flexible accumulation—relocation of the production process both through offshoring factories and outsourcing jobs—has spurred increasing migration of women from rural areas to work in urban, coastal, export-oriented factories established by foreign corporations searching for cheap labor, low taxes, and few environmental regulations. As both local and national economies have continued to undergo rapid transitions, these women have had to negotiate between traditional gender expectations and the pressure to engage in wage labor to support themselves and their families (Mills 2003).

Impacts on Women in the Labor Force

Working women in various parts of the globe have experienced similar challenges at the volatile intersection of globalization and local realities (Fernandez-Kelly 1983; Mills 2003; Ong 1987; Safa 1995).

Carla Freeman's *High Tech and High Heels in the Global Economy* (2000) explores the gendered production processes in export factories on the Caribbean island of Barbados. Women work in the *informatics* industry: They do computer data entry of airline tickets and insurance claims, and they key in manuscripts for everything from romance novels to academic journals. Instead of toiling in garment or electronics sweatshops, these women enjoy working in cool, air-conditioned, modern offices. Freeman asks whether the comfortable conditions in the data-processing factories establish an improved position in the global economy for Barbadian women, or whether this new factory formation is simply another expression of women's exploitation through flexible accumulation.

Key distinctions separate the Barbadian informatics workers from those in other studies. They enjoy improved work conditions. As wives, mothers, and heads of households, rather than young, single, temporary sweatshop workers, they have won concessions from the company that include transportation, higher levels of job security, and more flexible work hours to care for their families. Freeman labels these women "pink-collar" workers because they fall between the blue-collar work done on the sweatshop factory floor and the white-collar work carried out in the higher-wage environment of the front office.

Despite the improved working conditions and social status for Barbadian women working in informatics, the company owners strive to extract maximum efficiency from them. Supervisors walk the floor and observe through glass windows to ensure continual surveillance. Managers calculate the keystrokes of each computer terminal. Wages are no higher than those of the typical sweatshop worker and in some cases are lower. The skills of data entry are not transferable to higher-wage clerical work. Women often need to take on additional work sewing, selling in the market, or working in beauty salons to support their families.

MAP 8.5
Barbados

Globalization is reshaping the lives of working women as corporations search the world for cheap labor, low taxes, and fewer environmental restrictions. But are women reshaping globalization? (*clockwise from top left*) Women labor in an automobile factory in Juarez, Mexico; an electronics factory in Penang, Malaysia; an international call center in Barbados; and a pharmaceutical plant in Puerto Rico.

Freeman explores the ways in which the Barbadian women express their agency in the face of the informatics factory controls. These women use their status working with computers in air-conditioned offices to negotiate a different class status in the local community. They use clothing to fashion their local identities as well. Indeed, the women workers are preoccupied with fashion: They wear colorful, tailored skirt-suits with jewelry, high heels, and the latest hairstyles. With their clothes, these women perform a professional and modern gender identity that enhances their local reputations and distinguishes them from other low-wage workers in garment and textile factories.

Freeman's research adds to scholarly findings that women factory workers are not simply victims of the exploitative practices of flexible accumulation. Instead, by engaging these capitalist practices directly, women assert their own desires and goals in ways that transform the interaction between the local and the global (England 2002; Richman 2001).

Gendered Patterns of Global Migration

Globalization spurs the migration of women seeking to support themselves and their families, moving as never before within and between countries in a largely invisible flow. Tens of millions of women each year leave their homes and travel to urban areas to seek jobs in cities and export-processing factories in their own countries. Millions more leave developing countries in search of work abroad to support their families back home.

As an alternative to finding jobs in export-processing factories, many women immigrants work as nannies, cleaning ladies, maids, or home health aides in North America, Europe, Asia, and the Middle East. In so doing, they fill the shortage of what is known as "care work" in wealthier countries. This "global care chain" makes caregiving an international occupation in which the capacity of the world's poor—especially the world's poor women—to care is imported from the developing world to fill the expanding care deficit of the wealthy (Ehrenreich and Hochschild 2004). Without these immigrant care workers, many other women would be unable to go to work themselves (Hondagneu-Sotelo 2001).

Pei-chia Lan's (2006) study of Filipino and Indonesian care workers laboring for newly rich families in Taiwan reveals the ways women—both employers and workers, madams and maids—create new flows of global migration that destabilize traditional gendered and patriarchal roles in surprising ways.

As Taiwan's economy has expanded, first-generation Taiwanese career women, many from newly middle-class, dual-income families, have opted to meet their traditional filial and patriarchal family obligations as mother, wife, and daughter-in-law by hiring transnational migrant women domestic workers to do what was expected of their mothers in previous generations. Consuming transnational domestic labor—specifically the care work of Filipino and Indonesian women—allows them to move into the male workforce while still satisfying traditional expectations of womanhood.

In contrast, Filipino and Indonesian women convert their transnational migration and domestic labor into remittances that provide the major source of support for families at home. In the process, they assert new status roles as primary breadwinner, though their absence—often for years at a time—severely limits their ability to fulfill more traditional roles of mother, wife, and daughter. Lan calls these immigrant domestic workers "global Cinderellas"—women who dream of escaping poverty and finding freedom through care work abroad, yet whose emancipation is built upon oppression and exploitation within their employer's home. Lan warns that even as these Cinderellas become the primary

MAP 8.6
Taiwan, the Philippines, and Indonesia

national exports of their home countries, their longed-for happy ending is primarily a fairy tale trapped by the unequal power relations central to the transnational flow of care workers.

Barbara Ehrenreich (Ehrenreich and Hochschild 2004) has suggested that the primary resource extracted from the world's poorer nations today is no longer oil, gold, or agricultural products. It is love. But while immigrant women care for the children and elderly of families in relatively wealthy countries, their absence creates a care deficit for their own children and elderly family members. This deficit serves to restructure the patterns of family, kinship, and care in the women's home countries (Chang 1998).

Anthropologists, whether studying gender, sexuality, kinship, race, ethnicity, religion, or any other cultural construct, seek to understand the rich diversity of human bodies and human lives, both past and present, to unlock the presuppositions that reside in mental maps of reality. As we analyze gender, we strive to unmask the structures of power that create unequal opportunities and unequal access to rights and resources along gender lines. These inequalities are far from natural, essential aspects of human life and human community. Rather, they are cultural constructs established in specific historical moments and cultural contexts. Through a careful analysis and exposure of gender as a culturally constructed system of power—not fixed and natural patterns of human relationship—anthropologists hope to participate in opening possibilities for all humans to live to their full potential.

Thinking Like an Anthropologist: Broadening Your View of the Cultural Construction of Gender

In the chapter opener, we considered the intersection of gender and power in the U.S. military reflected in the experience of Captain Kristen Griest and Lieutenant Shaye Haver, the first women to complete the United States Army Ranger School. Their story illuminates larger dynamics at work throughout the U.S. military and other cultural institutions as expectations of the roles of men and women, the performances of femininity and masculinity, and stratification along the lines of gender undergo dramatic shifts and changes. The December 2015 opening of combat roles to women did not resolve these tensions in the military. Despite dramatic increases in the number of women serving in the U.S. military and the opening of most military jobs to women, over the past few years the military has been engulfed in a major scandal at the intersection of gender and power. According to a 2014 study by the Rand Corporation, commissioned by the U.S. military, as many as 5 percent of active-duty women have been sexually assaulted, as have 1 percent of men. The study also found that women soldiers are so reluctant to report these crimes that only 25 percent of these cases come to light and 62 percent of women who do report sexual assaults say they face retaliation within their units for doing so. Others assume that the military justice system, in which commanding officers, primarily men, decide whether cases should go to a court-martial, will not treat them fairly. Eventually, the report found, 90 percent of assault victims are involuntarily discharged.

Why is this kind of gender-based violence so prevalent in the U.S. military or anywhere in U.S. culture? What are the underlying assumptions about gender—what it means to be a man or woman, boy or girl, masculine or feminine—that lead to power being exercised in these destructive ways? And why does such a powerful institution allow it to continue?

As you reflect on these issues, consider how the big questions that have organized this chapter may help you analyze the situation more deeply:

- Are men and women born or made?
- Are there more than two sexes?
- How do anthropologists explore the relationship between gender and power?
- How is globalization transforming gender roles and stratification?

Anthropologists consider gender to be a central element in every aspect of human culture, including education, the workplace, sexuality, health, family, religion, politics, sports, and individual identity formation. Throughout this chapter we have explored how anthropologists examine the complex role of gender in crucial contemporary debates, social movements, and political struggles around the world.

Having read this chapter, are you able to take a fresh look at gender in your own life? Perhaps you can begin to see how unique cultural expectations of femininity and masculinity have shaped your ways of thinking and behaving—your interactions with family, friends, romantic interests, classmates, and coworkers. Perhaps you can see how culturally constructed notions of gender have been replicated in patterns of inequality in cultural institutions ranging from education to the workplace. And perhaps you can imagine how stereotypes and gender ideologies like the sperm and the egg or Man the Hunter, Women the Gatherer provide the rationale for maintaining patterns of inequality and stratification. Try to go through the next week with these tools in your anthropological toolkit and see how your view of the world, particularly the gendered world, might be transformed.

Key Terms

For Further Exploration

Brault, Brigitte, and the Aina Women's Filming Group. 2003. *Afghanistan Unveiled*. Women Make Movies. After the fall of the Taliban, young women document the experiences of women in Afghanistan.

Calling the Ghosts: A Story about Rape, War and Women. 1996. Directed by Mandy Jacobson and Karmen Jelincic. Bowery Productions. Jacobson and Jelincic document the experiences of women in Bosnia-Herzegovina and Croatia.

The Codes of Gender. 2009. Directed by Sut Jhally. Media Education Foundation. Jhally uncovers how contemporary advertising shapes masculine and feminine displays and poses in American popular culture.

Davis, Georgiann. 2015. *Contesting Intersex: The Dubious Diagnosis*. New York: NYU Press.

Disappearing World TV series. 1990. "The Trobriand Islanders of Papua New Guinea." Directed by David Watson; consulting anthropologist, Annette Weiner. Granada Television International.

Ehrenreich, Barbara, and Arlie Russell Hochschild, eds. 2004. *Global Woman: Nannies, Maids, and Sex Workers in the New Economy*. New York: Holt Paperbacks.

Hondagneu-Sotelo, Pierette. 2001. *Domestica: Immigrant Workers Cleaning and Caring in the Shadows of Affluence*. Berkeley: University of California Press.

InterACT: Advocates for Intersex Youth. http://interactadvocates.org

Intersex Society of North America. 2013. www.isna.org

Killermann, Sam. *Understanding the Complexities of Gender*. Comedian and Social Justice Advocate Killermann discusses gender identity and performance. TedxUofIChicago. https://www.youtube.com/watch?v=NRcPXtqdKjE

"Pointlessly Gendered Products". http://pointlessly genderedproducts.tumblr.com/ and https://www.pinterest.com/socimages/pointlessly-gendered-products/. These two blogs collect user-submitted photos of unnecessarily gendered products and advertising.

The Middle Sexes: Redefining He and She. 2006. HBO Undercover Video.

Transparent. Television series produced by Amazon about a family whose father transitions to a transgender woman.

United Nations Development Program, Sustainable Development Goals, Goal 5: Gender http://www.undp.org/content/undp/en/home/sdgoverview/post-2015-development-agenda/goal-5.html

Emma Sulkowicz, a Columbia
University student, carried a
mattress across campus for
nine months to protest the

CHAPTER 9
Sexuality

At Columbia University's graduation ceremony in May 2015, Emma Sulkowicz lugged a 50-pound, dark blue, extra-long twin mattress across the platform to receive her diploma. Carrying the mattress—the kind Columbia uses in its dorms—was the final act of a nine-month-long senior project for her visual arts degree called "Carry That Weight," designed to protest the university's refusal to expel the male student she accused of raping her in her dorm room. She carried the mattress with her wherever she went on campus all year. By her own rules she was not allowed to ask for help carrying it, though she was allowed to accept help when offered. The *New York Times* art critic Roberta Smith (2014) described the performance as "a woman with a mattress, refusing to keep her violation private, carrying with her a stark reminder of where it took place."

Following Sulkowicz's lead, in October 2014 Columbia students carried twenty-eight mattresses onto campus, one for each of the plaintiffs who had filed a federal Title IX complaint alleging that the university discouraged students from reporting sexual assault, that sanctions were too lenient, and that perpetrators were not removed from campus, leaving survivors to encounter their attackers in dormitories and classrooms. The students were fined $471 to clean up the mattresses left outside the president's home. By November, a group called Carry That Weight organized a national day of action during which students carried mattresses on 130 campuses, joining an increasingly effective anti-rape movement that is working to shatter the silence about widespread sexual assaults and demand that colleges and universities provide safe campus environments.

Surveys reveal that as many as one in five women will experience some form of assault while a college student (Fisher, Daigle, and Cullen 2010;

Sanday 1990). In response, college administrations are scrambling to address the crisis, under mandate by Title IX of the Education Amendments of 1972 to ensure gender equality in federally funded institutions. In September 2014 the University of California instituted an affirmative consent policy for sexual encounters between students on all of its campuses. Such policies, originally pioneered by Antioch College in Ohio in the early 1990s, require more explicit communication between sexual partners, including a clear "yes" at every step of the encounter. This shift in the standards of consent from "no means no" to "only yes means yes" has now been adopted at over 1,400 institutions of higher education in the United States, reflecting a growing effort to bring the resources of educational institutions to bear on the troubled intersection of sexuality and power in American culture.

What are your own experiences of the intersection of sexuality and power? Have you heard stories like Emma Sulkowicz's on your own college campus? Sexuality is a profound aspect of human life, one that stirs intense emotions, deep anxieties, and rigorous debate. The U.S. population holds widely varying views of where sexuality originates, what constitutes appropriate expressions of sexuality, and what its fundamental purpose is. It is fair to say that our cultural norms and mental maps of reality are in great flux, and have been for several generations, in response to theological shifts, medical advances, and powerful social movements promoting the equality of women and gay, lesbian, bisexual, and transgender individuals.

Sexuality involves more than personal choices about who our sexual partners are and what we do with them. It is also a cultural arena within which our desires are expressed, socialized and even thwarted. And it is an arena in which people debate ideas of what is moral, appropriate, and "natural" and use those ideas to create unequal access to society's power, privileges, and resources. Indeed, conflicts about sexuality often reveal the intersections of multiple systems of power, including those based on gender, religion, race, class, and kinship.

Anthropologists have a long but uneven history of studying human sexuality. Bronislaw Malinowski (1927, 1929) and Margaret Mead (1928, 1935), like other early anthropologists writing in the 1920s and 1930s, considered human sexuality a key to understanding the cultures they studied, so they wrote extensively about their research findings of human sexuality across cultures. Mead's work with young people in the islands of the western Pacific challenged the assumption that U.S. attitudes about gender roles and expressions of sexuality were universal traits immutably fixed in human nature. Rather, anthropological research began to reveal the vast scope and diversity of human sexuality across time and space and the broad arc of potential human sexual expression. After World War II, however, anthropological interest turned away from explicit attention to sexuality and focused instead on related issues of marriage, kinship, and the family. Since the mid-1980s, sexuality has reemerged as a key concern in anthropology, paralleling a rise of interest in the wider academic community spurred by the successes of the U.S. women's movement and the emergence of gay and lesbian studies in the 1980s (Weston 1993) and queer theory in the 1990s (Boellstorff 2007, Boellstorff and Howe 2015; Weiss 2011). Recently, anthropological scholarship has more intently considered the diverse expressions of sexuality in cultures worldwide, including Western cultures and the ways those expressions are being shaped by the intersection of local practices and globalization.

In this chapter we will examine the extensive body of work that anthropologists have compiled primarily in this latter period. In particular, we will consider the following questions:

- What is sexuality and where does it come from?
- What is the scope of human sexuality when seen in a global perspective?
- How has sexuality been constructed in the United States?
- How is sexuality an arena for working out relations of power?
- How does globalization influence local expressions of sexuality?

Sexuality is all around us in U.S. culture. Here, a Calvin Klein billboard uses sexuality to sell underwear. Where have you encountered sexuality today?

Despite all the sexuality in the air, especially in the media, Americans often struggle to find a common language with which to discuss it (whether in their personal lives, their families, their communities, the political arena, or the classroom) and often lack the theoretical and analytical frameworks to add depth to emotionally heated conversations. By the end of this chapter you should have a broader understanding of the vast diversity of human sexuality across cultures. You should be able to discuss the role of nature and culture in shaping human sexuality. Furthermore, you should be able to recognize how norms of sexuality are created and used to organize the way cultures work. And you should be able to incorporate anthropological insights as you seek to better understand the role of sexuality in your own life and in your relations with others.

What Is Sexuality and Where Does It Come From?

Text three friends and ask them to define sexuality. You will most likely get three very different responses. Perhaps this is not surprising in a culture where sexuality is omnipresent but rarely discussed carefully. In 1998, U.S. president Bill Clinton famously said of his liaison with White House intern Monica Lewinsky, "I did not have sexual relations with that woman." He chose those words presumably because he and Lewinsky had not had intercourse. But did they have sex? Such careful word choice by a sitting president giving testimony under oath reveals the challenges of defining behavior that is not only a physiological process but also a cultural construction whose meaning can vary widely.

Consider the following data. A survey of college students in a large midwestern university, with results published in 2006, asked: "Would you say you 'had sex' with someone if the most intimate behavior you engaged in was . . . ?" The survey results showed that even college students do not agree about what "having sex" means. Kissing (2 percent) and petting (3 percent) clearly did not constitute having sex for almost all respondents. Oral "sex" (40 percent) constituted sex for many but not most. For 20 percent of respondents, anal penetration did not constitute having sex. Fully 99.5 percent of respondents indicated that vaginal intercourse did constitute having sex (Sanders and Reinisch 2006). As this study makes evident, even within one population group—college students at one university—there is disagreement over the meaning of the most physical aspects of sexual relations.

For the purposes of this chapter, we will define sexuality from two key perspectives. First, **sexuality** is the complex range of desires, beliefs, and behaviors that are related to erotic physical contact, intimacy, and pleasure. Second, sexuality is the cultural arena within which people debate ideas of what kinds of physical desires and behaviors are morally right, appropriate, and "natural" and use those ideas to create unequal access to status, power, privileges, and resources.

sexuality: The complex range of desires, beliefs, and behaviors that are related to erotic physical contact and the cultural arena within which people debate about what kinds of physical desires and behaviors are right, appropriate, and natural.

"Birds Do It, Bees Do It": The Intersection of Sexuality and Biology

The famous 1928 Broadway show tune by Cole Porter asserts, "Birds do it, bees do it. Even educated fleas do it. Let's do it, let's fall in love." Is it really that simple? Clearly, biology plays a key role in shaping sexuality, for sexuality includes distinct physiological processes. But how much of human sexuality is shaped by our nature? As we will see, exactly how our genetic inheritance shapes our desires, attractions, identities, practices, and beliefs is quite complicated and subject to heated debate.

People sometimes think that sexuality is the most "natural" thing in the world. After all, every species must reproduce or face extinction, right? Therefore, many assume that the sexual instincts and behaviors of other animals provide an indication of the natural state of human sexuality unencumbered by the overlays of culture.

Yet research reveals that human sexuality is actually a distinct outlier in the animal kingdom. In his article "The Animal with the Weirdest Sex Life" (1997), scientist and author Jared Diamond suggested that human sexuality is completely abnormal by the standards of the world's estimated 8.7 million animal species and 5,400 mammal species. Diamond identified many ways in which humans differ from most other mammals, including the following examples:

- Most other mammals live individually, not in pairs, and meet only to have sex. They do not raise children together, and usually the males do not recognize their offspring or provide paternal care. In contrast, most humans engage in long-term sexual partnerships and often co-parent the couple's joint offspring.
- Most mammals engage in public sex, whereas humans, as a rule, have sex in private.
- Most mammals have sex only when the females of the species ovulate, at which time they advertise their fertility through visual signals, smells, sounds, and other changes in their behavior. Human women, however, may be receptive to sex not only during ovulation but also at other times during their menstrual cycle.
- Humans are one of the few species to have sex face to face.
- Possibly most intriguing, humans, dolphins, and bonobos—a variety of ape—are the only mammals that have sex for fun rather than exclusively for reproduction. In fact, in contemporary U.S. culture, humans seem to do it mostly for fun.

Bonobos, dolphins, and humans are the only mammals that have sex for fun rather than exclusively for procreation.

By the standards of most mammals (including great apes, to whom we are most closely related), we humans are the sexual outliers. Despite the common belief that clues to the essentials of human sex drives and behaviors may be found in "nature," Diamond makes clear that humans have developed a sex life that lies far outside the natural framework of that of our mammal relatives. If other animals' sex lives do not provide clues to the roots of our sexuality, what can human biology tell us about the genetic and hormonal roots of sexual desire and sexual behavior?

One school of thought, which draws heavily on evolutionary psychology, focuses on the ways in which human evolution has created biological drives that are embedded in the genes that shape the human brain and control the body's hormones. These drives work automatically—instinctively—to ensure the reproduction of the species. Human sexuality is thought to rely heavily on the expression of these biological drives.

Physical anthropologist Helen Fisher draws upon many of these ideas to explore the complex biological roots of human sexuality in her book *Why We Love: The Nature and Chemistry of Romantic Love* (2004), particularly the relationship of body chemistry to human sensations of love. Fisher suggests that through evolution humans have developed a set of neurochemicals that drive an "evolutionary trajectory of loving" (93). These neurochemicals guide us through three distinct phases of falling in love: finding the right sexual partner, building a relationship, and forming an emotional attachment that will last long enough to raise a child. First, testosterone—found in both women and men—triggers the sense of excitement, desire, arousal, and craving for sexual gratification that we call "lust." Then our bodies release the stimulant dopamine, and possibly norepinephrine and serotonin, to promote the feelings of romance that develop as relationships deepen. Eventually the hormones oxytocin and vasopressin generate the feelings of calm and security that are associated with a long-term partnership; Fisher calls these feelings "attachment." These phases, she suggests, are built into our biological systems to ensure the reproduction of the human species, and they play key roles in shaping human sexuality.

Genetic science, despite remarkable developments that include the ability to map the human genome (the whole human genetic structure), still has limitations as a predictor of individual human behavior, including sexual behavior. Yes, the frequency of certain behaviors in the human population may suggest an underlying biological component. But it is extremely difficult to directly trace links between specific genes and specific behaviors. So, for instance, despite widespread popular discussion of the topic, geneticists have not been able to identify a "straight" gene or a "gay" gene or any cluster of genes that determines sexual orientation.

Furthermore, we know that genes do not work in isolation from their surroundings. As discussed in Chapter 2, humans are a biocultural species, shaped by the interaction of genes, environment, and culture. Our bodies and minds, which are not fully formed at birth, bear the imprint of this interaction. Beginning in the womb, our genes interact with the nutrients, sounds, emotions, and diseases that surround and infuse us. The exact effects of the interaction of biology, culture, and environment are extremely difficult to measure, and this is particularly true in relationship to complex human sexual desires and behaviors.

Even within the parameters of Fisher's study, we cannot predict a particular man's level of sexual desire for a particular partner by measuring his level of testosterone. Attraction, desire, and even lack of interest are not only biologically driven but also triggered by a vast array of cultural factors—including responses to the potential partner's age, religion, class, race, education, and employment prospects—or previous positive or negative experiences that may shape the body's physiological response to certain stimuli. So, although biology clearly plays a role in human sexuality, exactly how it manifests itself in each individual and how it interacts with the environment and culture is not as clear as many popular descriptions of sexuality suggest.

Sexuality and Culture

A second school of thought, one we will consider in more detail throughout the rest of this chapter, focuses on the ways in which the people, events, and physical and cultural environments around us shape—or construct—our sexual desires and behaviors. These feelings and actions may have roots in human evolution, but they are shaped by our experiences and surroundings. So, for instance, humans are enculturated from birth to channel sexual feelings and desires into

How do people, events, and the cultural environment around us shape our sexual desires and behaviors? (*clockwise from top left*) Advertisements featuring sex and love; (*right*) Plaintiff "Jim" Obergefell speaks on June 26, 2015, after U.S. Supreme Court rules same-sex couples have a constitutional right to marry; (*bottom left*) a sex education class at Kealing Junior High School, Austin, Texas.

a limited number of acceptable expressions. Culture shapes what people think is natural, normal, and even possible. Parents, family, friends, doctors, religious communities, sex education classes, the media, and many other individual and institutional actors all play a role in shaping the way we imagine and express our sexuality and what those expressions mean to others. Thus, culture both guides and limits, encourages and thwarts our sexual desires and imaginations.

Constructionists also trace the ways in which, through culture, human groups arrange the diversity of human sexuality into a limited number of categories that are imagined to be discrete (such as homosexual and heterosexual, gay and straight), thereby masking the actual diversity and fluidity of human expressions of sexuality. Where an individual is assigned within these categories has direct consequences for his or her life chances. The meaning certain sexual desires and behaviors acquire in a particular culture has the potential to affect access to social networks, social benefits, jobs, health care, and other resources and to make people vulnerable to discrimination, marginalization and violence (Harding 1998; Ore 2010).

It is important to note that the perspectives of evolutionary biology and cultural constructionism discussed in this section need not be mutually exclusive. Rather, they reflect different research emphases into the roots and contemporary expressions of human sexuality.

What Is the Scope of Human Sexuality When Seen in a Global Perspective?

A look at human sexuality over time and across cultures reveals significant diversity in (1) how, where, when, and with whom humans have sex, and (2) what certain sexual behaviors mean. This diversity challenges Western culture-bound notions and suggests alternative options for reinterpreting assumed cultural categories of sexuality. The discussions that follow offer examples of alternative constructions of sexuality in Suriname, Nicaragua, and Japan.

Same-Gender "*Mati* Work" in Suriname

In the *Politics of Passion* (2006), cultural anthropologist Gloria Wekker explores the lives of black, working-class Creole women in the port city of Paramaribo, Suriname, a former Dutch colony on the northern coast of South America. Writing about the sexual choices Surinamese women make, Wekker (like Roger Lancaster and Anne Allison in the studies described below) challenges the dominant thinking about sexual identity in Western scholarship and social movements by describing a much more flexible and inclusive approach specific to the local Paramaribo context.

MAP 9.1
Suriname

Wekker's study focuses on *mati*—women who form intimate spiritual, emotional, and sexual relationships with other women. Wekker estimates that three out of four working-class black women in Paramaribo engage in "*mati* work" at some point in their lives, establishing relationships of mutual support, obligation, and responsibility with other women—sometimes living in the same household, sometimes separately, and often sharing in child rearing. In contrast to Western notions of fixed, "either/or" sexual identities, *mati* may engage in sexual relationships with both women and men—sometimes simultaneously, sometimes consecutively. Their relationships with men may center on having children or receiving economic support, but frequently *mati* choose a "visiting" relationship rather than marriage in order to maintain their independence.

Born in Suriname and trained as an anthropologist in the United States and the Netherlands, Wekker also writes about the transfer of *mati* work to the Netherlands. In recent decades, young Surinamese women have emigrated from the former colony to its former colonizer in search of economic opportunities. There, *mati* work has often developed in relationships between young immigrants and older black women of Surinamese parentage who have established Dutch citizenship. Wekker describes these relationships as often fraught with complicated power dynamics involving differential age, class, and citizenship status. Yet she notes that this *mati* work does not parallel European ideas of lesbianism.

Wekker pursues this distinction between conceptualizations of sexuality in Suriname and Europe in greater detail as she develops her analysis of *mati*

Women join a parade in the port city of Paramaribo, Suriname, on the northern coast of South America.

work in Paramaribo. What steps, she asks, must anthropologists take to understand sexual relationships between people of the same gender cross-culturally without distorting what these relationships mean in their actual lives? Wekker argues that Western scholarship mistakenly links all sexual acts between individuals of the same gender to a notion of "homosexual identity"—a permanent, stable, fixed sexual core or essence, whether inborn or learned, that is counterposed to an equally fixed and opposite heterosexual identity. In the Western framework, a person is "either/or." The *mati* of Paramaribo, Wekker argues, approach their sexual choices very differently, regarding sexuality as flexible behavior rather than fixed identity. Their behavior is dynamic, malleable, and inclusive—"both/and"—rather than exclusive.

Wekker urges students of sexuality to not impose Western views about sexuality—what she considers "Western folk knowledge"—on the rest of the world but to understand sexuality in its local reality with the goal of rethinking same-gender behavior in cross-cultural perspective. Rather than thinking of one uniform expression of same-gender sexual behavior, she recommends focusing attention on the variation of people's behaviors. Furthermore, thinking cross-culturally, she argues that research and analysis of same-gender sexuality must recognize that the identical physical sexual acts between same-gendered people may be understood in multiple ways and have vastly different social significance in different cultures and historical periods (Wekker 2006, 1999; Brown 2007; Stone 2007). This point is also taken up by the following study of male sexuality in Nicaragua.

Machismo and Sexuality in Nicaragua

Cultural anthropologist Roger Lancaster explores similar themes in *Life Is Hard: Machismo, Danger, and the Intimacy of Power in Nicaragua* (1994), in which he considers expressions of sexuality in a working-class neighborhood in Managua, Nicaragua, during the 1980s. In particular, he examined the concept of machismo—which can be defined as a strong, sometimes exaggerated performance of masculinity. This concept, which Lancaster sees as central to the Nicaraguan national imagination, shapes relationships not only between men and women but also between men and other men. Machismo creates a strong contrast between aggression and passivity. "Real" men—masculine men—are aggressive. But a real man's macho status is always at risk. Machismo must be constantly performed to retain one's social status.

Lancaster was particularly intrigued by the way machismo affects the sexual relations between men. Generally, in U.S. culture, any man who engages in a same-gender sexual behavior is considered gay. But in the Nicaraguan community that Lancaster studied, only the men who passively receive anal intercourse are pejoratively called *cochon*—"queer, faggot, gay." The *machista*, the

MAP 9.2
Nicaragua

penetrator, is still considered a manly man—an *hombre-hombres*—under the rules of machismo. For it is the *machista*'s role to achieve sexual conquest whenever possible with whoever is available. The active partner acts out machismo, enhancing his status by dominating a weaker person. Among Nicaraguan men, the intersection of sexuality and power creates a culturally constructed system of arbitrary and unequal value for male bodies in which machismo privileges the aggressive, assertive *machista* penetrator over the passive, receptive, penetrated *cochon*.

Lancaster points out that in Nicaragua the same acts that in the United States would be seen to reveal one's "essential" homosexuality—desire for and sexual activity with someone of the same sex—are interpreted differently. In fact, active, aggressive men enhance their masculinity and macho status even if they engage in same-gender sexual activity (Lewin 1995; Perez-Aleman 1994; Rouse 1994).

Sexuality and Pleasure in Corporate Japan

In Tokyo's fashionable Roppongi district, elegant hostess bars attract groups of white-collar "salary men" for evenings of high-priced entertainment organized and paid for by their employers at elite Japanese corporations (who may spend up to 5 percent of company budgets on entertainment). These are not sex clubs. But they are still part of the commercialized sex industry—only selling the idea of sex, not physical sex. In her ethnography *Nightwork: Sexuality, Pleasure, and Corporate Masculinity in a Tokyo Hostess Club* (1994), anthropologist Anne Allison draws on four months of fieldwork in one club to explore the relationship between sexuality, masculinity, and Japan's capitalist corporate culture. At the clubs, hostesses serve as the focal point of the party. They pour drinks, light cigarettes, flatter, and banter to enhance the clients' pleasure. Discussion of the hostess is also a central feature of the party, as men engage in sexual banter and innuendo about her personal and physical attributes, especially her breasts.

Despite the highly charged sexual atmosphere at the club, Allison suggests that corporate trips to hostess clubs are not primarily about sex. Rather, gathering in these spaces, outside the office and outside the home and family life, is about stimulating and channeling these men's sexual desire to strengthen corporate culture and office relationships. All the talk about breasts is not about heterosexuality but about building homosocial relationships with other men. Sexual innuendo transforms women hostesses into sexual objects—a status seemingly all men agree about—and turns men's laughter and banter into a unifying process of male identity construction and bonding. Ideally, difference and discord in the workday can be dissolved into sexual conversation after hours. Allison suggests that in the highly ritualized expression of male dominance

MAP 9.3
Tokyo

and male privilege performed in the hostess bars, the service purchased is not the eroticization of the woman but the eroticization of a man. The hostess does not deliver a sex act but through her banter, service and submissive role instead projects an image of the potent and pleasing man who is powerful and desirable. Ultimately this nightwork, whether performed by the hostess or by the men desperately attempting to have fun in an atmosphere of forced camaraderie and pretend sexuality long after the regular work day is over, fosters a particular form of masculinity—corporate masculinity—that serves the interests of contemporary Japanese businesses by channeling men's sexuality and desire into work (Curtis 1996; Davidson 1997; Ogasawara 1995).

The studies in Suriname, Nicaragua, and Japan are representative of the vast array of cross-cultural research that cumulatively has been called the "ethnocartography of human sexuality" (Weston 1993), mapping the global scope of diverse human sexual beliefs and behaviors. This ethnocartography marks a period in the anthropology of sexuality that built on the premises that (1) cross-cultural attention to the practices and beliefs of others can yield a deeper analysis of one's own culture, and (2) awareness of the broad panorama of human life offers opportunities for reexamining what seems normal and natural in one's own cultural practices. After reading about these studies, in what ways are you challenged to rethink your own conceptions of human sexuality?

We turn now to considering the unique construction of human sexuality in the United States.

How Has Sexuality Been Constructed in the United States?

Anthropology strives to make the often unconscious patterns and practices that frame our daily lives conscious so that we can examine them, make clearer assessments about how culture shapes our imaginations, expectations, and opportunities, and consider a more complete range of possible options.

In many of the studies discussed throughout this chapter, we see expressions of sexuality that do not fit the dominant Western model that limits discussion to two categories: **heterosexuality**, or attraction to and sexual relations between individuals of the opposite sex; and **homosexuality**, or attraction to and sexual relations with members of the same sex. At times in Western cultures this heterosexual-homosexual binary may be supplemented by discussions of **bisexuality**, or attraction to and sexual relations with members of both sexes, and **asexuality**, or lack of erotic attraction to others of either sex. But these latter categories are less frequently discussed. As we will see, historical and cross-cultural research suggests that the dual-category system of heterosexuality and homosexuality has a uniquely Western cultural history.

heterosexuality: Attraction to and sexual relations between individuals of the opposite sex.

homosexuality: Attraction to and sexual relations between individuals of the same sex.

bisexuality: Attraction to and sexual relations with members of both sexes.

asexuality: A lack of erotic attraction to others.

The Invention of Heterosexuality

Popular conversations about sexuality in the United States often focus on same-gender sexuality. This may not come as a surprise. As discussed in Chapter 6, contemporary conversations about race tend to center on the experiences of being black, Hispanic, or Asian and avoid discussing being white, even though whiteness is the central racial category around which all others have been organized. Likewise, in popular discussions and academic studies of sexuality, talk of different-gender eroticism (heterosexuality) is often overwhelmed by discussions of same-gender eroticism (homosexuality). This emphasis has left heterosexuality largely forgotten and unmarked. In recent years, the anthropology of sexuality has worked to shift scholarly attention to focus on the norm (heterosexuality) and the process by which the particular expression of heterosexuality prevalent in U.S. culture today became the norm (D'Emilio and Freedman 1998).

Historian Jonathan Katz (2007) argues that heterosexuality as it is practiced and understood in contemporary U.S. culture is a fairly recent invention. The respected *Oxford English Dictionary Supplement* lists the first U.S. usage of the term in 1892. Because words provide clues to cultural concepts, Katz suggests that the lack of earlier citations in popular or scientific venues in the United States indicates that heterosexuality had not achieved widespread cultural currency in the nineteenth century.

Does this mean that women and men in the United States were not engaging in opposite-gender sexual activity prior to the invention of this word? Katz suggests instead that heterosexuality as we think of it is not the same as reproductive intercourse between a man and a woman. Instead what we call "heterosexuality" today is a particular arrangement between the sexes that although not excluding reproductive intercourse, also involves ideas about the practice and purpose of sex that have not always been socially authorized. So, for instance, the early references to heterosexuality often referred to it as a perversion of the natural order because of its association with sex for pleasure rather than for procreation. The nineteenth-century Victorian ideal of sexuality, heavily influenced by Christian teachings, considered sex to be for procreation alone. Sex for pleasure represented a danger to the purposes of God. Masturbation—clearly nonprocreative—was considered a life-threatening, depleting form of self-abuse.

Only in 1892 did the translation of German psychiatrist Richard von Krafft-Ebing's influential work *Psychopathia Sexualis* first introduce to the U.S. scene the modern sense of "heterosexuality" as erotic feelings for the opposite sex and "homosexuality" as erotic feelings for the same sex. This marked a significant shift in the scientific community, supported by a growing number of medical doctors, toward the new idea of sexuality for pleasure rather than exclusively for

Studies by sexologist Dr. Alfred C. Kinsey (*right*), pictured with his research staff in 1953, challenged common assumptions about U.S. sexual practices.

procreation. The rapidly expanding number of newspapers, books, plays, films, restaurants, bars, and baths associated with the rising consumer culture in the early twentieth century reinforced the gradual shift toward the sex-for-pleasure concept.

Sexology A scientific study of sexuality, called *sexology*, began to emerge in the United States in the late nineteenth century. These studies played a central role in the establishment of heterosexuality as the dominant erotic ideal and in the gradual process of dividing the U.S. population into distinct heterosexual and homosexual groups. In the twentieth century, studies led by Alfred Kinsey, Shere Hite, and William Masters and Virginia Johnson used interviews, questionnaires, observation, and participation to explore the sexual lives of thousands of primarily white U.S. residents. Their studies produced surprising results. Kinsey and later sexologists found that human sexuality did not fit into simplistic categories. Same-gendered attraction, fantasies, and experiences were much more common than previously thought. Furthermore, sexual behaviors could shift over the course of a lifetime, spanning both heterosexual and homosexual activity. Rather than finding a sharp dichotomy between heterosexuality and homosexuality, research revealed diversity, flexibility, and fluidity, along a continuum of sexual behavior (Hubbard 1990).

Despite their arguments for the recognition of diversity and fluidity in human sexual behavior, sexology studies contributed to the establishment of heterosexuality as the dominant erotic ideal in U.S. culture and reinforced the emerging popular and scientific consensus that because it was the sex most people were having, heterosexuality was the functional norm for human sexuality (Hubbard 1990; Katz 2007).

Over the course of a century, heterosexuality gradually came to be seen as the norm—the presumed "natural" state—against which to judge all other expressions of sexuality. Today cultural notions of sexuality are in flux, yet a particular version of heterosexuality continues to be constructed and contested.

Within this context, we now consider the role of weddings in shaping contemporary conceptions of human sexuality in the United States.

"White Weddings"

White Weddings: Romancing Heterosexuality in Popular Culture (2008), a study by sociologist Chrys Ingraham, is not a book about wedding ceremonies. It is about wedding culture and what the author calls the "wedding industry"—the vast network of commercial activities and social institutions that market 2.1 million weddings a year in the United States. The wedding industry and the wedding culture, Ingraham argues, provide insights into how U.S. culture gives meaning to marriage and, in the process, constructs contemporary understandings of heterosexuality.

Constructing Heterosexuality It's hard to turn on the television, log on to the Internet, or check out at the local grocery store without encountering some reminder of U.S. society's fascination with weddings. Bridal magazines, popular tabloids, television shows, and commercials in every medium saturate the culture with images of a spectacle of excess that will, they promise, lead to everyone's fairy-tale ending of "happily ever after." Wedding consultants push wedding announcements, bridal showers, wedding halls, floral arrangements, diamond rings, rehearsal dinners, receptions, gifts and favors, caterers, photographers, bands, limousines, and glamorous honeymoons to romantic destinations. Wedding registries orchestrate the delivery of just the right gifts of kitchenware, china, household furnishings, and every appliance imaginable. The average bridal gown (mostly made in third world garment shops by women who will never have a white wedding), including alterations, headpiece, and veil, will cost $1,357 (2014 figures). The average U.S. couple will spend more than $31,213 (in 2014) on their "big day." Altogether, the annual $80 billion wedding industry wields enormous social and economic power.

Ingraham reminds her readers that brides are not born. They are made. Every girl in U.S. culture, almost from birth, is bombarded with cultural symbols and messages about what it will take to have her very own white wedding. Barbie dolls and other toy-industry favorites model the perfect bride, complete with accessories (including Ken?) for the perfect white wedding. Disney movies, feature films, and television shows celebrate weddings as key life moments (and central plot devices) and essential cultural symbols. Every broadcast season features a spate of elaborate made-for-television weddings, especially on shows struggling in the ratings.

From childhood, girls are tutored in preparation for the "you may kiss the bride" moment, learning to apply makeup, wear high heels, send valentines, go on dates, and select a prom dress. Boys learn to buy flowers and corsages, wear tuxedos, pay for dates, lead during the first dance, buy an engagement ring, and initiate sex. But no matter where you think human sexuality originates, it is clear that these behaviors do not occur in nature. They are constructed in culture. The wedding industry and wedding culture—the romantic idealization of the wedding ritual—enculture boys and girls, men and women, about what to do, when, and with whom, in order to lead up to that perfect day. Weddings, Ingraham suggests, and the elaborate rituals that lead up to them over a

What is your idea of a perfect wedding? Here, a woman adjusts a bridal gown at a wedding fair in Bucharest, Romania, where the wedding industry has grown despite an economic crisis.

lifetime, are not only exuberant public celebrations of romantic love. Weddings are also key cultural institutions through which we learn what it means to be heterosexual.

Inequality and Unequal Access What do weddings tell us about the construction of heterosexuality in U.S. culture? Building on recent feminist scholarship, Ingraham suggests that white weddings, and the marriages that result, offer insights into the gendered power dynamics embedded in the normative patterns of heterosexuality that have developed since the late nineteenth century. These power dynamics disadvantage women while being largely obscured by the idealism and romance that U.S. culture wraps around these institutions. Historically, the institution of heterosexual marriage included legal stipulations that effectively made women the economic and sexual property of their husbands. This assumption continues to be ritualized in contemporary U.S. weddings by the father "giving away" the bride to her soon-to-be husband, exchanging the woman between two men.

Today patterns of inequality are not legally sanctioned but still significant. In the home the gendered division of labor means that frequently the woman carries a double workload as a wage earner while simultaneously bearing primary responsibility for domestic work and child rearing. In the workplace, usually still dominated by male leadership, women receive unequal pay for equal work, are promoted less often than men, and are targets of sexual harassment.

Ingraham selected the book title *White Weddings* to highlight the issues of class and race that also are embedded in the workings of the wedding industry and the fairy tale of the wedding ritual. White weddings are not available to all. The women sewing wedding dresses, the young men mining diamonds, and the staff serving dinner on the Caribbean honeymoon island cannot afford a white wedding. Nor does the industry depict a diverse population in its advertising, insinuating that white weddings are primarily for white folks. Actually, most Americans cannot afford the average U.S. wedding; they incur significant debt for the ceremony and the honeymoon to launch their marriage.

Ingraham suggests that the idealized version of weddings and married life—full of love, purity, morality, and affluence—maintains an illusion of well-being in patterns of relationship between men and women that, in reality, may or may not be present. Our romance with this illusion (what the author calls the *heterosexual imaginary*), so heavily promoted by the wedding industry and the institutions of wedding culture, misleadingly encourages us to assume that the patterns of heterosexuality that we have inherited are natural, timeless, and unchanging. In reality, they are culturally constructed, recently invented, and malleable. As such, humans have the ability to make their own choices about the organization of their most intimate relationships, about the way the division of labor will be shaped between men and women: how family responsibilities are shared, gender roles assigned, and economic and cultural resources allocated.

This process of contestation is already under way, with significant cultural implications. Women's increasing economic independence, the necessity for two-career households to support the family, the presence of feminist and gay rights movements, the legal recognition of same-sex marriages, the availability of contraception and abortion, rising divorce rates, and the strengthening of laws against domestic and sexual violence all challenge the heterosexual norms. The cultural renegotiation of socially acceptable patterns of relationship and sexuality leaves very few in the United States untouched (Ingraham 2008; Milkie 2000; Siebel 2000).

Placed in historical perspective and in light of our anthropological perspectives on the fluidity and malleability of human sexuality, perhaps we can view these shifts not as some new and surprising contestation of age-old "natural" patterns of sexuality, but as the most recent rethinking of human sexuality

How are contemporary understandings of sexuality being shaped by the highly symbolic ritual of marriage? Here, a couple exchanges rings at their wedding ceremony.

THE SOCIAL LIFE OF THINGS
Diamonds: Sex, Love, and Status in a Little Rock

How did diamonds—ordinary objects of compressed carbon—become associated with romance, sex, and glamour? Ninety percent of U.S. women own at least one diamond. The United States is the largest diamond market, followed by China and India. Eighty percent of U.S. marriage engagements are sealed with a diamond engagement ring. How do anthropologists make sense of this as we consider cross-cultural expressions of sexuality? Let's consider the social life of diamonds through the work of anthropologist Susan Falls (2014).

① Diamonds flow through a sprawling global production chain managed by a handful of powerful companies like De Beers of South Africa. Diamonds are hard to find, are difficult to mine, and require sophisticated skills to cut and set into rings, but they generate over $72 billion in annual sales. "Blood diamonds" have been implicated in the purchase of weapons used to fuel civil conflicts in developing nations, but most diamonds are produced, circulated, and marketed legally. Their journey illuminates unequal economic relations between people along the commodity chain, including miners, producers, and consumers.

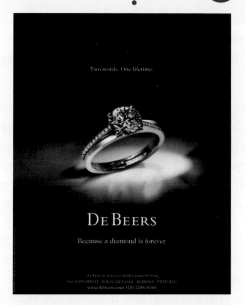

2 In the early twentieth century, De Beers hired an advertising agency to create an American middle-class market for diamonds. Their strategy was to associate diamonds with glamour, wealth, status, love, sex, and romance. Elaborate campaigns placed diamonds into movies, fashion advertisements, and pop culture books and declared that "A Diamond is Forever." Wedding brochures promoted diamond rings, of the right size and price, as an essential element of any engagement.

 3 Marketing firms have not been able to control the cultural interpretation of diamonds. Everyone who has a diamond ring has their own story to go with it. These unique, dramatic, and creative stories, involving romance, desire, family, gender, sexuality, beauty, love, and loss, resist the mass-marketed, mass-produced, and mass-consumed diamond rings. Instead, these personal stories endow rings with deep meaning and value that reflect the complex web of human relationships and experiences that shape local lives in a global age.

We express ourselves and learn about others in many ways, including through material culture, the things we make and use. Diamond rings, with their high symbolic value, provide insights not only into the processes of global capitalism but also into the local processes and creative strategies we use to express individual and local meaning.

- Ask if your family has a diamond. Can you piece together its biography, its social life? Was it a purchase or a gift? What stories are associated with it, and what does it mean to its owner? Do you know where the diamond came from?
- Do you associate diamonds with love, romance, sexuality, luxury, glamour, or status? Would you expect to give one or receive one at your engagement? Why? How do you see a diamond ring intertwined with sexuality?

in U.S. culture. If so, we might then be better prepared to analyze the underlying intersections of sexuality and power in our own personal and political lives.

How Is Sexuality an Arena for Working Out Relations of Power?

As we have noted, sexuality is more than an expression of individual desires and identities. French philosopher and social scientist Michel Foucault (1978) described sexuality as "an especially dense transfer point for relations of power." By this he meant that in every culture, sexuality—like race, ethnicity, class, and gender—is also an arena in which appropriate behavior is defined, relations of power are worked out, and inequality and stratification are created, enforced, and contested.

Indeed, cultural institutions ranging from governments to religious bodies attempt to regulate many aspects of sexuality. These aspects include marriage and divorce; monogamy and polygamy; age of consent; definition of incest; reproductive rights; the rights of gay men, lesbians, bisexuals, and transgender persons; pornography; and prostitution. A consideration of "who is allowed to do what with whom and when" exposes the intersections of sexuality and power in a culture. Attention to intersectionality—the way systems of power interconnect to affect individual lives and group experiences—offers a fundamental shift in the way social scientists study inequality and stratification, including the way we think about sexuality. In this section we consider several case studies that reflect on these intersections historically and in contemporary life, globally and in the United States.

Colonialism and Intersections of Sexuality, Race, Class, and Nation

Cultural anthropologist Ann Stoler explores sexuality as an arena for working out power relations. Her book *Carnal Knowledge and Imperial Power* (2010) is a historical study of the ways sexuality served as a tool for enforcing social boundaries under European colonialism. In particular, Stoler explores the strategies that European colonizers used to control the sexual practices, or carnal knowledge, of people under their rule. By controlling sexuality, colonizers sought to establish clear boundaries of European identity and thereby protect their rights to the profits of colonialism and their privileges as members of what they considered to be the dominant race.

Through extensive historical research on colonial activities from the early 1600s into the twentieth century, Stoler reveals the essential role of intersections of sexuality, race, class, and nationality for understanding the colonial enterprise. Questions of "who bedded and wedded whom" were not left to chance in the colonies of Spain, Portugal, France, England, or Holland. Leading corporations such as the Dutch East India Company painstakingly wrote, clarified, and implemented rules for sexual liaisons and marriage relations. For example, in the two centuries from 1622 to 1822, the Dutch restricted the immigration of European women to Asia. Bachelor European male employees were recruited but then prohibited from marrying women of the colonies. Instead, these male employees were encouraged to live with imported slaves or native concubines—but not to marry. Colonial legislation ensured that these women, along with the children of their liaisons, would have no right to claim citizenship in the colonial homeland or any rights and privileges as spouses or children of colonial subjects.

Later, when restrictions on the immigration of European women were lifted, their domestic, economic, political, and sexual lives in the colonies were restricted in gender-specific ways. Physical and social boundaries between European women and native men were hardened to discourage racial mixing. Colonized men, in particular, were portrayed as a sexual danger to the racial purity of women of the colonial community, despite the nearly total absence of reports of sexual violence by native men against European women.

Who bedded and wedded whom was not left to chance in European colonies. Physical and social boundaries in all areas of life were hardened to discourage racial mixing of colonists with the colonized, as depicted in this photo, circa 1940, of a Dutch colonialist family eating in Java, Indonesia, while a group of Indonesian waiters attend to them.

Sexuality and Power on Campus: Creating a Code of Sexual Conduct

Sexuality is more than an expression of individual desires and identities. It is also a highly contested arena in which appropriate behavior is defined and relations of power are worked out. What are your personal rules for sexual conduct? How do you expect others to treat you in intimate situations? What are your expectations about a healthy intersection of sexuality and power?

All colleges now have sexual offense policies or sexual harassment policies that spell out their expectations for how men and women on campus should behave toward one another. The high incidence of sexual harassment and date rape has forced colleges to become more explicit in expressing their expectations and more proactive in ensuring that all students understand what constitutes appropriate and inappropriate behavior.

Federal legislation has mandated that colleges be much more transparent about conditions on campus and develop avenues for addressing allegations of sexual violence. These policies include guidelines for filing complaints and responding to charges that are brought within the university community.

Consider drafting a code of sexual conduct for your college, either on your own or with classmates. Include clear expectations for behavior, requirements for training

members of the community, and procedures for addressing breaches of the code. In preparation, ask several classmates about their rules for intimate encounters on campus. How explicit are they in negotiating with their sexual partner? 61% of men believe women give consent non-verbally through body language. Only 10% of women say they give consent through body language cues. Have your classmates encountered this difference and how have they addressed it? Do your classmates know the college's protocols for reporting sexual abuse? Do they know about campus resources for victims of sexual assault? What kind of support would they like or expect to receive if they were victims of sexual assault?

In drafting your code of sexual conduct, be sure to consider the many different groups on campus your code would apply to. How would it account for different perspectives shaped by gender, sexual orientation, culture, age, religion, race, or ethnicity? Compare your policy to what your college actually has in place. You will be able to find your college's policy on its website. How do the two differ? Why do you think the areas of similarity and difference arise? If you find your college's policy inadequate, consider strategies you can take as an individual or with others to effect change.

Gender-specific sexual sanctions, especially as they related to race, delineated lines of power between European men and women in the colonial endeavor. Colonial administrators considered this strict control of sexual practices crucial to maintaining distinct communities of Europeans with clear racial and class boundaries.

The colonial boundaries that were intended to distinguish communities of colonizers from their colonial subjects were, in reality, much more complicated, fragile, fractious, and fluid than intended. The children of mixed-race relationships, for instance, posed a challenge to the preferred rules of colonization and threatened to blur the colonial divide. Because all mixed-race children shared some European heritage, decisions about their status as citizens or subjects often hinged on more than their perceived race. Often what mattered most was their parents' class position within the colonial enterprise. Many mixed-race children whose parents were of lower-class status were abandoned by the colonial powers. In most cases, however, boundaries between the colonizers and the colonized proved unenforceable. Stoler points out that in the Dutch-controlled colonial territory of Java, nearly 75 percent of those granted European legal status by 1900 were of mixed race, revealing a significant blurring of intended boundaries.

Stoler's analysis of European colonial practices indicates that attitudes toward sexual practices are not always shaped solely by carnal desires. Systems of economic, political, and colonial power exert significant influence on the ways desires are expressed and understood as sexuality intersects with dynamics of race, class, and nationality. These dynamics remain evident today, as we will see in the following discussions.

Intersections of Race and Sexuality for Black Gay Women

As previously discussed, one's sexual identity is shaped by its intersection with other dynamics of power, including race, class, gender, age, and religion.

Mignon Moore's study *Invisible Families* (2011) explores the impact of the intersection of race and sexuality on the identities, relationships, and families of black gay women in the United States. Moore notes that, historically, race has framed black women's political, economic, and religious identities (see also Dill 1983; Higgenbotham 1992). And whereas many middle-class white lesbian couples experience sexuality as the primary framework that shapes their identity, many in the black lesbian community (including African American, Afro-Caribbean, and African immigrant women) find that race—perhaps as much as, if not more than, sexuality—is the primary framework that shapes their identity.

In an interview with Moore, Zoe Ferron (a pseudonym), an African American woman born in 1960 in Brooklyn, New York, reflected on how the identities of race, gender, and sexuality described her:

> If I had to number them one, two, three? Probably Black and lesbian—real close, to be honest with you. I don't know which would come up as one. Probably Black. Woman last. . . . Because that is just what it is. People see your Blackness, and the world has affected me by my Blackness since the very inception of my life. . . . My sexuality is something that developed later on, or I became aware of later on, [because] I think *it's always been what it's been*, but I think that it was just something that developed in

my psyche. But being Black is something that I've always had to deal with: racism since day one and recognizing how to navigate through this world as a Black person, and even as a Black woman. (Moore 2012, 33)

The intersection of race and sexuality becomes particularly meaningful as black gay women participate in black or gay communities that define themselves around just one of these statuses.

Moore notes that prior to the 1980s, gay sexuality in racial minority communities was rarely articulated in public settings. And only infrequently was it recognized as a component of the community's larger experiences of discrimination and struggle. Instead, openly gay sexuality was perceived to flout notions of "respectability"—virtue, modesty, discipline, responsibility—that had developed within the black middle class and that its leadership promoted as important tools to combat racist stereotypes in the workplace, political arena, and family life (Shaw 1996; Wolcott 2001). Moore points to a strong reluctance during that period by gay blacks to challenge community expectations about respectability by creating families together.

In the intervening years, same-gender sexuality has become an increasingly public issue in U.S. culture through prominent debates about same-sex marriage, the rights of gay men and lesbian women to adopt children, and the rights of lesbians and gay men to serve openly in the military. At the same time,

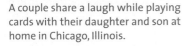

A couple share a laugh while playing cards with their daughter and son at home in Chicago, Illinois.

recognition of same-sex relationships and families has increased in the black community, and black political and religious leaders have begun to address issues related to gay sexuality as matters of civil rights and fairness. Relationships once hidden from families and communities have gradually moved into the public sphere, where the participants can be celebrated as gay women and men and can openly form unions and raise families.

How do the women in Moore's study navigate the black middle-class politics of respectability in order to both live their sexuality openly and maintain strong community connections? Moore suggests that by risking the disruption of this particular version of respectability, black women who live openly as lesbians—forming families, getting married, becoming mothers, and raising children—offer an alternative manifestation of respectability at the intersection of sexuality and race.

Can you see how the intersection of race and sexuality may differentially affect one's life choices and opportunities? In your own life, how is your sexuality shaped by its intersection with other systems of power—perhaps age, gender, race, class, or religion?

Sex, Disability, and Social Justice in Denmark and Sweden

Anthropologists Don Kulick and Jens Rydstrom explore the intersections of state power and sexuality in their book, *Loneliness and Its Opposite: Sex, Disability, and the Ethics of Engagement* (2015), focusing on the constraints and potential for sexuality for severely disabled people in Denmark and Sweden. In recent decades the disability rights movement has successfully advocated for access to physical spaces, jobs, social services, and other public arenas where people with disabilities have commonly faced discrimination and marginalization. But the more private realm of the erotic lives of people with disabilities has more often than not been ignored or viewed with discomfort or anxiety. Should a person with severe disabilities hope to have a meaningful sex life? And how can that be possible for someone who needs assistance to perform most basic life activities such as eating, bathing, and going to the bathroom?

Denmark and Sweden are two liberal welfare states with similar cultural histories, considered to be sexually progressive and at the forefront of the global movement for disability rights. Both countries commit significant portions of their budgets to social services (30 percent) and provide disability pensions, housing in group homes, or personal assistance to those who desire to live independently. But these two neighboring countries take distinctly different approaches to the erotic lives of people with disabilities. In Denmark their sexuality is acknowledged, discussed, and facilitated. In Sweden, as in the overwhelming majority of countries around the world, the erotic lives of people with disabilities are denied, repressed, and discouraged. Their desires for sexual

MAP 9.4
Denmark and Sweden

"I want a family—a marriage, children, the whole thing. 'Family' is happy is strong." Nick Hogan of Australia, one of an estimated seven million people around the world with Down Syndrome. What can we do to support people with disabilities as they form attachments with other people, including attachments that involve sexual pleasure and love?

pleasure are ignored. These adults with disabilities are commonly treated as children whose erotic desires and sexual behaviors are seen as inappropriate or even dangerous to their own well-being.

Kulick and Rydstrom's study focuses specifically on severely disabled people, including those with intellectual and physical disabilities, limited mobility in their limbs, and limited verbal language abilities who live in group homes. In Sweden staff are trained to discourage the erotic lives of their residents, to never "wake the sleeping bear"—meaning to avoid all mention of sexuality—and to shut down erotic feelings when they do arise. In stark contrast, the group homes in Denmark promote welcoming attitudes and affirmative policies regarding sex. Denmark supports a network of advocates, sexual advisors, social workers, medical professionals, educators, and counselors who work toward recognizing and facilitating the sexual desires and practices of people with disabilities. The government sponsors an eighteen-month training course to become a sexual advisor. An elaborate set of national *Guidelines about Sexuality—Regardless of Handicap* discusses how these advisors can support people with disabilities to engage in activities such as having sex with a partner, masturbation, or purchasing sexual services from a sex worker.

Ultimately, Kulick and Rydstrom are most interested in the impact of state policies on the lives of women and men with disabilities and their potential to develop, explore, and thrive as sexual human beings. Kulick and Rydstrom frame this as an ethical question—a matter of social justice. While few would oppose accessibility to public spaces, social services, and jobs for people with disabilities (though funds to realize those goals are often in short supply), sex is often another matter completely. But what can we do to support people with disabilities as they form attachments with other people, including attachments that involve sexual pleasure and love? And how can we foster the circumstances that allow each individual to realize a life of human dignity? This, Kulick and Rydstrom argue, is the true measure of a just society.

How Does Globalization Influence Local Expressions of Sexuality?

Globalization has significantly influenced local expressions of sexuality, and this effect is evident in many arenas. For example, time-space compression (see Chapter 1) is facilitating the movement of people—particularly men—within countries and across national borders in search of sexual pleasure. In addition, disruptions of local economies are pushing women to find wage labor to support themselves and their families. And international campaigns for gay and lesbian rights, often initiated in Western countries, are shaping a global conversation about sexuality and the human rights of sexual minorities worldwide. At the same time, groups opposing gay and lesbian sexuality are promoting their own agendas on a global platform.

These transformations suggest that individual expressions of sexuality and local understandings of sexuality are undergoing dramatic shifts as they intersect with economic policies, immigration practices, and political movements at the national, regional, and international levels influenced by processes of globalization (see Curtis 2009). The following studies offer insights into the potential for close linkages between your life and the lives of men and women around the world through the arena of human sexuality. This is an arena that most of us view as deeply personal but that today crosses national borders in the company of economic flows, immigrant journeys, international tourism, and global rights campaigns.

sex tourism: Travel, usually organized through the tourism sector, to facilitate commercial sexual relations between tourists and local residents in destinations around the world.

MAP 9.5
Dominican Republic

sex work: Labor through which one provides sexual services for money.

Beach Resorts, Dominican Women, and Sex Work

The current era of globalization has seen a dramatic rise in **sex tourism**—trips organized through the tourism sector to facilitate commercial sexual relationships between tourists and local residents in destinations around the world, including Brazil, Costa Rica, the Dominican Republic, Cuba, Kenya, the Philippines, and Thailand. Built on the infrastructure of the tourism industry (including airlines, hotels, restaurants, and local transportation), today sex tourism involves millions of sex workers in a multibillion-dollar industry.

Cultural anthropologist Denise Brennan's ethnography *What's Love Got to Do with It?* (2004) explores the impact of globalization on Sosua, a beautiful beach town on the northern coast of the Dominican Republic in the Caribbean. Sosua has become a prime destination for white male European sex tourists. Internet advertisements and chat rooms draw them in with images of beautiful beaches, luxurious accommodations, and inexpensive sex with Afro-Caribbean island women. The globalized tourism industry provides a seamlessly integrated product, as package tours purchased in Europe bundle airfare, hotels, meals, and entertainment. Corporate owners of the resort hotels are frequently the same foreign airline companies that recruit and deliver the tourists to Sosua.

Yet the booming industry does not benefit everyone. Despite the allure of development through globalization, little of the sex tourism money reaches local Dominican hotels, restaurants, or other businesses. Local workers still toil for low wages, while European nationals are brought in by the resorts to fill well-paid management positions. Over the years, the well-funded foreign tourist hotels have largely undermined the local tourist industry: They monopolize tourists' expenditures by providing all-inclusive package tours, thereby depriving local businesses of income from the tourist trade. In fact, most of the tourist money never leaves the travel companies' home bank accounts in Europe.

Sosua also attracts young women who migrate from across the Dominican Republic to seek opportunities through the sex trade that flourishes around the luxury hotels. These mostly poor, rural, black women hope to reap some of the benefits of globalization, too, through **sex work**—that is, providing commercial sexual services to foreign tourists. If white European sex tourists have fantasies of sexual pleasure with exotic native women, the women of the Dominican Republic have their own fantasies. They believe that the money they earn will help release them and their families from the hardships of life in their largely rural, underdeveloped country. Even more fantastical, they hope to marry one of these tourist men—who they imagine will help them acquire a European visa, take them away, and enable them to escape their world of poverty and limited opportunities. If they can find romance along the way, all the better.

Brennan describes how sex work is more than a survival strategy for these women. Sosua's sex workers have developed an advancement strategy. In essence, they are working to make the trans-national links created by foreign investment come alive for themselves just as for the European tourists. Brennan's careful story-telling depicts women who are not power-less victims of sexual violence and exploi-tation in the sex tourism industry; instead, they actively attempt to create a better life for themselves through it.

Unfortunately, the globalization deck seems stacked against these women. For one thing, prostitution is not legal in the Dominican Republic. With no legal pro-tections, sex workers frequently become the victims of extortion and harassment by local police. On a larger scale, globaliza-tion affects sex tourists and sex workers in radically different ways, providing completely different possibilities for fulfilling their fantasies. Marriage, a visa to Europe, and financial security rarely materialize for the women in Sosua. Instead, globalization as expressed through sex tourism reproduces and rein-forces the unequal relations that existed previously between men and women of different nationalities. In doing so, it also reinforces inequality along lines of gender, race, class, and nationality. At its roots, sex tourism relies on these inequalities of the globalized economy to satisfy the fantasies of tourists from developed countries and to maximize profits for corporate shareholders.

"Anthropologists Engage the World," on pages 342–343, highlights cultural anthropologist Patty Kelly and her research among sex workers in Mexico. It provides another example of the complicated ways in which sexuality intersects with other dynamics of power and the flows of globalization.

A European tourist walks with a local woman along a strip of night-clubs and hotels in the beach resort of Boca Chica, Dominican Republic, known as a hot spot for commercial sex tourism.

Sexuality, Language, and the Effects of Globalization in Nigeria

The tendency of globalization to intensify connections across national bound-aries may generate opportunities for greater cooperation on issues of mutual concern affecting people in disparate parts of the world. But this capacity to bridge barriers also has the potential to homogenize—to shape global dis-courses that blur distinctions and smooth over differences—in a way that may put local indigenous expressions at risk.

In *Allah Made Us: Sexual Outlaws in an Islamic African City* (2009), lin-guistic anthropologist Rudolf Gaudio presents an ethnographic study of the language practices of *'yan daudu*, feminine men in the northern Nigerian (Hausa-speaking) city of Kano. *'Yan daudu* are one group of *masu harka*, a code term for "people who do the deed"—that is, men who have sex with other men. *'Yan daudu* are men who act like women: They cook, serve food, sing, dance, or work as prostitutes. Over the years, their role has been publicly recognized in northern Nigerian culture. But with the introduction of strict Islamic sharia law, which forbids same-gender sexuality, in recent years *'yan daudu* have faced increased persecution, harassment, and marginalization because of their gender and sexual nonconformity. As international campaigns for gay rights intersect with Nigerian culture, the resulting conversations risk drawing local expressions of human sexuality into a national and international debate that links them to so-called Western decadence and new forms of colonialism considered unacceptable by the Nigerian government.

Unlike most Western conceptions of sexuality, *masu harka* and *'yan daudu* do not see homosexual behavior as incompatible with marrying women, forming families, and having children. Nor do they necessarily consider their sexuality incompatible with their Muslim faith. Gaudio met many who are observant Muslims and some who have taken the *hajj*, a pilgrimage to the Muslim holy city of Mecca that is required of every believer who can manage the journey. For some of these men, the pilgrimage to Mecca may enable them to establish status and respectability in the international arena that they could not achieve on their own at home, where many other Nigerians consider them to be outlaws and deviants.

MAP 9.6
Nigeria

Globalization's Homogenizing Influence *'Yan daudu* sexual practices in northern Nigeria are complicated by the effects of globalization. Most African countries achieved their independence from European colonial powers in the 1960s and 1970s, and memories of those incursions are still fresh in Africans' collective memory. Moreover, the awareness of new forms of economic, military, political, and cultural domination that have emerged since the end of colonialism are ever present. Like many Africans, many Nigerians regard homosexuality as part of the wave of Western influences that have been flooding their country and continent for well more than a hundred years.

Most national governments in Africa do not consider the practice of homosexuality as authentically African—certainly not the way homosexuality is framed in international scholarly and activist discourse. These governments see the push for recognizing gay sexual rights as a human right as simply a new front of Western imperial domination. One exception to this perspective is South Africa, where gay rights were included in the new constitution of 1994.

Gaudio's ethnography of *masu harka* shows diverse expressions of sexuality on the local level. The presence of *'yan daudu*, for example, challenges the notion that Africa is devoid of indigenous sexual minorities. But the emergence of an international movement for gay rights threatens to undermine the diversity of local expressions of human sexuality. Gaudio notes that Western scholars and international activists often presume that the international movement's categories can be applied with relative ease from one linguistic and cultural setting to another. However, forcing the conversation into restrictive, binary categories of heterosexuality and homosexuality endangers the continued existence of local sexual expression by placing those indigenous expressions into a debate about foreign influence, imperialism, and so-called Western decadence.

The emerging anti-gay rhetoric unifies Muslim fundamentalist, Christian orthodox, and evangelical groups. It threatens to close off the possibility of recognizing the diversity of sexual desires, practices, and identities of individuals and local communities that may have previously operated outside the Western-oriented, homosexual-heterosexual framework. In so doing, it reveals the power of globalization to introduce narrower, homogenizing perspectives on the many and varied expressions of human sexuality found in cultures around the globe (Gaudio 2009; Harris 2009; Leap 2010).

In this chapter we have considered the vast scope and diversity of human sexuality across cultures, time, and space. The sexual dimensions of human diversity in turn challenge us to expand our imaginations about the potential for human sexuality available to us. But as we have seen throughout this chapter, human sexuality is more than the personal choices we make about our sexual partners and how we express our erotic desires. The anthropological lens and a global perspective have enabled us to see that sexuality is a complex relationship between individuals as well as between individuals and the larger culture. We have examined how elements of human sexuality are culturally constructed—formed in relationship to particular people, cultural norms, and expectations. Rather than representing sharply drawn, fixed, and oppositional identities representing two discrete categories, sexuality is diverse, flexible, and fluid.

But we have also seen that the construction of human sexuality—how it is perceived and valued—is a highly contested process. Debates rage and decisions are made about human sexuality that affect people's life chances and access to power, privileges, rights, and resources. Certain rights or benefits may be granted or restricted based on assumptions about sexual preferences or sexual behavior. Given this reality, within anthropology sexuality has become a key cultural location for analyzing, understanding, and contesting stratification and inequality, including the ways sexuality intersects with other systems of power, such as race, gender, ethnicity, nationality, religion, kinship, and class.

Have international debates about human sexuality put local expressions at risk? Here 'yan daudu dance at a party in Kano, Nigeria. The men's faces have been disguised to conceal their identities.

Patty Kelly
Sex Work, Power, and Globalization in Mexico

How might an anthropologist study sexuality in an age of globalization? Cultural anthropologist Patty Kelly conducted fieldwork in a Mexican brothel.

Sex work is legal in one-third of the states of Mexico. The Zona Galactica brothel, where Kelly conducted her fieldwork, is located in Chiapas in southern Mexico. Sex work there is legal—run and regulated by the state. To study and analyze commercial sex in a globalizing world, Kelly spent a year with the Zona Galactica's 140 women sex workers, their clients, and the government administrators who run the brothel.

Kelly arrived in Chiapas during a time of popular unrest. Dramatic economic changes associated with globalization and supported by the Mexican government were disrupting the agricultural life of rural farmers, or *campesinos*. Pushed off their land by large-scale agribusiness, many were migrating to cities in search of work but finding themselves competing with other rural migrants and poor urban dwellers for the same low-paying jobs in factories, as servants, or in the informal economy.

The Zona Galactica created an alternative employment option within the local service economy that in many cases provided a more secure, predictable, and better-paid living. At the Zona Galactica, Kelly found that some women were satisfied with their jobs. They could set their own hours, decide their own rates, and choose what services they would provide. Others would have preferred doing other work if they could have found it. But all the women used the brothel to make a decent living, get health care, build a sense of community, and develop a sense of dignity. The patrons who visited the brothel were mostly local working-class men, along with a few truckers passing through the area. As a result, the sex workers often forged relationships with their customers over time. Such relationships enabled the women to negotiate better terms and work with more dignity. Overall, Kelly found

that these women held more open-minded and practical attitudes about sexuality than even their middle-class Mexican female counterparts.

At the Zona Galactica, Kelly built a particularly strong relationship with Lydia, who eventually became the central figure in her ethnography. Kelly's book, *Lydia's Open Door: Inside Mexico's Most Modern Brothel* (2008b), is a vivid account of life and work in the sex trade. It sets this topic amid the larger struggles against impoverishment, landlessness, and political upheaval that the women of southern Mexico face every day. Key to Kelly's portrayal are the heartfelt interactions with Lydia, who became her friend and key informant; Lydia taught Kelly about the life of a sex worker but also invited Kelly home to her shantytown on the hilly outskirts of the city to generously share holiday meals far beyond her means.

Sadly, Lydia died of HIV/AIDS shortly after Kelly's fieldwork stay and before the book's publication. Kelly was moved by the way Lydia's fellow sex workers honored her memory, including pooling their money to purchase a coffin so that Lydia's twin sons would not have to give their mother a pauper's funeral. Kelly reflects that it is these

Anthropologist Patty Kelly celebrates her birthday with a cake at her field site—a brothel in Chiapas, Mexico.

moments of community and solidarity that exemplify the lives of sex workers in the Zona Galactica.

Kelly's writing challenges stereotypes about prostitution by examining sex work in the Zona Galactica as one type of work in a wide spectrum of women's labor. Though rarely framed in this way, she notes that women often use their bodies, intimacy, and sexuality to perform various kinds of gendered work. Sometimes women's use of sexuality is explicit, as with Lydia and her colleague sex workers. But sexuality also comes into play in other kinds of workplaces. Waitresses dress, act, and talk in a sexualized manner, hoping that the allure of sexuality will bring them bigger tips. Most restaurants and many offices hire female receptionists in the belief that the women's sexuality will please the customers and clients. Sexuality is also on display in corporate offices in negotiations over roles, promotions, and power in the hierarchy. By seeing the women of the Zona Galactica within the broader spectrum of sexuality in work, Kelly urges her readers to understand the choices made by the women of the brothel without passing moral judgments. Can we consider sex work as a reasonable way for poor women living in the economic scarcity of the Chiapas region of southern Mexico to earn a living and support their families?

Kelly encourages a rethinking of the U.S. public policy debate over the criminalization of sex work. "Legalizing and regulating prostitution as the Mexican state has done in the Zona Galactica has its own problems—it stigmatizes sex workers (mostly by requiring them to register with the authorities), subjects them to mandatory medical testing that is not always effective, and gives clients and workers a false sense of security (with respect to sexual health and otherwise). But criminalization is worse. Prostitution will continue, even if illegal. But when criminalized, women will have fewer protections and less control over their work as they are forced to conduct it in the shadows."

In an editorial published by the *Los Angeles Times* and syndicated nationally, Kelly (2008a) built on her experiences in Mexico to take the bold step of advocating the decriminalization of sex work in the United States: "I have met hundreds of men who have paid for sex. Some seek any kind of sex; others want certain kinds of sex; a few look for comfort and conversation. Saying that all sex workers are victims and all clients are demons is the easy way out. Perhaps it's time to face this fact like adults (or at least like Mexico)—with a little less moralizing and a good deal more honesty."

> "*Legalizing and regulating prostitution has its own problems. . . . But criminalization is worse.*"

Reflecting on the value of fieldwork and the study of anthropology, Kelly offers, "Anthropology is a unique way to see such vitally important aspects of ordinary people's lives. The ethnographic methods brought me closer to the perspectives of the people I lived and worked with. I was able to use concepts from geography, gender theory, and political economy to analyze sex work in Zona Galactica. I think anthropology allows us to see the world differently, to recognize that long-held individual and collective beliefs can be changed if we come to understand each other in a more relative sense. Really, only by exposing ourselves to other people's way of life can we hope to achieve this kind of examination of ourselves and our own culture."

Thinking Like an Anthropologist: Sexuality in Your Life
Sexuality is all around us. Turn on the television, search the Internet, check out at the grocery store, or drive down an interstate highway, and you will find sexuality all around you in reality shows, websites, magazines, and billboard advertisements. At times in U.S. culture, the presence of sexuality is so pervasive as to be overwhelming. In such an environment, how do you begin to make sense of what sexuality means for you on a personal level and for U.S. culture on a political level?

Remember to consider the big questions that have organized this chapter:

- What is sexuality and where does it come from?
- What is the scope of human sexuality when seen in a global perspective?
- How has sexuality been constructed in the United States?
- How is sexuality an arena for working out relations of power?
- How does globalization influence local expressions of sexuality?

Think again about the story that opens this chapter. In what ways do sexuality and power intersect on your college campus? If, as anthropologist Eric Wolf argues (see Chapter 2), every relationship is embedded in complex dynamics of power, how do you navigate intersections of sexuality with gender, age, class, race, or religion? Has your college or university created opportunities to discuss matters of sexuality?

Certainly, attention to sexual violence on college campuses has increased. Terms such as *date rape* and *domestic violence* have become part of the national conversation (see also Chapter 8), and many colleges and universities have implemented policies on sexual harassment and sexual conduct. Still, many women experience sexual harassment, violence, and rape while in college (Fisher, Daigle, and Cullen 2010; Sanday 1990). While these policies attempt to address extreme expressions of the intersection of power with sexuality, conversations about sexuality can be far more wide-ranging.

Until recently, most sexual offense policies have started with the assumption that "*No* means *no*." Most legal definitions of rape have assumed that if a woman does not consent or is incapable of consent for any reason, then any sexual activity with her is considered rape. But more recently, affirmative consent policies have been developed that require consent to be an ongoing process and verbal consent to be obtained with each new level of physical intimacy.

An affirmative consent policy requires a dramatic shift in thinking about intimate sexual encounters. It also commands a new attention to shifting the power dynamics that underlie current patterns of gender and sexuality in the culture at large. Imagine if all forms of coercion—physical and psychological coercion; the pressure of norms, obligations, and expectations; and the fear of ridicule or abandonment—were removed from the equation, enabling people to engage in sexual intimacy only when they really wanted to. What if "yes" really meant "yes" (Friedman and Valenti 2008)?

Although anthropology may not be able to help you decide whom to date or when to do what and where, it does offer a set of tools—perspectives and insights—that may help you think more clearly about what it all means, what the cultural frameworks are within which you negotiate your desires and decisions, and what your full range of options may be when you consider your sexuality within a global perspective. Questions of sexuality run deep in U.S. cultural conversations. Having thought through key issues of sexuality from an anthropological perspective, are you better prepared to engage in the debates and advance the conversation?

Key Terms

sexuality (p. 314)

heterosexuality (p. 322)

homosexuality (p. 322)

bisexuality (p. 322)

asexuality (p. 322)

sex tourism (p. 338)

sex work (p. 338)

For Further Exploration

Columbia University. 2013. Go Ask Alice. www.goaskalice .columbia.edu. Columbia University's health service website provides reliable and accessible information about health, including sexuality, sexual health, and relationships.

The Education of Shelby Knox. 2005. By Marion Lipschutz and Rose Rosenblatt. Cine Qua Non/InCite Pictures. Documentary about a teenager from a Southern Baptist family in Lubbock, Texas, who takes a True Love Waits (chastity) pledge but eventually becomes an activist for comprehensive sex education.

It Gets Better Project. 2010. www.itgetsbetter.org. This website was created by sex advice columnist Dan Savage with his partner, Terry, in the wake of several well-publicized cases of young people bullied into suicide. Intended to inspire hope for LGBT youth facing harassment, the site features videos of moral support from political figures and entertainers who remind teenagers tormented by others about their sexuality that it indeed does get better.

LaFont, Suzanne. 2002. Constructing Sexualities: Readings in Sexuality, Gender and Culture. Upper Saddle River, NJ: Prentice Hall.

Schwartz, Pepper, and Virginia Rutter. 1998. The Gender of Sexuality: Exploring Sexual Possibilities. Lanham, MD: Altamira Press.

Southern Comfort. 2001. Directed by Kate Davis. Next Wave Films. A poignant documentary about the life of Robert Eads, a female-to-male transsexual living in rural Georgia. The painful tragedy of Eads's story is that he is dying of ovarian cancer and is denied treatment by two dozen doctors who feared harm to their reputations.

Stop Raping Our Greatest Resource: Power to Women and Girls of Democratic Republic of Congo. 2013. http://drc.vday.org. Hundreds of thousands of women in eastern Congo have been victimized by rape used as a weapon in the ongoing warfare in this African country. This website includes videos, photographs, and descriptions of women's efforts to break the cycle of violence and establish a women's shelter and leadership training school.

ONE FAMILY. NO AI

Who is family? The success of the television series *Transparent* reveals a growing openness to shifting American notions of family—what anthropologists call kinship.

OGIES.

CHAPTER 10
Kinship, Family, and Marriage

In season one of the Amazon television series *Transparent*, Mort, a retired professor of political science, who is transitioning to Maura, walks in on his daughter Amy—wife of Len and mother of two children—making out with Tammy, her ex-college girlfriend, now married to her second wife and raising a child in that relationship. Maura comes out to her daughter and says that after years of dressing up as a man she is finally able to be who she has known herself to be since the age of five. The series follows the stories of this family as Maura comes out to her children, ex-wife (who is caring for a second husband with Alzheimer's), and grandchildren and builds a new set of supportive relationships with people taking the same journey. The children wrestle with learning that the person they knew as their father is transgender and navigate their own complicated journeys toward creating family and meaningful relationships.

Though created by Jill Soloway as a television comedy-drama, *Transparent* is inspired by the story of her father who came out as transgender just a few years ago and offers a reflection on the shifting notion of family in the twenty-first–century United States. The show's critical and financial success reveals a growing willingness to engage the emerging new configurations of the relationships we sometimes call "family" and that anthropologists have explored under the category of *kinship*. Who is "related" to whom? Who decides? Is kinship biological or chosen? Who actually constitutes a family?

Humans live in groups. As a species, we rarely live alone or in isolation. Kinship is perhaps the most effective strategy humans have developed to form stable, reliable, separate, and deeply connected groups that can last over time and through generations.

Kinship is the system of meaning and power created to determine who is related to whom and to define their mutual expectations, rights, and responsibilities. Of course, humans also form groups through work, religion, education, and politics. But none compare to the power of families and kinship networks to provide support and nurture, ensure reproduction of the next generation, protect group assets, and influence social, economic, and political systems.

Kinship groups are often assumed by many in Western cultures to have a biological basis and to arise around the **nuclear family** of mother, father, and children. But when we examine these assumptions in a cross-cultural context, they show themselves to be a Euro-American ideal that not even those cultures have realized. Kinship groups come in a variety of shapes and sizes: We trace our connections through biological ancestors. We create kinship relations through marriage and remarriage. We adopt. We foster. We choose families of people who care about us. Sometimes we even imagine everyone in our nation to be part of one big, related, kinship community.

In the twenty-first century, we are vividly aware of new forms of family life as kinship relations shift, closing off familiar patterns and opening up new ones. The image of a family with mother, father, and two kids gathered around the dining room table every evening for a home-cooked meal and conversation may be familiar as a cultural icon, but for many people the experience of family is more complicated as families are made, taken apart, reconstructed, and blended. Gay and lesbian couples and their families are achieving increased acceptance and official recognition. New reproductive technologies—including artificial insemination, in vitro fertilization, and surrogacy—continue to stretch our ideas of kinship and families by showing how human culture, through science and technology, is shaping biological relationships.

Although the term *kinship* may be unfamiliar to you, the subject material is not. Through kinship studies, anthropologists examine the deepest and most complicated aspects of our everyday lives—our relationships with people closest to us, including our mothers, fathers, brothers, sisters, grandparents, cousins, husbands, wives, partners, and children. These are the people we live with, eat with, count on for support, and promise to take care of when they are in need. We pour our emotions, creative energy, hopes, and dreams into these relationships. Many of the most emotionally vibrant moments of our lives—from joy and love to anger and pain—occur at the intersection of individual and family life: birthdays, holiday celebrations, shared meals, weddings, illnesses, and funerals. Through kinship, we see our lives as part of a continuum. We look back to see the history of the people we come from, and we look ahead to imagine the relatives and families yet to be.

At the same time, kinship is deeply intertwined with forces beyond the everyday activities of family and home. In our families, we also learn basic patterns of human behavior—how to treat one another, how to act in groups, how to navigate differences of age, gender, ethnicity, and sexuality. This enculturation shapes our lives outside the household, including the ways we think about gender roles, the division of labor, religious practices, warfare, politics, migration, and nationalism. Because cultural norms, values, and social structures can always be changed, kinship and family also become places of contestation, experimentation, and change that reflect and shape debates within the larger culture.

The study of kinship is one of anthropology's unique innovations for thinking about how culture works. In this chapter, we will explore the following questions about kinship:

- How are we related to one another?
- Are biology and marriage the only basis for kinship?
- How are ideas of kinship linked to the nation-state?
- How is kinship changing in the modern world?

We will examine the many strategies people use to form kinship groups, and we will consider the implications of kinship's changing expressions in the twenty-first century. By the end of the chapter you should be ready to interpret your own family tree—not just by creating a list of relatives, but also by considering how those ties are formed and the role that kin play in shaping who you are as an individual and as a member of society. You will also be prepared to understand and analyze the ways debates about kinship shape important aspects of our individual and collective lives locally, nationally, and globally.

How Are We Related to One Another?

Who are you related to? As we saw in Chapter 5, all humans are closely related genetically, sharing more than 99.9 percent of our DNA. Despite this close biological "kinship" among all humans, closer to home we tend to organize our personal relationships more specifically through systems of common biological descent, marriage, love, and choice. As you will discover throughout this chapter, cultures have a variety of ways of organizing kinship relationships. Some will be familiar to you, and others will not. All are equally valid.

Descent

One way that humans construct kinship groups is by tracking genealogical descent. In **descent groups**, primary relationships are with certain consanguineal relatives (what U.S. culture refers to as "blood" relatives). These would include your mother, father, sister, brother, grandparents, children, and grandchildren,

descent group: A kinship group in which primary relationships are traced through certain consanguineous ("blood") relatives.

as well as your uncles and aunts who are your parents' siblings—but not your uncles and aunts who are married to your parents' siblings. Descent groups are often imagined as long chains of connections from parent to child that reach back through many generations to a common ancestor or group of ancestors and forward to imagined future generations.

Early anthropological studies through the mid-twentieth century assumed the descent group to be central to the social structure of most nonindustrial cultures outside Europe and North America (Evans-Pritchard 1951; Fortes 1949; Malinowski 1929, 1930; Radcliffe-Brown 1950). Anthropologists of that period expected to find extended descent groups that stretched back over many generations and worked together. Such groups were considered key to understanding each culture's economic, political, and religious dynamics because of the way kinship underlies large social networks extending beyond the immediate family into all aspects of cultural life. We will consider one classic example, the Nuer, in the following section.

In contrast, most European and North American cultures do not use descent to organize social groups. Although we may keep track of our ancestors over a few generations, we do so bilaterally—through both the mother's and the father's relatives—and generally we have not constructed large social networks based on kinship connections. In the United States, perhaps the Rockefeller, Kennedy, and Bush families might loosely qualify as descent groups. They stretch back over a few generations, tracing roots to a much more recent common ancestor (either John D. Rockefeller, Joseph Kennedy, or Prescott Bush); and although now subdivided into smaller segments, they still maintain strong enough connections to function together at times on common economic, social, political, or ritual activities and projects. But such descent groups are extremely rare in North America.

Anthropologists distinguish two types of descent groups: lineages and clans. **Lineages** can clearly demonstrate genealogical connections through many generations, tracing the family tree to a founding (apical) ancestor. **Clans** likewise claim connection to a founding ancestor, but they do not provide the same genealogical documentation. Descent groups may be *matrilineal*, constructing the group through female ancestors, or *patrilineal*, tracing kinship through male ancestors. Both matrilineal and patrilineal patterns reflect *unilineal* descent because they build kinship groups through either one line or the other. In contrast, *ambilineal* descent groups—including Samoans, Maori, Hawaiians, and others in Southeast Asia and the Pacific—trace kinship through both the mother and the father. This alternative pattern is sometimes called *cognatic* or *bilateral*.

Most people in the world practice patrilineal descent as their primary strategy to track kin group membership. At the same time, most people still build kinship networks bilaterally through both parents, even when tracing descent unilineally. Are you aware of how your own family traces descent?

lineage: A type of descent group that traces genealogical connection through generations by linking persons to a founding ancestor.

clan: A type of descent group based on a claim to a founding ancestor but lacking genealogical documentation.

The Nuer of Southern Sudan The Nuer people of southern Sudan in northeast Africa constitute a classic representation of the descent group. British anthropologist E. E. Evans-Pritchard studied this group in the 1930s (Evans-Pritchard 1951). At the time of his research and until the later part of the twentieth century, the Nuer were primarily a pastoral, cattle-herding people that moved between settlements throughout the year to adapt to rainy and dry seasons. The Nuer constituted a patrilineal descent group: Both boy and girl children were born into the group, but membership could only pass to the next generation through the sons who inherited membership through their fathers. Nuer clans were *exogamous*—meaning that marriages within the group were not permitted. Large clans were divided into lineages, although lineages were extensive enough to spread over several villages.

Cattle were the center of Nuer economic life. They were owned by men, but they were milked by women as well as by boys who had not yet come of age and been initiated into the descent group. A successful marriage proposal often required the groom to provide cattle in exchange for the bride.

What does a descent group look like? (*clockwise from left*) A chief (standing) and his sons, photographed by Bronislaw Malinowski; they represent the core of a patrilineal descent group in the Trobriand Islands. (*top right*) A Kennedy family portrait, Hyannis, Massachusetts, 1930s, including, seated second from left, future U.S. attorney general Robert Kennedy; center, future U.S. president John F. Kennedy; and second from right, family patriarch Joseph Kennedy Sr. (*bottom right*) A Bush family portrait at the White House, 2005, including, seated from right, Florida Governor Jeb Bush, U.S. President George H. W. Bush, and fourth from right U.S. President George W. Bush.

FIGURE 10.1 Kinship Naming Systems
Early anthropologists identified only six general patterns worldwide for classifying relatives when beginning with the ego's generation: Eskimo, Hawaiian, Sudanese, Omaha, Crow, and Iroquois.

SOURCE: *From Dennis O'Neil, "Kin Naming Systems: Part 1, The Nature of Kinship," http://anthro.palomar.edu /kinship/kinship_5.htm.*

ESKIMO

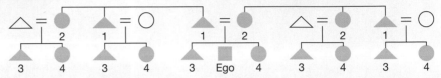

1 = Father	5 = Brother
2 = Mother	6 = Sister
3 = Aunt	7 = Cousin
4 = Uncle	

The Eskimo kinship naming system is the most common in Europe and North America. Only members of the nuclear family are given distinct terms. Aunts and uncles are distinguished from parents but not by side of the family. All cousins are lumped together.

HAWAIIAN

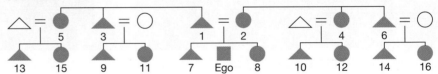

1 = Father and father's brothers	3 = Brothers and male cousins
2 = Mother and mother's sisters	4 = Sisters and female cousins

The Hawaiian system is the least complicated. The nuclear family is deemphasized, and relatives are distinguished only by generation and gender.

SUDANESE

The Sudanese kinship system is the most complex. Each category of relative is given a distinct term based on genealogical distance from ego. There can be eight different cousin terms, all of whom are distinguished from ego's brother and sister.

MAP 10.1
The Nuer Region of East Africa

The patrilineal kinship structures of clans and lineages provided the primary structure for Nuer political and economic activity. In the villages, the lineages collectively owned land, fisheries, and pastures. Ceremonial leadership of Nuer group life was organized under sacred ritual leaders, but these individuals did not control the social networks built around kinship and cattle, so they were not the driving force in Nuer culture (Stone 2009).

Searching for Kinship Patterns As early anthropologists gathered kinship data from cultures worldwide, they developed a limited number of general categories that facilitated comparison. Despite vast geographic distances and language differences, only four primary systems were identified to classify relatives in the parental generation: *lineal, bifurcate merging, generational,* and *bifurcate*

OMAHA

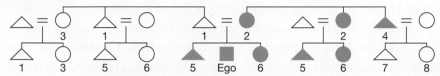

1 = Father and father's brothers
2 = Mother and female on mother's side
3 = Females on father's side
4 = Males on mother's side
5 = Male siblings and parallel cousins
6 = Female siblings and parallel cousins
7 = Male cross cousins
8 = Female cross cousins

The Omaha, Crow, and Iroquois naming systems trace kinship through unilineal descent—either patrilineally or matrilineally—so distinguishing between cousins takes on importance. The Omaha system is typical of kinship patterns traced through patrilineal descent.

CROW

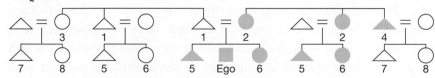

1 = Father and father's brothers
2 = Mother and mother's sisters
3 = Female on father's side
4 = Male on mother's side
5 = Male siblings and parallel cousins
6 = Female siblings and parallel cousins
7 = Male cross cousins
8 = Female cross cousins

The Crow system is typical of kinship patterns traced through matrilineal descent.

IROQUOIS

1 = Father and father's brother
2 = Mother and mother's sister
3 = Female on father's side
4 = Male on mother's side
5 = Male parallel cousins
6 = Female parallel cousins
7 = Male cross cousins
8 = Female cross cousins

The Iroquois kinship system can be traced either matrilineally or patrilineally. Note the same term is used for father and father's brother and for mother and mother's sister, reflecting shared membership in lineages.

collateral. When beginning with the ego's generation (the ego being the central character and starting point in tracing kinship relationships—for example, you in your own family tree), anthropologists found only six different ways of organizing relatives, in which the variation centered on the classification of siblings and cousins. Each of these six were named after a key group in which the pattern occurred: Eskimo, Hawaiian, Sudanese, Omaha, Crow, and Iroquois (Figure 10.1).

Generalized systems of kinship classification can be very useful for identifying and comparing broad patterns of social structure. But anthropologists have found that actual, local kinship patterns do not always match the generalized models. The ways in which human groups trace connections between generations—in other words, how they construct genealogies—can be messy and far from exact. Genealogies are full of gaps, interruptions, disruptions, uncertainties, and imagined or assumed connections. Some groups have extensive genealogies, but even these carefully constructed records may be partly mythical and based on limited recollections or partial history. In contrast, other groups have extremely shallow genealogical memories that span only two or three generations. Segments of these descent groups may no longer live together or act together. Other relatives may have been forgotten or excluded from the main line through conflict. Political, economic, and/or military upheaval, colonial interventions, and the establishment of modern nation-states may have disrupted collective memory and records. Or kinship patterns may have changed over time as groups adapted to external pressures. As a result, these groups' knowledge of individual ancestors and even whole generations may have been lost.

Once again, the Nuer are an excellent example. Despite representing one of the six key cross-cultural variations in kinship studies (Sudanese), their day-to-day kinship practices did not exactly match the clear patrilineal descent model that might be imagined on a Nuer family tree. Evans-Pritchard determined that the Nuer inherited formal group membership through patrilineal descent, but he and Kathleen Gough (1971), who revisited the study a generation later, found that most Nuer individuals continued to trace kinship relations through both parents. These bilateral kinship relationships created by marriage were often just as important as those created through descent. Specifically, while women married into the Nuer descent group and produced children for that group, they also provided their children with close connections to kin on the mother's side, particularly the mother's brother. This pattern often occurs in patrilineal groups.

When Gough revisited Evans-Pritchard's original study, she suggested that local events in the 1930s may have affected Nuer kinship practices at the time. During the time of Evans-Pritchard's research in the 1930s, the Nuer were resisting British colonial occupation of the Sudan. In addition, they were involved in a conquest of the neighboring Dinka ethnic group. Additional intense conflicts existed among Nuer groups. Gough suggests that these tensions, conflicts, and disruptions may have intensified Nuer attention to kinship and marriage patterns as they attempted to reinforce group identity and assimilate outsiders. Gough also suggests that the particular expressions of kinship recorded by Evans-Pritchard may have been adaptations to political

The Nuer, of the Sudan, are a classic representation of a descent group. (*top left*) A Nuer man, his sons, and cattle outside the family homestead, 1930s. (photo by E. E. Evans-Pritchard). (*top right*) A Nuer family homestead, 2007. (*bottom left*) Nuer men leaping (beside Evans-Pritchard's tent) in a dance that often took the form of mock battles between village groups. Dances accompanied marriages and provided courtship opportunities for Nuer youth. (*bottom right*) Nuer women dancing in the bride's family homestead at a contemporary Nuer wedding.

and economic conditions rather than an entrenched, changeless kinship norm (Gough 1971; see also Stone 2009).

Kinship, Descent, and Change in a Chinese Village As Gough found in her Nuer study, political factors can shape efforts to construct kinship—a pattern I also uncovered in my own research in a Chinese village. When I conducted fieldwork in the late 1990s, I thought I had found a classic, Nuer-style patrilineal descent group. Ninety percent of the men in the village had the surname Chen and traced their origins back to the founding Chen—the apical ancestor—who they believed had settled in the area more than 700 years earlier. The village children, boys and girls, were all named Chen. But the Chen daughters were all to be married out to men in neighboring villages. The Chen men were to marry women from the same neighboring villages who would move in with them at home. The Chen family temple was the largest ancestral hall in the village and served as the center for venerating Chen ancestors. Until the 1960s, village lands, including agricultural plots and fisheries, were held in common by the Chen lineage, which acted like a small corporation. Male elders allocated access to the collectively owned village property to the other males in the descent group during an annual lineage meeting.

The village appeared to be a textbook case of a patrilineal Chinese descent group. But kinship is always a bit more complicated and interesting than anthropologists first imagine. In the late 1960s, family and temple ancestral records were destroyed as part of a chaotic and brutal national political movement known as the Cultural Revolution—a modernization campaign promoted by the Chinese government to throw out the old and bring in the new. Only in the 1990s did political and economic conditions improve enough for local villagers to consider reconstructing their lost records. An older village member who had become a university professor in the provincial capital accepted the task of writing and publishing a local village history book called a *zupu* ("gazetteer"). His research included an effort to reconstruct the village genealogy and the Chen line of descent. Funding came from villagers working abroad, particularly in the United States.

When the research was complete, however, the devastating impact of the Cultural Revolution became apparent. Without written records, the reconstructed genealogy relied primarily on oral histories stored in the memories of village elders. Many vividly recalled their parents' and grandparents' generations. Some had heard stories of a few prominent Chen villagers whose earlier travel, business success, or scholarship had made them famous in the villagers' collective memory. Of course, the apical ancestor, his sons, and a few of their immediate descendants had been remembered. Unfortunately, most of the generations prior to 1900 had been left blank. The genealogical details, if they

MAP 10.2
Fuzhou

had ever existed, had been destroyed during the Cultural Revolution.

Migration has also challenged the Chen descent group's ability to maintain kinship connections, especially in the context of the current global age. In fact, fully 70 percent of the villagers—most between the ages of eighteen and fifty—have left China since the early 1980s to seek their fortunes in the United States, Japan, South America, Canada, Europe, and the Middle East. Some return to visit their hometown. Most marry and have children in their new host country. According to the rules of the patrilineal descent group, all children born to villagers working abroad still belong in the descent group, and males can pass on that membership to the next generation. But faced with such a massive out-migration and global diaspora of the lineage, how would they keep track as villagers migrated halfway around the world?

Chinese family ancestral hall outside Fuzhou, China, built with money sent by villagers working abroad.

New York is the primary international destination for the village's immigrants. There, with the support of village leaders in China, immigrants have created a village hometown association to rebuild and strengthen hometown kinship ties. The association enables villagers to reconnect, provide mutual support, share information, and use their kinship networks to improve their immigrant experience. Association leaders also keep track of fellow villagers, their marriages, and their offspring. They report these developments back to the Chen family elders in China for proper recording. Through this process, long-held village strategies for kinship formation and group building are adapting to the challenges of wide-scale international migration, spurred by globalization. Modern communication and transportation technologies are enabling Chinese villagers to innovatively extend their notions of patrilineal descent, both spatially beyond China's national boundary and temporally forward into the future.

Certainly the forces of globalization, including migration and time-space compression, are placing stress on kinship systems worldwide. This is occurring as members of kinship groups relocate temporarily or permanently to nearby factories or jobs in other countries to seek improved economic and educational opportunities or to avoid natural disasters and political upheavals. Although generalized kinship categories developed by an earlier generation of anthropologists have provided insights into broad patterns of kinship, anthropologists who study kinship today confront more fluid kinship patterns maintained through flexibility and creativity.

THE SOCIAL LIFE OF THINGS
Respecting the Ancestors: Chinese Lineage Records and Grave Rituals

Across cultures, family groups have many elaborate ways of tracing their kinship. In the United States, some families may have old documents, pictures, or family Bibles. More recently people have turned to online ancestry programs and even mail-in DNA tests (Chau 2006; Guest 2003).

1 In Chinese culture, lineages have traditionally compiled a genealogy book, called a *zupu*. This book constructs a family tree (primarily through the male line), records the clan's origins, and highlights illustrious members. Though this genealogical recordkeeping in China has been disrupted by politics and increasing internal and international migration, many lineages, especially in China's rural areas, where 60 percent of the population live, remain attentive to their kinship relations both in current generations and past.

2 Religious beliefs and rituals play a vital part in traditional Chinese kinship practices. Ancestors are important and active figures in Chinese popular religion, and the current generation is obligated to perform certain rituals of veneration. Foremost among these rituals is Qing Ming, or the annual Grave Sweeping Festival held each spring, when relatives visit their ancestors' grave sites, sweep (clean) them, and make offerings.

③ During Qing Ming, relatives clean and decorate the grave site, bring food offerings, and burn paper representations of money and household items—even paper homes and cars. It is believed that ancestors will need these things in the afterlife. Ancestors who are not remembered may return as Hungry Ghosts, wandering the countryside, making trouble for the living. Offerings may be left outside temples and homes at specific times during the year to ward off the unhappy and hungry ghost ancestors, or fireworks may be set off to scare them away.

A revival of traditional Chinese practices, including genealogical recordkeeping and religious rituals that venerate the ancestors, has spread across China in recent decades, surprising many both inside and outside China who thought these practices would disappear with modernization and political pressure. In the process, kinship networks have been revitalized and strengthened, particularly in rural areas where kinship relations often play important roles in economic and political success (Chau 2006; Guest 2003).

- Does your family have a formal system to track its ancestry?
- What practices does your family have for remembering and venerating your ancestors? Do you tell stories at family gatherings, display family portraits, or hand down family heirlooms like clothes, jewelry, books, or furniture from generation to generation?

Marriage and Affinal Ties

A second way humans form kinship groups is through marriage—what anthropologists refer to as **affinal relationships**. Unlike the construction of kinship groups through descent, which links direct genealogical ancestors and descendants, marriage builds kinship ties between two people who are (usually) not immediate biological kin. Marriage also creates a relationship between the spouses' respective kinship groups, called "in-laws" in U.S. culture. The new kinship group created through marriage is linked through affinity and alliance, not through shared biology and common descent.

Something like marriage exists in every culture, but its exact form and characteristics vary widely—so widely, in fact, that it is difficult to say that any one characteristic is universal. **Marriages** create socially recognized relationships that may involve physical and emotional intimacy, sexual pleasure, reproduction and raising of children, mutual support and companionship, and shared legal rights to property and inheritance. The bond of marriage may also serve to create connection, communication, and alliance between groups.

Marriages take many forms, including arranged marriages and companionate marriages. **Arranged marriages**, orchestrated by the families of the bride and groom, continue to be prominent in many cultures in Asia, the Pacific, the Middle East, and Africa. Arranged marriages are even common among some religious groups in the United States and, in a sense, among some segments of the upper class who send their children to elite private schools to meet future partners and encourage in-group marriage. These traditional marriages ensure the reproduction and continuation of the kinship group and build alliances with other kin groups. Thus the couple's parents may view the economic and political consequences of marriage alliance as being too important to the larger kinship group to be left to the whims of two young people. In this context, marriage becomes a social obligation and a symbol of commitment to the larger group rather than a mechanism for personal satisfaction and fulfillment. Alliance marriages of this sort require extensive negotiation to balance the needs of the group and the intimate personal feelings of the individuals being married. Bonds of affection may develop in an arranged marriage, but this is not the primary goal.

What about Love? Today marriage patterns are changing rapidly. Younger generations are increasingly thinking of love, intimacy, and personal pleasure—not social obligation—as the foundation on which to build families and kinship relations. Love—and what anthropologists call **companionate marriages**, which are built on love—is the ideal to be achieved. (Chan 2006; Gregg 2003; Inhorn 1996; Rebhun 1999; Wardlow 2006; Yan 2003).

Jennifer Hirsch's (2007) study of love in a small western Mexican town examines the rise of companionate marriage at the intersection of love and

---

affinal relationship: A kinship relationship established through marriage and/or alliance, not through biology or common descent.

marriage: A socially recognized relationship that may involve physical and emotional intimacy as well as legal rights to property and inheritance.

arranged marriage: Marriage orchestrated by the families of the involved parties.

companionate marriage: Marriage built on love, intimacy, and personal choice rather than social obligation.

globalization. In response to migration, economic exchange, and the time-space compression of communication technology such as telephones and the Internet, love and intimacy are being transformed as globalization links a poor, rural community with its wealthy neighbor to the north, the United States. The population of Degollado, Jalisco—21,000 people according to the 2010 census—varies according to the season. In the spring and summer, many residents migrate north of the border to do agricultural and construction work in the United States. When they return in the winter, they bring back dollars, baseball hats, electronics, and trucks. In a festival atmosphere, young girls promenade around the plaza in the hopes of evoking a marriage proposal. "The economy of love is intricately interwoven with the political economy of migration" (Hirsch 2007, 94).

In interviews with local women residents and those who had relocated to the United States, Hirsch found a distinct shift in the description of marriage. For older women, love came from living well together, and successful marriage involved fulfilling one's roles and obligations: men brought home the money; women cooked, washed, cleaned, and raised the children. In contrast, younger women measured a good marriage relationship by its level of intimacy and trust, as well as by mutually pleasurable sex. But Hirsch also found that companionate marriage and the emphasis on love do not lessen inequality in marriage or tensions about who earns the money and who gives the orders. Instead, the emphasis on love appears to provide a modernizing sheen to continuing gender inequalities by glossing them over with sexuality and intimacy.

On a global scale, changing notions of marriage are combining with expanding economic opportunities for women to spur a rapid rise of divorce

Young people's ideas about marriage and intimacy in Degollado, Jalisco, Mexico, are shifting under the influence of globalization. In the Procession of Absent Sons each winter (*right*), residents of Degollado welcome home those who migrate north of the U.S. border to work, part of a festival atmosphere in which young people explore possibilities for love and marriage.

MAP 10.3
Degollado

MAP 10.4
Brazil

and marriage dissolution. Melanie Medeiros's (2014) ethnographic study of the small town of Brogodo in the rural interior of Northeast Brazil reveals the local impact of these transformations. Populated by Afro-Brazilian descendants of slaves and plantation workers, Brogodo's economy shrank drastically in the early twentieth century because of the decline of the mining industry, leaving residents to rely primarily on small-scale farming and remittances from relatives in urban areas. When the adjacent area was declared a national park in 1985, however, the growing eco-tourism industry generated better-paying local jobs, particularly for women who were recruited to work as receptionists, waitresses and housekeepers. Economic opportunities for men were more limited, as positions as tour guides went primarily to bilingual outsiders. Medeiros's fieldwork in Brogodo found that 40 percent of couples in local households surveyed were separated or divorced and that 95 percent of those dissolutions occurred at the request of women. Interviews confirmed that women's increased economic independence, combined with shifting expectations about gender roles and marriage, was driving up the rate of marital dissolution in Brogodo.

Cross-cultural ethnographic research reveals diversity in local expressions of companionate marriage but shows that young people around the world increasingly frame marriage in terms of love, in contrast to the marriage patterns of their parents (Hirsch 2007). Consider for a moment how your own views on marriage compare to those of your parents and grandparents.

Monogamy, Polygyny, and Polyandry Cultural rules, often inscribed in law, may determine who is a legitimate or preferred marriage partner. They may even determine how many people one can marry. Historically, some cultures, such as the Nuer of the Sudan or the Brahmans of Nepal, practiced **polygyny**—several marriages involving one man and two or more women. In a few cultures, including the Nyar of India and the Nyimba of Tibet and Nepal, **polyandry** has been common—marriages between one woman and two or more men. Most marriages in the world demonstrate **monogamy**—marriage (usually) between one man and one woman, though, as of 2017, twenty-two countries also legally recognize same-sex marriages, as we will discuss later in the chapter.

Even where monogamous marriages are the norm, it is common for people to marry more than one person in their lifetime. How does this happen? Marriages may be interrupted by divorce or death. In these cases, individuals who marry again reflect a process called *serial monogamy* in which monogamous marriages follow one after the other.

Incest Taboos Just as some form of marriage exists in essentially all cultures, likewise all cultures have some form of **incest taboo**, or rules that forbid sexual relations with certain close relatives. Such taboos relate to nuclear family

polygyny: Marriage between one man and two or more women.

polyandry: Marriage between one woman and two or more men.

monogamy: A relationship between only two partners.

incest taboo: Cultural rules that forbid sexual relations with certain close relatives.

members: parents and children, siblings, and grandparents and grandchildren. Incest taboos also affect marriage patterns. A few historical examples of brother-sister marriage exist: among the Inca of Peru, among certain traditional Hawaiian groups, and among ancient Egyptian royalty (perhaps to preserve family control over wealth and power). But these cases are rare. Incest taboos universally prohibit marriage between siblings and between parents and children. But can a person marry a cousin? Let's explore that question more closely.

Beyond the nuclear family, incest taboos vary from culture to culture. In some contemporary cultures, including parts of China, India, the Middle East, and Africa, *cross-cousins* (children of a mother's brother or father's sister) are preferred marriage partners, but *parallel cousins* (children of a father's brother or a mother's sister) are excluded. Even in the United States, incest rules regarding marriage between cousins vary from state to state. Nineteen states allow *first-cousin* marriages (between the children of two siblings). More distant cousins are not excluded from marriage under U.S. law. No other country in the Western world prohibits first-cousin marriage. Moreover, although it is illegal in the United States to marry a *half-sibling* (a brother or sister with whom one shares a parent), this is not illegal in many other cultures. Can you think of anyone in your family or a friend's family who is married to a cousin?

Even though the incest taboo is universal, its origins are unclear. Some scholars have suggested that the taboo arises from an instinctive horror of sex with immediate family members that developed during our evolutionary history (Hobhouse 1915; Lowie 1920). But studies of primates do not reveal a consistent incest taboo that humans might have inherited (Rodseth et al. 1991). Furthermore, if this instinctive horror existed, then it seems likely that humans would not need to create taboos to restrict incest.

Other theories have addressed the issue from different perspectives. For example, anthropologist Bronislaw Malinowski (1929) and psychologist Sigmund Freud (1952) both suggested that incest taboos might have developed to protect the family unit from sexual competitiveness and jealousy, which would disrupt cooperation. However, neither scholar could substantiate this claim with historical or contemporary ethnographic data. Another theory suggests that incest taboos arose out of concern that inbreeding would promote biological degeneration and genetically abnormal offspring (Morgan 1877). However, incest taboos predate the development of population science and the understanding of human genetics.

Even using contemporary genetic information, the science does not support the assumptions behind the incest taboo. For instance, incest does not create defective genes. If a harmful trait runs in the family, systematic inbreeding will increase the possibility of the defective gene being passed along and amplified in the gene pool. But long-term systematic inbreeding over many generations has few actual historical human examples. Genetic studies of consanguineous unions (between "blood" relatives) show some increased risk of congenital defects, but only within the studies' margin of error. These risks are actually less than the risk of congenital defects in children whose mothers are over the age of forty; yet this older population is not prohibited from marrying or giving birth (Bennett et al. 2002). Therefore, despite the universal existence of incest taboos, the extent of the taboos varies widely and no consensus exists as to their origins or exact purpose.

Other Marriage Patterns Beyond explicit incest taboos, all cultures have norms about who is a legitimate or preferred marriage partner. In some groups, including most descent groups, marriage tends to reflect **exogamy**, meaning marriage to someone outside the group. Other groups practice **endogamy**, requiring marriage inside the group. Although kin group exogamy is more prevalent, endogamy exists in numerous cultures. It is practiced, for example, within the Indian caste system and within whole ethnic groups, as evidenced by both historical and contemporary U.S. marriage patterns.

In the United States, we practice *kindred exogamy*: we avoid, either by force of law or by power of tradition, marriage with certain relatives. At the same time, we also follow clear patterns of class, race, and religious endogamy. Indeed, most marriages occur between people of the same economic class, the same religious tradition, and within the same "race" (U.S. Census Bureau 2010). As noted in Chapter 2, interracial marriages were outlawed for most of U.S. history, and only in 1967 did the U.S. Supreme Court rule that antimiscegenation laws are unconstitutional. Although interracial marriage is legal today, intense patterns of racial endogamy continue.

Most monogamous marriages occur between one man and one woman, but there are important exceptions, including female marriage among the Nuer of the Sudan and the Nandi of Kenya. Today same-sex marriage has gained increasing acceptance globally, being recognized in the Netherlands (2001), Belgium (2003), Spain (2005), South Africa (2006), Norway (2009), Sweden (2009), Argentina (2010), Iceland (2010), Portugal (2010), Denmark (2012), France (2013), Brazil (2013), Uruguay (2013), New Zealand (2013), the United Kingdom (2014), Luxemborg (2015), Ireland (2015), Greenland (2016), Colombia (2016), and Finland (2017). In North America, Canada legalized same-sex marriages in 2005. In the United States, as of June 2015 same-sex marriages are legal in all fifty states.

Whether arranged or not, and whether monogamous, polygynous, or polyandrous, same or opposite gender, marriages may be accompanied by an exchange of gifts—most commonly, bridewealth and dowry—used to formalize and legalize the relationship. Though most contemporary Western cultures view marriage as an individual matter entered into by a couple who are

exogamy: Marriage to someone outside the kinship group.

endogamy: Marriage to someone within the kinship group.

romantically in love, in many non-Western cultures marriages focus on the establishment of strategic alliances, relationships, and obligations between groups—namely, the bride's kin and the groom's kin. Bridewealth and dowry gifts formalize and legalize marriages and establish the relationship between these groups.

Bridewealth—common in many parts of the Middle East and Africa, where it often involves the exchange of cattle, cash, or other goods—is a gift from the groom and his kin to the bride's kin. Often thought of as a means to compensate her family for the loss of the bride, bridewealth agreements also establish reciprocal rights and obligations of the husband and wife, give legitimacy to their children, and assign the children to the husband's family. Even with the exchange of bridewealth, though, marriages may not always remain stable. Incompatibility, infertility, and infidelity can threaten the marriage agreement and trigger a return of the bridewealth. In this way, bridewealth can stabilize the marriage by establishing a vested interest for both extended families in the marriage's success (Stone 2009).

bridewealth: The gift of goods or money from the groom's family to the bride's family as part of the marriage process.

Through a **dowry**, the bride's family gives gifts to the husband's family at marriage. Common in India, a dowry may be part of a woman's family inheritance that the woman and her new husband can use to establish their household. In many cases, dowries may be seen as compensation to a husband and his family for taking on the responsibility of a wife, perhaps because of women's relatively low status in India or because upper-class and upper-caste women are

dowry: The gift of goods or money from the bride's family to the groom's family as part of the marriage process.

not supposed to work. Today gifts often include personal and household items. Compulsory dowries are no longer legal in India (since 1961). But dowries are still quite common as part of the public process of transferring rights and legitimizing alliances. In some unfortunate instances where the dowry is considered insufficient, the bride may become the victim of domestic violence. In extreme cases this may lead to the murder or suicide of the bride, sometimes through bride burning or self-immolation. Such practices have come under severe criticism and are the target of human rights campaigns by groups inside India and in the international community that are committed to protecting the rights and lives of Indian women (Stone 2009).

Are Biology and Marriage the Only Basis for Kinship?

Cross-cultural ethnographic research reveals diverse strategies for constructing kinship ties that do not require direct biological connection or marriage alliances. As you will see, the range of strategies underscores the fluid, socially constructed aspect of kinship in many cultures.

Houses, Hearths, and Kinship: The Langkawi of Malaysia

Among Malay villagers on the island of Langkawi, studied by Janet Carsten in the 1990s, kinship is not only given at birth but also is acquired throughout life (Carsten 1997). The Langkawi house and its hearth—where people gather to cook and eat—serve as places to construct kinship. In particular, Langkawi kinship is acquired through co-residence and co-feeding. In the local thinking, "blood" and other bodily substances are formed by eating food cooked at home. Other bodily substances, explicitly breast milk and semen, are regarded as forms of blood. Thus, a husband and wife gradually become more similar by living and eating together. Sisters and brothers have the closest kinship relationship in childhood because they grow up in the same household eating the same food; but as they marry and move out of the shared home, their "blood" becomes less similar.

The Malay ideal is to marry someone close in terms of genealogy, geography, social status, or disposition. But perhaps because of the Langkawis' history of mobility, as well as the arrival of settlers in their outlying region of the Malay state, local notions of kinship have allowed new people to become close kin by living and eating together. For example, many children in the community have grown up spending significant time in homes with adults other than their birth parents. This fostering has been common for nieces, nephews, grandchildren, and others who are welcomed into the foster family and treated on an equal basis with those born into the family.

MAP 10.4
Langkawi

In addition, Langkawi understandings of fostering have often included expressions of hospitality in the community, whether one is a short-term or long-term visitor, a visiting student, or a distant relative. Villagers assume that all those who live together and eat together, regardless of their backgrounds, gradually come to resemble one another physically. The ideal guest—successfully fostered—stays for a long time, becomes part of the community, marries a local person, and raises children. In this way, the individual fully enters the kin group. This flexible process has built kinship relations that do not require the connection of biology or marriage. Instead, "[h]ouses and their hearths are the sites of the production of kinship" (Carsten 1997, 128; Carsten 2004; Peletz 1999; Stone 2009).

Among the Langkawi in Malaysia, kinship is created by sharing meals prepared in the family hearth and living together in the same house. (*left*) Langkawi children eat together near the family kitchen. (*right*) A Langkawi child and her maternal great-grandmother sit together, becoming kin, on a house ladder.

Cousins by Choice: Asian Youth in Southall, England

Who are your cousins? Are they all biologically related to you? Not necessarily. For example, the youth in Southall, an ethnically diverse suburb of London, England, call one another "cousin" as a way to build strong connections across ethnic, religious, and cultural boundaries. These connections enjoy the strength of kinship and friendship combined.

Southall, sometimes referred to as Britain's South Asian capital, is home to Sikhs (the majority), Muslims, Hindus, Caribbean immigrants, and whites (primarily Irish). In Britain, these ethnic minority communities are often viewed as separate groups made up of people who are essentially the same and who pass down their cultures from generation to generation without significant change.

MAP 10.5
London

Dana Davis
Battered Women and Fictive Kin

Dana Davis's research in a shelter for battered women, recounted in her book *Battered Black Women and Welfare Reform* (2006), offers insights into the creative process that people use to construct fictive kinship relationships during times of need.

"Since most of the women spent up to three months at the shelter, they came to know each other very well, and the relationships they developed lasted well beyond shelter life. Because the escalation of violence in women's lives caused family ties to disintegrate, women . . . attempted to re-create the family that was lost due to violence" (Davis 2006, 154).

Reflecting on her fieldwork, Davis recalled, "Doing research in the battered women's shelter was very intense. But it was amazing to be around people who at least at that moment had made the decision to leave a battering relationship. They were actually feeling phenomenally empowered. But then felt disempowered as a result of their encounter with the welfare system."

Davis's fieldwork took place immediately after the 1996 passage of the U.S. federal Personal Responsibility and Work Opportunity Reconciliation Act (PRWORA). This legislation sought to restructure the welfare system by limiting the length of time recipients could receive benefits, imposing stricter conditions for food stamp eligibility, reducing assistance to immigrants, and instituting recipient work requirements. In the case of the shelter women, these policies were applied without regard to their experience of violence and abuse, the actual availability of jobs, or the women's efforts to keep their children safe. From Davis's perspective, many of the law's requirements made it more difficult for women in the shelter to access the governmental support they and their families needed. In addition, Davis found that the women experienced a racism deeply intertwined with public welfare programs and in the actions of program administrators. As a result, after experiencing violence in their personal lives, the women felt they faced a kind of structural violence—violence enacted by the welfare system and its staff. Confronted by these conditions, women turned to the construction of fictive kin to create their own social safety net.

"I always think of fictive kinship as rooted in Carol Stack's work. But I also experienced that process in my own life, having 'sisters' and 'aunts' and 'uncles' who became part of my extended family, people for whom there were mutual obligations. The battered women actually had a structure of who could be who in their networks. People employed at the shelter became uncles and aunts. By naming them that, they then did things that were against shelter rules, including going to people's houses, babysitting their kids, doing stuff for them. When they left the shelter, women named other women in the shelter 'sister.' They informally adopted other people's children. The relationships came with mutual obligations for food, money, and services. Some women couldn't afford to get

Anthropologist Dana Davis

a phone when they moved out to their own apartments. But another woman would get the phone, and someone who was her 'sister' could use that phone number when looking for a job. They were constantly negotiating kinship relationships. They were also negotiating psychological reparative relationships because of the violence and disconnections they had experienced."

Reflecting on her intimate work with women in the shelter during her research, Davis remembered, "There were people I helped individually. I bought food. I went with women to social services. I used my knowledge about human rights violations to urge women to file human rights complaints when they were experiencing what they perceived as demoralizing forms of structural violence when they went to the welfare office.

"What I found so fascinating was the things that women expected me to do as a result of their perception of my power. In fact, I did have more power than they did. Informants are pretty savvy. They know the research world and they wanted me to tell people stuff—meaning policy makers and people who could give the women some immediate relief from their desperation. And they didn't want me to clean it up, which is a slightly awkward and different dilemma.

"One woman was bulimic. She would just stick her finger down her throat to vomit and get people's attention, which she learned to do in foster care when she was being sexually abused. Then she wanted me to go to the department of housing to talk to the director about her bulimia and ask the director to help get her an apartment.

"It's hard to imagine having to go generate the performance of another person's pain. But the women wanted me to translate their experience. I didn't think twice about it at the time. I went right over to the housing department and spoke to the director—who was really quite nice—and I said, you know, this woman, she's going to start gagging and throwing up unless she gets a house. Of course it didn't help her get a house, but I did what she asked me to. It wasn't until I began writing about how desperate the circumstances made these women, that I understood more deeply why they were completely fine with the sensationalization of their experiences. It's all about how you manage depravation through revelation. How you tell your story.

"In hindsight, I would say that I didn't do research on battered women, per se. I would say I did research on neoliberalism [see Chapter 12]. Since the women were experiencing the direct effects of U.S. welfare reform policies, I was really looking at the impact of privatization and neoliberalism, through the lens of battered women. I was talking to real people about something that is ideological and economic and global while at the same time very personal. My research on battered women sat at the intersection of neoliberalism, race, and gender, and at the intersection of intimate violence and structural violence."

In talking about what she hopes for anthropology students, Davis said, "I want students to think outside their own boxes. Anthropology has an accumulation of ethnographic data that helps us see things differently. But anthropology doesn't just help you understand the diversity of the world. It should help you think critically about your own perceptions of the world. Every conversation about cultural anthropology needs to work back to the question, 'How do you now interpret yourself and your community's behavior?'"

> *Anthropology doesn't just help you understand the diversity of the world. It should help you think critically about your own perceptions of the world.*

Youth in Southall, outside London, call one another "cousin" to build connections across boundaries of ethnicity, religion, and race.

In contrast, Southall youth are creating more diverse, inclusive notions of community and culture, connection, and kinship. According to anthropologist Gerd Baumann, who studied Southall youth in the 1990s, these young people are less locked into the dominant ideas of ethnic, cultural, and religious difference and are more open to the possibility of a connected Asian community. "Cousins are friends who are kin and kin who are friends," said one of the youths Baumann interviewed (1995, 734). A cousin may be related by biology or through choice. Southall youth may encourage their parents to let them go out because they are going out "with their cousins." Or they may line up cousins for protection against possible street violence because family takes care of family. In the process, Southall's youth are expanding the idea of kin across boundaries of religion, ethnicity, and culture.

Why has the kinship term *cousin* been so successful for constructing kinship ties in Southall? Because *cousin* is common in many of the languages and immigrant cultures represented in the community, people of diverse backgrounds share some common expectations about what being a cousin means. Biological cousins, like any biological alliances, are not always reliable in times of intense need. So the possibility of adding other, more trustworthy, cousins to one's kinship network is very attractive. And success in constructing cousins has led to further experimentation. In Southall, the power of *cousin* derives from the blurring of lines of kinship and friendship. Kinship carries a sense of obligation and loyalty; friendship affords the power of choice and preference. Together they generate a blend of moral expectations that establishes a unique foundation for relatedness. Using the term *cousin* provides an opening to build connections, alliances, and deep relations among people of often extremely different backgrounds (Helweg 1998; Shaw 1998).

MAP 10.6
Chicago

Creating Kin to Survive Poverty: Black Networks near Chicago, Illinois

Kinship can even be a means to survive poverty, as Carol Stack's *All Our Kin: Strategies for Survival in a Black Community* (1974) demonstrates. This ethnography is a classic in anthropological kinship studies. Through deep involvement in an impoverished urban African American community called the Flats in a town outside Chicago, Stack uncovered residents' complex survival strategies based on extended kinship networks.

Although the federal government's 1965 Moynihan Report "The Negro Family: The Case for National Action" had branded the black family as disorganized, dysfunctional, and lost in a culture of poverty of its own making (see Chapter 11), Stack found otherwise. She uncovered a dynamic set of kinship networks based on mutual reciprocity through which residents managed to survive conditions of intense structural poverty and long-term unemployment.

These kinship networks included biological kin and *fictive kin*—those who became kin. They stretched among households and across generations, extending to include all those willing to participate in a system of mutual support. Members provided child care. They loaned money to others in need. They took in children who needed a foster home for a while. They borrowed clothes. They exchanged all kinds of things when asked. They cared for one another's sick or aging family members. Despite survival odds stacked against them in a community with few jobs, dilapidated housing, and chronic poverty, residents of the Flats succeeded in building lifelines for survival through their extended kinship networks (McAdoo 2000; Taylor 2000).

For another look at black women's strategies for establishing kin relationships, see "Anthropologists Engage the World" on pages 368–369.

How Are Ideas of Kinship Linked to the Nation-State?

References to the nation often invoke metaphors of homeland, motherland, fatherland, and ancestral home. These concepts consolidate political force and build a sense of common nationality and ethnicity. Indeed, Benedict Anderson, in *Imagined Communities* (1983), marvels at the ability of nation-states to inspire a common national or ethnic identity among people who have never met, most likely never will meet, and have little in common socially, politically, or economically. Yet many people feel so connected to their country that they are even willing to die for it. How does this idea of the "nation" gain such emotional power? Janet Carsten (2004) suggests that nationalism draws heavily on ideas of kinship and family to create a sense of connection among very different people.

Like membership in many families, citizenship in the nation generally derives from birth and biology. Citizenship may be conveyed through direct descent from a current citizen. Another key pathway to membership in some nations, available to immigrants and other outsiders, like membership in many other families, is through marriage. Over time, members of the nation come to see themselves as part of an extended family that shares a common ancestry and a deep biological connection. As the boundaries blur among kinship, nationalism, and even religion, these powerful metaphors shape our actions and experiences (Carsten 2004). The next two sections illustrate how experiences related to the concepts of kinship and the nation can differ dramatically from one culture to another.

YOUR TURN: FIELDWORK

Mapping Kinship Relationships: Tracing Your Family Tree

Kinship is constructed. Exactly how it is constructed can vary from culture to culture. For example, families can be formed on the basis of biology, marriage, and/or choice. Thus strategies for building kinship and identifying relatives can be complicated. In this exercise, you will trace your family tree. Keeping in mind what you've read in this chapter, let's see what you can learn about how your family has constructed kinship relationships.

Getting Started

Here is an abbreviated list of symbols used to create a genealogical kinship chart. The chart starts with a key individual, the central character, who is referred to as the "ego" and serves as the starting point in tracing kinship relationships. In your family tree, you are the ego.

What does your family's kinship network reveal about your family history that you didn't know before?

Symbol	Meaning	Symbol	Meaning
Characters		*Kin Abbreviations*	
Δ	male	M	mother
○	female	F	father
□	individual	B	brother
	regardless of sex	Z	sister
/ (ⵄ, Ø)	deceased	H	husband
▲, ●, ■	ego of the	W	wife
	diagram	D	daughter
		S	son
		C	cousin

Symbol	Meaning
Relationships	
=	is married to
≠	is divorced from
~	cohabitates with
≁	is separated from / does not cohabitate with
		is descended from
⊓ (⊓)	is the sibling of
⊙	adopted-in female
△	adopted-in male

Research Strategies

In gathering information about your family history, many sources are available. Interview family members. Search family records to see what might already exist. Old family papers and record books can be very useful. For instance, family Bibles often have records written in them, and photographs may have names or dates noted on the back. Search for family burial plots; census and voter rolls; birth, marriage, and death certificates; wills; land deeds; and immigration and military records. Consult genealogy websites, and consider using an online program that allows members of your family to add information to your tree.

Kinship Language in Comparative Perspective

Language can tell you a lot about kinship. Anthropologists compare genealogical kin types to various cultures' actual kinship terms. For example, Americans use the term *uncle* to cover a wide range of kin, including a mother's brother (MB), a father's brother (FB), a mother's sister's husband (MZH), and a father's sister's husband (FZH). In this context *uncle* does not differentiate biological descent from marriage relationships, nor does it distinguish by age.

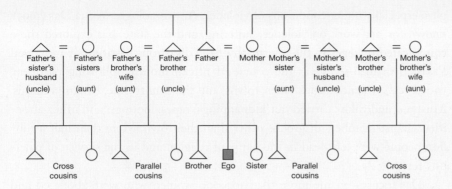

FIGURE 10.2 Nuclear Family Kinship Chart

This typical kinship chart of a nuclear family is labeled both with genealogical kin type and with the culturally specific kinship terms used in the United States. Your family may not fit this pattern, but it provides a place to start building your own family tree.

In contrast, Chinese terminology calculates kinship much more carefully. It distinguishes paternal and maternal relatives as well as birth order within generations and biological versus affinal descent. The Chinese do not have a generic term for "uncle." Instead, unique terms denote a father's older brother as opposed to his younger brother. A distinction also exists between a father's brothers and a mother's brothers, as well as between a father's sister's husband and a mother's sister's husband.

Father's older brother: *bofu* 伯父
Father's younger brother: *shufu* 叔父
Father's sister's husband: *gufu* 姑父
Mother's brother: *jiufu* 舅父
Mother's older sister's husband: *yifu* 姨父

Kinship terminology reflects different calculations within the culture about the role of these relatives in the life of the ego. In much of China, the extended family (*jia* 家) and lineage (*zu* 族) have played a pervasive role in economics, politics, and religion. As a result, kinship roles and obligations are carefully traced and implemented.

As you develop your own kinship chart/family tree, try using kin types rather than kin terms to make your family tree as specific and informative as possible. The simplicity of contemporary U.S. kinship terminology reflects the dominant role of the nuclear family that focuses on father, mother, and children as the key kinship relationships. Uncles and aunts, regardless of their genealogical kin type, play a limited role in child rearing, economic support, and inheritance. With kinship calculated bilaterally (that is, with equal weight on the mother's and the father's sides of the kinship chart), there is no need to differentiate kinship terminology at this level.

Interpreting Your Family Tree

Families are more than lines on a family tree. Families represent stories, interesting people, power dynamics, even mysteries. What story does your family tree tell? Your family tree reflects educational patterns, geographic relocations, and inheritance flows. It has grown and been pruned through biology, marriage, and choice. Some branches likely are well preserved, and others might be missing. Who has been cultivating and pruning the tree and who has the records now? As a budding anthropologist, you are interested in what patterns your family tree reveals.

MAP 10.7
Punjab

Muslims, carrying their possessions, flee India for Pakistan as riots spread following the partitioning of India in 1947.

Violence, Kinship, and the State: Abducted Women in Western Punjab

The relationship between kinship and the nation-state can be highly complex, especially under conditions of violence. Anthropologist Veena Das (1995), known for her work on violence, suffering, and the state, has explored these complicated linkages in the aftermath of the disastrous partition of India and Pakistan in 1946–47. Over the course of fifteen months following partition, widespread violence struck cities, towns, and the countryside. Fanatic Hindus, Muslims, and Sikhs carried out kidnappings, rapes, lootings, and other atrocities against members of groups other than their own. More than half a million people were left dead in the name of religion and in the service of patriotic fervor.

Das focuses on the more than 100,000 women who were abducted and the many more who were raped during the mayhem. Their abduction and rape created a moral and practical crisis, both for families and for the state. Within families of West Punjab, where most of the abuses occurred, kinship norms traditionally placed high values on purity and honor to help regulate sexuality. Thus, women who were violated and abducted during the violence were seen to bring shame on themselves and their families. In fact, Das documents widespread stories, particularly among men, who honored the memory of women relatives who chose death rather than sexual violation. These women were considered heroic martyrs.

After the conflict, the governments of both countries set a high priority on recovering the "sisters and daughters" who had been abducted so they could be restored to their families of origin. Over several years, however, numbers of abducted women had married, become pregnant, borne children, and even converted to their abductor-husbands' religion. Yet the return of these women and children became a matter of national honor. The Indian and Pakistani governments passed legislation invalidating their marriages and conversions and forced them to leave their new families behind.

Despite each state's sense of victory in restoring its national kinship honor, the women's families of origin did not always share this satisfaction. For example, many returning women were quietly married off to any relative who would take them. Their children—conceived during abduction—were rarely claimed as legitimate kin. Both the women and children were left out of family genealogies and stories.

Overall, the return effort yielded contradictory outcomes. The state celebrated the return of abducted sisters, daughters, and their children as a sign of the restoration of the national family and the upholding of its paternal role to protect its family members. But the state's actions conflicted with local kinship norms. Family honor was not restored by the return of the abductees, but rather was compromised by the sexual violations these women had experienced. Although the state sought the return of its rightful members as an act of purification to restore national honor, local families, confronting the abducted women's perceived pollution, sought to restore family honor by pushing the women away and silencing their stories. In these contradictory outcomes, we see how kinship can serve as an arena in which other structures of power exert domination.

Reproducing Jews: Issues of Artificial Insemination in Israel

In another nation as well, Israel, we can see how women serve as key players in defining and maintaining kinship connections. Susan Kahn's (2000) ethnography *Reproducing Jews: A Cultural Account of Assisted Conception in Israel* provides a dramatic contemporary example of the powerful intersection among reproduction, kinship, religion, and the state. For historical and religious reasons, Jewish women in Israel feel great pressure to reproduce the family and the nation. Israel's national health policies heavily favor increased reproduction. The national health insurance, for instance, subsidizes all assisted reproductive technologies. It does not promote family planning services to prevent pregnancy. Today the country has more fertility clinics per person than any other nation in the world, and it was the first to legalize surrogate motherhood.

MAP 10.8
Israel

Kahn's study examines a small but growing group of single Jewish mothers who are giving birth through artificial insemination. Because Jewishness passes down matrilineally from mother to child, what happens when a child is conceived through assisted reproductive technologies? These matters are of vital importance to the reproduction of Judaism and the state of Israel and, thus, are subject to intense debate by Jewish rabbis and Israeli state policymakers alike. Some scenarios are straightforward. For instance, in the eyes of the Israeli state any offspring conceived through artificial insemination and born to unmarried Jewish women are legitimate citizens. The line of descent and religious inheritance through the mother is clear. As evidence, the state provides these unmarried mothers with a wide range of support, including housing, child care, and tax breaks.

But other scenarios spur complex disagreements about religion and nationality. What is the effect on citizenship and religious identity when non-Jewish men donate sperm to Jewish women? Who is considered to be the father—the sperm donor or the mother's husband? When Jewish women carry to term eggs

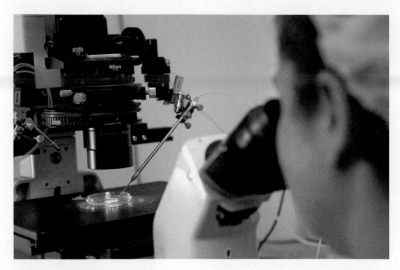

What is the relationship between kinship and the nation-state? A lab technician looks through a microscope while fertilizing egg cells at a fertility clinic in Tel Aviv, Israel.

from non-Jewish women, who is considered to be the mother—the donor of the egg or the woman who carries the egg to term? The situation is equally complicated if a non-Jewish surrogate mother carries the embryo of a Jewish woman that was fertilized by a Jewish man through in vitro fertilization.

Much is at stake in these arguments for the Jewish religion and for the state of Israel. The decision about kinship in these cases of assisted reproductive technologies intersects with heated debates about how Judaism is reproduced and how Israel is populated. In fact, the decision has implications not only for the Jewish religion but also for notions of ethnic and national belonging and for the pathways to legal citizenship in the state of Israel (Feldman 2001; Finkler 2002; Nahman 2002; Stone 2009).

How Is Kinship Changing in the Modern World?

Kinship patterns are rapidly changing around the world in response to cultural shifts, changing gender roles, new imaginations of marriage, technological advances, and processes of globalization.

The Nuclear Family: The Ideal versus the Reality

The nuclear family concept acquired a particular history in Western industrialized cultures. This occurred as families adapted to an economic system that required increased mobility to follow job opportunities wherever they might lead. Though people are born into a **family of orientation** (in which they grow up and develop life skills), when they reach adulthood they are expected to detach from their nuclear family of orientation, choose a mate, and construct a new nuclear **family of procreation** (in which they reproduce and raise their own children). These "detachable" nuclear family units are extremely well adapted to a culture that prioritizes economic success, independence, and mobility over geographic stability and intergenerational continuity. In many ways, this view of the nuclear family has become entrenched as the standard against which to judge other family forms (Schneider 1980).

Historical studies suggest that the place of the nuclear family as the cornerstone of U.S. culture may be more myth than reality (Coontz 1988, 1992). Although the nuclear family came into prominence during a unique period

family of orientation: The family group in which one is born, grows up, and develops life skills.

family of procreation: The family group created when one reproduces and within which one rears children.

of economic expansion after World War II, before that time it had not played a major role in the kinship history of the United States. The idealized nuclear family of the twentieth century did not exist for the early colonists and only emerged as a result of industrialization in the nineteenth century. Even at its height in the mid-twentieth century, participation in the nuclear family model was far from universal. It was limited to a minority of Americans, particularly those in the white middle class (Carsten 2004; Coontz 1988, 1992; Stone 2009).

Current kinship patterns in the United States are changing rapidly, just as they are in many other parts of the world. In a wide variety of newly constructed family forms and kinship networks, biology is becoming less central and personal choice is becoming more important (Figure 10.3). Families are creatively renegotiating kinship after divorce. Blended families are constructing new relationships to include step-parents, step-children, step-siblings, multiple sets of grandparents, and extended households of former spouses. Unmarried couples are living together. Same-sex couples are having or adopting children. Families are supplementing biological connections and affinal marriage connections with alternative family forms based on friendship, respect, and mutual support. New reproductive technologies are yielding families of choice through in vitro fertilization, artificial insemination, and surrogacy. These patterns cut across all social classes and ethnic groups and reflect new residential and interpersonal relationships that contrast sharply with the imagined privacy and separation associated with the nuclear family ideal.

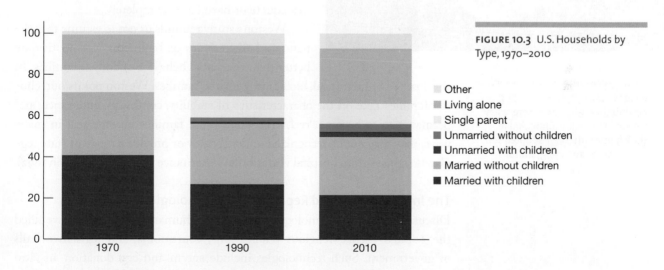

FIGURE 10.3 U.S. Households by Type, 1970–2010

- Other
- Living alone
- Single parent
- Unmarried without children
- Unmarried with children
- Married without children
- Married with children

SOURCE: *U.S. Census Bureau. 2014. "Families and Living Arrangements." http://www.census.gov /hhes/families/data/families.html*

Chosen Families

Kath Weston's (1991) ethnographic study of the construction of gay and lesbian families in San Francisco in the 1980s, *Families We Choose*, provides an example of creating kinship through choice. For many gay men and lesbians, "coming out" is a uniquely traumatic experience, especially when the revelation of one's sexuality and life choices generates hostility from close friends and family. When parents, siblings, and other close relatives cut off the kinship ties that U.S. culture suggests should be permanent and enduring, gay men and lesbians have turned to chosen families instead.

Not surprisingly, chosen families come in many shapes and sizes. Gay and straight friends, biological children, children adopted formally and informally, and former lovers all can become kin. Close friends can become family. Support networks and caregivers can take the place of biological kin and become kin themselves. Weston finds this to be a particularly common experience for those who provide care through intense illness, such as AIDS. Love, compassion, and the hard work of care over time make kinship very real in chosen families. This is a crucial development, especially when biological kin ties are inadequate or have failed completely.

Weston's study reminds us not to assume that the natural characteristics of biological kinship ties are better than the actual behavior of chosen families. In the absence of functional, biologically related families, Weston points out, chosen families take on the characteristics of stability, continuity, endurance, and permanence to become "real." Yet while these families become real in many ways, they may not be recognized under the law or provide a range of state regulated rights—from hospital visitation to inheritance (Bolin 1992; Lewin 1992).

The Impact of Assisted Reproductive Technologies

Discussions of new technologies that assist in human reproduction have filled the popular media, religious publications, courtrooms, and legislative halls of government. Such technologies include sperm and egg donation, in vitro fertilization, surrogacy, and cloning. Their emergence raises questions about the rights of parents and of children born with this assistance, as well as the

Increasingly people are creating kinship through choice. Here, a gay couple in Chengdu, China, share their home with their adopted son, daughter-in-law, and grandson.

impact of these innovations on our ideas and experience of kinship and family. Culture, in the form of medical technology, is now shaping biology. The long-term implications for kinship are unclear but deserve consideration (Franklin 1997).

Reproductive technologies are not new. Most, if not all, cultures have had techniques for promoting or preventing conception or enabling or terminating pregnancy. These have included fertility enhancements, contraceptives, abortion, and cesarean surgeries. Over the last thirty years, technological developments have opened new avenues for scientific intervention in the reproductive process and the formation of kinship. DNA testing can now determine the identity of a child's father with remarkable certainty, erasing uncertainty about paternity. Medical tests can now identify the sex of unborn children, a practice that has become problematic in parts of India and China where a strong cultural preference for male children has led to early termination of many female fetuses (Davis-Floyd & Dumit 1997). Across the globe, when reproductive technologies become increasingly specialized, the implications for cultural constructs such as family and kinship become progressively more complex.

Families of Same-Sex Partners

Gay and lesbian couples are not new in U.S. culture, but recently they have become more open about their sexual orientation and their relationships. At the same time, many other people are having an increasingly open discussion about gay men, lesbians, and same-sex marriage. Television shows and movies routinely include gay characters. Celebrities like Elton John, Jillian Michaels, and Neil Patrick Harris raise children with their same-sex partners. The United Methodist Church ordained its first openly gay bishop, Karen Oliveto, in 2016. And when a high school in Louisiana canceled its senior prom in 2010 rather than allow a graduating student to bring her girlfriend as her date, a group of parents organized an alternative prom so the girls could attend. These examples demonstrate a growing recognition of same-sex relationships in numerous U.S. cultural arenas.

However, the cultural debate about homosexuality and same-sex marriage in the United States is intense and by no means settled. Within the debate we can see the contestation of cultural norms and values. Opponents raise concerns that these alternative kinship patterns will cause the breakdown of the traditional family and that the acceptance of homosexuality will lead to social disorder.

Julia Troxler (*right*) and new spouse Barbara Schwartz (*center*) celebrate their wedding in Atlanta, Georgia, in 2015, just hours after the U.S. Supreme Court ruled same-sex marriage a constitutional right.

Drawing on generations of cross-cultural research on kinship, marriage, and the family, in 2004 the American Anthropological Association issued the following statement:

> The results of more than a century of anthropological research on households, kinship relationships, and families, across cultures and through time, provide no support whatsoever for the view that either civilization or viable social orders depend upon marriage as an exclusively heterosexual institution. Rather, anthropological research supports the conclusion that a vast array of family types, including families built upon same-sex partnerships, can contribute to stable and humane societies. (American Anthropological Association 2004)

From an anthropological perspective, these discussions about same-sex marriage illustrate the changing patterns of kinship in the United States. Looking cross-culturally, we see that there is no single definition of marriage, but many. As anthropologist Linda Stone notes, "From a global, cross-cultural perspective, those who seek same-sex marriage are not trying to redefine marriage, but merely to define it for themselves, in their own interests, as people around the world have always done" (Stone 2009, 271).

Transnational Adoptions

The process of adoption—the legal transferring of children for parenting purposes—and the experiences of adopted children and their families offer further insight into the social construction of kinship and the creation of chosen families. At the same time, the recent rise in transnational adoptions offers insights into the influence of globalization on the construction of kinship across national borders.

Global Trends and Structural Players In the United States, by 2008 inter-country adoptions represented 12.8 percent of all adoptions, the third largest source after adoption by relatives and those organized through a U.S. child welfare agency. Fully 17,416 out of 135,813 adoptions in 2008 were arranged across national borders. By 2014 the total number of intercountry adoptions had dropped to 6,441 as many countries established more restrictive adoption guidelines. The top five "sending" countries were China (2,040), Ethiopia (716), Ukraine (521), Haiti (464), and South Korea (370). Globally, not all countries permit international adoption of their children. Even those that do allow such adoptions, such as China and Korea, have well-established rules and strict procedures (Kim 2010). In contrast, Guatemala, in 2007 the second largest sending country, significantly curtailed its adoption program in response to abuses that include the trafficking of children bought or stolen from their Guatemalan birth parents (U.S. Department of Health & Human Services 2012). In 2013, Russia banned adoptions of Russian children by U.S. citizens.

It is no surprise that the power of government offices, welfare agencies, immigration departments, and other institutions shapes the movement of people based on age, nationality, gender, and class. In this context, the exchange of babies creates a global market in which children in certain countries become commodities for consumption by parents in other countries. Research by sociologist Sara Dorow explores this complicated intersection of economics, politics, national identities, race, gender, and class created through the adoption process.

In *Transnational Adoption: A Cultural Economy of Race, Gender, and Kinship* (2006), Dorow traces the journey of Chinese children adopted by U.S. parents as they cross geographic, cultural, ethnic, and class divides. Most children adopted from China have been abandoned in public spaces or secretly delivered to orphanages by Chinese parents struggling to navigate the contradictory pressures of (1) a strong cultural preference for sons and (2) government-enforced family planning policies that until 2015 sought to limit families to one child. In traditional Chinese exogamous marriage patterns, daughters marry out into another family. Sons then provide the only guaranteed source of long-term labor and financial security, especially for rural families.

China provides no legal channel for parents to put their children up for adoption. As a result, Dorow estimates that several hundred thousand abandoned babies, almost all girls, are in the care of Chinese orphanages at any given time. An even larger number have been adopted by Chinese families in China through informal processes. Moreover, fully 90 percent of intercountry Chinese adoptions are girls.

Dorow advocates a comprehensive and global view of the process—a view that incorporates cultural norms and values, the political contexts of the sending and receiving countries, economic factors, and a vast array of institutions and individual actors that combine to create a new form of international immigration. Dorow's multi-sited, global ethnography traces the paths of the children through the adoption process and their encounters with a complicated array of orphanages, administrators, government offices, tourist hotels, adoption agencies, translators, facilitators, advocacy groups, social workers, support groups, adoptive families, and the children themselves. All play a role in a circuitous, expensive (adoptive families pay $35,000 on average), and public process of creating the intimate experience of kinship.

Is a "Clean Break" Possible? One attraction of Chinese adoptions is the imagination of a "clean break" between the family of birth and the family of adoption. Public records of biological parents rarely exist for abandoned Chinese babies, significantly curtailing the likelihood of later attempts to reclaim the children or reestablish contact. The new parents become indisputably permanent and legal parents. And with the passage of the 2001 U.S. Child Citizen Act, children adopted abroad are automatically granted U.S. citizenship upon their return with citizen parents to the United States. The Act dramatically streamlines the process of adoption, citizenship, and, in the eyes of adoptive parents, assimilation into their new families, culture, and nation. Many adoptive parents also believe that Asian children are more easily assimilated into white families than children of Latino, Native American, or African descent, including African American babies—thus facilitating the "clean break" from country and culture of origin.

But Dorow's research questions whether such a clean break is possible. Where do adopted Chinese babies belong? Born in China, are they Chinese? Adopted by U.S. families, are they American? Are they Chinese American? How are Chinese girls made kin?

Dorow traces the many strategies that adoptive parents and their children take to navigate the space that adoptive children inhabit between U.S. and Chinese culture. They participate in Chinese cultural celebrations, maintain contact with Chinese orphanages, participate in support groups or groups of children adopted from the same agency, and even make return visits to China. Such activities help to restore a sense of history in the face of the many silences and gaps related to birth parents, birth family, ancestry, and home village. Still, Asian children of white parents are frequently marked as nonbiological kin. "Are these your real kids?" adoptive parents are often asked. Friends and neighbors, classmates and teachers still read race and kinship in the bodies of these adopted children (Yngvesson 2003).

Dorow challenges all those "touched by adoption"—the extended network of people who are affected by adoption and whose lives affect the adoption experience—to "reimagine an intimate geography of difference" (Dorow 2006, 269) that can better bridge the contradictions of race, class, family, and nation. The adoption process creates possibilities for transformative new patterns of kinship and belonging. By looking beyond the borders of difference, transnational and transracial adoption holds out possibilities to reimagine a global kinship focused on belonging rather than dislocation (Dorow 2006; Kim 2007; Volkman 2005).

Today, changes in the nuclear family, the rise of families of choice, the increase of same-sex marriages, advances in assisted reproductive technologies, and the expansion of transnational adoptions are reshaping views of kinship and family in the United States and globally. These changes do not necessarily

Globalization is shaping kinship as families are constructed across national borders. Here, couples from the United States wait at the U.S. embassy in Guangzhou, south China, to get visas for their newly adopted Chinese children.

indicate an improvement or decline of family life or moral values. However, they do reveal a shift of kinship patterns away from a biologically defined, nuclear family model toward other models based on choice, flexibility, and fluidity (Stone 2009; Coontz 1992).

While debates will continue over changing patterns of marriage and family, from an anthropological perspective one point is undeniable: Marriage, family and kinship are cultural constructs, and as such they are subject to change. You are certain to see even more change in these arenas during your lifetime.

Thinking Like an Anthropologist: Kinship in Personal and Global Perspective

We experience kinship all the time, although we may not use that term to describe it. Kinship is close to home, for it comes alive in the people we live with, eat with, play with. It is vital as we experience the most dramatic periods of our personal lives. You will continue to make kinship and family relationships—perhaps through marriage, having children, and choosing close friends who ultimately become family. Thinking like an anthropologist can help you to better understand these experiences. And in today's globally interconnected world, having an understanding of the vast diversity of kinship patterns may help you navigate relationships with classmates, friends, family, and colleagues. As you do so, keep in mind the questions that have guided our discussion in this chapter:

- How are we related to one another?
- Are biology and marriage the only basis for kinship?
- How are ideas of kinship linked to the nation-state?
- How is kinship changing in the modern world?

In thinking about the complex family relationships described in the chapter opener, how can we apply this chapter's ideas to better understand their situation and, more generally, any future changes in the constructs of kin and family? Who is related to whom? Who decides? Is kinship primarily biological, or can family be chosen? Who constitutes your own family? As you traced your family tree, did you see that kinship is not only about creating a list of relatives but also about understanding the many ways those ties are formed and the role that kin play in shaping you as an individual and as a member of society? These tools of anthropological analysis will become increasingly important to you as you engage changing concepts of kinship in cultures across the globe during the twenty-first century.

Key Terms

kinship (p. 348)

nuclear family (p. 348)

descent group (p. 349)

lineage (p. 350)

clan (p. 350)

affinal relationship (p. 360)

marriage (p. 360)

arranged marriage (p. 360)

companionate marriage (p. 360)

polygyny (p. 362)

polyandry (p. 362)

monogamy (p. 362)

incest taboo (p. 362)

exogamy (p. 364)

endogamy (p. 364)

bridewealth (p. 365)

dowry (p. 365)

family of orientation (p. 376)

family of procreation (p. 376)

For Further Exploration

Bridewealth for a Goddess. 2000. Film by Chris Owen, with Andrew Strathern. Ronin Films. An elaborate religious ritual in the Western Highlands of New Guinea in which men seek protection through marriage to a powerful goddess.

Coontz, Stephanie. 1988. *The Social Origins of Private Life: A History of American Families* 1600–1900. New York: Verso.

———. 1992. *The Way We Never Were: American Families and the Nostalgia Trap*. New York: Basic Books.

———. 1997. *The Way We Really Are: Coming to Terms with America's Changing Families*. New York: Basic Books.

Holtzman, Jon D. 2000. *Nuer Journeys, Nuer Lives: Sudanese Refugees in Minnesota*. Boston: Allyn & Bacon. As a result of the civil war in Sudan, some Nuer refugees now live in Minnesota. Holtzman discusses changes in Nuer lifestyle since Evans-Pritchard's time and in the context of global migration.

"The Complicated Chinese Family Tree." 2013. bit.ly/191waB3. Humorous YouTube video elaborating Chinese kinship terms in just four minutes.

The Nuer. 1971. Produced by Robert Gardner and Hilary Harris for The Film Study Center at Harvard University. CRM/McGraw-Hill Films. Classic film portraying the traditional, cattle-centered life of the Nuer of Sudan.

Saheri's Choice: Arranged Marriage in India. 2002. Films for the Humanities and Sciences, Princeton, NJ. A contemporary arranged marriage seen through the life story of an Indian girl.

Labor and community activists call for Michigan Governor Rick Snyder to resign over the Flint water contamination crisis.

CHAPTER 11
Class and Inequality

In January 2016, National Guard troops deployed to Flint, Michigan, distributing bottled water to residents who for nearly two years had unsafe water flowing out of their taps. In April 2014, the emergency manager appointed by Michigan's governor to tackle Flint's fiscal crisis had switched the source of drinking water from Lake Huron to the highly corrosive and historically polluted Flint River. The city's failure to implement corrosion control measures then caused lead to leach out of aging water pipes into residents' drinking water.

Widespread complaints and public protests of foul smelling orange-brown water, rashes, hair loss, abdominal pains, and other health problems were dismissed by city and state officials who offered assurances that the water was safe to drink. It was not.

Only when a Flint pediatrician, Dr. Mona Hanna-Attisha, and researchers from Virginia Tech in September 2015 reported widespread incidents of children testing positive for elevated lead levels did officials begin to react, and then only after more weeks of denial. Lead is a known neurotoxin, and lead poisoning can severely affect children's physical and mental development. Its effects are irreversible.

Under mounting pressure, in October 2015 officials returned Flint's water supply to its Lake Huron source. But using bottled water for drinking, cooking and bathing has become a daily routine for Flint residents in a city with a severely damaged water system. The long-term effects of Flint's public health emergency are unknown.

How could such a water crisis—more often associated with megacities in the global South—have been created in one of the wealthiest countries in the world? What made Flint particularly vulnerable?

MAP 11.1
Flint

Flint, about an hour's drive north of Detroit, was once a prosperous working-class city at the center of the Industrial Revolution. Birthplace of General Motors and the United Automobile Workers union, its population peaked at almost 200,000 in 1960, and as late as 1978 GM employed nearly 80,000 residents. But over the next forty years Flint was gutted by deindustrialization and flexible accumulation as GM relocated jobs overseas in search of cheaper wages, fewer environmental restrictions, lower taxes, and greater profits. Today Flint is one of the country's poorest cities. Its majority African American population has dropped to under 100,000, and fewer than 8,000 GM jobs remain. The city's poverty rate is over 40 percent and its median household income is $24,679.

As anthropologists have long noted (Wittfogel 1957), the circulation of water is not a strictly natural process involving oceans, lakes, streams, evaporation, clouds, and rain. Increasingly, the circulation of water intersects with human systems of power to become a *hydro-social process*. Nature intersects with dams, canals, irrigation systems, pipes, pumps, faucets, drains, and sewers. Technicians manage its circulation. Politicians allocate resources for its infrastructure. On a global scale, the distribution of water reveals the distribution of social power along intersecting lines of class, race, gender, and age (Harvey 1996, 2003). Who has access to it, controls its flow, and organizes its distribution? According to the United Nations and the World Health Organization, 663 million people in the world lack access to safe drinking water, 1.8 billion people use a water source contaminated by fecal matter, and each year 340,000 children die from related diseases (World Health Organization, 2015b). In Flint, the hydro-social process led to the poisoning of the city's water supply.

The water crisis in Flint offers particular insights into the complicated workings of class and inequality in U.S. culture. Of all the systems of stratification and power, class may be the most difficult to see clearly and discuss openly. In previous chapters we have considered stratification along lines of race, ethnicity, gender, and sexuality. In this chapter we will explore the systems of class and inequality that exist in the United States and elsewhere: how they are constructed, how class intersects with race and gender, and how inequality affects individuals' life chances.

class: A system of power based on wealth, income, and status that creates an unequal distribution of a society's resources.

By **class** we refer to a system of power based on wealth, income, and status that creates an unequal distribution of the society's resources—usually moving wealth steadily upward into the hands of an elite. Systems of class stratify individuals' life chances and affect their possibilities for upward social mobility.

In this chapter we will consider the following questions:

- Is inequality a natural part of human culture?
- How do anthropologists analyze class and inequality?

- How are class and inequality constructed?
- What makes class and inequality largely invisible?
- What is caste, and how are caste and class related?
- What are the effects of global inequality?

By the end of the chapter, you will understand how systems of class work and how they affect your life chances and those of others. You may also be motivated to engage in efforts to change systems of inequality if you so choose. As you prepare for a career in the global economy and a life in this global age, being able to analyze the effects of class and inequality will prove an essential tool in your anthropological toolkit.

Is Inequality a Natural Part of Human Culture?

Inequality exists in every contemporary culture, though it may be organized in very different ways. Each society develops its own patterns of stratification that differentiate people into groups or classes. Such categories serve as the basis for unequal access to wealth, power, resources, privileges, and status. As discussed in earlier chapters, these systems of power and stratification may include race, ethnicity, gender, and sexuality. In addition, systems of social class create and sustain patterns of inequality, structuring the relationships between rich and poor, between the privileged and the less well off. But are stratification and inequality intrinsic to human culture?

Egalitarian Societies

As we will consider further in Chapter 12, for thousands of years, until the development of agriculture approximately 10,000 years ago, the primary human economic and social structure was hunting and gathering. This type of structure has promoted **egalitarian societies** based on the sharing of resources to ensure group success with a relative absence of hierarchy and violence within or among groups. Most modern humans who have ever lived have been hunter-gatherers.

Archaeological evidence suggests that human evolutionary success relied on cooperation and the sharing of food, child rearing, and hunting-and-gathering responsibilities, not on hierarchy, violence, and aggression. After all, building a system of **reciprocity** in which group members equally share the bounty of the moment has long-term benefits for sustaining the group. Members can then expect the generosity to be reciprocated (Knauft 1991). Although contemporary economic relations tend to be organized around the exchange of money for services, patterns of reciprocity still exist. You may take class notes for someone who returns the favor—reciprocates—at a later date. You may give someone a ride or walk their dog or share your lunch with the understanding that at some point in the future your favor will be reciprocated. In these instances, members of our extended "group" share their resources of time, food, or other amenities for the long-term benefit of sustaining the group. Can you think of other ways you engage in reciprocity with people in your group? (See Chapter 12 for a longer discussion of reciprocity.)

Anthropologists have studied egalitarian societies among contemporary hunter-gatherer groups such as the Ju/Hoansi of Africa's Kalahari region (Lee 2003), as well as the Canadian Inuit and the Hadza of Tanzania (Marlowe 2010), among many others. Efforts to establish more-egalitarian systems of economic and social relations have also occurred within highly stratified societies. The Amish (Hostetler 1993) and Hutterite (Hostetler 1997) communities in the United States are good examples on a small scale.

Hutterites, a small Christian sect, live primarily in rural North American communities and make their living mostly through agriculture. They own all property collectively and provide for individual members and families from the community's common resources. Families live in separate homes owned collectively by the community and take their meals in a common dining room. The Amish, also a small North American Christian group, are known for their simple lifestyle and their rejection of labor-saving devices that might make them less reliant on the community. The Amish, while owning private property, maintain a cooperative economic and social structure that revolves around the church, based heavily around reciprocity. Perhaps the best-known example

egalitarian society: A group based on the sharing of resources to ensure success with a relative absence of hierarchy and violence.

reciprocity: The exchange of resources, goods, and services among people of relatively equal status; meant to create and reinforce social ties.

is the distinctive Amish practice of collective barn raising in which the entire community gathers to rapidly erect a barn for one family, an act of reciprocity that is returned many times over as barns are raised throughout the community over the years.

Ranked Societies

Anthropologists also recognize **ranked societies**, in which wealth is not stratified but prestige and status are. In these societies, positions of high prestige—such as chief—are largely hereditary. Because only certain individuals can occupy these positions, the social rank of the society is set regardless of the skills, wisdom, or efforts of other members.

Chiefs usually do not accumulate great wealth, despite their high prestige. In fact, their lifestyle and standard of living may not vary significantly from those of any other member of the group. Group members offer gifts of tribute to the chief, but these are not kept and hoarded. Instead, the chief redistributes the tribute to group members. This act of gift giving—a form of **redistribution**—ensures his or her prestige while also preserving the well-being of all group members. The chief's rank and status are reinforced not through accumulation of wealth but through reciprocity and generosity. Ranked societies have existed in most parts of the world, but anthropologists have most carefully studied those in the islands of the South Pacific (Petersen 2009) and along the Pacific Northwest coast of North America (Boas 1966).

One redistribution ceremony famous in the field of anthropology is the **potlatch** practiced among the Kwakiutl of the Pacific Northwest. Among this Native American group, the chief would establish and reestablish

ranked society: A group in which wealth is not stratified but prestige and status are.

redistribution: A form of exchange in which accumulated wealth is collected from the members of the group and reallocated in a different pattern.

potlatch: Elaborate redistribution ceremony practiced among the Kwakiutl of the Pacific Northwest.

claims to prestige and status by holding an elaborate feast and gift-giving ceremony—a potlatch. He would give guests all of his personal possessions, including supplies of food, cooking pots, blankets, weapons, and even boats. What was not given away might be destroyed as a sign of the chief's great capacity. The more elaborate the gift giving, the more status and rank the chief gained in the community. The chief's generosity also applied pressure on his guests to reciprocate in like manner, or even more elaborately in a later ceremony (Boas 1966). In a practical sense, the potlatch served to distribute key community resources of food and clothing broadly among group members. As a ritual ceremony, it represented a tradition among the Kwakiutl and other ranked societies in which social status is established not by wealth and power, but by the prestige earned via one's capacity for generosity (Boas 1966).

Contemporary patterns of cooperation, sharing, collaboration, and reciprocity draw on patterns of behavior central to human evolutionary success

Women of the Makah Nation on the U.S. Pacific Northwest coast prepare salmon steaks for a potlatch, a communitywide redistribution ceremony and feast.

over millions of years. In contrast, social patterns of entrenched hierarchy and stratification emerged much more recently in the human story.

The extreme stratification in today's world is a fairly recent development. Anthropologists trace its roots to the rise of intensive agriculture and populous market towns, where relatively small groups of elite merchants and landholders were able to accumulate wealth. Stratification and inequality became more pronounced in industrialized capitalist economies over recent centuries, and this uneven development appears to be accelerating under the forces of globalization, further concentrating wealth in the hands of the few. Still, countries such as Norway, Sweden, and Denmark have made efforts to narrow stratification through a system of redistribution that combines taxation of wealth with generous social benefits. Even the United States, the country with the most extreme inequality of any current advanced industrialized country (Stiglitz 2012), also uses a progressive tax rate, requiring higher-income earners to pay a moderately higher tax rate to more equally disperse the costs of government services.

The anthropological literature reveals that inequality itself is not inherent and natural to human groups and extreme inequality is a recent development. We will further explore the development of stratification and inequality in the current era of globalization via analysis and statistical evidence throughout this chapter and in Chapter 12.

How Do Anthropologists Analyze Class and Inequality?

We turn now to consider four key theorists of class and inequality. European social philosophers Karl Marx and Max Weber, writing in the nineteenth and early twentieth centuries in the context of the Industrial Revolution, are separated by a century from French sociologist Pierre Bourdieu and U.S. anthropologist Leith Mullings, whose late twentieth-century writings are based in the context of a much more complicated and advanced capitalist economic system.

Theories of Class

Each theorist discussed here has responded to the unique social and economic challenges of his or her time and offers key analytical insights that allow anthropologists today to more deeply investigate the realities of class and inequality. As you read about each theorist, consider how you might apply their key concepts to understanding the social class relationships and inequality in our opening story about the Flint water crisis.

Karl Marx: Bourgeoisie and Proletariat Karl Marx (1801–1882), perhaps the most widely read theorist of class, wrote against a background of economic change and social upheaval. During the nineteenth century, rapid economic changes and new government policies brought massive social upheaval and dislocation to western Europe. As the Industrial Revolution swept through the area, government policies restricted poor rural families' use of common village lands. (In England, these were called Enclosure Acts, because they enclosed the commons.) Deprived of access to land they had depended on for farming, grazing, and gathering, rural people migrated to urban centers to seek jobs in the expanding industrial factories.

Marx's analysis of the increasing inequalities in the emerging capitalist economy of nineteenth-century Europe distinguished between two distinct classes of people. The **bourgeoisie**, or capitalist class, owned the **means of production**—the factories, machines, tools, raw materials, land, and financial capital needed to make things. The **proletariat**, or working class, lacked land to grow their own food, tools to make their own products, and capital to build workshops or factories. Unable to make their own living, they sold their work—their labor—to capitalists in return for wages.

Marx identified labor as the key source of value and profit in the marketplace. Owners sought to constantly increase their income by forcing workers to toil faster, longer, and for lower wages, thereby reducing the cost of production and increasing the difference between the production cost and the sale price. The surplus value created by the workers could then become profit for the owner. In this relationship, capitalists increased their wealth by extracting the surplus labor value from workers. Recognition of these two fundamentally different positions within the economy—two different classes—was essential to Marx's understanding of power relations in a culture.

Today anthropologists apply Marx's ideas to analyze class and power in contemporary society while acknowledging that capitalism has grown much more complex since Marx's time. Intense competition has grown among capitalists, notably between those in the manufacturing and financial sectors. Small-business owners and farmers now own the means of production, technically making them part of Marx's bourgeoisie, but they do not possess the same access to capital as others in that class. The working class—the proletariat—is divided, with conflicts along lines of race, gender, and ethnicity. Moreover, increasing global circulation of capital is drawing local cultures and communities into class-based relationships that were not present even a generation ago.

Many contemporary social scientists recognize a middle class of professionals and managers (white-collar workers) that has emerged between capitalists and the working class (blue-collar workers). But others who take a more strict Marxist view of class argue that professionals and managers are still members of the proletariat (Buck 2009; Durrenberger and Erem 2010). They

bourgeoisie: Marxist term for the capitalist class that owns the means of production.

means of production: The factories, machines, tools, raw materials, land, and financial capital needed to make things.

proletariat: Marxist term for the class of laborers who own only their labor.

may have more power in the workplace and substantially higher incomes, but they still sell their labor to the bourgeoisie. These managers, government officials, military, police, and even college professors receive special privileges from the bourgeoisie. But it is worth the price to gain the cooperation of this middle class in organizing, educating, and controlling the working class, thereby maximizing the extraction of profits by the capitalist class.

Along with Friedrich Engels, Marx wrote the *Communist Manifesto* (1848) as a political pamphlet urging workers to recognize their exploited class position and to unite in order to change the relations between proletariat and bourgeoisie emerging in the capitalist system. Marx noted, however, the extreme difficulty for workers to develop a class consciousness—a political awareness of their common position in the economy that would allow them to unite to change the system. Why? Because their continuous struggle simply to make ends meet, as well as the creative means used by the bourgeoisie to keep the proletariat divided, works against a unified challenge to the stratification of society.

Max Weber: Prestige and Life Chances Max Weber (1864–1920), like Marx, wrote against the backdrop of economic and social upheavals in western Europe caused by the expansion of capitalism during the Industrial Revolution. In analyzing the emerging structures of stratification, Weber added consideration of power and prestige to Marx's concern for economic stratification of wealth and income. By **prestige**, Weber referred to the reputation, influence,

prestige: The reputation, influence, and deference bestowed on certain people because of their membership in certain groups.

and deference bestowed on certain people because of their membership in certain groups (Weber [1920] 1946). Thus certain occupations may hold higher or lower prestige in a culture—for instance, physicians and farm workers. Prestige, like wealth and income, can affect life chances. Prestige rankings affect the way individuals are treated in social situations, their access to influential social networks, and their access to people of wealth and power (Table 11.1).

Weber saw classes as groups of people for whom similar sets of factors determine their life chances. By **life chances**, Weber referred to the opportunities that individuals have to improve their quality of life and realize their life goals. Life chances are determined by access not only to financial resources but also to social resources such as education, health care, food, clothing, and shelter. Class position—relative wealth, power, and prestige—determines access to these resources. According to Weber, members of a class share common life chances, experiences, and access to resources, as well as similar exposure and vulnerability to other systems of stratification. For Weber, however, class stratification doesn't just happen. Instead, he suggests that the state holds the monopoly on the legitimate use of force, and class-based societies and elite control of the means of production would not be possible without the exercise of state power through police, tax collectors, and even the military.

Pierre Bourdieu: Education and Social Reproduction Pierre Bourdieu (1930–2002) studied the French educational system to understand the relationship among class, culture, and power ([1970] 1990). Throughout much of the world, education is considered the key to upward social mobility within stratified societies. **Social mobility** refers to one's change of class position—upward or downward—in stratified societies. Theoretically, the *meritocracy* of education—whereby students are deemed successful on the basis of their individual talent and motivation—should provide all students an equal opportunity. Instead, Bourdieu's research uncovered a phenomenon of **social reproduction** in the schools: Rather than providing opportunities for social class mobility, the educational system helped reproduce the social relations that already exist by passing class position from generation to generation in a family.

What factors in schools work against the meritocratic idea and instead serve to limit a person's life chances? First, a family's economic circumstances make a difference. But Bourdieu identified two additional key factors: *habitus* and cultural capital.

Bourdieu described ***habitus*** as the dispositions, self-perceptions, sensibilities, and tastes developed in response to external influences over a lifetime that shape one's conceptions of the world and where one fits into it. *Habitus* is taught and learned from an early age and is culturally reinforced through family, education, religion, socioeconomic status, and the media. It is not fixed

life chances: An individual's opportunities to improve quality of life and realize life goals.

social mobility: The movement of one's class position, upward or downward, in stratified societies.

social reproduction: The phenomenon whereby social and class relations of prestige or lack of prestige are passed from one generation to the next.

***habitus*:** Bourdieu's term to describe the self-perceptions, sensibilities, and tastes developed in response to external influences over a lifetime that shape one's conceptions of the world and where one fits in it.

TABLE 11.1 Comparative Perceptions of Prestige in the United States and China

Rank	United States	Score	China	Score
1	Physician	86.1	Mayor	92.9
2	Lawyer	74.8	Government minister	91.4
3	Computer scientist	73.7	University professor	90.1
4	University professor	73.5	Computer engineer	88.6
5	Physicist	73.5	Judge	88.3
6	Chemist	73.3	Court prosecutor	87.6
7	Chemical engineer	73.3	Lawyer	86.6
8	Architect	73.2	Engineer	85.8
9	Biologist	73.1	High-ranking governmental or political party member	85.7
10	Scientist	73.1	Scientist	85.3
11	Dentist	71.8	Translator	84.9
12	Judge	71.5	Revenue officer	84.9
13	Engineer	70.7	Social scientist	83.9
14	CEO	70.5	Doctor	83.7
15	Geologist	69.8	Computer software designer	83.6
16	Psychologist	69.4	Writer	82.5
17	Aerospace engineer	69.2	Reporter	81.6
18	Manager, medicine and health	69.2	Real estate developer	81.5
19	Clergy	69.0	Director/manager of state-owned enterprise	81.3
20	Civil engineer	68.8	Manager of investment company	81.1

SOURCE: **United States:** National Opinion Research Center. 2009. *General Social Surveys, 1972–2008: Cumulative Codebook*. Chicago: University of Chicago. publicdata.norc.org; **China:** Xinxin Xu. 2013. "Changes in the Chinese Social Structure as Seen from Occupational Prestige Ratings and Job Preferences." Translated by Yihan Feng. *Sociology Research* 3.

or predetermined, but it is so deeply enculturated and embedded that it becomes an almost instinctive sense of one's potential. *Habitus* emerges among a class of people as a set of common perceptions that shape expectations and aspirations and guide the individual in assessing his or her life chances and the potential for social mobility. Life decisions—for instance, the choice of college education or career—are made on the basis of the individual's *habitus*.

To get a sense of the pervasiveness of *habitus*, think for a moment about your own situation. Why have you chosen to attend college, and this particular college? What major are you pursuing? Might certain concerns of class or money be influencing your educational and career paths? How might this *habitus* also influence your choice of friends, activities, and, perhaps someday, a marriage partner?

Cultural capital is another key to the social reproduction of class. Bourdieu defined **cultural capital** as the knowledge, habits, and tastes learned from parents and family that individuals can use to gain access to scarce and valuable resources of society. For example, family wealth can create cultural capital for children. With enough money, parents can provide their children with opportunities to travel abroad, learn multiple languages, take music lessons, join sports clubs, go to concerts and museums, have enriching summer experiences, and build social networks with others who have similar opportunities. The less wealthy may pass along existing cultural capital through inexpensive activities like reading, while others may divert additional financial resources toward cultural-capital-building activities for their children. These opportunities build the social skills, networks, and sense of power and confidence that are essential for shaping class position and identity in stratified societies. Family wealth enables children to perpetuate cultural capital, including high motivation and a sense of possibilities that are crucial for academic success. Schools reward cultural capital. In the process, schools reproduce social class advantage.

The U.S. public school system is heavily influenced by cultural capital. From an early age, students are split into separate tracks based on standardized test performance and teacher evaluations. Around sixth grade, for example, students are separated into the mathematics track that will lead either to Advanced

cultural capital: The knowledge, habits, and tastes learned from parents and family that individuals can use to gain access to scarce and valuable resources in society.

Children build cultural capital at the Metropolitan Museum of Art in New York City.

Placement Calculus their senior year in high school or to remedial or regular math. Selective colleges often screen positively for applicants with AP Calculus credits. As a result, decisions made in sixth grade affect students' college possibilities. Did you know this? Some people with cultural capital do know. A study of middle-school math groups in Boston public schools revealed the way mathematics tracking tends to reproduce class in the classroom. Of the students in the accelerated math track, 56 percent had fathers with a doctorate or other professional degree, and 33 percent had fathers with a master's degree. Just 5.6 percent had fathers with only a high school degree. Of the students in remedial math, 48 percent had fathers with a high school diploma or less (Useem 1992).

How would you assess your own level of cultural capital? Be aware that cultural capital can also shape the way others see you. Do you have the social skills, experiences, and exposure to travel, music, art, and language that will make you seem an appropriate fit for a particular workplace? While employers will take into account a candidate's skills, they will also, intentionally or not, assess how comfortable they themselves are around the candidate. Can you identify ways in which your level of cultural capital would provide an advantage or disadvantage in scenarios such as succeeding in a job interview, obtaining health care, finding an apartment, or getting a date?

Leith Mullings: Intersectionality among Race, Gender, and Class In recent years, Leith Mullings's work on intersectionality has led anthropologists to reexamine class by analyzing the deep connections among class, race, and gender. Building on the field's long history of holistic ethnographic studies of local communities, Mullings offers an intersectional approach: She asserts that class, in the United States and many other areas, cannot be studied in isolation but, instead, must be considered together with race and gender as interlocking systems of power. **Intersectionality** provides a framework for analyzing the many factors—especially race and gender—that determine how class is lived and how all three systems of power and stratification build on and shape one another.

In the 1990s Mullings led a study, The Harlem Birth Right Project, on the impact of class, race, and gender on women's health and infant mortality. The study focused on central Harlem, at that time a vibrant, primarily African American community in northern Manhattan, New York City (Mullings 2005b; Mullings and Wali 2001). Of particular concern, infant mortality rates in Harlem were twice the rate of New York City's overall. Previous studies (e.g., Schoendorf, Hogue, and Kleinman 1992) had demonstrated that at all class levels African American women in the United States have more problematic birth outcomes than white women of similar class. Even college-educated African American women experienced infant mortality at twice the rate of

intersectionality: An analytic framework for assessing how factors such as race, gender, and class interact to shape individual life chances and societal patterns of stratification.

college-educated white women. This observation suggested that factors other than education and social status were at work.

Mullings's research team gathered data through participant observation in community organizations and other sites in Harlem, as well as through surveys, in-depth interviews, and life histories with pregnant women and women with children. On the basis of their data, the team examined how the underlying conditions of housing, employment, child care, and environmental factors, as well as the quality of public spaces, parks, and even grocery and retail stores, might affect the health outcomes being reported in Harlem, where both working-class and middle-class women lived. Since the early 1990s, Harlem has been hard hit by dramatic changes in New York City's economy. Manufacturing jobs with middle-class wages have been lost to flexible accumulation (see Chapters 1 and 12), as New York City–based companies relocate production overseas. Meanwhile, job growth in the metropolitan area has occurred in the high-wage financial sector and in the low-wage service sector. Throughout the 1990s, government social services were cut back while public housing and transportation were allowed to deteriorate.

The effects on working-class and middle-class women in Mullings's study were notable, with increased physical and mental stress, especially for pregnant women. For working-class women, inadequate, overpriced, and poorly maintained private and public housing forced many mothers and their children to be constantly on the move, searching for affordable housing and sharing living spaces with friends and relatives to make ends meet. The need to regularly fight for needed repairs drained time and energy from hard-working women holding multiple low-wage jobs while juggling work and child care. A shortage of steady, well-paying jobs meant that women had very little income security or benefits, so they often pieced together a living from multiple sources. Middle-class women, many of whom were employed in the public sector, were also increasingly subject to layoffs as local governments downsized. The study also found that heavy pollution in the Harlem area, including airborne pollutants from a sewage treatment plant and six bus depots, contributed to elevating the child asthma rate to four times the national average (Mullings 2005b; Mullings and Wali 2001).

The Harlem Birth Right Project illustrates a powerful application of the intersectional approach to understanding class and inequality. It reveals how inequality of resources (class), institutional racism, and gender discrimination combine to affect opportunities for employment, housing, and health care in the Harlem community. It also shows how these factors link to elevated health problems and infant mortality.

Mullings points out the many forms of collaboration that women in Harlem use to resist these structures of inequality and survive in their chosen

MAP 11.2
Harlem

community. Calling this the *Sojourner syndrome*, she links the agency of contemporary African American women to the life story of Sojourner Truth. Truth was born into slavery in the late 1790s and was emancipated in 1827 after experiencing physical abuse and rape and watching many of her children be sold away from her. Subsequently she became an itinerant preacher for the abolition of slavery, building coalitions with white abolitionists and later participating in the early women's rights movement. The stories of the women in Harlem today, like Sojourner Truth's, reflect the determination and creativity required to overcome interlocking constraints of racism, sexism, and class inequality.

Applying Theory to Practice: Analyzing Class in the Flint, Michigan, Water Crisis

Let's return to the story at the beginning of the chapter. Can you see ways to apply the theoretical concepts introduced by Marx, Weber, Bourdieu, and

Leith Mullings
Analyzing Intersecting Systems of Power

Leith Mullings first encountered anthropology as an undergraduate at Queens College, City University of New York, during the civil rights movement. Now a distinguished professor at the City University of New York Graduate Center and past president of the American Anthropological Association, Mullings has become well known for her work on intersectionality — analyzing the intersection of race, class, and gender — which she has put to work in her ethnographic fieldwork, including a groundbreaking project on health disparities in Harlem, New York.

"One reason I became interested in the Harlem project was the opportunity to undertake a study that embraced community collaboration in research. Community collaboration refers to involving the community in guiding research in a wide variety of ways.

"For example, the researchers formed a Community Advisory Board (CAB), composed of people who lived or worked in Harlem. The CAB suggested that instead of recounting the data in the traditional format — unemployment, female-headed households, numbers of people on welfare — that we report the same data in a more positive way — for example, how many people are employed, how many are not on welfare. In other words, to emphasize the strengths of the community.

"The CAB also advised us to consider the ways people resisted and the ways people attempted to overcome the circumstances they found themselves in. For instance, they suggested that we do ethnography in Housing Court. There I encountered Harlem women on their own, bravely confronting the lawyers of their landlords in order to hold on to shelter for themselves and their children. That was one of the ways in which we discovered how much insecure housing negatively affects health and well-being.

"The CAB also pointed us to the lines at Legal Aid as people tried to prevent their children from being placed in the problematic special education track. Filing complaints of police brutality and job discrimination, or informing the City about landlords who did not provide heat or hot water, are all ways people tried to better their lives that are not obvious to the casual observer. They don't show up in the news. They don't show up in the statistics. Major social movements such as the civil rights movement or people marching against police brutality may make the news. The day-to-day struggles people wage are often not apparent. We may not have directly encountered this without community collaboration."

Since its popularization in the early 1980s, intersectionality has become a key theoretical approach within anthropology and other social sciences but one that requires careful analysis of local realities. "What is not addressed in many statements of intersectionality is how to analyze the intersection of race, class, and gender. What is their relationship? In some circles it has become a mantra. Many scholars reiterate Race, Class, Gender: Intersectionality. But the real work lies in understanding how at a particular moment these three indices of inequality articulate.

Anthropologist Leith Mullings

"I believe that class is prefigurative. Race and gender have various degrees of salience in different historical conditions, societies, or locations.

"Sometimes one trumps the other. For example, in the contemporary United States, gender subordination results in some limitations for elite women. But in most instances, class trumps: access to huge resources allows them all kinds of privileges and freedom unimagined by most men or women.

"To put intersectionality to work, when you read a newspaper, encounter situations, or interact with people, think —and this is a hard concept —what are the axes of stratification that affect the opportunities of the people involved. Start by thinking about whiteness, for instance: What are the privileges that whiteness brings, whatever the class? What obstacles do people of different classes, races, and / or genders confront? What does it mean in their lives? What does that mean for their opportunities?

"Take something so minor as trying to get a taxi. It is often difficult for black people of any class to catch a cab in New York City. A cab driver will frequently pass a black person by to pick up a white person. Race is the first thing the drivers see. Taxi drivers cannot always read class. People do not always "wear" their class. A number of elite black people have had trouble getting cabs, famously the actor Danny Glover or former New York City mayor David Dinkins. But as an older black woman, I can get a taxi to stop

> "*To put intersectionality to work, when you read a newspaper, encounter situations, or interact with people, think, 'What are the axes of stratification that affect the opportunities of the people involved?'*"

more often than my son Michael, a tall, good-looking, dark-skinned black man, who can rarely get a cab to stop. The intersection of gender and race make it more difficult for him to get a taxi.

"These are daily inconveniences. But think about how it works on a broader level: trying to find a job or housing, or even to purchase a car. White and black 'testers' with virtually identical resumés and qualifications have been sent to job interviews; 20 to 25 percent of the time blacks and Latinos were 'treated less well' and often not called back for interviews or offered lesser jobs and lower pay than their counterparts with the same qualifications. Studies (see Marable 2000) have demonstrated that African Americans with financial circumstances identical or superior to whites have been denied loans or are offered mortgages with less favorable terms."

In thinking about anthropology as a toolkit for life, Mullings offers the following observation: "Anthropology is important because anyone living in today's world will have to learn to live with many different kinds of people. We live in a global, transnational world in which few places are isolated. Anthropology also encourages looking beneath the appearance to the underlying structure. You don't have to become a professional anthropologist. But it is a way of being in the world. It is an important lens through which to understand today's world. In the end this is what makes us anthropologists, eyes wide open."

Mullings to analyze the water crisis in Flint and the economic and social dynamics at work in that community? Can you recognize a stratification of classes based on control over the means of production as Marx suggested? Where do a child with lead poisoning, the pediatrician, the university researchers, the emergency manager, the National Guardsmen, the governor of Michigan, and the CEO of General Motors fit? How do you assess the differential life chances of those connected by the water crisis? How does class affect their life chances for education, health, and financial security? Does prestige play a role in differentially shaping their life chances? How do *habitus* and cultural capital affect the social mobility of each person? And how do systems of stratification such as race, gender, and class intersect in this context? Because class is so rarely discussed in U.S. culture, these questions may seem difficult to pursue. But by asking these questions about the circulation of water—or any cultural activity, group, or institution—you begin to develop the tools necessary to think like an anthropologist.

How Are Class and Inequality Constructed?

The United States' national myth tells of a "classless" society with open access to upward social mobility for those who are hardworking and talented, including the potential to rise from rags to riches in a single generation. This is the cultural story we tell, but is it reality? In fact, in the United States one's life chances are heavily influenced by the class position of one's family—the financial and cultural resources passed from generation to generation. What are the chances that a child affected by lead poisoning in Flint will someday grow up to be the president of General Motors or governor of the state of Michigan?

In the fall of 2011, issues of class and inequality burst into U.S. national headlines as the Occupy Wall Street (OWS) movement established encampments in cities across the country and made famous their slogan, "We Are the 99%." OWS pointed to the increasing inequality in the United States and the growing advantages of the wealthiest. Though OWS spurred conversations about class and inequality, including significant attention in the 2016 U.S. presidential campaign, class has been and continues to be one of the most mystifying concepts in U.S. culture. In fact, most people do not have an accurate picture of where they and their families fit into the nation's class structure. Do you think you do? A 2015 Gallup poll showed that 71 percent of Americans consider themselves to be middle or working class. Only 1 percent of respondents considered themselves to be upper class and 13 percent upper-middle class; 15 percent considered themselves to be lower class (Gallup 2015).

Both quantitative and qualitative research reveal that stratification by class is very real and significantly affects people's life chances. Class stratification in the United States is not new. The signers of the Declaration of Independence and drafters the U.S. Constitution were among the richest men in the thirteen colonies at that time, having built their wealth largely on the labor of enslaved Africans on land taken from Native Americans. George Washington was one of the largest landholders and slaveholders. In the southwest, labor was provided by conquered people in a system established under Spanish colonialism and continued after the territory's annexation by the United States, a system that rivaled the oppression of blacks in the American South and East. As the young nation's territories spread westward, opportunities for upward social mobility were plentiful for certain immigrant portions of the population, but not for Native Americans, blacks, and most women. Access to wealth, power, prestige, and the resources of U.S. society were stratified not only by race and gender but also by class. Income and wealth inequality narrowed after World War II as an economic boom spurred a growing middle class, particularly among European Americans. Government benefits such as the GI Bill for returning soldiers created opportunities for a new segment of the population to attend college and own homes, and labor unions forced employers to improve pay and working conditions. But since the mid-1970s, inequality has been increasing as income and wealth have concentrated at the upper end of the economic spectrum.

Ethnographic Studies of Class in the United States

Anthropologists have studied the construction of class and its effects across the spectrum of U.S. culture—in rural, urban, and suburban settings and in relationship to race and gender. Ethnographic studies like those presented here explore class and income inequality in local contexts and their impact on the life chances of real people in local communities.

Poor Whites in Rural Kentucky In *Worked to the Bone: Race, Class, Power, and Privilege in Kentucky* (2001), anthropologist Pem Davidson Buck provides a dynamic introduction to intersectionality. She analyzes the intersections of class, race, and gender through the history of the poor white population in two rural Kentucky counties. Here, the privileges often associated with whiteness in the United States have been severely limited by class. Buck traces the development of an economic system built on tobacco cultivation, coal mining, and manufacturing that has created a class hierarchy in which "sweat is made to trickle up" (13). In other words (reflecting Marx's theory), the surplus value of workers' labor drains upward into the hands of successive layers of elites.

According to Buck, numerous historical events and processes contributed to this development. The construction of race in Kentucky through slavery, sharecropping, and Jim Crow legislation served to persuade European laborers that they should value their whiteness and attach their primary identities

MAP 11.3
Kentucky

with the white elite rather than build solidarity with laborers of other races. The dispossession of Native Americans from their land consolidated elite control over the territory's natural resources. Later, poor and working-class whites were enticed by the elites with promises of white privilege to view all newcomer groups (such as Jews, Catholics, Irish, and later immigrants) with suspicion as outsiders, ethnic "others," and "white trash," rather than as potential allies in the struggle for fair value, wages, and compensation for their work.

Buck writes about life in central Kentucky from a personal perspective. She and her husband bought land in the rolling farm country, choosing to not pursue careers but to try to live off of the land. They grew food in their garden, raised goats and dairy calves, and took various jobs shoveling corn or stripping tobacco on a large farm to make ends meet. He eventually took a job with a plumbing and heating supply company, and later they started a small plumbing and heating business of their own. All told, they spent twelve years living under the poverty line and producing most of their own food. Reflecting on her time in central Kentucky, Buck writes:

> It was while fixing plumbing leaks, lying on my back under kitchen counters, soldering pipes while wedged between bottles of cleaning fluids, that I learned about the view from under the sink. I often found myself in fairly wealthy homes, looking up from under the sink at the lady of the house and thinking about her life. She had furniture I could not afford, dressed her children from stores I never entered, and complained about leaking plumbing at a time when what few pipes we had in our own house froze and burst with remarkable regularity. (Buck 2001, 2)

It is this view "from under the sink" that Buck brings to her analysis—the view of the farmhands, handymen, factory workers, and students struggling to make ends meet despite endless hours of back-breaking work. It is the view of people who see clearly how their sweat trickles up to enhance the lives and economic success of others who are already better off.

Buck places Kentucky's economic development within the context of national economic trends and the global economy. Whiteness has been a continuously evolving smokescreen, she claims, adjusted and readjusted to the changing needs of the elites as the drainage system has been reorganized:

> We are presently in . . . a period of intense competition, this time between elites around the world struggling to control the global economy. The consequences of that struggle are now filtering into the middle class, although they have been affecting people lower

in the drainage system since the late 1970s. Whiteness no longer provides protection from the consequences of policies that make larger and larger portions of the United States into a Third World labor force. Nor does middle-class status provide complete protection. (221–22)

Through her analysis, Buck—who drew on her own middle-class cultural capital to escape poverty—draws connections between class and race in U.S. culture. The construction of class, as she chronicles in her reflections on her community in central Kentucky, has relied on a complex manufacturing of what it means to be white. But as the local economy of the rural United States becomes further integrated into the global economy, and as the sweat of local workers trickles further and further up, even the privileges of whiteness are not enough to protect those who live at or below the poverty line and whose fingers are already "worked to the bone."

Downward Mobility: The Middle Class and the Working Poor Wealth and poverty mark the extremes of a fluid class continuum, but the expected trajectory up the ladder—the core of the so-called American dream—often eludes U.S. families. Social mobility does not always involve movement up the class ladder. News stories, television shows, movies, newspapers, and magazines rarely publish articles about the downwardly mobile. This is a "hidden dimension of our society's experience because it simply does not fit into our cultural universe" (Newman 1999, 9). Instead, our cultural narrative is a story of a meritocracy where "worthy individuals rise to the top and the undeserving fall by the way side" (243).

Katherine S. Newman has written extensively about the vulnerabilities of the U.S. middle class and the obstacles to success for the working poor. In *Falling from Grace: Downward Mobility in the Age of Affluence* ([1998] 1999), Newman explores the economic and psychological struggles of 150 families who strive to maintain their class position in U.S. culture. She interviewed managers, air traffic controllers, factory workers, and displaced homemakers (women and men who have worked primarily in the home but are no longer financially able to continue); she traced their vulnerability to moving down the economic ladder as a result of job losses, relocation of jobs overseas, and divorce (Kingfisher 2001).

What are the effects on the psyche when hardworking, moral individuals spiral downward—that is, when they "fall from grace"? Newman notes that many do not blame the failure of the economic system; instead, they blame their own failure, personal defects, and unworthiness.

In *No Shame in My Game: The Working Poor in the Inner City* (1999), Newman asks why, in a nation of great prosperity and wealth, people who work full time are still poor. She examines obstacles facing the working poor—those who often work more than full time to make ends meet and for whom minimum-wage jobs are not enough to pull themselves or their families out of poverty. Many people in the United States believe that urban poverty is a result of lack of motivation, welfare dependency, and a poor work ethic (see "The 'Culture of Poverty': Poverty as Pathology" on page 415); but Newman challenges this vision as a gap in our understanding of urban environments and inner-city economies. In these milieus she has found a broad array of hardworking citizens for whom hard work does not pay off, who struggle to provide for their families, who are one paycheck away from financial disaster. According to Newman, the main determinant of class position and social mobility is not one's work ethic, but structural barriers that have created an increasing gap between the life chances of the well educated and highly skilled and those of high school dropouts (see "Poverty as a Structural Economic Problem" on page 415) (Durrenberger 2001; Wacquant 2002).

Wealth, Inequality, and Wall Street Although many anthropologists study the most marginalized members of a culture, a number of research projects have "studied up" (Nader 1972; Savage and Williams 2008): They have investigated power elites and cultural decision makers ranging from elite scientists (Gusterson 1996) and Wall Street executives (Tett 2010) to government officials (Brash 2011). In *Liquidated: An Ethnography of Wall Street* (2008), anthropologist Karen Ho relates how she went to work in a Wall Street investment bank to understand the inner workings of Wall Street in the 1990s during one of its biggest boom periods. Why, she asks, in a time of record corporate profits and soaring

Ten Chairs of Inequality

To dramatize the distribution of wealth in the United States, find ten friends and ten chairs. Each chair will represent 10 percent of the nation's wealth, and each person will represent 10 percent of the population. Place one friend in each chair to visualize what an even distribution of wealth would look like. Ask yourselves what the ideal distribution of wealth should be and arrange yourselves in the chairs accordingly. Now ask what you think the actual distribution is and rearrange yourselves again. To visualize the actual distribution of wealth, pick one of your friends and give her seven chairs. This shows the proportion of wealth held by the top 10 percent of the population. In fact, if your friend's arm represented the top 1 percent of the population, her arm alone would have more than three chairs (about 33 percent). Your other nine friends get to share the remaining three chairs. But to make the exercise even more accurate, place one of your friends on the floor with no chair to represent the 10 percent of the population with negative wealth—more debt than assets.

How does it feel to be in the group of nine or to be the one person in the top 10 percent? What is it like to be the one person sitting on the floor? This exercise reveals the dynamics of the stratification of power through wealth in U.S. society. But it also offers potential insights into social mobility. What are the chances that any of the nine people sharing three chairs will be able to move into a situation in which they have seven chairs? What conditions would need to exist for that social mobility to happen? There clearly could be more equality. Can you imagine being frustrated enough to revolt and take a few chairs by force? What keeps you from doing it?

For further consideration of class and inequality, consider viewing the YouTube videos "Wealth Inequality in America" and "Global Wealth Inequality" cited in the For Further Exploration section at the end of the chapter.

Ten Chairs of Inequality

Source: Adapted from Tamara Sober Giecek. 2013. "The Ten Chairs." Teaching Economics As If People Mattered. www.teachingeconomics.org

stock prices, do we see rapid downsizing, layoffs, and dismantling of the social safety net? She focuses on the surprising fact that when corporations lay off workers and downsize, not only do the companies' stock prices go up but the stock values of the investment banks go up as well.

What is the corporate culture of
Wall Street investment banks? Did
it contribute to the 2008 financial
crash?

Ho points to a transformation of the corporate culture of Wall Street: The desire for profits is not new; what is new, she finds, is a disconnect between what is considered best for the corporation and what is best for most of its employees. Today employees seldom benefit from corporate success. Instead, the benefits go to stockholders. Ho suggests that a "new cultural code for doing business" on Wall Street—characterized by a relentless search for unending profits and combined with government deregulation of the financial services industry—rewards efforts to make money, not to make goods and services. Witness in recent years the willingness of commercial banks and investment houses to bundle and resell so-called toxic assets, exposed in the book and feature film *The Big Short* and the documentary *The Inside Job*, including the high-risk mortgages that played a key role in the 2008 market meltdown and Wall Street collapse. Ho claims that Wall Street participated in its own dismantling through mergers and liquidations within the financial community itself as large companies consumed smaller ones, downsized, and laid off employees to maximize their own stock values. Ho regards the collapse of Wall Street banks and investment houses in 2008 not so much as a surprise or anomaly, but as a predictable result of Wall Street culture, values, and workplace models.

Despite the U.S. national myth of a classless society, quantitative and qualitative research studies expose the depth of inequality and stratification as well as the obstacles to social mobility. Although class stratification is not new, historical research suggests it is also not inevitable. By examining both statistical and ethnographic material, anthropologists seek to reopen a conversation about the roots of inequality—the obstacles to greater opportunity, social mobility, and improved life chances in a culture that is reluctant to discuss class.

A Look at the Numbers

Economic statistics provide a sobering picture of inequality in the United States today. They also reveal the increasing concentration of income and wealth at the top rungs of the class ladder. In reviewing statistics related to class, we examine both income and wealth.

Income Income is what people earn from work, plus dividends and interest on investments along with rents and royalties. (A *dividend* is a payment by a corporation to its shareholders of a portion of corporate profits. *Interest* is a fee paid for the use of borrowed money—for example, interest paid on a bank savings account. *Rent* refers to payment to an owner as compensation for the use of land, a building, an apartment, property, or equipment. *Royalties* are income based on a percentage of the revenue from the sale of a patent, book, or theatrical work paid to the inventor or author.) Table 11.2a shows a breakdown of average household income in the United States for 2014. Do you know where your family fits in the national income range? Review the accompanying charts to get an idea of your family's position and how it may have changed over the years.

Income patterns reveal the way power is distributed in a society. As Table 11.2b illustrates, income distribution among the U.S. population shows a heavy concentration at the top. Although the median income in the United States in 2014 was just over $53,000 (meaning that half of the nation's households earned more than that and half earned less), the top 5 percent of

income: What people earn from work, plus dividends and interest on investments, along with rents and royalties.

TABLE 11.2 Income Disparities in the United States

a) AVERAGE U.S. HOUSEHOLD INCOME BY PERCENTAGE OF THE POPULATION, 2014

Percentage of U.S. Population	Household Income Range
Top 5%	Above $206,568
Top 20%	Above $112,262
Second 20%	$68,213–$112,262
Middle 20%	$41,187–$68,212
Fourth 20%	$21,433–$41,186
Bottom 20%	Less than $21,432

b) DISTRIBUTION OF TOTAL U.S. HOUSEHOLD INCOME, 1967 VERSUS 2014

	Top 5% of Population	Top 20% of Population	Bottom 40% of Population	Bottom 20% of Population
1967	16.3%	43%	15%	4.1%
2014	21.9%	51.2%	11.3%	3.1%

SOURCE: U.S. Census Bureau, 2015. Historical Income Tables: Income Inequality, Tables H-1 and H-2 All Races. www.census.gov/hhes/www/income/data/historical/inequality/index.html

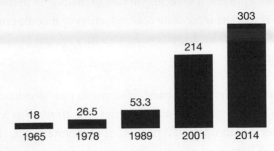

FIGURE 11.1 Ratio of average U.S. CEO Pay to Average Worker Pay, 1965–2014

SOURCE: www.epi.org

households received 21.9 percent of all income. The top 20 percent received 51.2 percent of all income, while the bottom 20 percent received only 3.1 percent. The bottom 40 percent totaled only 11.3 percent of all income. These gaps have widened substantially over the past four decades.

Furthermore, the gap between people at the top end of the income scale and the average worker has dramatically increased over the past five decades (Figure 11.1). Between 1978–2014, the average pay for corporate CEOs increased by almost 1000 percent. The typical worker's pay increased only 11 percent. In 1965, the salaries of corporate CEOs averaged eighteen times the pay of an average worker. By 2014 that number had skyrocketed to an astonishing 303 times the average worker's pay. In comparison, the ratio in the United Kingdom was 84 to 1 and in Japan 67 to 1. The typical worker at McDonalds or Starbucks needed to work for six months to earn what a CEO at a top American corporation earned in one hour. In 2012, in the United States, as many as 17,685 people earned $10 million or more. The top 400 earners averaged $335 million.

Wealth Wealth is another key indicator of the distribution of power in a society. By **wealth** we mean the total value of what someone owns—including stocks, bonds, and real estate—minus any debt, such as a mortgage or credit card debt. If wealth were evenly distributed, every U.S. household would have had $498,800 in 2010 (Board of Governors of the Federal Reserve System 2012). But wealth is not evenly distributed, as Table 11.3 shows.

Wealth is even more unevenly distributed than income, and the widening gap has multiple causes. First, shifts in the U.S. tax code have lowered the top tax rate from 91 percent in the years from 1950 to 1963, to to 39.6 percent beginning in 2014, allowing the wealthy to retain far more of their income (Tax Policy Center 2015). Second, wages for most U.S. families have stagnated since the early 1970s. Moreover, credit card, education, and mortgage debt have skyrocketed. Finally, the collapse of the housing market beginning

wealth: The total value of what someone owns, minus any debt.

TABLE 11.3 Distribution of Private Wealth in the United States, 2013

Percentage of Population*	Percentage of Private Wealth
Top 3%	54%
Next 7%	21%
Bottom 90%	25%

*Total U.S. population in 2013 = 310,000,000.

SOURCE: Federal Reserve Board Survey of Consumer Finances. 2014. Cited in inequality.org /wealth-inequality

in 2007 dramatically affected many middle-class families who held a significant portion of their wealth in the value of their home. By 2014, 16.9 percent of all homeowners owed more on their mortgages than their homes were worth (Zillow 2014).

Despite our society's cultural images of the United States as a nation of stockholders, Wall Street as a democratizing institution, and the stock market as a place of economic empowerment, the actual distribution of stocks in the U.S. population tells another story. The top 1 percent of all U.S. households owns 38.3 percent of all stocks. The top 10 percent owns roughly 81 percent. Fully 50 percent of U.S. households own no stocks. Even among those who do hold stocks, most own them through pension and retirement funds, where they are not accessible for general use.

In another surprising statistic about the transfer of wealth from generation to generation, only 1.6 percent of Americans receive $100,000 or more in inheritance. Another 1.1 percent receives $50,000 to $100,000. Ninety-two percent of the population receives no inheritance whatsoever (Domhoff 2012).

Wealth is also stratified by race, as Table 11.4 shows. Reflecting the devastating long-term effects of slavery and Jim Crow segregation on the African American community, as well as the difficult immigration experiences of most

TABLE 11.4 Median* Income and Wealth by Race in U.S. Households, 2011

Race	Median Income	Median Wealth (Net Worth)
White	$53,340	$110,500
Black	$33,137	$6,314
Hispanic	$38,818	$7,683

*Median = the number separating the top half from the bottom half of the distribution.

SOURCE: U.S. Census Bureau. 2012. Table 1. www.census.gov; U.S. Census Bureau. 2011. "Net Worth and Asset Ownership of Households." www.census.gov

of the U.S. Hispanic population, white households have accumulated fifteen times the net worth of black and Hispanic households.

Most Americans struggle to identify the distribution of income and wealth in the United States and to locate their position within it (Norton and Ariely 2011). After reviewing the quantitative data on income and wealth stratification in the United States, can you identify pieces of information that were particularly surprising to you? Does the statistical picture correspond with the picture of U.S. society that you imagined? Do you have a clearer sense of where you and your family currently stand?

The Roots of Poverty

Why do people live in poverty in the United States—one of the wealthiest countries in the world? The actual roots of poverty—part of the same system that creates wealth—must be clearly understood if the experience of poverty is to be eliminated or ameliorated.

A 2014 report of the U.S. Census Bureau found 46.7 million people—14.8 percent of the U.S. population—living in poverty (U.S. Census Bureau 2015). The 48.8 million people living in poverty in 2012 was the largest number in the fifty-five years that poverty statistics have been tracked. Just over twenty percent of U.S. children live in poverty. The 2016 U.S. government's poverty line for single adults stood at $11,880 in pretax income and $24,300 for a family of four. How could a family of four (or two or three for that matter) eat, pay rent, keep heat, water, and electricity turned on, have clean clothes, and care for even the most rudimentary dental or health needs on $506 per family member per month? The U.S. poverty line calculations, developed in 1964, are widely considered to be unrealistic in today's economy; instead, most scholars calculate a poverty line at 50 percent higher to be a more useful representation of people's standard of living.

Poverty rates vary by race (Figure 11.2). Hispanics have a 23.6 percent rate, representing 13,104,000 people. Non-Hispanic whites are at 10.1 percent, with 19,652,000 people below the poverty line. The black poverty rate is 26.2 percent, which includes 10,755,000 people. The Asian poverty rate is 12.0 percent, or 2,137,000 people (U.S. Census Bureau 2015). Our discussions of the history and contemporary expressions of race and racism in the United States in Chapter 6 helped shed light on these disparities. Despite prevalent media representations of inner-city poverty among communities of color, it is important to note that the largest group of the nation's poor are white and live in rural and suburban areas, as represented in the work of Pem Buck.

Anthropologists and other social scientists have articulated numerous theories to explain poverty's origins and persistence. In the United States, two key theories have focused on poverty as pathology and poverty as a structural economic problem.

FIGURE 11.2 Percentage of People in Poverty within Racial Groups, 2014

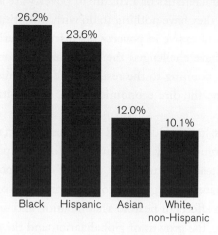

26.2%

23.6%

12.0%

10.1%

Black | Hispanic | Asian | White, non-Hispanic

SOURCE: www.census.gov

The "Culture of Poverty": Poverty as Pathology

Theories of poverty as pathology trace ongoing poverty to the personal failings of the individual, family, or community. Such theories—which most anthropologists reject—see these failings as stemming from a combination of dysfunctional behaviors, attitudes, and values that make and keep poor people poor. Anthropologist Oscar Lewis called this a "culture of poverty." His research in Mexico (1959) and the United States (1966) suggested that certain ways of thinking and feeling lead to the perpetuation of poverty among the poor. Lewis argued that children growing up poor in a highly class-stratified economic system were particularly vulnerable to developing feelings of marginality, helplessness, and dependency that would shape their value system, worldviews, aspirations, and character and make it difficult for them to escape poverty.

Lewis's work focused primarily on the impact of poverty in the developing world. But his research and theory of a culture of poverty became attractive to policymakers in the United States. Although many scholars, including anthropologists, discredited this theory on the grounds that it blamed the victims of poverty for structural problems beyond their control, the theory formed the basis of key social policies during the latter part of the twentieth century (Wilson 1987).

Poverty as a Structural Economic Problem

Many anthropologists have critiqued the "culture of poverty" theory, beginning with a series of essays edited by Eleanor Burke Leacock (1971), and have proposed instead that poverty is a structural economic problem. If there are no jobs, inadequate education and health care, and systematic failure to invest in the infrastructure of impoverished neighborhoods and communities, then poverty cannot be changed by changing attitudes and values. What are often considered to be characteristics of a culture of poverty are actually characteristics of poverty itself; they have nothing to do with the attitudes, values, and life choices of those forced to live in poverty. As discussed earlier, Leith Mullings (2005b) and others have challenged the depiction of a complacent and ghettoized underclass by pointing to the resilient and determined efforts made by the poor to overcome the dire economic, social, and political conditions that they face.

Anthropologists Judith Goode and Jeff Maskovsky (2001) challenge the culture of poverty argument by questioning its focus on poor communities as isolated spheres. Instead, they trace the roots of contemporary poverty in the United States to the impact of global economic processes on the nation's economy, particularly the effects of flexible accumulation and uneven development.

How is flexible accumulation shaping U.S. inequality? Laid-off factory workers of the closed Doosan Bobcat plant, Bismarck, North Dakota, symbolically leave behind steel-toed work boots in the parking lot as they exit the plant for the final time.

The growth of globalization and the expansion of global capitalism, they argue, have launched an economic restructuring in which corporations ship high-paying, blue-collar manufacturing jobs overseas in search of cheaper labor, lower taxes, and fewer environmental restrictions. The U.S. workforce has become more polarized between highly educated, well-paid professionals and managers and undereducated workers who struggle with low pay, no benefits, and little job security. U.S. government policies and programs designed to regulate the economy, protect the most vulnerable, and provide opportunities for social mobility have been reduced, including public education, housing, and investment in infrastructure—roads, bridges, water systems, and power grids.

Goode and Maskovsky warn that as poverty and inequality grow, those most deeply affected—including the one in five U.S. children who live in poverty (U.S. Census Bureau 2015)—remain largely hidden and disappear from national awareness. In response, they encourage a new awareness of the many ways in which poor people engage in collective and individual strategies to survive. They call for anthropologists to engage in ethnographic research that contributes to the grassroots efforts of the poor (Anglin 2002; Checker 2005, Dudley 2000; Goldstein 2016; Speed 2007). In addition, they call for adequate public investment in affordable housing, health care, education, and nutrition programs to create a framework whereby individual initiative can more readily lead to upward mobility.

Discussions about the root causes of poverty continue today in both popular conversations and policy circles. Intense debate continues, for instance, on the appropriate role of government in addressing problems of persistent poverty. Arguments often draw on the distinction between seeing its roots in a culture of poverty or in a long-term structural problem of exclusion built into government policies and economic practices. Can poverty be addressed through improved housing, provision of health care, education, and the creation of living-wage jobs (the structural causes), or must perceived patterns of dependency on government programs and services be addressed to confront an underlying culture that holds people back? You will encounter these questions in conversations with classmates and coworkers, and you will influence these debates at different points in your life—perhaps as you undertake community service as a college student or later as you participate in the U.S. political process.

What Makes Class and Inequality Largely Invisible?

As previously discussed, the U.S. national origin myth (see Chapter 7) consistently promotes themes of meritocracy and social mobility as central to U.S. national identity. Despite this claim to a culture of equal opportunity, the review of economic data in this chapter has revealed the existence of class and inequality in U.S. society as well as the disturbing reality that inequality is increasing. Even with the statistical evidence of class in America, attention to this pattern of stratification historically has been minimal and inequality remains largely invisible. Why?

The Role of the Media

Anthropologist Gregory Mantsios (2003) suggests that the media play a significant role in hiding class stratification in the United States by largely ignoring it. In an analysis of news articles, Mantsios found that only one in every 500 *New York Times* stories addressed poverty. In a broader review, using the *Reader's Guide to Periodic Literature*, Mantsios found that only one article in every 1,000 addressed poverty. Instead, the media focus on promoting a narrative of the United States as a meritocracy and an egalitarian society. At the same time, poverty and class divisions are described as strange and abnormal—as aberrations of true American life, not as a reflection of the structure of the nation's economic system.

Class is particularly invisible in U.S. television programming. Programs rarely portray poverty. Poor people are absent or ignored. Instead, the typical television series presents a homogenized version of the upper middle class designed to represent "everyone." Living in a generic upper-middle-class neighborhood, everyone is a cop, a doctor, a lawyer, or a business executive. Even those with blue-collar jobs are portrayed as middle class. Everyone is well off and, if not rich already, aspiring to be so. Among the cool young people who inhabit these communities, difference and stratification arise from beauty and sexuality, not from jobs, income, or wealth (McGrath 2005). Working-class, blue-collar workers and their jobs—supervised, unskilled, or semiskilled labor—are portrayed as increasingly outmoded and irrelevant in the global economy, even though 61 percent of all U.S. workers hold blue-collar jobs. It's no wonder, then, that the poor are rarely seen.

Voluntary Isolation

In addition to the media's reluctance to show the hard realities of poverty, we can identify a tendency in part of the population to isolate itself from exposure to the lower class. Anthropologist Setha Low has explored the recent development of gated communities—neighborhoods protected with walls, gates, security guards, entry codes, and key cards designed to control the social environment. As Low points out in *Behind the Gates: Life, Security, and the Pursuit of Happiness in Fortress America* (2004), wealthy and middle-class residents create these enclaves, now estimated to represent 10 percent of all homes in the United States, to ensure spatial distance from others whom they consider less desirable.

Forty years ago, before the rise of gated communities, members of these middle and upper-middle classes led a massive flight from urban areas to the suburbs in an attempt to distance themselves from the poverty, crime, and decay associated with city life. Today residents who can afford homes in gated communities—including retirees and commuters who work in the city—attempt to enhance their sense of safety by extending their isolation and insulation. Wealth and income allow this particular segment of U.S. society to wall themselves off from others, providing the illusion of enhanced security while reinforcing the replication of cultural capital through interactions limited to a certain class of the population.

Low suggests that in many ways the gates and walls may be counterproductive. By increasing isolation, the gates also produce fear. Life lived behind the walls is life lived in an enclave as if under siege—constantly guarded and locked up, protected from dangers real and imagined. Furthermore, the walls and gates not only shut others out but also shut residents in. In this way walls and gates increase social segregation, limit interaction across classes, deter broad-based civic engagement, and inhibit social connectedness, ultimately undermining the very efforts to create safety through community that the walls and gates were originally intended to promote and secure (Polanco 2014; Sullivan 2006; Walklate 2005).

The Consumer Culture

The consumer culture provides yet another explanation for the invisibility of class in the United States. Despite falling incomes over the past thirty years, many families have been able to pay for necessities and maintain at least the experience of a middle-class lifestyle. They accomplish this by working more (especially women, who have entered the workforce in increasing numbers), borrowing money in mortgages against the value of their homes, running up credit card debt, and taking out more student loans to pay for their own or their children's college education.

Though income and wealth have not increased for the vast majority of the nation's population, people have been able to consume as if they were upwardly mobile—at least until the collapse of the housing bubble in 2007 and the meltdown of financial markets beginning in late 2008. At that point, banks began to foreclose on homes that were no longer worth as much as the owners had borrowed against them. Credit card interest rates skyrocketed, and credit lines were reduced. Still, total credit card debt in 2016 was $762 billion (Board of Governors of the Federal Reserve System 2016a), a sign of the extent to which the population continues to consume as if it were middle and upper class even when annual income does not support this lifestyle. Fully 56 percent of U.S. households carried a balance on their credit cards, with an average of over $16,000 per indebted household in 2016. Perhaps more surprising, in 2010 student loan debt surpassed total credit card debt for the first time, climbing to $1.3 trillion in 2016 and revealing the shifting burden of educational expenses into long-term debt (FinAid 2016). Total mortgage debt in 2015 stood at a staggering $13.8 trillion (Board of Governors of the Federal Reserve System 2016b). These sobering statistics reveal the ways consumer spending has been supported by mortgage, credit card, and education debt, thereby masking the growing inequalities of income and wealth in the United States (Williams 2004).

The role of class is rarely discussed but is present everywhere in U.S. society, as is the attempt to "consume" class. In *Consuming the Romantic Utopia: Love and Cultural Contradictions of Capitalism* (1997), sociologist Eva Illouz suggests that even love and romance are shaped by class—both by financial capital and by cultural capital. As a college student, you experience this tension all the time. Dating is expensive. Romance takes time and money. How do you show you are in love? The rituals of love—the acts that are expected to show affection and cultivate romance—depend on the ability to shop and buy. You need the right clothes, haircut, makeup, perfume or cologne, shoes, birth control. You need a gym membership to stay fit or diet pills to stay skinny. The rituals of romance, including food, drinks, movies, gifts, and travel, all require money. A romantic dinner out is expensive.

Class even shapes our choice of romantic partners. We often think of love as a spontaneous act of emotion, good chemistry—a matter of the heart. But why do we feel that connection? Research shows that people are likely to marry someone of their own race (see Chapter 2). Discounting Hollywood movies, how likely is it that you would marry someone outside your class? Finding someone of a similar background who has the same cultural capital and knows the same language and symbols of romance—someone of the same class— strongly influences our choices of romantic partners. What has your own experience been in this regard?

As you develop your skills as a budding anthropologist, clearly seeing the outlines of class and its effects on you and the people around you may require extra effort. Media—from movies to television to the press—largely ignore the existence of income inequality and the gaps between wealth and poverty. Consumption patterns, fueled by deep indebtedness through credit cards, home mortgages, and educational loans, mask class differences at least on the level of acquisition of consumer goods. Perhaps this cultural tendency to mask class and inequality—to make them invisible—is one reason that the abrupt rise of the Occupy Wall Street movement in the fall of 2011, with its class-revealing slogan "We Are the 99%," surprised many people. But perhaps the same tendency to make class invisible explains why the movement fell so quickly from the media's public eye once protesters were removed by police from the spaces they physically occupied in parks and town squares. Their removal continues a long historical pattern of crackdowns against labor unions, anti-war demonstrators, civil rights protesters—even against residents of Ferguson, Missouri, after the shooting of Michael Brown—as the state, as Weber pointed out, reserves the monopoly on the use of force in order to keep the class structure in place. In a time of increasing inequality in the United States and around the world, a careful consideration and analysis of class will prove to be a crucial tool in your toolkit as you attempt to understand the complexities of the global world in which you live.

What Is Caste, and How Are Caste and Class Related?

Caste, like class, is a system of stratification. It organizes members of a culture into hierarchically ranked groups with unequal access to the rewards and privileges of society. **Caste** is commonly, though incorrectly, considered a closed system of stratification with deep historical roots, inherited, assigned at birth,

caste: A system of stratification most prominently found in India.

Visvamitra Visits Vasishtha's Hermitage, Kulu, Punjab Hills, 1700 depicts representatives of all four Hindu varna, or castes: Vasishtha—the hermit *Brahmins*; Visvamitra-*Ksyatriyas*—the soldier/rulers; *Vaisyas*—the agricultural workers/merchants; and *Shudras*—the laborers and artisans.

passed down from generation to generation with rigidly enforced boundaries among caste groups. As we will see, it also shares characteristics of fluidity and change more commonly associated with systems of class.

Caste in India

The most carefully described example of caste exists among the Hindus of India. Their complex caste system reflects the influences of religion, Indian social and economic relations, the nation's experience of colonialism, and recent processes of globalization.

Textbook descriptions of India's caste system trace its origins back 2,000 years to Hindu religious texts, rituals, and beliefs that divided the population into four *varna*, or castes. Each caste was associated with particular occupations and was ranked according to its purity in following Hindu ritual practices. *Brahmins* were scholars and spiritual leaders. *Ksyatriyas* served as soldiers and rulers. *Vaisyas* were agricultural workers and merchants. *Shudras* worked as laborers and artisans.

Completely outside and below these castes were other marginalized groups, including the "Untouchables," or **dalits** (literally, "broken people"). *Dalits* were assigned the most spiritually polluting work: cleaning latrines, collecting garbage, tanning leather. Social and religious stigma led to their physical separation from the rest of the community. They were considered so polluted that they were forbidden to use upper-class wells or temples. Members of the upper classes believed that simply touching a *dalit* would contaminate them; even touching a *dalit*'s shadow was considered unclean.

dalits: Members of India's "lowest" caste; literally, "broken people." Also called "Untouchables."

These religious beliefs have provided a rationale for an inflexible system of inequality and stratification, locking people into a caste for life. Though the caste hierarchies were established on religious principles, the resulting system established powerful long-term political, economic, and social implications.

Recent scholarship (Prashad 2001) explores a more complicated history of the Indian caste system than most textbooks present. Studies of local Indian communities suggest that caste has no uniform expression across India. The nation has an immense geographic range and a diverse population, with more than 4,600 distinct ethnic groups in a total population of over 1.2 billion people. Patterns of stratification within those communities could not be traced to a uniform application of ancient Hindu ritual texts. Instead, patterns of stratification vary widely. Caste has served not only as a cultural, religious, or political system but also as a structure for organizing economic exploitation.

Although caste predates European expansion into India and British colonial rule, the arrival of the Portuguese in 1498 and later British colonial efforts radically reshaped the system and made it more rigid. Colonial land laws removed certain groups, particularly *dalits*, from their ancestral lands and put them to work as street sweepers and leather workers. Segregation of employment groups created a stereotyped version of caste relations. By replicating in the Indian caste system patterns of class that were prominent in England, the British colonial power reshaped Indian castes as a mechanism for administering

MAP 11.4
India

Indian boys and men of the Untouchables, or *dalits*, working with hides in a lime pit at a tannery, circa 1946.

the enormous colony and extracting wealth generated there for the benefit of the British Empire (Prashad 2001).

India's caste system continues to change. Discrimination on the basis of caste is now illegal, having been outlawed in the constitution written after India gained independence in 1949. *Dalits* and other oppressed groups are now provided special protections and affirmative action programs to overcome the effects of centuries of exploitation. In the political realm, caste identity and consciousness have at times served for mobilizing allies and votes. In 1997, India elected its first *dalit* president, K. R. Narayanan. Caste distinctions have been blurred, especially in some urban areas.

India's recent economic transformations mean that new occupations and social mobility are undermining the power of caste boundaries to maintain a system of stratification. But the deep inequalities of the caste system persist, and changes are uneven. In public settings, caste boundaries are breaking down—for instance, in inter-caste dining. But in private—for instance, in arranged marriages—and particularly in rural areas, caste patterns remain strong. Moreover, the historical advantages of higher-caste groups have not been dismantled; this is especially evident in rural areas, where 68 percent of the population lives. Most of India's 201 million *dalits*—one-sixth of the population—continue to be agricultural workers who live in poverty. Few live in cities. The vast majority are illiterate, and only a handful participate in the industrial workforce or other Indian economic sectors (such as technology, telecommunications, and finance) that are becoming more integrated into the global economy.

Demonstration for women's rights and *dalit* rights in Bangalore, India, 2009, highlighting the intersection of gender and caste.

From Caste to Class

As India participates more fully in the global economy, certain sectors of the economy and certain regions of the country, particularly urban areas, are seeing the hierarchy of caste shift toward a hierarchy of class, beginning a transition from a society organized by an ascribed status to one organized by an achieved status. Yet, despite these economic changes and *dalit*-led movements for civil rights at the local, regional, and even national levels, the nation's deeply rooted inequalities continue to preserve power and privilege for the upper classes while inhibiting most *dalits* and lower-caste members from participating fully in the country's economic and social life (Deliege 2011; Guilmoto 2011).

Globally, the spread of globalization and worldwide market economies has been speeding the transition from caste systems to class systems. After all, capitalism and the forces of globalization mean that workers must be able to move freely from place to place in response to changing economic conditions. Workers have to be able to transition within professions to match up with changing jobs. The rigidity of a closed caste system stands in stark contrast to and in direct conflict with the demands of the global economy. The rigidity of the caste-based, ascribed status hierarchy is gradually shifting to a class-based (achieved) status system. Yet patterns of inequality remain extremely slow to change.

What Are the Effects of Global Inequality?

Globalization has produced unprecedented opportunities for the creation of wealth, but it has also produced widespread poverty. This uneven development is a central characteristic of the global capitalist system. Because it affects every corner of the world, it will be increasingly important for you as a global citizen to understand its impact.

Street Vendors in the Global Economy

Anthropologist Daniel Goldstein (2016) explores the contours of class and inequality for the poorest and most vulnerable people in today's globalized economy in his study of street vendors in the enormous Cancha outdoor market in Cochabamba, Bolivia. Today's global economic transformations have led to historic levels of poverty in the world's poorest cities as rural dwellers with limited job opportunities and no state safety net move to urban areas in search of survival and security for themselves and their families. Goldstein's ethnographic research focuses specifically on vulnerable street vendors and their small-scale commercial activities—what scholars call the informal

MAP 11.5
Cochabamba

economy, the underground, and sometimes illegal, system of buying and selling that parallels the official economy. In many poor countries like Bolivia—the poorest in Latin America—and particularly in urban centers like Cochabamba, the informal economy has become the majority of the economic activity.

The bright, colorful, and dynamic Cancha marketplace is the largest of its kind in Bolivia. Thousands of long-term merchants, known as *fijos*, sell their wares from narrow stalls in the market's central pavilion. At the same time, thousands of street vendors, locally known as *ambulantes*, rove the surrounding, traffic-clogged streets and packed sidewalks, alleyways, and passageways hawking food, drink, watches, radios, DVDs, men's briefs, hardware, soap, cosmetics, bananas, rice—any small, portable item that might attract the attention of a local shopper or visiting tourist. While stall vendors and street vendors alike contribute to the dynamism and success of the market, their experiences stand in stark contrast. Tensions between the groups runs high. Their furious competition for sales ensures that. But the *fijos* and *ambulantes* operate on unequal playing fields. For stall vendors, their fixed, permanent and legal locations at the center of the market provide a more secure position in the local economy. Their stability and legal status create conditions for economic success and the potential, if all goes well, for upward economic mobility.

The street vendors of the Cancha, in contrast, work under much more tenuous and vulnerable conditions. They are harassed by police, insulted by motorists and pedestrians, preyed upon by shoplifters and muggers. State laws explicitly prohibit them from selling on the street. And yet thousands do. Though enforcement of these laws is inconsistent, street vendors daily risk fines and arrests as they struggle against the poverty facing their families. But their "in between place" of informality and illegality makes street vendors particularly vulnerable, exploitable, and insecure. And when corrupt government officials simultaneously sell space to vendors on the street and sidewalks while authorizing police crackdowns and fines, they turn street vendors' vulnerability into a source of profit.

Goldstein argues that the marked growth of informal urban economic activity worldwide is produced not by the informal workers themselves, but by the way economic and political conditions are created and regulated by the state. What may appear to the outsider as chaotic, disorderly, even criminal and

The informal economy—small-scale, underground, and sometimes illegal—has become the primary economic activity in many poor countries. Here, street vendors and stall vendors compete for customers at the sprawling Cancha outdoor market in downtown Cochabamba, Bolivia.

dangerous, is not random at all. Rather, the state and its representatives create and benefit directly from the conditions of informality and illegality that turn urban small-scale entrepreneurs into criminals. Inconsistently enforced laws and regulations applied to the urban poor—an increasingly common pattern in the contemporary global economy—only increase workers' experience of uncertainty, insecurity, and vulnerability.

Despite the chaos and disorder built into the informal activity in the Cancha, Goldstein's ethnography reveals the determined efforts of street vendors—poor urban small business people—to scrabble together a living against the odds in the only way available to them—as precarious owners of the streets and sidewalks of the informal city.

Class and the Circulation of Water in Mumbai, India

Eight thousand miles from Flint, Michigan, poor people in Mumbai, India, also navigate a water crisis affecting the city's most marginalized communities. Sixty percent of Mumbai's 20.5 million people are poor urban settlers evicted from the city center or arriving from rural areas. With no permanent, legally recognized residence, the city's rules provide no legal rights to Mumbai's water. Anthropologist Nikhil Anand (2011a, 2011b, 2012) explores the strategies Mumbai's poor use to stake their claim to a hydraulic citizenship—a right to water—as they seek to make reliable homes for themselves and their families.

Purchasing bottled water as a private commodity is prohibitively expensive. So everyone must access Mumbai's municipal water in some fashion. With limited financial capital, Mumbai settlers mobilize social capital—relationships with friends, employers, clients, siblings, water officials, and fictive kin—to find points of access. They stage protests and write petitions. And they surreptitiously connect to public water mains late at night or early in the morning. Anand tells the story of accompanying a friend to connect to the water supply at 4:30 in the morning, waiting in a long line for his allotted water distribution. In the pre-dawn darkness Anand's friend—a housekeeper at a luxury downtown hotel—tells a painfully ironic story of his own, recounting a recent request from his manager to turn off the tap of a guest who had left it running when he went out. Anand notes how class structures are made visible as poor Indian laborers travel across the city, passing shanties and luxury buildings, seeing poverty and wealth and remembering having turned off a running hotel tap while standing in line for water. Urban infrastructure plays a key role in establishing these patterns of class stratification and inequality, structuring into the relationships between citizen and state conditions of marginality and illegality.

MAP 11.6
Mumbai

Cities are made possible by the circulation of water in city pipes. But what kind of a city? The complex assemblages of water pipes in Mumbai tell a story and enable an analysis of how marginality is created. Here we see not the marginality of the rural poor living on the edges of national and international economic activity. Instead, we see marginality at the center of the nation-state, in India's largest city and through its most essential matter—water. Relations of power come into focus as Anand traces the circulation of water in the city. Mumbai's municipal water system returns a hefty profit to the city yet its managers and political decision makers are unable to provide a steady and safe supply to settlement dwellers—its most vulnerable population. What is citizenship if it does not include the right to water? Does disconnection of water mean disconnection of citizenship? Anand's research offers insights into the creative, persistent, informal, and even illegal strategies Mumbai's poor settlement dwellers use to resist the city's water rules and renegotiate the terms of their hydraulic citizenship in the face of an infrastructure managed to create and reinforce their conditions of class stratification and inequality.

Thinking Globally about Inequality

Statistics reveal the extremes of uneven development described in the ethnographic studies of Cochabamba and Mumbai. For example, in 2016 the world had 1,810 billionaires, up from 937 billionaires in 2010 (Dolan and Kroll 2016); yet, with the exception of China, global poverty has increased over the past twenty years. Today 40 percent of the world's population live in poverty, defined by the United Nations as income of less than $2.00 per day. Nearly 1 billion people live in extreme poverty, surviving on less than $1.25 each day (United Nations 2015). The U.N. has calculated that if household wealth were divided equally on a global basis, using 2000 data each household would have roughly $20,000. Instead, the report found that 2 percent of the world's population owns more than half of all wealth on the entire planet. The wealthiest 20 percent of the world's population receive 75 percent of the total global income (Davies et al. 2007).

The Gini index developed by the World Bank provides a global picture of inequality by comparing the per capita gross national income—total income produced by the economic activity of a state—of the world's economies. The World Bank classifies countries as high income ($12,746 or more per person), upper middle income ($4,126 to $12,745), lower middle income ($1,046 to $4,125), or low income ($1045 or less). According to the Gini index, the gap between rich and poor countries has grown in recent years and continues to widen (Figure 11.3). Although the index provides a comparison of country averages, it does not take into account inequality within countries. Even the poorest countries

THE SOCIAL LIFE OF THINGS
Landfills, Waste, and Social Inequality

We all encounter waste every day, whether it's our trash, old fast-food wrappers, or what goes into our toilet. But where does it go? Anthropologist Josh Reno (2016) worked for nine months in a sanitary landfill on the outskirts of Detroit, Michigan to understand the social life of waste and the complex social relations of class and inequality it forms as it moves from production to consumption to disposal.

1 The United States generates more waste than any country in the world. Yet our system of mass waste removal system is largely invisible. Landfills redistribute dangerous material from densely populated urban areas and concentrate them elsewhere, transferring the risk of leakage, pollution, contamination, and ill health to poor rural communities and communities of color. The construction of landfills transforms neighborhoods and ecosystems, remaking the surface of the Earth and endangering the surrounding air, water, and soil.

2 Waste disposal has become a measure of modernity all around the world. The availability of sanitation and clean water marks a clear distinction of class and status. In the United States, waste disposal is central to removing waste and signs of decay that can so easily intrude on middle-class expectations of order and cleanliness. Imagine the disorder and decay—and the damage to your social status—if you stopped taking out the trash or flushing the toilet for a few weeks.

3 Waste disposal involves a complex network of workers: trash collectors, recycling sorters, truckers, regulators, landfill managers, mechanics, bulldozer operators, and common landfill laborers. Waste workers are commonly stigmatized for their work with our garbage, but Reno challenges us to recognize them as essential care workers. By caring for mass waste—removing filth and decay—waste workers indirectly care for us, creating the conditions for cleanliness, health, and order but also striving for or maintaining a middle-class lifestyle.

If you follow the contents of your garbage bag, recycling bin, or toilet, they will lead you to people and places most of us never consider. A careful analysis of the social life of waste reveals connections often disguised and provides another insight into the complex web of social relationships in American culture.

- Do you know where your trash goes?
- Do you know the hands your waste passes through from your home to the landfill, recycling station, or incinerator?
- Why do you think the waste removal system has been made almost invisible in the United States?

FIGURE 11.3 The World by Income, 2016

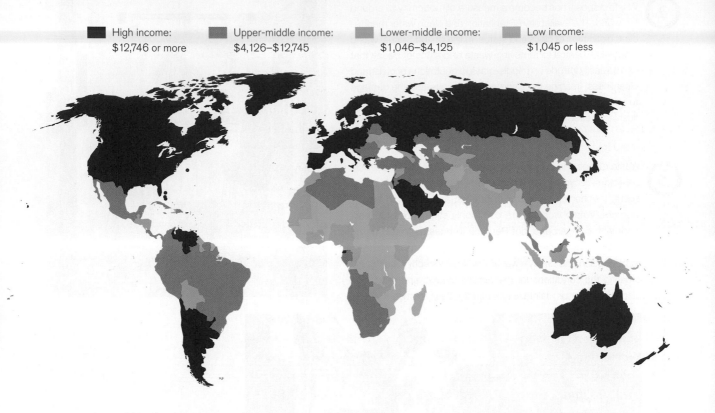

High income: $12,746 or more

Upper-middle income: $4,126–$12,745

Lower-middle income: $1,046–$4,125

Low income: $1,045 or less

SOURCE: The World Bank. 2016. Country and Lending Groups. data.worldbank.org

have an elite organized around political, economic, or military power. The richest countries, as we have seen in the United States, have an increasing number of people living in poverty. What does this mean in concrete terms?

Growing global inequality affects the life chances of the world's population on many fronts, including hunger and malnutrition, health, education, vulnerability to climate change, and access to technology. Hunger is indeed a global problem. Although there is enough food in the world to feed everyone, it is unevenly distributed. Every day 870 million people go hungry—one out of every eight—and 200 million children under age five are malnourished (World Food Programme 2013).

Health and mortality are also serious problem areas. Preventable infectious diseases such as malaria, measles, and HIV/AIDS kill millions each year in poor countries. People are more likely to die in infancy in low-income countries—and are eleven times more likely to die at birth than in wealthy countries. Moreover, people live longer in high-income countries, averaging a seventy-eight-year life span compared to fifty-eight in low-income countries (World Food Programme 2013).

Access to education, a gateway to economic advancement, is also uneven. Basic literacy varies widely between high- and low-income countries. In addition, the digital divide prevents the majority of the world's inhabitants from participating in technological advances that are transforming the world's economy.

Climate change also affects the rich and poor unequally. Those with financial and political resources can buy safety, living outside areas that are vulnerable to natural disasters. A recent example from the United States underscores this point: Anthropologist Neil Smith (2006), when examining the effects of Hurricane Katrina on the people of New Orleans, called it an "unnatural disaster" because the storm's most severe effects were caused by the government's failure to adequately build and maintain the city's levee system, not by the storm itself. New Orleans residents experienced Katrina's effects unevenly along lines of class as well as race and gender.

Throughout this chapter we have explored the complexity of class stratification and inequality both within the United States and globally. Despite the centrality of class-based stratification in the dynamics of globalization and its powerful effects on individuals' life chances and possibility for social mobility, class arguably remains the most overlooked of the systems of power we have considered in this textbook. Careful attention to the theoretical approaches to class adopted by anthropologists, including ethnographic research and data analysis, will position you to more fully engage issues of income and wealth inequality as you participate in a rapidly globalizing world.

Thinking Like an Anthropologist: The Dynamics of Class through Water and Beyond

In our chapter-opening story, we began to tease out the dynamics of class through the story of Flint, Michigan's water crisis. Water is essential to human life. Humans need a steady supply of quality water every day. Yet people in Flint, and others around the globe, struggle to gain access to safe and abundant water. What is for many in the United States an afterthought—a drink of water—has become one of the most highly contentious issues of our time. What is too often thought of as a natural process—the circulation of water—has now become a hydro-social process, shaped and determined not only by rainfall and topography but increasingly by infrastructures, technological skills, and political decision makers. And as we have seen in this chapter, in Flint and Mumbai, inequalities in the distribution of water often map directly onto inequalities in class, race, gender and ethnicity.

Having read this chapter, you are now better prepared to analyze the water crisis in Flint through the lens of class. For underneath the decision to switch water supplies, the orange-brown water and corroded pipes lies a set of unequal relationships. And these differences—starkly revealed by the health consequences of water management decisions—translate into significantly different access to services, resources, and life chances. Our discussion in this chapter has expanded from Flint's water crisis to explore the following questions:

- Is inequality a natural part of human culture?
- How do anthropologists analyze class and inequality?
- How are class and inequality constructed?
- Why are class and inequality largely invisible?
- What is caste, and how are caste and class related?
- What are the effects of global inequality?

As systems of class stratification create widening inequality, your ability to perceive, analyze, and discuss class will become increasingly important. Class affects life chances in almost all realms of culture, including infrastructure, the restaurant industry, universities and other elements of the education system, health care, religious organizations, housing, government services, and many others that you can identify. How do these systems of class and inequality affect your own life chances and those of the people closest to you? As you consider these issues, you may be motivated to engage in efforts to reshape systems of inequality. Certainly, as you prepare for a career in the global economy and a life in this global age, being able to analyze the effects of class and inequality will be an essential tool in your anthropological toolkit.

Key Terms

class (p. 388)
egalitarian society (p. 390)
reciprocity (p. 390)
ranked society (p. 391)
redistribution (p. 391)
potlatch (p. 391)
bourgeoisie (p. 394)
means of production (p. 394)
proletariat (p. 394)
prestige (p. 395)
life chances (p. 396)
social mobility (p. 396)
social reproduction (p. 396)
habitus (p. 396)
cultural capital (p. 398)
intersectionality (p. 399)
income (p. 411)
wealth (p. 412)
caste (p. 420)
dalits (p. 421)

For Further Exploration

Class Matters. 2005. New York: Times Books. www.nytimes
.com/pages/national/class/index.html. A year-long
series of articles and features (print and online)
and interactive graphics (online) developed by
the *New York Times* to explore the impact of class
in U.S. culture.

Domhoff, G. William. 2012. *Who Rules America?* http://
sociology.ucsc.edu/whorulesamerica/power/wealth
.html. Website by sociologist William Dumhoff
explores issues of wealth and power.

Economic Policy Institute. 2013. *The State of Working
America*. http://stateofworkingamerica.org. The
Economic Policy Institute's annual publication.

FinAid. "Student Loan Debt Clock." www.finaid.org
/loans/studentdebtclock.phtml.

"Global Wealth Inequality" https://www.youtube.com
/watch?v=uWSxzjyMNpU

Inequality.org. www.inequality.org. A website established
by the Institute for Policy Studies, a Washington, D.C.–
based think tank focusing on economic inequality.

Roosevelt, Franklin Delano. 1944. "Economic Bill of Rights"
(speech). www.youtube.com/watch?v=3EZ5bx9AyI4.
Roosevelt's proposal for a "second bill of rights"
for U.S. citizens.

Statistic Brain. "Credit Card Debt Statistics." www
.statisticbrain.com/credit-card-debt-statistics/.

Stiglitz, Joseph. 2012. *The Price of Inequality: How Today's
Divided Society Endangers Our Future*. New York:
Norton.

The Take. 2004. By Naomi Klein and Avi Lewis.
Documentary about Argentine auto parts workers
taking over an abandoned factory and putting it back
into production themselves.

United Nations. 1948. The Universal Declaration of Human
Rights. www.un.org/en/documents/udhr
/index.shtml. The Declaration was established in 1948,
in the aftermath of the atrocities of World War II, to
articulate an international agreement about what
fundamental rights should be available to all humans.

United Nations. "Sustainable Development Goals: 17 Goals
to Transform Our World." http://www.un.org
/sustainabledevelopment/. The U.N. established 17
goals toward eliminating global poverty by 2030.

"Wealth Inequality in America" https://www.youtube
.com/watch?v=QPKKQnijnsM&spfreload=10

Yes! 2013. www.yesmagazine.org. Magazine that
provides in-depth analysis of global economic and
environmental issues, stories about real people
confronting these challenges, and suggestions for
how to become engaged in finding solutions.

The world is changing rapidly in the twenty-first century. People are on the move, spurred by changes in the global economy, political systems, communication and transportation infrastructures, and more. At Tongi Station on the outskirts of Dhaka, Bangladesh, hundreds of people sit on the roof of an overcrowded train to travel homeward for Eid al-Fitr, a Muslim festival marking the end of the fasting month of Ramadan.

Where does your chocolate come from? A young man on an eastern Côte d'Ivoire farm breaks cocoa pods to extract the beans used to make chocolate.

CHAPTER 12
The Global Economy

Do you know where your last chocolate bar came from?

Today's global economy is a complex network of exchanges and connections that reach far beyond the candy machine outside your classroom or the store across the street. A piece of chocolate, a cup of coffee, or an iPhone can link the wealthiest resident of a world capital or a student at an elite college to a subsistence farmer in Africa or a factory worker in China. In today's world we are all deeply connected. Let's use the chocolate bar to illustrate this point.

Côte d'Ivoire, West Africa, exports 40 percent of the world's cocoa, which is used to make chocolate. Much of the country is covered in tropical forest, amid which are plantations carved out by farmers using hand tools. Seven million Côte d'Ivoirians make a living farming cocoa and coffee. Although the global price for cocoa—set on the commodities market in New York City—is relatively high, Côte d'Ivoire's farmers see little return for their work. The bulk of the profits go to transnational agricultural corporations, such as U.S.-based Cargill and Archer Daniels Midland (ADM) and the Swiss firm Barry Callebaut. These corporations buy cocoa beans and process them into chocolate products to be eaten worldwide. Few local farmers in Côte d'Ivoire have ever eaten a chocolate bar.

In recent years, Côte d'Ivoire has been riven by poverty, civil war, and conflict over cocoa and coffee revenues. In a fiercely contested election in 2010, Alessane Ouattara defeated incumbent Laurent Gbagbo for the presidency. Gbagbo's regime had relied on high taxes on cocoa and coffee farmers to subsidize its excesses and to fund Gbagbo's paramilitary hit squads. The election of Ouattara, a former deputy director of the

MAP 12.1
Côte d'Ivoire

International Monetary Fund (IMF), gave Côte d'Ivoirians hope of a more secure and prosperous future. But Gbagbo refused to acknowledge his loss in the election and remained ensconced in the presidential palace. By clinging to power and stirring ethnic violence, Gbagbo pushed the country toward civil war.

To undercut Gbagbo's financial base, Ouattara called on international corporations to embargo Côte d'Ivoire's coffee and cocoa exports, claiming that Gbagbo used profits from the sales to fund his armed resistance. Giant U.S. agribusiness corporations eventually pledged to cooperate, but they refused to allow independent inspection of their exports. Many nongovernmental organizations (NGOs) charged that Côte d'Ivoire was circumventing the embargo by shipping its coffee and cocoa overland to neighboring Mali and Burkina Faso, which were reselling the goods to the same corporations.

As fighting between Gbagbo's and Ouattara's supporters escalated in 2011, the French military, returning to its colonial role, stormed the airport outside Abidjian, the country's economic capital and primary port. The French had established a colony in Côte d'Ivoire in 1840 to enter the ivory trade and build coffee and cocoa plantations. Even after Côte d'Ivoire's independence in 1960, however, the French maintained a strong economic and military presence there. In the hopes of limiting violence in the civil war, France joined with the United Nations to create a demilitarized zone stretching across the country. French and U.N. soldiers then isolated the presidential palace, still occupied by the

What role have chocolate revenues played in the recent conflict in Côte d'Ivoire? Here, soldiers loyal to newly installed president Alassane Ouattara patrol after the arrest of former president Gbagbo.

defeated Gbagbo, until forces loyal to new president Ouattara ousted Gbagbo from the residence and arrested him. Despite continuing hostility between supporters of Gbagbo and Ouattara, in 2012 the country's economy began to recover (Monnier 2013; North 2011). In recent years, cocoa production has stabilized, France and China have launched large infrastructure projects, and the International Cocoa Federation is moving its headquarters from London to Abijian. Laurent Gbagbo was tried by the International Criminal Court for crimes against humanity and war crimes.

The conflict in Côte d'Ivoire reveals many of the complex dynamics of today's global economy: (1) the interconnectedness of farmers in rural West Africa with chocolate eaters and coffee drinkers worldwide; (2) the tension-filled relationship between nation-states and transnational corporations; (3) the strategic military interventions, often by former colonial powers, that serve to police local political affairs and global economic flows; (4) the power of global financial markets to determine the price of coffee and cocoa, and thus the quality of life of small farmers; and (5) the link between consumers and producers through global commodity chains that have blurred notions of distinct national territories.

To fully understand the modern world economy, we must examine the concept of an economy as well as the historical developments that underlie today's global economy. In this chapter we will explore the following questions:

- What is an economy, and what is its purpose?
- What are the roots of today's global economy?
- What role has colonialism played in forming today's global economy?
- What is the relationship between the nation-state and the corporation in the global economy?
- What are the dominant organizing principles of the global economy today?
- How does today's global economy link workers with consumers worldwide?
- Is today's global economic system sustainable?

By the end of the chapter you should be able to analyze the major economic patterns of the contemporary global economy and assess its underlying principles. Armed with this information, you will be better prepared to make choices about your own lifestyle as a consumer and to engage in debates about how to create a sustainable economic system as the growing human population places increasing pressure on Earth's resources.

What Is an Economy, and What Is Its Purpose?

economy: A cultural adaptation to the environment that enables a group of humans to use the available land, resources, and labor to satisfy their needs and to thrive.

At the most basic level, an **economy** is a cultural adaptation to the environment—a set of ideas, activities, and technologies that enable a group of humans to use the available land, resources, and labor to satisfy their basic needs and, if organized well, to thrive. Thus, an economic system is a pattern of relations and institutions that humans construct to help collectively meet the needs of the community. Of course, today the concept of an economy seems much more complicated. But what is an economy at its core?

Production, Distribution, and Consumption

Anthropologist Yehudi Cohen (1974) refers to an economy as a set of adaptive strategies that humans have used to provide food, water, and shelter to a group of people through the production, distribution, and consumption of foodstuffs and other goods. In the following sections, we will explore the varied ways humans have produced, distributed, and consumed as part of their economic activity. In particular, we will consider distinctive modes of production, ranging from food foraging to industrialism; general patterns of distribution and exchange; and the emergence of a global economy that has transformed both production and distribution, as well as patterns of human consumption.

From Foraging to Industrial Agriculture: A Brief Survey of Food Production

Over the course of history, humans have developed various economic strategies to survive in diverse environments. Cohen (1974) suggests five primary adaptive strategies that developed at different times and places: food foraging, pastoralism, horticulture, agriculture, and industrialism. By reviewing these strategies, we begin to understand that the current consumption-based global economy—with its emphasis on industrial production (even in agriculture), consumption, and technology—is only one of many possible variations.

Food Foraging Before the domestication of plants and animals around 10,000 years ago, all humans were **food foragers**. They made their living by hunting, fishing, and gathering nuts, fruit, and root crops; in fact, humans evolved into our current physical form as food foragers. Mobility was key: small, egalitarian groups followed the movement of large animals and the seasonal growth of fruits, vegetables, and nuts to secure their survival. Throughout human history, food foragers have ranged over a remarkable variety of habitats, from the most hospitable to the most extreme.

food foragers: Humans who subsist by hunting, fishing, and gathering plants to eat.

Today fewer than 250,000 people make their primary living from food foraging. Most food foragers now incorporate farming and the domestication of animals. The remaining food foragers often live in the most marginal of Earth's environments—cold places, forests, islands—where other economic activity and other strategies for food production are not sustainable. Recent food foragers include the Inuit (Eskimos) of Canada and Alaska, Native Australian aborigines, and inhabitants of African and South American rainforests.

Two classic ethnographies examine recent food forager communities. Richard Lee's *The Dobe !Kung* (1984) explores the history and life patterns of the *!Kung san* people living in the Dobe region of the Kalahari Desert in southern Africa. Also, Colin Turnbull's *The Forest People* ([1961] 2010) considers the Mbuti and Efe people living in tropical forests along the equator of Central and East Africa in what is now the Congo; they hunt elephants and other big game with spears, bow and arrow, and large nets. Robert Gordon's ethnography *The Bushman Myth: The Making of a Namibian Underclass* (1992) undermines stereotyped images of contemporary hunter-gatherers as pristine surviving relics of the Stone Age. Instead, Gordon describes their ethnic diversity and many languages, their early involvement in copper mining and trade, and their resistance to colonial settler practices of ethnocide and domestication that forced them into marginalized areas and reserves in present-day Namibia.

Pastoralism, Horticulture, and Agriculture Cohen identifies three adaptive strategies for food production in nonindustrial societies: pastoralism, horticulture, and agriculture. The earliest evidence of food production can be traced to approximately 11,000 years ago in the region surrounding the Tigris and Euphrates Rivers (the Fertile Crescent) in what is modern-day Iraq. These strategies for food production led to more permanent human settlements that facilitated the development of tools and pottery and the specialization of human trades.

Pastoralism involves the domestication and herding of animals for food production. Goats, pigs, sheep, cattle, llamas, horses, and camels may be raised and herded to support the family or extended community (although pastoralism today is often combined with hunting and gathering and horticulture). Pastoralism usually involves herders moving livestock seasonally between high- and low-altitude grazing areas—a process referred to as *transhumance*—while other community members remain at home. The Nuer of Sudan, studied by E. E. Evans-Pritchard (see Chapter 10) and more recently by Sharon Hutchinson (1996), are perhaps the best-known group for whom pastoralism (paired with small-scale agriculture) was a key component of their economic strategy.

Horticulture is the cultivation of plants for subsistence through a nonintensive use of land and labor. Horticulturalists use simple tools such as sticks and hoes to cultivate small garden plots. Land is generally rotated in and out of use to exploit more fertile ground. Horticulturalists frequently employ *slash and burn agriculture*—also called "swidden farming"—to clear land for cultivation, kill insects that may inhibit crop growth, and produce nutrient-rich ash that serves as fertilizer. Communities that rely on horticulture tend to be fairly sedentary, remaining close to their sites of food production. Horticulture is frequently combined with hunting, gathering, and pastoralism to provide the communities' basic needs.

In addition to the Fertile Crescent, early evidence of agricultural activity exists in Pakistan's Indus River Valley, China's Yellow River Valley, and the Nile Valley of Egypt, as well as in Mexico, the American southwest, and the Andes region of South America. **Agriculture** requires an intensive investment in farming and well-orchestrated land-use strategies. Irrigation, fertilizer, draft animals, and machinery such as plows and tractors provide the technology and labor for successful agriculture. Irrigation systems may include the terracing of hillsides and the channeling of rainfall and natural watercourses through carefully constructed pathways in an elaborate manipulation of natural resources. Through agriculture, humans produce enough food on permanently cultivated land to satisfy the immediate needs of the community and to create a surplus that can be sold or traded.

Exact catalysts for the emergence of agriculture alongside hunting and gathering and pastoralism are unclear. But the effects of increased food production promoted a more sedentary lifestyle, an increased population size, and the founding of permanent settlements and population centers. Towns and cities created markets to facilitate local and long-distance trade of agricultural

pastoralism: A strategy for food production involving the domestication of animals.

horticulture: The cultivation of plants for subsistence through nonintensive use of land and labor.

agriculture: An intensive farming strategy for food production involving permanently cultivated land.

surpluses and craft products. Specialists such as blacksmiths, carpenters, stone-cutters, and weavers established small businesses in market towns to serve the surrounding territories.

Whereas hunter-gatherer societies tended to be largely egalitarian, the rise of intensive agriculture in nonindustrial cultures led to social stratification. Social distinctions included large landholders, wealthy merchants, and owners of small businesses, as well as peasants and landless tenants working on large farms and estates as wage laborers. Anthropologists consider *peasants* to be small-scale rural farmers whose agricultural surpluses are transferred upward to support the dominant elites and others who do not farm but whose goods and services are considered essential (Wolf 1966).

Industrial Agriculture Intensive agricultural practices began with the introduction of plows, draft animals, and irrigation. But recent years have seen the rise of **industrial agriculture**, which involves a massive mechanization of farming and the mass production of foodstuffs. In fact, in the twentieth century, agricultural production shifted from individual farms and farmers to large corporate-run farms, or agribusinesses, that rely on the intensive use of machinery (such as tractors and combines), irrigation systems, pesticides, and fertilizers.

industrial agriculture: Intensive farming practices involving mechanization and mass production of foodstuffs.

As the world's population continues to expand, pressure to increase global food production intensifies. Recent decades have seen remarkable progress in feeding the world population. Although portions of the world continue to face famines and food shortages, these are not a result of inadequate food production but, rather, of unequal distribution of the food that is produced.

Despite increased food production, industrial agriculture and agribusinesses have yielded complicated results. For example, chemical fertilizers and pesticides pose dangers to workers and to local water resources. Antibiotics that keep poultry and livestock healthy in industrial production facilities seep into the human food chain. Genetic engineering reduces crop diversity, making crops more susceptible to harsh weather and pests in the long term. Food irradiation poses potential safety and health hazards. Overall, industrial agriculture requires extremely high energy input to support machinery, irrigation, pesticides, fertilizer, and transportation costs. In many cases, more calories—units of energy— are required in the production process than the food actually provides when it is consumed.

Over the last fifty years, the introduction of industrial agricultural practices by transnational corporations has transformed the role of small farmers and peasants in the global economy. Agribusinesses in many parts of the world have pushed many formerly self-sufficient, small-scale farmers off the land in order to mechanize the preparation of fields, planting of seeds, application of fertilizers and pesticides, and harvesting. As a result, even though the

A Chinese-owned farm in Angola, southern Africa, produces corn for export to China, a reflection of industrial agriculture in today's global economy.

industrialization of farming has yielded dramatic increases in global food production, fewer people work in agriculture, and the displaced rural populations are moving to urban centers in search of wage labor.

Despite the advances in pest- and weather-resistant crop varieties and the dramatic recent increase in output, world food production faces increasing stress today. For example, global climate change is creating less-predictable growing conditions, and rapid population growth is straining available food supplies. As a result, wealthy food-importing nations such as China, Korea, Japan, India, and Saudi Arabia are buying up agricultural land and water resources in the fertile nations of Africa (ranging from Egypt to the Sudan to the Congo and Angola) to ensure exports of wheat, rice, and corn to support their own populations. With such activity by foreign countries, will Africa's countries be able to feed themselves in times of environmental and economic instability (Brown 2011a)?

All adaptive strategies are subject to the limitations of the natural environment. **Carrying capacity** is the number of people who can be supported by the resources of the surrounding region. The carrying capacity of land for food foragers, pastoralists, horticulturalists, or lower-intensity agriculturalists is more locally limited. But in most cases, farming generates a higher carrying capacity than food foraging because the labor-intensive activity of farming supports more extensive human settlements.

Given the expansion of industrialism, including industrial agriculture, the impact of economic activity has more global consequences today. What is Earth's carrying capacity? Can the planet support our projected population growth and consumption of natural resources? Can our contemporary economy

carrying capacity: The number of people who can be supported by the resources of the surrounding region.

meet current human needs, given the planet's carrying capacity? We will consider these questions as we explore the modern world economic system over the remainder of this chapter.

Distribution and Exchange

All cultures have developed patterns for the distribution and exchange of goods and information produced by their members. In fact, the exchange of goods and ideas appears to be central to the workings of culture, establishing patterns of interaction and obligation among people. Anthropologists recognize three main patterns of exchange: market exchange, reciprocity, and redistribution. All are embedded in the everyday workings of almost every cultural group.

Market Exchange Today, patterns of distribution and exchange are heavily influenced by economic markets that facilitate the buying and selling of land, natural resources, goods, services, labor, and ideas. Contemporary markets range in size and scope from village markets in India to the New York Stock Exchange on Wall Street. Though some people may **barter**—that is, exchange goods and services one for the other—most contemporary economic transactions are based on an exchange medium, or some form of money. In recent human history, the medium of exchange has varied. Items such as salt, precious stones, shells, livestock, precious metals such as gold or silver, coins, and most recently paper money and digital transfers of money have served to make payments for goods and services. By 2,000 years ago, coins had become a common method of exchange in urban centers in Asia, Africa, and Europe and along long-distance trade routes, facilitating the expansion of trade across vast distances (Davies 2005; Wolf 1982).

barter: The exchange of goods and services one for the other.

Reciprocity **Reciprocity** involves an exchange of goods and services among people of relatively equal status. Such exchanges, including gift giving, create and reinforce social ties between givers and receivers, fulfill social obligations, and often raise the prestige of the gift giver. For example, the sharing of food resources, whether in earlier hunter-gatherer groups or among contemporary families, builds a sense of community, fulfills social obligations to the group, and raises the prestige of the provider. Anthropologists identify three types of reciprocity defined by the social distance between exchange partners: generalized reciprocity, balanced reciprocity, and negative reciprocity (Sahlins [1974] 2004; Service 1966).

reciprocity: The exchange of resources, goods, and services among people of relatively equal status; meant to create and reinforce social ties.

Generalized reciprocity encompasses exchanges in which the value of what is exchanged is not carefully calculated and the timing or amount of repayment is not predetermined. Generalized reciprocity is common among close kin or close friends, serving as an expression of personal connection while reinforcing family and social networks. You may often experience generalized reciprocity without recognizing it: offering to take someone to the airport without expecting exact or timely reciprocity; borrowing a pen or sheets of paper; offering some of your food to a friend. Likewise, parents provide for their children—food, shelter, education, clothes, protection—without calculating the value or expecting repayment on predetermined terms. They give these gifts out of a sense of love and responsibility. Any expectation of reciprocity tends to be general, not specific—looked for in the form of love or respect rather than a specific amount of cash.

Balanced reciprocity occurs between people who are more distantly related. This type of exchange includes norms about giving, accepting, and reciprocating. The giver expects the gift to be accepted and then to receive something in return. The recipient has an obligation to accept the gift (or is otherwise considered rude or ungrateful) and reciprocate promptly with a gift of equal value. The goal of exchanges based on balanced reciprocity is to build and maintain social relationships, often beyond the immediate kin group. A classic example is the gift exchanges of the Trobriand Islanders' Kula Ring discussed in Chapter 3. Contemporary examples might include gifts between friends and close associates, such as birthday presents, dinner invitations, or even picking up a round of drinks after work. Participants in these relationships of exchange have an obligation to reciprocate and to do so proportionally to the gift that they have received.

Negative reciprocity refers to a pattern of exchange in which the parties seek to receive more than they give, reaping a material advantage through the exchange. Whereas general and balanced reciprocity are based on relationships of trust and familiarity, negative reciprocity occurs among people who are strangers, antagonists, and enemies with opposing interests. Through hard bargaining, cleverness, deception, or cheating, the parties hope to minimize their cost and maximize their return. Extreme cases of negative reciprocity may include the use of force to achieve one's goals despite an imminent threat of retaliation. Familiar contemporary examples include email scams that offer to share an inheritance if recipients send their bank account information; Wall Street investment managers who offer high returns but ultimately steal their clients' money; or predatory mortgage lenders that offer housing loans at interest rates the borrower cannot afford to repay, ultimately taking the borrower's money and home through foreclosure.

Redistribution Finally, **redistribution** is a form of exchange in which goods are collected from the members of the group and reallocated in a different pattern. Redistribution requires the collected goods to flow through a central location—a chief, a storehouse, or a central government—where it can be

redistribution: A form of exchange in which accumulated wealth is collected from the members of the group and reallocated in a different pattern.

sorted, counted, and redistributed. In small-scale societies, redistribution brings prestige to the community leader as food and goods collected from the leader's supporters are reallocated for supporting the general populace or establishing alliances with outside groups. A classic example in the anthropological literature is the potlatch (see Chapter 11). You have experienced redistribution directly if in your family those who work outside the home share their wages with those who do not in order to provide all members with food and shelter. And if you receive a paycheck for a job, your taxes are part of the U.S. government's system of redistribution.

Redistribution may increase or decrease the inequality of wealth and resources within a group. In fact, many cultures have **leveling mechanisms**— practices and organizations that level out resources within the group. In the United States, for example, as in many other nation-states, redistribution is enacted through local, state, and federal tax codes. The government collects money (more from those with greater resources) and then reallocates and redistributes the nation's wealth to provide services (for example, the military) and

What are our expectations for exchanging gifts and favors? (*top left*) A family sits down for breakfast in Afghanistan, an expression of *generalized reciprocity*. (*bottom left*) A birthday party represents a form of *balanced reciprocity*, exchange designed to build and maintain social networks. (*right*) Wall Street investment manager Bernard Madoff, convicted in 2009 of bilking investors of $65 billion through the promise of high returns, an example of *negative reciprocity*.

leveling mechanism: Practices and organizations that reallocate resources among a group to maximize the collective good.

infrastructure (for example, roads and bridges). Leveling mechanisms enact a cultural commitment to the collective good that seeks access to safety, health, education, food, and shelter for all group members irrespective of class.

The extent and direction of redistribution is constantly debated. How much should successful people contribute to ensure that other members of society have an opportunity to be successful as well? Patterns of redistribution may also shift wealth upward. For instance, the U.S. government has used taxpayer money to rescue failing Wall Street financial firms during the 2008 market crash and to subsidize profitable oil companies and agribusinesses. The government also assesses lower taxes on capital gains on investments—a benefit accruing largely to the wealthy—than on income earned from wages.

Having reviewed general concepts of production, distribution, and exchange, we now turn to the roots of today's global economy. It has fundamentally transformed patterns of production, distribution, exchange, and consumption and the ways humans interact through economic systems.

What Are the Roots of Today's Global Economy?

Recent centuries have intensified the integration of all humanity into an interconnected global economy. Although images from *National Geographic* magazine or Discovery Channel programs often imply that human history is a story of isolated tribes with little or no outside contact or exchange, anthropological research tells a different story. It is one of connection and encounter, not isolation.

Economic anthropology—the study of human economic activity and relations—views the world through the lens of movement rather than through the perspective of fixed and discrete groups. The key characteristics of today's global economy are mobility and connection. But not all of these connections have been smooth and easy. Many have been—and still are—contentious and unequal.

Early Long-Distance Trade Routes

In 1492 Christopher Columbus sailed from Spain in search of a sea route to Asia. Many scholars regard Columbus's voyage as the symbolic beginning of the modern world economic system. His journey across the Atlantic certainly launched the encounter between Europe and the Americas. But by that time, European elites were already aware that China and India dominated world economic activity. Europe stood on the periphery.

More than 2,000 years ago, long-distance trade routes connected Asia, the Middle East, Africa, and Europe in a dynamic international network

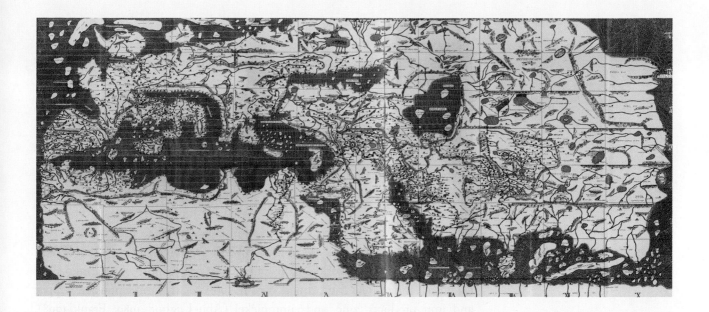

of economic exchange (Abu-Lughod 1989; Braudel [1979] 1992; Frank 1998; Schneider 1977; Wolf 1982). Camel caravans traveled along the Silk Route from China through India and the Middle East. From there, overland trade routes led into North Africa and Europe, energizing Mediterranean ports such as Alexandria, Venice, Rome, and Constantinople. In the first millennium C.E., sea routes extended trade along the Arabian Peninsula and down the eastern coast of Africa. Regular maritime trade linked coastal regions around the Indian Ocean, China, and Southeast Asia. Arab traders had established trade routes, economic exchange relations, and local communities throughout Asia. Camel caravans moved gold, salt, and slaves from West Africa across the Sahara to North Africa and the Middle East. An Arab slave trade predated the European transatlantic slave trade by 700 years, transporting slaves of diverse origins from West and North Africa, the Mediterranean, Persia, England, Ireland, and eastern Europe at different times between the eighth and the nineteenth centuries (Lydon 2009).

Movement was slow, but long-distance trade moved luxury items such as silk, spices, tea, and gunpowder across vast territory encompassing Asia, the Middle East, Europe, and Africa. Marco Polo traveled the Silk Route from Venice to China and back again along already-existing land and sea trade routes. His journey took twenty-four years (1271–1295). Ibn Battutah, an Islamic scholar/official from Morocco in North Africa, began a pilgrimage to Mecca in 1325 and traveled to Constantinople, the Middle East, Southeast Asia, and China as well as West Africa before returning home in 1349. Tales of Marco Polo and Ibn Battutah's travels have been preserved, but most likely they reflect

Long-distance trade routes have connected Asia, the Middle East, Europe, and Africa for over 2,000 years. The Tabula Rogeriana, a map of trade routes through northern Africa, Europe, the Indian Ocean, and much of Asia, was written in Arabic and attributed to the Arab geographer Muhammad al-Idrisi, 1154.

the experiences of many others who also journeyed along long-distance trade routes long before Columbus sailed west from Spain in 1492.

In 1405, eighty-seven years before Columbus voyaged to the Americas, a seven-foot-tall admiral named Zheng He set sail from Fuzhou, China, with a fleet that would have dwarfed Columbus's three ships. Fully 317 ships and 27,870 sailors made the first of seven voyages between 1405 and 1433, sponsored by China's Ming emperor. Zheng He's fleets visited thirty-seven countries throughout the South Seas of Asia, the Middle East, and down the eastern coast of Africa, linking into existing patterns of trade, exchange, and connection. At each stop Zheng He's fleet encountered the far-reaching networks of overseas Chinese that had existed for hundreds of years. His voyages illustrate the extensive global economic system that already existed by 1400 and China's pivotal role as the world's economic powerhouse (Frank 1998). China led the world in the production and export of silk, porcelain ceramics (china), tea, fruit, drugs, cotton, tobacco, arms and powder, copper and iron products, zinc, and cupronickel (Abu-Lughod 1989; Frank 1998). Before long, Europe's elite were seeking greater access to China's desirable commodities.

European Traders Buy Their Way In

By the time Columbus sailed in 1492, Europe's elite needed more than a shorter trade route to Asia to enter the world economy. They needed a way to buy themselves in. Although China wanted or needed very little from the West, Europeans increasingly sought its export commodities. As a result, European trade in Asia created surpluses for China, whose exports constantly surpassed its imports. China demanded payment of all deficits in silver and gold, setting off an intense global competition for these scarce resources.

As a result, acquisition of silver and gold was high on the Europeans' agenda in the Caribbean and the Americas. They systematically plundered the Mayan and Aztec kingdoms as well as the indigenous populations as they conquered the South American continent. Local populations were forced into slave labor to extract precious minerals, as at the lucrative silver mines in Peru. Between 1500 and 1600 the supply of silver in circulation in Europe increased eightfold (Robbins 2013). The gold and silver plundered from the Americas enabled Europeans to buy a seat on the economic train based in Asia. As a result, between 1500 and 1800, massive quantities of silver flowed eastward across the globe to China. By the mid-1800s frustrated by the drain on their national treasuries, European powers moved to alter their trade imbalance with China through military action. This action began with the first Opium War in 1839, in which Britain forced China to accept opium grown on British plantations in India in lieu of silver (Frank 1998; Spence 2013).

What Role Has Colonialism Played in Forming Today's Global Economy?

Europe's global economic engagements between 1500 and 1800 relied primarily on extensive maritime trade within the existing global economic system. The American colonies were an important exception. They served as a harbinger of colonial expansion in the rest of the world in the nineteenth and early twentieth centuries. In fact, the European conquest of the New World—the Caribbean and the Americas—launched an era of colonialism that eventually touched every corner of the globe.

Under **colonialism**, European powers redrew the map of the world and fundamentally reorganized the political and economic balance of power on a global scale. Europeans' advanced military weaponry and strategies, developed through years of continental warfare and naval battles, gave them an advantage that enabled them to dominate others in the colonial era. Beginning in the 1500s, European colonialism played a pivotal role in establishing the framework for today's global economic system.

colonialism: The practice by which a nation-state extends political, economic, and military power beyond its own borders over an extended period of time to secure access to raw materials, cheap labor, and markets in other countries or regions.

The Triangle Trade

The **triangle trade** that emerged in the 1500s among Europe, Africa, and the Americas involved an extensive exchange of goods, people, wealth, food, diseases, and ideas that transformed economic, political, and social life on both sides of the Atlantic (Figure 12.1). It also brought western Europeans the resources they needed in order to grow their national economies and expand their role in international trade.

triangle trade: The extensive exchange of slaves, sugar, cotton, and furs between Europe, Africa, and the Americas that transformed economic, political, and social life on both sides of the Atlantic.

Sugar Europeans established a plantation economy in the Caribbean and South America to produce sugar for export to Europe. Although sugarcane was originally domesticated in the South Pacific, early merchants had carried sugar along trade routes through India, the Middle East, and the Mediterranean. Columbus had carried sugar to the Caribbean, which, along with Brazil, offered an ideal climate for sugarcane cultivation. But now, plantation production transformed sugar from a luxury item to a key component of the European diet. Sugar also sweetened three other key commodities in the triangle trade—all stimulants (drugs)—coffee, tea, and cocoa (Mintz 1985).

Slaves The expansion of sugarcane plantations by the Spanish and Portuguese could not be sustained by the local populations in the Caribbean and South America because they were decimated by European diseases and the grueling conditions of forced labor. So plantation owners turned to the African

FIGURE 12.1 The Triangle Trade

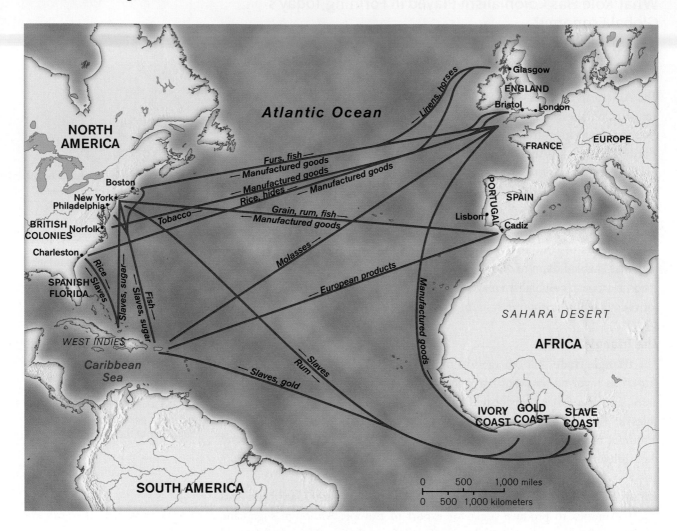

slave trade to supply their labor needs. Between the sixteenth and eighteenth centuries, millions of Africans were sold into slavery and transported across the Atlantic to work on sugarcane plantations in the Caribbean and South America. Later, rising demand for cotton for England's textile industry required more laborers for cotton plantations in the southern region of what is now the United States. This pressure further stimulated demand for enslaved Africans. Many—perhaps millions—died in the traumatic passage across the Atlantic, and millions more died in inhuman conditions of incarceration and slavery after arriving in the Americas.

Slavery has existed at many times in human history, often based on differences in religion or ethnicity or involving prisoners of war. Evidence reveals that at the time of the Europeans' arrival in West Africa in the sixteenth century, an active slave market already existed (Alexander 2001). Europeans and others, including Arab traders from the Middle East, linked into it to purchase enslaved people. But the enslavement of Africans in the Americas drew on a unique framework in which skin color served as the marker for enslavement. The uncompensated labor of enslaved Africans, extracted under brutal conditions, subsidized the economic growth and development of Europe and the American colonies for more than 350 years.

Furs In North America, the fur trade, particularly in beaver pelts, pulled the continent into the global economy. European trappers established trading relationships with Native Americans, swapping beaver pelts for European finished products such as guns, metal tools, and textiles. The fur trade was not as lucrative as the Asia trade in spices, silk, or porcelains, but an active European market for fur coats and hats created steady demand.

The production and consumption of beaver fur transformed North America. The European demand for fur drove the European expansion deeper into the North American continent. Native American settlement patterns were severely disrupted, as were local agricultural practices and economic activities. Conflicts between the British and French drew indigenous populations into colonial wars. European germs devastated a population that had no immunity to European diseases (Wolf 1982).

Beginning in the early seventeenth century, the fur trade pulled North America into the global economy. European fur traders barter with Native Americans in this engraving after a detail from Gauthier and Faden's "Map of Canada," 1777.

The decimation of the indigenous populations in North and South America and the Caribbean (estimated by some scholars to be as many as 15 million people), combined with the relocation of millions of Africans and the arrival of millions of European immigrants, transformed the human population of the New World over a period of a few centuries. Furthermore, the large-scale migration of Europeans and the forced migration of Africans had lasting repercussions on their home communities as well. The conquest of Native American lands, genocide of indigenous people, and enslavement of Africans relied on intertwined ideologies of racial supremacy, patriarchy, and religious destiny to establish, expand, and justify a hierarchy of exploitation central to the European colonial enterprise. (Robbins 2013; Truillot 1994; Wolf 1982).

The Industrial Revolution

The **Industrial Revolution** in the eighteenth and nineteenth centuries drove the next phase of European colonial activities. As European economies, led by Great Britain, shifted toward machine-based manufacturing, the new industries relied heavily on the raw materials, cheap labor, and open markets of the colonies. Numerous factors contributed to this phenomenon.

The Colonies' Essential Role In the emerging capitalist economy, the globalizing effects of improved communication and transportation drew together the lives of rural farmers and miners in the colonies with factory workers in industrializing nations. Urban textile factories in England replaced home-based systems of manufacturing and pulled rural peasants into urban wage-based jobs. Cheap cotton from plantations in the southern United States and India stimulated production. The steam engine, iron making, and new forms of power generation increased industrial production. Larger and faster steam-powered ships transported significant quantities of raw materials, food, and finished products from port to port. And railroads provided transportation between port cities and interior areas, moving rural workers to urban factories, raw materials from mines and farms to ports, and finished products to markets across continents.

At the same time, Europe's expanding cities, combined with growing colonies, provided markets for goods produced in Europe's factories. The huge profits from the transatlantic triangle trade provided the capital infusion necessary to fund Europe's industrial transformation.

Competition under Capitalism Industrial expansion of the capitalist economy created intense competition among European countries for raw materials, cheap labor, and markets. Throughout the nineteenth and early twentieth centuries, Great Britain, France, the Netherlands, Belgium, Russia, and Japan all raced to divide nonindustrial regions of the world into colonies that would

Industrial Revolution: The eighteenth- and nineteenth-century shift from agriculture and artisanal skill craft to machine-based manufacturing.

secure their economic growth. In the process, European countries redrew the political map of the world and restructured the global economy to serve their expanding industrial activities.

Colonial spheres of influence were established over much of Asia, Africa, and the Middle East. In Asia, British military intervention forced China into a series of unequal treaties that granted Great Britain and later the United States, France, and Germany special rights to trade and legal protection within China. (These privileges continued until the communist revolution in 1949.) Hong Kong and Macau were ceded to the British and Portuguese, respectively. By the late nineteenth century, Japan began to establish Asian colonies, first in Taiwan (1895) and eventually including most of East Asia, including the eastern seaboard of China. (Japan's colonial enterprise was only ended by its 1945 defeat in World War II.)

The colonial division of Africa was extremely abrupt. In 1884–85, fourteen countries gathered at the Berlin Conference in Germany to negotiate a settlement in the competition for African resources. Representatives of Germany, Portugal, France, and England took the lead—accompanied by Spain, Russia, Belgium, Turkey, and the United States—in carving up the African continent into fifty colonies. No African representatives were present.

Previously, only coastal Africa had been colonized. Eighty percent of the continent was still locally controlled. But the Berlin Conference forced a division of people and resources in the interior, drawing new political boundaries along natural features such as rivers, mountains, and ports without regard to ethnicity, language, history, village, or family. These boundaries have continued to shape political, economic, and cultural life in Africa long after African liberation movements brought an end to colonialism following World War II (see the Rwanda discussion in Chapter 7).

Anti-Colonial Struggles

Local populations resisted colonialism with mixed success. Independence movements used strategies of rebellion, resistance, and negotiation to achieve their goals. These included nonviolent actions such as those led by Mohandas Ghandi in the Indian struggle against British colonialism, as well as violent uprisings such as those in the Algerian quest for independence discussed in the next section. Frequently, external factors such as wars, economic crises, and international pressures aided independence movements by creating conditions for their success.

National Independence Movements In the Americas, independence movements on both continents brought changes. The United States declared independence from Great Britain in 1776, eventually winning independence through the Revolutionary War. The people of Haiti, a highly profitable Caribbean French colony known for its sugarcane, coffee, cocoa, indigo, and cotton plantations, declared independence in 1804 and became the first independent former colony to be ruled by people of African descent. In Latin America, Brazil declared independence from Portugal in 1822. By 1825, most of Spain's colonies in South America had achieved independence.

In Asia, Japan not only successfully resisted European colonial efforts but also established its own colonial enterprise. It occupied Taiwan for fifty years (1895–1945), Korea for thirty-five years (1910–1945), and China beginning with the invasion of Manchuria in 1931 and expanding to much of eastern China through World War II. During the war, the Japanese military overran European and American colonies in Asia, including Indonesia, Malaysia, Vietnam, Cambodia, Laos, Burma, Hong Kong, and the Philippines.

Ultimately, World War II created conditions for the success of national independence movements and the collapse of the colonial system. For example, Japanese occupation destroyed much of the European colonial infrastructure in Asia and inspired organized national resistance movements. These forces led efforts toward national independence when the war ended. On a global scale, the war-ravaged economies and political institutions of the European colonial powers could no longer sustain their colonial enterprises, especially in the face of organized resistance movements. Between 1945 and 1990, more than one hundred former colonies gained their independence.

The Algerian Experience Gillo Pontecorvo's riveting film *The Battle of Algiers* (1965) captures universal aspects of the brutal anti-colonial struggle through the lens of the Algerian movement for independence from France. The French, who were active colonialists in West and North Africa, ruled Algeria from 1830 to 1962.

Set in the Algerian capital, *The Battle of Algiers* focuses on the narrow streets of the Casbah, the old Turkish city within Algiers. This area became the site of violent conflict between pro-independence guerrillas of the National Liberation Front (NLF) and the French military. Between 1954 and 1962, two million young Frenchmen served as soldiers in Algeria. More than 20,000 died. Unable to convince the French to withdraw, the NLF launched terrorist attacks against the French settler population, setting off bombs in public places and killing French policemen. In retaliation, French paratroopers stormed the Casbah, sealing in the Algerian population and ferreting out NLF leaders and supporters through interrogation, torture, assassination, and bombings.

After independence, ties between the two countries remained complicated. Independence brought massive migration from Algeria to France. More than one million French colonial settlers, along with Algerian Muslims who served as soldiers in the French military, were "repatriated" (relocated) to France for

MAP 12.2
Algeria

Algerian residents do battle against the colonial French military in *The Battle of Algiers*, 1965.

their safety. In succeeding years, many poor rural Algerians also migrated to France to find work in the expanding postwar economy.

In Algeria, *The Battle of Algiers* has become popular as a tale of the anti-colonial struggle that threw off French control after 132 years of colonial administration. But in France, screening of the film was not allowed until 2001, thirty-six years after its release. Its graphic portrayal of French troops created discomfort with French complicity in the widespread torture of Algerian nationalists. The torture included beatings, electric shock, waterboarding, and extrajudicial killings. The French commander in Algiers during the uprising called these techniques a "cruel necessity" in the battle against the terror tactics of nationalist guerrillas (Harries 2007).

Pontecorvo's film reflects a brutal but not uncommon path toward independence at the end of colonialism following World War II. In 1980, Zimbabwe became the last African country to achieve independence from the European colonial powers. In Asia, however, only toward the end of the twentieth century did Britain return Hong Kong (1997) and Portugal return Macau (1999) to China. But as we have seen in the opening story about Côte d'Ivoire, and as we will see throughout the remainder of this chapter, despite the formal end of the colonial era, patterns of relationship established under colonialism—from migration and economics to military involvement—continue to influence both former colonies and colonizers.

The Modern World Economic System

With the end of the colonial era, many people believed that the former colonies—wealthy in natural resources and freed from colonial control—would see rapid economic growth. But such growth, as well as diminished poverty and the possibility for income equality, has proved to be elusive. Why have patterns of inequality established under colonialism persisted into the current era?

Conflicting Theories **Modernization theories**, which became popular following World War II, predicted that with the end of colonialism poor countries would follow the same trajectory as the industrialized countries and achieve improved standards of living. Certainly, the rise of industrial capitalism in Europe beginning in the late eighteenth century had spurred spectacular advances in production and a sense of optimism in the possibilities for dramatic material progress—in other words, **development** (Larrain 1989). As decolonization approached, politicians and economists in industrialized nations began to strategize about how to develop the economies of the colonies of Britain, France, Portugal, and other European powers (Leys 1996). The modernization model was assumed to be the key. Progress, modernization, and industrialization would be the natural path of economic development throughout the global capitalist economy, though this process would need nurturing through foreign aid and international investment.

After World War II, policy theorists and planners believed that scientific and technological expertise could help replicate the European and North American style of development across the globe. Through an array of new international aid agencies and financial institutions, such as the World Bank, the IMF, and the U.N., wealthy nations worked with emerging national governments in former colonies to develop programs they hoped would stimulate growth, alleviate poverty, and raise living standards. Development projects often emphasized state investment in infrastructure as an engine of economic growth, focusing on the construction of ports, roads, dams, and irrigation systems (Cowen and Shenton 1996).

The underlying philosophy of post–World War II development efforts put faith in the inevitability of human progress: With the right economic policies and economic stimulation, all or most societies would follow the same trajectory toward greater accumulation and standards of living. This faith in universal progress assumed that development efforts would facilitate shifts from poverty to wealth by transforming local economic activity from agriculture to industry; from subsistence lifestyles to capital accumulation and mass consumption; from kinship-based social and economic relations to contract-based ones; and, ultimately, from tradition to modernity. In many early development efforts,

---

modernization theories: Post–World War II economic theories that predicted that with the end of colonialism, less-developed countries would follow the same trajectory toward modernization as the industrialized countries.

development: Post–World War II strategy of wealthy nations to spur global economic growth, alleviate poverty, and raise living standards through strategic investment in national economies of former colonies.

anthropologists helped tailor projects to local needs as they designed, implemented, and evaluated programs to alleviate poverty and human suffering (Edelman and Haugerud 2005).

But by the 1960s, scholars began to question the Western development model. Despite the end of colonialism, less-developed countries, even those with rich natural resources, did not experience modernization and economic growth. Many local and national economies remained stagnant or lost ground in the international economy. Many countries took on increasing international debt to keep their economies stable in the postcolonial era.

At this time, **dependency theory** emerged as a critique of modernization theory. Scholars from Latin America, in particular, argued that a new kind of colonialism—**neocolonialism**—had emerged (Cardoso and Faletto 1969; Frank 1969). Dependency theorists argued that despite the end of colonialism, the underlying economic relations of the modern world system had not changed. These scholars introduced the term **underdevelopment** to suggest that poor countries were not poor because of some fundamental structural flaw (such as inadequate natural resources), but because participation in the global economy left them underdeveloped. The global economy was still structured to extract resources from less-developed countries and transfer them to developed, industrialized countries. Thus, dependency theorists argued, underdeveloped countries should break their dependency on the global economic system and build up and protect their own self-sufficient national economic activities.

Core and Periphery Immanuel Wallerstein (1974) introduced to these debates a *modern world systems* analysis. Wallerstein characterized the nations within the world economic system as occupying core, semiperiphery, and periphery positions (Figure 12.2). The **core countries**—primarily industrialized former colonial states—dominate the world system, extracting cheap labor and raw materials from periphery countries and sending them to the industrialized core. Finished products, with value added in the manufacturing process, are then returned to markets in the periphery. Core countries control the most lucrative economic processes, including the financial services sectors.

Periphery countries—among the least developed and least powerful nations—serve primarily as sources of raw materials, agricultural products, cheap labor, and markets for the economic activities of the core. Established patterns of economic, political, and military relationship ensure the steady transfer of wealth, natural resources, and human resources from the periphery to core, contributing to underdevelopment. **Semiperiphery countries** occupy a middle position. They may have developed some industry, draw resources from the periphery, and export manufactured products to the core and periphery, but they lack the economic and political power of the core.

dependency theory: A critique of modernization theory arguing that despite the end of colonialism, the underlying economic relations of the modern world economic system had not changed.

neocolonialism: A continued pattern of unequal economic relations despite the formal end of colonial political and military control.

underdevelopment: The term used to suggest that poor countries are poor as a result of their relationship to an unbalanced global economic system.

core countries: Industrialized former colonial states that dominate the world economic system.

periphery countries: The least-developed and least-powerful nations; often exploited by the core countries as sources of raw materials, cheap labor, and markets.

semiperiphery countries: Nations ranking in between core and periphery countries, with some attributes of the core countries but with less of a central role in the global economy.

FIGURE 12.2 The Core/Periphery Division of the World

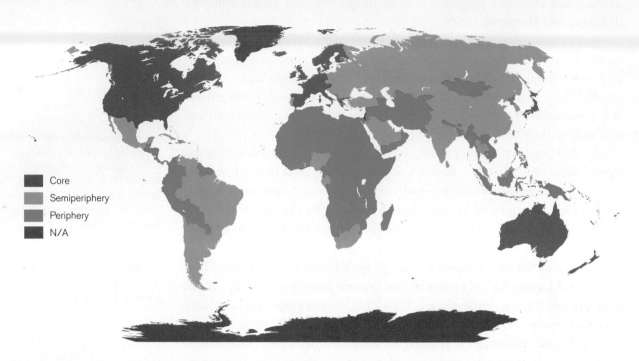

Core
Semiperiphery
Periphery
N/A

Core and periphery are not necessarily geographically isolated from one another. Wallerstein suggests that peripheral areas often exist within core countries as pockets of poverty amid generally high standards of living. In the United States, the Appalachian mountain region (see the discussion of Pem Buck's book *Worked to the Bone* in Chapter 11) might be considered a periphery within a core country: It has abundant natural resources of coal, timber, and water but intense poverty, poor education and health care, and limited infrastructure. Core areas also exist within periphery countries. These include urban centers (ports and capital cities), dominated by the economic, military, and political elite, that provide linkages between core countries and the often more rural people in the periphery. Abidjian, Côte d'Ivoire, could be considered a core area within a periphery country, serving to connect rural cocoa farmers and the global chocolate trade.

Over the past forty years, globalization has complicated the neat categories of Wallerstein's theory. Capital, goods, people, and ideas flow less predictably today between a geographically defined core and periphery. But the realities of uneven development and entrenched inequality persist. Over 80 percent of the world's population still live in developing nations decades after the end of colonialism. The failure of the dominant economic development strategies since World War II to advance the economic conditions of most former colonies,

Where does your iPhone come from? The journey of an iPhone illustrates Wallerstein's concepts of core, semiperiphery, and periphery. (*clockwise from right*) A worker at a rare earth mine in Inner Mongolia; rare earth elements are vital to the manufacturing of electronics, including iPhones. Factory workers at the Foxconn plant in Shenzhen, south China, where many iPhones, iPads, and other Apple products are made. Footballer Francesco Totti takes a selfie after scoring a goal against S.S. Lazio.

combined with dramatically uneven development, has raised significant questions about the appropriate strategies for addressing structural imbalance in the global economy and related problems of poverty, hunger, illness, and environmental degradation going forward.

Development In recent years development has become contentious within the field of anthropology. Although development remains a foundational strategy of powerful international organizations as well as most governments of poor nations, many scholars question its ultimate goals and beneficiaries (Escobar 1991, 1995; Ferguson 1997; Gupta and Ferguson 1997). In response, broader indices have been created to more holistically evaluate the effects of development strategies by augmenting the previous reliance on strictly economic measures such as gross domestic product. One such measure is the U.N. Development Program's Human Development Index, which considers improvements in life expectancy, literacy, formal education, political participation, and access to basic resources (Edelman and Haugerud 2005).

Despite disagreements within anthropology about the overall effectiveness of development strategies, today many anthropologists work in the field of development, at the World Bank, U.N. agencies, the Inter-American Development Bank, and smaller development-oriented NGOs. But the failure of dominant approaches to development to significantly alleviate global poverty has led other anthropologists to explore alternatives. These approaches include efforts to localize projects and de-link them from the global marketplace; draw on community and indigenous knowledge; establish fair trade markets; and deepen local involvement in economic and policy decisions. These efforts are often linked to local social movements, NGOs, and civil society groups; they focus on developing practical experiences for raising living standards that can then be expanded to broader contexts (Cavanaugh, Wysham, and Aruda 2002).

What Is the Relationship between the Nation-State and the Corporation in the Global Economy?

Over the past hundred years, the corporation has increasingly challenged the nation-state (which dominated the colonial era) for supremacy in the global economy. We can trace this change through the history of two economic models that dominated the U.S. economy (and beyond) during the twentieth century.

From Fordism to Flexible Accumulation

In 1914 Henry Ford, the founder of Ford Motor Company, a U.S. automobile manufacturer, experimented with a new strategy for profit making within the industrializing economy of the United States. Ford is famous for refining the factory assembly line and the division of labor that facilitated efficiency in industrial mass production. Perhaps equally significant, at a time when many U.S. manufacturers were exploiting immigrant workers with low wages and long work hours to maximize profits, Ford took a different approach.

Ford made several key innovations. Most important, he introduced a $5, eight-hour workday—a living wage that he hoped would create a worker who was loyal to the company, dependable on the job, and cooperative with management in the grueling, repetitive work environment of the assembly line. Ford also believed that every Ford worker should be able to buy a Ford car. Higher wages and shorter hours, he felt, would create a new pool of consumers with the income and leisure to purchase and enjoy a car. Ford sought to form a new social compact between labor and capital that would benefit his corporation. These were the central aspects of **Fordism**.

Fordism took hold firmly after World War II with growing cooperation among corporations, labor, and government. The latter stepped in to regulate corporate responsibility for worker health and safety and, eventually, environmental impact. An income tax structure with high marginal rates for the very wealthy moderated the growth in income inequality. Wages and benefits, along with corporate profits, rose steadily through a long post-war boom that drove a rapid expansion of the middle class through the early 1970s.

However, industrial economic activity in the late 1960s and 1970s began to shift away from the Fordist model toward what geographer David Harvey (1990) has called "strategies of flexible accumulation." At this time, corporate

Fordism: The dominant model of industrial production for much of the twentieth century, based on a social compact between labor, corporations, and government.

profits faced increasing pressures as European and Japanese economies recovered from the devastation of World War II and the "tiger" economies of newly industrializing nations (such as South Korea, Taiwan, Hong Kong, and Singapore) entered global competition. An oil crisis in 1973 further strained economic production in core countries, and a simultaneous global recession left many corporations seeking new strategies to enhance their profits.

Flexible accumulation refers to the increasingly flexible strategies that corporations use to accumulate profits in an era of globalization. In particular, these strategies include *offshoring* (relocating factories anywhere in the world that provides optimal production, infrastructure, labor, marketing, and political conditions) and *outsourcing* (hiring low-wage laborers in periphery countries to perform jobs previously done in core countries). By so doing, corporations could bypass high production costs, organized labor, and environmental laws in the core industrial cities and core countries.

Under flexible accumulation, corporations—even highly profitable ones—began to eliminate jobs in old core industrial centers such as New York, Chicago, and Detroit. Instead, they opened factories "offshore" in places such as Mexico, the Caribbean, South Korea, and Taiwan. In the 1980s they began to relocate factories to China to take advantage of even lower wages, lower taxes, and weaker environmental restrictions. Today Walmart has more than 7,000 factories in China producing goods for its stores worldwide. Recent strikes by Chinese workers demanding higher wages and better working conditions have led some corporations to relocate again, opening new factories in Thailand, Cambodia, Vietnam,

flexible accumulation: The increasingly flexible strategies that corporations use to accumulate profits in an era of globalization, enabled by innovative communication and transportation technologies.

Who answered your last call for tech support? Here, a call center agent in the Philippines talks to a client in the United States, an example of how jobs are being outsourced from core countries to low-wage destinations under flexible accumulation.

global cities: Former industrial centers that have reinvented themselves as command centers for global production.

and Bangladesh. Over the past forty years, strategies of flexible accumulation have transformed the local factory assembly line into a global assembly line.

Global Cities To manage global production, corporations created international headquarters. As part of this process, a number of old industrial centers reinvented themselves as command centers for global production. This phenomenon began with New York, Tokyo, and London and subsequently included Los Angeles, Chicago, Miami, Hong Kong, Sydney, Paris, Amsterdam, and Buenos Aires. All of these cities had experienced the loss of industrial manufacturing in the 1970s and 1980s. Now these **global cities** (Sassen 2012) provide corporations with the physical infrastructure and human resources required to run a corporate headquarters: local transportation, international airports, regional rail networks, reliable power grids and water supplies, and modern communication systems, as well as skilled accountants, lawyers, information technology specialists, and marketers.

Outsourcing of Jobs

New communication technologies have enabled corporations to outsource many jobs to developing areas. Since the 1990s, companies have been outsourcing software design, airplane reservations, data processing, radiology readings, and data analysis. The call center industry—those people at the 800 numbers we call for help with an electronic device or to make rental car and airline reservations—has been aggressively pursuing low-cost options across the globe.

Call centers once located in Kansas and Nebraska now operate in India and the Philippines. They attract college graduates with English language skills who earn 30 to 50 percent of what a U.S. worker would earn for the same job. Recently, call centers in the Philippines have been expanding as Indian centers shift to the development of information technologies and software that require a higher level of education. With over a million call center workers, the Philippines has surpassed India to become the largest call center operator in the world—for now (Patel 2010).

Under flexible accumulation, corporations will continue to search for the lowest costs through offshoring and outsourcing. They will follow the money trail to countries with pockets of low-wage English speakers, whether in China, Vietnam, Egypt, Mexico, Eastern Europe, or South America.

What Are the Dominant Organizing Principles of the Global Economy Today?

Flows of capital, goods, and services associated with flexible accumulation have built on old colonial patterns and have made use of advances in transportation and communication technologies (time-space compression). But other forces also help move all people and nations toward one free market with minimal barriers. These forces include powerful international financial institutions, and international and regional trade agreements. Drawing on an economic philosophy called "neoliberalism," these institutions and agreements have created a strong international financial and policy framework, one that promotes an even deeper integration of nations and local communities into the contemporary global economy.

Capitalism, Economic Liberalism, and the Free Market

The work of the Scottish economist and philosopher Adam Smith (1723–1790) and the British economist John Maynard Keynes (1883–1946) provided key intellectual counterpoints that have shaped economic debates about the functioning of capitalism in the twentieth century. In *The Wealth of Nations* (1776), Adam Smith promoted economic liberalism through his ideas of laissez-faire ("leave it alone") capitalism. In Smith's view, free markets and free trade, being liberated from government intervention, would provide the best conditions for economic growth: They would unleash competition to maximize profits. In contrast, Keynes later argued that capitalism would work best when the government had a role in moderating the excesses of capitalism and ensuring the basic welfare of all citizens (Keynes [1936] 2007).

U.S. president Franklin Delano Roosevelt relied on Keynesian economic philosophy in his approach to the Great Depression of 1929–1941. His administration initiated government programs such as the Works Progress Administration to put unemployed Americans back to work, and the Social Security program to ensure the basic welfare of all American people, especially the elderly and most vulnerable.

After World War II, leading Western governments applied Keynesian economic philosophy in rebuilding their war-torn economies and establishing development projects to stimulate growth in former colonies. Keynesian economics began to lose popularity in the 1970s in the wake of a global recession. But today it maintains a role in certain government policies—those that (1) stimulate economic activity through public investment in infrastructure projects and the employment of civil servants while also (2) seeking to regulate the excesses of corporate and financial activities and moderate the most extreme effects of capitalism on the population through the provision of a social safety net and investment in health, education, and housing.

Neoliberalism

Economic liberalism, building on Smith's philosophy, has reemerged since the 1970s as a guiding philosophy for the global economy. This **neoliberalism**, associated with conservative fiscal and political policies in the United States, views the free market—not the state—as the main mechanism for ensuring economic growth. Neoliberal policies focus on promoting free trade on a global scale, eliminating trade barriers, and reducing taxes, tariffs, and most government intervention in the economy. Neoliberalism promotes the privatization of public assets (such as publicly owned utilities and transportation systems) and an overall reduction, if not privatization, of government spending on health, education, and welfare.

Since the 1980s, powerful international financial institutions have promoted neoliberal policies. These institutions are the International Monetary Fund (IMF), the World Bank, and the World Trade Organization (WTO), which was founded in 1995 to replace the Global Agreement on Trade and Tariffs (GATT). The Allied nations established the IMF and the World Bank after World War II to regulate financial and commercial relations among the industrial powers. The IMF and the World Bank were also charged with providing loans for modernizing national economies ravaged by the war; in this role they often subsidized national development efforts, including infrastructure projects such as ports, roads, dams, and irrigation systems. Particularly since the 1980s, IMF and World Bank programs have promoted free trade, free markets, and reduction of the state's role in local and international economics.

Structural Adjustment During the 1980s and 1990s, global financial institutions emphasized structural adjustment loans as a key, though controversial, mechanism to address poverty and development in poorer nations. Structural adjustment loans seek to stabilize a country's long-term economic development. They require fiscal austerity measures, a reduced role for the state in the economy, and a restructuring of national trade and tariff policies so as to create freer access to local markets. These loans also require receiving governments to (1) eliminate agricultural and manufacturing subsidies and price supports on essential commodities such as food and oil; (2) reduce government spending on health, education, and social services; (3) privatize state-owned enterprises; and (4) deregulate financial and labor markets.

In the 2001 documentary film *Life and Debt*, filmmaker Stephanie Black explores the recent economic history of the Caribbean island of Jamaica. Her research examines the effects of IMF and World Bank structural adjustment programs on the day-to-day life of Jamaicans and on the Jamaican government's efforts to establish economic independence after 300 years of British colonialism (1655–1962).

Since the withdrawal of British financial support at the end of colonial rule, Jamaica's government has had to turn to international lenders to provide short-term cash infusions to support basic services. The loans and their high interest rates carry requirements to restructure the Jamaican economy, reduce price supports for basic foods, cut back on education and health-care spending, and reduce barriers to international trade—all strategies intended to stabilize the economy and enhance growth through participation in global trade. But the promised benefits failed to materialize. Jamaica's local economic production in key agricultural sectors has in fact been undermined by subsidized, low-cost imports—for instance, subsidized milk products from the United States. Jamaica has ultimately become saddled with more than $13.7 billion in external debt (2013) that it does not have the capacity to repay.

MAP 12.3
Jamaica

Pros and Cons of Neoliberal Policies Debates continue over the effectiveness of neoliberal policies. The failure of IMF and World Bank policies to avert economic crises in Asia and Latin America in the 1990s called into question the long-term benefits of neoliberal policy prescriptions on a global scale. In particular, there is skepticism in many countries over the notion that facilitating competition and profit making through free trade, free markets, and privatization promotes improved economic opportunities for most of the world's people. Much of Latin America has repaid debts to the IMF and has rejected neoliberal economic strategies. The World Social Forum, an annual international meeting of social movements and NGOs, explores alternatives to neoliberal economic policies and the negative aspects of globalization.

In Europe, several nations (Greece, Spain, Portugal, and Ireland) have struggled to adapt to mandates for austerity imposed by the IMF and the European Central Bank in return for loans made to stabilize their national economies. Widespread protests by affected workers have threatened the stability of national governing coalitions that agreed to the externally imposed restrictions. Leaders of underdeveloped countries, scholars, and activists have argued that these policies are the centerpiece of an ever-evolving global economic system that promotes uneven development and ensures that wealthy countries remain wealthy and poor countries remain poor (Krugman 2015; Sachs 2005; Stiglitz 2010).

What are the best steps to build a healthy economy? Here, protestors in Greece demonstrate against government austerity measures.

The (In)stability of the Global Financial Markets in the Twenty-First Century

In late 2008 the United States experienced the worst financial collapse in over seventy years. Over the next several years, in the U.S. alone, five trillion dollars of pension money, real estate values, 401K retirement plans, savings and bonds disappeared. Eight million people lost their jobs. Six million people lost their homes to foreclosure. At the center of the crisis was a massive credit bubble created by millions of high risk mortgages and other complex new financial instruments including credit default swaps (CDS) and synthetic collateralized debt obligations (CDO)—more generally called credit derivatives. Financial derivatives are essentially contracts based on (derived from) some other asset—commodities, interest rates, credit, foreign exchange rates, equities and mortgages. In the years leading up to 2008, bankers seeking new investment vehicles for their clients bundled millions of individual mortgages into new financial instruments—derivative contracts—that could themselves be traded, bought, sold, exchanged and insured. People buying the derivatives were making a bet on the future value of the new asset. In her ethnography, *Fool's Gold: The Inside Story of J.P. Morgan and How Wall Street Greed Corrupted Its Bold Dream and Created a Financial Catastrophe* (2009), anthropologist and financial journalist Gillian Tett explores the roots of the derivative market and actions by bankers, government regulators and ratings agencies that led to the 2008 financial collapse. Of particular interest to anthropologists are the flawed cultural assumptions of the banking industry—for example, about the market's ability to regulate itself—that obscured the underlying realities of the credit bubble and eventually threatened the entire global financial system.

The U.S. financial collapse of 2008 and its subsequent impact on other countries indicate a significant shift in the global economy in which the circulation of capital has become the principal means of generating profits. As we have discussed, flexible accumulation has disrupted the earlier Fordist mode of industrial production, offshoring and outsourcing jobs from core countries to developing countries in search of increased profits, cheap labor, low taxes and limited regulations. But under flexible accumulation commodity production has grown slowly in recent decades while outsourcing production has created more risks and instability from events in countries beyond corporate control. Anthropologists of finance suggest that circulation of capital is now the driving force behind the global expansion of capitalism in the twenty-first century. Accumulated global capital reserves have increasingly been moving toward the creation of financial products and the construction of new infrastructures to facilitate their circulation. As a result, while the total gross domestic product of the global economy was estimated to be 77 trillion dollars in 2014, the face value of derivatives circulating through the global financial markets is now estimated to be between 700 trillion and 1 quadrillion dollars. (Bank of International Settlements 2016)

Banking, which was a sleepy industry in the 1970s focused on savings, bonds, and mortgages, has been transformed. In addition to the creation of complex financial derivatives, banks have also launched corporate finance units, global capital desks, and have spun off hedge funds. Financial technicians have been trained, logistical support services have been developed, and new communication technologies have been invented—the internet, microchips, wireless systems, high-speed data transmission, real-time inventory assessments—that permit instantaneous, around-the-clock global trading. Global capital markets and the firms that service them, based predominately in Europe and the United States, increasingly shape economic and political realities in every part of the world, from corporate board rooms to local economies. Their activities directly affect the price of food and gas, the ability to borrow money to start a small business or buy a home and the ability of the nation-state to provide social welfare support in local communities around the world. As a result, the ability of the nation-state to regulate what occurs within its borders is being steadily eroded in this era of increasing globalization. (LiPuma and Lee 2004, Zaloom 2006, Ho 2008)

The debate over neoliberal and Keynesian economic strategies continues to rage in the United States and globally. Many economists (Stiglitz 2008, 2009) have pointed to the U.S. government's deregulation of derivatives in the 1990s—consistent with neoliberal economic policies—as key to the increased speculation and risk-taking that led to the 2008 financial collapse. During the crisis itself, however, the U.S. government engaged in a number of Keynesian-style interventions: moving to guarantee bank deposits and shore up major financial institutions and corporations threatened by economic collapse;

Gillian Tett
Anthropology's Fresh Lens on the Global Economy

Anthropologist Gillian Tett is one of the keenest observers of the global economy today. As a journalist and U.S. Managing Editor of the *Financial Times*, Tett was one of the few to identify and warn of the unsustainable financial practices that led to the collapse of derivative and mortgage markets in the financial crisis of 2008. She gives credit to her training as an anthropologist. Two years of ethnographic research at J.P. Morgan from 2005–7, published in *Fools Gold* (2009), revealed an insular culture that blinded the financial services industry to its own flawed assumptions. Her book *The Silo Effect* (2015) expands that analysis to the role of culture in shaping contemporary globalization.

"In today's society, we have this incredible paradox that we live in a world that's more interconnected than ever before. And yet our jobs, our lives, our thinking, and

Anthropologist Gillian Tett

our economic structures encourage a tunnel-vision and tribalism—a fragmentation. We end up living in a customized world where we define our information content, our friends, and our identities around ourselves. And, the deeper we get trapped in these tunnels, these silos, and this tribalism, the less we understand how the world works and the more vulnerable we become to risks.

"When I went into reporting on finance in 2005, I went into a world that was initially quite alien to me. I didn't know much about derivatives. I wasn't an expert. I treated trying to understand the derivatives world exactly like I had treated my Ph.D. research in Tajikistan, which was to just immerse myself in this new world. Talk to everybody. Make connections. Try to look at what people were talking about and the gap between rhetoric and reality.

"The more I delved into it, the more I became aware that the whole financial world was beset by these incredible intellectual contradictions. And the whole thing struck me as being incredibly unsustainable. The only reason that the people involved in finance couldn't see how dangerous it was, was because they were complete insiders who had lost any sense of perspective.

"When I first went to the big annual derivatives conference I tried to think about what people weren't talking about. It occurred to me that they weren't talking about real people being at the end of any of their borrowing chains. They had this vision of finance which was all about numbers. People had largely been taken out of the equation. That wasn't just of interest to me from a moral perspective. It had a very practical perspective: people who are devising sub-prime securities and re-packaging mortgages had completely taken their eye off the ball of the people who are at the end of the equation (i.e. the borrowers). They weren't bothering to ask the most obvious question: Were people going to repay their loans? As the film *The Big Short* showed, if you were doing an intro to anthropology class ethnography project at the time and walking around neighborhoods, you would have instantly said: 'This whole thing is crazy!' But they were trapped in this tunnel vision. So, they were incredibly blind to the risks that were looming. I would say I was able to see it a bit more clearly because I had a fresh pair of eyes.

"The financial crisis shows very, very clearly what happens if you remove attention to the human and to culture from your understanding of the world, and why anthropology is so important for everybody to study. You cannot explain the world just through an algorithm or spreadsheet or a Profit and Loss statement. What happened in finance is true of every single sector of business and economics today. Time and again, businesses blow up because they knock out any sense of culture.

"Globalization is occurring at a very rapid pace, but a very uneven pace. If you're trying to sell any products, you're dealing with massive cultural difference and you can't just presume that your customers are going to behave like you do. Then your employees you work with will have huge cultural differences. And you can't assume that they're going to behave like you think they should. The paradox is that with globalization we have a very closely integrated system but at the same time all of our business and social practices constantly push us into incredible blindness and tribalism.

"Technological change is also upending almost everything we do both on a social front and on a business front. Disruption is everywhere. People today have this illusion that technology is a cultural—without cultural content—and is changing our lives in an a cultural way. They think computers are just sort of there, without culture. But they've failed to realize that actually the way we use computers, the internet, or social media, and the way this disruption occurs is absolutely rooted in cultural patterns. If we're not careful, what technology tends to do is actually solidify and reinforce the existing cultural biases that we have. The faster technology takes over our lives and changes our lives, the more we actually need to think about culture. Otherwise we get onto these train tracks and don't question stuff.

"The biggest challenge for business is not just disruption, it's also convergence. You've got different people, business sectors, geographies, product lines, and processes collapsing together very, very fast. And one of the biggest single problems any big company faces is that they have their internal structures and culture organized in such rigid buckets that they can't keep pace with the change outside. You see that pattern over and over again.

> **"The financial crisis shows what happens if you remove attention to the human and to culture from your understanding of the world.**

"If you don't think about culture you could blow yourself up. Seriously. You'll miss huge risks. And if you do think about culture you may spot huge opportunities. Being stuck in a little mental tunnel and cultural tunnel, silos of your own creation, makes you blind to risks and to opportunities. That's really the central, core thesis of my book *The Silo Effect*.

"I think that anthropology is an amazing discipline, but it's not defined by the content or the object of its study. It's defined by the process by which it goes around trying to understand the human condition. Anthropology is about realizing the value of studying the 'other,' a different culture. It's not just that it helps you to understand how an alien culture operates. But it gives you fresh lenses to look back at yourself, and look at yourself, and try to understand how you operate. We need more of that in today's world."

keeping interest rates near zero to stimulate economic recovery; and temporarily cutting Social Security taxes to put cash in the pockets of consumers.

In the aftermath of the crisis, followers of Keynesian economics—often associated with political liberals and moderates—argued for greater regulation of financial markets, increased consumer protections, an expanded health-care safety net, and heavy investment in infrastructure projects to put people back to work. Followers of neoliberalism—primarily associated with political conservatives—sought lower taxes, smaller government, faster debt repayment, and reduced regulation to stimulate economic activity by businesses. Crucial debates continue over efforts to address growing economic inequality, repair crumbling infrastructure, stabilize the future of Social Security, Medicare, and Medicaid, implement the Affordable Care Act (Obamacare) and reduce government support for higher education. Have you experienced any of the effects of these debates, perhaps in reduced government funding of your high school, college, or university or expanded health-care access?

How Does Today's Global Economy Link Workers with Consumers Worldwide?

Through much of recent human history, markets have been places where farmers and craftsmen, traders and consumers exchange products, ideas, information, and news, linking local communities to one another and to communities at greater distances, enabling all to benefit (Polanyi [1944] 2001). Today local markets are more deeply integrated as social and material commodities often flow across national borders (Hannerz 1996). Although **commodity chains**—the hands an item (commodity) passes through between producer and consumer—used to be primarily local, globalization has extended their span across territories and cultures, intensifying the connection between the local and global in ways previously unimaginable (Haugerud, Stone, and Little 2000). Tsukiji Fish Market, the largest fish market in the world today, is a prime example, as described in the Social Life of Things box.

"Friction" in the Global Economy

To examine the complicated movement of commodities, people, ideas, and money in the global economy, cultural anthropologist Anna Tsing (2005) has focused on what she names "friction"—the messy and often unequal encounters at the intersection of the local and the global, including the role of transnational corporations, international development agencies, local and national governments, and global trade regulations. She examines the destruction of rainforest in Kalimantan, Indonesia, on the island of Borneo. Recently the

commodity chains: The hands an item passes through between producer and consumer.

dense tropical forests and swamp lands have been clear-cut and burned to satisfy a global demand for timber, to open lands for mining, and to create agricultural land for palm oil plantations. (Palm oil is a common ingredient in foods, cosmetics, household products, and biofuels.) Today, transnational corporations use uncontrolled burns to clear rainforests at the rate of an equivalent of three hundred football fields each day.

Tsing's ethnography focuses on the complex interactions and frictions among the many players in Kalimantan. We can list some examples:

- International corporations seek profits for shareholders by conducting widespread logging and mining to feed an expanding global market.
- Indonesia's military dictatorship conspires with corporations to gain a share of profits.
- Local residents resist destruction of their native lands. Other residents participate with the corporations in hopes of getting rich.
- Indonesian environmental activists link local residents to international networks of NGOs working on environmental and human rights campaigns.
- Foundations based in the West invest in development projects to improve the living conditions of those affected by landscape conversion and to promote community-based natural resource management.
- U.N. meetings in New York address the impact of environmental degradation on quality of life.
- Scholars study conditions on the ground and the forces driving the multiple global projects that touch down in Kalimantan.

Tsing's notion of friction pushes anthropologists to recognize that the global interconnections associated with the world systems model are complicated and full of tension. Indeed, encounters between powerful economic forces and corporate actors, on one hand, and real-life individuals, households, communities, and regions, on the other hand, are often awkward, unstable, and unequal. They bring people together across different cultures, social and economic statuses, and worldviews. In Tsing's study of Kalimantan, the transformation of the natural environment brings into friction dozens of players with different motivations. She argues that ethnographers must address the total array of global connections—both the flows and disjunctures—that shape local realities (Tsing 2005; McKay 2006).

Chinese Restaurants and the Global Economy

The global movement of people is also full of friction. Have you ever wondered why chicken with broccoli is so cheap in your local Chinese restaurant? Or how

THE SOCIAL LIFE OF THINGS
Tracing the Global Tuna Trade

What can a spicy tuna roll at your local sushi restaurant tell us about the workings of the global economy? Anthropologist Ted Bestor's (2004) study of Tsukiji Fish Market in central Tokyo, Japan, brings to life the tale of the transnational tuna trade and, with it, the power of today's global markets and commodity chains.

(1) Standing in the heart of downtown Tokyo, Tsukiji Fish Market is the center of a massive global trade in seafood. Each day 60,000 traders gather to auction bluefin tuna from Maine, eel from southern China, octopus from West Africa, salmon from Canada, and shellfish from California.

2 Tsukiji's seafood makes its way into restaurants, supermarkets and homes across Japan, feeding Tokyo's 22 million people and many more throughout the country.

3 The Japanese people's desire for sushi and sashimi has established Japan as the world's main market for fresh tuna. But rising demand has led to overfishing and decimation of the local Japanese tuna fishery. To meet Japanese demand, the search for the perfect tuna has now expanded to the North Atlantic, the Mediterranean, and Australia. The tuna commodity chain—the hands an item (commodity) passes through between producer and consumer—extends far beyond Japan's territorial waters to previously unconnected places and people. Tsukiji Market has become command central for this intricate global trade in tuna and other seafood.

A highly integrated network of fisherman, buyers, and shippers is key to the tuna trade. Fishing boats returning from the northern Atlantic Ocean with their catch of bluefin tuna dock at marinas along the eastern seaboard of Canada and the United States. There they meet with Japanese buyers who assess the quality of the catch. The sale is based on the latest prices on the Tokyo market. High-quality tuna is packed in ice, and refrigerated trucks deliver it to an airport to be shipped to Tokyo for the next day's market at Tsukiji.

As we have discussed in this chapter, Wallerstein's world systems theory helps us analyze an integrated, but increasingly complicated, global economy through which goods, money, ideas, and even people (or, in this case, tuna) flow from periphery to core. But in the story of tuna and sushi, Bestor notes that assumptions of a fixed core and periphery, as well as expectations of a predictable flow of raw materials, are called into question. In this story Japan is the core. The Atlantic seaboards of North America and Europe are the periphery as natural resources flow to consumers at the center of the global market and at the end of the global commodity chain (Bestor 2001, 2004; Jacobs 2005; Stevens 2005).

- Do you eat sushi? Have you wondered where the raw fish comes from and how it gets to your local restaurant or market while still fresh? The next time you see sushi displayed for sale, consider asking the store manager or restaurant owner about the commodity chain that links a fisherman to your dinner.

the Chinese restaurant workers got to the little town or big city where your college is located? The answer lies along a street called East Broadway in Chinatown on the Lower East Side of Manhattan. There an entire migration industry draws Chinese immigrants from the rural villages of the Fuzhou area of southeastern China to New York City and sets them on the move again to a Chinese restaurant near you.

Located along East Broadway are a cluster of services that facilitate the movement of Chinese immigrants. These services provide for their daily needs as they make their way from a rural Chinese economy built around farming and fishing to a U.S. restaurant economy in one of the world's most developed countries. Offices for immigration lawyers, English language classes, driving schools, and producers of legitimate and illegitimate documents stand alongside doctors' offices, pharmacies, clothing stores, and gambling parlors. East Broadway's human smugglers help undocumented immigrants make their way across national borders. Phone card sales booths help workers keep in touch with family back in China. MoneyGram and Western Union wire-transfer offices send money back to family members in the home villages. Key to this migration industry are two dozen employment agencies that match newly arrived workers with Chinese restaurants across the country and another dozen long-distance buses that deliver Fuzhounese to those restaurants.

This global flow of Fuzhounese is fraught with frictions. Chinese smugglers charge more than $80,000 to bring a person to the United States, leaving immigrants with huge debts that may take years to repay. Restaurant owners rely on vulnerable, underpaid workers to make their profit margins on inexpensive dishes such as chicken with broccoli. Workers often live and work in the restaurants, putting in twelve- to fourteen-hour days, six or seven days a week. They suffer from emotional stress and the physical strain of grueling work, plus the isolation of living in a foreign land. New York's Chinatown becomes a place for rest and recuperation between stints at a far-off restaurant. The so-called Chinatown buses provide the link that moves workers between out-of-town jobs and the support system of the migration industry along East Broadway. As many as 50,000 individuals are circulating through this Chinese restaurant industry at any given time.

The movement of rural men and women from Chinese villages to the far reaches of the United States illustrates the deep interconnectivity of people in the modern world economic system. The demand for inexpensive Chinese food in Omaha, Nebraska, can pull a young Chinese farmer across an ocean to help fill the demand of a global labor market and pursue her dream of wealth and happiness for herself and her family. That is the story behind your next dish of chicken with broccoli (Guest 2011).

The Travels of a Chocolate Bar

Anthropologists have often traced the movement of commodities such as silver, sugar, fur, tea, and coffee to reveal the global connections—political, economic, military, and social—that link producers and consumers, rural and urban communities, and people and nations on opposite sides of the world. For example, Sidney Mintz's classic work *Sweetness and Power: The Place of Sugar in Modern History* (1985) explores the way sugar historically transformed economic and social relations among Europe, Africa, and the Americas. In general, the movement of commodities illuminates the human dimensions of globalization that are often obscured by distance and marketing. Do you know where your chocolate, tea, coffee, and sugar come from? Who made these products? What are their lives like? How are you connected to the people who harvested those crops in another part of the world?

To return to our opening story, consider writing a biography of a chocolate bar. Buy one and put it on your desk. What are the ingredients? Where do they come from? Start with cocoa, the primary ingredient, and Côte d'Ivoire, which produces more than 40 percent of the world's cocoa. Ask yourself the following questions:

- What are the working and living conditions of the people who produce the cocoa?
- How is it produced? Are child laborers involved?
- How do the producers get the cocoa to market?
- How are the prices set?
- Which international corporations dominate the chocolate trade? Who regulates it?
- How is chocolate marketed?
- Where did you buy it?
- How much profit does a store owner make on a bar of chocolate?
- Are there hidden costs that are not included in the price you paid? Consider underpayment of labor; environmental impact; government subsidies that are direct (to the company) and indirect (infrastructure such as roads, ports, bridges, and water systems); and the health-care costs created by harvesting, transporting, processing, or eating the food. How are these costs obscured?

For further information, research government reports, industry or company materials, advocacy organizations, journalistic reports, and scholarly articles. For example, read the report *Hot Chocolate* (2007) produced by Global Witness. If you would rather research your morning cup of coffee than your afternoon bar of chocolate, start by watching the documentary *Black Gold: Wake Up and Smell the Coffee* (2006).

Where does your chocolate bar come from?

Is Today's Global Economic System Sustainable?

Today we have an economic system of astounding complexity. Our economic activity surpasses anything we might have imagined even fifty years ago. The global economy integrates all of the world's people to one extent or another into a global system of exchange. But does it work well for everyone? What are the criteria we might use to assess its effectiveness?

Successes and Failures

The global economy has achieved remarkable success over the past sixty years. For example, gross national income of the global economy rose from around $1 trillion in 1960 to nearly $77.6 trillion in 2014 (International Monetary Fund 2014). The same period saw a 50 percent increase in school enrollments and a drop in infant mortality rates of more than 60 percent. And life expectancy nearly doubled over the last century, reaching 70 years in 2012 (World Health Organization 2015).

But the outlook is not all rosy. In 2015 the world had nearly 1 billion people going hungry each day and living in extreme poverty. Over three million children under five die of malnutrition each year (United Nations 2015). Clearly, global inequality continues to increase. Is the current trajectory of the global economy sustainable? And what can anthropologists contribute to addressing these questions?

The Human Ecological Footprint

Since at least the time of the earliest human settlements and the development of farming and pastoralism, humans have had an impact on their local environments. Human impact increased with an expanding population and was accelerated by the Industrial Revolution. Over the past sixty years, we have transformed our relationship with nature, and now our impact is being felt on a planetary scale. Scientists have begun calling this period of Earth's history the Anthropocene to reflect the ways humans are reshaping the physical contours of the planet.

The U.N. estimates that the world population, which was 2.5 billion in 1950, will increase from 7.3 billion in 2015 to 11.2 billion by 2100 (United Nations Department of Economic and Social Affairs, Population Division 2015). Each day, we add 220,000 people. Each day, human consumption increases while available natural resources decrease. How will we sustain an almost 50 percent increase in global population when current resources are already overused? As this crisis deepens, how will your life be directly affected? What personal and collective strategies can you imagine for addressing the emerging problems?

Accelerating climate change is already evident, and the human contribution to the environmental crisis is clear. Agricultural yields are being affected

Can Earth sustain the current global economy? Here, demonstrators in the 2014 New York Climate Change March warn that investments in carbon-generating oil companies may backfire and flood Wall Street.

by rising temperatures and increased greenhouse gases in the atmosphere. Food shortages are increasing despite intensive farm mechanization, chemical fertilizers, and pesticides. Carbon emissions from burning oil and gas are heating the planet and acidifying the oceans. At the 2015 global climate conference in Paris, France, 196 nations endorsed an agreement that acknowledged the need to cut global emissions drastically to hold the overall increase in global temperatures below 2 degrees Celsius (3.6 degrees Fahrenheit). Meeting this goal was recognized as essential to avoid a global ecological catastrophe. Global temperatures have already risen eight-tenths of a degree Celsius, two-thirds since 1975, and humans continue to pour record amounts of carbon into the atmosphere (McKibben 2010, 2012; Kolbert 2014).

The scramble for natural resources—especially freshwater, oil, and coltan (a scarce metal ore used in cell phones and other electronic devices)—pits wealthy nations against poor nations. The ice sheets in the Himalayas that provide drinking water for billions of people in Pakistan, India, Burma, and Indo-China are shrinking from global warming. Underground aquifers that provide freshwater to billions more in China and the Middle East are being depleted faster than nature can replenish them. Environmental trends do not bode well for the global economy using today's technologies.

Humans have a huge ecological footprint. Production, distribution, and consumption have been transformed in the contemporary global economy (Table 12.1). And consumerism is driving a dramatic expansion of the human ecological footprint. Studies suggest that as early as 1980 humans began to use more resources than the planet could regenerate. Today, our consumption of the world's resources has stretched above 60 percent over sustainable levels. In

TABLE 12.1 Energy Consumption in Selected Countries, 2011

Country	Total[a]	Per Capita[b]
World	520.3	74.9
China	103.7	77.5
United States	97.5	312.8
Russia	30.4	213.4
India	23.5	19.7
Japan	20.9	164.1
Germany	13.5	165.4
Canada	13.4	393.7
Brazil	11.9	60.2
France	10.8	165.9
United Kingdom	8.4	134.5

[a]Total consumption figures are in quadrillion Btu.

[b]Per capita consumption figures are in million Btu.

SOURCE: U.S. Energy Information Administration. International Energy Statistics. www.eia.gov/

other words, at our current rate of consumption, it would take 1.6 Earths to sustain our rate of resource consumption and absorb our pollution using prevailing technologies. By the year 2030, estimates suggest we would need two planets to sustain our economic activity. This is what scientists call "ecological overshoot," which occurs when human demands on nature exceed the planet's ability to provide. The results are depletion of freshwater systems, the buildup of carbon dioxide in the atmosphere, collapsing fisheries in the oceans, and diminishing forest cover (Global Footprint Network 2016).

World on the Edge

Time is short. Scholars in many fields are asking if we have come to the crisis point where our model of economic growth is leading to ecological collapse. Our current economic system risks pushing us closer to the edge. Although most residents of wealthy countries have been shielded from the worst effects of these changes, people in poorer countries, particularly in coastal and low-lying regions, are already hard hit. For example, as we will discuss in Chapter 14, Bangladesh's coastal flood plain has been repeatedly inundated with monsoons, flooding, and devastating erosion. Even the United States is experiencing an increased incidence of droughts, heat waves, and damaging storm fronts.

Perhaps the biggest test of the global economy and its underlying principles will be its sustainability. Can we sustain the current pace of economic growth? Is it within the planet's carrying capacity? Is it reasonable to think that through modernization all people will attain a middle-class lifestyle when we

know that if everyone on the planet had the same ecological footprint as an American, the global lifestyle would require five Earths to support?

If we are on the edge, we are not yet over the cliff. But significant changes are needed in order to reestablish the balance between humans and our planet. We must slow population growth. We must stabilize the global climate by rapidly shifting from petroleum-based, carbon dioxide–producing energy sources to renewable fuels such as wind and solar power. Perhaps most fundamental, we need to reassess the culture of consumption that considers the acquisition of capital as a measure of self-worth and compensates for a lack of capital by buying on credit. In the twenty-first century, we will need to redefine the key threats to the future of humanity (Korten 2001, 2015). These are not terrorism but population growth, climate change, hunger, water shortages, costly oil, poverty, rising food prices, the collapse of nation-states, and a lack of will to address these challenges urgently (Brown 2011a, 2011b; Worldwatch Institute 2015).

As a student, you can engage these issues on an individual and an institutional level. You can conserve energy and water, plant trees, use public transportation or a bike rather than a car, reduce how much you consume, and consider the hidden costs in all products that you buy. You can educate yourself about the threats to the future of your friends, family, and future generations. Beyond changes in your lifestyle, you can engage these issues through the institutions around you. Challenge your college to conserve energy, recycle, invest in solar and wind power on campus, invest its endowment in renewable energy companies rather than carbon-generating oil companies, and offer courses on the relationship between economics and the environment. Find creative ways to engage religious institutions, local governments, stores, and corporations to adjust their institutional practices and cultures. Change, whether personal or institutional, is not easy. But it may not be a choice.

Thinking Like an Anthropologist: Situating Yourself within the Global Economy

Globalization of the world economy has transformed the way we live. If you wish, you can touch just about anyone anywhere in the world in the next twenty-four hours by phone, email, or air travel. Communication and transportation advances have enabled companies to move their production facilities around the world in search of lower labor costs, lower taxes, and fewer environmental restrictions—what we call "flexible accumulation." Factories move offshore to make clothing and electronic goods. Offices spring up around the world to process X-rays, book airline reservations, and offer technical support. These new global factories and global assembly lines mean that much of what we eat, wear, drive, and communicate with has traveled across national borders and oceans to reach our table, closet, driveway, or desktop.

As you analyze the global economy and your connection to it, consider again the questions we raised at the beginning of the chapter:

- What is an economy, and what is its purpose?
- What are the roots of today's global economy?
- What role has colonialism played in forming today's global economy?
- What is the relationship between the nation-state and the corporation in the global economy?
- What are the dominant organizing principles of the global economy today?
- How does today's global economy link workers with consumers worldwide?
- Is today's global economic system sustainable?

Our opening story of chocolate in Côte d'Ivoire highlighted both the complexities of the global economy and the connections it facilitates among people, states, and corporations worldwide. Chocolate—like coffee, tea, sugar, a laptop, or a smartphone—reveals both (1) the incredible potential of our globalized economy to create connections, and (2) the unwelcome consequences of globalization that lead to imbalances and inequalities.

We have asked whether the global economy works well. Is it sustainable? How can we ensure the adequate distribution of resources necessary for human life—food, clean water, shelter, and health care? These are questions you will have to answer in your lifetime. And you will answer them by the life choices you make. For, with the continuing intensification of globalization, we are all connected in a web of constraints and opportunities. Your engagement with the global economy may not be constrained by poverty, illiteracy, or violence, but it could be constrained by cultural expectations—for instance, group and peer pressure about what you need to do to fit in, dress well, eat right, and travel from place to place. Do you really have the choice in U.S. culture to not consume? How you address these constraints and opportunities will make a difference.

The good news is that there are many points at which to intervene in the current patterns of the global economy, whether you work to save the forests, recycle, support fair trade, reevaluate your consumption patterns, organize to support the rights of workers around the world, or become an engineer focusing on clean manufacturing or a scientist developing renewable energy sources. Thinking like an anthropologist will help you to analyze your choices in a more informed and responsible way.

Key Terms

economy (p. 440)
food foragers (p. 440)
pastoralism (p. 442)
horticulture (p. 442)

For Further Exploration

The Battle of Algiers. 1965. Directed by Gillo Pontecorvo. Allied Artists Corporation. Riveting film about Algerian anti-colonial struggle against France.

The Big Short. 2015. Directed by Adam McKay. Feature film about the origins of the 2008 financial crisis.

Even It Up: Time to End Extreme Inequality. 2014. Oxfam Report. https://www.oxfam.org/sites/www.oxfam.org/files/file_attachments/cr-even-it-up-extreme-inequality-291014-en.pdf

Fish Is Our Life. 1994. Directed by Peregrine Beckman. Documentary Educational Resources. Companion to Theodore Bestor's book *Tsukiji: The Fish Market at the Center of the World.*

Global Footprint Network. www.footprintnetwork.org. Assess your global footprint.

Global Witness. 2007. *Hot Chocolate: How Cocoa Fueled the Conflict in Côte D'Ivoire.* www.globalwitness.org/sites/default/files/pdfs/cotedivoire.pdf. Report on chocolate in Côte d'Ivoire.

Inequality for All. 2013. Directed by Jacob Kornbluth. 72 Productions. Documentary. Former U.S. Labor Secretary Robert Reich explores U.S. and global inequality.

Inside Job. 2010. Directed by Charles Ferguson. Representational Pictures. Oscar-winning documentary film about the US financial industry leading up to the 2008 financial crisis.

Life and Debt. 2001. Directed by Stephanie Black. Tuff Gong Pictures. Documentary on the effects of the global debt crisis on Jamaica.

Roger & Me. 1989. Directed by Michael Moore. Dog Eat Dog/Warner Bros. Documentary about the deindustrialization of Flint, Michigan, as General Motors closed its automobile factories in an early stage of flexible accumulation.

The Story of Stuff. 2007. By Annie Leonard. www.storyofstuff.org. An online animated documentary film exploring the contemporary cycle of production, distribution, and consumption, and its impact on the global environment.

350.org. www.350.org. Movement of grassroots environmental activists, including student chapters on college campuses across the United States.

Twelve Years a Slave. 2013. Directed by Steve McQueen. Feature film on the effects of the triangle slave trade.

United Nations Human Development Report 2015. http://hdr.undp.org/sites/default/files/2015_human_development_report.pdf

Yes! Magazine. www.yesmagazine.org. Alternative strategies for a sustainable world.

Hungarian soldiers and police seal off a major border crossing from Syria used by Syrian, Iraqi, and Afghan refugees.

CHAPTER 13
Migration

On an early August morning in 2015, seventy-one refugees from Syria, Iraq, and Afghanistan crowded into a smuggler's truck near the Serbian border for the five-hour ride across Hungary into Austria. Their ultimate destination: economically prosperous and politically stable countries in northern Europe and Scandinavia. Two days later, police found the truck abandoned in the emergency lane of a highway just east of Vienna. All of the occupants—trapped inside—were dead, the inner walls of the truck damaged by victims desperate for fresh air and a way out. The sealed truck had no ventilation. Its refrigeration unit was off. All the refugees, including four children, had died of asphyxiation in the summer heat within 90 minutes of beginning the journey before being abandoned on the side of the road.

Tens of thousands of refugees embarked on similar perilous journeys to Europe in 2015 and 2016, crowding into train stations, climbing border fences, boarding unstable rubber rafts, overloading boats, cars, trucks, and vans, and walking thousands of miles to escape war-torn and strife-ridden countries in the Middle East and North Africa. Their stories reveal the dramatic and sometimes tragic realities of migration today—why people leave home, how they travel, and why they choose certain destinations over others—and shed light on the unprecedented levels of migration, both voluntary and involuntary, reshaping the contours of the human population today. In Syria alone, faced with brutal civil war, violence, and collapsing health, safety, and education infrastructures, 13.5 million people were displaced between 2011 and 2016. Of these, 6.5 million remain within Syria's borders. But 4.8 million have sought refuge abroad, including 1.9 million in neighboring Turkey, 1.1 million in Lebanon, 629,000 in Jordan, 250,000 in Iraq, and 130,000 in Egypt. Nearly half a million have fled to Europe.

MAP 13.1
Hungary

As we will see, patterns of migration are expanding across the globe, spurred by the process of flexible accumulation, time-space compression, and uneven development of the contemporary global economy. Migration itself is stretching the network of human interaction and creating new opportunities for encounter and exchange, linking cultures, ideas, and institutions while creating opportunities for people to relocate and expand beyond long-term networks of kinship and religious, political, and ethnic identities.

The death of Syrian, Afghan, and Iraqi refugees crossing through Eastern Europe in search of safety and economic opportunities is a devastating tragedy, but the migration story of these refugees is not unique. Their journeys play out on overcrowded boats, trains, planes, and buses and by foot in every country, bringing individuals from their home communities to new places in search of work or refuge from hostile conditions. The tragedy in Hungary highlights the massive and often precarious global movement of people, and it raises fundamental questions about migration in today's world:

- Why do people move from place to place?
- Who are today's migrants?
- Where do people move to and from?
- How is immigration affecting the United States today?

With so much migration, it is often hard to remember that each journey encompasses the hopes and dreams of one person, his or her family, and perhaps an entire community. This chapter introduces many of the concepts, themes, and dynamics that anthropologists consider when examining the interconnections between migration and globalization, as well as case studies of specific immigrant groups and individuals. By the end of the chapter, you will be able to apply these perspectives to understand the important migration process that is transforming individual lives and our world in the twenty-first century.

Why Do People Move from Place to Place?

Humans have been on the move since our species' earliest days, seeking out better living conditions for themselves and their families. Humans eventually migrated out of Africa across continents into the Middle East, Europe, and Asia; they ultimately crossed oceans and land bridges to reach Australia and the Americas. Humans have moved in search of better hunting grounds, pastures, fields, natural resources, and climate. They have moved to avoid conflict, violence, predators, and natural disasters. Some, such as early explorers Marco Polo of Italy (1254–1324) and Ibn Battuta of Morocco (1304–1369), traveled along

long-distance trade routes that linked much of the world well before Columbus's time. Others were forced to move against their will—for example, to serve the needs of colonialism on plantations and in mines, including millions in the transatlantic slave trade. Clearly, movement is a fundamental characteristic of the human experience.

The past thirty years have seen one of the highest rates of global migration in modern history, not only between countries but within them as well. The powerful effects of globalization have stimulated migration from rural areas to urban areas and from less-developed countries to more-developed countries. At the same time, time-space compression (see Chapter 1) has transformed the migration experience: Rapid transportation and instantaneous communication enable some migrants to travel more cheaply and quickly, and to still stay connected with folks back home, in ways that were impossible for earlier migrant generations. Flexible accumulation also stimulates migration by disrupting local economic, political, and social relationships while linking local communities to global economic processes. In 2015 the United Nations estimated that there were 243 million international migrants, plus hundreds of millions more internal migrants moving within their own national borders (United Nations Department of Economic and Social Affairs, Population Division 2015). The Chinese government estimates that more than 230 million people migrate internally in that one country alone (Liang 2012).

But why do people migrate? And why do they choose certain destinations? These decisions are rarely random or frivolous. In fact, most people in the world never migrate. Only 3 percent move beyond national borders. With 7 billion people on the planet today being drawn into an ever-thickening web of global interactions, we might ask why so few people are migrating. And with such uneven distribution of wealth and standards of living in the contemporary global economy, why are so few people moving to make a better life?

My own research, published in *God in Chinatown: Religion and Survival in New York's Evolving Immigrant Community* (2003), focuses on migrants from towns and villages near Fuzhou in southeastern China. In recent years, these individuals have come in large numbers: first to New York to work in Chinese restaurants, garment shops, nail salons, and construction trades; and now spreading across the United States as they open take-out restaurants and all-you-can-eat buffets. As much as 50–70 percent of the population in many towns and villages has migrated out, and hundreds of thousands of them have come to and through New York City.

Of the more than 1.3 billion people in China, why have people from the Fuzhou City area decided to migrate out of China? And why do so many go to New York City? The conditions are the same for Fuzhounese as they are for many rural people in China—small incomes, difficult farm labor, limited

MAP 13.2
Fuzhou City

opportunities for upward mobility or education. And the attraction of New York City—in this case, the tremendous need for low-wage workers—exists in many big cities, not only in the United States but also in countries much closer to China.

In the back of a Chinese restaurant in New York City, I interviewed Chen Dawei, age nineteen, who had come from Fuzhou one year earlier and whose story sheds light on the Fuzhounese immigrant experience:

> I didn't really want to go to America. But everyone else my age had already gone. I didn't want to seem stupid. My parents really wanted to send me. They have a little shop on the main street. We aren't poor. But we don't make much money either. Making $1,500 a month as a delivery man for a Chinese restaurant in the United States sounds really good when your family is lucky to make that much in a whole year back home. I really didn't want to go. But people kept calling to say how well they were doing. Both of my uncles were already in the U.S. Lots of people were sending money back home. And people who got green cards would come back and build a nice home for their family.
>
> So my dad arranged with a snakehead (smuggler) to send me to New York. It cost $65,000. We borrowed some from my uncles. And some from friends who had already gone to New York. The rest we borrowed at really high interest. It will probably take me four or five years to pay it all off.
>
> My trip was easier than a lot of my friends'. At least I didn't have to spend time on a boat or get smuggled across the border from Mexico. The snakeheads got me a tourist visa to Hong Kong. Then they took me to Thailand, Turkey, and Amsterdam. I flew into JFK Airport. The snakeheads had arranged a visa from a fake company, so I didn't have any problem getting through immigration. Do I like it here in New York? It's kind of boring. Since I've been here I've been working non-stop. Mostly in Chinese restaurants, six days a week. New York, Milwaukee, Asheville, and Maryland. Lots of places. I've got to pay off my debt, so I keep working. I send some money home to my parents when I can. Someday I want to open my own restaurant.

Can you identify the factors influencing Chen's departure from China, his choice of New York as a destination, and the shape of his migrant journey? In fact, the decision to migrate requires the confluence of a variety of factors—factors that anthropologists identify as pushes and pulls, bridges and barriers.

East Broadway, Chinatown, New York, the central business district for new immigrants from Fuzhou, China.

Pushes and Pulls

The decision to migrate and the chosen destination are often shaped by **pushes and pulls**. People are *pushed* to migrate from their home community by poverty, famine, natural disasters, war, ethnic conflict, genocide, disease, or political or religious oppression. Even some development policies may push people to move: For example, some may have to relocate to make room for a hydroelectric dam that is essential to the country's economic development. (This has been the case in areas throughout the world, including Panama's Bayano dam, China's Three Gorges dam, and Malaysia's Batang Ai dam.) Those who are forced to migrate are often termed "refugees." Other people are pushed to migrate by a lack of opportunities in their home community. Indeed, the uneven development in the global economy stimulates much of today's global migration. Frustrated by their inability to achieve life aspirations and meet the needs of their families at home, many people seek opportunities elsewhere. Still others migrate to keep up with successful immigrant neighbors who send money back home to support family, build a house, or pay for family members' education (Portes and Rumbaut 2006).

Destinations are not chosen randomly, nor are all destinations equal. When considering migration, people are *pulled* to certain places by job opportunities, higher wages, educational opportunities for themselves and their children, access to health care, or investment opportunities. Family and friends who have already migrated provide encouragement and connections. At the same time, media such as television, music, and film, along with powerful advertising, promote the desire to live a Western middle-class, consumer-oriented lifestyle. The

pushes and pulls: The forces that spur migration from the country of origin and draw immigrants to a particular new destination country.

manufacturing of this desire (see Chapter 2) sweeps across the globe to motivate people who dream of fulfilling this vision by moving abroad. China and India alone hold 37 percent of the world's population (2.6 billion together), and their rapidly expanding economies have drawn hundreds of millions into the search for a middle-class lifestyle and its status symbols—a television, a car, and a refrigerator. Indeed, at the beginning of the twenty-first century, more and more people are eagerly entering the globalizing world economy.

Bridges and Barriers

bridges and barriers: The factors that enable or inhibit migration.

Immigrants also encounter **bridges and barriers** that influence who moves and where they go. Despite strong pushes and pulls, migration is not a journey easily undertaken. There are many barriers to such movement. Migrants need a high level of motivation and a good deal of ingenuity to get started. Migration often requires learning a new language and adapting to a new culture. It means leaving family, friends, and religious communities. And it can be expensive, requiring upfront expenditures for passports, visas, and transportation, as well as fees paid to recruitment firms or smugglers. Even though globalization has promoted an increased movement of goods, money, and information, the free movement of people is still discouraged. Governments go to great lengths to regulate borders (with varying degrees of success), using passports, visas, border patrol agents, and immigration inspectors to determine who may leave and who may enter.

What bridges enable the migration flow of Fuzhounese as they seek to relocate tens of thousands of miles across the Pacific Ocean, and what barriers must they overcome? Chen Dawei's story highlights some of these important

bridges and barriers. Consider the following aspects of his story, all of which illustrate bridges. Like most immigrants, Fuzhounese come to New York City because someone from their family or hometown is already there. Family and friends create **chain migration** as networks of people who have already immigrated to a new place encourage and support other immigrants who follow. They may share information, loan money, or even support visa applications and sponsor legal migration. Moreover, communication technology stimulates the exchange of information between earlier immigrants and those considering the journey. Phone calls, videos, letters, emails, and wire transfers of money all link sending and receiving areas. Geographic proximity or distance makes certain journeys more or less difficult and precarious (in this sense, it can act as either a bridge or a barrier). Contiguous borders are easier to cross. But as in the Fuzhounese case, expanding transportation networks and increasingly inexpensive international flights facilitate migration along certain corridors.

Yet immigrants cannot randomly cross borders, for official barriers stand in their way. Most noticeable are government immigration policies that regulate borders and place restrictions on who comes in and out of the country. To address this problem, in many countries legal immigration is brokered through recruitment agencies that negotiate between workers and employers to arrange visas and travel. These recruiters channel qualified professionals into high-skill jobs such as nursing or information technology as well as low-skill jobs such as domestic work, agriculture, construction, and factory work. When the need for workers cannot be met legally, smugglers guide undocumented working-class immigrants, like Chen Dawei, across national borders under the radar of governments.

Global migration today takes many forms. (*left to right*) Women line up outside an employment agency in Manila, Philippines, seeking jobs as domestic workers in Middle Eastern countries. Croatian Serb refugees flee Bosnia and Herzegovina in 1995. A camp for Somalis displaced by drought and famine, in Mogadishu, Somalia, 2011. A family scavenges in the ruins of their home in Fengjie, China, one of many towns eventually submerged by the massive Three Gorges dam.

chain migration: The movement of people facilitated by the support of networks of family and friends who have already immigrated.

hometown associations:
Organizations created for mutual support by immigrants from the same hometown or region.

In some immigrant flows, supportive organizations such as **hometown associations** (organizations created for mutual support by immigrants from the same hometown), religious communities, or refugee placement groups encourage migrants, sponsor immigration, and help to resettle newcomers in the receiving country. Other bridges for immigration include media (such as television and film) and advertising that familiarize immigrants with particular destinations. Immigration can also be influenced by political connections between countries based on colonial histories, or by current patterns of aid and investment and cultural ties such as religion and language.

Remittances and Cumulative Causation

Individuals generally do not make migration decisions on their own, as in Chen Dawei's case. Who migrates and where they go is usually a group decision embodying the family's hopes and dreams entrusted to one member considered most likely to succeed. Family resources are assembled to support the migration. Sacrifices are made as husbands, spouses, or children are sent ahead to establish an economic foothold and diversify the family's opportunities. Once settled, the immigrant sends home income in **remittances** (resources transferred from migrants working abroad to individuals, families, and institutions in their country of origin).

remittances: Resources transferred from migrants working abroad to individuals, families, and institutions in their country of origin.

Remittances have a significant impact on migrants' families, communities, and even national economies. These include both economic (monetary) resources and social remittances such as ideas, behaviors, identities, and social capital (Levitt 2001). Globally, economic remittances in 2015 were estimated to be $582 billion, including $432 billion sent by migrants to developing countries, although they are often undercounted because of the widespread informal transfers of cash through friends, family, and other middlemen (World Bank 2016). Most remittances support the basic needs of families back home—food, shelter, and education—but they may also support public works and institutions in the local community. Immigrants contribute to infrastructure projects such as senior centers, schools, roads, and water systems. They support hometown associations, churches, temples, and mosques. A smaller percentage of remittances are invested in business enterprises. For many labor immigrants, remittances guarantee a place to return to if things don't work out or for their retirement years. In these cases, remittances provide not only an economic foundation but also an investment in social status.

cumulative causation: An accumulation of factors that create a culture in which migration comes to be expected.

In many communities worldwide, like the areas around Fuzhou, China, so many of these factors come together that immigration has actually become a way of life. It reflects a dynamic called **cumulative causation**, in which migration comes to be expected. On a visit to a rural town outside Fuzhou, I was

A woman and her daughter send a remittance to family through an agent at a general store just north of Dhaka, capital of Bangladesh.

invited to give a lecture at an English-language prep school. Since the 1980s, as many as 70 percent of the residents in this area have emigrated to the United States. The forty teenagers in my classroom were all excited to have a native English speaker to practice with, and as an anthropologist I am always happy to have a chance to learn more about the local culture. "Why are you studying English?" I asked them. "To go to America!" they answered. When I opened their textbook, I found it filled with chapters on typical Chinese restaurant phrases: *Do you want fried rice or white rice? Do you want your chicken and broccoli spicy or not spicy?* The students were all preparing not only to go to America, but to work in Chinese restaurants there! For these young people, as for Chen Dawei, immigration is more than just a possibility. Because their communities harbor a culture of migration, these young people may prepare for this likelihood for years. As they grow up they expect to follow their parents and siblings, uncles and aunts, and neighbors and friends in leaving home in search of a better life through immigration.

Each immigrant's journey is unique in some way. Yet each journey entails certain elements that can be helpful in analyzing the migration process. If you or someone in your family is an immigrant, or perhaps someone else you know, how might the key concepts of pushes and pulls, bridges and barriers help you to understand their immigrant journey more deeply? As you consider Chen Dawei's story of migration and his challenges upon arriving in the United States, do you think his journey was worth it?

Who Are Today's Migrants?

Globally, immigration includes people from a wide variety of class backgrounds, ranging from refugees fleeing war or natural disaster, to unskilled workers with little education, to well-educated doctors and elite corporate businesspeople. The immigration debates raging on evening news programs in the United States might give the impression that all migrants to the United States are poor, undocumented, and from Mexico. But these impressions would be wrong. Most migrants to the United States do not fit this description. Migration to the United States is a journey more frequently undertaken by those with education, job skills, and financial resources—and the motivation—that set them apart from the majority of their fellow citizens. Even those who come illegally tend to have skills and education levels above their home country's national average. Indeed, the rigors of the migration process self-select the brightest and the best (Portes and Rumbaut 2006).

Types of Immigrants

To begin to analyze the migration experiences of so many people in so many parts of the world, immigration scholars often focus on immigrants' economic roles, whether as laborers, professionals, entrepreneurs, or refugees. Although not applicable to every immigrant journey, these categories delineate certain patterns that constitute a general framework for analysis and comparison.

labor immigrants: Persons who move in search of a low-skill and low-wage job, often filling an economic niche that native-born workers will not fill.

guest worker program: A policy that allows labor immigrants to enter a country temporarily to work but denies them long-term rights and privileges.

Labor Immigrants **Labor immigrants**, like the Fuzhounese, move in search of low-skill and low-wage jobs, filling economic niches that native-born workers will not fill. Labor immigrants constitute the majority of migrants in the world today. They may be legal or illegal, but they are drawn by employment opportunities that, though limited, provide jobs at higher wages than are available in their home economies. In many countries, labor immigrants enter under temporary **guest worker programs** that grant the right to work for limited periods but deny long-term rights and privileges.

In the United States, labor immigrants are key to the success of agriculture, restaurants, hotels, garment production, and meat processing. Have you ever thought about who launders the hotel sheets and towels, cuts up the chicken in your grocery poultry section, picks the peaches at the fruit stand, or washes the dishes in your local diner? Have you ever wondered why you can eat Chinese food at such reasonable prices? Labor immigrants, legal and illegal, are part of our everyday lives. Without them, many businesses would have to close their doors or raise wages (and thus prices) and offer benefits to attract native-born workers.

Indonesian women migrant workers return home from Saudi Arabia. Excluded from citizenship or permanent residence there, many experienced exploitative work conditions.

Saudi Arabia, like other Gulf states, has a severe shortage of workers for low-skill jobs. In fact, the nation meets its labor needs by recruiting laborers from Egypt, Pakistan, India, Sri Lanka, Nepal, and the Philippines. Egypt alone sends approximately 2.7 million citizens abroad to work each year, more than 900,000 to Saudi Arabia. In Saudi Arabia, labor immigrants' working conditions can be quite difficult. They are not allowed to become permanent residents or citizens. They must have signed binding contracts before entering Saudi Arabia and may not switch jobs or leave the country without their employer's permission. Many times, the employer holds their passports to ensure compliance. Because this practice puts the employer in a position of tremendous power over the workers, there have been many complaints about abusive practices. In particular, many women domestic workers have charged that employers keep them employed against their will under abusive conditions. As temporary workers, with limited legal rights, they are vulnerable to exploitation. Despite these problems, hundreds of thousands of Egyptians continue to immigrate to Saudi Arabia in hopes of improving their own and their families' economic situation.

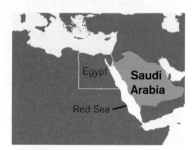

MAP 13.3
Saudi Arabia

Professional Immigrants **Professional immigrants** are highly trained individuals who move to fill economic niches in middle-class professions marked by shortages in the receiving country. A key component of the professional immigrant category is university students trained in Western-style professions who lack opportunities to implement their training at home. This migration is often referred to as a **brain drain**, for many of the most highly skilled

professional immigrants: Highly trained individuals who move to fill economic niches in a middle-class profession often marked by shortages in the receiving country.

brain drain: Migration of highly skilled professionals from developing/periphery countries to developed/core countries.

THE SOCIAL LIFE OF THINGS
Mexican Migrants and the Things They Carry

Each year hundreds of thousands of undocumented immigrants attempt to cross the U.S.–Mexico border. Politicians unleash fiery rhetoric about border-crossers, but what is their actual journey like? Anthropologist Jason DeLeón (2015), an archaeologist by training, explores their experiences by examining their archaeological footprint—the things people carry and leave behind along the way.

1 The U.S.–Mexico border stretches 1,954 miles. Only 20 percent has a wall. Nearly 40,000 border patrol agents, motion sensors, infrared cameras, drones, and a multi-billion-dollar budget—plus the wall—make crossing the border difficult, especially in and around urban ports of entry. When ladders, ramps, and tunnels prove ineffective, the wall pushes people east and west to the outskirts of town where the desert serves as a natural barrier.

2 The desert, with its snakes, wild animals, and risk of heat stroke, dehydration, and fatal encounters with drug smugglers, is the most lethal weapon the U.S. Border Patrol has to keep out migrants. A migrant's successful journey, and perhaps their lives, depends on packing the right supplies. They prepare for the desert crossing at staging areas on the Mexican side of the border like the one pictured here. Each purchases a backpack and carefully loads it with food cans, bottles of water, camping supplies, extra socks, foot powder, a first aid kit, garlic to ward off snakes, and a Bible or religious amulet. A successful journey, and perhaps their lives, depends on packing the right supplies.

(3) The journey across the desert is difficult and uncertain—a struggle between life and death. Religious shrines dot the landscape at key resting points as migrants leave offerings to ensure a safe journey: necklaces, religious icons, votive candles, crosses, prayer beads, and images of the Virgin of Guadalupe.

(4) Migrants may discard their belongings. Backpacks, shoes, socks, and water bottles may be broken or empty; food, beverages and extra clothes may be too heavy to carry when exhausted; medication, electronics, deportation slips, and bus tickets may be forgotten when individuals are startled or detained by border patrol agents. Many of the things that people drop are valuable objects not meant to be left behind: pocket Bibles, family photos, and love letters. Together they tell stories of migrants that are often ignored in conversation about border crossers.

Danger, death, violence, and suffering are woven into the journeys of people trying to cross the U.S.–Mexico border. Hundreds die in the crossing every year. Their stories, along with the stories of those who successfully make the journey and those who are apprehended and deported, come alive in the social life of the things they leave behind.

- What do you carry in your pocket as you begin your journey though each day? A wallet, a cell phone, a set of keys?
- Do you carry anything that you don't really need? Why?
- What would people learn about you if you left them behind?

professionals trained in developing (periphery) countries are enticed by wages and other opportunities to relocate to developed (core) countries (See Chapter 12). This migration is doubly devastating: Not only are the talents of these professionals lost to the home country, but so is the investment in their education and training.

In the United States today, professional immigrants include doctors, nurses, engineers, and information technology specialists, among others. Hospital corporations in developed countries establish recruitment centers in developing countries to attract health-care professionals and prepare them for immigration to fill shortages. Nursing schools in the United States, for instance, cannot train enough nurses to staff the nation's hospitals and expanding nursing-home facilities. As a result, tens of thousands of Filipino, Indian, and Caribbean nurses and doctors have come to the United States as professional immigrants. In fact, hospitals in Africa face a critical shortage as health-care professionals are recruited to fill shortages in Europe. These middle-class immigrants move not only to gain better salaries but also to enjoy better working conditions.

Significant numbers of Indians have come to the United States as professional immigrants. Already prepared for relatively privileged positions in India, these are ambitious, middle-class people with training in economics, medicine, nursing, engineering, or management. Once in the United States, if they receive the proper credentials, they work in these fields; moreover, their children attend college and often focus on science, information technologies, engineering, business, law, or medicine. If unable to obtain the proper credentials, professionals from other countries may face the prospects of downward mobility in the immigration process, working in less desirable jobs for a short period or permanently.

social capital: Assets and skills such as language, education, and social networks that can be mobilized in lieu of or as complementary to financial capital.

One distinct advantage that professional immigrants bring is a combination of social capital and access to financial capital. **Social capital** (language skills, education, and social and kinship networks) enables them to quickly enter the U.S. economy. Access to financial capital (either their own money or funds borrowed through extended family networks) provides resources for success as professionals or entrepreneurs. Many professional immigrants choose to launch entrepreneurial careers in small, local, family-run retail stores, hotels, or motels in the United States (Lessinger 1995).

Another kind of professional immigrant emerges at the extreme upper end of globalization activity. The expansion of transnational corporations requires elite professional immigrants who are willing to relocate for long periods or to routinely travel from country to country as part of the workweek. These professional immigrants, sometimes called "cosmonauts" because of their constant, jet-set movement through Earth's atmosphere, constitute a small fraction of the global migration flow, but they have caught the attention of many scholars and

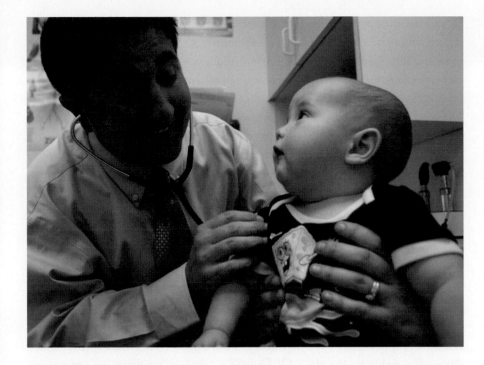

journalists because they represent the hyperactivity of movement made possible by contemporary globalization (Ong and Nonini 1997).

Entrepreneurial Immigrants **Entrepreneurial immigrants** move to new locations to conduct trade and establish businesses. On a global scale, Chinese entrepreneurs are perhaps the most famous for practicing the art of buying and selling: They establish businesses as merchants, restaurateurs, and small shopkeepers in countries worldwide. Immigrant entrepreneurs often use ethnic connections to mobilize the financial capital needed to start businesses. They borrow from family and friends. Revolving loan funds are common in these communities as networks of immigrants pool resources that are borrowed at interest, repaid, and borrowed again.

In addition, ethnic connections nurtured in ethnic neighborhoods link entrepreneurs with co-ethnic labor migrants. These connections enable the entrepreneurs to find the cheap labor they need in order to compete in the U.S. marketplace. The connections also provide labor immigrants with avenues to use their social capital to locate jobs in an ethnic economy—where immigrants work in businesses owned by co-ethnics—that may not be available to them in the mainstream economy. However, sometimes these connections have a downside: Such co-ethnic relations may also open opportunities for more-established immigrants to exploit newcomers under the guise of ethnic solidarity (Guest and Kwong 2000).

entrepreneurial immigrants: Persons who move to a new location to conduct trade and establish a business.

MAP 13.4
Dubai

In her ethnography *Impossible Citizens* (2013), anthropologist Neha Vora writes about the community of Indian immigrant entrepreneurs in Dubai, a dynamic and glamorous Middle Eastern global city in the United Arab Emirates (see the Social Life of Things feature in Chapter 7). Historically Dubai has been a key center of maritime trade across the Arabian Sea and Indian Ocean. Dubai's Indian population, dating back over 100 years, traces its roots to these trade networks. While Dubai's gleaming skyscrapers reflect its oil wealth and booming finance and tourism sectors, the city's Indian community occupies the dense downtown neighborhood of Old Dubai. For many, the area feels like an extension of India rather than the Middle East. Indian immigrant stores and businesses, including in the long-standing Indian-run gold business, anchor this vibrant enclave. Its street life—sounds, smells, foods, clothing, language use, and religious practices—evokes a way of life from another place and culture. In fact, India is only a short plane ride away, and the regular movement of people, money and goods between India and Dubai gives this diasporic community a transnational feel.

Despite the historical roots of this large and vibrant community, Dubai's Indian immigrants, like other foreigners in the United Arab Emirates, are denied citizenship rights by the state. Of Dubai's 2.5 million residents, 89 percent are noncitizens, including 1.5 million South Asians. Many are second-, third-, and fourth-generation residents yet are considered temporary "guests." Indian entrepreneurs, professionals, laborers, and their families make up the largest group. Vora documents how this exclusion from rights-based citizenship exposes Indian immigrants to race and class inequalities and even human rights violations. Lower-class laborers—key to Dubai's recent construction boom and economic growth—are particularly vulnerable.

Vora also explores Indian middle-class entrepreneurs' efforts to resist this exclusion and their attempts to create an alternative framework for citizenship and belonging rooted in the economic realm rather than the political. Though not citizens, Indian entrepreneurs are granted the right to own a business and use their economic activity to participate in the economic, social, and political structuring of Dubai society. But their success is not without complication and compromise. Indian entrepreneurs are also granted the right to employ other immigrants and actively use ethnic and national networks to recruit and employ migrant laborers from India. Vora notes that while this practice clearly enhances the political, social and economic status of Indian entrepreneurs, the co-ethnic exploitation of Indian immigrant laborers also contributes to the marginalization of their co-ethnics in Dubai's highly stratified economy.

Entrepreneurial migrants have been on the move for thousands of years along local, regional, and long-distance trade routes. Contemporary globalization has only increased the volume of entrepreneurial activity and enhanced entrepreneurs' ability to engage in their trade in places farther from home.

Refugees A fourth type of immigrant, **refugees**, are people who have been forced to migrate beyond their national borders because of political or religious persecution, armed conflict or other forms of violence, or natural or human-made disasters. To be officially recognized as refugees under international treaties, they must usually demonstrate to a foreign government a well-founded fear of persecution or physical harm. The United Nations estimated a total of 19.5 million refugees worldwide in 2014 (United Nations High Commissioner for Refugees 2015).

Although refugee status technically applies to those who seek asylum in another nation, the experiences of **internally displaced persons** can be just as devastating. These migrants' experiences mirror those of international refugees, except they take place in the migrants' own countries. As highlighted in the chapter opener, millions of Syrian refugees have fled to Europe and neighboring countries while millions more remain internally displaced within the country. Worldwide, the United Nations estimated 38.2 million internally displaced persons in 2014 (United Nations High Commissioner for Refugees 2015).

Because of increasing globalization, refugees are arriving in unexpected places. When political anthropologist Catherine Besteman arrived in the small village of Banta, Somalia in 1987 to conduct fieldwork, she had no way of anticipating that she would reconnect with many of the same villagers twenty years later as they resettled in Lewiston, Maine, refugee survivors of a brutal Somalian civil war that began in 1991. Unlike Banta, a community of 500 subsistence farmers living in mud and grass huts along the Jubba River in southern Somalia, Lewiston, about an hour from where Besteman teaches at Colby College, is a former mill town where textile and shoe factories have been shuttered by deindustrialization and flexible accumulation. Its 35,000 residents were 96 percent white, largely of French-Canadian ancestry. The city had not asked to become a place of refugee resettlement, and residents and officials were caught off guard when Somali refugees began arriving in 2001 looking for safety, a low cost of living, and a place to re-create their community support structures.

Drawing on her personal encounters across continents and generations, Besteman's ethnography, *Making Refuge* (2016) tells the story of the torturous international journey of Somali Bantu immigrants, including a deadly escape through the desert, and years in dismal and violent Kenyan refugee camps before arriving in the United States. Her intimate portraits in word and image depict their efforts to rebuild shattered lives, families, and communities and make a refuge for themselves in a new and foreign country. The encounters of

MAP 13.5
Lewiston, Maine and Somalia

Thousands of Somali refugees have become a force for renewal in Lewiston, Maine. (*Clockwise from top left*) Somali shops and restaurants now line the formerly deteriorating main street. Somali families have renovated old houses; and integrated into local cultural life, from schools to soccer leagues.

refugees and long-term residents, also captured by Besteman, challenge popular U.S. narratives that warn of a destructive clash of civilizations and cultures when immigrants become neighbors. Instead, in Lewiston immigrants and locals work together in complicated and creative ways to reshape Somali immigration into a force of renewal for the city. The urban landscape has been transformed over a decade. Today, Somali shops, groceries, restaurants, immigrant organizations, and a mosque line the main street and have revitalized Lewiston's formerly deteriorating downtown. Fifteen percent of the population is now Somali. Crashes and clashes have occurred around language, schools, youth, cultural practices, zoning, and religion. But so have connections, mutual transformations and "border-crossings" of many kinds. Change, however, has not been a one-sided affair. Yes, rural, subsistence farmer Somali refugees are adapting to a new society. But their new Lewiston neighbors are also adapting to new ways of being in the world that immigrants bring.

Women and Immigration

Just as the current global age is experiencing increased migration, it is also seeing larger numbers of women in all four immigrant categories. This is a result of economic globalization. For example, as discussed in Chapter 8, the growth of export processing zones has feminized global factory work as women migrate both within their countries and across national boundaries. By 2015, according to U.N. statistics, 118 million women immigrants were living abroad, nearly matching the 126 million immigrant men (United Nations Department of Economic and Social Affairs, Population Division 2015). In some receiving countries, such as the United States, women immigrants are now in the majority.

Anthropologists have been at the forefront of research about women immigrants, challenging scholars in all fields to see migration as a *gendered process*— one that affects both men and women, but often in distinctly different ways. Just as women reshape immigration patterns, the immigration experience also reshapes gender roles and gender relations (Hondagneu-Sotelo 1994; Mahler and Pessar 2001). Through migration, many women enhance their economic and social status as they take jobs, expand social networks, access social institutions, and gain new personal freedom. As a result, not just women but also husbands, children, parents, and other kin must adjust to shifting gender roles and family patterns. Also through migration, some immigrant men may lose status in public and domestic spheres—perhaps through diminished economic power, an unfamiliar status as a racial or ethnic minority, or being undocumented in their new country. In these ways, migration has a transformative effect on gender roles for both women and men.

Recently, anthropologists and other immigration scholars have turned particular attention to the complicated lives of women labor immigrants—both legal and illegal, both those migrating by choice and those forced to migrate through sex and labor trafficking. The increasing numbers of domestic workers are particularly vulnerable, often experiencing domestic violence and sexual abuse. But they are also particularly powerful, holding a central financial role in supporting their families back home and in providing the hard currency that developing countries need in order to repay global debts (Constable 2007). Pierrette Hondagneu-Sotelo's ethnography *Doméstica* (2001), for example, examines Mexican and Central American immigrant women who work as nannies and housekeepers in Los Angeles. This is an area where urban and suburban homes are joining factories as the primary places for new immigrants to find work. As the globalizing economy places ever-greater time pressure on the managerial class, they are hiring immigrant laborers to mow their lawns, clean their homes, and care for their children. The low-wage, off-the-books labor of Mexican and Central American immigrants, particularly women, has become so prevalent that it goes unnoticed as they subsidize the lifestyles of middle- and upper-class working families (Sassen 1998).

Donde está Spot? Elas Tarazona, an immigrant from Central America, works as a nanny for a U.S. family and teaches Spanish as a second language to William.

An Immigrant Interview

Interview an immigrant of any age, gender, and nationality. Ask to hear his or her immigration story. Listen for the key migration concepts discussed in this chapter: pushes and pulls, bridges and barriers, and immigrant type. Ask about the person's incorporation experience in the new country, and explore immigration-related issues such as gender and the second generation. How are gender roles different in the new country? What are the expectations of members of the second generation, and how does their life differ from that of their immigrant parents? Analyze this story, and then synthesize it in a short essay using the first person.

Immigrant Generations

The children of immigrants have also been the focus of a growing body of research. Both scholars and public policy experts are carefully observing how this expanding population will become part of U.S. culture (Kasinitz et al. 2008; Portes and Rumbaut 2001; Zhou and Bankston 1998). Immigration scholars generally distinguish among first-, 1.5-, and second-generation immigrants. The first generation comprises immigrants who left their home countries as adults. Their children born and raised in the new host country are the second generation. The term *1.5 generation* refers to children born in the home country who then migrate with their parents and grow up in the new host country. Depending on the age at migration, these children experience a doubly complex enculturation process, negotiating two cultures during adolescence and often serving as cultural brokers for their parents—for instance, translating between English and their home-country language.

Anthropologist Ana Aparicio explores the local community-organizing and political activism of second-generation Dominicans who are now teenagers and young adults in the Washington Heights area of New York City. Unlike their parents, whose identity and political activity included both the Dominican Republic and New York, the second generation is deeply engaged in New York's local issues because that is where they were raised and educated. In her ethnography, *Dominican-Americans and the Politics of Empowerment* (2006), Aparicio highlights how these young activists have mobilized their own community to address issues of education, police brutality, civic participation, and the lack of services and public investment. These second-generation young people also resist the typical racial-ethnic classifications found in U.S. society. As we discussed in Chapter 7, these people negotiate their identity situationally, moving back and forth among being Latino, Dominican, black, or more generally people of color. This sophisticated awareness of racial hierarchies and power enables them to build coalitions and organize across racial-ethnic lines, particularly with Puerto Rican and African American New Yorkers.

Where Do People Move To and From?

Globalization has transformed the spatiality of the world economy and has intensified the volume and types of movement occurring within and across political boundaries (Trouillot 2003). But not every country is equally affected by today's global flow of migrants. Some are primarily sending countries; others are primarily receiving countries. Moreover, not all migration occurs across borders. Thus a truly global perspective on migration must include both international and internal migration.

International Migration

International migrants, or migrants who cross borders, exist across the globe, but they largely relocate to more-developed countries. Of the 243 million international migrants in 2015, 76.1 million (31 percent) lived in Europe, 75.1 million (31 percent) in Asia, and 54.5 million (22 percent) in North America. Only 8 percent of international migrants lived in Africa, and 3 percent each in Latin America and the Caribbean and Oceania (United Nations Department of Economic and Social Affairs Population Division 2015). Figure 13.1 shows the primary migration flows for receiving and sending countries.

FIGURE 13.1 Contemporary Global Migration Patterns

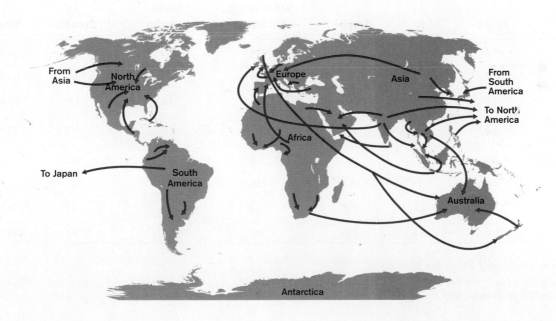

Reflecting strong trends of the past forty years, nearly 20 percent of all international migrants live in the United States. The U.S. total of nearly 45 million foreign-born residents in 2013 was the highest total of any nation in the world, and migration to the United States has continued at an average rate of 1.2 million annually since 2000 (U.S. Census Bureau 2012). Other countries, however, have a much higher percentage of immigrants in their population than the 13.1 percent of the foreign-born U.S. population. As of 2015, 32.3 percent of Saudi Arabia's 31.5 million people was foreign-born, primarily guest workers who do not have permanent legal status. Ireland's foreign-born population in 2015 was 15.9 percent; Canada's, 21.8 percent; Israel's, 24.9 percent; Australia's, 28.2 percent; Switzerland's, 29.4 percent; Hong Kong's, 38.9 percent; Kuwait's, 73.6 percent; and the United Arab Emirates', 88.4 percent (United Nations Department of Economic and Social Affairs, Population Division, 2015). Table 13.1 presents data on migrant populations in absolute numbers.

Malian Migrants: Reshaping Globalization from the Ground Up Though international movements of people between continents and across oceans often capture public and scholarly attention, today significant movement occurs between neighboring countries. In *Migrants and Strangers in an African City*

TABLE 13.1 Migration Stock by Major Area of Origin and Destination, 2015 (in millions)

Origin	DESTINATION						
	Africa	Asia	Europe	Latin America and Caribbean	North America	Oceania	Total
Africa	16.4	4.1	9.2	0.0	2.3	0.5	32.6
Asia	1.2	59.4	20.2	0.3	15.5	3.0	99.8
Europe	1.0	6.9	39.9	1.3	7.5	3.0	59.6
Latin America and Caribbean	0.0	0.4	4.6	5.9	24.6	0.2	35.8
North America	0.1	0.5	1.0	1.3	1.2	0.2	4.3
Oceania	0.0	0.1	0.4	0.0	0.3	1.1	1.8
Other	2.0	3.6	0.8	0.3	3.1	0.1	9.8
TOTAL	20.6	75.1	76.1	9.2	54.5	8.1	243.7

Note: Numbers may not always add up due to rounding.

SOURCE: *United Nations Department of Economic and Social Affairs, Population Division. 2015. Trends in International Migrant Stock: Migrants by Destination and Origin. www.un.org/*

(2012), anthropologist Bruce Whitehouse examines the large-scale migrations happening within Africa as people move in response to poverty and uncertainty. Whitehouse focuses on migrants from Mali, a large West African nation of 17 million people. Though landlocked, Mali's position at the center of regional trade networks crisscrossing West and North Africa has a long history. Today Malians, along with hundreds of thousands of other West Africans, increasingly have been on the move. Some have settled in developed Western countries such as France, Spain, and the United States, or in Asian cities such as Dubai, Bangkok, Hong Kong, and Guangzhou. Most, however, have relocated within the African continent—notably to Senegal, Côte d'Ivoire, Burkina Faso, Gabon, Congo, and South Africa.

MAP 13.6
Mali and Republic of the Congo

Whitehouse begins his ethnography with the story of a small town in southern Mali that he calls Togotala. The town lies on an arid plain between desert to the north and forest to the south. The harsh environment brings regular drought and then a three-month rainy season during which torrential downpours threaten to erode the area's fragile soil. With agricultural production being inadequate to meet the immediate needs of the Togotala population, and with no development assistance from the Malian government, the community has a history of producing merchants who enter the regional trade networks in order to send remittances home to support their families and the community at large. The influence of merchant remittances is evident in the larger cinderblock homes that have been constructed in Togotala's central district, a school for children in grades 1 to 9, a water tower run by solar power to pump water to communal faucets throughout the town, a landline phone system, a health clinic, and several modern mosques. These local developments are concrete testimony to Togotala's deep connection to the world beyond its borders, and they hint at the creative individual responses that literally bring home the benefits of the global economy.

Twice daily, battered buses arrive in Togotala carrying goods and passengers and providing the town's primary link to the outside world. A ride south to Mali's capital, Bamako, connects Togotala's merchants to an extensive transport network through which they can reach more-distant destinations. Whitehouse traces some of Togotala's residents southward to a large Malian community in Brazzaville, capital of the Republic of Congo. A port city of 1.5 million residents on the northern bank of the Congo River, Brazzaville serves as the country's administrative, manufacturing, and financial center. It is also a transfer point for agricultural products, wood, rubber, and other raw materials coming from upriver onto the Congo-Ocean railroad that links Brazzaville to the seaport of Pointe-Noire. French colonialists originally brought West Africans to Brazzaville in the 1800s to serve as soldiers, porters, laborers, and messengers. But West Africans succeeded in creating parallel economic networks of

Jason De León
Backpacks, Baby Bottles, and Tattoo Guns: The Stuff of Migrant Journeys

In his innovative ethnography, *Land of Open Graves: Living and Dying on the Sonoran Desert Migrant Trail* (2015), anthropologist Jason De León brings a four-field anthropological approach to documenting the experiences of Mexican migrants crossing the U.S./Mexico border. His attention to the details of their journeys as he accompanies migrants—their stories, their religious beliefs, their physical bodies, their use of language, and the stuff they carry—brings to life the violence, brutality, courage, and humor of the border crossing experience and the human consequences of U.S. immigration policy.

De León's attention to stuff—from backpacks and shoes to religious icons and baby bottles—has broken new ground in anthropology, bringing the skills of archaeology into the contemporary and interweaving them with strong ethnographic framing. "I was always really interested in archaeology as a kid. I had visited archaeological sites in Mexico when I was young and those things really stuck with me. As an undergrad at UCLA, the four-field focus really laid the groundwork. But before I knew what archaeology was, objects really fascinated me. The history of individual objects—what I would call my archaeological sensibility—really pervades everything else that I do anthropologically.

"As someone who was trained as an archaeologist, I've found that an archaeological approach can tell you a lot about things that perhaps language, biology, and ethnography can't really speak to. I've really come to believe in the power of the object to help tell a story.

"At the beginning of my research I thought, okay, I'm going to the Arizona desert, I'm going to see a lot of stuff out there, and I'm going to use this training in archaeology to try and understand that process. But I didn't have a very good understanding of material culture and what these objects could and couldn't tell me about historical and contemporary moments. Today my interest in archaeology is focused on how it can help me address a particular question. That's why for me the four-field approach is so helpful. I can borrow from whoever I want in anthropology depending on the scenario.

"Some people say, 'Objects don't lie'. I'm like, of course objects lie. Objects lie all the time. People manipulate the archaeological record in so many ways, for various reasons. So I think this idea that the object itself can speak for people, I think that is really dangerous territory.

"I worry about robbing the voices of people themselves through this archaeological kind of authority. I think it's especially true for undocumented people. Here you've got a group of folks who don't have a very upfront political voice, who often aren't able to tell their own stories. So any person from the outside can come in and say, 'Hey, check out this stuff that I found in the desert, let me tell you all about this experience.' That really bothers me.

"I think objects can do important social, cultural, political work. We've done different exhibits and displayed stuff in different ways. But we want to present these objects in conversation with the ethnographic data. People can really empathize with baby shoes or baby bot-

Anthropologist Jason De León

tles or backpacks. But they have a hard time empathizing with the folks who actually left that stuff behind. So the challenge has really been to take those objects and say, these objects don't tell their own story. These objects tell stories about people's experiences.

"At the end of the day, my goal has always been to try to stay true to the people. I always try to put them first. Do the objects help me do that? Sometimes they do. Do other approaches help humanize them? Sometimes they do. But at the end of the day I wanted the story to be told through their voices."

Recently De León has shifted his research away from the U.S./Mexico border to Chiapas, in the south of Mexico, where an entire migration industry has grown to facilitate the movement of people, many from Central America, across Mexico on their way to the U.S. border. "When I went to Chiapas I decided I didn't want to work inside the migrant shelters anymore. So I decided to hang out outside. What I found was a whole different set of people who were involved in the migration process who had really been ignored. There is a bit of archaeology still. But right now it's about smugglers and the border patrol with a greater focus on the visual. I think both the smuggler voice and the law enforcement voice were missing from my book. How do I humanize smugglers? How do I humanize the border patrol? And how do I take on a whole new methodological approach that focuses on the visual?"

De León's fieldwork continues to interweave an interest in objects and things but now with an increasing interest in the visual. His revealing photographs, some displayed on his website (www.jasonpatrickdeleon.com), focus not on people's faces but on the little details of an immigrant's life. "What's in the wallet? Does one's wallet tell me more than their face? Focusing on those little details really adds to the richness of the ethnographic detail. I think photographs of people's faces can be really limiting. And I like the mystery of not knowing what a person looks like. Often I can't show their picture because I'm concerned for their safety and I don't want to out them by photographing their face. But what can you learn about them from looking at their hands? Or the things they carry in their backpack? Are there other details that can add to the richness? So I'm always asking, 'Hey, what's in your pockets? What's in your backpack? Let me take a picture of your shoes.'

I've really come to believe in the power of the object to help tell a story.

"I think sometimes migrants think these pictures are a little strange. But occasionally I can have a more in-depth discussion about the objects, and the objects become an inroad to some other topic. 'Okay, well, show me your tattoo gun.' Then I'm thinking about how the tattoo gun connects up to perceptions of the body or violence or the state.

"People are attuned to objects in very unique, specialized ways. I'll just say, 'Look, I'm just so fascinated by the way you guys use stuff!' And then the stuff becomes a window into all kinds of processes."

De León is also the director of the Undocumented Migration Project at the University of Michigan and leads a field school for students each summer in Mexico, part of his commitment to preparing students to think anthropologically and live more fully in today's world. "If you can do a field school, if you can do something that will get you, not just travelling, but getting into the field and doing some work with people, it is a life changing experience. It has been for me."

Entrepreneurial immigrants from Mali have built a vibrant community in Brazzaville, Republic of Congo.

merchants, traders, laborers, blacksmiths, leatherworkers, and traditional storytellers—economic networks that survived the end of colonialism in 1960. Today a large community of Malians, mostly Muslim, work in Brazzaville as importers, shopkeepers, street vendors, entrepreneurs, and merchants in the diamond and jewelry trades.

Despite their long history in Brazzaville, Malians are treated as outsiders and strangers, segregated by language, social organization, and religion. Under these conditions, a strong connection to home enables the migrant Malians to resist the experience of exclusion from key local spaces, whether political, economic, social, or religious. Whitehouse easily portrays why people seek employment outside Togotala. More difficult to understand is why they come back so frequently and continue to be active in Togotala economics, politics, and social life.

From the perspective of Malian life in Brazzaville, the choice to maintain an intense and direct connection to home becomes more understandable. The connection enables them to maintain a sense of place and belonging despite the local marginalization and in the face of increasing mobility and spatial separation from their families and home community.

Migrants, including the merchants of Togotala and other entrepreneurs across Africa, reveal creative individual responses to the intensification of interaction that is occurring worldwide. Actions by migrants whose stories are often ignored in the grand narrative of globalization reveal the determined, entrepreneurial strategies that local people use to bring the benefits of the global economy to their communities and to reshape globalization from the ground up.

Internal Migration

internal migration: The movement of people within their own national borders.

Whereas international migration involves migration across borders, **internal migration** refers to the movement of people within their own national borders. For example, disruptions of rural life such as farm consolidation by agribusiness or development projects such as dams and roads stimulate migration. In addition, urban-oriented development programs and the establishment of large-scale export processing zones in developing countries have provided the pulls for significant internal migration from rural to urban areas to fill the new labor needs. (This is the case in countries such as Mexico, Guatemala, Brazil, South

Korea, China, Thailand, and Bangladesh.) Moreover, women workers, sought after by factory owners in export processing zones, constitute a high proportion of internal migrants.

Advantages and Disadvantages of Internal Migration in China China today is gripped by economic transformations and the widespread migration—both internal and international—that often accompanies such change. Since the early 1980s, the country has been rapidly modernizing, experimenting with a mixture of capitalism and state control of key sectors of the economy. As a result, private investment and private ownership are on the rise. They have combined with direct investments by overseas Chinese and massive state investment in infrastructure to spur the growth of China's cities, particularly in coastal provinces. The construction boom and the growth of industry in cities, along with the increasing income disparity between urban and rural dwellers, has pulled seasonal and long-term labor migrants from rural to urban areas. Downtown areas of both large and small cities have seen the emergence of day-labor pools as these migrants shop their physical labor for wages, which are scarce in rural areas (Liang 2012; Solinger 1999; Zhang 2001).

MAP 13.7
Shenzhen

Special economic zones for export processing have been springing up along China's coasts since 1982 in an effort to attract foreign investment and boost industrial production (Solinger 1999). Shenzhen, once a sleepy border village between Hong Kong and Guangzhou (Canton), is perhaps the most vivid example of this policy. Today it is one of China's leading manufacturing centers for exported goods, providing easy access to Hong Kong's port and transportation hubs as well as drawing tens of thousands of internal migrants to work in its factories. Shenzhen's economic success, however, also reveals the vulnerable position of low-wage migrant laborers in developing countries as they sweat on factory floors at very low wages and with few environmental or safety protections. Studies show evidence of internal migrant laborers returning to their rural hometowns with long-term physical illnesses and injuries from their sweatshop work (Chang 2008).

Shenzhen also reveals the vagaries and economic logic of globalization's flexible accumulation strategy. For nearly three decades China's factories, situated in export processing zones, have provided lower-wage labor, lower taxes, and fewer environmental restrictions than other developing countries in Asia and Latin America. Jobs and production have expanded as these conditions attract foreign investment and draw internal migrants. But as China's economic conditions have improved and workers have become better organized, many in the workforce are unwilling to work for extremely low wages and under brutal conditions. As a result, wages have been creeping up. Recent trends show factories now shifting out of China to Bangladesh, Thailand, Cambodia, and

Laos as globalization facilitates the search for export processing zones that will provide cheaper labor and other lower production costs.

Transnational Migration: Effects on Families and Communities Back Home

In another phenomenon of globalization, time-space compression—notably, advances in communication and transportation—has transformed the migration experience by tying migrants more closely to their families and communities back home. The dominant story of previous generations often had migrants leaving one country and settling permanently in a new country, largely cutting off ties with their country of origin and assimilating to the new home country. But for many migrants today, relocating no longer entails the abrupt rupture of ties between sending and receiving communities. Many migrants travel back and forth, send money through Western Union, talk regularly with family and friends by telephone, and share videos and movies. Phone cards that provide hours of service for $10 or $20 have replaced the $1-a-minute international calls of a generation ago.

This practice of maintaining active participation in social, economic, religious, and political spheres across national borders has been called **transnationalism** and its participants *transnational immigrants*. Recent research on earlier waves of migration reveal a level of transnationalism evident even one hundred years ago as European immigrants to the United States exchanged letters and money, made return trips, arranged marriages, and supported family migration across the Atlantic (Foner 2000). Contemporary globalization has intensified the webs of interaction, lowered the cost of travel and communication, and speeded up the exchange of people, information, and money, thereby enabling some migrants to enjoy a lifestyle that spans national borders.

Ethnographer Robert Smith (2006) has documented the transnational political lives of Mexicans living on Long Island, New York, who maintain deep involvement in their hometown in Puebla, Mexico. These immigrants have established a hometown association in Long Island that raises money for school construction, road repair, and other infrastructure projects back home in Mexico. Leaders of the hometown association keep in regular contact with fellow villagers in Long Island and actively solicit their support for the needs of the home community. These villagers, who may be citizens of both the United States and Mexico, also actively participate in local Mexican politics. They vote. They lobby. They meet with Mexican officials who visit the United States. And some based in Long Island actually serve on their Mexican community's town council, flying to Mexico for meetings and bringing the concerns of other transnational Mexican migrants into the affairs of their hometown.

transnationalism: The practice of maintaining active participation in social, economic, religious, and political spheres across national borders.

Return Migration

Return migration refers to immigrants who, having settled in a new receiving country, reverse course and return "home," sometimes in the same generation and sometimes in later generations. In the early twentieth century, for example, hundreds of thousands of Japanese migrated to Brazil, Peru, Argentina, and other Latin American countries to escape a deep economic recession and to avail themselves of expanding economic opportunities in new lands. Despite being marginalized as foreigners, the Japanese immigrants settled in, learned new languages, built homes and businesses, and established families. Decades later, in the early 1990s, nearly 250,000 of the 2 million Nikkeijin—overseas Japanese—living in Latin America returned to Japan, pushed by an economic downturn and pulled by a severe labor shortage in Japan.

Confronted by manufacturing industries collapsing for lack of workers, and unable to attract native Japanese to jobs that young people especially considered unappealing, the Japanese government established preferential immigration policies—bridges—for the Nikkeijin, assuming that they would integrate better than migrant workers from China, Korea, India, and Iran. Indeed, the Nikkeijin, many of whom had maintained a strong sense of Japanese identity in Latin America, saw an opportunity for economic success in a return to what they considered their homeland. Much to their surprise, though, the returning Nikkeijin did not receive a warm welcome. Instead many permanent Japanese viewed them as "foreigners," as intruders and cultural strangers.

Brazilian Japanese: Creating a New Ethnic Niche after Return Migration

In *Brokered Homeland* (2002), Joshua Hotaka Roth examines the return migration experiences of these Japanese Brazilians. Roth documents not only the ways in which Japanese policies and practices intensified the Nikkeijin marginalization, but also the Japanese Brazilians' creative responses to their rejection by mainstream Japanese society. Roth's research reveals how a wide array of mediating institutions—employers, labor brokers, politicians, journalists, and government agencies—established barriers to Nikkeijin reentry into Japanese life. For instance, although they were legal immigrants and visa holders, few Brazilian Japanese held Japanese citizenship. As a result, the government denied them access to a wide range of public services generally available to the Japanese population, including health insurance, pensions, social welfare, and unemployment insurance.

Faced with often intense cultural and structural marginalization, a few Nikkeijin returned again to Latin America. Still others continued to travel back and forth as "transnational commuters" or "yo-yo migrants" (Ishi 2003). But most Brazilian Japanese remained in Japan. Counter to their original intentions of reintegration into Japanese culture, now many of them have strategically

MAP 13.8
Japan and Brazil

accentuated their Brazilian identities, constructing their own cultural forms and a unique ethnic community. Carving out their own ethnic niche, Japanese Brazilians—many unattached to Brazilian culture while residing in Brazil—have embraced Brazilian cultural forms in Japan: waving Brazilian flags, dancing the samba, and joining Brazilian musical bands. More significant, they have launched Japanese Brazilian businesses and local media outlets, even constructing a cultural center to teach Brazilian music and dance in the community.

Over time, Roth notes, Japanese Brazilians are becoming a permanent ethnic group in Japan. These migrants, who are the children and grandchildren of Japanese born in Japan, have returned to contribute to an increasingly multicultural homeland, enriching Japanese culture in the process. As the Japanese Brazilian return migrants establish their own identity in Japan, Roth predicts that these new cultural forms may even eventually become part of what it means to be Japanese (Goodman 2004; Howell 2004; Yamanaka 2003).

How Is Immigration Affecting the United States Today?

Immigration is one of the most controversial issues in the United States today. "Build a wall with Mexico," some say. "Ban Muslim immigrants," say others. Still others advocate deporting 15 million undocumented workers and their families. The U.S.–Mexico border is increasingly defended and militarized, becoming one of the most heavily guarded borders in history. The U.S. Congress is unable to pass comprehensive immigration legislation. And vulnerable immigrants are targeted with hate crimes and violence. All the while, we benefit from immigrants working in back-breaking low-wage jobs other Americans will not do in agriculture, meatpacking, construction, restaurants, and the hospitality industry. Americans are clearly struggling with the implications of immigrants coming to the United States in numbers not seen since the last great wave brought Italians and eastern European Jews from 1880 to 1915. As many as one million immigrants may enter the United States legally each year. Hundreds of thousands more enter illegally.

Although migration has always been a part of the U.S. national origin story, the country's record is mixed, as a deep ambivalence about immigration has often come to the fore. Are you and your family immigrants? Where do you think immigrants should fit in the nation's story going forward?

Immigration and the National Origin Myth

Immigration is a central component of the U.S. national origin myth. Many people in the United States like to trace their national roots to the pilgrims who landed on the *Mayflower* at Plymouth Rock in Massachusetts in 1620, migrating to these shores to escape religious persecution in Europe. Two hundred years

(*left*) Minuteman volunteers armed with binoculars and pistols watch the U.S.–Mexico border near Bisbee, Arizona, for signs of undocumented immigrants, 2005. "Future generations will inherit a tangle of rancorous, unassimilated, squabbling cultures with no common bond to hold them together, a certain guarantee of the death of this nation as a harmonious 'melting pot.' The result: political, economic and social mayhem."—from About Us at www.minutemanproject.com. (*right*) A young boy demonstrates outside the Supreme Court during oral arguments of *United States v. Texas*, a challenge to President Obama's immigration plan. "If the United States is 'a country of immigrants,' why are so many people worked up about new immigrants today? My family works hard. Most of my classmates are immigrants. We're the future of America!"—eighteen-year-old student, Baruch College, The City University of New York.

later, the Irish fleeing the 1840s potato famine arrived to help build the country's roads, canals, and transcontinental railroad. Germans, Italians, and eastern European Jews followed in the late nineteenth and early twentieth centuries, escaping political and religious persecution and economic instability while searching for the fabled streets paved with gold. The "melting pot" received these immigrants, and the Statue of Liberty lifted its torch in New York harbor in welcome. The words of Emma Lazarus's poem are indelibly etched in the popular imagination as a symbol of that era and of the nation's generosity toward and reliance upon immigrants:

> *Give me your tired, your poor,*
> *Your huddled masses yearning to breathe free,*
> *The wretched refuse of your teeming shore.*

Send these, the homeless, tempest-tost to me,
I lift my lamp beside the golden door!

Of course, the actual immigrant story is more complicated. Certainly, immigration provided new opportunities for many new arrivals. But they did not arrive in an empty land. For the indigenous population of the Americas, immigration brought not opportunity but destruction. Nor did all those who came to the Americas come of their own free will.

The Spanish settled the southeastern area and explored the southern reaches of the continent all the way to California long before the Plymouth or Jamestown settlements sprang up. But today the Spanish language they left behind is considered a foreign language. Subsequently, the massive westward internal migration led by European immigrants was facilitated by the rapid spread of infectious diseases and by a state-sponsored genocide of Native American peoples. Moreover, the African slave trade, driven by a need for labor in the sugar, cotton, and tobacco plantations of the South, forced the involuntary migration of millions of Africans to the United States, where they worked as slaves without compensation to build a nation. And the Irish, viewed as poor, Catholic, and racially inferior, were targeted in the 1840s and 1850s with gang violence and ostracism. From 1882 until 1943, under the federal government's Chinese Exclusion Acts, the Chinese were the only immigrant group excluded on the basis of national origin (see Chapter 6). Clearly, the nation was not entirely welcoming to all newcomers.

The anti-Chinese sentiment codified in the Chinese Exclusion Acts marked a shift in American attitudes toward immigrants as earlier arrivals from Britain and France looked down even on later European arrivals, specifically those from southern and eastern Europe, as watering down the original "stock" of the U.S. population. In 1921, following the peak of Italian (largely Catholic) and eastern European (largely Jewish) immigration, Vice President Calvin Coolidge stated, "America must be kept American," signaling his desire to limit future immigration from those regions. In 1924 the U.S. Congress passed the National Origins Act, which severely restricted immigration from all but western and northern European countries. Subsequently, the intense period of globalization and labor migration at the end of the late nineteenth and early twentieth centuries came to a halt, followed by a period of protectionism, isolationism, and nationalist fervor that lasted until 1965.

Immigration since 1965

The United States Immigrant and Nationalities Act of 1965 radically changed the country's immigration policies, creating a rising tide of immigrants arriving again on the nation's shores. Coming from a vast array of countries and cultures,

by their sheer numbers and diversity they are transforming cities, suburbs, and rural areas and are affecting schools, religion, politics, and health care. In cities such as New York and Los Angeles, the foreign-born immigrant population is close to 40 percent. Together with their U.S.-born children, this group constitutes more than 20 percent of the U.S. population (U.S. Census Bureau 2012).

Today's immigrants differ in many ways from those of a century ago. Post-1965 immigration—particularly the unprecedented numbers from Latin America and the Caribbean, but also from Asia, Africa, and the Middle East—has transformed the nation's racial-ethnic composition. Prior to 1950, fully 90 percent of immigrants were from Europe. By early in the twenty-first century, 50 percent were from Latin America and 25 percent were from Asia, areas where globalization has produced especially uneven results (Suarez-Orosco 2003). See Table 13.2 for a comparison of immigrants' countries of origin in 1900 versus 2013.

Other demographic trends are revealing as well. In 2001 Hispanics surpassed African Americans for the first time as the largest minority group

Despite the prominence of immigrants in the U.S. national origin myth, the country has not entirely welcomed all newcomers. (*left*) Chinese migrants came to the U.S. West Coast in the 1850s to work in agriculture, mining, and railroad building but gradually came to be perceived as "The Yellow Peril"—dangerous competition with European immigrants for jobs. (*top right*) "Where the Blame Lies": In this 1891 anti-immigration cartoon, Uncle Sam surveys an immigrant horde in New York Harbor. (*bottom right*) The crowded intersection of Orchard and Hester Streets on New York City's Lower East Side, 1905.

TABLE 13.2 Ten Largest Foreign-Born Populations in the United States, 1900 and 2013

1900	2013
1. Germany	1. Mexico
2. Ireland	2. China
3. Canada	3. India
4. Great Britain	4. Philippines
5. Sweden	5. Dominican Republic
6. Italy	6. Cuba
7. Russia	7. Vietnam
8. Poland	8. South Korea
9. Norway	9. Colombia
10. Austria	10. Guatemala

SOURCE: *1900 data from U.S. Census Bureau. 1999. "Profile of the Foreign Born Population in the United States: 1997," www.census.gov/; 2013 data from DHS Office of Immigration Statistics, "U.S. Lawful Permanent Residents: 2013." Retrieved from http://www.dhs.gov/*

in the United States. Asians have shown the most rapid growth, increasing eightfold from 0.5 percent to 4 percent since 1960. The number of professionals and the changing settlement patterns also distinguish today's immigrants. Though many immigrants arrive with limited education or skills, a higher proportion now already have professional skills and college degrees, drawn to the United States by knowledge-intensive sectors of the economy. Fully 50 percent of today's immigrants continue to settle in traditional gateway cities such as New York, Chicago, Los Angeles, San Francisco, Houston, and Miami; but some are also finding jobs and settling in middle America—from the Rocky Mountains to the Great Plains to New England, including rural areas and suburban enclaves (Foner 2003).

Immigrants from the Middle East have changed the religious and cultural landscape of many parts of the United States over the past thirty years. In *All American Yemeni Girls: Being Muslim in a Public School* (2005), education scholar Loukia K. Sarroub examines the educational experiences of the children of immigrants from Yemen, a small oil-rich country near Saudi Arabia. Along with other, larger numbers of Middle Eastern immigrants, these Yemenis have settled in Dearborn, Michigan. Though their parents live much as they did in Yemen, the Muslim teenage girls navigate multiple worlds and systems of belief as they make their way through the Dearborn public schools. They are simultaneously Yemenis, Muslims, Americans, daughters of immigrants, and high school students. With their bodies covered except for face and hands, they negotiate a balance among their homes, mosques, and schools as they try to be "good Muslim women," "good Yemeni daughters," and "good Americans." Sarroub's ethnography reveals the challenge facing the nation's public schools in this era of intense immigration and the crucial role of public education as a place for immigrants to explore what it means to be American.

Debates over Inclusion

Never before has the United States received immigrants from so many countries, with such a variety of economic and social backgrounds and so many motivations for migration. In fact, the diversity of the current immigrant population challenges fundamental assumptions about how newcomers are incorporated into the host society. How much multiculturalism and cultural diversity are desirable? To what extent should the dominant culture accommodate the newcomer, and to what extent should immigrant groups change to match the dominant culture? In the United States, these questions generate heated debates on topics as varied as the use of English as an "official" language, public school holidays, parental and child rights, religious practices, farm labor conditions, and health practices. The following examples are just a small sample of the broad range of issues under debate.

A Santería Church in Florida Consider the legal case of *Church of the Lukumi Babulu Ayea v. City of Hialeah* in Florida. A legal battle erupted in 1987 when the town of Hialeah passed laws to ban animal sacrifices after learning that Cuban and Haitian immigrants intended to start a Santería church there. The church's religious rituals would include slaughtering goats, chickens, pigeons, ducks, and turtles. Santería, a religion that is common in parts of the Caribbean, combines elements of Catholicism and West African spiritualism. Worshippers communicate through trances and spirit possessions with powerful spirits called Orishas, who play an active role in the worshippers' lives. Animal sacrifices are considered essential to please these Orishas, to facilitate communication with them, and to ensure support from them.

After public hearings in which some residents condemned the Cuban and Haitian immigrants as sinners who needed to be saved by Jesus, the Hialeah city council passed an ordinance criminalizing the killing of animals outside slaughterhouses for any purpose other than food consumption. The council made explicit exemptions, however, for Jewish ritual slaughter and for hunters, exterminators, and local farmers, among others. After a six-year court battle, the U.S. Supreme Court ruled in favor of the Cuban and Haitian congregation, stating that "although the practice of animal sacrifice may seem abhorrent

Practitioners prepare for a religious ritual at the Church of the Lukumi Babulu Ayea, a Santería congregation started by Cuban and Haitian immigrants in Hialeah, Florida. The U.S. Supreme Court ruled that the city of Hialeah could not ban the church's animal sacrifices.

to some, religious beliefs need not be acceptable, logical, consistent, or comprehensible to others in order to merit First Amendment protection" (cited in Shweder 2003, 280). The Court further ruled that the city could not make laws designed to discriminate against the religious practices of one particular group (Shweder 2003).

Fresh Fruit, Broken Bodies: Migrant Farm Workers What rights and protections should migrant farm workers, many of whom are undocumented, have in the United States? Anthropologist Seth Holmes' *Fresh Fruit, Broken Bodies* (2013) reveals the consequences when Americans' unresolved debates and deep ambivalence about immigration become painfully inscribed on bodies of Mexican migrant farmworkers. While their labor provides fresh fruit and produce to the American table, they simultaneously remain invisible to the majority of the population. Holmes traces the perilous journey of indigenous Triqui workers from Oaxaca, Mexico, across the highly militarized U.S.–Mexico border to central California and northwest Washington State to help produce the greatest bounty of food the world has ever seen.

As an anthropologist and a medical doctor, Holmes turned his gaze particularly to the impact of harsh physical and emotional conditions on the bodies of these farmworkers. Laborers work in the fields all day, bent over or kneeling. They are regularly exposed to carcinogenic pesticides. They suffer verbal abuse, are shortchanged for their work, and live in substandard housing conditions. Strawberry pickers with whom Holmes worked gathered 51 pounds per hour to earn $7.16—the Washington State minimum wage. Accompanying workers to health clinics in the U.S. and Mexico, Holmes observed firsthand how their brutal, backbreaking work led to long-term disabilities, especially injured knees, feet, joints, hips, and other repetitive-stress injuries. And when they could no longer continue, they returned home to Mexico to be cared for by their families there.

Holmes' ethnography raises crucial questions about the place of undocumented workers in American culture. While debates over inclusion and exclusion rage, millions of immigrants continue to provide indispensable labor to the U.S. food system at great cost to themselves and their families. Failure to resolve these debates leaves undocumented workers vulnerable to entrenched disparities organized around race, language, and immigrant status and played out along the border, in the fields, and on workers' bodies. Holmes's work raises alarms over the increasing invisibility of farmworkers despite the daily presence of the fruits of their labor in American lives. It is this invisibility, Holmes suggests, that allows social inequality and suffering to become normalized and naturalized and the workers' realities to be kept at a distance from our kitchens and tables.

Thinking more broadly about immigration, how far do you think a host society should go to accommodate newcomers? Where is the proper line between the melting pot's assimilationist approach and a multicultural approach (see Chapter 7)? Some scholars (e.g., Brimelow 1995) argue that the United States receives too many immigrants, that the melting pot is overflowing, and that the nation's cultural unity is at risk. Yet studies of the immigrant second generation (the children of immigrants) have shown their deep integration into mainstream U.S. culture. Children of immigrants, with few exceptions, fully incorporate into their parents' country of choice and feel little allegiance or connection to their parents' country of origin (Portes and Rumbaut 2001).

Today the United States continues to be one of the top destinations for international migration, both documented and undocumented. Labor immigrants, professional immigrants, entrepreneurs, and refugees arrive in the country ready to work and contribute to the economy and overall society. But immigrants bring diversity of beliefs and practices as well, a diversity that has the potential for reshaping the dominant patterns of cultural thinking and action. How do you assess the risks and benefits? How is immigration directly affecting your life?

Thinking Like an Anthropologist: Assessing the Advantages and Disadvantages of Migration

As you encounter the challenges and opportunities of migration—studying with classmates from other countries, working with people in multinational corporations, socializing or working with immigrants, reading about immigrant experiences in the newspaper, debating immigration policies, or yourself being a migrant away from home inside or outside your native country—thinking like an anthropologist can help you to better understand these experiences.

Now that you have read this chapter, how would you apply its ideas and analysis to gain a more complete understanding of the tragic deaths of Syrian, Afghan, and Iraqi refugees in our opening story? Reconsider for a moment the key questions posed at the beginning of the chapter:

- Why do people move from place to place?
- Who are today's migrants?
- Where do people move to and from?
- How is immigration affecting the United States today?

Then reconsider the chapter's opening story. Why are Syrians, Afghans, and Iraqis leaving home and making the dangerous trek across Europe? What are the pushes and pulls, the bridges and barriers? Who actually migrates? How does their migration affect their families and home communities? Can these migrants become part of the cultures of their receiving countries? Then remember that the migration journeys from the Middle East and North Africa to Europe are reenacted in countless other migration journeys across the globe.

Refugees and other immigrants are a product of our current world order and disorder. And, as we discussed in Chapter 12, globalization stimulates migration by creating uneven development: Some areas develop rapidly and others fall behind. These areas may be in close geographic proximity, such as Syria and Europe or the United States and Mexico. They may also be far apart, such as New York City and Fuzhou, China. They may be linked by common language, religion, regional transportation and communication networks, and complicated political histories. Regardless of distance and national boundaries, globalization facilitates the movement of people, particularly to satisfy the pulls of the labor market. But these seemingly overwhelming migration flows are quite controversial. Some people, particularly in developed countries, see immigration as threatening to their "way of life." Anti-immigrant sentiment is strong in the United States, Europe, Australia, and Japan, which are all immigrant-receiving areas. Despite the increasingly free flow of goods, services, and money around the globe, national immigration policies have resisted the flow of people. As you practice thinking like an anthropologist, how do you think this tension within globalization will be resolved?

Key Terms

pushes and pulls (p. 489)

bridges and barriers (p. 490)

chain migration (p. 491)

hometown associations (p. 492)

remittances (p. 492)

cumulative causation (p. 492)

labor immigrants (p. 494)

guest worker program (p. 494)

professional immigrants (p. 495)

brain drain (p. 495)

social capital (p. 498)

entrepreneurial immigrants (p. 499)

refugees (p. 501)

internally displaced persons (p. 501)

internal migration (p. 510)

transnationalism (p. 512)

For Further Exploration

American Immigration Council. www.immigrationpolicy .org Provides research and data about U.S. immigration.

A Day without a Mexican. 2004. Directed by Sergio Arau. Xenon Pictures. A film about what happens in California when all the Mexicans disappear for a day.

De Leon, Jason. 2015. *The Land of Open Graves: Living and Dying on the Migrant Trail.* Berkeley: University of California Press.

Ho, Christine G. T., and James Loucky. 2012. *Humane Migration: Establishing Legitimacy and Rights for Displaced People.* Boulder, CO: Lynne Rienner Publishers.

The Internal Displacement Monitoring Centre. www .internal-displacement.org. Online source of current information about internally displaced persons.

Lost Boys of Sudan. Documentary film (2004, directed by Megan Mylan and Jon Shenk, Actual Films/Principe Productions) and book (by Mark Bixler, 2006, Athens: University of Georgia Press) about a group of more than 20,000 boys displaced and orphaned during the Sudanese civil war from 1983 to 2005.

The Migration Policy Institute. www.migrationpolicy .org An independent, nonpartisan, nonprofit think tank in Washington, D.C. dedicated to analysis of the movement of people worldwide.

The Other Side of Immigration. 2009. Directed by Roy Germano. Roy Germano Films. Explores the Mexican side of the Mexico–U.S. migration.

Pew Research Center on trends in Hispanic immigration in the United States. www.pewhispanic.org.

United Nations Department of Economic and Social Affairs, Population Division. www .unpopulation.org. Extensive data on international migration.

United Nations High Commissioner for Refugees. www .unhcr.org/statistics/populationdatabase. Online source of current information about international refugees.

Bangladeshi young people march to protect the Sundarbans coastal forest, home to farmers, fisherfolk, as well as the endangered Royal Bengal Tiger. What political activity have you been part of?

CHAPTER 14
Politics and Power

"The Sundarbans is our mother. We won't let it be destroyed."
"We will give our blood and our lives but not the Sundarbans!"

Over 1,000 young people—students, workers, and civil society activists—chanted these words as they marched more than 100 miles over four days in the spring of 2016 from the Bangladesh capital, Dhaka, to the vast Sundarbans tidal forest on the low-lying Bangladesh coast. Their march protested the environmental hazards of constructing two giant coal-fired power plants just a few miles upstream from this World Heritage site. The Sundarbans' mangrove trees, mudflats, and wetlands stretch along the vast coastal delta where the Ganges, Brahmaputra, and Meghna rivers reach the Bay of Bengal and provide protection from frequent storm surges and tidal flooding for 40 million people in southern Bangladesh. Thousands of farmers and fisherfolk call the Sundarbans home, as do endangered Royal Bengal Tigers, freshwater river dolphins, and thousands of other indigenous plant and animal species. When climate change is already raising sea levels, why would the government agree to build more fossil fuel plants to spew more pollutants into the air and water of a fragile ecosystem, the protestors asked? And why build them on land already vulnerable to coastal flooding

The Sundarbans campaign is just one of many ways people around the world today are taking action in an unprecedented global political movement to halt and reverse climate change and global warming.

Just a few months earlier, representatives of 196 nation-states gathered at the United Nations 2015 climate change conference in Paris, France, to discuss plans to limit human-generated greenhouse emissions and global warming. Simultaneously in Paris, thousands of demonstrators and activists from women's groups, indigenous rights organizations, antipoverty coalitions, and environmental movements gathered to pressure national governments to honor their pledges to keep fossil fuels in the ground; to demand that fossil fuel companies be held responsible for environmental damage; and to expand the global movement of local environmental actions to stop global warming and climate change.

In the U.S., students on over 400 campuses have launched campaigns to push for divestment of school endowment funds from fossil fuels. At the University of California, three years of student demonstrations by Fossil Free UC, a group of students, faculty, and alumni, led to the divestment in 2015 of $200 million of shares in companies profiting from coal and tar sands, the largest divestment in the United States to date. In the spring of 2016, six years after the fossil-free movement started at Swarthmore College in Philadelphia and at the same time as the Sundarbans campaign in Bangladesh, student-led divestment actions on campuses included demonstrations, teach-ins, and social media organizing. The dramatic occupation of university administration buildings, presidents' offices, and investment management offices—as well as over sixty student arrests—brought increasing public attention to student political activism and challenges to institutional power.

Power is often described as the ability or potential to bring about change through action or influence—either one's own or that of a group or institution. Indeed, power is embedded in all human relationships, whether that power is openly displayed or carefully avoided—from the most mundane aspects of friendships and family relationships to the myriad ways humans organize institutions and the structural frameworks of whole societies (Wolf 1982).

The Greek philosopher Aristotle spoke of humans as political animals. By this he meant that we live with other people in communities through which we strive to organize ourselves to achieve the good life—not as hedonists seeking the maximization of individual pleasure, but as a collective partnership (*koinonia*) seeking the good life, virtue, and beauty through community. Politics, then, is the mobilization of people's beliefs into collective action. The presence of politics and relations of power in the ebb and flow of daily life is a central focus of anthropological study. Although uprisings and demonstrations may draw attention to the most public, dramatic, and sometimes violent aspects of politics, anthropologists also consider the multiple local forms of politics—the careful political interactions and activities that occupy much of daily life and are essential in making a community a decent place to live (Gledhill 2000; Kurtz 2001; Lewellen 2003).

Throughout this book we explore power and its intersections with culture. We work to unmask the structures of power built on ideologies of race, gender, ethnicity, and sexuality and the institutions of kinship and religion. We

also examine the power dynamics of the world economy and the stratifications of class. In this chapter, we explore power as it is expressed through political systems and processes: the way humans have organized themselves in small groups, the role of the state in national and international politics, and the ability of people (nonstate actors) to engage in politics and exercise power through individual action and social movements outside the direct control of the state. We consider the historical and contemporary approaches that anthropologists have taken toward these crucial issues and the ways in which globalization is shifting the dynamics of power and politics on local and global levels. In particular, we will examine the following questions:

- How have anthropologists viewed the origins of human political history?
- What is the state?
- How is globalization affecting the state?
- What is the relationship among politics, the state, violence, and war?
- How do people mobilize power outside the state's control?

While reading this chapter, you will analyze many expressions of politics and the ways in which aspects of power are expressed locally and globally today. You will consider how political anthropology can help you think more deeply about your own expressions as a political creature, including the ways you negotiate human relationships on the interpersonal, group, community, national, and global level. You will examine the changing role of the state in local, national, and global affairs and the ways humans mobilize collectively through social movements to challenge the power of the state and the effects of globalization by advocating for social change and human rights. Finally, you will consider an anthropological debate about the roots of violence in human culture. The skills you acquire in this chapter will be valuable additions to your toolkit for living as a political actor and an engaged citizen in today's global world.

How Have Anthropologists Viewed the Origins of Human Political History?

Over the course of history, humans have organized themselves politically by using flexible strategies to help their groups survive and make their communities a better place to live. Our earliest human ancestors appear to have evolved in small, mobile, egalitarian groups of hunter-gatherers. It is in these types of groups that core human characteristics and cultural patterns emerged.

For nearly a century, beginning in the late 1800s, anthropologists studying politics and power focused primarily on small-scale, stateless societies, attempting to understand human political history through the political activities of contemporary hunter-gatherers, pastoralists, and horticulturalists. But beginning in the 1960s, as nation-states emerged to dominate political activity on a global scale, the anthropological gaze shifted significantly to encompass more complex, state-oriented societies and the process by which local settings are politically incorporated into a larger context.

The specialization called *political anthropology* took clear shape after World War II as anthropologists such as Meyer Fortes and E. E. Evans-Pritchard (1940), as well as other British social anthropologists (e.g., Gluckman 1954; Turner 1957), examined the local political systems of Africa. Others looked closely at the political systems of the Middle East and Asia (Barth 1959; Leach 1954) and the indigenous people of the Americas (Redfield 1941; Wallace 1957). These highly detailed studies of local political systems rarely placed the communities in a larger context, despite being conducted at a time when colonialist powers had imposed nonindigenous governing structures in much of the world.

As they undertook these studies of politics in many cultures, anthropologists attempted to create a common language, a typology that would

Qaanaaq, Greenland, dog teams and Inuit hunters traveling to a hunt. Once food foraging was the primary way of life for humans and our ancestors, but today food foragers are limited to the most remote areas of the planet.

enable them to communicate across cultural areas and compare and contrast their findings (Gledhill 2000; Lewellen 2003). The political anthropologist Elman Service (1962) famously classified the vast and varied world of political systems into four basic types: bands, tribes, chiefdoms, and states. Although infrequently used today, this framework shaped a generation of anthropological thinking about political systems. Service proposed that political systems develop through a natural, evolutionary progression from simple to complex and from less integrated to more integrated, with patterns of leadership evolving from weaker to stronger. Subsequently, when states emerged as the dominant political actors on the world stage, the examination of bands, tribes, and chiefdoms, anthropologists hoped, might provide insights into the origins and fundamental nature of the state.

Bands

Anthropologists have used the term **band** to describe small, kinship-based groups of food foragers who move over a particular territory while hunting and gathering. Through archaeological evidence and the study of a few remaining band societies, anthropologists have identified key characteristics of band organization and leadership. A band might range in size from twenty to several hundred people depending on the time of year and the group's hunting and ritual cycles. Bands break up and re-form regularly in response to conflicts among members and the formation of new alliances.

Small, close-knit bands served as the primary way of life not only for our human ancestors but also for the entire genus *Homo*, including *Homo habilis*,

band: A small kinship-based group of foragers who hunt and gather for a living over a particular territory.

HOW HAVE ANTHROPOLOGISTS VIEWED THE ORIGINS OF HUMAN POLITICAL HISTORY? **529**

Homo erectus, and early *Homo sapiens*. As a result, evolutionary biologists suggest that life in the band shaped the development of our earliest human characteristics and cultural patterns.

Politically, bands are highly decentralized, with decisions made primarily by consensus. Leaders emerge for a task at hand (organizing the hunt, moving the campsite, negotiating a conflict), with their leadership position resting on their skill, knowledge, generosity toward others, and level of respect within the band. With limited resources to compete for, bands have minimal stratification of wealth and power. But perhaps more important, bands required active cooperation among diverse groups of relatives and nonrelatives in order to successfully adapt to an unpredictable and shifting landscape. In turn, these early patterns may have embedded in humans a tendency toward egalitarian social and political organization rather than hierarchy.

In his book *Hierarchy in the Forest: The Evolution of Egalitarian Behavior* (1999), evolutionary biologist Christopher Boehm explores what life in bands can tell us about whether humans are fundamentally hierarchical or egalitarian. Drawing on ethnographic studies of contemporary and historical hunter-gatherer bands as well as archaeological findings, Boehm argues that the sharing of scarce resources, including food, was for hunter-gatherer bands the most economically efficient—indeed, essential—economic strategy. And this strategy could only be sustained through egalitarianism. Cooperative gathering of foods, coordinated game hunting, and reciprocal sharing went hand in hand with resisting hierarchy and domination as successful adaptations for humans living in hunter-gatherer bands. As a result, over the course of human evolutionary history, hunter-gatherer bands and tribal communities generated an egalitarian ethos that promoted generosity, altruism, and sharing while resisting upstarts, aggression, and egoism.

In hunter-gatherer and other small-scale communities, which served as the political and economic framework for much of human existence, members invest an enormous effort to suppress hierarchy and enhance cooperation. The resulting egalitarianism made the hunter-gatherer lifestyle possible as people worked as a group to assert dominance over anyone who tried to establish himself or herself as a leader. While other close primate kin—and perhaps humans themselves— may instinctively form social dominance hierarchies (that is, patterns of interpersonal domination) with alpha individuals presiding over them, the evidence of egalitarian hunter-gatherer societies provides a crucial insight into an alternative or complementary pattern that emerged during the time human interaction was shaped by life in small bands. Boehm argues that this social environment lasted long enough to shape innate human tendencies toward cooperation. Although hierarchical tendencies are present in egalitarian social systems, evidence reveals that hierarchical tendencies are regularly balanced out and even overcome as the weak work together to compensate for, and even dominate, the strong in order to create egalitarianism and effective community.

Despite serving as the predominant economic, social, and political structure over the course of human evolution, by the mid-twentieth century only a few bands of food foragers remained. These groups were living in the most remote areas of the planet: the rain forests of South America, the arctic tundra of North America, and the deserts of Africa and Australia.

Tribes

The term *tribe* is frequently used in contemporary media when describing conflict among groups within a state. Media coverage of civil wars or internal conflicts—particularly in parts of Africa, the Middle East, Asia, and the Pacific—frequently refers to tribal conflicts, tribal warfare, tribal factions, rifts, and alliances. In these instances, *tribe* is usually a reference to a loosely organized group of people acting together, outside the authority of the state, under unelected leaders and "big men"/"strong men" and drawing on a sense of unity based on a notion of shared ethnicity.

Most popular references to tribes carry connotations of primitive, uncivilized, and violent people who engage in conflict based on "ancient" tribal factions and hatreds. These faulty characterizations reflect the ethnocentric perspectives of observers who operate from inside a state framework. Their characterizations perpetuate the deeply problematic evolutionary assumption that less-complex political organizations are naturally less effective, stable, rational, and civilized.

As originally formulated (Service 1962), the term *tribe* referred to a culturally distinct population, often combining several bands, that imagined itself as one people descended from a common ancestor and organized around villages, kin groups, clans, and lineages. Tribes appear to have emerged between 10,000 and 12,000 years ago as humans began to shift from food foraging to pastoralism and horticulture. Like bands, tribes are largely egalitarian, with a decentralized power structure and consensus decision making. Leaders do emerge, sometimes called "village heads" or "big men" (Sahlins 1971), who garner the support of followers in several villages. But their power is limited. It is built and maintained through the leaders' personal achievements—such as success in war, conflict resolution, group organizing, and generosity of feasts and gifts—rather than awarded through political institutions.

Anthropologists have identified confederacies of tribes in Central Africa and on the Central Plains of North America that worked together to coordinate hunting, preserve the peace, or defend against perceived outside threats. Perhaps most famous is the Iroquois Confederacy formed by five distinct but closely related indigenous groups in the northeastern United States and Canada: the Mohawk, Oneida, Onandaga, Cayuga, and Seneca. Although the Iroquois Confederacy

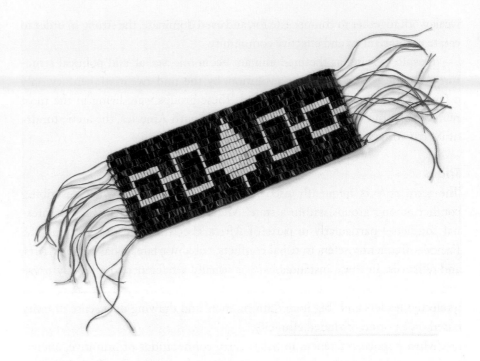

A replica of the eighteenth-century Hiawatha belt that records the agreement of the first five nations of the Iroquois Confederacy to live in peace (Smithsonian object no. 269056). The center tree symbol represents the Onondaga, where Hiawatha, the peacemaker, planted the Tree of Peace under which the leaders of all five nations buried their weapons of war.

tribe: Originally viewed as a culturally distinct, multiband population that imagined itself as one people descended from a common ancestor; currently used to describe an indigenous group with its own set of loyalties and leaders living to some extent outside the control of a centralized authoritative state.

chiefdom: An autonomous political unit composed of a number of villages or communities under the permanent control of a paramount chief.

appears to have predated European colonial activity in the Americas, confederacies are often formed at the demand of colonial powers, which prefer to deal with defined political groups rather than people on the move with shifting leadership and allegiances. The confederacy structure enabled colonizers to streamline the process of colonial control for trade and treaty making (Snow 1994).

In recent centuries, independent tribal peoples have largely been eliminated; they have been conquered and incorporated into the nation-states that have come to dominate the global political landscape. Today no groups operate totally outside the framework of the state. Even a weak state or a failed state directly influences all those living within its borders. In this context, today we might define a **tribe** more accurately as an indigenous group of people with its own set of loyalties and leaders living to some extent outside the direct control of a centralized, authoritative state. In many cases, current discussions use the term *ethnic group* instead of *tribe* (Ferguson 2011).

Chiefdoms

Within Elman Service's evolutionary typology of political systems, the **chiefdom**—an autonomous political unit composed of a number of villages or communities under the permanent control of a paramount chief (Carneiro 1981)—represented a transitional form between the simpler political structures of tribes and the more complex political structures of states. As in bands and tribes, the social relations of the chiefdom were built around extended kinship networks or lineages. The chiefdom might encompass thousands of people spread over many villages.

Unique to chiefdoms, leadership was centralized under a single ruling authority figure—a chief who headed a ranked hierarchy of people, asserted political control over a particular territory, and held the authority to make and enforce decisions. In parts of Polynesia, for instance, chiefs functioned as full-time political specialists, resolving conflicts and organizing collective economic activity. The permanent position of chief endured from generation to generation, often passing through direct descent and inheritance from father to son or through other kinship relationships. Religious rituals and beliefs often served to confirm the chief's authority.

Through feasts and festivals such as the potlatch (see Chapter 11), the chief gathered a portion of the collective bounty of the chiefdom's harvest or hunt and redistributed the communal wealth to the populace, thereby symbolically and practically reinforcing his or her central role among the people. Though group members' access to power and resources depended on their hierarchical relationship to the chief, the process of redistribution served a central role in moderating inequality and limiting conflict within the chiefdom.

Micronesia: Adapting Political and Social Structures to an Island Ecology

As mentioned early in this section, humans have always applied flexible strategies to improve life in their communities. In *Traditional Micronesian Societies* (2009), political anthropologist Glenn Petersen explores the creative adaptation of Micronesian social and political structures to the particular ecological challenges of island life. Micronesia is an archipelago of thousands of mostly small islands in the South Pacific that are often separated by hundreds of miles. The islands are extremely fertile, with abundant fresh water, food, vegetation, and marine life. Normally, they are ideal places to live and can support a sizable population relative to their land mass.

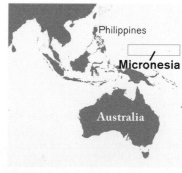

MAP 14.1
Micronesia

But the islands are also highly susceptible to catastrophic storms and droughts generated by fluctuating weather patterns over the Pacific. Droughts can easily devastate the vegetation and population of smaller islands. And the storm surge associated with a direct strike by a typhoon can inundate the typical Micronesian island, which is a coral atoll less than fifteen feet above sea level. Such a surge can completely saturate the island's gardens with saltwater, causing a disaster that may require several years of intensive labor to rehabilitate. Although the frequency of devastating droughts or typhoons is unpredictable, their occurrence every twenty years or so has made an indelible mark on Micronesian political and social structure.

Petersen documents how over time Micronesians have developed an elaborate social and political organization that enables them to survive and quickly recover from natural disasters. Because of the distance between islands and the irregularity of weather patterns, devastation on one island may not touch neighboring islands. Thus Micronesian social and political structures allow survivors to travel to other islands to find relief and support from extended kinship-based networks while they rehabilitate gardens at home. Key to this arrangement are the matrilineal clans widely dispersed among multiple islands that systematize the relations of reciprocity needed to overcome natural catastrophes.

Every Micronesian is a member of both a local lineage and a dispersed clan that includes local lineages on many islands. During times of catastrophe, this dual political and social system provides a highly effective adaptation to natural disasters. Even when faced with personal tragedy and the destruction of home and garden, each Micronesian is able to rely on interpersonal networks on other islands for survival and assistance. Each Micronesian knows that he or she can move in with relatives on another island or may be expected to invite displaced relatives into his or her own home while they reconstruct their gardens, homes, lineages, and lives. This kind of support can be found on islands large and small. In fact, on larger, higher islands that are less vulnerable to drought and typhoon, feast making is central to lineage and community life. Feasts, which feature the sharing and redistribution of community surpluses, such as the potlatch discussed in Chapter 11, enable individuals and groups to build prestige. But they also serve as mechanisms for supporting families, lineages, and communities in times of crisis.

Violence and Conflict Resolution in Micronesia Petersen takes particular note of the impact of the Micronesians' elaborate social and political structures on the patterns of violence and conflict resolution within their society. Micronesian culture celebrates the warrior role, holding warriors and martial skill in high regard. In fact, a central role of the chief involves preparing the group for warfare and conflict. Warfare is always seen as a possible, sometimes unavoidable means for resolving disputes. The potential for conflict over scarce resources intensifies during times of natural disaster, drought, and flood. But Petersen argues that Micronesians employ these capacities for organized violence as deliberate strategies for maintaining peace. Preparing for war serves as a deterrent, reminding people of the potential costs and spurring the development of an extensive repertoire of ways to avoid warfare and violence.

Thus, while Micronesian culture places elaborate emphasis on the role of warriors and martial skill, these are, in the language of the central island Pohnpei, considered *tautik* ("little service"). Held in greater honor in traditional Micronesian culture are what the Pohnpeians call *taulap* ("great service"): generosity of spirit, duty to one's kin, and the ability to produce food and

other goods in quantities that enable gift giving and feasting. These values are reflected and embedded in the elaborate social and political structures of dispersed matrilineal clans that provide a nonviolent means for moving people from resource shortage to resource availability, even during times of great crisis.

Micronesian islanders confront the effects of natural disasters—like this home destroyed by a typhoon (*left*)—with creativity, signs of aesthetic beauty, and flexible kinship structures. In this context, generosity of spirit, duty to one's kin, and the ability to produce food and other goods in quantities that enable gift giving and feasting (*right*) are held in higher esteem than martial skill or the role of the warrior.

Putting Typologies in Perspective

Though the typology of bands, tribes, chiefdoms, and states provided a basis for cross-cultural comparison, Service's framework has frequently proven too simple to capture the complexity and diversity of political practices and institutions that are reflected in ethnographic studies and the archaeological record. For instance, evidence now clearly suggests that across human history, groups of bands, tribes, and chiefdoms were never as isolated or homogenous as mid-twentieth-century anthropologists proposed. In contrast, today we argue that movement, encounter, exchange, and change have been the hallmarks of human groups, both small and large, throughout human history.

Nor could twentieth-century political systems always be considered trustworthy representations of the human past, recent or distant. Certainly, by the time anthropologists began to enter the field in the late nineteenth century to document and classify people and their political systems, European colonial expansion—including often violent encounters—had transformed peoples and their political structures across the globe. Colonialism, the slave trade, the conquest of indigenous peoples of the Americas, military activity, missionary efforts, and global trade deeply influenced every political arrangement, from the most populous urban setting to the most rural village. It is safe to say that anthropologists have not observed a band, tribe, or chiefdom that has not been influenced by colonialism, the power of the state, and the forces of globalization. And today no political arrangement of band, tribe, or chiefdom can operate outside the pervasive influence of the state.

What Is the State?

As states took on an increasingly central role in shaping the local communities that anthropologists traditionally studied, political anthropologists turned their ethnographic attention to the state itself. Today we typically define the **state** as an autonomous regional structure of political, economic, and military rule with a central government authorized to make laws and use force to maintain order and defend its territory.

Anthropologists link the origins of the state to the rise of agriculture. With fixed settlements, elite specialists emerged to manage increasingly complex economic activity (Wittfogel 1957) and warriors emerged to defend agricultural surpluses from marauders (Carneiro 1978). The ability of these local elites to collect taxes and tribute in increasingly unequal and stratified societies also supported aggressive efforts to consolidate smaller, autonomous villages into states, a process through which, political scientist Charles Tilley suggests, "war made the state and the state made war" (1975, 42). Some loosely configured states existed as early as 5,000 years ago in Mesopotamia and Egypt, and somewhat later in China, Japan, the Indus Valley (which became parts of modern-day India, Pakistan, and Afghanistan), and portions of the Americas. Throughout most of human history, however, people organized themselves primarily through less centralized, flexible bands, tribes, and chiefdoms.

The global landscape of contemporary states that now dominates local, regional, and international affairs reflects the impact of Western expansion over the past 500 years, particularly European imperial and colonial expansion (see Chapter 12). European colonialists deployed economic, political, and military force to redraw the political borders of much of the world to meet colonial economic needs. In this process, the colonial powers carved states and territories out of geographic areas inhabited by indigenous groups who were previously organized along lines based more on local kinship, political, and economic relations.

Most of the states in the world today did not exist before World War II—certainly not in their current configurations. In fact, few states are older than the United States, which officially formed in 1783. Most gained independence from colonial rule only in the decades immediately following World War II. By 2015, there were 196 independent states in the world.

state: An autonomous regional structure of political, economic, and military rule with a central government authorized to make laws and use force to maintain order and defend its territory.

The Modern Western-Style State

The type of state that has emerged since the sixteenth century, built largely on a Western model and expanded through colonization and globalization, developed with certain unique characteristics (Giddens 1985). Unlike earlier forms of the state, such as China's, which had relatively porous borders and loose administration, modern states feature a central administration designed to penetrate the everyday social life of its citizenry. A standing army asserts control over a carefully defined territory. Administrative, communication, and military infrastructures define and enforce the state's borders. The state, rather than a big man or chief, serves as the source of laws and law enforcement. People of all classes within the bounds of the state acquire an identity as citizens who owe allegiance primarily to the state, not to local networks based on kinship, religion, or ethnicity (Asad 1992).

Externally, modern states compete economically and militarily with other states for resources and territory. Internally, each state seeks to establish a monopoly on the legitimate use of force within a territorial domain (Weber 1919). For example, it enlists citizens' cooperation and pacifies resistance through expanded administrative power in police forces, the judicial system, tax collection, and regulatory regimes (Giddens 1985). It also accomplishes these objectives via surveillance techniques and institutions such as prisons, hospitals, and asylums, through which individuals classified as deviant from the cultural norm are removed from mainstream society and disciplined (Foucault 1977).

One unique contribution of political anthropologists to the study of the state has been a focus on the processes of the state rather than its institutions and structures. Despite the illusion that the state is fixed, cohesive, and coherent, states are in fact constantly being shaped and reshaped by elections, political campaigns, court rulings, creditors, legislation and executive orders as well as through daily interactions with individuals, communities, nonstate institutions, social movements, and other states. From this perspective, we can see that states are actually quite fluid, contested, and even fragile (Sharma and Gupta 2006).

How does the state become the ultimate authority within a particular territory? Anthropologists suggest that the state becomes real in the imaginations and experiences of people as it is encountered in a particular space. This spatialization of the state (Ferguson and Gupta 2002)—the perception that the state fills a particular space, encompasses all aspects of culture, and stands above all other elements of the society—is produced through mundane bureaucratic state practices. The state is encountered in everyday acts of governance: policing, mail delivery, tax collection, mapping, surveys, issuance of passports, jury duty, voting, notarization, distribution of food to the poor, distribution of pension checks to

When does the state become real to you? Consider the particular spaces in which you encounter the state. (*from left to right*) Police officers patrol New York City's Pennsylvania Station; a courtroom in Santa Fe, New Mexico; a voting booth in Ciudad Juarez, Mexico; the construction site of a bridge over the Danube River between Romania and Bulgaria; a street in Melbourne, Australia, where firefighters race to an emergency.

hegemony: The ability of a dominant group to create consent and agreement within a population without the use or threat of force.

the elderly. Through these routine and repetitive acts, the state comes to feel all-encompassing and overarching—a dynamic that Ferguson and Gupta call "vertical encompassment." Representations of the state on the television and radio, as well as in the newspapers or movies, all contribute to the construction of the state as concrete and real. These representations reinforce the conception of the state as the primary institutional form through which people experience social relations—family, community, civil society, economic exchange.

Aspects of State Power

The rituals and routines of the state also include overt practices of coercion. In fact, political philosopher Max Weber argued in 1919 that the fundamental characteristic of a state is its ability to establish a monopoly on the legitimate use of force in a particular territorial domain (Parsons 1964). States exert coercive power not only through military and police forces but also through the guarding and regulating of borders, the determining of criteria for citizenship, and the enforcing of discipline through rules, regulations, taxation, and the judicial system.

State power is also established through **hegemony**, which is the ability of a dominant group to create consent and agreement within a population without the use or threat of force (Gramsci 1971). How is this done? As discussed in Chapter 2, cultural institutions of government, media, schools, and religions shape what group members think is normal, natural, and possible, thereby influencing and limiting the scope of human action and interaction. Group members develop a way of seeing the world—a set of beliefs about what is normal and appropriate—that subconsciously limits their life choices and chances. As discussed in Chapter 7, states reinforce this hegemony by promoting intense feelings of nationalism (a sense of shared history, culture, language, destiny, and purpose, often through invented traditions of holidays, parades, national songs,

public ceremonies, and historical reenactments) to promote the perception of the state as a unified entity.

The hegemonic aspect of power can make group members discipline their own behavior, believing and acting in certain "normal" ways (often against their own interests), even without threat of punishment for misbehavior (Foucault 1977). Within the hegemony of ideas, some thoughts and actions actually become unthinkable and undoable. Others seem reasonable, necessary, and desirable; these include collective actions for the greater good of the "nation," even going so far as killing and being killed. Some modern states, however, are unable to gain the cooperation of their populace through consent and must resort to coercion. Where do you see this dynamic at work in the world today?

How Is Globalization Affecting the State?

Today globalization presents serious challenges to the state, particularly in terms of flexible accumulation, time-space compression, and expanding migration. The boundaries of the state—its influence and control over internal and external affairs—appear to be shrinking in the face of pressures related to globalization and the neoliberalizing global economy.

International Nonstate Actors Challenge State Sovereignty

In a global economy with increasing flows of people, money, goods, and ideas, state borders are becoming more porous. As a result, states are increasingly struggling to control who and what enters and leaves their territories. State sovereignty—the right of the state to maintain self-determination within its borders—is being challenged by powerful international nonstate actors.

"Kayakctivists" who oppose Royal Dutch Shell's plans to drill for oil in the Arctic Ocean, attempt to block Shell's Polar Pioneer drilling rig in Seattle's harbor. With a narrow summer window for arctic drilling, every day of delay reduces potential environmental damage.

civil society organization: A local nongovernmental organization that challenges state policies and uneven development, and advocates for resources and opportunities for members of its local communities.

As discussed in Chapter 12, international financial institutions such as the World Bank, the International Monetary Fund, and the World Trade Organization, backed by the world's most developed economies, are pressuring states to adopt neoliberal economic policies. These policies include free markets; free trade; the free movement of goods, capital, and ideas; and access to local markets for transnational corporations. Furthermore, to receive development loans from international financial institutions, developing countries are required to privatize state-owned infrastructure such as ports, water systems, utilities, and transportation and to reduce state funding for social services, health care, and education. Neoliberal economists suggest that these changes, while lessening the state's ability to control what flows across its borders, will enhance the state's ability to compete in the global economy.

Economic restructuring promoted by international financial institutions and implemented by the state has yielded a flourishing of civil society. This is evident in the phenomenon of people joining together to form local organizations and movements to protest the social upheaval and uneven development that has accompanied the institution of neoliberal economic policies. These nongovernmental organizations (NGOs), sometimes called **civil society organizations**, have become key players in challenging state policies and in creating space through which activists can work together to access resources and opportunities for their local communities.

Civil Society Organizations Gain a Global Reach

One key strategy of civil society organizations—which many states have viewed warily—has been to join forces with transnational movements and networks to transform local problems and conflicts into part of a global project for rights and resources. By linking up with groups outside their national borders, local civil society organizations are able to join forces with other activists, networks, and campaigns, such as Amnesty International, Human Rights Watch, Africa Watch, or World Vision and even international agencies like the United Nations. These linkages enable the civil society organizations to advocate for local environmental concerns, demilitarization, women's rights, LGBT rights, human rights, and indigenous rights—issues that also transcend the borders of the state.

Communication and transportation advances associated with time-space compression—from cell phones to Facebook, Twitter, and YouTube—facilitate the formation of these transnational networks. This process not only promotes the flow of observers, advisors, and participants in meetings and conferences but also stimulates global information flows of on-the-ground developments and organizing strategies. Working together, the international coalitions mobilize international sentiment and bring pressure to bear on nation-states to address problems occurring within their borders. In this way, the coalitions challenge the ultimate claims of state sovereignty over affairs within state borders.

Tanzania: The Maasai Demand Political Rights and International Recognition Anthropologist Dorothy Hodgson documents the rise of civil society organizations in Tanzania, East Africa, in *Being Maasai, Becoming Indigenous: Postcolonial Politics in a Neoliberal World* (2011). The Maasai have traditionally lived as seminomadic pastoralists raising cattle on the open rangelands of Tanzania and Kenya. Marginalized within their own nation, first by colonial governments and later by the postcolonial state established after independence from Britain in 1961, the Maasai live on the economic and political periphery. They suffer from low levels of education, limited access to health care, and high levels of poverty.

MAP 14.2
The Maasai

Though the Maasai lifestyle has been changing and pastoralist economic patterns have been diversifying to include cultivation, trade, and wage labor, the Maasai have remained largely invisible to state planners. These bureaucrats have viewed the Maasai rangelands as "unoccupied" and have frequently sold or leased them to investors and developers.

Spurred by increasing land loss and impoverishment, beginning in the 1990s Maasai and other pastoralists in northern Tanzania began to create NGOs in an attempt to assert their political rights to resources and recognition and to represent themselves in negotiations with state and international

entities. More than 100 NGOs were created in slightly more than a decade. Key to their strategy was a decision to represent themselves as "indigenous" in order to build alliances in the international indigenous rights movement. The move generated hostile responses from their own government, which had sought to downplay any ethnic divisions within the country. But the claim of indigenous rights established the Maasai as prominent actors with the United Nations and other international human rights bodies and attracted millions of dollars of funding for the NGOs from a wide array of international organizations focused on the plight of "first peoples."

Unfortunately, the rapid influx of outside funding and attention generated tremendous internal tensions in the Maasai community. Rifts developed among activists along lines of gender, generation, and class, and between the younger educated men who tended to run the NGOs and the rural, uneducated, grassroots communities they represented. By the early 2000s, Maasai NGOs strategically shifted themselves away from identification with indigenous rights. Instead, they cultivated a new reputation as advocates on the issue of livelihood: What cultural rights, land rights, political recognition, and services were necessary to preserve the pastoralist livelihood of the Maasai people? Through this shift, they successfully struck a new balance between two goals. They continued to advocate for Maasai political rights in relationship to the state government. But they also developed a new identity as civil society organizations dedicated to serving their people through the delivery of services and economic resources.

Hodgson (2001, 2005), a long-time observer of Maasai culture with a deep knowledge of northern Tanzania, reflects on the broader significance of these creative and often challenging projects. She notes that the Maasai efforts to address impoverishment and marginalization reveal central trends and tensions prevalent in many developing nations as local communities explore avenues for political action in a local context shaped both by the legacies of colonialism and by contemporary neoliberal economic and political policies (Homewood 2012; Lesorogol 2012).

What Is the Relationship among Politics, the State, Violence, and War?

Perhaps no use of power is more troubling and challenging than violence, the "bodily harm that individuals, groups and nations inflict on one another in the course of their conflicts" (Ury 2002, 7). Conflict happens on the playground, in the classroom, in the boardroom, and on the battlefield. As we look globally today, we seem to be experiencing a period during which violent conflict is not sporadic, but permanent—a time of continuous war in one place or another involving extraordinarily sophisticated tools and weaponry (Waterston 2009).

Are Humans Naturally Violent or Peaceful?

Underlying many discussions and debates about politics, war, and peace is the question of whether humans are naturally violent or peaceful. Is there something in the human evolutionary past that predisposes modern humans to behave in a particular way when confronted with conflict?

The main arguments can be simplified into three generalizations. First, organized human violence can be seen as a natural expression of the inherent human condition. In this view, human aggression and violence may be attributed to physiological factors such as testosterone, DNA, and neural wiring.

A second conception of violence considers humans to be inherently peaceful. In this view, violence arises through cultural practices and patterns that overwhelm basic human nature. A third scenario places the roots of human violence in between nature and culture. So, for instance, humans may be naturally prone to violence but culturally capable of avoiding it. Or humans may be naturally peaceful and only culturally provoked into forsaking their nature. Or these two alternatives are evenly matched. As described earlier, for instance, Micronesians develop and display their capacities for organized violence as a deliberate means for maintaining peace, believing that preparation for war actually serves as a deterrent to war and a reminder of the detrimental effects of violence.

Challenging the Myth of Killer Apes and Aggressive Humans Some who see contemporary violence as a legacy of our evolutionary past point to a common myth about aggressive primates and killer apes as evidence. If aggression, competition, and violence are part of our primate relatives' evolutionary development, they argue, then these impulses must be deeply ingrained in human nature as well. According to this view, natural levels of aggression, competition, and violence linked to genes and hormones must be generated internally and instinctively released in social relations. Conflict, then, naturally drives individuals farther apart into competing groups.

Physical anthropologist Frans de Waal (2002), reviewing studies of living primate macaques, chimpanzees, and bonobos, points out patterns of behavior that directly challenge this myth. (See also Chapter 5's Anthropologists Engage the World.) De Waal notes, for instance, that for social animals such as primates, this pattern of conflict and distancing would lead to everyone living alone, yielding an ineffective pattern of social relationships for individuals who rely on social cooperation for survival. In the primate social groups de Waal has reviewed, a far more complicated dynamic emerges in times of conflict. Rather than increased distance, reconciliation occurs on a regular basis. In fact, increased attraction is regularly observed between opponents after fights. Researchers have identified this reconciliation mechanism in twenty-five separate primate groups, revealing powerful inclinations toward reconciliation among individuals who have a great deal to lose if their relationship deteriorates. Among bonobos, a primate group closely related to humans on a genetic level, sex is used to resolve conflicts. Bonobo conflicts and tensions occur in all combinations of female and male. So do reconciliations. Bonobos have a high rate of reconciliation and a low rate of violence.

De Waal suggests that among primates there are various options for resolving conflicts, including avoidance, tolerance, and aggression. These options are used at various times depending on the situation, the partner, and the stakes. According to de Waal, primate studies indicate that "aggression [is] not . . . the product of an inner drive but . . . one of the options that exists when there is a conflict of interest" (24). Ultimately, researchers may find that aggressive primate behavior has a genetic component; but this component does not operate in isolation, nor is it necessarily dominant. Equally natural among primates are mechanisms for cooperation, conflict resolution, rechanneling of aggression, and reconciliation (de Waal 2002).

Margaret Mead and the Invention of Warfare Margaret Mead explored the difference between the human instinct for violence and the cultural institution of war in her article, "Warfare Is Only an Invention—not a Biological Necessity" written in 1940, during World War II. She presents ethnographic examples of people who do not go to war to settle disputes, thereby undermining the

theory of a universal biological imperative for warfare. She also describes the wide variety of reasons people go to war—not only for land and loot but for prestige and women—that can be satisfied without violence. In the end, Mead comes down firmly on the side of war as a cultural invention. And a bad one at that. What then are we to do about this invention? According to Mead (1940):

> If we despair over the way in which war seems such an ingrained habit of most of the human race, we can take comfort from the fact that a poor invention will usually give place to a better invention. For this, two conditions at least are necessary. The people must recognize the defects of the old invention, and someone must make a new one. Propaganda against warfare, documentation of its terrible cost in human suffering and social waste, these prepare the ground by teaching people to feel that warfare is a defective social institution. There is further needed a belief that social invention is possible and the invention of new methods which will render warfare as outdated as the tractor is making the plow, or the motorcar the horse and buggy. A form of behavior becomes outdated only when something else takes its place, and in order to invent forms of behavior which will make war obsolete, it is a first requirement to believe that an invention is possible. (19-22)

Can your generation invent an alternative to war—a new way to resolve conflicts without violence?

The State and War

Political anthropologists actively explore the complicated cultural processes through which war is invented, learned, and enacted (Besteman 2002; Besteman and Cassanelli 1996; Farmer 2003; Ferguson 2002; Gusterson 1996, 2004; Lutz 2001; Waterston 2009). Over the past 100 years, war has become far more than waging hand-to-hand combat or pulling a trigger at close range—actions that we might associate with aggression driven by hormones. Instead, modern warfare is considerably more premeditated and calculated, relying on computers, satellites, missiles, GPS tracking, and airborne drone strikes.

Today anthropologists study a highly militarized world in which war seems normalized and permanent. Warfare has become one of the most visible of all human political institutions that reveals the state's pursuit of power. As we will see in Carolyn Nordstrom's work later in this chapter, warfare can no longer be viewed as a local military phenomenon. Indeed, modern warfare is embedded in a global system of war making. This fact pushes anthropologists to study the intersection of multiple factors that play a role in constructing warfare as a reasonable means for resolving conflicts. These factors may be as disparate as economic stratification, ethnic identity formation, migration, weapons manufacturing and trade, the imbalance between weak states and strong states, and resource shortages involving oil, water, and land (Nugent and Vincent 2004).

Militarization A growing body of anthropological literature has focused on **militarization**—the contested social process through which a civil society organizes for the production of military violence (Lutz 2004; see also Bickford 2011; Geyer 1989). Catherine Lutz, an anthropologist of militarization, in *Homefront: A Military City and the American Twentieth Century* (2001), describes how the processes of militarization include not only the production of material objects such as bullets, bombs, tanks, planes, and missiles but also the glorification of war and those who make war, as states seek to shape their national histories and political culture.

Lutz warns that left unchecked, militarization threatens to shape other aspects of cultural institutions to its own ends. For example, it influences research in physics, information technology, and psychology; it affects national budget priorities; it affects discussions and debates about gender and sexuality, race and citizenship, privacy and security; and it limits what can be discussed in the news, online, or in the classroom.

Sociologist C. Wright Mills, in his classic study *The Power Elite* (1956), warned that building an expansive military structure and the industrial capacity to support it—a military industrial complex—ultimately would lead to a "military definition of reality" in which human interactions would be seen through the logic of warfare and violence. War would become the "common sense of the nation." The central elements of this militarized thinking include cultural

militarization: The contested social process through which a civil society organizes for the production of military violence.

assumptions that defense is the first need of every organism; that human beings are naturally aggressive and territorial; that force is the primary means to get things done in the world; and that if one weapon creates security, then a thousand weapons create more security. The fact that these assumptions seem reasonable to many people in a society were evidence to Mills of the power of militarized culture to shape the way people think.

Lutz (2004) suggests that ultimately, militarization creates a kind of hegemony of thinking: It limits what is perceived as normal and natural, what can and cannot be said or done. It identifies some people as allies and others as enemies. It dehumanizes and demonizes to make hating and killing seem logical, normal, and appropriate.

Constructing Soldiers, Constructing War Are soldiers born or made? Is it possible that if war must be constructed, soldiers must be constructed, too? In *Fallen Elites* (2011), Andrew Bickford explores the process of militarization, particularly the process by which soldiers are made—and unmade—by the state. Bickford's work sheds light on how states make soldiers in order to make war.

MAP 14.3
Germany

Bickford studied the life histories of military officers and border guards of the former East Germany who have been living in postunification Germany since the fall of the Berlin Wall in 1990. Originally stationed by the U.S. military as a soldier on the front lines in Berlin toward the end of the Cold War in 1984, Bickford returned after reunification as an anthropologist. He found himself at interviews, meals, and meetings sitting across the table from his recent enemies, some of whom readily admitted that given the opportunity, in the earlier era they would have shot and killed him without hesitation. After all, he had been a member of the U.S. military—an enemy. Now demobilized by the unified German military, however, these formerly powerful elites of the hardline communist East German military participated in Bickford's anthropological study. How could matters of life and death have shifted so easily?

No one is born a soldier, argues Bickford. As the demobilized East German officers in Bickford's study reveal, soldiers who are made can also be unmade. Soldiers do not come prepackaged and ready to fight, kill, and die. Instead, individuals must be made into soldiers through processes of enculturation that teach them to fear, hate, and kill—processes that define particular people as the enemy, as a dangerous, mortal threat.

Because soldiers become the flesh-and-blood actors performing on behalf of the state, Bickford notes how crucial it is for the state to construct a powerful ideal of the soldier—an ideal imbued with characteristics of courage, honor, strength, and duty. This ideal becomes the preeminent symbol of the state and its power. In the process, the hero soldier comes to represent the ideal citizen who embodies the state's key values and worldview.

How does popular culture glorify war and those who make war? A woman walks by an advertisement for the video game "Call of Duty: Black Ops III".

The construction of soldiers as model citizens happens in numerous ways. States formally honor the memory of soldiers—individuals who were fathers, grandfathers, brothers, uncles, husbands, boyfriends (and less often but no less honorable, mothers, grandmothers, sisters, aunts, wives, girlfriends). States also promote the character of soldiers, representing in mythologized language and ritual their heroic deeds in defense of the state: their service as strong and virtuous warriors, protectors, and conquerors—indeed, as powerful agents of life and death, yet also as simple men and women with a job to do to protect their families, their nation, and its way of life. Creating the ideal of the soldier, argues Bickford, is essential to the process of militarization, linking that ideal to notions of citizenship, national identity, and the honor and legitimacy of the state.

Exploring the Complex Life of Dangerous Things

Anthropologist and physician Paul Farmer suggests that to understand how deeply war and violence have become insinuated into human culture, anthropologists must trace the complicated life of "dangerous things" (Farmer 2010; Waterston 2009). Try this mental exercise: Think of an object of war—perhaps a bullet, a gun, a landmine, a remote sensing device. Imagine its dangerous life. When it reaches the battlefield, how did it get there? Consider how it is designed, tested, manufactured, paid for, and delivered. Who sells it?

In the case of war, the dangerous object is embedded in a network of actions and decisions. Who sends soldiers into battle? Who chooses the enemy? Who provides the food, hospitals, toilets, cafeterias, and health-care supplies to support the soldiers? How is intelligence gathered and surveillance conducted? How is the public convinced or required to provide funding and other support for this process?

What role do movies, video games, holidays, parades, and memorials play in creating an environment in which violence is perceived as a reasonable means to resolve conflict? How do we learn to hate certain people and not others—enough to consider firing a bullet at them?

When we carefully consider the life of a dangerous object such as a bullet, we can begin to see the complex cultural production of the act of firing a gun that goes far beyond any instinctive need to resolve conflict through violence.

Anthropology on the Front Lines of War and Globalization

The fact that today's world is rife with conflict presents anthropologists with many opportunities to study current cases of warfare and violence in the context of pressures from globalization. Anthropologist Carolyn Nordstrom's work exemplifies contemporary anthropological contributions to this kind of study. Nordstrom focuses on the real, messy, local experiences of violence, resistance, survival, and creativity in actual communities where war occurs, not in the comfortable offices and remote institutions of military officials and political leaders. At the same time, she turns a spotlight on the complex web of local and foreign interactions and actors that drive war and make warfare a global phenomenon.

Mozambique Between 1989 and 1996, Nordstrom made multiple visits to war-torn areas of Mozambique, a southeast African country wracked by a fifteen-year civil war after independence from Portugal that claimed a million lives, mostly civilian. To reach rural and forested regions, she traveled with bush pilots making airlifts into war zones. In contrast to typical journalistic war reports, Nordstrom experienced firsthand the low-intensity conflict called "terror warfare," perpetrated by rebel guerrillas and Mozambican government soldiers, that targeted the country's civilian population through military attacks, hunger, and displacement.

MAP 14.4
Mozambique

These destructive forces of warfare targeted the basic structures of Mozambican community life: hospitals, schools, and government offices, as well as teachers, health-care professionals, religious authorities, and community leaders. By destroying and disrupting the institutions, practices, and key practitioners of local culture, the forces of violence sought to destroy the local population's political will.

In her ethnography of civil war in Mozambique, *A Different Kind of War Story* (1997), Nordstrom recounts the determined creativity that local populations used to combat this terror and violence. In one village heavily targeted and frequently overrun by troops of both armies, most community leaders and service providers had fled as refugees to avoid potential assassination. Most

THE SOCIAL LIFE OF THINGS
Drones and Remote Control Warfare

For over fifteen years the United States military and Central Intelligence Agency have been using weaponized drones—unmanned aircraft—to conduct highly secretive targeted killings in the warzones of Afghanistan and Iraq and against terrorists in countries like Somalia, Yemen, and Pakistan. The U.S. public knows little about drones, how they are used, who controls them, or who their targets are. In *Drone: Remote Control Warfare* (2016) anthropologist Hugh Gusterson explores how drones are quietly reshaping the practice of warcraft, blurring the lines between civilians and combatants, intimacy and distance, policing and warfare.

(1) How does it feel to operate a remote-control drone? As drones circle miles above their prey, operators may sit in air-conditioned rooms thousands of miles away tracking their victim on a video screen, sometimes for days, before launching an attack. From CIA headquarters in Virginia or an Air Force station in Nevada, the drone strike is quick, clean, and bloodless—no sound, smell, taste, or texture. The operator acts as executioner, with godlike power over life and death.

2 Victims and local residents experience the drone attack differently than drone operators. Without warning, missiles descend from the sky, erupting with violent and deadly force. Survivors tell of smoke, screams, the smell of burning, the ground trembling beneath them, the pain of shrapnel wounds, and the enduring grief in the aftermath. How do they know the drone will not return? The safe predictability of life has been permanently destroyed.

3 Advocates of drone attacks emphasize their effectiveness: accurately targeting their prey while minimizing civilian casualties. Opponents warn that combatant and civilian casualties have been severely underreported. They worry about slippage in drone missions from military operations to policing efforts— policing the world from the sky at the U.S. President's sole discretion, even when warfare is not legally authorized. And some world leaders condemn the breach of sovereign territory. Do acts of war conducted without warlike activity or U.S. human cost make the move to war far too easy?

A drone, even a weaponized drone, is simply a machine. But the social life of a drone—how it is deployed, targeted against combatants and noncombatants, and deployed in accordance with or against international law; how it affects operators, victims, and a nation's democratic institutions—raises complex ethical and political questions that an anthropology of things brings into sharper focus.

- Do you know how many times the U.S. launches a drone attack in any given week, the number of people killed, the number of unintended deaths, or the countries where airstrikes have occurred?
- Have you ever heard or read a firsthand account from victims of a drone strike? If not, why?
- Why do so few protest the U.S.'s use of weaponized drones?

What is the life of a dangerous thing like a rifle, a bullet, or a bomb? (*clockwise, from top left*) The Colt Defense factory in Hartford, Connecticut, makes the M16 and M4 rifles, the rifles of choice of the U.S. military; a gun poised and ready, in a refugee camp in Lebanon; the Eleventh International Defence Industry Fair, in Istanbul, Turkey, in 2013, which attracted 781 companies from 82 countries.

resources and infrastructure had been destroyed. During the first severe attack on the village, however, one remaining health-care practitioner gathered up as many medical supplies as she could carry and hid in the nearby bush until the soldiers left. Though the soldiers knew her name and searched for her, the villagers kept her secret, kept her safe. On the front lines of battle, soldiers passed through the village regularly in subsequent months. Yet the health worker remained, hiding her medical supplies, living a nomadic life on the outskirts of the area, and being protected by the villagers, who continued to carry their ailing members to her for treatment.

These actions by the health worker and the villagers are emblematic of the creativity that Nordstrom's research finds to be the most potent weapon against war—the determination to survive and resist, to continually refashion and reconstruct one's self, community, and world. Nordstrom concludes her ethnography by suggesting that if, as early political philosophers such as Thomas Hobbes proposed, violence is the "natural state" of human affairs when political institutions collapse, then war-torn regions such as Mozambique should be rife with scenes of aggression, acts of self-preservation, and individual attempts at survival in a dog-eat-dog world. Instead Nordstrom consistently found people who resisted and defeated the political violence of war by attending to the day-to-day matters of their community—sharing food, healing wounds, repairing lives, teaching children, performing rituals, exchanging friendship, rebuilding places, and creatively reconstructing the everyday patterns that constitute a meaningful life (Englund 1999; Honwana 1999; Richards 1999).

A Comparative Study In a later book, *Shadows of War* (2004), Nordstrom makes the case that standard notions of local wars fought by local actors over local issues are largely fiction. Through a comparative study of war and violence in Mozambique, Sri Lanka, South Africa, and Angola, she instead traces the extensive global networks of individuals and industries that feed and fuel local violence and war. Mercenary soldiers, foreign strategists, arms suppliers, businesspeople, black marketeers, smugglers, humanitarian relief workers, researchers, propagandists, and journalists all circle the globe, moving from one war to the next. Multi-trillion-dollar international financial networks support warfare. Illegal drugs, precious gems, weapons, food supplies, military training manuals, and medicines are products moved by international networks of legitimate and illegitimate businesses and agencies that profit from the business of war.

Thanks to globalization, the business of war now operates on a worldwide scale. It influences both the architects of war, who primarily engage the battle from a distance, and the people who suffer the consequences on a war's front lines. Discussing the local people affected by the business of war, Nordstrom notes that theirs are not the typical war stories recounted in the media. When war is portrayed only through the prism of weapons, soldiers, territory, and strategic interests won or lost, a more significant reality is ignored: the heroic efforts of people on the front lines who resist and maintain life in the face of violence and death (Finnstrom 2005).

How Do People Mobilize Power outside the State's Control?

Systems of power, including the state, are never absolute. Their dominance is never complete. Even when a culture's dominant groups and institutions are very powerful in terms of their ability to exercise force or to establish control through hegemony, they do not completely dominate people's lives and thinking. Individuals and groups with less power or no power may still contest the established power relationships and structures through political, economic,

With globalization, an extensive network of individuals and industries circles the globe from one war to the next. (*clockwise, from top*) United Nations High Commissioner for Refugees workers distribute blankets to Syrian refugees along the Jordanian-Syrian border, 2012; members of the media mark their flak jackets as gunfire rings out near the Tripoli Hotel in Lebanon, 2011; an Australian mercenary trains rebel recruits in Myanmar.

religious, or military means and challenge and change cultural norms, values, symbols, and institutions. This power is a potential that anthropologists call **agency**.

In such displays of human agency, we see the way culture becomes the realm in which battles over power are waged; where people contest, negotiate, and enforce what is considered normal and what people can say, do, and even think. Because of human agency, cultures do not remain rigid and static. They change.

Efforts to change cultural patterns take various forms, which we will consider further. Human agency may be expressed through individual strategies of resistance, such as the "weapons of the weak" discussed in Chapter 2, collective efforts such as social movements, and alternative institutions to the state such as those based on religion.

Social Movements

Social movements are collective, group actions in response to uneven development, inequality, and injustice that seek to build institutional networks to transform cultural patterns and government policies. Social movements engage in contentious politics, usually outside the mainstream political process, to address specific social issues, although they usually do not seek to overthrow the social order. The study of social movements is interdisciplinary, engaging not only anthropologists but also sociologists, political scientists, and historians (Edelman 2001).

Recently, the anthropological analysis of social movements has focused on the responses of local communities to the forces of globalization. Factors such as the worldwide movement of capital and production through flexible accumulation, the increasing migration within and across national borders, and rapidly increasing yet uneven rates of development have spurred the emergence of social movements as local communities organize to protect their land, environment, human rights, and cultural identities in a changing economic and political context. Simultaneously, time-space compression has facilitated increased communication and cooperation among individuals, social movements, and NGOs, thus creating opportunities for a "globalization from below" (Falk 1993, 39).

As part of this phenomenon, as we discussed earlier in terms of Hodgson's ethnography of the Maasai, actors who operate outside the formal institutions of the state and beyond the control of dominant global financial entities (such as the World Bank, the International Monetary Fund, and the World Trade Organization) use social media and social networking to build transnational activist networks and alliances. Through these mechanisms, their combined efforts address inequality, environmental degradation, and human rights abuses (Juris 2008; Nash 2005). Within the past several years, for example, social

agency: The potential power of individuals and groups to contest cultural norms, values, mental maps of reality, symbols, institutions, and structures of power.

social movement: Collective group actions that seek to build institutional networks to transform cultural patterns and government policies.

Activists in Kathmandu, Nepal, demand constitutional protections for "Dalits" who have been systematically marginalized by the region's caste system.

movements from Tunisia to Egypt to Syria and New York have relied heavily on social media to challenge political, economic, and military systems of power. In the following sections, we consider several types of social movements: rural peasants in Costa Rica and urban Occupy Wall Street protestors seeking greater economic egalitarianism.

Rural Social Movements In the last thirty years, rural social movements have drawn anthropologists' attention as farmers engage in creative political struggles to resist the impact of globalization on their land, livelihood, and way of life. As one example, Marc Edelman's *Peasants against Globalization* (1999) examines the activism of the rural poor in Costa Rica, Central America, during the 1980s and 1990s. Edelman recounts a story that reflects the beleaguered experience of rural agricultural workers elsewhere across the globe in recent decades.

Having gained independence from Spain in 1821, Costa Rica is one of the most politically stable countries in the Americas. By the early 1980s, Costa Ricans had built a strong, economically self-sufficient democracy and taken the radical step of abolishing the nation's military in order to invest in programs of national development. Such programs aimed to provide education, health care, tariff protections for local products, and price supports for basic foodstuffs to ensure a basic livelihood for all citizens. The programs also provided government-backed loans to farmers to stabilize agricultural production.

MAP 14.5
Costa Rica

Exploring the Balance of Power in Human Relationships

Human political engagements encompass every relationship in our lives. You don't have to be running for elected office or participating in a social movement to be involved in politics. Every relationship has a power dynamic. In some, you have power over the other person. In others, someone has power over you. Or the dynamic of power may shift back and forth depending on the circumstance.

Make a list of all the relationships and interactions you have in the course of a day: with family, friends, teachers, students, employers, coworkers, shop owners, waiters, government officials. Or watch a television show or a movie and observe the relationships of power represented there. Now describe the way power is balanced in each relationship you experience or observe. How is power organized? Can you see the intersections of age, gender, income, race, religion, sexuality, and/or citizenship? What political negotiations are present in these relationships? Consider how these political dynamics were established and how they might be changed. Must they continue indefinitely as they are?

During the mid-1980s, however, Costa Rica was drawn into the civil wars of its neighbors, serving as a key ally of the United States on the Central American peninsula as war and upheaval spread in Nicaragua, Guatemala, and Panama. Simultaneously, a debt crisis affecting most of Latin America shook Costa Rica's economy and spurred rapid inflation. Under the auspices of providing foreign aid to an ally, the U.S.-sponsored Food for Peace program delivered massive quantities of subsidized corn, wheat, and rice—purchased from U.S. farmers—to the Costa Rican market. The subsidized food, however, undercut Costa Rican farm prices, making it increasingly difficult for local farmers to sell their own products at the price needed to break even.

Ultimately, these changes in the Costa Rican food market drove many small-scale farmers out of business, lowered the country's overall food production, and ended its history of food self-sufficiency. Structural adjustment loans offered by the International Monetary Fund and the World Bank to help Costa Rica through the crisis required the government to eliminate price supports, tariff protections, and government-backed loans while drastically reducing investments in health care and education. These measures further deepened the country's crisis.

Edelman retells the stories of local, small-scale farmers—often called "peasants" in the anthropological literature—and their national umbrella group, UPANACIONAL, as they fought these threats to their way of life. The peasants marched, blocked highways, and held street demonstrations. They built alliances with wealthy farmers, lobbied national politicians, and promoted charismatic activist figures into national prominence to speak on their behalf. In fact,

A farmer holds a puppet of Costa Rican president Laura Chinchilla during protests in the capital, San Jose, over new property taxes on agricultural land, 2012.

the rural farmers that Edelman depicts challenge many traditional stereotypes of peasants. In the face of difficulties tied to both national and international policies, they reveal themselves to be worldly, outspoken, forward thinking, creative, persistent, and proud, refusing to be silenced or sidelined.

The climax of the Costa Rican peasants' collective action and direct pressure tactics came as several dozen farmers and movement leaders occupied government buildings in June 1988. At the conclusion of the standoff, the activists were arrested; however, the negotiated settlement extracted a government commitment to provide access to low-interest credit for Costa Rica's rural farmers. This was a significant victory in response to the peasants' demands. Edelman concludes that the Costa Rican peasants may not have stopped the effects of globalization on their nation's rural population, but through collective action they were able to soften the harshest blows (Gudmundson 2001; Welch 2001).

Occupy Wall Street Anthropologists seek to understand how social movements arise, mobilize, and sustain themselves. Even though conditions of inequality and injustice are widespread in many parts of the world, the activation of movements for social justice occurs in only certain situations. Anthropologists have investigated the material, human, cognitive, technical, and organizational resources necessary for social movements to succeed (McAdam, McCarthy, and Zald 1996). Recent attention has turned to the **framing process** of movements—specifically, how shared meanings and definitions arise to motivate and justify collective action.

framing process: The creation of shared meanings and definitions that motivate and justify collective action by social movements.

Actions by the Occupy Wall Street movement beginning in September 2011 illustrate the role of the framing process. How did Occupy protestors capture the attention of a nation (and beyond) and build a consensus for social action? What factors led to their success? Organizers of the movement had been involved in planning well before September 2011. The financial crisis of 2008, precipitated by reckless speculation on the part of big banks and investment companies, had created an underlying instability in the U.S. economy and intensifying recriminations in the political sphere. But when protestors occupied Zuccotti Park near Wall Street in lower Manhattan three years later, they needed other strategies to capture people's attention and imagination. There were two keys to their success, both related to framing. First was the framing of the movement as simultaneously virtual and physical. And second was a framing of their cause under the banner "We Are the 99%."

Anthropologist Jeffrey Juris, who studied Occupy Boston, has examined both the core identity of the Occupy movement and the cultural and technological mechanisms that sustained its momentum. The interplay between virtual and physical forms of protest has been key. Social media drew a diverse group of people with shared concerns—in this case, over economic inequality—into shared physical spaces. Listservs, websites, and collaborative networking tools facilitated new patterns of protest that built on and resonated with more traditional forms. Social media served a key role in keeping the physical outdoor protests and occupations alive, vibrant, and relevant. In the process, not only did the physical occupations become a protest tactic, but also the "physical and communal embodiments of the virtual crowds of individuals aggregated through the viral flows of social media" (Juris 2012, 269).

Another key to Occupy's success rested on framing the movement's cause under the banner "We Are the 99%." With this simple phrase, Occupy Wall Street gradually focused public discourse on questions of the fundamental fairness of the U.S. and global economy in light of rapidly growing conditions of inequality over the past forty years that have steadily transferred wealth from 99 percent to 1 percent of the nation's population. Despite growing calls by political leaders and media critics demanding that Occupy Wall Street activists put forward specific policy proposals to address the problems they were decrying, the movement steadfastly refused. Instead its members focused on the underlying issue of inequality framed in their motto, "We Are the 99%."

Activists recognized that sustaining a consensus for action would depend not only on the underlying economic conditions and openness of the political system to change, but also on the movement's ability to continue to successfully frame its identity. However, Juris suggests that movements such as Occupy Wall Street can pursue multiple paths. While continuing to develop alternative models of democratic self-organizing that directly challenge state

policies, such movements can also recognize the possibility for indirectly shaping policy debates by influencing wider political discussion. Writing in the spring of 2012, Juris noted that Occupy Wall Street had already contributed to a shift in public discourse. The framing process of Occupy has successfully highlighted growing inequality and the influence of financial and corporate interests in the economy and politics. At the same time, Occupy has functioned as a laboratory for the production of alternative forms of democracy and community (Juris 2012). Where have you encountered this framing of the 99 percent and the 1 percent in discussions on inequality?

Alternative Legal Structures

In addition to overt social movements and subtle, nonovert forms of resistance, it is possible to challenge structures of power in an arena where the state usually holds clear authority: in matters of the law. But how do people organize alternative legal structures outside the direct control of the modern state? What gives authority and legitimacy to alternative structures if they are not enforceable by the state's coercive power? Legal anthropologist Hussein Ali Agrama spent two years conducting ethnographic research on local courts and councils in Cairo, Egypt, to explore these questions (Agrama 2010, 2012).

Islamic Fatwa Councils in Cairo, Egypt Agrama compared the operations of two key local sources of legal authority: (1) the Personal Status courts operated by the Egyptian state and (2) the Al Azhar Fatwa Council, independently established in 1935 and one of the oldest and most established centers of Islamic authority. In the busy and crowded Personal Status courts, Egyptians of all walks of life appear before a judge, an official of the state, who makes legally binding rulings that draw on the Egyptian Constitution and legal codes that are based on the principles of Islamic Sharia (law). In the equally busy and crowded Fatwa Council, held in a spacious room located at the main entrance to the Al Azhar mosque, seekers approach Islamic legal scholars and interpreters of Islamic law, or muftis, for religious answers about matters of daily life. The muftis respond freely with legally nonbinding answers to anyone who asks. Their decision is called a "fatwa"—a response to a question about how to live ethically and rightly.

MAP 14.6
Cairo

In comparing these two court systems, Agrama encounters a startling dynamic. Both deal with an overlapping set of issues heavily focused on matters of marriage, sex, divorce, reconciliation, and inheritance. Both draw their decisions from Islamic Sharia, although the Personal Status courts engage Islamic law through the Egyptian Constitution and legal code, whereas the muftis refer directly to Sharia and other Islamic traditions in their fatwas. What interests Agrama is that despite these basic similarities, the petitioners' responses to the authorities' rulings are markedly different. The legally binding judgments of the Personal Status court are generally looked on with great suspicion. People go to great lengths to avoid the consequences of the court's decisions despite the state's ability to coerce obedience to its judgments. In distinct contrast, the Fatwa Council exercises great authority even though seeking decisions from the Council is not obligatory, a fatwa is not legally binding, and once issued, a fatwa does not have to be obeyed. In fact, petitioners can seek more than one fatwa on the same issue if they wish. But Agrama's research finds that petitioners take fatwas very seriously, following the decisions even if they entail great difficulty or unhappiness—this despite no identifiable institutional enforcement mechanism.

What accounts for the differentiation between Personal Status courts and the Fatwa Council? And how does a given fatwa acquire its authority without the threat of coercive force like that which the state makes available to the Personal Status courts? To understand the authority of the fatwa, Agrama explores the complex interactions and expectations between seekers of fatwas and the muftis that issue them. Contrary to popular impressions, fatwas are not merely designed to dispense points of correct doctrine in obedience to prescriptions found in Islamic Sharia. Rather, the mufti seeks to apply Islamic tradition and law to resolve particular problems, identify an effective solution, and point the seeker toward a path forward. The process includes significant perplexities and uncertainties: The fatwa seeker arrives perplexed by his or her life situation, and at least initially the mufti is uncertain about how to respond. In

David Vine
Militarization at Home and Abroad

Anthropologist David Vine, professor at American University, studies U.S. militarization and its impact on people around the world and in the United States. His book *Base Nation: How U.S. Military Bases Abroad Harm America and the World* (2015) documents the effect of the more than 800 U.S. military bases operating outside the United States. Their global footprint shapes not only U.S. military interventions, but the lives of local people, U.S. military families, indigenous populations, and the environment. The cost to the U.S. national budget alone, Vine estimates, is around $100 billion a year.

Vine became interested in militarization in graduate school while conducting research for a group of exiles from the island Diego Garcia in the Indian Ocean. "In the late 1960s, the U.S. and British governments forcibly removed this entire indigenous people, the Chagossians, from Diego Garcia to create a major U.S. military base. They were simply dumped in exile, deported to the islands of Mauritius and the Seychelles with no resettlement assistance. Unsurprisingly, they became deeply impoverished, and despite that, over the last almost fifty years now, they've been struggling to get back to their homeland and get proper compensation for what they've suffered. That opened my eyes to the world of U.S. military bases overseas and the damaging effects of so many of them.

"Ethnographic skills were very helpful in allowing me to live with the Chagossians, participate and research their daily lives, and see the ways in which their lives have been deeply damaged by living in exile. But I was also interested in not just looking at the ways the Chagossians have suffered but understanding why my government, the U.S. government, decided it needed a military base in the middle of the Indian Ocean and why it was appropriate to exile the entire people. I became part of a growing group of anthropologists who have studied U.S. foreign policy, U.S. military policy and policy makers, and done so

with ethnographic methods." Vine's research became his book *Island of Shame: The Secret History of the U.S. Military Base on Diego Garcia* (2009).

But what of the impact of U.S. militarization on the United States itself? "I don't think people understand how much tax-payer money we are pouring into the military. By some estimates it's around a trillion dollars annually— at least half the discretionary budget of the government. I think the Pentagon today—the U.S. military—has become a fourth branch of government. It controls such a large portion of the budget in this country and has so much power—easily as much as the legislative or judicial branches.

"President Eisenhower coined the term 'military-industrial complex'. I think it's a useful way of under-

Anthropologist David Vine

standing the combined power of the military, the military services, and the military contractors that build weaponry. Members of Congress are also part of this system that has exerted tremendous power in our daily lives and shapes, in often invisible but powerful ways, our political lives, economic lives, even our spiritual and cultural lives."

Vine warns about the ways even students have become militarized—embedded in this system of militarization. "I think Eisenhower's military-industrial complex speech should be required reading. He pointed out that every billion dollars spent on a bomber is money that is being taken from someone who's unclothed, who's going hungry or is poorly educated. Today, the reason undergraduates are going into so much debt—one reason college costs so much and secondary schools are in such poor shape—is because we've poured so much of our tax money, our national wealth, into the military and not into schools, hospitals, housing, and infrastructure.

"In the post-9/11 era, we're spending money at a rate like we were at the height of the Cold War when we were faced with another superpower with nuclear arms. Now we face no such enemy and our military spending in many ways has become counter-productive. It has actually inflamed tensions in many cases. This is where bases come in. They've outraged local populations who—not surprisingly and understandably—don't want their lands occupied by U.S. bases and U.S. troops. All that money is not, generally speaking, making us safer. In many ways, it's actually making us less safe."

Students can take steps to de-militarize themselves, Vine suggests, "first by starting to become aware of the influence of the military and the glorification of war in your lives. Perhaps even with the clothes you wear, like the camouflage that's pervasive in our fashion. And then in the media you consume. Perhaps ask yourself why war games involving mass killing are so popular and how that's shaping our lives and how we think about the world and even shaping our brains. Another dimension of militarization of popular culture is Hollywood. Look at how popular violence is in media, including movies and TV. Begin to become aware of how war and violence are celebrated. And certainly begin to pay attention to money that's being invested in war and the military and begin to talk with friends and neighbors and family about the choices that our political leaders are making with our tax dollars, taking money from our schools, hospitals, infrastructure, and housing.

> *Research has shown time and again that military solutions are not effective ways to solve international problems.*

"There are other direct actions that people can take, beginning with opposing any future wars or military interventions. Research has shown time and again that military solutions, military responses are not effective ways to solve international problems. They're certainly not effective solutions to terrorism. And get involved in efforts to move money from the military budget to the civilian side of the budget. Research has shown that money invested in health care and education and infrastructure creates many more jobs than the equivalent amount of spending in the military."

Vine has actively worked to resist efforts to militarize anthropology as a co-founder of the Network of Concerned Anthropologists. "We created this group in response to efforts by the military and CIA to recruit anthropologists into the War on Terror and to serve in Afghanistan and Iraq. They became in some cases armed anthropologists. This is a direct violation of our professional code of ethics to *do no harm* to the people and other animals with whom we do research. Anthropologists organized to oppose this effort to recruit other anthropologists and we were quite successful."

Fatwa Council at the Al Azhar
Mosque, Cairo, Egypt.

this context, the mufti typically begins by asking for further information in an attempt to fully understand the context and facts as presented. The fatwa seeker approaches the mufti with the hope that he will have the skills to point the way out of the trouble, to offer a way forward—to discern and speak the right words.

In the end, both seeker and mufti share a collective responsibility for the success of the fatwa: The mufti must be sure to speak the right words, and the seeker must apply them correctly. Although the consequences of an incorrect fatwa may be most damaging for the seeker during his or her lifetime, the mufti is believed to bear responsibility for the outcome in the hereafter. Ultimately, the fatwa is pronounced in order to put the questioner on the right path forward, to offer direction and facilitate a journey on which the seeker can advance within the range of doctrine toward a Muslim ideal. Agrama suggests that it is careful and personal navigation of these complexities that engenders trust and conveys legitimacy on the muftis and their fatwas.

Despite the overarching presence of the state (Ferguson and Gupta 2002) and, in this case, the explicit presence of a state-run court, individuals and communities consistently seek alternative frameworks of authority through which to organize their lives. Agrama's study of the bustling Al Azhar Fatwa Council in Cairo provides one compelling example and sheds light on local practices of the fatwa—practices that are increasingly popular within Egyptian society and the Muslim world more generally, yet are frequently misunderstood in the West.

In the opening story of the Sundarbans march, Paris climate change demonstrations, and U.S. student fossil fuel divestment campaigns, as well as in the ethnographic examples presented throughout this chapter, we have seen the remarkable diversity of strategies that humans use to exercise power through the medium of politics. Although political upheaval in North Africa and the Middle East readily draws the focus of the world media, Agrama's work in Cairo reminds us that human political activity occurs at many different levels during the course of daily life. Whether through the politics of the state, acts of war, social movements, or small-scale resistance that James Scott (1985; see Chapter 2) labeled weapons of the weak, we have considered how anthropologists examine power and politics and the cutting edges of political activism that will continue to draw their interest in the future.

Thinking Like an Anthropologist: Applying Politics to Daily Life and Beyond

In each chapter of this book, we have investigated how human cultures construct, engage, and negotiate systems of power. We have considered the role of influential ideologies and structures of race, gender, ethnicity, class, kinship, and religion. In this chapter, we have explored how power is expressed and organized through political systems and processes. Politics exist in every human relationship and every community, large or small. People are constantly negotiating the interpersonal and institutional balances of power.

As we saw in the chapter-opening stories, politics is not necessarily separate from daily life. We don't have to run for political office or start an online petition to be involved in politics. At its most basic level, politics encompasses all of the ways we organize ourselves to achieve what we most desire for our community: our family, friends, classmates, fellow citizens, the environment and fellow inhabitants of planet Earth. As you learn to think like an anthropologist about politics and power, remember the opening questions that we have used to frame our inquiries:

- How have anthropologists viewed the origins of human political history?
- What is the state?
- How is globalization affecting the state?
- What is the relationship among politics, the state, violence, and war?
- How do people mobilize power outside the state's control?

If, as it appears, humans do not have an overwhelming and uncontrollable biological drive toward aggression and violence, then unlimited avenues open up to explore strategies for addressing problems that confront us today. These strategies include cooperatively engaging the challenging issues of our schools, communities, nations, and world and developing political responses that take into account the unique cultural dynamics of local communities and specific groups.

In this era of globalization, local political action can have global implications. Certainly the challenge of climate change creates opportunities for political action on a global scale. There are no climate-endangering activities anywhere in the world that do not directly affect all of the humans on the planet. But how quickly can activists, investors, civil society groups, and governments coalesce around strategies to address this existential challenge?

As a new generation of social activists around the globe develop social networking and social media strategies for expressing their concerns and attempting to influence the systems of power and politics, the networked nature of these movements also means that you, as a college student, have every possibility of becoming an anthropologist who engages the world.

Key Terms

band (p. 529)
tribe (p. 532)
chiefdom (p. 532)
state (p. 536)
hegemony (p. 538)
civil society organization (p. 540)
militarization (p. 546)
agency (p. 555)
social movement (p. 555)
framing process (p. 558)

For Further Exploration

Checker, Melissa. 2005. *Polluted Promises: Environmental Racism and the Search for Justice in a Southern Town.* New York: NYU Press.

Eye in the Sky. 2015. Directed by Gavin Hood. Film about a drone strike against suspected terrorists in Nairobi, Kenya.

Gusterson, Hugh. 2016. *Drone: Remote Control Warfare.* Boston: MIT Press.

How to Start a Revolution. 2011. Directed by Ruaridh Arrow. www.howtostartarevolutionfilm.com. Documentary featuring Gene Sharp and his impact on social movements and uprisings around the world.

Mead, Margaret. 1940. "Warfare Is Only an Invention—Not a Biological Necessity." In *Approaches to Peace: A Reader in Peace Studies,* edited by David P. Barash, 19–22. New York: Oxford University Press, 2000.

Nordstrom, Carolyn. 2004. *Shadows of War: Violence, Power, and International Profiteering in the Twenty-First Century.* Berkeley: University of California Press.

Sharp, Gene. 1993. *From Dictatorship to Democracy: A Conceptual Framework for Liberation.* East Boston, MA: Albert Einstein Institution. Nearly 200 methods of nonviolent resistance from rude gestures to mock funerals.

Ury, William. 2002. *Must We Fight? From the Battlefield to the Schoolyard, a New Perspective on Violent Conflict and Its Prevention.* San Francisco, CA: Jossey-Bass.

Vine, David. 2015. *Base Nation: How U.S. Military Bases Abroad Harm America and the World.* New York: Metropolitan Books.

What is religion? Pope Francis, head of the Roman Catholic Church, addresses a joint session of the U.S. Congress in 2015.

CHAPTER 15
Religion

Entering the United States Capitol to a standing ovation from lawmakers, Pope Francis—dressed in a simple white robe adorned with a silver cross necklace—processed through the assembled senators and representatives before mounting the raised dais to address the joint session of the U.S. Congress. Francis, leader of the world's 1.2 billion Roman Catholics—the world's largest religious denomination—arrived on Capitol Hill in the midst of a U.S. tour that electrified much of the nation in late September 2015.

Since his election as the 266th Pope in March 2013, Francis—formerly known as Jorge Mario Borgoglio, an Argentinian Jesuit and son of Italian immigrants—had revitalized the papacy, rejecting many of the elaborate fineries associated with his position, traveling the world to speak on pressing issues of the day as diverse as the Armenian genocide, the conflict between Israelis and Palestinians, and the atrocities of the Islamic State, and calling for renewed attention to poverty and climate devastation. The Pope's personality, theological openness, and direct actions struck such a chord that both *Rolling Stone* and *The Advocate* featured him on their covers, *Time* magazine and *Vanity Fair* named him Man of the Year, and *Forbes* placed him at the top of a list of the World's 50 Greatest Leaders.

In Washington, some politicians called on the Pope to stick to spiritual matters. The Pope instead continued to integrate theological reflection, social analysis, and calls for action. While some politicians were advocating building a wall on the U.S.–Mexican border, the Pope reminded the assembled leaders that they were all immigrants or descendants of immigrants and had nothing to fear. He advocated protection of life at every stage, including abolishing the death penalty and the reduction of armed conflict. He called for an end to the sale of weapons to people intent on violence, an arms trade driven by "money drenched in blood, often innocent blood." And in a chamber sharply divided on the issue of climate change, the Pope came down clearly on the side of climate science and the need for immediate action.

Only months earlier, in an elaborate reflection on the environment, *Laudato Si'*, the Pope lamented increasing pollution of the planet, global warming, a lack of clean water, loss of biodiversity, and an overall decline in human life and breakdown in society. But he went further, declaring the warming of the planet and expanding global poverty to be symptoms of a greater problem: the developed world's indifference to the destruction of the planet in pursuit of short-term economic gains. The resulting culture of consumerism—a "throwaway culture"—too easily discards unwanted items and unwanted people.

For many, the Pope's bold proclamations seemed out of place for a spiritual leader. But for Pope Francis, the integration of theology, social analysis, and action in addressing the pressing issues facing humanity only continued a long tradition of papal leadership on matters of importance to the church's followers and the world.

Religion plays a central role in human life and human culture. Through the study of religion, anthropologists engage some of the deepest, most difficult, and most enduring human questions—about meaning, difference, power, love, sexuality, mortality, morality, human origins, and kinship. Religion has been a central interest of anthropologists since the beginning of our field (Frazer 1890; Tylor 1871). Research about religious beliefs and practices worldwide has explored an amazing diversity of beliefs, symbols, rituals, myths, institutions, religious experts, groups, deities, and supernatural forces. As you read about diverse religions in this chapter, some beliefs and practices may seem quite familiar. Others may be surprising or unexpected. Many might stretch your basic assumptions of what religion is and does.

Religion offers a rich vein of material for exploring the complexity of human culture, including systems of belief and systems of power. It is perhaps the hottest topic in the world today as globalization brings different traditions, beliefs, and practices into contact. In the United States, immigration over the past five decades has transformed the religious landscape (Figure 15.1). Temples, mosques, gurdwaras, and retreat centers now join churches and synagogues in small towns and big cities across the country. College campuses, too, reflect an expanding religious diversity. And while some politicians have called for sweeping bans on Muslim immigrants, at the local level, as people of different religious traditions encounter one another in neighborhoods, schools, and other public institutions, lively debates take place about education, zoning, health care, public security, and civil rights. These encounters create the

FIGURE 15.1 Religion in the United States

Extensive public polling in the United States reveals shifts in religious demographics in response to globalization and immigration patterns. In particular, the United States is experiencing a decline in the total percentage of Protestant Christians that parallels a growth in Catholic Christians from Latin America; Muslims from the Middle East, South Asia, and Africa; Orthodox Christians from Eastern Europe and the Middle East; Hindus from India; and Buddhists from China, Southeast Asia, and East Asia.

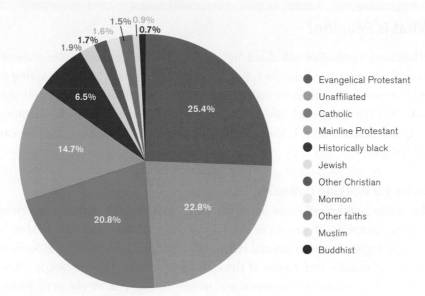

● Evangelical Protestant
● Unaffiliated
● Catholic
● Mainline Protestant
● Historically black
● Jewish
● Other Christian
● Mormon
● Other faiths
● Muslim
● Buddhist

SOURCE: Pew Forum on Religion & Public Life. 2015. "America's Changing Religious Landscape." www.pewforum.org

potential for tension and misunderstanding on school boards, zoning committees, and town and city councils, as well as in civic associations and even college classrooms. But they also offer opportunities for interfaith encounters, learning, and engagement. An anthropological understanding of religion can help you to navigate and engage this changing landscape.

In this chapter, we will consider the anthropological approach to understanding the many groups, beliefs, and practices that are called "religion." In particular, we will examine the following questions:

- What is religion?
- What tools do anthropologists use to understand how religion works?
- In what ways is religion both a system of meaning and a system of power?
- How is globalization changing religion?

By the end of the chapter you will be able to investigate and analyze religion using the tools of an anthropologist. You will be better able to understand religion in your own life, in the growing religious pluralism of the United States, and in diverse religious expressions around the world. These skills will be increasingly valuable tools for living and working in the twenty-first century.

What Is Religion?

When anthropologists talk about "religion," what are we really talking about? Since the beginning of the discipline, anthropologists have been attempting to create a universal definition that might apply to all religions' local manifestations. But the vast global diversity of unique local expressions makes defining religion a difficult task. Is there something present in all cultures that we can call "religion"?

Seeking a Working Definition

The unique anthropological approach to religion begins with the everyday religious practices of people in their local communities. Through fieldwork, anthropologists focus on the real religious worlds in which humans experience religion physically and express it through their actions. We may study a religion's history, theology, scriptures, and major figures, but we do so to understand their meaning and significance in the life of a community of people. Religion is not theoretical in people's daily activities. People make sense of the world, reach decisions, and organize their lives on the basis of their religious beliefs. Starting from these beginning principles, anthropologists also explore the myriad ways religion intersects with other systems of power, whether economics, politics, race, gender, or sexuality. And we explore how local religious expressions may be connected to larger religious movements or institutions.

Anthropologists have compiled a vast and diverse set of data on religious beliefs and practices worldwide. But are there any common characteristics that apply in every situation? In general, we find that all local expressions of religion combine some, but not necessarily all, of the following elements:

- Belief in powers or deities whose abilities transcend those of the natural world and cannot be measured by scientific tools.
- Myths and stories that reflect on the meaning and purpose of life, its origins, and humans' place in the universe.
- Ritual activities that reinforce, recall, instill, and explore collective beliefs.

- Powerful symbols, often used in religious rituals, that represent key aspects of the religion for its followers.
- Specialists who assist the average believer to bridge everyday life experiences and the religion's ideals and supernatural aspects.
- Organizations and institutions that preserve, explore, teach, and implement the religion's key beliefs.
- A community of believers.

As a working definition, we might then say that a **religion** is a set of beliefs and rituals based on a unique vision of how the world ought to be, often focused on a supernatural power and lived out in community. (For an overview of the distribution of adherents to major world religions today, see Figure 15.2. Considering the range of religions shown there, perhaps you can begin to imagine the challenge inherent in creating a working definition to cover such a broad spectrum.)

As social scientists, anthropologists have largely been uninterested in questions of any religion's ultimate truth or falsity. Instead we understand that religious worlds are real, meaningful, and powerful to those who live in them. Our task is to carefully make those worlds come alive for others by capturing their vivid inner life, sense of moral order, dynamic public expressions, and interactions with other systems of meaning and power—whether those religious expressions occur in a remote Chinese village temple or the most famous Catholic cathedral in Rome (Bowie 2006).

religion: A set of beliefs and rituals based on a unique vision of how the world ought to be, often focused on a supernatural power and lived out in community.

FIGURE 15.2 Religion in Global Perspective

This chart shows estimated relative distribution of adherents to the major world religions. It is worth noting, however, that few countries collect data on religious beliefs and practices; as discussed in the chapter, local religious expressions may not neatly fit these categories.

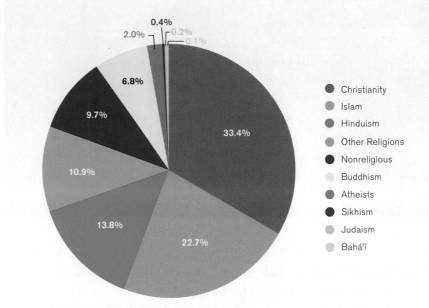

- Christianity
- Islam
- Hinduism
- Other Religions
- Nonreligious
- Buddhism
- Atheists
- Sikhism
- Judaism
- Bahá'í

SOURCE: CIA World Factbook, 2014. www.cia.gov

Local Expressions and Universal Definitions

Attention to local religious expressions complicates anthropologists' efforts to create a universal definition of religion. In a religious studies course, you would likely use a textbook that allocates one chapter for each of the largest world religions, including Christianity, Islam, Hinduism, Buddhism, Chinese religion, Sikhism, Judaism, and others. Each chapter might include an overview of the religion's history, theology, scriptures, major figures, and formal institutions. Under such an approach, drawing broad comparisons among the major religions can prove helpful in providing a general picture of the world's most established religious traditions and in understanding each religion's ideal expression. At the same time, it may obscure the creative and flexible ways people actually practice their religion that may diverge from the ideal.

Indeed, local expressions and creative adaptations are often at the heart of anthropological research because they reveal how people make a religious tradition come alive in their own context. Let's consider Islam for a moment. Muslims and non-Muslims alike generally regard Islam as highly uniform wherever it is practiced—as a religion that would consistently manifest its core characteristics and definition regardless of location. For example, all Muslims are expected to follow the Five Pillars of Islam: making a declaration of faith, saying prayers five times a day, performing acts of charity, fasting during the holy month of Ramadan, and undertaking a pilgrimage to Mecca. In addition, all Muslims revere the authority of the Quran and the Prophet Muhammad. But on the local level, Muslims frequently expand these formal borders and develop modes of popular expression that may include distinctive devotional practices, life-cycle rituals, marriage customs, ritual clothing, and forms of veiling.

Awareness of the ways in which Muslim life and religious practice vary locally can offer an important insight to an anthropologist conducting research or to anyone seeking to build relationships across religious boundaries. The examples that follow illustrate the possibilities for local variation within a religious tradition that is often assumed to be universal in its expressions.

A Muslim Saint Shrine Across India, certain popular expressions of Islam push the boundaries of what many people would consider traditional Islam. One example is Husain Tekri, a Muslim saint shrine, or *dargah*, named in memory of the martyred grandson of the Prophet Muhammad. (A **martyr** is a person who sacrifices his or her life for the sake of his or her religion.) Pilgrims from across northern India come to this shrine to remember Husain Tekri, to venerate the Muslim saints, and to participate in healing rituals. (A **saint** is an individual considered exceptionally close to God who is then exalted after death.) Husain Tekri is part of the religious healing circuit of northern India

martyr: A person who sacrifices his or her life for the sake of his or her religion.

saint: An individual considered exceptionally close to God and who is then exalted after death.

Hindu and Muslim pilgrims at the Husain Tekri shrine in northern India breathe in incense to access the healing powers of the shrine.

along which both Hindu and Muslim pilgrims travel as they seek the saint or deity with the specific power to cure their ills.

Pilgrims to Husain Tekri may stay for a day or settle in nearby lodges and remain for days, months, or a year. They come in search of healing from suffering, illness, and financial ruin and for relief from the presence of evil spirits (*haziri*). The main daily ritual activity is the burning and distribution of *loban*—rocklike chunks of incense sold at the shrine and thrown onto red-hot coals eight times a day. As the white smoke of *loban* billows from the braziers, pilgrims—both men and women—are engulfed in the cloud, breathe in the smoke, symbolically consume the *loban*, and absorb its potency. Through pilgrimage and the ritual consumption of *loban*, pilgrims access the healing powers of the shrine. There, they believe, the power and mercy of the martyred Husain and his family enable them to escape their sick bodies, their mental anguish, and the malevolent spirits possessing them.

Surprisingly, pilgrims to the shrine of Husain Tekri are of many religious backgrounds, not only Muslim but also Hindu, Sikh, and Jain. Seeking healing across religious lines is actually a common occurrence in many parts of India, as pilgrims of various faiths try multiple religious systems to find the most successful means of healing, especially for illnesses beyond the powers of mainstream medicine (Bellamy 2011; Flueckiger 2006).

Amma's Healing Room Also in India, another local practice involves the healing powers of just one individual: a woman named Amma. In a small courtyard in the southern Indian city of Hyderabad, this Muslim healer meets forty or fifty patients a day. They come to her for healing from all manner of mental, spiritual, and physical illnesses brought on by evil spirits and forces.

As at the saint shrine of Husain Tekri, people of many faiths come to Amma—Hindus, Muslims, even a few Christians—directed by word of mouth or drawn to her healing room by the green flag of a saint shrine flying above the courtyard. They come to be cured of illnesses that seem beyond the power of their medical doctors or that require treatments beyond their financial means. At a low table in her healing room, surrounded by dozens of patients and disciples, Amma listens to each patient's problems and writes healing charms and remedies (such as verses from the Quran, numbers, or names of God) on an amulet, often a small fabric pouch or metal box hung on the right upper arm or around the neck for spiritual protection.

Amma's healing room crosses seemingly rigid boundaries of religious categories. In one sense, it does so in terms of the ease and comfort with which practitioners of various faiths seek healing in the same place. In another sense, it does so because a female Muslim healer takes a position of spiritual leadership that in Islam would usually be reserved for men (Flueckiger 2006).

Amma (*right*), a Muslim healer, in Hyderabad, India, writes out charms and remedies at her healing table for pilgrims afflicted by mental, spiritual, and physical illnesses.

The examples above suggest that what are often considered clearly defined, universally uniform, and consistent world religions actually can be flexible and innovative at the local level. Certainly the pilgrims of Husain Tekri and the visitors to Amma's healing room consider their practices to be mainstream local religious activity. From an anthropological perspective, such local expressions of religion are no less complete, meaningful, or true than those taught in the most elite Muslim madrassa, Buddhist monastery, or Christian school of theology.

What Tools Do Anthropologists Use to Understand How Religion Works?

Anthropologists have developed a set of key insights about how religion works that serve as a toolkit for understanding religion as we experience it in our fieldwork. These concepts may prove useful to you in thinking about religion in your own life and in your community, nation, and the world.

Anthropological theories of religion have been deeply influenced by the ideas of nineteenth- and twentieth-century social scientists Émile Durkheim, Karl Marx, and Max Weber. All three examined the connection between religion and the political and economic upheavals of their time: an Industrial Revolution that spurred massive shifts in land tenure patterns throughout western Europe; large-scale rural-to-urban migration; and high levels of unemployment, poverty, and disease. Through their writing, Durkheim, Marx, and Weber reshaped the study of religion, moving from the theological and cosmological orientation that dominated pre-twentieth-century European and North American thinking to focus on the role of religion in society. These thinkers inspired generations of anthropologists who have expanded and refined their theories.

Émile Durkheim: The Sacred and the Profane

Émile Durkheim (1858–1917) was a French sociologist who explored ideas of the **sacred** (holy) and the **profane** (unholy), as well as the practical effects of religious **ritual**. His work in these areas has provided key analytical tools for social scientists seeking to understand common elements in different religious movements and the practical application of religious ideas in the social life of religious adherents.

Developing the notion of a fundamental dichotomy between sacred and profane, Durkheim defined religion as "a unified system of beliefs and practices relative to sacred things, that is to say, things set apart and forbidden—beliefs and practices which unite into one single moral community called a Church, all those who adhere to them" ([1912] 1965, 62). Durkheim saw religion as ultimately social—something practiced with others—not private or individual. Through the collective action of religious ritual, group members reaffirm, clarify, and define for one another what is sacred and what is profane. Durkheim's famous study *Elementary Forms of Religious Life* (1912) examined the religious beliefs and practices of indigenous Australians, which he and others believed to be the most primitive culture of the time and, thus, closest to religion's original forms. The indigenous "elementary" religious beliefs and practices, he believed, could reveal the most basic elements of religions and shed light on religion's evolution into present forms.

As western European societies experienced radical transformations in the late nineteenth and early twentieth centuries, Durkheim turned to the rising problem of *anomie*—an alienation that individuals experience when faced with physical dislocation and the disruption of social networks and group values. He wondered how society would overcome this crisis and reestablish its essential cohesion. Durkheim argued that religion, particularly religious ritual, plays a crucial role in combating anomie and addressing larger social dynamics of alienation and dislocation by creating social solidarity, cohesion, and stability. He saw religion as the glue that holds together society's many different pieces. Through ritual, Durkheim believed, society is able to regenerate its sense of social solidarity and connection. Ritual defines and reinforces collective ideas of the sacred and profane. Thus, through ritual, the community's sense of cosmic order is reaffirmed, its social solidarity is regenerated, and the group's continued survival and growth are ensured.

sacred: Anything that is considered holy.

profane: Anything that is considered unholy.

ritual: An act or series of acts regularly repeated over years or generations that embody the beliefs of a group of people and create a sense of continuity and belonging.

French sociologist Émile Durkheim.

Durkheim's work has influenced many anthropologists who have explored the role of ritual in religions and in the wider society. As we will see, the focus on how religion is lived out daily and enacted through ritual has become a cornerstone of the anthropological approach to the study of religion.

Religion and Ritual

Anthropologists of religion have paid particular attention to the role of ritual. They are aware that religion is not so much talked about as it is *performed* in public displays, rites, and rituals—not so much thought about as *danced* and *sung*. Rituals embody the beliefs, passions, and sense of solidarity of a group of people. They make beliefs come alive. When performed repeatedly over years and generations, rituals, as Durkheim suggested, create a sense of continuity and belonging that defines a group and regenerates its sense of solidarity, history, purpose, and meaning.

Rites of Passage French ethnographer and folklorist Arnold van Gennep (1873–1957) first theorized a category of ritual called **rites of passage** that enacts a change of status from one life stage to another, either for an individual or for a group (van Gennep 1908). Religious rites of passage are life-transition rituals marking moments of intense change, such as birth, coming of age, marriage, and death.

Audrey Richards (1899–1984), a pioneering British woman in early male-dominated British anthropology, observed and recorded one such rite of passage in 1931 among the Bemba people of Zambia, Central Africa. Their elaborate ritual, called the *chisungu*—a coming-of-age ceremony for young teenage

rite of passage: A category of ritual that enacts a change of status from one life stage to another, either for an individual or for a group.

(*left*) Anthropologist Audrey Richards at work in Zambia, ca. 1931. (*right*) Girls kneeling during the *chisungu*, a coming-of-age initiation ceremony among the Bemba people of Zambia. Have you experienced a coming-of-age ritual or other rite of passage?

MAP 15.1
Zambia

liminality: One stage in a rite of passage during which a ritual participant experiences a period of outsiderhood, set apart from normal society, that is key to achieving a new perspective on the past, future, and current community.

communitas: A sense of camaraderie, a common vision of what constitutes a good life, and a commitment to take social action to move toward achieving this vision that is shaped by the common experience of rites of passage.

women after first menstruation and in preparation for marriage—was danced in eighteen separate ceremonies over one month in a ritual hut and the surrounding bush. Over fifty special *chisungu* songs and forty different pottery emblems were involved. The *chisungu*, exclusively a women's ritual, was performed to provide magical protection to the girl and her family from the physical dangers of puberty and the magical dangers associated with the first act of intercourse in legal marriage. Within the rituals, older women also passed down the songs, sacred stories, sacred teachings, and secret lore of the Bemba womanhood, marking a clear change of status within the tribe from girl to woman (Richards 1956).

Victor Turner (1920–1983) built on Richards's pioneering work to explore why rituals and rites of passage are so powerful across religions and cultures. Drawing on his own research in Africa and on extensive comparison of cross-cultural data, Turner theorized that the power of ritual comes from the drama contained within it, in which the normal structure of social life is symbolically dissolved and reconstituted. He identified three primary stages in all rites of passage. First, the individual experiences *separation*—physically, psychologically, or symbolically—from the normal, day-to-day activities of the group. This may involve going to a special ritual place, wearing special clothing, or performing actions such as shaving one's head. The second stage, **liminality**, involves a period of outsiderhood during which the ritual participant is set apart from normal society, existing on the margins of everyday life. From this position the individual can gain a new perspective on the past, the present, or the future and thereby experience a new relationship to the community. The final ritual stage, *reaggregation* or *reincorporation*, returns the individual to everyday life and reintegrates him or her into the ritual community, transformed by the experience of liminality and endowed with a deeper sense of meaning, purpose, and connection to the larger group (Turner 1969).

Turner believed that all humans experience these rites of passage and that the experiences shape their perceptions of themselves and their community. Through them, he asserted, humans develop **communitas**: a sense of camaraderie, a common vision of what constitutes the good life, and perhaps most important, a commitment to take social action to move toward achieving this vision. Turner felt that the universal practice and experience of ritual reveals at the root of human existence an underlying desire for community and connection. Based on his cross-cultural investigation of the practice of rituals and rites of passage, Turner suggested that at the center of all human relationships there is a deep longing for shared meaning and connection, not a desire for self-preservation or material gain.

Have you experienced a rite of passage such as van Gennep, Richards, and Turner describe? Perhaps you have traversed these ritual stages of separation,

liminality, and reincorporation at some point in your life—at a coming-of-age ceremony in your own religious tradition, or at a wedding or funeral. If so, can you recall the feeling as you put aside the mundane rhythms of everyday life, entered a liminal space set apart from normal society (perhaps in a church, synagogue, mosque, temple, gurdwara, wedding hall, or funeral parlor set aside for sacred rituals), and then reentered the regular flow of the world with a new outlook or thinking a bit more deeply about the meaning of life? Perhaps, then, you also have an idea of the sense of communitas that Turner suggests emerges from these common experiences that all humans share at some point in their lives.

Pilgrimage Turner applied his thinking about rites of passage to the study of religious pilgrimage, which he considered to be a unique form of religious ritual. Pilgrimage rituals, like those to Muslim saint shrines in northern India discussed earlier, exist in religions around the world. In a **pilgrimage**, adherents travel to sacred places as a sign of devotion and in search of transformation and enlightenment. For example, all Muslims are obliged to perform, if life circumstances allow,

Pilgrims circumambulate the Kaaba in Al Masjid al-Haram, the most sacred mosque in Islam, during the *hajj*, in Mecca, Saudi Arabia.

pilgrimage: A religious journey to a sacred place as a sign of devotion and in search of transformation and enlightenment.

the *hajj* pilgrimage to Mecca. Jews, Christians, and Muslims all have pilgrimage sites in Jerusalem. Many Hindus travel to the holy city of Varanasi (Benares) to bathe in the Ganges River. Daoists climb Mount Tai in eastern China. The pilgrimage journey, Turner suggested, involves the same process of separation, liminality, and reincorporation associated with other rites of passage. Similarly, pilgrimage creates a shared sense of communitas among those who undertake the journey, even if years or entire generations separate the pilgrimages.

For Turner (1969), life in society is a process of becoming, not being; it is a process of change. He maintained that rituals, pilgrimages, celebrations, and even theatrical performances facilitate this process and have the potential to initiate and foster change, not only in the individual but in the larger culture as well.

"The Abominations of Leviticus" The British anthropologist Mary Douglas (1921–2007), like Richards and Turner, began her studies of ritual in Africa. Subsequently, she applied her insights to Western cultures by drawing parallels between the ceremonies and ritual practices of African cultures and those of Christianity and Judaism. In *Purity and Danger* (1966), Douglas explored the ways that Durkheim's notions of sacred and profane—for Douglas, purity and danger—are deeply embedded in Western traditions.

In a famous chapter called "The Abominations of Leviticus," she examined the ritual practices of Jewish dietary laws. She approached this study with the following questions: Why are some animals considered clean and others unclean in God's eyes, according to the Book of Leviticus in the Hebrew scriptures? Do these practices reflect medical concerns about eating pork that might be infected by trichinosis? Do they reflect ethical guidelines about the treatment of animals? Are they arbitrary religious prescriptions? After concluding her study, Douglas argued instead that these codes reflect a deep-seated desire for order in the midst of the social chaos that confronted the Hebrew people of that time.

Historically, in the period when the dietary codes were written, the Hebrew people struggled with their return from captivity and exile. The codes helped define the community and make clear who was a Jew and who was not. In this way, they protected the community from the dangers of foreign influence. How could they create order out of chaos? And how could they keep God's commandments constantly in mind? The dietary laws, Douglas suggested, are a command to be holy. Thus, they became a metaphor of holiness. Keeping the dietary laws daily became a ritualized meditation—a reminder of the holiness of God, who is always present in their lives.

Douglas maintained that keeping the Jewish dietary laws plays the same role today. The ritual rules of dietary discipline serve as a regular reminder of who God is and who the individual is in relationship to God. These rituals are a kind of meditative practice that regularizes moments of liminality in the course of daily life. Are there similar practices or requirements in your religious tradition that serve as a reminder, a command to be holy? Do you observe religious dietary restrictions? Do you wear certain clothes or jewelry? Do you wear a cross or a bindi or a hijab? Do you style your hair in a certain way? Are you called to daily prayer during the day or at night? Do you say a prayer before meals? If you answer yes to any of these questions, perhaps you can personally assess Douglas's insights. And perhaps you have a sense of the power that ritual action can hold in a person's or a group's daily life.

Karl Marx: Religion as "the Opiate of the Masses"

Karl Marx (1818–1883) was a German political philosopher. He is primarily known for his *Communist Manifesto* (with Friedrich Engels, 1848) and *Capital* (1867), a radical critique of capitalist economics emerging in western Europe in the nineteenth century (see Chapter 11). However, Marx was also highly critical of the role of religion in society, famously calling religion "the opiate of the masses" (Marx and Engels 1957). What did he mean?

German political philosopher Karl Marx.

In a time of economic upheaval and intensifying social stratification, Marx warned that religion was like a narcotic: It dulled people's pain so they did not realize how serious the situation was. Religion, Marx argued, played a key role in keeping the proletariat—the working poor—from engaging in the revolutionary social change that he believed was needed to improve their situation.

Marx's statement that religion is "the opiate of the masses" fits within his larger social analysis. He believed that throughout human history, economic realities have formed the foundation of social life and have generated society's primary dynamics, including class stratification and class struggle. He called this economic reality the "base." In his view, the other institutions of culture (including family, government, arts, and religion) arise from and are shaped by economic reality and the deep tensions of economic inequality and class struggle.

The role of these institutions, including religion, according to Marx, is to mask the material conditions and exploitation at the economic base and to contain—or provide a controlled release for—the tensions generated by class difference and class conflict. Religion, which Marx also called "the sigh of the oppressed," could provide to the downtrodden a sense of consolation that the sufferings of this life would end and be rewarded in heaven, thereby offering divine justification for the economic status quo. In Marx's view, religion provides an opiate—a painkiller—to undermine the masses' impulses to resist exploitation and change the social order.

Marx's overall focus on economics and power has pushed anthropologists to consider the relationship between religion and power. Contemporary studies move beyond Marx's idea that religion is merely an illusion that blinds people to economic realities. Studies like those of Adam Chau (2006), Robin Root

(2009), and Charlene Floyd (1996) (considered later in this chapter), while not drawing directly on Marxist theory, examine how religion can play a complex role in systems of power—both by exercising power through economic resources and the mobilization of religious personnel, and by resisting systems of oppression through alternative ideas, symbols, and resources.

Religion and Cultural Materialism Anthropologist Marvin Harris (1927–2001) built on Marx's analysis of the base, or infrastructure, and the way in which the material conditions of a society shape its other components. Harris's theory of **cultural materialism** argued that material conditions, including technology and the environment, determine patterns of social organization. In this view, human culture is a response to the practical problems of earthly existence. In *Cows, Pigs, Wars, & Witches* (1974), Harris turned this perspective toward many perplexing questions of why humans behave in certain ways—including why Hindus venerate the cow, Jews and Muslims abstain from eating pork, and some people believe in witches. Harris proposed that these practices might have developed in response to very practical problems as people sought to adapt to the natural environment.

Have you ever wondered why cows are considered sacred in India? Harris approached this question not through personal immersion in the worldviews of Indian Hindus, but rather by exploring larger environmental forces—the cultural ecology—that might promote this cultural practice. If you visit India you will find zebu cows—a scrawny, large-humped cattle species found in Africa and Asia—wandering freely about city streets and rural areas. These cows randomly eat food from market stalls, graze on sidewalk shrubs, and defecate indiscriminately. In a country with deep pockets of poverty and malnutrition, why are these cows left to roam and not slaughtered for nutritious, protein-rich dinner beefsteak?

Eating beef is prohibited in Hinduism, as is eating all meat. The cow, in Harris's view, became a symbolic representation of *ahimsa*—the practice of non-violence and respect for the unity of all life that is key to Hinduism, Buddhism, and Jainism. How this tradition began is unclear, but today the holy mother cow is a symbol of health and abundance, and its image appears throughout Indian culture in media such as posters, movies, and carvings. The symbol also has a literal presence on streets and in fields.

Harris suggests that religious prohibitions protecting the cow have overwhelming practical applications in a culture that relies on agricultural production. Cows, after all, produce calves that grow up to be oxen, which Harris calls the tractor, thresher, and family car of the Indian agricultural system. Without an ox, a family has no way of planting, harvesting, preparing, or transporting its crops. Without an ox, a family loses the capacity to farm and eventually loses its land. Cows also produce vast quantities of dung, almost all of which can be recycled into

cultural materialism: A theory that argues that material conditions, including technology, determine patterns of social organization, including religious principles.

MAP 15.2
India

A sacred cow lies unperturbed and undisturbed in a busy intersection of Varanasi, India. Why is the cow sacred in India?

fertilizer and cooking fuel. Religious dedication to *ahimsa* protects this resource even under the most difficult economic conditions. No matter how hungry the family may be in one season, keeping the cow alive ensures long-term survival.

For Harris, religiously based practices that appear to function in opposition to sound nutritional practices or economic development strategies may in fact be very rational cultural adaptations to the surrounding ecology. In India, the cow is extraordinarily useful. Its protection, especially during difficult economic times, may be essential to the long-term stability and survival of the Indian people and culture.

Think about any other religion, perhaps one you already have an affiliation with. Can you apply the perspectives of Marvin Harris's cultural materialism to any of its practices and beliefs? Can you begin to imagine how certain material conditions of everyday life may have shaped patterns of religious belief and practice?

Max Weber: The Protestant Ethic and Secularization

Max Weber (1864–1920), a German sociologist, philosopher, and economist, considered religious ideas to be a key for understanding the unique development of

German sociologist and philosopher Max Weber.

societies worldwide and the rise of industrial capitalism, particularly in western Europe. Why, he asked, did this highly rationalized, systematized, and industrial form of capitalism emerge in Europe and not in another part of the world?

Unlike Marx, who considered that economics ultimately shapes society, Weber believed that ideas, including religious ideas, can be equally powerful. His book *Sociology of Religion* (1920) was the first sociological attempt to compare the world's religions. In it, Weber suggested that Asian religious beliefs and ethical systems had stood in the way of capitalist economic growth there and had kept Asian economies from developing along the western European path. China, India, and other cultures had developed aspects of modern capitalism even earlier than western Europe did; but without a certain kind of ideological support, a more advanced capitalism had not evolved in Asia. Weber suggested that economic innovations alone could not explain the different paths.

In *The Protestant Ethic and the Spirit of Capitalism* (1905), Weber suggested that the ascetic values of self-denial and self-discipline that developed in western European Protestantism provided the ethic that was necessary for capitalism to flourish. Certain Protestant sects, including Calvinists, felt that it was important to express their religious beliefs and values in a daily lifestyle of thrift, discipline, and hard work. In these ideas, Weber found evidence of the ethical and psychological framework necessary for the success of industrial capitalism. He did not dismiss the role of economics in shaping the social dynamics of western Europe, but he argued that ideas, including religious ideas, may at times equally influence the economic direction of a society.

Also key to the development of Western capitalism, according to Weber, was an increasing systematization and rationalization of religious ideas. As Western Christianity evolved, this increasing rationality brought a decline of practices based on tradition, ritual, and magic. Weber saw these developments echoed in society at large: Rationalization led to bureaucracies with clear, intellectual, and systematized rules that replaced tradition, sentiment, and charisma as the operating system in social institutions. Weber imagined an evolution of rationalization in religion that led from (1) traditional religion based on magic and led by shamans to (2) charismatic religion based on the persuasive power of prophets such as Buddha, Jesus, and Moses and, finally, to (3) rational religion based on legal codes of conduct, bureaucratic structures, and formally trained religious leaders. He anticipated that this evolutionary process would be almost inevitable. But he warned that as society became more rationalized, it also risked becoming more secular—less religious—and thus losing the very spirit that had driven its success and development.

Scholars have debated Weber's secularization thesis for many years (Asad 1993; Berger 1999; Casanova 1994; Stark and Bainbridge 1985). Certainly in western Europe today, religious identification among native-born residents continues to sink to record lows. In contrast, the United States stands as a striking exception to this pattern in industrialized countries, as religious beliefs and practices remain strong in both the native-born and the immigrant populations. Polls consistently show that nearly 90 percent of the U.S. population believe in God, and about 80 percent identify with a particular religion (Pew Forum on Religion & Public Life 2015). Even the assumed separation of church and state in the United States is far from absolute. Battles continue over the teaching of evolution in the science curriculums of public schools, fans at public high school football games in Texas rise to recite the Christian Lord's Prayer, and crowds at New York's Yankee Stadium stand during the seventh-inning stretch for a moment of silence to remember those serving in the U.S. military and then sing "God Bless America." In these instances, religious sentiments infuse public and political life, and public rituals of civil society take on sacred status (Bellah 1980).

Moreover, widespread revivals of religious ideas, organizations, and movements around the world in the face of increasing modernization—and at times in resistance to the homogenizing influences of globalization and Western culture—provide additional evidence that modernization does not always lead to secularization.

Shamanism

Throughout much of human history, the religious needs of human communities have been served by **shamans**—part-time religious practitioners with special abilities to connect individuals with supernatural powers or beings. More formal religious organizations with trained specialists and elaborate moral rules and ritual practices are fairly recent in human history, spanning 2,000 to 3,000 years at most with the rise of Hinduism, Buddhism, Judaism, Christianity, and Islam. The term *shaman* derives from the name given to healing specialists among the seminomadic people of Siberia, but it has since been applied to healers, spiritualists, witches, and witch doctors in cultures worldwide.

Shamans live as part of the local community, participating in daily activities and work, but are called on at times to perform special rituals and ceremonies. They often gain their powers through special training or experience, passing through a journey or test of spirit such as illness, isolation, physical pain, or an emotional ordeal. Through rituals involving prayers, meditation, songs, dance, pain, or drugs, shamans enter a trance, often at will. While entranced, they implore deities and powers to take action or to provide special knowledge and power that may assist individuals or the community at large: healing, medicinal advice, personal guidance, protection from illness or other attack, fortune telling, and control over the weather.

shamans: Part-time religious practitioners with special abilities to connect individuals with supernatural powers or beings.

MAP 15.3
South Korea

Anthropologist Laurel Kendall studied both the public and private rituals of women shamans in a small rural community in South Korea. In the opening scene of her book, *Shamans, Housewives, and Other Restless Spirits* (1985), Kendall describes a *kut*—a public shamanistic ritual. This event was officiated by several women shamans who, through a dramatic performance involving costumes, music, dances, and trancelike states, called upon local gods, deceased ancestors, and related spirits, including warriors and generals. The shamans pleaded, cajoled, and bribed them to help those in the present world address problems with troublesome children, drunken husbands, economic struggles, illness, and other maladies and fight off threats by meddling ghosts and spirits. Each shaman invoked certain deities with whom she had developed a special relationship, and they in turn inhabited her during the ritual trances, dances, songs, and mediation. During such events, deities often weep, lament, and console the living through the words and actions of the shamans.

Kendall notes that public shamanistic rituals represent a professionalization of Korean household religion. Whereas trained and initiated shamans lead public rituals, in the home untrained and uninitiated women frequently engage the same deities and spirits on behalf of their husbands and children in an attempt to diagnose and heal the family's ills—from disease to crop failure. In this Korean household religion—a complex blend of elements of Buddhism, Daoism, and Confucianism—both shamans and housewives, Kendall argues, take on the role not only of ritual specialists but also of creators of meaning for their families and communities (De Vos 1987; Kendall 1985, 1988; Spencer 1987).

Although the role of the shaman is generally associated with small agricultural or seminomadic societies, shamans today often relocate to contemporary urban settings along with their immigrant communities. A variation of the shaman role also occurs in more formal religious organizations, as trained religious specialists there seek to (1) intervene with their deities on behalf of adherents or (2) assist adherents in practices of prayer and meditation through which they seek healing or guidance.

Religion and Magic

Anthropology has a long history of studying cultures where magic is practiced and witches are real. **Magic** involves the use of spells, incantations, words, and actions in an attempt to compel supernatural forces to act in certain ways, whether for good or for evil. Magic is part of cultural practices in every part of the world. And religion, almost everywhere, contains some components of magic.

In *The Golden Bough* (1890), anthropologist James Frazer (1854–1941) distinguishes between imitative magic and contagious magic. **Imitative magic** involves a performance that imitates the desired result, perhaps manipulating a doll or some other representation of the target of magic in the belief that

magic: The use of spells, incantations, words, and actions in an attempt to compel supernatural forces to act in certain ways, whether for good or for evil.

imitative magic: A ritual performance that achieves efficacy by imitating the desired magical result.

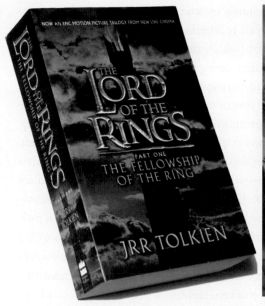

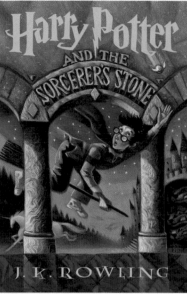

The success of J. R. R. Tolkien's *Lord of the Rings* trilogy and J. K. Rowling's *Harry Potter* series has revealed a vast appetite in Western culture for magic, witches, and wizards, at least in their fantastical literary and cinematic form.

the action will have direct imitative effect. **Contagious magic** centers on the belief that certain materials—perhaps clothing, hair, fingernails, teeth—that have come into contact with one person carry a magical connection that allows power to be transferred from person to person.

In this section we consider the work of E. E. Evans-Pritchard, who sought to understand witchcraft and magic in East Africa; Paul Stoller, who apprenticed with a sorcerer in West Africa; and George Gmelch, who traces the belief in magic in contemporary U.S. society.

contagious magic: Ritual words or performances that achieve efficacy as certain materials that come into contact with one person carry a magical connection that allows power to be transferred from person to person.

E. E. Evans-Pritchard: Rethinking the Logic of Magic

E. E. Evans-Pritchard (1902–1973), a British anthropologist who conducted extensive fieldwork in Africa's southern Sudan region, challenged Weber's rationalization thesis that assumed modernization and the rise of science would bring increasing rationality in a culture and its religious practices, thereby leading to a decrease in practices of magic. Instead, Evans-Pritchard's research among the tribal Azande people from 1926 to 1930 found that their use of magic was not an irrational expression but a component of a highly organized, rational, and logical system of thought that complemented science in understanding the way the world works.

In *Witchcraft, Oracles and Magic among the Azande* (1937), Evans-Pritchard describes in careful detail the elaborate religious system of the Azande in which magic, witchcraft, and poison oracles are central elements in daily life and conversation. The Azande trace all misfortunes to witchcraft. Their witchcraft does not involve rituals, spells, or medicines. Instead it is a psychic power that may be used consciously or unconsciously by a witch—a woman or a man—to cause misfortunes or death. Witchcraft is inherited from a parent, and a witch's body contains a witchcraft substance (which the Azande described to Evans-Pritchard as an oval, blackish swelling or bag near the liver) that cannot be detected during life but can be found during an autopsy.

Magic among the Azande, in contrast to witchcraft, is performed consciously through rites, spells, the preparation of herbal medicines, and other magical techniques. Magic has its own power and can be used to combat witchcraft. If people perceive that magic is being deployed against them, they may consult a witch doctor—almost always a man—who will use magic and medicines to try to thwart the work of the witch. Witch doctors are formally taught the knowledge of rituals and medicines as they are initiated into what amounts to a professional association. In the most extreme cases—those involving matters of life and death, and those that have ended up in court—the witch doctor may consult a poison oracle. As described to Evans-Pritchard, the poison oracle is created by administering a dose of poison to a chicken, and its subsequent death or recovery exposes the innocence or guilt of the accused witch. Poison oracles may also be used to ascertain answers to questions posed by the witch doctor to resolve the case. The witch identified as the source of the evil witchcraft is then asked to cease the witchcraft but may claim ignorance and proceed to plead with his or her own stomach—the location of the witchcraft in the body—to stop.

Witchcraft, Oracles and Magic among the Azande is considered one of the outstanding works of anthropology in the twentieth century. It not only stands as an exquisitely detailed ethnography but also provides the basis for rethinking the role of magic in society. Evans-Pritchard challenges the ethnocentric views of Western scholars who dismiss magical practices as irrational and illogical when compared to modern, rational, Western scientific strategies for accumulating knowledge of the external world. He contends instead that Azande ideas that may seem exotic, strange, and irrational to Europeans in actuality formed consistent, comprehensive, and rational systems of thought within the context of the Azande's daily lives and social structures.

Among the Azande, magic explained things that did not make sense otherwise, particularly the experience of misfortune; it provided an alternative theory of causation that supplemented the theory of natural causation. Magic helped explain what could not be explained by scientific study of nature. Evans-Pritchard presented the case of a wooden granary structure that collapsed and injured several people seated underneath it. Science could explain how insects had damaged the wood, which led to the collapse. But science could not explain the misfortune of why the people who were injured were sitting in a particular location at a particular time. For the Azande, witchcraft and magic could explain the misfortune.

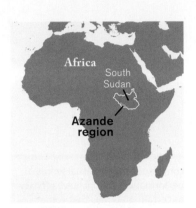

MAP 15.4
Azande region, South Sudan

Evans-Pritchard argued that the Azande saw no contradiction between witchcraft and empirical knowledge. For them, witchcraft and magic provided a rational and intellectually consistent explanation for what science cannot explain. Belief in witchcraft only appears inconsistent and irrational, Evans-Pritchard chided his Western colleagues, when they are arranged like museum objects on a shelf and examined outside the context of daily life.

Paul Stoller: *In Sorcery's Shadow* In the ethnography *In Sorcery's Shadow* (1987), anthropologist Paul Stoller and his co-author Cherl Olkes extend Evans-Pritchard's commitment to respect and understand others' systems of knowledge, even when they may at first appear irrational, unreasonable, and incomprehensible. Stoller takes Evans-Pritchard's work on magic and sorcery (another term for witchcraft) to a deeper personal level through direct engagement in the beliefs and practices of those he studied.

In the late 1970s Stoller arrived in the Songhay region of the Republic of Niger, West Africa, determined to learn about the role of religion in community life there. Through intensive fieldwork covering five visits over eight years, his deep involvement in a world of magic, spirits, sorcery, and spirit possession prevalent in the Songhay and surrounding regions eventually led him to be initiated as a sorcerer's apprentice. He memorized magical incantations. He ate special foods needed for his initiation. He ingested medicinal powders and wore magical objects to protect himself from antagonistic sorcerers. And he indirectly

A sorcerer preparing a written tablet for a customer in the Songhay region of Niger.

MAP 15.5
Songhay region, Niger

participated in an attack of sorcery that temporarily paralyzed the intended victim.

Stoller's fieldwork led him to reflect on the transformative and deeply personal experience of conducting research into people's religious worlds:

> For me, respect means accepting fully beliefs and phenomena which our system of knowledge often holds preposterous. I took my teachers seriously. They *knew* that I used divination in my personal life. They *knew* that I had eaten powders to protect myself. They *knew* I wore objects to demonstrate my respect for the spirits. They *knew* I had an altar in my house over which I recited incantations. They liked the way I carried my knowledge and power and taught me more and more. (1987, 228)

His fieldwork came to an abrupt end, however, when he experienced an attack by spirits sent against him by a powerful village sorceress. Suffering the debilitating physical effects of the sorceress's attack, Stoller fled the village and West Africa, returning home to the United States to finally rid himself of the illness:

> But ethnographers can go too far. They can pursue the other's reality too hotly, crossing a line that brings them face to face with a violent reality that is no mere epistemological exercise. If they know too much, they must swear an oath of silence. If they reveal what they shouldn't, they may be murdered. (1987, 229)

Not every anthropologist apprentices with a sorcerer or is attacked by one. In this regard, Stoller's experience as an anthropologist of religion is an outlier in the field. But the anthropological commitment to long-term, in-depth participant observation brings many of us into close contact with the beliefs, practices, and emotions of those whom we study, an intimacy that often reveals the vibrant power of religion in their lives that leaves one marked by the encounter. Is it possible to comprehend someone's religious beliefs and practices without accepting that they are real—at least for the believer?

George Gmelch: Baseball Magic If reading about the work of Evans-Pritchard and Stoller leaves you relieved that you live in a Western world that relegates belief in magic to children's books and movies, research by anthropologist and former minor league baseball player George Gmelch may surprise you. It turns out that beliefs and practices of magic are not so unfamiliar in U.S. culture.

Gmelch's study of baseball in the United States (1992) explores the rituals, taboos, and sacred objects of magic that are in almost constant use. He finds that they reflect the kinds of beliefs and activities that are prevalent in all sports.

Baseball players use charms such as special clothes or jewelry. Moreover, Gmelch found, players believe that good magic is contagious. If it worked before, and if the player uses the same ritual again, perhaps the magical conditions for success can be re-created. Thus, players repeat certain actions to help them succeed: Pitchers touch the bill of their cap, wear good-luck charms, or never touch the foul line between home plate and first base when moving between the pitcher's mound and the dugout. Batters wear the same shirt or underwear, or use the same movements over and over again in the batter's box, to capture the magic of previous success.

Have you ever noticed certain ritual-like movements while watching close-ups of batters and pitchers during televised baseball games or other sporting events? Do you yourself have special charms or practices or clothes that you believe will bring you good luck during games, exams, dates, and so on? What about jewelry or ornaments?

Magic rituals, taboos, and sacred objects are used constantly in American sports. (*left*) Boston Red Sox designated hitter David Ortiz adjusts his gloves before every swing, drawing on a notion of contagious magic to bring him good luck while batting. (*right*) Former New York Mets reliever Turk Wendell's magical practices included always leaping over the baseline when walking to the mound, brushing his teeth between innings, chewing black licorice while pitching, and wearing a necklace decorated with the teeth of wild animals he had hunted and killed.

In What Ways Is Religion Both a System of Meaning and a System of Power?

Many people in Western cultures think of religion as a system of ideas and beliefs that are primarily a personal matter. In the United States, for instance, doctrines asserting the separation of church and state promote an ideal of the separation of religion from politics. But as we saw in Chapter 2, any analysis of a cultural system that focuses solely on its underlying meanings risks ignoring the ways that power is negotiated within the system and how it engages other systems of power within the culture. This observation applies to our study of religion as well.

Religion and Meaning

Building on the themes of Max Weber's *Protestant Ethic and the Spirit of Capitalism*, anthropologist Clifford Geertz (1926–2006), in his essay "Religion as a Cultural System" (1973b), suggests that religion is essentially a system of ideas surrounding a set of powerful **symbols**. Hindus, for example, consider the cow sacred because by protecting it they symbolically enact the protection of all life. Other widely recognized religious symbols include the cross for Christians, the Torah scroll for Jews, and the holy city of Mecca for Muslims. For Geertz, each symbol has deep meaning and evokes powerful emotions and motivations in the religion's followers. Why?

These symbols acquire significance far beyond the actual material they are made of. Objects made of wood, metal, rock, or paper come to represent influential explanations about what it means to be human and where humans fit in the general order of the universe. Symbols, with their deep pool of meaning, create a sense of order and resist chaos by building and reinforcing a larger worldview—a framework of ideas about what is real, what exists, and what that means.

We can see symbols at work in various religious contexts. For Christians, the bread and wine served at the communion ritual are more than actual bread and wine. They symbolically recall the death and resurrection of Jesus, the power of God to overcome death, and the promise to Jesus's followers of everlasting life beyond the suffering of this world. Communion also recalls the fellowship of all Christian believers who share in the benefits of God's sacrifice, a sense of connection with people around the world. For Jews, the Torah scroll is more than a composite of paper and ink. It represents the holy word of God as revealed through the prophets, the story of a covenant between God and the people of Israel, an agreement that in return for faithfulness God will provide liberation from captivity, the establishment of a nation of people, and abundant life. For Hindus, the cow requires veneration because it represents the Hindu practice of *ahimsa*—nonviolence toward all living things. In a practical sense, this means that no leather may enter the temple and all shoes must remain outside the temple door. Even these acts are symbolic of Hindus' belief that all life is sacred and that attention to this fact will transform the practicing individual and lead to his or her reincarnation as a more sentient being.

Geertz comments that these symbols and their underlying conceptions of reality become so matter-of-fact in the religious context, expressed in familiar

symbol: Anything that represents something else.

rituals and doctrines, that believers feel their presence helps them move beyond mundane matters and experience what is "really real." Believers may have contact with the religious world only briefly or irregularly, especially in comparison with the ordinary world that they experience every day. Yet through the power of religious symbols, they feel that the religious world is truly real. Religious practice, ritual, and symbols provide access to that ultimate and sought-after reality.

Anthropologists encounter symbols and their powerful effects in numerous areas of our field, but the use of symbols in religious belief and practice is particularly pervasive and rich. As we will consider next, as anthropologists work to analyze the ongoing vitality of religion in today's globalizing age, understanding the ways symbols are constructed and given meaning and authority will be a valuable skill for navigating an increasingly interconnected world.

Religion and Power

Anthropologist Talal Asad, in his book *Genealogies of Religion* (1993), criticizes Geertz's explanation of religion. Asad bases his inquiry on questions such as these: How did religious symbols get their power? Who or what gave them their authority? What gives religion the power and authority to have meaning in people's lives? After all, Asad asserts, symbols do not have meaning in and

authorizing process: The complex historical and social developments through which symbols are given power and meaning.

of themselves. He suggests that religion and religious symbols are actually produced through complex historical and social developments in which power and meaning are created, contested, and maintained. What historical processes have given the cross, the Torah, the *hajj*, and the cow their symbolic power? Without understanding these particular **authorizing processes**, Asad claims, we cannot understand what really makes religion work.

Asad argues that most definitions of religion are not universal. Instead, he claims, they are the creations of Western scholars based on western European ideas of what religion is and how it works—in particular, the way Christianity has developed in relationship to the state. Such scholars look for Western ideas of religion in the spiritual and ritual practices of other cultures. Asad warns that these attempts to create a universal definition impede an understanding of religion in other parts of the world. For instance, he suggests that Weber's assumptions that religions become increasingly rationalized as societies modernize and that societies become increasingly secularized as a sharper separation develops between religion and the state are rooted in the way Western Christianity has developed—not in a universal pattern that we can assume exists in religions worldwide.

In the case of Islam, religious beliefs and political power are intricately intertwined in many countries, and national governments may seek to impose a version of Islamic religious law, the Sharia, through mechanisms of the state. Asad suggests that in these cases, Western understandings of the essential nature of religion that assume increasing secularization and separation of church and state may lead scholars and casual observers to dismiss other expressions of religion as irrational and backward. Instead, these other religious expressions are simply different—outside the normative definition of religion established in Western scholarship. Asad states that scholars of religion must beware the power of universal definitions to obscure local realities. They must carefully examine local expressions of religion, how those expressions developed over time, and what has given those expressions the power and authority to be so meaningful to believers (Asad 1993).

As you begin to think like an anthropologist of religion, try to examine religious symbols from the perspectives of both Geertz and Asad. As you consider religious symbols in the culture around you—perhaps in your own religious tradition—can you begin to appreciate the power of symbols to evoke intense emotions and motivations that put believers in touch with what feels "really real"? Can you begin to consider the ways in which particular symbols have been constructed, given meaning, and authorized through particular historical and cultural processes? The "Your Turn" exercise on page 606 will give you an opportunity to transform these new insights into analytical tools.

Blurring the Boundaries between Meaning and Power

The work of both Geertz and Asad has influenced contemporary anthropological research on religion. We now consider local examples of religious activities and organizations in which meaning and power are intertwined and the boundary between religion and other social systems of power is not rigid. As we consider these studies, can you begin to see how analyses of both meaning and power are essential in achieving a comprehensive picture of the role of religion in culture?

China's Religious Revival Since the 1990s, a religious revival has been spreading across China in urban and rural areas. After years of attempts by the Chinese government to eradicate religious practices, especially popular folk religious activities, today the Chinese population is rebuilding temples, restoring graves, and re-creating religious festivals. The Chinese state officially recognizes Buddhism, Daoism, Protestant Christianity, Catholicism, and Islam, and all are experiencing growth and revitalization. However, the most vibrant expansion of religious activity is among practitioners of Chinese popular religion—a tradition that incorporates elements of Buddhism, Daoism, and the veneration of family and village ancestors.

MAP 15.6
Shaanbei

The Black Dragon King Temple complex in Shaanbei, China, is the center of one such revival. Formerly a small, isolated shrine in the early 1980s, it is now a large temple complex with many buildings and year-round activity. The temple has become a catalyst for religious revival, the revival of folk cultural traditions, and the development of community economic activity. It also serves as a site for negotiating the relationships among popular religion, the Chinese state, and the surrounding rural agricultural society.

Village religious life throughout China today includes elaborate public funerals, weddings, grave sweeping, the burning of spirit paper money for ancestors, the avoidance of hungry ghosts (ancestors who have no family looking after them), and the seeking of favor from a wide variety of deities. Each village has at least one god, sometimes more, and the area's deities are ranked according to their *ling*, or magical efficacy (in other words, how well they are able to get the job done). People pray to these gods for practical benefits in times of trouble, to resolve conflicts, to protect the souls of sick children, to heal illnesses and maladies, to offer advice on matters ranging from matchmaking to business dealings, and to send rain in times of drought.

The village temples become the central location for praying, presenting offerings, buying incense and spirit paper money, performing public rituals, and hosting religious festivals. Villagers may pray to many gods—any they think may be able to help them. Visiting different temples and shrines in several villages is quite common; people believe this practice will not incite the wrath of jealous gods as long as individuals offer proper thanks when requests are successfully granted and problems resolved.

The revival of popular religious life has generated activities well beyond the temple. Temple festivals have spurred the rebirth of opera performances, storytelling, folk dances, and a wide variety of other folk cultural traditions. China's overall economic growth translates into increased donations as both local worshippers and visiting pilgrims contribute to temple renovations, sponsor rituals and festivals, and make gifts to honor the gods. Temple activities in turn generate income for the entire community.

Key to the Black Dragon King Temple's success is an active and effective temple leadership committee. At its head is Lao Wang, a visionary, energetic, and enterprising local resident. The temple association builds and maintains the temple and its structures, manages its funds, stages festivals, and negotiates with other social organizations and players. In addition, the temple leadership channels a portion of its economic proceeds to the construction of better roads, irrigation systems, and schools in the community. Such civic engagement has elevated the temple leaders' position in community affairs. In today's China, some people become part of the local elite by getting rich, whereas others are elevated through moral leadership. In this atmosphere, the temple leadership's economic activities and political influence have earned them status as part of the local elite. Through the success of their religious organization, the temple association—and particularly Lao Wang—has become the most influential nongovernmental organization in the area, a powerful civic organization operating completely outside the realm of the Chinese state.

The experience of the Black Dragon King Temple reveals the surprising power of popular religion in contemporary China. Rural religious communities are carving out spaces of civic activity apart from the operations of the Chinese government, reviving and re-creating rural traditions in the face of modernization and urbanization throughout China. They are reasserting and negotiating avenues of autonomy in what has been a highly centralized political system (Chau 2006; Guest 2003).

Religion and Revolution in Mexico Religion scholar Charlene Floyd's (1996) research on the role of the Catholic Church in a revolutionary movement in the Chiapas region of southern Mexico provides another example of how meaning and power are expressed in religion. Chiapas is one of the poorest states in Mexico, where most children do not finish primary school and many homes have no running water. The people are poor, but the land is rich: It holds large reserves of oil and natural gas, provides most of the country's hydroelectric power, and supports half of its coffee crop. The tension between an impoverished people on the one hand and rich natural resources extracted by Mexico's state and corporations on the other has not always found a smooth resolution.

MAP 15.7
Chiapas region, Mexico

Crowds attend the Black Dragon King Temple annual festival in rural Shaanbei, China. How would anthropologists examine the intersection of religion with other systems of power in this scene?

In the early hours of January 1, 1994, some of the poor people of Chiapas, calling themselves "Zapatistas" (after the Mexican revolutionary Emiliano Zapata), covered their faces with bandanas and ski masks, marched into four Chiapas cities, and declared in a dramatic manifesto, "Today we say enough is enough!" Stunned by the uprising, the Mexican government and the economic leaders of Chiapas quickly accused the Catholic Church of inciting the rebellion. In particular, they blamed one of the bishops of Chiapas, Samuel Ruiz García, and his *catequistas*, or lay teachers. But how could a Catholic bishop and a group of lay teachers be accused of inciting a rebellion? Did they actually do so? In considering these questions, we must explore the Church's role in Mexican society.

Today 90 percent of Mexicans identify themselves as Catholic, a faith that has been a key component of Mexican national identity ever since Spanish colonizers forcibly imported it 500 years ago. In certain periods of Mexican history, religion and politics have been closely aligned. For example, a Catholic priest, Father Miguel Hidalgo y Costilla, is credited with providing the initial spark for the Mexican independence movement in 1810. Calling on the name of Mexico's

THE SOCIAL LIFE OF THINGS
Balinese Water Temples

Travelers to the Indonesian island of Bali may encounter large, stone structures that look like religious temples. They *are* temples, but they are also the center of an elaborate, and crucial, part of how Indonesians feed themselves. For over 1,000 years Balinese farmers have engineered a complex agricultural system of rice terraces and irrigation systems managed by a network of hundreds of water temples in a process studied by anthropologist Stephen Lansing (1987).

1 At the beginning of the growing season, farmers fill terraced rice paddies in the hills and countryside. On a volcanic island, water flows swiftly down mountainsides through sharp, steep fissures. Over the centuries, Balinese have built an elaborate system of tunnels and canals to control water flow for farming. Bali's water temples carefully coordinate the distribution of this water to ensure the best conditions for growth while minimizing the habitat for rice-eating pests.

② Farmers who share irrigation water form a water temple to manage the canals and terraces. At monthly gatherings they give thanks to the island's water goddess and other local gods who make the rice grow and assemble to decide how and when they will plant in the coming season. Delegates from over 200 water temples journey to Bali's volcanic crater lake to bring offerings to the water goddess. They return home with water blessings for their local communities.

③ In the 1970s, the World Bank introduced a "green revolution" program in Bali to increase agricultural production through Western farming techniques, high-yield, fast-growing plants, chemical fertilizers, and pesticides. After only a few years of bumper crops, the program collapsed in near chaos, unable to control the island's rice-eating pests. Gradually, Balinese returned to the water temple system that had maintained an ecological balance between humans, land, water, and animals for centuries.

Balinese religious beliefs, drawing heavily on Hindu precepts, hold that everything is made by the Creator. Killing one thing disturbs all things. Attention to the whole ecological system is central to religious ritual and practice, a dynamic easily overlooked by economists, engineers, and development officials, who may disregard the intersection of religion and power in local community life in favor of technological advancement. Balinese water temples apply the practical and spiritual wisdom accumulated over centuries to the island's complex agricultural system.

- Why do you think it was so easy for economists, engineers, and development officials to overlook the important role of the Balinese water temples? What facets of Balinese life might they have missed?
- Why do you think the Balinese water temple system may have survived when other systems combining religion and power may have collapsed?

indigenous saint, the Virgin of Guadalupe, Father Hidalgo challenged his parishioners by asking, "Will you free yourselves?" Despite periods of alignment, Mexican history has seen ongoing tensions between the powerful institution of the Catholic Church (which has been one of Mexico's largest landholders) and the Mexican state. The Church has been involved in political movements in Mexico before, but did it have a role in the 1994 uprising in Chiapas? A quick look at recent Church history may shed light on this question.

In 1959 Pope John XXIII called for a Vatican Council to modernize the Catholic Church. By the end of this conference (1962–65), commonly called Vatican II, the Catholic Church had begun a dramatic revolution in theology and practice. In an attempt to redefine the Church as "the people of God" rather than an institution, Vatican II moved to make local congregations more accessible to the layperson. Congregations were allowed to worship in their own local language rather than Latin. Priests and lay members were encouraged to open the Church as a servant to the poor rather than an ally of the politically powerful.

Bishop Samuel Ruiz García, head of the Diocese of San Cristobal de las Casas in Chiapas, where the Zapatista uprising occurred, attended Vatican II and a subsequent meeting in 1968 of Latin American Catholic leaders. He returned to Mexico determined to implement the new theology of liberation: He would put the Church to work to better the life conditions of the one million primarily indigenous people in his diocese. The diocesan program for training lay teachers (*catequistas*) transformed its curriculum from a primary focus on Church doctrine, scriptures, law, liturgy, and music to include concerns of community life and social needs. By the time of the Zapatista uprising, the *catequistas* had grown from 700 to 8,000. Most were now elected by their local indigenous communities; they were deeply involved not only in traditional Catholic religious education but also in the empowerment of indigenous people in their struggles against poverty. *Catequistas* developed prominent roles as community and political leaders, accompanying their constituents in efforts to eradicate poverty and landlessness in Chiapas and to open the state's political process to greater participation from people at the grassroots.

Were Bishop Ruiz and the *catequistas* responsible for the 1994 Zapatista uprising? No accusations have been proven of a direct role in the Zapatista leadership. But did the theology of liberation, expressing the Catholic Church's desire for the empowerment of indigenous people and the elimination of poverty, provide moral support and practical training to communities engaged in this struggle? If so, then the Catholic Church of Chiapas provides an instructive example for anthropologists of how we must consider the role of religious ideas, symbols, and engagements with other systems of power to understand religion in all its fullness (Floyd 1996).

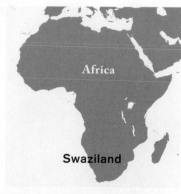

Catholic bishop Samuel Ruiz of San Cristobal in Chiapas, southern Mexico, and the church's network of *catequistas*, or lay teachers, have been accused by the Mexican government of inciting rebellion.

Swaziland's Churches: Religious Health Assets in Fighting HIV/AIDS

Research suggests that across Africa, religious organizations—particularly Christian churches—manage as much as 70 percent of all medical assets, including urban hospitals and rural health clinics (Root 2009). As the following discussion illustrates, the potential role of local congregations in health promotion in Swaziland reveals churches to be not only places of spiritual life but also significant health assets.

Swaziland is a small, landlocked, primarily agricultural country in southern Africa. It has one of the highest rates of HIV infection in the world, with 27.7 percent of Swazis between the ages of twenty-five and forty-nine testing HIV positive in 2014. As a result, life expectancy is only fifty-three years, and 45 percent of children under age eighteen live with neither parent. Swaziland has an estimated 6,500 local church congregations—one for every 183 people. In comparison, the country has one HIV testing and counseling facility for every 6,180 people and one antiretroviral treatment site for every 45,400 people. In this dire context, recent research (Root 2009) has been exploring the current and potential role of Christian churches not as places for worship and prayer, but as key community health assets. Fieldwork reveals that churches function as places where health can be promoted, treatment encouraged, and social, material, and spiritual support provided.

HIV infection among Swazi women is particularly high. Forty-nine percent of Swazi women ages twenty-five to twenty-nine are HIV-positive. And because Swaziland is an intensely patriarchal society, women's rights within the family are severely limited and their role in public affairs is even more

MAP 15.8
Swaziland

Dena Freeman
Religion and Development in an Ethiopian Village

Anthropologist Dena Freeman of the London School of Economics has spent over twenty years studying the cultural transformation of villages in the Gamo Highlands of southern Ethiopia. Her early research, which she wrote about in her first book, *Initiating Change in Highland Ethiopia (2002)*, focused on the dynamics of political and ritual transformation, while her more recent work has explored the intersection of local religious practices and economic development efforts.

"When I first did fieldwork in the mid-1990s, I lived out in a little village in a mud hut in the middle of nowhere, in a community that was really peripheral to capitalism. People were subsistence farmers. They had very little money. They would buy a bit of salt or a bit of sugar in the market. Occasionally they would sell a cow. But the main locus of their economy was non-capitalist." Religion, economics, politics, and kinship were all deeply intertwined in the village.

Six years later Freeman returned and was surprised by the rapid religious and economic changes, which she later wrote about in her book *Pentecostalism and Development* (2012). The number of Pentecostal Christians had grown from around ten percent to nearly seventy percent of the population. And the majority of the people were now engaged in growing apples as a cash crop. What had happened? And was there a connection between these two phenomena?

During that time a development NGO had chosen her highland village for a project growing apples. "Normally peasant societies are very resistant to change and new technologies. So why did so many people jump at this? Then I noticed that in my little neighborhood of the village alone, six out of seven of the farmers who had first experimented with apples were Pentecostals. In the village's traditional religion, relationships with the spirits are mediated by one's father, the lineage head, and the clan head through various ritual sacrifices and thus people are placed in a social hierarchy.

"In contrast, the Pentecostal message is rather liberating and somewhat revolutionary, especially to young men who were at the bottom of the traditional hierarchy. Pentecostalism encourages you to be independent, not dependent on your father or your elders like in the traditional system. And it calls the traditional religious practices devil worship. So these predominately young Pentecostal men—many of them educated by the churches—were desperately looking for ways to be independent from their fathers, who owned all the land and all the means of production. They were really ready for this apple project when it came and they jumped at the chance to get involved."

The early success of the first apple growers began to destabilize other community practices. "In the traditional system, when you start generating some wealth,

Anthropologist Dena Freeman

the elders come to you and tell you it's time to become initiated, to become *halak'a*. The initiation involves elaborate rituals and sponsoring huge feasts for everyone in the community.

"I actually think that the vast majority of traditional religious-economic type systems are essentially systems for redistributing wealth. The people who have more wealth basically trade their wealth for status in the community. And this keeps things in a kind of balance.

"Now with the Pentecostals, who were only a tiny minority of ten percent, they had already said that this is all devil worship and that they didn't want anything to do with it. So when the elders came to make them *halak'a*, they said no. And they kept their wealth.

"A year or two later when the next batch of farmers was chosen by the NGO, more people were interested, even ones who were not Pentecostal, because they had seen the success of the apple trade. When they made some money as well, the elders came to ask them to become *halak'a*. The only way that they could legitimately, and morally, say no was if they were Pentecostal and thus outside of the traditional system. It appears that an awful lot of people converted to Pentecostalism at that time.

"Once they started learning things in the church and becoming involved, for the vast majority of them it turned into something much deeper and much more meaningful. But the apples were the initial push."

Drawing on early social scientist Max Weber's work, *The Protestant Ethic and the Spirit of Capitalism*, about the role of Protestant ethical and moral ideas in the rise of western capitalism, Freeman develops a notion she calls a Pentacostal Ethic and the Spirit of Development.

"In the general dynamic of moving from a redistributive cultural system to something that morally allowed accumulation, I think the religion part is really important.

> **" *I think that's the magic of anthropology, the possibility of alternatives.* "**

A lot of development projects focus solely on the material things. Will it teach people new skills? Will it teach them new techniques? What they miss is the change in morality and values that I think Pentecostalism brings that is a very powerful mechanism for reformulating people's relationships with their community and family. Its ethical ideas make successful enterprise and individual accumulation seem moral, not simply selfish.

"In the pre-apple era, the traditional cultural system had various ways of keeping people happy. It was very communal. They worked hard, but it was with their friends and family, at a fairly relaxed pace. Work was interspersed with coffee drinking, and joking with your neighbors. Once people started getting into the apples, time became money. People drink coffee less because it takes up so much time. They still joke around, but they do it much less. The greetings are less. There are more conflicts. People now have things that they're worried will be stolen. Then people start building fences and having guard dogs.

"And what did they get in return? Everyone now wears shoes. More kids go to school. There are more plastic buckets. People have more changes of clothes. But are they happier in the long run?" Freeman remains a skeptic.

Freeman's traces her interest in anthropology to a backpacking trip through Africa, during college. "That really opened my eyes to the world—to different ways of living in the world and being in the world. I also began to see other people's cosmologies: other people's ideas of how the world was, how it worked, and what our places in it are. I began to imagine the possibility of alternatives, the possibility that the world I always knew and grew up in was not the only way the world was. That was very exciting intellectually and also very liberating for me. I still think that's the magic of anthropology, the possibility of alternatives."

YOUR TURN: FIELDWORK

Visit to a Religious Community

Choose a religious community that you would like to visit, either by yourself or with other members of your class. Contact the organization to arrange a visit at a time when you can participate in a public ritual, perhaps a worship service, festival, or parade. Be sure to find out what attire is appropriate for visitors.

During your visit, consider how the concepts introduced in this chapter can serve as tools for analyzing and understanding what you see.

1. Do you see examples of sacred and profane objects/acts during your visit (Durkheim)?
2. Can you recognize ways in which ritual promotes a sense of communitas by leading members through separation, liminality, and reincorporation (Turner)?
3. Is Marx's critique of religion as "the opiate of the masses" relevant to the event you attend?
4. Can you identify particular symbols (Geertz) unique to this religious community and determine their meaning? What do you think gives them their power and authority (Asad)?
5. How does power make itself evident during your visit? What power relationships do you observe?
6. Can you identify any ways in which globalization influences the religious beliefs and practices that you observe?

If appropriate, interview a religious leader and/or a member of the religious community during your visit. Use the interview to explore these questions further and to gain deeper insight into what you observe.

If you attend with other classmates, compare your reflections after the visit. Be sure to reread the appropriate sections of this chapter to see which concepts come alive in more detail now that you have observed the activities of a religious community from an anthropological viewpoint.

---

circumscribed. Gender inequality is stark. Even the family homestead can be a place of particular vulnerability, stigmatization, and discrimination for HIV-positive individuals. In this environment, it is very difficult for anyone to disclose their HIV symptoms and seek treatment (Whiteside et al. 2006).

In the midst of this health-care crisis, churches are complex social spaces. They can be sites for stigmatization, but they also provide alternative spaces for women to deal with their HIV infections. In fact, women make up the majority of churchgoers in Swaziland. Churches can provide networks of material support that women may not receive on their homesteads. Just as important, churches can promote alternative narratives of self-understanding that allow women to imagine disclosing their HIV status. Indeed, research shows that disclosure may be a key to treating and preventing the spread of disease. Women who disclose their HIV status in the church community have the possibility not to be shunned and dismissed. Instead, they may be called courageous for daring to make their problem public and asking for help. As a result, local church congregations in many locations where health clinics are rare and HIV testing is rarer still are becoming key avenues for health education, health promotion, and reduced stigma and discrimination.

These "religious health assets" (Cochrane 2006) play tangible and intangible roles in the public health enterprise, mobilizing the symbolic and material power of Christian communities to promote concrete interventions in the health outcomes of rural Swazis. Think back to the discussions of religious expression in China and Mexico, as well as your own visit to a religious community. In what ways do those different religious contexts exemplify the blurring of boundaries between meaning and power?

How Is Globalization Changing Religion?

The forces of globalization—especially migration and time-space compression—are stretching and shaping religions and religious practices. Increasing immigration sometimes means that whole communities—their beliefs, religious architecture, religious leaders, and even their gods—relocate across national boundaries. Travel is broadening the encounters of people of different faiths. At the same time, information about religion is more widely available, and communication technologies enable religious institutions to transform their strategies for cultivating and educating participants. Cities, especially those serving as immigrant gateways, are generally the focal point of this increasing encounter. It is here that new immigrants revitalize older religious institutions and construct new ones, often establishing deep ties to home and sophisticated networks of transnational exchange.

Revitalizing the Catholic Church in the United States

Throughout the United States, Catholic churches are being rejuvenated as immigration from heavily Catholic countries brings new membership, worship styles, social needs, and political engagements. A wave of rallies in major cities across the United States in 2005 in support of reform of U.S. immigration laws received key institutional and organizational support from local Catholic churches, with encouragement from the U.S. Catholic leadership. Indeed, the Church saw as a key human rights issue the reuniting of families across the border and eliminating opportunities for the exploitation of vulnerable, low-wage workers. At the same time, today's immigrants are reshaping the Church's future—just as immigrant waves from Ireland, Germany, and Italy did in the nineteenth century.

Mexican Catholicism in New York City In New York City, Mexican immigrants have reshaped many of the city's Catholic churches. Over the past twenty years, hundreds of thousands of Mexicans, many undocumented and the vast majority Catholic, have arrived in New York to work in low-wage jobs in restaurants, groceries, construction, and the nearby agricultural industry on Long Island. In the process, these immigrants have brought their home-country religious practices and particularly their devotion to Our Lady of Guadalupe. The miraculous appearance of the Virgin Mary, mother of Jesus, in 1531 on the Hill of Tepayac in what is now Mexico City in the form of an indigenous person has become a symbol of the Mexican nation and of the special blessings Mexicans have received from God.

Across New York's Catholic churches, images of the Virgin of Guadalupe are prominently displayed. Within parishes, Guadalupano committees have formed to meet new members' needs and political concerns. The root of these committees is Association Tepeyac, a Mexican Catholic immigrant organization created in New York by a Mexican Catholic religious order to advocate for immigrant rights, services, and legalization. Tepeyac draws on the symbolic power of the Virgin to galvanize its movement. In this context, the Virgin of Guadalupe links and mobilizes Mexicans more than language, ethnicity, social class, or common nationality. She is a symbol of Mexican national identity but also represents a universal Catholic commitment to human rights. The Virgin is venerated as a protector of the poor, oppressed, and weak. Tepeyac supports and links Guadalupano committees in local churches and takes the lead in advocating for immigrant rights, particularly a general amnesty for undocumented workers.

The arrival of Mexican Catholics has brought increased attention to the plight of undocumented workers and has built new symbolic and practical links across the U.S.–Mexico border. On December 12 each year since 2002, thousands of Mexican Catholic immigrants walk in procession down New York City's Fifth Avenue to St. Patrick's Cathedral to celebrate the Feast Day of Our Lady of Guadalupe. Organized by Association Tepeyac and the Guadalupano committees, the procession in New York is the culmination of a torch run that begins in the Basilica Church of the Virgin of Guadalupe in Mexico City. Each year, Mexican Catholic devotees carry a lit torch and a portrait of the Virgin across the U.S.–Mexico border, through the large Mexican immigrant populations across the southeastern United States (including in Alabama, Georgia, and North Carolina), and culminate their pilgrimage in New York City. Calling themselves "messengers of a people divided by a border," the torch runners combine an expression of religious devotion to the Virgin of Guadalupe with advocacy for the reform of U.S. immigration laws.

Through their devotional practices, Tepeyac and the Guadalupano committees articulate an alternative citizenship. This citizenship is not subject to

How are religious practices crossing national borders in a global age? Every year, Mexican Catholics carry a lit torch and a portrait of Our Lady of Guadalupe from Mexico City to New York, combining religious expression with political advocacy for reform of U.S. immigration laws.

the temporary and seemingly capricious laws of a foreign country. Rather, it is one in which all people are equal in the eyes of the Mother of God, represented in her manifestation as the Virgin of Guadalupe. Today, as globalization stimulates the international movement of people, nation-states may resist that movement through immigration policies that create disjunctures for family members living on opposite sides of a border or for undocumented immigrants living on the wrong side of the law. For these immigrants, as revealed in the story of Tepeyac and the Guadalupano committees, religion can provide both a symbolic and a material healing of the rift created by the states' response to globalization and cross-border flows of immigrants (Galvez 2009).

Relocating Rituals and Deities from the Home Country

Globalization is transforming the ritual practices of religious communities large and small as congregations adapt to their members' mobility and the lively flow of ideas, information, and money across borders. These dynamics have rapidly spread the religious practices of a small, local, Daoist village temple in rural China to New York and beyond through a network of Chinese restaurants opening across the United States. Today, thanks to globalization, the village temple's adherents and their local god have become international border-crossing immigrants.

Immigrant Chinese Gods A few years ago, I walked into a little temple just off Canal Street in Manhattan's Chinatown as part of a project to map the Chinese religious communities in New York City (Guest 2003). Women and men, young and old, crowded into the noisy and smoky old storefront space, lighting incense, chatting with old friends, and saying prayers at the altar. Most were from the same small village in southeastern China, outside the provincial capital of Fuzhou. They had opened this temple to continue their religious practices in the United States and to serve as a gathering place for fellow immigrant villagers who lived and worked in and around New York City. Here, immigrants can reconnect with friends and relatives from their hometown, participate in rituals of devotion to their deities, and build networks of fellow devotees they may not have known before arriving in New York.

For a highly transient population, the temple serves as a center for exchanging information about jobs, housing, lawyers, doctors, employment agencies, and more. It operates a revolving loan fund for members to pay off smuggling debts or start up a take-out restaurant. Through the temple, members contribute to building their home temple and support other charitable projects in their home community back in China. Despite the undocumented status of many of these immigrants, the temple provides a way to participate in civic activities and express themselves as contributing members of the community in much the same way that Tepeyac and the Guadalupano committees do for New York's Mexican immigrants.

I later visited the home village temple in China to learn about village life and local religious traditions. One evening as I prepared to leave, the master of the temple expressed disappointment that I had not been able to meet the temple's spirit medium, a young woman who had a special relationship with the village's local god. He explained that on the first and fifteenth day of each lunar month, the local god possesses her and speaks through her to interpret the villagers' dreams and answer their questions: What name should I give my child? What herbal remedy will cure my ill? Will this woman be a good match for my son? When should I try to be smuggled out of China to the United States? I shared the master's disappointment at this missed opportunity and readily accepted his invitation to return on a future visit.

A year later I did return. The spirit medium, however, was gone. She and her husband, the temple master informed me, had moved to the United States and were now working in a restaurant in a place called "Indiana." I was disappointed again, but I expressed my concern that their departure may have disrupted a key element of temple life. The master then told me this story:

> Actually she still does it—only now it's from Indiana. Our believers work in restaurants all over the United States and some are still here in China. When they want to ask the advice of the god, they just pick up their cell phones and call. The spirit medium keeps careful records of their questions and dreams. Then on the first and fifteenth of the lunar month, just as always used to happen when she was here, she goes into a trance. The god leaves our temple here in China and flies to Indiana to possess her. Her husband then asks all the questions and writes down the answers. When the possession is over, the god returns to our village, and the spirit medium and her husband return all the phone calls to report the wisdom of the god.

Perhaps the look on my face and my one raised eyebrow alerted the master to my initial skepticism. "We can feel the god leave here every time," he said. "Really. Why don't you believe that? In America you have lots of Christians who believe the Christian god can be everywhere in the world at the same time. Why can't ours?"

The more I thought about it, the more I wondered why the local god of a village in China couldn't also be in Indiana. As an anthropologist of religion, I was reminded once again that religious practices and beliefs in today's age of globalization continue to be fluid and adaptable. After all, humans are adaptable, and so are their cultural constructions. Religion is a vibrant example of this core anthropological insight.

Anthropology challenges us to understand the beliefs and practices of others from within their own cultural framework. By making the strange familiar, we may then also make the familiar strange. In other words, we may take what seems natural and normal in our own lives and see it through new eyes.

The study of religion often forces anthropologists to address personal issues of identity, belief, and objectivity in ways that many other areas of study do not. Is it possible to fully understand a religion without being a practitioner? Can someone remain objective if he practices the religion he studies? Anthropologists of religion consider these important questions when conducting fieldwork and writing about their experiences. Through any experience of intensive fieldwork we risk challenging, transforming, and possibly shattering our own worldviews even as we risk influencing those of the people we study. These dynamics are particularly volatile in the study of religion.

Thinking Like an Anthropologist: Religion in the Twenty-First Century

After reading this chapter, you should have a deeper understanding of some of the approaches anthropologists take to understanding the role of religion in people's lives and in communities large and small. These insights can serve as a toolkit as you consider expressions of religion in other countries and at home in the United States.

Think again about Pope Francis's address to the U.S. Congress that opened the chapter, and recall the key questions we have asked about religion:

- What is religion?
- What tools do anthropologists use to understand how religion works?
- In what ways is religion both a system of meaning and a system of power?
- How is globalization changing religion?

After reading the chapter, can you apply the writings of Durkheim, Marx, Weber, Geertz, and Asad to events in the real world? Can you see concepts of sacred and profane, ritual, rite of passage, communitas, symbol, and power emerge in religious expressions in your own life?

After his visit to the United States, Pope Francis continued his commitment to integrating theological reflection, social analysis and calls to action. In the summer of 2016 alone he lit candles and offered prayers at the World War II era Nazi-run Auschwitz-Birkenau concentration camp; urged the world to never forget the Ottoman genocide of 1.5 million Armenians during and after World War I; warned one million youth at World Youth Day in Poland against consumerism and complacency; and pressed for peace in Syria. While his visits and his words were often highly symbolic, his proclamations reverberated through the powerful institutions of the Catholic Church and its 1.2 billion members worldwide. As the spiritual and political head of the church, what role might Pope Francis's words and actions play in shaping political and economic developments in places around the world? Do you see other religious leaders who exercise both symbolic and material power? Where have religious language and symbols been used to mobilize political action?

Key Terms

religion (p. 573)

martyr (p. 575)

saint (p. 575)

sacred (p. 578)

profane (p. 578)

For Further Exploration

Dialogue at Washington High. 2007. By the Jewish-Palestinian Living Room Dialogue Group. Dialogue. Documentary film of Jewish and Palestinian teens who model connecting with the "other."

Lambek, Michael, ed. 2008. *A Reader in the Anthropology of Religion*, 2nd ed. Malden, MA: Blackwell.

Lansing, John Stephen. "Perfect order—recognizing complexity in Bali: John Stephen Lansing at TEDxNTV." tedxtalks.ted.com/video/Perfect-order-recognizing-compl.TEDx talk on Balinese Water Temples./

Morris, Brian. 2006. *Religion and Anthropology: A Critical Introduction*. New York: Cambridge University Press.

Number Our Days. 1977. Directed by Lynne Littman. Direct Cinema. Documentary film by anthropologist Barbara Myerhoff of creation of ritual in a Jewish senior center in California.

Pew Forum on Religion & Public Life. www.pewforum.org. This website explores the intersection of religion and public affairs in the United States and globally through surveys, demographic analysis, and social science research.

The Pluralism Project. www.pluralism.org. Twenty-year-long Harvard University project to document the changing U.S. religious landscape. Of particular interest, Case Studies in Religious Pluralism explore critical incidents of religious interaction in contemporary U.S. context.

Stoller, Paul, and Cheryl Oakes. 1987. *In Sorcery's Shadow: A Memoir of Apprenticeship among the Songhay of Niger*. Chicago: University of Chicago Press.

Gillette STADIUM

Junior Seau

1969 - 2012

Bank of America

 SBLI 0

DOWN TO GO BALL ON
1ST 10
QTR TIME
1 4:44 0

 VISA

 CROS
INSURAN

BUD

Retired NFL star Junior Seau committed suicide in 2012. An autopsy revealed he was suffering from chronic traumatic encephalopathy, a neurodegenerative brain disease caused by repeated hits to the head. Are our star athletes' bodies healthy?

CHAPTER 16
Health, Illness, and the Body

There is an incredible beauty to American football. Twenty-two men move across the field with precision, intuition, discipline, and creativity—men of immense size yet stunning speed, agility, quickness, and grace. How many years of practice, strength training, weightlifting, running, jumping, and special diets does it take these men to craft bodies so athletic, sharp-minded, healthy, and vibrant?

Americans watch a lot of football. I certainly have—first with my father and then with my son. In 2016, 1,800 players on thirty-two teams generated $13.3 billion in revenue for the National Football League, mostly from television contracts.

The quarterback drops back with the ball. Five linemen form a pocket of protection around him—shoulder to shoulder with teammates, head to head with opponents, hands, arms, feet flying. Five receivers fly downfield, eyes wide, adrenaline pumping, nimble, savvy, fleet driving quick cuts and sprints. Deep in the pocket, the quarterback lets go a perfect spiral like a rocket down the middle of the field as a racing receiver's body launches into the air at 100 miles an hour, horizontal, arms extended, fingers outstretched—just as the defensive back catapults his body for a perfectly timed collision.

And for a moment everyone holds their breath.

Everyone knows what could happen. Everyone is hoping it doesn't.

At that moment of exquisite gracefulness and athleticism everyone remembers that football is a brutal game and hopes that all the players come out of this encounter alive.

In 2002 Dr. Bennet Omalu, a Nigerian doctor, first diagnosed chronic traumatic encephalopathy (CTE) as the cause of death of fifty-year-old

Pittsburgh Steelers championship center Mike Webster. CTE is a degenerative brain disease caused by repeated head injuries that can only be detected after death. Twelve years later, after increasing reports of dementia, Alzheimer's disease, Parkinson's disease, and ALS in retired football players, dozens more CTE cases, and multiple suicides, the National Football League settled a class-action lawsuit brought by 5,000 retired players who accused the league of systematically hiding the dangers of concussions. Actuarial studies suggest 30 percent of NFL players will suffer from Alzheimer's disease or dementia, far above national averages. In 2016, in congressional testimony, an NFL representative admitted for the first time the clear scientific connection between football concussions and CTE.

Tune in again on a Sunday and look closely. The beauty and elegance come through. But between the plays, on the edges of the camera view, just before the cutaway to commercials, you may also see the broken noses, bloodied jerseys, swollen fingers, broken legs, torn ligaments, hanging heads, bandages, braces, crutches, casts, and concussions. Listen more closely for talk of the painkillers, the injections, the dementia, and the tragic suicides.

As we think as anthropologists about health, illness, and notions of the body across cultures, how do we make sense of bodies and health in American sports, and American football in particular? This most successful of U.S. cultural products has transformed play, exercise, and games that build healthy bodies into a multibillion dollar extravaganza in which bodies become entertainment and injuries and long-term health consequences almost invisible. How do we make sense of the NFL's efforts to obscure the scientific data linking football concussions with brain disease or the ways Americans' notions of health, illness, and the body may intersect with concepts of race and class to mask the harsh realities of this game? And why did it take a doctor from Nigeria to see clearly the injuries to bodies and brains in this classic American sport?

Conventional wisdom attributes health and longevity to a combination of "good genes" and good behavioral choices: eating right, not smoking, drinking in moderation, avoiding illegal drugs, exercising, and even flossing. These criteria mesh with core American values of individualism, personal responsibility, and the benefits of hard work and clean living. But are these factors sufficient to explain health and longevity—or the lack of it? Getting sick is a part of life. Everyone experiences colds, fevers, cuts and bruises, perhaps a broken bone. But some people get sick more often than others. Death and dying are part of life; but some people suffer more and die sooner, while others are healthier and live longer. Anthropologists are interested in knowing why.

In this chapter we will explore anthropologists' growing interest in health, illness, and the body. Although these concerns have deep roots in our discipline, the specialization of *medical anthropology* has grown immensely since the 1980s as anthropology's key research strategies—intensive fieldwork, extensive participant observation in local communities, and deep immersion in the daily lives of people and their local problems and experiences—have proven profoundly effective in solving pressing public health problems.

Medical anthropologists use a variety of analytical perspectives to examine the wide range of experiences and practices that humans associate with disease, illness, health, well-being, and the body—both today and in the past. We study the spread of disease and pathogens through the human population (known as epidemiology) by examining the *medical ecology*: the interaction of diseases with the natural environment and human culture. Looking more broadly, medical anthropologists use an *interpretivist approach* to study health systems as systems of meaning: How do humans across cultures make sense of health and illness? How do we think and talk and feel about illness, pain, suffering, birth, and mortality? *Critical medical anthropology* explores the impact of inequality on human health in two important ways. First, it considers how economic and political systems, race, class, gender, and sexuality create and perpetuate unequal access to health care. Second, it examines how health systems themselves are systems of power that promote disparities in health by defining who is sick, who gets treated, and how the treatment is provided.

Medical anthropology's holistic approach to health and illness—examining epidemiology, meaning, and power—assumes that health and illness are more than a result of germs, individual behavior, and genes. Health is also a product of our environment—our access to adequate nutrition, housing, education, and health care and the absence of poverty, violence, and warfare.

In this chapter we will explore the following questions:

- How does culture shape our ideas of health and illness?
- How do different cultural conceptions of the body affect health practices?
- How can anthropologists help solve health-care problems?
- Why does the distribution of health and illness mirror that of wealth and power?
- How is globalization changing the experience of health and illness and the practice of medicine?

By the end of the chapter you will understand how anthropologists approach the study of health, illness, and the body and how these concepts vary across cultures. You will be able to recognize how your own conceptions of health and illness are a cultural construction. You will be able to critically analyze both the systems of power that shape access to health care and the ways in which health systems create and exacerbate inequalities within and between populations.

How Does Culture Shape Our Ideas of Health and Illness?

health: The absence of disease and infirmity, as well as the presence of physical, mental, and social well-being.

What does it mean to be healthy? The World Health Organization proposes that **health** includes not merely the absence of disease and infirmity but complete physical, mental, and social well-being. This is a standard that few people in the world currently attain. Perhaps it is enough to be functionally healthy—not perfectly well, but healthy enough to do what you need to do: get up in the morning, go to school, go to work, reproduce the species. What level of health do you expect, hope for, and strive for? What level of health enables your culture to thrive?

Medical anthropologists have dedicated significant effort to document healing practices and health systems around the globe, from indigenous and tribal communities and urban metropolises to farming communities and groups of migrant workers. In the process, medical anthropologists have identified a vast array of ideas about the causes of health and disease, different notions of the body, and varied cultural strategies to address pain, treat illness, and promote health. One key finding is that these beliefs and practices are intricately intertwined with the way local cultures imagine the world works and the relationship of an individual's body to his or her surroundings.

disease: A discrete natural entity that can be clinically identified and treated by a health professional.

illness: The individual patient's experience of being unwell.

In assessing how disease and health conditions affect specific populations and how specific cultural groups diagnose, manage, and treat health-related problems, medical anthropologists have found it useful to distinguish between disease, illness, and sickness. A **disease** is a discrete, natural entity that can be clinically identified and treated by a health professional. A disease may be caused genetically or through infection by bacteria, a virus, or parasites. But the bacteria, viruses, or parasites are the same regardless of location or cultural context. Illness, however, is more than the biological disease. **Illness** is the individual patient's experience of being unwell—the culturally defined understanding of disease. It includes the way he or she feels about it, talks about it, thinks about it, and experiences it within a particular cultural context. Diseases can be observed, measured, and treated by sufferers and healers. But culture gives meaning to disease, shaping the human experience of illness, pain, suffering, dying, and death (Singer and Baer 2007).

sickness: An individual's public expression of illness and disease, including social expectations about how one should behave and how others will respond.

Sickness refers to the individual's public expression of illness and disease, including social expectations about how one should behave and how others will respond. Being sick may release the sick person from social obligations like work, school or parenting. But sickness also requires the patient to perform a certain "sick role" in order to receive the corresponding social support. In American culture this involves showing a clear wish to get well and willingness to cooperate with medial experts (from parents to doctors). If, for instance,

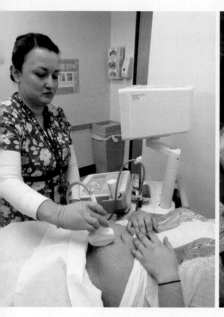

you are sick enough to miss class and expect to be released from schoolwork, the social agreement about sickness suggests that you should be resting at home and following a doctor's advice.

People recognize widely different symptoms, illnesses, and causes for health challenges and have developed widely different strategies for achieving and maintaining health. Though the stereotypical Western images of health care often revolve around doctors in white coats, dentists' chairs, hospitals, strong medications, and advanced technology (such as X-rays, MRIs, and CT scans), medical anthropologists have found that these are not the primary points of access to health care for most people in the world. Nor are they even the first point of access for most people in Western countries. Rather, before seeking the assistance of a trained medical professional, people everywhere apply their personal medical knowledge, their own strategies—often handed down within families or communities—for dealing with disease, illness, pain, and discomfort.

Ethnomedicine

Over the years, medical anthropologists have focused extensive research on **ethnomedicine**. This field involves the comparative study of local systems of health and healing rooted in culturally specific norms and values; it includes the ways in which local cultures create unique strategies for identifying and treating disease and conceptualizing the experience of health, illness, and the physical world.

Early research on ethnomedicine focused primarily on non-Western health systems and emphasized natural healing remedies such as herbs, teas, and

Globally, people have created a vast array of healing practices, all intricately intertwined with local cultural understandings of disease, health, illness, and the body. (*left*) A clinical assistant performs an ultrasound sonogram on a pregnant woman. (*right*) An Indian healer provides villagers with ayurvedic medicines.

ethnomedicine: Local systems of health and healing rooted in culturally specific norms and values.

massage; reliance on religious ritual in health practices; and the role of locally trained healers such as shamans, spirit mediums, and priests as health care professionals. The subdiscipline of **ethnopharmacology** emerged from efforts to document and describe the local use of natural substances, such as herbs, powders, teas, and animal products, in healing remedies and practices. But today, as we will see, even Western biomedicine, which emphasizes science and technology in healing but also reflects a particular system of cultural meanings, is considered through the lens of ethnomedicine. Today medical anthropologists use the concept of ethnomedicine to refer to local health systems everywhere (Green 1999; Saillant and Genest 2007).

Healing Practices of Tibetan Buddhism Applied in Northern India French anthropologist Laurent Pordié (2008) has documented one typical system of ethnomedicine—a variation of Tibetan medicine practiced in the sparsely populated Ladakh region of northern India. Roughly three times the size of Switzerland and straddling the northwestern Himalayas, Ladakh is home to 275,000 villagers, mostly Tibetans, living primarily in remote areas at altitudes up to 5,000 meters (16,400 feet). Their only health care is provided by approximately two hundred *amchis*, traditional healers whose healing practices are deeply rooted in Tibetan Buddhism.

Amchi medicine is based on achieving bodily and spiritual balance between the individual and the surrounding universe. *Amchis* diagnose ailments by asking questions of the patient, examining bodily wastes, and carefully taking the pulse. Recommended treatments include changes in diet and behavior—both social and religious—and the use of natural medicines made from local plants and minerals. Shaped into pills, these remedies are then boiled in water and taken by the patient as an infusion, or drink. Pordié reports that *amchi* treatments are effective for the vast majority of the Ladakhis' health problems, such as respiratory difficulty from the high altitude and smoke in dwellings, hypertension from high-salt diets, and psychological stress. *Amchis* do not perform surgery. Patients who need surgery are transported, if possible, to an urban area to be treated by a doctor trained in Western biological medicine.

Amchi medicine plays a vital role in the survival of Ladakhis. But the *amchis* and their healing practices are under threat from Westernization, militarization, and economic liberalization. For example, the Indian government strongly favors Western biological medicine over traditional ethnomedicine, though it is still unable to provide care to its dispersed rural population. The pervasive presence of the Indian military in response to civil unrest in the bordering Kashmir region inhibits the movement of *amchis* as they gather plants and minerals for natural medicines. In addition, urbanization and modernization, particularly market-oriented economic activity, have increasingly fragmented community

MAP 16.1
Ladakh

life. In the past, *amchi* healers bartered their services for help in plowing, harvesting, and raising livestock. The *amchis* then had time to forage for medicinal plants. But with the penetration of market-oriented economics even into the rural areas, the barter system has been undermined. *Amchis* must now run their therapeutic practices more like businesses, selling medicines and charging for services rather than bartering. Their time to gather medicines has become limited. And with increasing social mobility, the intergenerational transmission of *amchi* skills has been disrupted.

To address this challenge to the *amchi* system, Pordié and a French nongovernmental organization, Nomad RSI, have been working with local *amchis* to establish a coordinated system for growing medicinal plants and distributing them among far-flung villages. *Amchis* from across Ladakh now gather annually to share diagnosis and treatment strategies, and a school has been established to train new practitioners.

Although Tibetan medicine struggles in rural areas where it has been practiced for centuries, it is experiencing unprecedented prominence internationally. Pordié's study also considers how the local *amchi* system of healing is entering the global health arena. Over the last thirty years, as more Tibetans migrate abroad and carry their cultural and religious practices with them, Tibetan medicine has been embraced as an "alternative medicine." The international health market, particularly in Europe and North America, has welcomed

Tibetan medicine as natural, spiritual, and holistic, drawing as it does from indigenous, traditional practices, Buddhist moral values, and Tibetan ecological worldviews. *Amchis* and their practices of Tibetan medicine have become quite popular.

Pordié recounts the story of meeting one *amchi* who was returning from an international speaking tour:

> Impeccably dressed in crimson flannel trousers and a mustard yellow shirt, a Buddhist rosary clasped between the fingers of one hand and a passport replete with visas clutched in the other, the *amchi* from the mountains of the western Himalayas returns to his country after another visit to the United States of America, where for two months he had delivered his teachings on his centuries-old medical art. I meet up with him again in the airport in Delhi. . . . [T]he *amchi* invites me to accompany him to the nearest cybercafé. He wants to check his email immediately. He announces proudly that he is expecting an official invitation abroad. This man, who a few years earlier had marveled at my laptop computer, is today a confirmed Internet user. He even amiably makes fun of me when he notices my astonishment at the speed at which his messages appear on the screen. "You stayed too long in the mountains," he says, and bursts out laughing. (2008, 6–7)

With this portrait, Pordié warns against representing these cultures and their medical practices as artifacts in a museum. Instead, practitioners of what medical anthropologists call ethnomedicine hail from vibrant communities and use their healing practices to cure those at home while reinventing their traditions to engage today's world. Because it is perceived as traditional, Tibetan medicine is highly sought by people in the West. But this tradition has also been reinvented and reinterpreted to meet the contemporary medical needs of the Tibetan community and the healing desires of others far beyond their local borders:

> So, after all, why not the Internet for everyone? This mountain dweller with long hair tied in a chignon, a Tibetan physician by trade, a Tantric practitioner returning from the Americas with an ultra-bright smile and brand new spectacles . . . why shouldn't he communicate with I don't know which extremity of the planet thanks to a high-speed electronic connection? Why should this man remain trapped in the mountains, an image from a postcard or tourist's photo album, when his role is also to provide remedies for illnesses afflicting people elsewhere? (2008, 7)

In this era of globalization, this transnational *amchi* is just as authentic as the *amchi* prescribing healing remedies in a remote village in Ladakh.

Medical anthropologists have played a significant role in documenting the diverse forms of treatment and care as well as the complex medical epistemologies (ways of knowing) that have been developed by local cultures across the globe. As local systems have come into contact and adopted care and healing strategies from one another, these anthropological efforts have helped legitimize and advance their status in the global conversation about health and illness. From the perspective of medical anthropology, all medical systems constitute a form of ethnomedicine because they develop from and are embedded in a particular local cultural reality. And from the perspective of medical anthropology, we might also call all healers ethno-healers, practicing local health knowledge about disease, illness, and health. We now turn to consider why this may be true, whether the healer is an *amchi* or a cardiovascular surgeon.

Western biomedicine or alternative medicines? At a biotech company near Berlin, Germany, researchers develop natural remedies to complement biomedical treatments.

Biomedicine

Biomedicine is the approach to health that has risen to predominance in many Western cultures. **Biomedicine** seeks to apply the principles of biology and the natural sciences (such as physics and chemistry) to the practice of diagnosing diseases and promoting healing. Individual and institutional practitioners of biomedicine—whether doctors, pharmacies, hospitals, medical schools, or pharmaceutical companies—work to clinically identify discrete natural disease entities that can be diagnosed and treated by biomedically trained health professionals. The term *biomedicine* encompasses many local variations and a wide range of treatment practices. But the use of medication, surgery, and other invasive treatments is characteristic of biomedical healing practices (Baer, Singer, and Susser 2003; Saillant and Genest 2007).

biomedicine: A practice, often associated with Western medicine, that seeks to apply the principles of biology and the natural sciences to the practice of diagnosing disease and promoting healing.

Varieties of biomedicine occur across Western industrialized countries, as we consider later in our discussion of the anthropology of birth. For example, British doctors are far less concerned about elevated blood pressure and cholesterol counts than their counterparts in the United States. The German health system, which uses far fewer antibiotics than other Western health systems, recognizes two complementary approaches: *schulmedizin* ("school medicine"), which focuses on typical biomedical treatments, and *naturheilkunde* ("nature cure"), which draws on natural remedies. Biomedicine in the United States emphasizes the most extreme treatments—psychotropic drugs, antibiotics, cholesterol and blood pressure medications, C-section births, and hysterectomies. (Payer 1996).

Because biomedicine is closely linked with Western economic and political expansion, it has taken hold well beyond its original local cultural boundaries and has increasingly gained an aura of universality, modernity, and progress. But medical anthropologists have been careful to point out the ways in which, like

What Do You Do When You Get Sick?

Interview a classmate about his or her strategies for getting healthy or staying healthy. The following questions may help you to assess the person's understandings of health, disease, illness, and proper health care.

- *Whom do you call?* Do you call your mom, dad, doctor, pharmacy, health food store, pastor, friends, massage therapist, chiropractor, campus health center, hospital?
- *What strategies do you use to get well?* Do you sleep, drink orange juice, eat chicken soup, take vitamin C, get antibiotics? Do you starve a cold and feed a fever? Do you follow practices from a culture outside the United States?
- *What strategies do you use to relieve the pain?* Do you take medications for fever, headache, cough, and running nose, or do you let them run their course? Do you take over-the-counter pain relievers or get a doctor's prescription for something more powerful? Do you apply heat or ice? Do you ask for a massage?
- *How do you figure out what made you sick so you don't get sick again?* Do you wash your hands more often? Use hand sanitizer? Filter or boil your water? Consult an older adult, a doctor, or an online source such as WebMD?

- *When you are sick, how do you keep others from being infected?* Do you cover your mouth when you sneeze? Do you stop hugging and kissing your friends and loved ones? Do you take medications or other preparations more regularly?
- *How do you feel about getting sick?* What do you think getting sick says about you as a person? What does it say about you if you have certain symptoms: cold, fever, diarrhea, a sexually transmitted infection?
- *Is there a social cause of your illness or disease?* Is it from poor hygiene by others, lack of clean water, or improper food inspection or preparation? Does a stigma about the illness or disease keep you from seeking treatment? Is treatment too expensive for you? Is it too difficult for you to access health care (too far away)?

As you assess your classmate's replies, consider how their strategies may have been shaped by culture. How did they learn these things? What is the culture of information and communication about health, disease, and illness that shapes these attitudes and actions? Consider your own responses and compare. Can you imagine that someone from another culture might have very different strategies and responses, yet ones that are just as effective?

other ethnomedical systems, the epistemology (ways of knowing) and practice of Western biomedicine are rooted in a particular system of knowledge. This system draws heavily on European enlightenment values of rationality, individualism, and progress—values and ideas that are culturally specific and not universally held. The individual body is the focus of treatment. Diagnosis and treatment are based on rational scientific data. And there is a firm conviction that direct intervention through surgery and medications based on scientific facts will positively affect health.

Are There Other Global Health Systems?

Although Western biomedicine is intimately tied to Western culture and its values, anthropologists also acknowledge that with the spread of Western cultural influences, biomedicine has crossed beyond its cultural and regional boundaries to become a global health system now used in a wide array of countries as well as in international health agencies that engage in health promotion globally. But are there health systems other than biomedicine that function on a global level? Earlier in this chapter, we discussed the growing popularity of Tibetan medicine, especially in Europe and North America. Now let's consider Chinese medicine today as one health system with a long history, elaborate theories of health, illness and the body, a global reach, and proven effectiveness (e.g., Farquhar 1986; Scheid 2002; Zhan 2009).

Chinese Medicine Today In very general terms, Chinese medicine conceptualizes health as a harmonious relationship between Heaven and Earth, which are considered the major forces of the universe. An individual's *qi*—translated as "breath" or "air" and referring to an energy found in all living things—must be balanced and flowing in equilibrium with the rest of the universe for a person to be healthy. Illness occurs when the *qi* is blocked and the flow and balance are disrupted. In traditional Chinese medicine, health-care practices such as acupuncture, *tuina* (therapeutic massage), acupressure, moxibustion (the burning of herbs near the skin), and the consumption of healing herbs and teas promote health by restoring the free flow of *qi* along the body's meridians, or energy pathways (Farquhar 1986; Scheid 2002).

What are those purple circles on Olympic swimmer Michael Phelps' back and shoulders? Phelps, winner of a record 23 gold medals, is one of a growing number of athletes using the Chinese healing practice of cupping, a technique that places specialized cups on the skin, which, when heated, create suction to stimulate blood flow and healing.

In her book *Other-Worldly: Making Chinese Medicine through Transnational Frames* (2009), medical anthropologist Mei Zhan challenges many of the stereotypes of Chinese medicine, including the idea that it is somehow emblematic of an ancient Chinese culture, regionally limited with fixed healing practices that are the antithesis of, or merely "alternative" to, Western biomedicine. Instead, Zhan argues that Chinese medical practices vary widely even within China. Rather than undergoing a regimented and fixed set of health-care practices, patients participate in a dynamic health-care environment. Patients and doctors carefully negotiate treatments. And no good physician ever writes the same prescription twice, because the treatment must meet the needs of each specific patient (Scheid 2002).

Zhan notes three key historical moments over the past century that have significantly reshaped modern Chinese medicine. First, the early-twentieth-century expansion of Western biomedicine into China influenced the practice of Chinese medicine. Western biomedicine's emphasis on institution building, laboratory research, clinical and teaching practices, and even insurance policies reshaped Chinese medical thinking and practice. Today the everyday world of Chinese medicine includes interactions with biomedical professionals. Patients move back and forth between biomedicine and Chinese medicine.

Second, upon the founding of the People's Republic of China in 1949, the new Chinese government moved to institutionalize traditional Chinese medicine, subsidize research, formalize teaching, and establish a process for professional certification. The government widely promoted traditional Chinese medicine as a low-tech, low-cost approach to preventive care and trained and deployed "barefoot doctors" to promote health care in every rural Chinese community. The government also exported traditional Chinese medicine—including medicines, doctors, and health-promotion strategies—to the developing world, particularly Africa, to establish international ties of solidarity with other developing nations. This move marked a rapid expansion of Chinese medicine beyond China's national borders into the international arena.

Finally, Zhan documents the shift of Chinese medicine beginning in the 1980s from primarily a developing-world medical practice to one with established niches in developed countries. Traditional Chinese medicine has become popular

Chinese medicine is a globalized health system with its own internal logic for diagnosing disease and promoting healing. (*left*) Chinese diagram of meridians, or energy pathways, indicates potential sites of blockage that can be restored through treatment with acupuncture (*right*), massage, herbs, and teas.

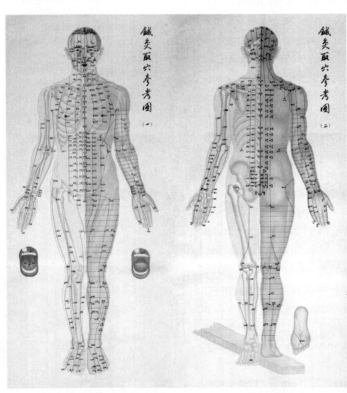

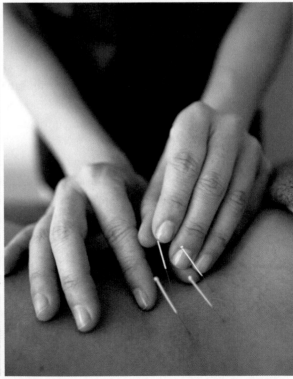

with cosmopolitan consumers in China, North America, and Europe, both as a preventive medicine and as an alternative treatment for illness when biomedicine proves ineffective. The flow of Chinese medical practitioners and Chinese medical knowledge have increased encounters with Chinese medicine, particularly along routes between Asia and Europe and across the Pacific Ocean. Throughout much of California, for example, acupuncture and Chinese herbal medicine have grown increasingly popular. They have gained a foothold in mainstream medical practices ranging from biomedical hospitals to medical schools, and they are increasingly covered by U.S. health insurance policies—a sign of their growing acceptance even within the predominant Western biomedical framework.

Zhan carefully demonstrates how Chinese medicine—often viewed as an ancient, culturally specific, fixed ethnomedicine "alternative" to Western biomedicine—has been relocated in both time and space to represent a modern, effective, globally respected body of health-care practices (Farquhar 1994; Scheid and MacPherson 2012; Zhan 2009).

How Do Different Cultural Conceptions of the Body Affect Health Practices?

We live in our bodies. We are embodied beings. Our bodies mediate all of our experiences of living in and encountering the world. But what exactly is a body, and what does the body signify?

Bodies are perceived, known, and understood in various ways by cultures and medical traditions around the world. Anthropological research has challenged the prevalent biomedical notion of the body as an isolated, natural, and universal object. Instead, anthropologists recognize the body as a product of specific environments, cultural experiences, and historical contexts. Culture has shaped the evolution of the human body and shapes individual bodies today. Culture shapes our experience of the world around us, including how we feel and how others feel about us. And health-care systems are a key site of contestation over the management of bodies.

Biomedical Conceptions of the Body

Nancy Scheper-Hughes and Margaret Lock (1987) recount a now-famous story of a challenging case that illustrates the powerful influence of cultural values on understanding the body in biomedical healing practices. At a teaching hospital, the case of a woman suffering chronic, debilitating headaches was presented to a lecture hall of 250 medical students. When asked about her ailment, the woman recounted that her alcoholic husband beat her, that she had been virtually housebound for five years while caring for her ailing and incontinent mother-in-law, and that she worried about her teenage son, who was failing high school. Then one of the medical students raised her hand and asked, "But what is the *real* cause of her headaches?" By this the student meant, What is the real *biomedical* diagnosis—what neurochemical changes in the individual's body created the pain? In the mind of the medical student, the patient's statements were irrelevant to the task of identifying the cause of her pain or determining a treatment. The student's biomedical training, with its focus on the individual body, science, and technology, had not prepared her to recognize that social experiences might produce embodied responses.

The Human Microbiome

Is a typical biomedical notion of the discrete, treatable, individual body really based in science? Recent scientific research suggests that our bodies are not as independent or as self-contained as we have thought. Researchers at the Human Microbiome Project have discovered that the human body, made up of 10 trillion cells, is also host to 100 trillion microbes—microscopic organisms such as bacteria, viruses, and fungi—that live on and within our bodies. Rather than being discrete biological entities, our bodies appear to be more like complex ecosystems (think tropical rain forests), habitats for trillions of different organisms living with us. Thus we can define the **human microbiome** as the complete collection of microorganisms in the body's ecosystem.

human microbiome: The complete collection of microorganisms in the human body's ecosystem.

These microbes are not random hitchhikers, opportunistic parasites, or dangerous outsider enemies of our bodies. They are deeply integrated into the ways our bodies work. Microbes help us digest food, synthesize vitamins, make natural antibiotics, produce natural moisturizer for the skin, guide the immune system, and spur the development of body parts (such as the intestines). Scientists suggest that we have evolved with these microbes as part of our personal ecosystem for promoting health and combating the pathogens that create disease in our bodies. We not only tolerate these microbes, we need them (Helmreich 2009).

Discoveries of the role of microbes in our bodies' experience of health and illness open the door to rethinking one of the central tenets of Western biomedicine—the notion of the discrete individual body—and offer new pathways for the innovative treatment of both common and rare diseases (Zimmer 2010, 2011).

The Body and Childbirth Across Cultures

The anthropology of childbirth provides one clear example of the cross-cultural variation of health beliefs and practices and understandings of the body. Childbirth is a universal biological event. Indeed, the physiology of childbirth—the biological process—is the same no matter where the birth occurs. But anthropological research shows that cultures around the world have developed unique practices and beliefs about pregnancy, delivery, and the treatment of newborns and their mothers that shape the way childbirth is understood and experienced. Different cultures conceptualize birth in different ways, and these shared understandings shape women's experiences. For example, a popular view of birth in the United States sees it as a medical procedure—what Robbie Davis-Floyd (1992) calls the "technocratic birth." In this view, women become patients—sick and helpless, seeking the assistance of a medical professional to resolve a dangerous life crisis. In contrast, in Holland birth is perceived as an entirely natural process; in Sweden, as an intensely personal and fulfilling achievement; in Yucatán, Mexico, as a stressful but normal part of life. These differing conceptualizations shape and justify the practices each culture puts into place to support, monitor, and control the birth process. Such practices include the location of the birth, the personnel who attend, the decision-making authority as the birth proceeds, and the expectations of pain and pain management. These differences underlie Brigitte Jordan and Robbie Davis-Floyd's (1993) study *Birth in Four Cultures*.

Birth experiences in Yucatán and the United States contrast sharply. Birth for many Mayan women surveyed in Jordan's study occurred in a small, dimly lit home with a dirt floor, attended by a local midwife using everyday materials, while family life continued around them. Mayan women rested in a hammock, considered the best position for labor, although in the final stages of pushing the women might sit astride a wooden chair turned on its side. The husband and the woman's mother were usually present throughout the entire process. Other women of the extended family, particularly those who had given birth before, might be present as well. During the final stages of labor, the husband and the woman's mother took turns sitting behind the woman, supporting her head and lifting her up toward the ceiling to relieve pressure from the contractions. In a difficult labor, other women would provide emotional and physical support, offering encouragement and participating in "birth talk" by urging, cajoling, and challenging the mother to finish pushing her baby out into the world. There were no drugs and no machines (Jordan and Davis-Floyd 1993).

In contrast, 98 percent of American births today occur in a sterile, brightly lit hospital with sophisticated equipment and the attention of highly trained medical professionals who enforce a strict separation of the laboring mother from family and daily life. The father may be present. Elaborate machinery monitors pregnancy and birth. Sonograms and amniocentesis assess the health of the fetus during pregnancy, and fetal heart monitors track the newborn's heartbeat and stress levels during delivery. Medications are sometimes administered through epidural injections near the spinal cord to deaden the mother's

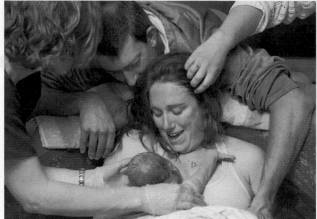

The physiological process of childbirth may be universal, but the experience of childbirth, including the approach toward pain, varies from culture to culture. (*left to right*) The Dutch view birth as an entirely natural process that often takes place at home with no pain medication. In Sweden, delivery rooms are quiet, comforting spaces where women decide on their own pain medication. In Yucatán, Mexico, women labor in a hammock or on a stool at home, surrounded by family and supported by a midwife. In the U.S. delivery room, women become patients admitted for a procedure in a sterile environment with lots of equipment.

pain. To advance childbirth during a difficult delivery, obstetricians may perform episiotomies, surgically widening the opening to the birth canal.

In 2014, one-third of all babies in the United States were delivered by Caesarean section, a surgical procedure by which the baby is removed directly from the mother's abdomen rather than through the birth canal. This number was an increase from 20.7 percent in 1996 (U.S. Centers for Disease Control 2012). This rate of C-sections is among the highest in the world, a fact that raises questions about whether these procedures are performed out of necessity or are influenced by cultural understandings of birth and the institutional pressures that shape health care in hospitals. Rates also vary from region to region in the United States, a reflection of the regional cultural variations in the practice of Western medicine rather than an indication of regional variation in rates of complications.

Can culture shape women's experience of pain during childbirth? Jordan notes that some women in every culture give birth without pain. But a certain amount of pain is expected in almost all cultures. What differs from one medical system to another is the way in which that pain is handled. Jordan's study explores the possibility that cultural expectations of pain during childbirth shape the actual experience and display of pain by laboring mothers.

The introduction of pain medication during childbirth is a recent phenomenon, emerging as part of twentieth-century medicine. Jordan's study found that the use of pain medication during labor is not consistent across cultures. In the United States, pain medication is administered at the discretion of the medical attendants and is often delayed lest the drugs slow the course of labor. Jordan also found that to receive medication, a woman must convince her physician that her pain is severe. Jordan suggests that this dynamic shapes the woman's experience of childbirth, drawing attention away from the delivery and more toward pain—both the experience of pain and the performance of

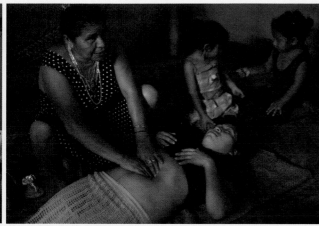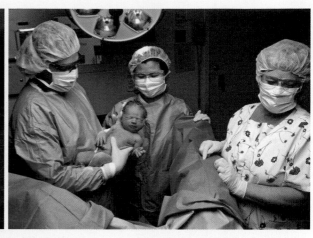

that pain. Obstetric wards in the United States, notes Jordan, as a result of this negotiation between patient and physician, have a relatively high level of noise, anxiety, and vocal despair bordering on panic during the birth process.

In contrast, obstetric wards in Sweden are characterized by quiet, intense concentration on the process of giving birth. Before labor begins, Swedish women are introduced to a variety of pain medicines, their benefits, and side effects. During labor the women themselves make decisions about how much, if any, medication to take and when. Women do not need to convince medical staff of the need for pain medication.

The Dutch view birth as an entirely natural process. They administer no pain medication during the normal course of labor, even in many of the same situations that would lead to the use of pain medication in the United States. The Dutch, like the Maya of Yucatán, are reluctant to interfere with the birth process, waiting for nature to take its course and trusting that women's bodies know best how to handle the process. Birth is not considered a crisis or a medical emergency.

In Yucatán, pain is seen as a natural and expected part of childbirth. It is not frightening. The work of labor is considered a normal part of life. In this view the suffering and pain will pass soon, especially if the mother works hard. Labor is considered a collective process—an experience shared by the woman's husband, mother, and female family members. The pain marks a significant yet normal part of the life experience.

Jordan reflects that the intense experience of childbirth reinforces key Mayan cultural values, particularly local understandings of the importance of hard work, endurance, and tolerance of difficulty. The Maya view these values and personal qualities as desirable in childbirth as well as in life. During the stress of childbirth, women display these qualities in the public sphere.

As you reflect on the anthropology of birth, consider what you have heard about your own birth. Where did it take place? Who was present? What was your mother's experience like? Consider interviewing your mother or another woman in your extended family about her experience giving birth. How does her experience vary from what you might have expected? How does it compare to those described in this chapter? Can you identify culturally specific approaches to pregnancy and childbirth that emerge in their stories?

The variation of cultural approaches to labor and childbirth—a common human biological activity—suggests the extent to which cultural concepts of the body, health, illness, and pain may shape every aspect of a medical system.

The Body and Disability

Anthropology's increasing attention to the body has been accompanied by a recent expansion of work on issues of disability— the embodied experiences of people with impairments as shaped by broader forms of social inequality (Ginsburg and Rapp 2013). Significantly, anthropologists have explored the ways disability is lodged not simply in the body but is socially defined specifically by the often painful and isolating encounters with social and material conditions that "dis-able" and impair people considered to be atypical in a particular culture. So, for instance people restricted to wheelchairs experience their impairment— are "disabled"—differently by the presence or absence of accessibility ramps.

Anyone can experience impairment and disability and most people will at some point in their lives. In fact, being "able-bodied" might be considered only a temporary condition. This is a distinctive quality of disabilities when compared to other systems of power and inequality that may affect only certain portions of a population. Disability may include sensory impairments to hearing and sight, limited mobility, epilepsy, autism and psychiatric illness, chronic pain or dementia related to aging, or result from a sudden illness like a heart attack, an accident or warfare. These disabilities may interact with other stratified systems of power to create additional vulnerabilities. Poverty, warfare, natural disasters, and unequal access to health care directly affect the experience of disability. Through groundbreaking cross-cultural ethnographic work (Kohrman 2005; Ingstad and Whyte 2007; Phillips 2011; Nakamura 2006; Friedner 2015), anthropologists have also explored how the lived experience of "dis-ability" varies widely within and between cultures. (See Kulick and Rydstrom's study on sexuality and disability in Chapter 9)

Anthropologists have written movingly about their own encounters with disabling conditions or those of close friends and family (Rapp and Ginsburg 2001). In the now classic *The Body Silent* (2001), noted anthropologist Robert Murphy constructs an ethnography of paralysis and paralytics in the U.S. culture through the story of his own journey from health to disability as a spinal tumor gradually brought on quadriplegia that left him wheelchair-bound. (Myers 1988; Kensigner 1988; Hirschfeld 1989) Murphy writes powerfully about his thoughts and feelings about his increasing immobility and marginalization, the pain and damage caused by other people's fears, myths and misunderstandings of disability, and the struggle for autonomy amidst increasing isolation and dependency in an American culture that highly values independence. But it is this struggle for autonomy, Murphy concludes, that represents the "highest expression of the human rage for life, the ultimate purpose of our species." (p. 230)

How Can Anthropologists Help Solve Health-Care Problems?

Anthropologists can apply research strategies and key theoretical concepts of our field to solve pressing public health problems, understand the spread of disease, and improve the delivery of health care. In fact, the work of an anthropologist may be just as crucial to explaining and resolving health challenges as that of a physician, epidemiologist, pathologist, or virologist. The following discussion illustrates this point through the groundbreaking efforts of anthropologists working in Haiti and Papua New Guinea.

Creating a Public Health System in Rural Haiti

When the American Paul Farmer first visited Cange, Haiti, in 1983, the remote village of one hundred families was one of the poorest places in one of the world's poorest countries. Most people in Haiti lived on $1 a day, but residents of Cange lived on less. Along with intense poverty, Farmer found a village overwhelmed by high levels of infant mortality, childhood malnutrition, typhoid, dysentery, HIV/AIDS, and tuberculosis. Many residents were water refugees, having been pushed off their land by the construction of a hydroelectric dam that flooded their valley to provide power to Haiti's cities and irrigation for large landholders and agribusinesses downstream. With the best farmland taken out of production by the dam's reservoir, the surrounding area suffered from widespread deforestation, soil erosion, and terrible health statistics (Farmer 2006).

Farmer's work in Cange, popularized in the best-selling biography *Mountains beyond Mountains* (Kidder 2003), began with the encouragement of a Haitian Anglican priest, Fritz Lafontant, who had been working in the area for years. In 1984, the year after Farmer's first visit to Haiti, he enrolled in Harvard's medical school and doctoral program in anthropology. He believed that anthropology would be essential to addressing the health needs of poor Haitians. The delivery of medicines and medical procedures would not be enough, he felt. Deeper questions would need to be asked: What made the people sick? How could they stay healthy after being treated? The basic approaches of an anthropologist—understanding the local language, norms, values, classifications of reality, and religious beliefs—would help a trained physician to think about health in the broadest possible sense.

MAP 16.2
Cange

How do you create an effective public health system? (*left*) People seeking health care in rural Haiti sleep outside following long journeys from their villages. (*center*) Patients receive direct treatment at a clinic. (*right*) Anthropologist Paul Farmer at the opening of a new teaching and primary care hospital in Mirebalais, north of Haiti's capital.

While at Harvard, Farmer immediately began to apply what he was learning, using the research strategies of anthropology and the professional knowledge of medicine to create a public health system for Cange. Living in the community and speaking the local language, Farmer engaged in a process of listening to the residents' needs and experiences and working with them to identify and treat their public health problems. First he recruited a few villagers to help him conduct a health census. Moving from hut to hut in Cange and two neighboring villages, the census takers identified the breadth of the residents' health problems and established a baseline by which to measure future success. To address the community's needs, Farmer launched Partners in Health, or Zanmi Lasante in the Cange language, with financial support from backers in the United States.

Zanmi Lasante began to create multiple lines of defense to protect the Cange villagers' health. Clean water came first. Because they lived on Haiti's central plateau, the villagers had been climbing down an 800-foot hillside to draw water from the stagnant reservoir created by the hydroelectric dam. Using old plastic jugs and calabash gourds, they had been carrying water back up the hill to their huts, where it sometimes sat uncovered for days. But now Father Lafontant recruited a construction crew from an Episcopal Church diocese in South Carolina to tap into an underground river to provide fresh water to the families at the top of the hill. Thereafter, Farmer and his associates noticed that the incidence of infant deaths began to drop almost immediately.

Sanitation and hygiene came next. Father LaFontant organized the construction of latrines (outdoor toilets) to improve human waste disposal and protect the water supply. He and Farmer raised money to replace the dirt floors and thatched roofs of the residents' crude lean-to homes with tin roofs and cement floors. An expanded village school provided a place to teach children to read and write and a place to teach the community about basic health practices. Malnourished schoolchildren received free meals with dignity. Childhood vaccinations dramatically improved health in the community.

Perhaps most significant, Zanmi Lasante trained local community members as community health workers. Being familiar with the local language, social structure, values, and religious beliefs, the community health workers were able to identify emerging health-care problems, administer vaccinations, and assist people in taking medications. The newly constructed health clinic and hospital of Zanmi Lasante served those who were too sick to be cared for at home. Over time, Zanmi Lasante became one of the largest nongovernmental health-care providers in Haiti, serving an area of 1.2 million people with more than 4,000 doctors, nurses, and community health workers. The success of Zanmi Lasante in addressing the health needs of the people of Cange grew directly from Paul Farmer's anthropological approach.

In an essay written during his fieldwork and medical practice in Cange, Farmer (1985) commented that anthropology must involve more than the careful observation of problems. If anthropologists stop there, they fail to use their full power. Anthropology must be a tool for intervention, he argued. Farmer's research and work in Cange explored how anthropology could tackle the day-to-day challenges of health on the ground—nutrition, clean water, prevention of illness, and promotion of health. Public health work could be guided and greatly improved by the strategies and theoretical concerns of anthropology. However, to truly make a difference, anthropology must be used not only to analyze and scrutinize a problem but also to turn research into action.

Connecting Kuru and Cannibalism in Papua New Guinea

One of the early pioneers in medical anthropology, Shirley Lindenbaum, investigated the origins and spread of a disease called *kuru* among the South Fore people of the Eastern Highlands of Papua New Guinea. By the 1960s, the incidence of kuru had reached epidemic proportions. Lindenbaum's work provided insights crucial to developing successful strategies for its control and eventual eradication.

MAP 16.3
Papua New Guinea

Kuru, translated as "tremble" or "fear" for the uncontrollable tremors that its victims experience, is an acute degenerative disease of the central nervous system. Lindenbaum and her partner, Robert Glasse, arrived among the South Fore in 1961 at the height of the kuru epidemic. Earlier researchers had hypothesized that kuru was a genetic disease, passed down among biological kin from generation to generation. But patterns of infection observed by Lindenbaum raised questions about its genetic origins. Men were rarely affected; the victims were primarily women and children of both sexes. Among this part of the population, kuru was common and fatal. To test the genetic hypothesis, Lindenbaum used her anthropological training to track potential genetic links to kuru.

Lindenbaum studied the kinship patterns of the South Fore, mapping kinship terms, creating kinship charts, and conducting participant observation within

David Simmons
Holistic Approaches to Understanding Health and Illness

Each summer for fifteen years David Simmons, professor of anthropology and public health at the University of South Carolina, has led a fieldwork training school in the Dominican Republic for U.S. students to learn first-hand about public health issues in a low-income country. Students take classes, work in urban and rural health clinics, immerse themselves in the local community, and see a broad spectrum of health and healing practices. And, says Simmons, "From the minute they step off the plane they see ways that people are treated differently according to socio-economic status, nationality, and perceived differences."

Students also explore the ways Dominicans navigate between ethno-medicine and biomedicine. In the cities, *botanicas*—small medical-religious-type shops filled with lotions, candles, and cards for saints with healing powers—form a key component of alternative medicine, particularly for people looking for luck, success in a cer-

tain endeavor or who are suffering from a particular malady they feel is more than a biological condition—perhaps malevolent forces that might be causing them misfortune or illness. In the countryside people who historically have not had access to biomedical doctors, nurses, or health promoters may turn to medicinal plants to make teas or compresses to treat their ailments.

"I think people are very pragmatic in terms of navigating between biomedicine, and complementary, alternative medicine. I don't think people necessarily see them in competition. Most people just see them as spheres of knowledge and practice that can overlap and build on one another. People are very comfortable moving back and forth. It's similar in some ways to the United States with acupuncture, yoga, and mindfulness mediation. I think it's part of the universal human condition that people look for holistic ways to make themselves feel better, whether that's through biomedicine or other alternative means."

Simmons' interest in medical anthropology and unequal health outcomes developed while conducting research in Nigeria, West Africa, for his master's degree on the traditions of orators—*griots*—and the importance of the spoken word in African churches that finds resonance in Black Churches in the United States. Living in a rural area with no running water or electricity, Simmons fell ill with malaria, dysentery, and a serious botfly larvae infestation. "The experience really sensitized me to health issues. As a relatively privileged outsider, of course I always had the option of leaving that place and ready access to health resources that the local community did not. That really got me thinking about health and the social causes of health inequalities."

Simmons' ethnography, *Modernizing Medicine in Zimbabwe: HIV/AIDS and Traditional Healers* (2012) focuses on the role of traditional healers in addressing the rapid spread of HIV/AIDS. "Zimbabwe had become ground zero

Anthropologist David Simmons

in the battle against HIV/AIDS in Africa. And in the press there was a lot of stigmatization of the African continent around HIV/AIDS. I really wanted to help push back against that. The consensus in the medical and public health literature really cast traditional healers as obstacles to combating the virus. They were portrayed as backwards individuals putting people at risk of contracting the virus by using unclean razor blades, not sterilizing their equipment or using their hands instead of gloves in their medical work—generally not taking the proper precautions when coming in contact with blood.

"But it was clear to me that the literature did not take into account non-biomedical approaches to understanding illness and disease. This needed a deeper ethnographic analysis. What is it the healers know about this disease? What do they think it is? Where do they think it came from? What are they doing to treat it? I began a partnership with the Zimbabwe National Traditional Healers Association—the national organization of traditional healers. I conducted over 200 interviews with different kinds of healers: spirit mediums, traditional birth attendants, herbalists, prophets. I found that regardless of their sub-specialty, many did have a biomedical understanding of the disease.

"But they also conceptualized the disease in broader, more holistic terms. They would say things like, 'This disease is really the result of Westernization. Our people are forgetting their culture, losing respect for the elders and ancestors, taking on Western ways, becoming more promiscuous and not taking care of family.' For them, the broader context explained why the disease was descending on Zimbabwe in the way that it was. Understanding

> *I think it's part of the universal human condition that people look for holistic ways to make themselves feel better.*

that broader conceptualization of an infectious disease like HIV/AIDS is very important in developing interventions that target traditional healers. From a public health perspective, if you don't understand the local perspective, your ability to put together a culturally appropriate, sustainable intervention will be compromised.

"If you're going to put together HIV/AIDS education workshops for traditional healers, you have to find ways to include the ancestral spirits. Having that healing spirit be present through a spirit medium to sanction the conversation is very important in developing these culturally appropriate sustainable interventions that healers feel they have a stake in. A top-down approach to health development really distances people and pushes them away, making it harder to get local stakeholder investment in the program.

"Anthropology is very well placed to look not only at the biological aspects of health—medical and physical anthropologists do that all the time—but also the broader social forces that can be embodied as biological events. Within public health there is much talk about the social determinants of health and understanding how socio-economic status and social policy—how things like racism, discrimination, classism and homophobia—actually get under peoples' skin."

"You know, as anthropologists, we have to ask ourselves, what is the big question that motivates all the different projects and activities over the course of our careers." For David Simmons, those questions focus on addressing concerns of power, disparity, inequality and an attention to social context in understanding the experiences of health and illness of local communities, whether in the Dominican Republic, Zimbabwe, or South Carolina.

families. Like Janet Carsten's study (see Chapter 10), Lindenbaum's research found that South Fore kinship was not strictly biological. Instead, it was very flexible, constructed among those who shared "one blood"—a concept created not by genetic inheritance but by eating together and residing in the same household. Even immigrants from other parts of Papua New Guinea could be incorporated into the kin group if they showed loyalty and observed local expectations and obligations. Lindenbaum concluded that kinship was not a reliable guide to genetic relationships, so she began to explore other potential factors in the spread of kuru.

Intensive fieldwork in the South Fore and neighboring communities documented political systems, agricultural production, gender roles, and ritual practices. Oral histories gathered from villagers throughout the highlands revealed that kuru had emerged only recently, around 1900, and had spread along a specific, traceable route, arriving in South Fore between 1930 and 1940. Kuru's rapid spread further ruled out a genetic basis for the disease. Instead, transmission patterns suggested that kuru might be an infectious disease spreading from person to person. But how did this occur?

Disease Transmission via a Death Ritual Of particular interest in Lindenbaum's fieldwork, the South Fore and other groups in the Papua New Guinea highlands practiced cannibalism, ingesting cooked human tissue. Specifically, as part of a mourning ritual for the dead, members of the kin group ate the bodies of their deceased relatives. Hypothesizing that the spread of kuru might be related to this ritual practice, Lindenbaum and Glasse collected the names of all those who had died of kuru and of all those who had consumed the body parts of deceased ancestors.

Although the practice was suppressed in the 1960s by the government and by Christian missionaries, the ingestion of cooked human tissue previously had been quite common among the South Fore. Because of this history, Lindenbaum and Glasse were able to collect extensive ethnographic data on the rules for consuming human flesh. The South Fore ate deceased ancestors, not enemies. They ate all body parts except the gall bladder, which was considered too bitter. While they did not eat ancestors who died of leprosy, dysentery, or certain other diseases, kuru forebears were looked upon favorably for ritual consumption. Not all Fore were cannibals. Most adult women consumed cooked human tissue, as did children of both sexes who ate what their mothers gave them. Few adult men ate flesh. Those who did never ate the bodies of women.

By correlating this data, the researchers found that the ritual guidelines matched the patterns of the epidemic's spread. This led to the conclusion that the infectious agent causing kuru was transmitted through the mortuary ceremonies as kin ate the bodies of their deceased ancestors and ingested the infection. Although kuru likely emerged spontaneously in the brain of one individual, the infectious agent that caused kuru was recycled and transmitted through the eating of deceased relatives' bodies, particularly the brain matter, spreading and amplifying within the communities of the South Fore and their neighbors over a relatively short period.

Through the careful anthropological research of Lindenbaum and Glasse, public health practices were developed to contain the spread of the kuru infectious agent. Combined with the elimination of cannibalism, the epidemic of kuru was alleviated and the spread of kuru stopped. Kuru has an extremely long gestation period in the infected person, so the last case was diagnosed in 2009, nearly fifty years after the end of ritual ingestion of human tissue. That case is still being monitored (Lindenbaum 2009).

Why Does the Distribution of Health and Illness Mirror That of Wealth and Power?

Writing in the late 1800s, Rudolf Virchow, a renowned pathologist considered to be one of the ancestors of medical anthropology, asked why the distribution of health and illness appeared to mirror the distribution of wealth and power. Although anthropology from its inception has focused on concerns of health and illness, in recent years Virchow's question has become central to the critical medical anthropology approach to health and illness. If the distribution of health and illness cannot be explained solely on the basis of genetic vulnerabilities, individual behaviors, and the random spread of pathogens through a population, then what are the root causes of health disparities?

Health Transition and Critical Medical Anthropology

Over the twentieth century, much of the human population experienced dramatic improvements in health. Life expectancy rose significantly. Infectious diseases (with the exception of HIV) declined as the primary causes of death and were replaced by chronic diseases such as cancer and heart disease and by syndromes such as stroke. Unfortunately, despite improvements in global health statistics, local populations have not experienced the **health transition** equally. Inequalities of health—sometimes extreme—and unequal access to health care persist between local populations and within them.

Although overall human life expectancy increased from 31 years in 1900 to 70.5 in 2015 (from 49.2 in 1900 to 78.9 in 2015 in the United States), extreme differences exist among countries. As Table 16.1 shows, in 2015 Hong Kong ranked first in overall life expectancy at birth at 83.7 years. Swaziland ranked last of 200 countries, with an overall life expectancy at birth of 49.2 years. The United States ranked 42nd.

These statistics raise crucial questions about health disparities that are central to the concerns of critical medical anthropologists. If the United States is

health transition: The significant improvements in human health made over the course of the twentieth century that were not, however, distributed evenly across the world's population.

the richest and most technologically advanced country in the world, why is its population's average life expectancy shorter than that of people in forty-one other countries? Why is the average life expectancy of the population of Swaziland 30 percent below the global average?

critical medical anthropology: An approach to the study of health and illness that analyzes the impact of inequality and stratification within systems of power on individual and group health outcomes.

Critical medical anthropology examines health as a system of power. Specifically, it explores the impact of inequality on human health by examining (1) how economic and political systems, race, class, gender, and sexuality create and perpetuate unequal access to health care, and (2) how health systems themselves are systems of power that generate disparities in health by defining who is sick, who gets treated, and how. Critical medical anthropologists look beyond Western biomedicine's traditional focus on individual patients' problems; instead, they analyze patterns of health and illness among entire groups. Critical medical anthropologists search for the origins of these health disparities, the mechanisms that perpetuate them, and strategies for overcoming them (Baer, Singer, and Susser 2003; Budrys 2010).

Each of us develops our own individual way of thinking about health, including strategies for treating disease and illness and addressing other threats to our well-being. On an individual level, we may each choose from a set of home remedies and cures passed along from family and friends. But on a structural level, our universe of options is not of our own making. The available choices are far from equal for each of us. For example, consider the following questions: What kind of health insurance do you have? Do you have health insurance at all? Do you have access to clean water, childhood immunizations, nutritious food, clean air, and exceptional health-care facilities? Do you have a choice of doctors? Do you have social networks to help identify the best doctors to treat your particular problems? Are your home and neighborhood safe from violence and war? After you answer these questions for yourself, think about how the president of the United States would answer them. Think about how a resident of Cange, Haiti, would answer them.

Patterns of inequality in a culture create patterns of inequality in health care. Health practices and policies in turn create and reinforce patterns of inequality. We might actually say that illness can have social origins in poverty, violence, fear of violence, and discrimination based on race, ethnicity, gender, sexuality, and age. Illness and disease can result from cultural patterns of inequality and the distribution of health-care resources within a population (Schulz and Mullings 2006).

Staff Attitudes Affect Health-Care Delivery in a New York Women's Clinic

Various systems of power—including economics, politics, race, class, gender, and sexuality—shape the distribution and accessibility of health-care resources (Chapman and Berggren 2005). In *Reproducing Race* (2011), legal scholar and

TABLE 16.1 Global Life Expectancy by Country

Country (state/territory)	Rank	Life Expectancy at Birth (in years)
Hong Kong	1	83.7
Japan	2	83.3
Italy	3	82.8
Switzerland	4	82.7
Singapore	5	82.6
Iceland	6	82.3
Spain	7	82.3
Australia	8	82.1
Israel	9	82.1
Sweden	10	81.9
Netherlands	17	81.3
Germany	21	80.7
United Kingdom	28	80.5
United States	42	78.9
Mexico	56	76.5
China	70	75.4
Egypt	119	70.8
World average		70.5
India	144	67.5
Laos	151	65.5
Papua New Guinea	165	62.3
Haiti	166	62.3
Nigeria	193	52.3
Swaziland	200	49.2

United Nations Department of Economic and Social Affairs, Population Division. 2015. "World Population Prospects, the 2015 Revision." http://esa.un.org/unpd/wpp/

MAP 16.4
New York City

anthropologist Khiara Bridges examines the ways in which race, class, and gender intersect to shape the delivery of health care in a women's health clinic at a famous trauma hospital on Manhattan's East Side. This facility provides prenatal, delivery, and postpartum checkups and services to pregnant women who are poor. The women's health clinic of Alpha Hospital (a pseudonym), which also serves as a top-tier teaching hospital, treats an incredibly diverse population of patients, including some whites but mostly people of color. Because of their economic status, all patients qualify for the U.S. federal government's Medicaid program.

In contrast to the patient population, physicians working in Alpha's women's health clinic are predominantly white. Most medical staffers are women of color but of immigrant backgrounds. Tensions exist between these groups. During a year and a half of fieldwork, Bridges documented the stereotypes and prejudices expressed by physicians and medical staff about their patients. In a Medicaid-supported women's health clinic, women of color are already treated in ways that non-Medicaid patients would not be. For example, because the government has categorized Medicaid patients as an "at risk" population whose exceptional health issues require special treatment, these women are subjected to interviews, counseling sessions, intrusive procedures, and invasive examinations that non-Medicaid pregnant women do not undergo. In addition to the exceptional institutional requirements, Bridges raises the possibility that physicians' racial attitudes may contribute to the health disparities experienced by patients who are women of color.

Bridges's research documents a racist oral tradition within the medical profession that features stories and folklore about black women's bodies. One common theme centers on the supposedly unique strength and hardiness of black women and other women of color, who, often referred to as more "primitive" by health workers, were assumed to be able to endure more intense pain and overcome more hardship in medical procedures than other women.

Bridges presents these troubling anecdotes in relationship to statistics that show significant racial disparities in infant and maternal mortality. In the United States, black babies are nearly two and a half times more likely to die as infants than white babies. Black women are three times more likely than white women to die from complications of pregnancy and childbirth. In New York City, they are five times more likely to do so!

Are these women and infants dying because they are poor or because they are black? Bridges suggests that the mortality rates reflect more than poverty. Studies consistently show that racial and ethnic minorities in the United States receive lower-quality health care. But even when ruling out variables such as insurance status, income, age, and severity of medical condition, black women and infants have higher mortality rates than whites with similar profiles.

Bridges notes a deep reluctance within Western medicine to invade physicians' privacy by interrogating their human frailties. Perhaps as a result, the

How might dynamics of race, gender, age, and class affect the medical care that patients receive in a hospital, clinic, or doctor's office?

existence of physicians' racism is never addressed in the larger medical literature. But based on the patterns of behavior she observed at Alpha Hospital's women's health clinic, Bridges argues for the need to explore the possibility that physicians' views regarding patients of color may lead to different treatment during pregnancy and childbirth, disparate health outcomes, and higher infant and maternal mortality rates (Bridges 2011; Chapman and Berggren 2005).

How Is Globalization Changing the Experience of Health and Illness and the Practice of Medicine?

The current era of worldwide interconnectedness associated with globalization is bringing profound changes to individuals' experience of health and illness and to the practice of medicine. Various facets of medical migration, as well as global humanitarian efforts and encounters among multiple systems of healing, make today's era of globalization unique.

Medical Migration

The small town of De Leon Springs and its crystal clear lake on Florida's eastern coast bear the name of the Spanish explorer Juan Ponce de León. Legend tells that he entered Florida in 1513, at the beginning of an earlier period of

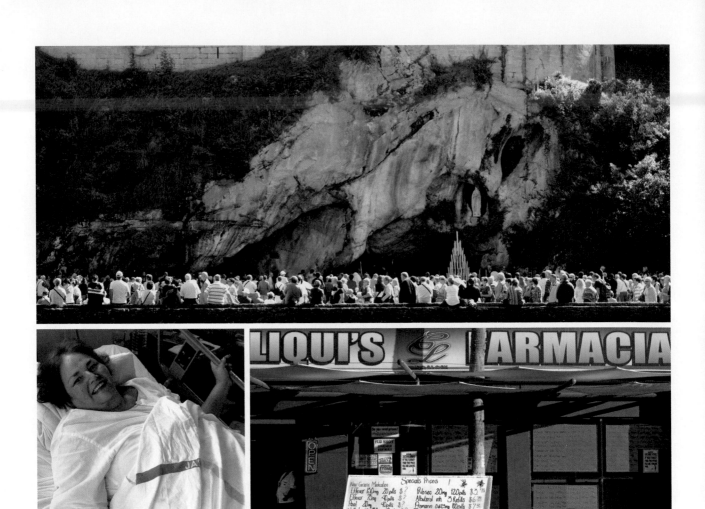

Globalization has spurred many forms of medical migration. (*clockwise from top*) Crowds seek healing at the sacred grotto sanctuary of Our Lady of Lourdes in France. Thousands of Americans cross the border from Arizona to buy prescription drugs at Mexican pharmacies for a fraction of their U.S. cost. A school bus driver, Edna Harsha, from Minnesota, traveled to Bombay, India, for hip replacement surgery.

globalization, looking for the fountain of youth, which was rumored to restore the vitality of anyone who drank from it. But while Ponce de León sought a fountain of youth, his transatlantic voyage, like those of other European explorers, merchants, and colonialists, introduced an array of foreign diseases to the population of the Americas—a medical migration with devastating effect.

Globalization today has launched a new and intensified era of **medical migration**—not only of disease but also of health-care systems, diagnoses, and treatments (Roberts and Scheper-Hughes 2011), with both positive and negative results. Medical treatments and technologies cross national borders as vaccines have been introduced worldwide to treat previously fatal or debilitating illnesses such as polio, tuberculosis, measles, mumps, rubella, tetanus, typhoid, and diphtheria. Antibiotics treat bacterial infections. Pesticides inhibit the spread of disease-carrying insects. At the same time, diseases migrate on a global scale. HIV/AIDS knows no national boundaries. Medical researchers travel with their scientific knowledge and technology in search of subjects for medical research and experimental clinical trials. Images of youth, health, and beauty (as well as consumer products that purport to provide and prolong them) infuse global media, even though their benefits are as fleeting as the promised restorative powers of the fountain of youth.

Medical travelers cross borders in search of cures and therapies for every condition possible, from heart disease to obesity, failed organs, infertility, and sexual dysfunction. Senior citizens travel from the United States to Canada and Mexico to buy lower-priced generic drugs that are unavailable or unaffordable at home. The wealthy travel on tourist visas to impoverished countries to receive organ transplants. The poor travel without documents to wealthy countries to receive basic health care. Surgeons and patients migrate. So do body parts (see Scheper-Hughes's work in Chapter 3) and medicines (both legally and illegally). Many medical travelers search for alternative cures outside the world of biomedicine, including Chinese or Indian treatments for chronic ailments such as cancer or diabetes. Muslims, Christians, Buddhists, Daoists, and Hindus make pilgrimages to sacred shrines, holy mountains, and healing waters. They bathe in the Ganges River in India, scale Mount Tai in China, and pray to the Virgin Mary at the Sanctuary of Our Lady of Lourdes in France.

Global Humanitarianism and Egypt's Village Girls

In the twentieth century, most global humanitarian initiatives were implemented by nation-states and coordinated by special bodies like the World Health Organization (WHO) or the United Nations' Children's Emergency Fund (UNICEF). But today private-sector actors like philanthropic agencies and nongovernmental organizations (NGOs) are reshaping public health interventions worldwide under the umbrella of humanitarianism, development, and security (Biehl and Petryna 2013).

Anthropologist Rania Sweis (2012) examines the impact of one such program, The Village Girl Youth Project (VGYP). The first large-scale humanitarian initiative targeting adolescent village girls in Egypt, VGYP mobilizes middle-class donors in Europe and North America to support efforts to protect and liberate village girls. These girls are portrayed as vulnerable, suffering, confined to their homes, denied education, and victims of patriarchal oppression that forces them into domestic work and early childhood marriages. Through direct interventions the project hopes that village girls can be freed from traditional roles, taught about their rights, and prepared to be future leaders of their country. Outdoor sports are considered essential to the program, as the

medical migration: The movement of diseases, medical treatments, and entire health-care systems, as well as those seeking medical care, across national borders.

THE SOCIAL LIFE OF THINGS
Pharmaceutical Drugs in Nigeria

Many of us visit the local pharmacy to fill a prescription for an antibiotic or asthma, acid reflux or ADHD (attention deficit/hyperactivity disorder) medication. We expect the drug to be pure, accurately labeled, effective, and predictably priced. This is not the reality for many people in the world. Kristin Peterson's (2015) research explores what happened in Nigeria when international pharmaceutical companies abandoned the country and the innovative strategies local Nigerians have used to fill the gap.

① Big pharmaceutical companies set up business in Nigeria in the 1970s and early 1980s, manufacturing and distributing branded pharmaceuticals for the expanding Nigerian middle class. But a civil war, an oil bust, and policies of economic austerity drove Nigeria's economy into near ruin. Pressured by financial investors, pharmaceutical companies abandoned Nigeria in the 1980s, leaving Nigerians to fill the pharmaceutical shortfall.

② Over the past twenty years, Idumota, one of Nigeria's largest marketplaces, has become the key point for drugs entering Nigeria and moving into West Africa's drug distribution network. Local entrepreneurs have transformed the local streets, alleyways, intersections, and tight passageways into locations for pharmaceutical sales. And Idumota's traders have replaced pharmacists as dispensers of pharmaceuticals to those with health needs.

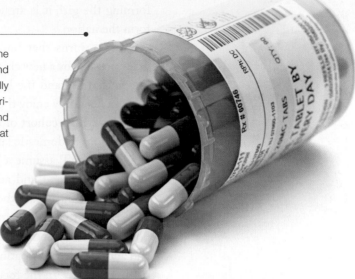

(3) In an unregulated market, the source and quality of the drugs sold in Idumota is hard to verify. European and North American manufacturers have been gradually replaced by Indian ones and by Chinese raw materials compounded by local Nigerians. Brand-name and generic drugs can be purchased in the market, but at least 30 percent are fakes.

(4) In Nigeria's pharmaceutical market, people are left to manage their own risk. Entrepreneurs manage the risk of an unregulated, cash-based and haphazardly policed drug market where prices fluctuate wildly and quantity and quality of supply is unpredictable. Consumers are left to manage the risk not just of disease, but of the supposed cure, which may do them more harm than good.

Like people all over the world, Nigerians work hard to prevent disease and return to health once sick. But their obstacles are daunting. An examination of the social life of pharmaceuticals in Nigeria reveals that the heart of the problem lies in the gap between people's medical needs and the available treatments. This discrepancy leaves both entrepreneurs and consumers in Nigeria to hustle, struggle, and innovate to bridge that divide.

- If you take any prescription medicine, do you know where it is made and by whom? If not, why?
- Because of the price of prescription drugs, many people in the United States, like those in Nigeria, are left to hustle and innovate to receive the treatment they need to be healthy. What strategies could you use in this situation? What are the risks you would face?

emancipation of a girl's body is seen as key to emancipation of the girl. Transforming the girl, it is argued, can transform the village and eventually transform the nation.

Sweis warns that humanitarian development projects such as this one, made possible by a new era of globalization, may fall short of their goals because they misunderstand the local culture of the people they are intended to help. Girls in her study enjoy the sports, for instance, and they build new social relationships with a cohort of village friends. But the program does not alter their involvement in domestic labor or early childhood marriage. Humanitarian projects like VGYP assume a Western notion of adolescence as a separate period between childhood and adulthood: a time of play, learning, and exploration before the work of adulthood begins. But youth is not a fixed category with global relevance. Instead, it is mediated by local culture and realities. In areas of poverty, children and youth constantly cross the boundary between childhood and adulthood, participating in household work, caring for children, and working in the fields. In the focus on teaching girls' rights, Sweis warns, humanitarian organizations often miss the more profound everyday conditions of poverty that create these realities in the first place, affecting the girls' households on a daily basis, keeping them and their friends out of the public school and out of local processes of growth and development.

Multiple Systems of Healing

The current era of medical migration has spurred the encounter of multiple systems of healing, including ideas of health and illness that overlap and often conflict. The intersection of multiple cultural approaches to healing, called **medical pluralism**, often creates tensions, especially in the encounter between Western biomedicine and other cultural patterns of health and illness. But the engagement also provides opportunities for additional alternative and complementary choices and medical options to emerge (Lock 1993, 2002).

medical pluralism: The intersection of multiple cultural approaches to healing.

Colliding Cultures: Hmong Refugees and the U.S. Health-Care System

Anne Fadiman's *The Spirit Catches You and You Fall Down* (1997) captures the intensity and danger of cross-cultural medical encounters through the story of the Lees, a Hmong refugee family from Laos in Southeast Asia. The Lees settled in the city of Merced in California's agricultural Central Valley in the 1980s. More than 150,000 Hmong refugees fled Laos in the 1970s and 1980s. Many had fought clandestinely with the United States on the losing side of wars in Vietnam and Laos. More than 12,000 Hmong eventually settled in Merced, a city of only 61,000 people.

The Lees' fourteenth child, Lia Lee, was born on July 9, 1982, apparently a healthy, happy baby. But at three months of age, her seizures began. At first, her family comforted her and cared for her at home. Her uncontrollable convulsions on October 24 led the family to Merced Community Medical Center (MCMC), a small county hospital but also a teaching hospital where first-year residents from the University of California–Davis train in family practice. The October 24 visit began a long and painful encounter—a collision—between the Lee family and the U.S. health-care system.

Unbeknownst to the doctors at MCMC, the Lees had already diagnosed Lia's illness as *qaug dab peg*, which translates into English as epilepsy. Familiar with *qaug dab peg* in their own cultural context, the Lees were ambivalent about their daughter's illness. The seizures, they knew, could be dangerous. But among the Hmong, those suffering from *qaug dab peg* were held in high esteem. Many became powerful shamans—traditional healers and community visionaries. The Lees had come to the hospital for their daughter to be healed, but they also wondered about her potentially auspicious future.

MAP 16.5
Laos

Also unbeknownst to the MCMC doctors, the Lees knew what had caused Lia's illness and how to treat it. She suffered from soul loss. Her older sister had allowed the front door of their small home to slam, and the loud noise had scared Lia's soul away. An elaborate ritual of soul-calling conducted by a Hmong shaman could trap the lost soul and return it to Lia's body. But her seizures on that October night were overwhelming, and her parents feared that she would die without immediate care.

By the time the Lees arrived at the hospital, the seizures had stopped. With no clear symptoms to treat, the doctors were at a loss. The hospital had no translator, and the Lees spoke no English. The resident on call misdiagnosed the remaining symptoms as an infection, prescribed medication, and sent the family home. Unfortunately, the prescription and medication instructions were written in English, which the Lees could not understand. Lia Lee was misdiagnosed at the hospital again on November 11. Finally, on March 3, 1983, the family arrived with Lia still convulsing. A young family member who spoke some English translated. The resident on call diagnosed the cause as epilepsy. Then the child was subjected to a battery of invasive tests, including a spinal tap, a CT scan, a chest X-ray, and blood work—none of which the hospital staff could adequately explain to Lia's parents. The child had experienced five months of seizures small and large without proper diagnosis and medication, and now she endured a terrifying night at the hospital.

Between the ages of eight months and four and a half years, Lia Lee was admitted to MCMC seventeen times and made more than one hundred outpatient visits for treatment of her seizures. Over the same period, her doctors prescribed fourteen different medications in different combinations and dosages, changing her prescription twenty-three times—all with a family unfamiliar with English, Western medical practices, or the U.S. system of weights and measures needed to determine the proper dosage.

The collision of cultures escalated when doctors decided that Lia Lee's ongoing seizures were caused by her parents' failure to comply with the medication prescriptions. This, the lead doctor determined, qualified as child neglect and child abuse. Acting on the doctor's concerns, the county courts ordered Lia Lee removed from her parents' custody and placed in foster care so that her medicines could be properly administered. The doctors thought they were acting to protect the child. Her parents, however, unable to understand the medical, legal, or moral logic of removing a child from her family and convinced that they were doing everything in their power to care for their daughter, could only imagine that they were being punished for some unknown reason.

The courts eventually returned Lia Lee to her parents after nearly a year in foster care. Her condition had not improved. Her parents, in fact, felt that her cognitive abilities and social skills had deteriorated during the year away. Despite the parents' efforts to comply with Lia's drug regimen, another series of catastrophic epileptic seizures landed her in MCMC again and finally in a children's hospital in nearby Fresno. Treatment of the seizures was ultimately ineffective. Despite what hospital staff considered heroic measures, Lia was left with the dramatically reduced brain activity that doctors call a "persistent vegetative state." Doctors removed all life support and feeding tubes. She was returned to MCMC and finally to the Lees' home.

Considering her lingering fevers, the medical professionals expected her to die. But Lia's parents placed her in soothing herbal baths, fed her, carried her with them, slept with her in their bed, and continued the elaborate Hmong rituals of soul-calling to return her to health. Though her brain activity never returned, Lia did not die. Her parents were convinced that all the medicines the doctors had forced on her had left her in this condition. (Indeed, Fadiman found some evidence suggesting that Lia's massive final seizure may have been caused by a hospital-acquired infection.) They hoped that their traditional healing methods might still return her lost soul to her body.

Bridging Cultural Divides via Illness Narratives Fadiman's interviews found that the parties in this cross-cultural health encounter held vastly different views of what had occurred. Most of the doctors criticized the parents as uncooperative. They debated whether this stemmed from cultural barriers, lack of intelligence, or character flaws that kept them from caring properly for their daughter. Many saw the parents as ungrateful for all the effort and resources that had been expended on their daughter's case. Few made any attempt to ask the Lees how they understood Lia's illness and how they would treat it. In contrast, the Lees considered most of the medical staff to be uncommunicative, arrogant, cold, and punitive; they also described the medical procedures Lia had undergone as invasive, culturally inappropriate, and ineffective. They never understood how the government could take their beloved daughter from them to be put in the care of strangers.

The conflict between the Lees and the MCMC staff reflected broader misunderstandings between the Hmong community and the hospital's medical staff. These misunderstandings were based on language barriers, cultural barriers, varied interpretations of what health and illness mean, and different strategies for taking care of ill family members. The Lees never understood the biomedical assessment of epilepsy as a misfiring of brain cells caused by an electromagnetic storm in their daughter's head. The doctors never understood the Lees' assessment of *qaug dab peg* as caused by soul loss, treatable through the healing traditions of their local community.

At the conclusion of her research, Fadiman contacted a preeminent medical anthropologist, Arthur Kleinman of Harvard University. Kleinman, a specialist in cross-cultural issues in health and illness, has been instrumental in formulating a concept of collecting illness narratives as a way to bridge cultural divides in treating illness and promoting health (Kleinman 1988). **Illness narratives** are the personal stories that people tell to explain their illness. The narratives reveal the psychological, social, and cultural aspects that give illness its context and meaning. These stories can provide healers with an essential framework for developing treatment strategies that will make sense to the patient and have the greatest chance of success. To elicit the illness narrative, Kleinman suggests asking the following questions:

1. What do you call the problem?
2. What do you think has caused the problem?
3. Why do you think it started when it did?
4. What do you think the sickness does? How does it work?
5. How severe is the sickness? Will it have a short or long course?
6. What kind of treatment do you think the patient should receive? What are the most important results you hope the patient will receive from this treatment?

Kleinman argues that in order to provide effective treatment, "you need to understand that as powerful an influence as the culture of the Hmong patient and her family is on this case, the culture of biomedicine is equally powerful. If you can't see that your own culture has its own set of interests, emotions, and biases, how can you expect to deal successfully with someone else's culture?" (Fadiman 1997, 261).

Would Lia Lee's treatment would have been effective had the MCMC medical staff asked the family to provide this illness narrative—the cultural framework through which they viewed the cause and potential treatment of her illness? Doing so might have provided an avenue to engage the family in a

Foua Yang weeps as she talks about her daughter, Lia Lee, who died on August 31, 2012, at the age of 30 after a lifelong struggle for health. A collision of two cultural approaches to healing left her severely wounded in childhood.

illness narratives: The personal stories that people tell to explain their illnesses.

cooperative treatment process. Through that process, multiple systems of healing and concepts of health and illness might have intersected to create a multifaceted approach to healing for Lia Lee.

Encounters of distinct medical systems like that experienced by Lia Lee and her family in the California health-care system will only increase as globalization continues to break down barriers to the flow of ideas, people, diseases,

TOOLKIT

Thinking Like an Anthropologist: Health in the Individual and in the Global Population

The human body is a spectacularly sophisticated organism. Its 10 trillion cells constitute complex cardiovascular, pulmonary, and digestive systems made up of muscles, ligaments, organs, veins, and arteries, all shaped and guided by approximately 20,000 protein-coding genes that form our DNA sequence. The body, which has evolved over millions of years, enables us to interact with one another, reproduce our species, and adapt to the remarkable variety of environments found on Earth.

Healthy bodies are produced through a complex interaction between genetics and culture. As we saw in Chapter 5, the human genetic code provides a basic framework for the body's growth, but culture and the natural environment influence how our bodies actually develop. Nutrition, disease, and exercise, along with our collective human health-care practices, affect what we look like, how we feel, how well we live, and how long we live. Even the human mind is not fully formed at birth. Nutrition, stimulation, affection, and trauma after birth continue to shape the contours of the brain.

When medical anthropologists consider issues of health, they think about both the individual body and the social body. As discussed in this chapter, we humans and our individual bodies do not live in isolation. Nor is our health created in isolation. We live in relation to one another as part of a social body—a collection of individuals whose health is tied to the success of the group as well (Scheper-Hughes and Lock 1987). The health of the football players discussed in the chapter opener, like the health of Lia Lee, is directly related to the health of those

around them, to understandings of bodies, and to the system of health care created and shared by the larger culture in which they live.

As you think more about health and illness—perhaps your own personal experiences or those of people around you—remember the big questions we have been exploring:

- How does culture shape our ideas of health and illness?
- How do different cultural conceptions of the body affect health practices?
- How can anthropologists help solve health-care problems?
- Why does the distribution of health and illness mirror that of wealth and power?
- How is globalization changing the experience of health and illness and the practice of medicine?

After reading this chapter, are you able to apply these questions to specific situations?

As we have seen, medical anthropologists examine the diverse strategies that cultures have developed to protect and promote the health of the body. And they work to apply the methodological and analytical tools of anthropology to enhance and expand health care in the face of increasing global health inequalities. Debates about health and illness are all around us: Will all fifty U.S. states expand Medicaid eligibility for the poor as envisioned by the 2010 Affordable Care Act? Will the law address women's reproductive health needs? Will the Medicare eligibility age be raised, making it harder for seniors to find health medical treatments, and health practitioners from one world region to another. These encounters will continue to challenge and expand our notions of disease, illness, and health care. As we have seen in this chapter, medical anthropologists are deeply engaged in the analysis and understanding of these transitions and in the articulation of strategies to develop and promote sophisticated, people-centered, and holistic approaches to the challenges of health and illness.

coverage? Will your college or university adequately fund its student health center to provide for all of a student's health needs? Who sets the health center's policies and budget? Would you consider joining or supporting an organization like Paul Farmer's Partners in Health (see p. 633) to help address the health-care needs of people in another part of the world? How will you engage these debates? Thinking like an anthropologist can help you better understand and address these issues, whether they present themselves as your own personal issues of health and illness, those of your friends and family, or the health of the global human population.

Key Terms

For Further Exploration

Amchi Medicine. www.rolexawards.com/profiles /laureates/laurent_pordi. Short video about *amchi* medicine in India and the work of French anthropologist Laurent Pordié.

The Business of Being Born. 2008. Directed by Abby Epstein. Barranca Productions. www.thebusinessofbeingborn .com. Documentary examining childbirth practices in the United States.

Fadiman, Anne. 1997. *The Spirit Catches You and You Fall Down: A Hmong Child, Her American Doctors, and the Collision of Two Cultures*. New York: Farrar, Straus, and Giroux.

Go Ask Alice. www.goaskalice.columbia.edu. Columbia University's health website designed specifically for college students.

Kidder, Tracy. 2003. *Mountains beyond Mountains: The Quest of Dr. Paul Farmer, a Man Who Would Cure the World*. New York: Random House.

Nomad RSI. www.nomadrsi.org. French nongovernmental organization founded by Laurent Pordié that supports *amchi* medical practices in Ladakh, India.

Pandemic: Facing AIDS. 2003. HBO. Five 30-minute films exposing the worldwide AIDS epidemic with stories from Thailand, Brazil, India, Uganda, and Russia.

Partners in Health. www.pih.org. Paul Farmer's global health organization.

Society for Medical Anthropology. www.medanthro.net. lists films and resources for the study of medical anthropology.

WebMD. www.webmd.com. Online health information.

Youth in a Brazilian shantytown have constructed a miniature city where they reenact their complex urban world in an elaborate game started in 1997.

CHAPTER 17
Art and Media

In a favela, or shantytown, set on a steep hillside above Rio de Janeiro, Brazil, a remarkable 4,000-square-foot miniature model of the city overlooks the sprawling metropolis below. Known as Morrinho ("Little Hill"), this virtual urban world began as a children's game in 1997 and today draws the attention of government officials, filmmakers, development agencies, and artists from around the world.

Working and playing together with other neighborhood kids, two brothers began to construct the miniature city out of discarded bricks, tiles, mortar, and borrowed masonry tools. As the game gradually grew in size and complexity, streets began to emerge, followed by homes, restaurants, stores, hospitals, and police stations. Each of the children began to inhabit the game, making avatars for themselves from bottle caps and batteries. The streets came alive with human interactions: friendships and fights, games and business. The constructed city took on a life of its own, yet it was a life that reflected and illuminated human relations and social conditions in the favela and the city of Rio.

Today thousands of avatars placed within the miniature city engage in an elaborate dramatization of community life. They live and die, work and play, break the law and make love. Battles rage between gangs and with police. Brazilian pennies have become currency, exchanged in the game for goods and services, motorcycle rides, and bags of drugs. Each youth controls his or her avatar and portion of the model.

Anthropologist Alessandro Angelini has conducted ethnographic fieldwork in this miniature world and the surrounding community since 2008. He notes the ways in which Morrinho has developed significance beyond the interactive model city, particularly as the youths' manipulation

Art? Play? Politics? All are expressed in the reconstruction of Morrinho, a virtual urban world in a Brazilian favela (*left*) begun as a children's game but now a national and international destination. Youth from Morrinho have even re-created their favela as art installations in cities abroad, including London (*right*), where they integrated miniatures of St. Paul's Cathedral, Big Ben, the London Eye, and the London "tube" subway.

of miniature urban life has cast a spotlight on the intersection of poverty, class, power, kinship, identity, the state, and politics. For instance, Morrinho has drawn the attention of Brazilian political authorities. The community—now well known in Rio and beyond—became one of the first favelas to receive state infrastructure improvements, including sewage systems, housing, road paving, lighting, pathways, and railings. The community was also one of the first to be targeted with increased police presence and paramilitary security forces as the government sought to pacify and eliminate any undesirable elements.

Morrinho has also drawn the attention of artists and activists, crossing a boundary between play, creative expression, politics, and art. Tourists visit from Rio and beyond. Filmmakers document the story of the miniature city and its surrounding community through artistic films shown at international festivals. A small group of Morrinho's originators have been invited on multiple occasions since 2004 to reproduce a model of Morrinho at art festivals in cities such as Barcelona, Paris, Vienna, Munich, Venice, and Innsbruck, as well as in places in Holland, Colombia, and East Timor. Collaborating with local underprivileged youth from South London in the summer of 2010, the group created an installation of Morrinho at a prominent Brazilian arts festival in England, while adding to their miniature city certain elements of London—Big Ben, prisons, and other features important to London youth. In these settings what began as a game is admired as art, not as play (Angelini 2016).

In this chapter we will explore the array of human creative expression and interaction that anthropologists consider when exploring the world of art. Humans express themselves creatively and interact meaningfully through the visual and written arts, movement, sound, and more. An anthropological approach to art may include attention to paintings, drawings, design, weavings, photographs, film, sculpture, architecture, dance, music, songs, games, sports, clothing, cuisine, and even virtual online design and creativity. In addition, we will consider the intersection of art and globalization, art and politics, and art and media as technologies such as television, radio, film, and Internet-based social media establish new venues for creative expression and new avenues for communicating and engaging those expressions. In particular, we will consider the following questions:

- What is art?
- What is unique about how anthropologists study art?
- What is the relationship between art and power?
- How do art and media intersect?

By the end of the chapter you will have gained an understanding of the unique approach that anthropologists take to the study of art, the many ways in which art reflects and transforms culture, and the ways in which globalization and new forms of media are transforming art and its dissemination.

What Is Art?

Anthropologists define **art** broadly as all the ideas, forms, techniques, and strategies that humans employ to express themselves creatively and to communicate their creativity and inspiration to others. Art may include a vast array of music, songs, stories, paintings, plays, design, sculpture, architecture, clothing, food, and games. But art is not limited to the artist.

art: All ideas, forms, techniques, and strategies that humans employ to express themselves creatively and to communicate their creativity and inspiration to others.

The Anthropology of Art

Art is both created and received. Cooking and building, fashion and oratory, decorating and dressing, sewing and play all represent media through which artists and audience communicate. Through these often dynamic encounters, art takes its shape not only in creation but also in perception. In the chapter-opening story, for example, the full impact of the game created by the young people of Morrinho emerges in the interaction of those who are creating it with those who are perceiving it, interpreting it, and making it come alive for the community—a community that stretches far beyond local boundaries.

When thinking anthropologically about art in its global context, it is helpful to first consider some of the common but flawed assumptions that Western traditions have developed about how to evaluate what is and is not art. In particular, we will examine how the anthropology of art challenges commonplace notions of (1) a distinction between fine art and popular art, (2) the existence

of a universal art aesthetic, and (3) the assumption of qualitative differences between Western art and so-called primitive art.

Fine Art versus Popular Art Art in Western traditions has often been associated with notions of "high culture" or "fine art," especially elite representations of visual and performance arts experienced in formal venues. Paintings and sculptures displayed in museums and art galleries; operas, symphonies, and ballets performed in recital halls; musicals and plays performed in theaters; fashion shows on runways; and fine cuisine prepared in expensive restaurants fit a view of **fine art** as the province of the elite. Such art is often evaluated and portrayed in contrast to **popular art**—less refined and less sophisticated creative expressions associated with the general population—in the same way that high culture might be simplistically compared to popular culture.

From an anthropological perspective, however, art is not the sole province of the elites or professional artists. Art is integral to all of human life. As such, it can be expressed through elaborate performances in specialized venues as well as through routine activities in mundane settings. Later in this chapter, for example, we will explore powerful expressions of art in such diverse media as Australian indigenous paintings, Haitian marching bands, and African American children's games. Seen from a broad anthropological perspective, any members of a group can create and experience art.

The significance of art cannot be underestimated as anthropologists consider the full expression of human life. All creativity expressed through cultural products such as songs, paintings, dance, architecture, clothing, games, and food carries rich deposits of information about culture as a system of meaning and

fine art: Creative expression and communication often associated with cultural elites.

popular art: Creative expression and communication often associated with the general population.

as a system of power. In fact, the very distinction between fine art and popular art may have more to do with political choices and hierarchies of power than with an intrinsic character of the art itself. Who decides, for instance, what will be performed in an opera house or displayed in a national museum? Who directs and who funds the selection, acquisition, and presentation (Thornton 2009; Werner 2006)? Can you identify other cultural dynamics of power and stratification—perhaps race, gender, class, religion, or sexuality—that might be reflected in these decisions and representations of what is fine art and what is popular art? (Marcus and Myers 1995; see Perkins and Morphy 2006; Schneider and Wright 2006.)

Considering Aesthetics across Cultures The human encounter with art entails an aesthetic experience—broadly speaking, the perception through one's senses in contrast with the perception through intellect and logic. Western art traditions, specifically those in Europe and North America, have tended to focus primarily on the aesthetic value of art and on a particular concept of aesthetics associated with certain standards of beauty, creativity, and innovation that are presumed to represent the most refined expressions of a group's culture. But is there a universal art aesthetic found across cultures that informs what people consider to be art and not art? Is there a **universal gaze**—an intrinsic way of perceiving art—that guides the ways people respond to art? Anthropologists of art have been deeply involved in this debate.

The Western concept of a universal art aesthetic traces back to the German philosophers Immanuel Kant (1724–1804) and Georg W. F. Hegel (1770–1831). They suggested that nature creates a universal aesthetic in humans—particularly a sense of what is beautiful—and that it establishes the foundation

universal gaze: An intrinsic way of perceiving art—thought by many in the Western art world to be found across cultures—that informs what people consider to be art or not art.

of a universal gaze through which all art can be seen. Through this universal gaze, art can provide viewers with a "transcendental" aesthetic experience, lift them out of the day-to-day, and transform their vision of the world (Stoller 2003).

A presumption of a universal art aesthetic was prevalent in much of the Western art world throughout most of the twentieth century. Reflecting this, Western art institutions, particularly those focusing on fine art, strove to reinforce this aesthetic experience through their style of presentation. Beginning in the last half of the twentieth century, curators displayed art in a minimalist manner, perhaps only accompanied by a piece's title, date, and name of artist, in an attempt to allow the art to speak for itself. Neutral, objective presentation encouraged the contemplation of objects removed from their worldly context, including their social and economic conditions of production, marketing, and consumption. Similarly, architects designed the physical spaces of Western art galleries and museums to symbolize this universal aesthetic, constructing high ceilings, bare white walls, and open areas that offered unique spaces for experiencing objects' transcendental qualities. The intent was for people to experience art as art—the intrinsic aesthetic of art objects re-created through a universal gaze.

Anthropologists of art have actively challenged the widespread belief in and representation of a universal art aesthetic. Not all cultures have the same aesthetic. Perceptions of beauty, imagination, skill, and style vary widely across cultures, as do approaches to artistic ideas, objects, and practices. In fact, what many people have considered to be a universal aesthetic has frequently proven to be a unique product of Western history and culture (Alexander 1996; Alpers 1991; Karp and Lavine 1991; Price 1989).

The expectations of art and the cultural frameworks for perceiving art may also vary from place to place and even within different cultures. Art may be viewed as beautiful and inspirational: A painting, sculpture, dance, or song may bring pleasure and joy to those who experience it. But the perception and response to art is not limited to only those emotions. Art may also shock, terrify, horrify, or anger its audience. Like other key elements of culture, art is deeply embedded in the processes of enculturation that shape the observer's perceptions, expectations, and experience when evaluating art.

To further illustrate the vast range of possible aesthetic perspectives, consider the following simple contrasts. Whereas Western art traditions may emphasize innovation and originality—creating something entirely new— other traditions may celebrate improvisation on already-existing themes (Boas 1927; Price 1989). In such traditions, artistic value is created as the artist explores variations on established themes (Vogel 1991). Likewise, whereas many Western cultures may idealize the artist as an individual genius—as a cultural outsider

How does the presentation of art—for instance, in this minimalist gallery—affect your experience and understanding of it?

separated from mundane daily life—other cultures may prioritize engagement with the audience and interaction with the community as the highest aspects of artistic expression. In such instances, the artist may be celebrated for playing a central role in the community's life rather than for his or her individual behavior (Perkins and Morphy 2006).

Beyond "Primitive" Art Western art traditions have often created a problematic distinction between Western art and so-called primitive art. Early anthropologists played key roles in the nineteenth and early twentieth centuries in building great ethnographic museum collections to store and display the art and life ways of "other" cultures for a Western audience, though these treasure troves were often acquired through the colonial encounter (that is, taken rather than purchased or borrowed).

The Western art world became interested in what came to be known as "primitive art" in the early twentieth century. At that time, modernist European artists such as Pablo Picasso began to incorporate African and Oceanic art features and themes into their own work, though largely without reference to the art's original cultural context. In the twentieth century, museums and galleries mounted prominent displays, dioramas, and collections of "primitive" art itself (typically, the art of Africa, Oceania, and Latin America).

In contrast to the anthropological approach to world art, which seeks to understand the development and meaning of local art forms within their unique and complex cultural contexts, the tendency in Western art traditions to draw clear distinctions between Western and "primitive" art reinforced the perception of a hierarchy of world art and an evolutionary trajectory in its development from simple to complex, primitive to civilized. The tendency to display art from other cultures without reference to its original context or meaning reinforced the stereotypes about non-Western people and their relationship to Western civilization.

Anthropologists of art (as well as economic anthropologists and political anthropologists) reject an evolutionary framing and evaluation. As noted, through their research and writing, as well as through direct engagement with Western art institutions, anthropologists of art have been instrumental in challenging and transforming the ways museums and other institutions of art depict non-Western cultures and their creative expressions. These anthropologists have also been encouraging an ethnographic turn toward a thorough contextualization of the processes and meaning of art as it emerges in each local context, investigating art's "social life" as it moves beyond local borders, and even reconsidering Western art within its own indigenous, local cultural context (Alexander 1996; Alpers 1991; Karp and Lavine 1991; Price 1989).

Art in Human History

An examination of art in human history provides a crucial context for our deliberations as we consider the question "What is art?" Although common images of our human ancestors may not depict them as artists, the expanding archaeological record reveals a deep historical connection between humans and art that reaches back tens of thousands of years. Art appears to be a fundamental aspect of what it means to be human. Though the archaeological record of human artistic work expands dramatically around 40,000 years ago, clear evidence has emerged of human creative expression dating back at least 100,000 years.

MAP 17.1
South Africa

Blombos Cave, South Africa Archaeological discoveries over the past two decades in South Africa's Blombos Cave—set high in a cliff overlooking the Indian Ocean—reveal that as early as 75,000 years ago, anatomically modern humans were making finely crafted stone weapon points, carving tools out of animal bones, and engraving symbols on blocks of a red stone called ochre. The treasure trove of artifacts, initially discovered in 1993 by Norwegian archaeologist Christopher Henshilwood and colleagues, provides the earliest evidence of what could be considered artistic expression by our modern human ancestors.

In 2008 Henshilwood's team uncovered what amounts to a 100,000-year-old painters' workshop: bone tools for mixing paint, stones for pounding and grinding, yellow and red ochre for color. The ochre would have been blended with fat, charcoal, and mammal-bone marrow to form a paint mixture. The bone tools retained traces of red ocher. Samples of the reddish material were still attached to the interior of two large abalone shells used to mix the paint (Henshilwood et al. 2011; Larsen 2014).

Archaeologists are uncertain what the paint was used for, but they suggest that this isolated cave served as a kind of artists' studio to prepare material for use on the body, on clothing, or in ritual ceremonies. The extensive use of paint may, in turn, indicate an early capacity for symbolic thought. Unlike weapons and tools, which could be used to hunt or build or protect the group, the utilitarian value of paint is less clear. Though perhaps applied to the skin or clothing as camoflauge for hunting, paint might also have been used symbolically to convey a social message, perhaps in a group's social or ritual practices beyond the immediate group. Finds from this early date suggest that humans had already developed a rudimentary knowledge of chemistry and engaged in complex social practices, including the long-range planning required to find, store, and combine the materials found in Blombos Cave. And, perhaps most significant, the finds push back the date of the earliest indications of human capacity for symbolic thought.

A comprehensive study of artifacts gleaned from various African sites reveals the gradual emergence of human artistic expression that later spread to other world regions. Recent archaeological evidence suggests that our human ancestors in Africa may have become cognitively and behaviorally "modern" as early as 300,000 to 400,000 years ago. Later, the development of bone and stone tools—along with the processing and use of pigment, art, and decoration at sites across Africa and from various eras—suggests that our human ancestors in Africa gradually assembled the package of modern human behaviors associated with art, eventually carrying them to other regions of the world (McBrearty and Brooks 2000).

Paleolithic Cave Paintings in Europe Perhaps the best-known examples of early art outside Africa are the spectacular Paleolithic cave paintings that have been discovered in areas of southern France (Lascaux Cave and Chauvet-Pont-d'Arc Cave) and northern Spain (Altamira Cave). The artwork dates from 32,000 to 10,000 years ago. The early artists elaborately depicted reindeer, bison, mammoth, horses, lions, and other animals prevalent in that period. Carved human figurines, jewelry, ritual objects, and bone and ivory carvings accompany elaborate burial sites found in the caves.

The cave art reveals highly developed artistic skills, including the incorporation of the contours of partially sculpted cave walls to provide a sense of dynamism and movement in the paintings. Analysis of the paintings reveals that the

The connection between humans and art reaches back tens of thousands of years. Here, archaeologists excavate a 100,000-year-old "artists' studio" in Blombos Cave, South Africa, with artifacts in the foreground.

MAP 17.2
Spain and France

This elaborate wall painting in Lascaux Cave, France, depicting horses, bison, mammoth, and lions and dating between 32,000 to 12,000 BCE, reveals the highly developed artistic skills of our immediate ancestors.

cave art was not the work of a few individuals or small groups but rather developed over a 20,000-year period through the efforts of many different artists who reused, modified, and painted over the artwork of their predecessors (Herzog 2010; Larsen 2014).

The purpose of the cave paintings is not clear. Our ancestors may have utilized them in storytelling, recordkeeping, rituals, ceremonies, or perhaps all of these. Despite the uncertainty over their purpose, it is clear that the complexity of materials, subjects, and symbolism reveals an elaborate social life and an advanced level of cognitive development that does not fit contemporary stereotypes of "cavemen" living during the most recent ice age in Europe.

Whether through a 100,000-year-old painters' studio in southern Africa, Paleolithic cave art in southern France, or a fine art museum in a contemporary global city, we see that art is integral to all of human life. It can be expressed in elaborate displays or through simple craftwork. But through these events, objects, and expressions, anthropologists can gather crucial insights into people and their cultures. Anthropologists bring a unique perspective to the study of art. As we will explore in the following section, one of these unique contributions lies in careful ethnographic analysis and attention to the cultural production and transaction of art. This focus illuminates the complex social life of art as it is produced and exchanged between people and across geographic spaces and cultural boundaries.

What Is Unique about How Anthropologists Study Art?

Anthropologists' unique approach to art includes particular attention to how art is embedded in a community—how art connects to social norms and values and economic and political systems and events. Who makes it and why? What does it mean to the people who create it and to those who perceive it? What are its functional and inspirational roles? As ethnographers, anthropologists of art attend not only to the form of the art itself—its designs, movements, and sounds—but also to its context. We consider not only the creative production of a piece of art but also each work's unique and often complex history as it journeys through human culture. After all, as we will see, art is embedded in everyday exchanges, social networks, business negotiations, and other struggles over profit, power, and prestige.

The Ethnography of Art

Placing art in context has become more complicated and interesting in recent years. Today, in an era of intensifying globalization, local art is created in a global landscape. Local art practices, objects, and events intersect with global movements of people and ideas. Art is often a key juncture through which local communities engage the global economy (Kopytoff 1986). Within this global "artscape" (Appadurai 1986), the creation of local art may provide not only a means of economic activity but also a venue to demonstrate cultural skills and values and to assert local cultural identity in the face of rapid change (Perkins and Morphy 2006). As a result, contemporary anthropologists of art explore the journeys of objects across boundaries and the implications of the "traffic in culture" for both those who produce art and those who consume it (Marcus and Myers 1995; Schneider and Wright 2006; Venbrux, Rosi, and Welsch 2006).

Let's consider a few case studies that illuminate contemporary anthropological approaches to the study of art through ethnography.

The Trade in West African Art

In *African Art in Transit* (1994), anthropologist Christopher Steiner explores the dynamic role of art in human culture through an ethnographic study of art traders in Abidjan, the main port city of Côte d'Ivoire in West Africa. Abidjan's art traders, mostly Muslims, serve as middlemen in the flow of African art between its creators (mostly rural villagers) and its consumers (Western tourists and international art collectors).

Within this flow, itinerant African traders circulate among upcountry villages, purchasing wooden carvings and clay figurines. The traders sometimes buy unique ritual items and family heirlooms directly from individuals, but generally they acquire mass-produced objects from artisan workshops that cater to

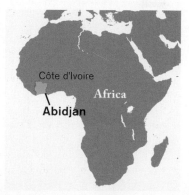

MAP 17.3
Abidjan

the tourist and export art trade. The traders then sell to urban dealers, small and large, who resell the pieces to street hawkers, market stands, and upscale galleries. Within this milieu, Steiner investigates the intricate business practices and networks that link traders, suppliers, and consumers. And he details the elaborate production, presentation, description, alteration, authentication, and pricing of local art pieces within an increasingly globalized art market driven by tourists, Western and non-Western art dealers, and art connoisseurs.

As is true in all art markets, whether for carvings, paintings, fabrics, jewelry, or cuisine, an object's aesthetic value translates into a monetary value. Steiner examines the process by which West African art objects acquire value as they move through the art market. For example, how does a piece of carved wood become a desired object for purchase and collection? In Côte d'Ivoire, it is primarily a few Western tourists and art dealers who determine these values. For the most highly valued objects, an influential and wealthy elite of dealers, scholars, collectors, and exhibitors establishes their worth.

Key to the creation of value in the African art market is the perception of art objects as "authentic" or "genuine." Indeed, buyers and collectors are drawn to objects perceived to be of a certain origin and initial use. In turn, Côte d'Ivoire's local traders actively engage in the construction of **authenticity**—the perception of an object's antiquity, uniqueness, and originality within a local culture. Art objects are dirtied, artificially aged, stained, made to appear "primitive" to Western eyes, and altered to fit the buyers' ideals. Local traders tell stories about the objects' origin, meaning, and use to enhance the impression of authenticity. For tourists, traders create stories that appeal to the buyers' aesthetic tastes and desires to acquire a genuine, authentic object. For high-end collectors, traders provide an elaborate market history—a description of when, where, and how the object was collected, as well as its origins. Most of these stories, Steiner finds, are fabricated to meet the tastes of Western consumers and thereby raise the objects' value.

Many traders are highly skilled at constructing the illusion of discovery, uniqueness, and authenticity as they work to enhance their economic success in the art trade. Steiner recounts visits to local markets with Western collectors. At the front of a sprawling market, small booths and stands overflowed with local art objects. Of the first items encountered, none would hold interest for the tourist or collector. Later, a trader might lead the customer deeper into the market, down narrow, winding, dark alleys and into enclosed stalls and tents. Inside these dimly lit spaces, traders would hesitantly reveal objects tucked away in antique-looking wooden chests and cabinets. Here, customers would suddenly express keen interest, feeling they had discovered something more authentic than what the average tourist might find. Only then would they agree to pay higher prices. Steiner reveals that many art objects purchased

authenticity: The perception of an object's antiquity, uniqueness, and originality within a local culture.

What makes art "authentic"? A woodworker in West Africa makes carved figurines for market.

in this way were identical to objects displayed in booths on the outskirts of the market. Only the traders' performance had changed, demonstrating their mastery in conveying the characteristics of discovery, uniqueness, and authenticity that are central to consumers' aesthetic expectations.

The aesthetic values of Western tourists and collectors, expressed in their consumption patterns, significantly influence the production, marketing, and display of West African art. In fact, West African art traders continually move between local and global art markets, communicating between image creators and image consumers, between artists and audiences. In this context, the production of art does not occur solely for art's sake but is part of an economic strategy that engages multiple levels of the art market. Steiner notes, "West African traders leave each negotiation with a new sense of the aesthetic sense of the Western buyers, a sense that the traders and manufacturers must be closely in tune with as they go about their business of making a living in a rapidly globalizing world and in their niche in a rapidly globalizing art market" (1995, 164). In this way, West African art traders play a sophisticated role in a global art market. They serve as cultural brokers and mediators who communicate Western desires to the native artists and who promote a particular image of African art and culture to the West (Beidelman 1994; Gell 1995; Zilberg 1996).

Think about your own perception of art. What makes a piece of art "authentic" in your eyes?

Transforming West African "Wood" and "Mud" into Global Art In recent years, facilitated by increased migration and enhanced global transportation and communication systems, West African art traders have extended their business networks across the Atlantic Ocean to New York and throughout the United States. As a result, the long-distance trade of West African artwork, particularly "wood" (carved statues and masks) and "mud" (terra-cotta clay figurines), is leading to encounters between cultures and commerce at the intersection of two worlds (Stoller 2003).

The hub of the West African art trade in the United States is New York City—in particular, a multistory building on the west side of Midtown Manhattan called the Warehouse. The Warehouse is packed with stalls and shelves and display tables, each overflowing with "wood" and "mud." Every day, moving vans unload newly arrived shipments from West Africa while others onload pieces to be distributed by itinerant traders across the United States. West African traders cater to a wide array of clients: high-end art collectors, middle-class shoppers, and low-end street markets. High-end collectors search the New York galleries and art shows for what they consider fine art. At the same time, male and female West African art traders crisscross the country delivering mass-produced art objects for sale at boutiques, street markets, flea markets, and cultural festivals. They even deliver directly to some individual clients. The traders rely on networks of "cousins" and other fictive kin who provide housing, marketing advice, cultural interpretation, and shared transport in an extension of practices developed in West African long-distance trade networks.

The production of West African art for consumption in the United States leads to a mutual transformation of artistic meaning, aesthetics, and economic practice. It also provides a context within which an ethnologist can address the following questions: What exactly is art? What is considered aesthetically pleasing in each culture? What communicates? What moves people? What inspires people? What sells?

Stoller reflects on the power of global flows of people, art, and ideas to shape worlds of work and worlds of meaning. The introduction of West African art pieces into Western art worlds expands Western cultural notions of art

and beauty. Simultaneously, Western notions of art affect West African patterns of production and marketing, including what traders will buy from artisans in the mud and wood workshops in towns and villages throughout West Africa.

Moreover, on a practical level, these encounters at the crossroads of immigration and trade enable West African traders to meet their own social and economic obligations. They can pay off debts acquired in the immigration process and in starting up their small businesses. They can send remittances home to West Africa to support close family and extended kin groups. They can provide small amounts of start-up capital for rural and urban family enterprises. In the process of meeting these obligations, the traders themselves receive honor and respect from their home communities. Stoller expresses this insight candidly:

> As for the African art traders, many of them have a sophisticated comprehension of the aesthetic, economic, and political forces that drive the markets they attempt—often with great success—to exploit. In the end, the art that they sell has only a fleeting value. It is a material investment that enables many of them to meet their considerable economic and social obligations. (2003, 228)

The studies by Steiner and Stoller provide an insightful ethnographic analysis of the power of movement, encounter, and exchange to shape key aspects of human life, including categories such as art. By considering the production, marketing, and consumption of art within this framework, Steiner and Stoller challenge notions of ideal art types and universal standards of aesthetic beauty. They discuss how aesthetic perceptions, commonly viewed as timeless

How do wood and mud become art? West African traders have transformed a Manhattan warehouse into an African art market (*left*), full of stalls, shelves, and tables from which art is circulated to markets, vendors, galleries, and private collections across the United States, including this African art stall (*right*) at the San Diego, California, County Fair.

THE SOCIAL LIFE OF THINGS
Native Australian Painters Invent Traditional Art Forms

Do the words *invent* and *traditional* seem contradictory to you when used to describe artwork? Anthropologist Fred Myers (1986, 2002) explores the invention of traditional art by indigenous people in Australia.

1 Until the 1960s, the indigenous Pintupi-speaking people of the Australian Western Desert region were primarily nomadic hunter-gatherers. But by 1973 nearly all of them had been relocated by the national government to settlements in central Australia, where their social, political, and economic lives changed dramatically.

2 In 1971, the local population in the settlement of Papunya began to create a unique style of acrylic dot painting—a new art form—that captured the imaginations not only of tourists visiting Australian Western Desert towns but also of art collectors and gallery owners across Australia and worldwide. At that time a visiting Euro-Australian art teacher, concerned about high unemployment and poverty in the community, encouraged local people to paint traditional ritual designs on wood to make money from visiting tourists.

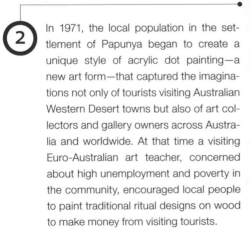

 Over time, local artisans drew upon designs and stories from indigenous religious traditions—including religious ceremonies, mythical narratives, body painting, cave painting, and sand stories—to invent new dot painting designs. Despite the art form's recent invention, the Pintupi proclaimed their designs to be "authentic," "traditional," and "true." In fact, they believe that the paintings have a power of their own, drawn from the indigenous mythology of the Dreaming, a sacred experience of creation among the Australian indigenous people. The claims of authenticity are crucial to elevating the value of their artwork on the Australian and global art markets.

 In just a few decades, this invented yet authentic art form, developed in desert towns by a people transitioning from a hunting-and-gathering lifestyle, has created a world of new possibilities for Australia's indigenous people. The transformation of paint, canvas, and wood from obscure ethnographic objects to fine art collected and displayed in major galleries and museums worldwide has enabled indigenous people to achieve economic growth—employment, wealth, land, and power; to establish an identity in the cultural milieu of the Australian people and state; and to paint their culture onto the global landscape. The Pintupi believe that their paintings have the power to transform the world. And in fact they have done exactly that.

- Can you begin to see how this study of Pintupi acrylic dot paintings offers insights into the relationships between traditional and newly developed art forms?
- How can the social life of Pintupi art shed light on the changing relationship between local markets and global art worlds?
- How has globalization reshaped the production, distribution, and consumption of art today?

and universal, can be constructed and negotiated in the encounters among humans—person to person, group to group, locally and globally.

What Is the Relationship between Art and Power?

Anthropologists do not approach art for art's sake. Instead, they inquire about the intersection of art with key systems of power such as race, ethnicity, class, gender, sexuality, politics, religion and economics (Marcus and Myers 1995; Perkins and Morphy 2006). Creative expressions, performances, and interactions through music, dance, song, museum displays, art events, and other art forms can produce venues for staging dynamic engagements with these systems of power, unmasking patterns of stratification, making the unconscious conscious, and opening space for alternative visions of reality (see Downey 2005; Dunham 1969; Shannon 2006). Artistic expressions enable people to explore and perform alternative identities to those that seem "normal" within the dominant culture. In some instances, as we will discuss in the case of the display of Middle Eastern and Islamic art, they may also create and reinforce stereotypes and misunderstandings.

In the following sections, including the Anthropologists Engage the World feature, we consider examples of creative artistic performances and events that challenge dominant ways of thinking and the underlying systems of power that support them.

Political Critique and Self-Affirmation

As we have noted, creative expression and engagement can take many forms and serve many purposes. As part of its role in reflecting a culture's social dynamics, art can sometimes function within the political arena. The following discussion explores how music, dance, and song enable a marginalized group to protest unequal power relationships and to assert a strong sense of identity despite that inequality.

Rara **Bands, Performance, and Politics in Haiti** In the six weeks leading up to Easter, *rara* bands take center stage in Haiti's rural and urban poor communities. Small ensembles of twenty or so musical revelers, singers, musicians, and dancers, dressed in elaborate, colorful, sequined or striped costumes, parade through the night. As they wind through rural and urban poor communities, they gather audiences along the way.

To the casual observer, the *rara* processions may appear to be unruly groups of revelers as band members march and sing, drum, and joke through the streets of urban centers and rural communities. Competition among bands is fierce, and heated battles frequently erupt when groups collide and "crash the *rara*" in

MAP 17.4
Haiti

the middle of the street, attempting to disrupt one another's performance. But, like small armies, *rara* bands are actually carefully organized and highly disciplined. For instance, members hold formal rank, wear prescribed costumes, and perform songs, dances, and rituals that are thoroughly orchestrated and choreographed. The distinctive performance of the *rara* band features a dynamic combination of bamboo wind instruments, drummers, singers, and dancers. Less complex *rara* bands may establish a rhythm through foot-stomping or hand-clapping. More elaborate bands might include a brass section.

In *Rara!: Vodou, Power, and Performance in Haiti and Its Diaspora* (2002), anthropologist Elizabeth McAlister documents the dynamic performances of *rara* bands that have become key features of Haitian culture. As an ethnographer, she situates them within the political and religious context of Haiti, revealing the complex layers of meaning and power that make *rara* music come alive for the poor and marginalized in Haiti's population. "*Rara* is about play, religion and politics and also about remembering a bloody history and persevering in its face. But at its most bare philosophical level, *rara* is a ritual enactment of life itself and an affirmation of life's difficulties" (2002, 23).

The vast majority of Haitians are poor peasants and urban dwellers who are excluded from political discourse and denied access to political and economic power. Every day they confront conditions of poverty, violence, and terror perpetrated by military and paramilitary forces intent on protecting the economic and political resources of the Haitian elites and their own political power. *Rara* bands and *rara* festivals open up a social space for popular religious and political expressions that might otherwise be silenced. This space enables Haiti's marginalized to contest the violence and political oppression of the present and the past through performances, processions, and song. McAlister reflects on the ways in which *rara* performances perform social critique, particularly through an elaborate interweaving of musical genres: Vodou prayers, obscene *betiz* songs, and politically pointed *pwen* songs.

Rara bands perform a type of religious "work" amid the appearances of all-night play. *Rara* festivals, processionals, and ceremonies, although conducted during the Christian season of Lent, publicly celebrate Vodoun religious culture. The participants sing, drum, pray, and enact religious rituals for Vodoun spirits as the bands stop at crossroads, cemeteries, and shrines, serving the spirit world and in the process celebrating the whole community around which these religious practices are built. The bands' work may include complex negotiations with supernatural spirits. In fact, *rara* bands may call on Vodoun spirits for protection and may, in return, be claimed by and drafted by *lwa*—Vodoun spirits—to work on their behalf.

Outside the religious rituals, *rara* bands perform two unique genres of songs as they move in procession. *Betiz* songs feature vulgar lyrics laced with sexual innuendo, obscenity, and profanity, creating a raucous environment—a form of popular laughter in the face of daily conditions. The more political messages and metaphors of *pwen* songs playfully open up a public conversation that indirectly critiques the political conditions of Haitian life. These songs use metaphor and musical misdirection to elude the wrath of military authorities and paramilitary forces.

Creating space for social protests and critique runs the risk of reprisal, even when performed through the raucous *rara* bands. McAlister recalls accompanying one band through Port-au-Prince on what appeared to be a normal night of *rara* revelry. After starting the evening with a religious ritual to invoke the presence of protective spirits, the band, attracting a large crowd, danced into the streets, moving quickly through the capital to the sounds of bamboo instruments, drums, and songs. Abruptly and without warning, McAlister recalls, the band leader switched the tune from a *pwen* critiquing the military to a raunchy *betiz*—but too late. A Haitian military attaché, apparently incensed by the band's political commentary, stepped from behind a pillar and opened fire on the *rara* band and its audience with a semiautomatic rifle. Perhaps protected by their accompanying Vodoun spirits, the band members peeled themselves off the pavement—unhurt—and raced down a side street out of harm's way.

Clearly, in this case the open space for political critique created by the late-night *rara* procession had limits. A member of Haiti's security forces had chosen to send a message of displeasure. The band's performance had captivated the wrong audience. Its song had not changed genres from *pwen* to *betiz* quickly enough to avoid potentially deadly discipline by a representative of Haiti's powerful elite. Nevertheless, after a rest and a few drinks, the *rara* band regrouped and, with McAlister still in tow, set off down another street, boisterously singing another *betiz* song (Averill 2003; Miller 2003; Neely 2005; Walls 2005).

Construction of Gender Identity through "Kinetic Orality"

Just as music plays a role in the religious and political expressions of Haitians, it can also influence the development of gender identity among young black girls. In the following discussion, we see how a musical form can both reflect a type of cultural continuity and also gain new meaning when adapted to a different context.

Black Girls' Playground Games and Musical Socialization When we think of kids jumping rope on the sidewalk or standing in a circle in the playground calling out rhymes and clapping to keep the beat, we may not automatically think of art. But in *The Games Black Girls Play* (2006), ethnomusicologist Kyra Gaunt explores the sophisticated musical forms that are taught and learned, particularly by young black girls, on the playground.

Gaunt, herself a gifted musician and an anthropologist trained in **ethnomusicology**—the study of music and culture (see Nettl 2005)—applies a unique combination of musical analysis and gender analysis in her study of games that black girls play. According to Gaunt, the girls' hand-clapping and rope-jumping games embody a unique musical genre that combines body movement and voice to produce what she calls a **kinetic orality**. Hand clapping, foot stomping, and highly percussive singing create a musical expression deeply tied to the body—a performance that does not rely on musical instruments but only on body and voice.

These performances may appear to be improvised on the playground, street corner, or schoolyard. But Gaunt argues that they are learned in an elaborate process of enculturation. Through this process, complex rhythmic syncopations, chants, call-and-response vocal patterns, dances, and melodies are transferred from generation to generation as central lessons of socialization for young African American girls. Gaunt challenges the stereotypes that attribute musical patterns and bodily movement in black children's games to biology. Instead, she traces the enculturation processes of what she calls "learned musical blackness" that begins at an early age as part of African American identity construction.

Gaunt also explores how black girls' games and songs influence the development of commercially popular music associated with the African American community—namely, hip-hop, soul, and rhythm and blues. In particular, she details the ways in which the rhyming, syncopations, dancelike gestures,

ethnomusicology: The study of music in cultural context.

kinetic orality: A musical genre combining body movement and voice.

melodies, and lyrics from black girls' game songs have been adopted from and borrowed by the commercial music of black male artists from the 1950s to the present. Although others have suggested that black girls' games and songs imitate music from radio and television, borrowing from genres such as rhythm and blues and hip-hop, Gaunt documents a dynamic circular relationship. Commercial songs may indeed be adopted, modified, and played within the girls' games and songs, but their games, musical styles, and group play are also sampled, borrowed, and appropriated by the popular music industry. Moreover, this occurs with a particular gender twist, as they are incorporated into music predominately associated with men and masculinity.

As an example of this borrowing, Gaunt documents how a common song in black girls' games, "Down, Down Baby," was appropriated into the chorus of the 2000 song "Country Grammar" by Grammy award–winning rap artist Nelly. Elements of "Down, Down Baby" appear not only in "Country Grammar" but in many other commercial music sources as well, including the 1988 Tom Hanks movie *Big*. In "Country Grammar," Nelly incorporates significant lyrical, rhythmic, melodic, and linguistic features of the game-song while revising the lyrics to fit commercial, masculine-centered mainstream hip-hop expectations.

By examining musical performance through the lens of gender, Gaunt raises important questions about the performance of gender and the patterns of interaction between women and men that are reflected through music. This is occurring as women transfer embodied music across generations as a form of socialization while men appropriate women's music for commercial purposes, often without attribution. Nelly's rewritten lyrics, complete with macho references to

being "cocked ready to let it go" and marijuana culture, stand in sharp contrast to the language and tone of girls' performances on the playground. Unlike many artists who have borrowed from girls' games, Nelly has publicly acknowledged the borrowing from a chant in a popular "children's game," although he fails to acknowledge girls as the primary performers of schoolyard songs.

Gaunt's examination of kinetic orality in the games black girls play opens a window on the dynamic process of identity construction, including the construction of racial and gender identities, that emerges at the intersection of play, performance, creative expression, and art (Jamison 2006).

Art Exhibitions and Displays of Power: Playing the Humanity Game

How might art exhibits, special events, and museum displays that are designed to educate, illuminate, and build bridges of understanding across cultures instead reinforce stereotypes and create and maintain narratives of difference and exclusion? After September 11, 2001, many local and national institutions, universities, and grassroots organizations in the United States for the first time organized Middle Eastern art exhibits and special events. Established art institutions increased displays of Middle Eastern and Islamic art, and art funders including the Rockefeller, Soros, Mellon, and Flora Family foundations contributed generously to underwrite the events and exhibits. All hoped to mobilize galleries and exhibit spaces to counter growing anti-Muslim rhetoric and rising talk of an inevitable "clash of civilizations" between Islam and the West. Art, they believed, would provide a unique venue for building bridges of cross-cultural understanding and an awareness of a common humanity. (Boas 1927; Buchli 2002; Kant 1790; Morgan 1877).

How have the rhyming, syncopations, dancelike gestures, melodies, and lyrics from black girls' game songs (*left*) shaped commercial music, like that performed by rap artist Nelly (*right*)?

Aimee Cox
Linking Movement, Performance, and Community Transformation

"I'm a black woman who grew up in the Midwest. For me, that is the lens through which I learned to see the world. As a young girl I became fascinated with the women in my family. My grandmother was born in 1898, had eleven children. Ten of them were girls. And some of them had really interesting pasts. Through those stories I was starting to understand that there was more to life and more to history than what I was learning in school.

"When I was applying to college, it dawned on me that what really interested me were all those other stories that were never told to me. Not just in my family, but what was left out of my educational process. I was searching so desperately for a history and an understanding of social processes that would help me place myself in the world. I felt like I was always missing."

Cox first encountered anthropology in an undergraduate introductory course at Vassar College. "That really opened the world for me. It allowed me to begin to see connections globally that I had never thought about."

She had been dancing since she was three years old, including studying classical ballet in high school at the College Conservatory of Music at the University of Cincinnati. While at Vassar, Cox spent a semester studying with the Dance Theatre of Harlem—the world's first black ballet company—and then spent a semester at the Alvin Ailey School to pursue modern dance. Eventually Cox danced professionally with Ailey II in New York City. Reflecting on those years, Cox recalls, "Through dance, through moving my body and telling stories through my body, I felt like that was a space where I had a certain type of voice and I could express myself. But I still felt limited. I was marrying modern dance and classical ballet. But I felt like I was telling the story in somebody else's language—classical ballet, for example."

That feeling began to change in graduate school as she explored the connections between anthropology and the performing arts—particularly through directing a homeless shelter in Detroit for young women ages 16 to 21 while conducting her doctoral fieldwork.

"When I came to graduate school, I had this vague idea that I was interested in studying how young women, low-income young women, who are seen as the most marginal people in society, find ways to navigate social systems. How do they find ways to survive, and in some ways be successful in the ways that they define success, despite all of these odds? What are the creative ways that they do that?

"I came into graduate school in anthropology and decided consciously, I was no longer a dancer, I was no longer an artist. I left that all behind because I did not, at that time, understand this whole world of performing. I think that had a lot to do with being a black woman, too, in higher education and not wanting to be seen as a performing body. I figured: I need to be an intellectual. But the minute I came to the homeless shelter, those young women would not allow me to leave that behind. They were dancing on their own—not trained, they were not taking classes—they were moving their bodies, choreographing for each other, making these connections across

Anthropologist Aimee Cox

their individual stories through dance and through writing. When I saw that, I said to myself, 'I need to start dancing again. I can't act like this is not a part of me.'

"It started off for them as kind of a creative healing space. They were frustrated at the end of the day by their struggles to survive in Detroit, and they started moving and dancing. I helped turn it into an artistic medium and a community, an educative creative space where they used those art forms to connect their stories. Then they realized, 'Oh, yeah! I'm not the only one who feels this way at the end of the day.' Through dance and storytelling they began to move from feeling their frustration and anger, to in-house community building, to political commentary."

In what eventually became the BlackLight Project, these women developed community workshops, training sessions, and street theater. "They did a lot of this on the street, because if they stayed in the shelter, no one would come and see it. Let's say they were at a bus stop in Detroit. And they'd have a hat, like street performers in New York City have a hat, saying that we're trying to collect some money. They would have the hat, and it would already be full with slips of paper with facts and stories, comments about the city, about the mayor at the time. They would start performing, and as the audience grew around them, they would stop; and in order for them to continue with the performance, one of those in the audience would have to take a piece of paper, read it, and start a discussion about it. So, in a small way, that was the way that these women used performance as more than just a spectacle, but also as a way to engage in a dialogue.

> "Through this kind of embodiment, something else opens up—a different space, a different way of seeing the world, a different language, and even a different sort of courage around thinking about possibilities.

"Through this kind of embodiment, something else opens up—a different space, a different way of seeing the world, a different language, and even a different sort of courage around thinking about possibilities.

"Up until then, I didn't really understand anthropology. I was getting a very traditional understanding in graduate school. But what I wasn't getting, and what no graduate student really gets until they get to the field, I think, is that explosion of what all this really means in the world. These women exploded anthropology for me.

"Performance, in many ways, is the foundation for culture. We perform language. We perform in everything we do. The narrative construct of performing, communicating, telling a story is very tied to anthropology, to cultural anthropology. To making connections, making something clear. In the specificity, for example, of an individual performer—or an individual piece of art—there's a larger story that we can all step into.

"Anthropology is more than just a discipline that studies some abstract notion of culture or power. It's a way to break apart problems. And that takes a real understanding of culture, of how social processes work, of our interconnectedness, of possibilities that are latently embedded in society. And that's what anthropologists are able to do creatively. We see those things. And we bring those things that are not readily apparent to the surface through our ethnographic work. Not because we're wired differently than anybody else, but because we've worked to see outside and inside at the same time, to reveal people to themselves. We give people possibilities to see themselves."

But did the art events have the intended effect?

Anthropologist Jessica Winegar, a scholar of Middle Eastern art and politics, suggests that in fact these art events may have had the opposite effect of what was intended. That is, they may have reinforced stereotypes and dichotomies rather than built bridges of understanding (see Marcus and Myers 1995; Price 1989). Winegar had a front-row seat to observe this phenomenon as virtual gallery operator for ArteEast, a nonprofit organization promoting cultural exchange between the United States, the Middle East, and North Africa. Drawing on her fieldwork in Egypt and her ethnography *Creative Reckonings: The Politics of Art and Culture in Contemporary Egypt* (2006), Winegar was surprised to discover that displays of Middle Eastern art in Egypt and the United States differed dramatically, with US art events presenting an extremely narrow slice of the Middle Eastern art world. Three selection biases were most frequent: historical art focusing on Islam's past achievements; music and rituals of Sufism, a mystical tradition within Islam, rather than mainstream orthodox Islam; and events featuring female Middle Eastern visual artists and filmmakers.

Why, wondered Winegar, were these the only categories considered "good Middle Eastern art" and selected for exhibition? Exhibitions largely ignored works celebrating contemporary orthodox Islam, despite the success of shows of art from Buddhist, Hindu, African, and Native American religious traditions. Male artists were seldom featured. Middle Eastern art such as abstract painting or sculptures with no explicit reference to Islam or the Middle East could have been shown but was not. Missing was art representing resistance to occupation, music critical of the United States or Israel, political cartoons and graffiti, graphic art from Islamic publications, or even the genre of martyr posters and videos—all representing cultural practices involving significant creativity. Winegar suggests that what the U.S. art market would bear—what would attract funders and audiences—was shaped not by some objective notion of art but rather by the post-9/11 political landscape of war in Afghanistan and Iraq and a War on Terror that had established Islam and the Middle East as the enemy.

Winegar warns that by focusing on certain limited categories of art as "good Middle Eastern art" worthy of exhibition, these events actually served to reinforce perceived differences. So while work by Middle Eastern women artists was popular, its representation played upon stereotypes of Middle Eastern women and assumptions about gender inequality in Islam. For instance, exhibits featuring Middle Eastern women artists were often presented and viewed as if critiquing Middle Eastern culture, particularly gender inequalities presumed to be derived from Islam. The artists themselves were often born in the Middle East but now residing in the West. While they were frequently viewed as human bridges of understanding, they were also seen as uniquely positioned

How do museums choose what to exhibit? Anthropologist Jessica Winegar critiques the narrow slice of Middle Eastern art considered appropriate for display: (*left*) more frequently displayed "good Middle Eastern art" like this photograph "Speechless" from the series Women of Allah by Shirin Neshat, an Iranian woman artist living in New York; and (*right*) less frequently displayed controversial pieces like "Suffurya," a display of ceramic sacks by Palestinian artist Mervat Essa, memorializing the depopulation and destruction of Al Biram, her family's village, and many other Palestinian villages in 1948 at the creation of the state of Israel.

and actively engaged in critiquing the culture from which they had come. In interviews with Winegar, audience members described the art as reflecting the submission of Middle Eastern and Muslim women and the desire of those women for freedom and liberty, even if these were not the intended meanings of the artist or presenter, or were clearly contradicted by the exhibition booklets or wall descriptions.

Is it possible that rather than bringing clarity to a complicated situation and building bridges of understanding, by framing so-called Islamic art to make it attractive, interesting, and palatable to funders and audiences, exhibitors actually reinforced the clash of civilizations and War on Terror frameworks? In the process of trying to accentuate common humanity through art—what Winegar calls "The Humanity Game"—could curators and funders' narrow selections have reinforced assumed oppositions between freedom and oppression, understanding and ignorance, civilization and barbarism? Winegar's research reveals the narrow limits imposed on the role of art as bridge builder and suggests that the potential of art to serve as an avenue for expressing and perceiving common humanity is severely limited by the political context in which art is selected, funded, marketed, and viewed (Winegar 2008).

How Do Art and Media Intersect?

Historically, anthropologists have carefully analyzed visual systems and visible culture as part of their ethnographic fieldwork. Art, media, material culture, and even museums become objects of anthropological inquiry. But visual media, including photography, film, television, videos, and web-based techniques, can

YOUR TURN: FIELDWORK

Conducting an Ethnography of Art

Throughout this chapter you have been developing your skills as an ethnographer of art, developing a set of concepts and analytical frames for thinking about what art is, what it means to artist and audience, how it moves, how it is valued by markets. In this exercise, you will apply those skills to the study of a piece of art of your own choosing.

Select a piece of art. It can be any object, event, or other expressive form. In this chapter we consider reproductions of urban life, wood carvings, mud sculptures, acrylic paintings, fashion, dance, music, processions, kids' games, documentary films, and museum displays. You might also choose a banquet, a parade, a festival, a concert, a religious ritual. Don't be constrained by your previously held notions of popular art or fine art.

Now get out your anthropological toolkit. Approach your piece of art as an ethnographer. Participate in it. Observe it. Assess its content. Interview the artist or the audience. Take notes, and be prepared to discuss your findings with a classmate. Consider the following to stimulate your thinking:

- As a form of communication, art is meant to evoke emotional responses (laughter, crying, melancholy, or joy) as well as intellectual responses to its shape, order, and form. The artistic message may be intended to teach or inspire, to engage in an exchange about values, goals, standards, and imagination of the artist and community. It may commemorate individuals, groups, events, or deities and attempt to create enduring messages or memories. Or it may seek to provoke action, influence events, or inspire social change, like the *rara* bands of Haiti. What do you think the artist was trying to say with his or her work?
- As you consider your object, event, or experience, take some time to carefully describe the

Can you see art in the performance of a skateboarder at a graffiti-covered park?

elements of the art. How do people interact with the art and why?
- Consider its history, its role in the local community, and its connections beyond the local community. Where did this piece of art come from? Has it moved across geographic space? Who paid for it, bought it, developed it? Can it be sold?
- See how it is embedded in relationships of power. Who told you it was "art"? Who controls it? If it is displayed, who designed the display and determined how it would be contextualized?
- How might the artwork you have chosen allow certain people to form or maintain relationships of power or assert particular ideas about how relationships of power are organized.

Compare notes with your classmates. With all the information you have gathered, see if you can collectively develop a universal definition of art. Try to limit yourself to one sentence. (Now you know how it feels to be a textbook author!)

also become tools of anthropological inquiry, drawing attention to the imaginative and sensory in a way ethnographic writing may not and opening up new possibilities for understanding the world.

Since the late nineteenth century anthropologists like Franz Boaz have incorporated photography and recorded film footage into their research, both to document their ethnographic projects and to provide visual support for their public educational work at home. Margaret Mead and her husband Gregory Bateson set new standards for integrating the visual into their work, taking 25,000 photos and 22,000 feet of film in Bali, Indonesia, between 1931 and 1938. With the technological advance of portable, synchronous sound cameras in the 1960s, ethnographic filmmaking entered a new and expansive era (Ruby and Banks 2011).

Just as globalization has intensified the worldwide movement of people, money, data, goods, and services, so globalization has transformed the flow of images and sounds through new media technologies (Askew and Wilk 2007). The anthropologist Arjun Appadurai (1990) calls this new formation a **global mediascape**: Global cultural flows of media and visual images enable linkages and communication across boundaries of culture, language, geography, economics, and politics in ways unimaginable one hundred years ago. Faye Ginsberg and colleagues (2002) have introduced the concept **media worlds**, to reflect more textured local realities and the tensions that exist when political, economic and visual worlds collide in the context of contemporary globalization.

Just as newspapers dominated the mediascape in the late nineteenth century, radio, audio recordings, film, television, and the Internet have shaped communication in the twentieth and twenty-first centuries. In contemporary culture the image, whether in photograph, film, or video, has replaced written texts as the primary educator. New forms of **social media**, including Facebook, YouTube, Twitter, Instagram, and Tumblr, have transformed communication for many people and computer- and Internet-based technologies serve as sources of pleasure and social engagement, not merely as tools for work (Boellstorff 2008).

Today, media reach every corner of the globe and permeate all aspects of daily life. Media are everywhere humans live and everywhere anthropologists work. In fact, it is fair to say that media are central to human life in the twenty-first century. The decentralized production and circulation of new media, facilitated by satellites, computers, and handheld communication devices, has undermined the old media empires and has challenged the state's ability to control media content and media flows. In turn, new media have facilitated opportunities for activism as indigenous and marginalized groups use photographs, film, text, and video to mobilize movements for social change and to challenge existing power structures (Askew and Wilk 2007; Ginsburg, Abu-Lughod, and Larkin 2002; Juris and Khasnabish 2013).

global mediascape: Global cultural flows of media and visual images that enable linkages and communication across boundaries in ways unimaginable a century ago.

media worlds: An ethnographic and theoretical approach to media studies that focuses on the tensions that may exist when visual worlds collide in the context of contemporary globalization.

social media: New forms of communication based on computer- and Internet-based technologies that facilitate social engagement, work, and pleasure.

Visual Images and Cultural Identity

Visual anthropology explores the production, circulation, and consumption of visual images, including photographs, film, television, and new media, focusing on the power of visual representations in art, performance, museums, and the mass media to influence culture and cultural identity (Hockings 2003). As you read the following discussion, you may be surprised to discover the power that photographs have to wield such influence.

National Geographic's Photographic Gaze

In a classic work of visual anthropology, *Reading National Geographic* (1993), anthropologists Catherine Lutz and Jane Collins examine the photographs of the popular U.S. magazine *National Geographic* to reveal the power of visual images to shape cultural perspectives and behavior. Launched in 1888, *National Geographic* has successfully blended science, art, photojournalism, and entertainment to become one of the most popular and influential U.S. sources of information about other cultures. Indeed, it collects "the world between its covers." At its peak, the reasonably priced magazine attracted more than ten million monthly subscribers (97 percent white and middle-class) and, with multiple reads in classrooms, lobbies, and doctors' offices, perhaps 40 million total viewers. *National Geographic's* beautiful photos of smiling people from around the globe have inspired world travel, scientific exploration, and even sexual fantasies for generations of U.S. readers.

National Geographic may at first glance appear to offer a straightforward presentation of evidence about human nature and the natural world. But Lutz and Collins, using the analytical frameworks of visual anthropology, ask how the particular "gaze" of *National Geographic* photographs may reflect the worldview of those behind the lens—that is, the magazine's owners, editors, photographers, and graphic designers. This gaze, the authors suggest, can shape the understandings of the magazine's readers as they think about humanity, the natural world, and their own culture's position in the global arena.

To investigate this claim, Lutz and Collins interviewed editors and readers and analyzed photographs from the magazine's nearly 600 articles published about non-Western topics between 1950 and 1986. The researchers asked: What messages did these images convey? What was their intent?

According to the magazine's mission statement, issued in 1915, "only what is of a kindly nature is printed about any country or people; everything unpleasant or unduly critical is to be avoided" (1993, 27). Indeed, underlying the exquisite photos of seemingly happy people, elaborate rituals, and exotic costumes, Lutz and Collins perceive a particular editorial perspective and philosophical worldview. They draw the following conclusion: "Clearly, photographic practice at *National Geographic* is geared to a classic form of humanism, drawing readers' attention through its portrayal of difference, and then showing that under the colorful dress and skin, as it were, we are all more or less the same" (1993, 61). Even though this editorial viewpoint—expressed in the **photographic gaze**—appeared neutral, it projected a particular perspective on human nature, the natural world, history, and difference.

In projecting an almost magical sense of unity, the magazine's photographic gaze tended to overlook key aspects of human history. Photographers and editors selected and framed images to limit political and economic contexts. Conflict, inequality, poverty, and hunger were downplayed or completely avoided. In keeping with this editorial approach, photos of the period under study rarely portrayed dramatic world events of the time. Struggles for decolonization, the Cold War, the Vietnam War, or movements for civil rights, women's rights, and gay rights in the United States were left out of the magazine's photographic gaze. Lutz and Collins note that the magazine's editorial choices consistently minimized diversity and difference, especially along the lines of race and gender.

The authors suggest that during the period they studied, the gaze of *National Geographic*'s images created a cultural lens that mediated U.S. readers' experience of the world and its diverse people. The photographs avoided images

How might the visual images of *National Geographic*—its photographic gaze—shape readers' perspectives on the world? What messages emerge from these photos? (*left to right*): An Egyptian girl and man sit in front of the Sphinx, Giza, Egypt (Nov. 1955); a Mayan man reads to a crowd from his Bible during Holy Week, Guatemala (March 1960); an Imperial Bodyguard member rides in a war game, Ethiopia (March 1964); a Swazi princess accepts a new suitcase at her wedding ceremony, Swaziland (Jan. 1978); and a highland girl gathers wild cosmos flowers near Lake Itasy, Madagascar (Oct. 1967).

photographic gaze: The presumed neutral viewpoint of the camera that in fact projects the perspective of the person behind the camera onto human nature, the natural world, and history.

that might disrupt readers' views of the world and the United States' place in it. Instead, as a primary source for U.S. middle-class information about the world, the magazine's gaze provided reassurance that (1) in essential ways the world that seems so diverse is actually quite familiar; (2) fundamentally, all is well with the world; and (3) the readers and their country play a benevolent role in world events. Here, Lutz and Collins suggest, the power of *National Geographic*'s photographs to shape the U.S. cultural worldview held deep implications for the way the magazine's primarily middle-class readers engaged debates about the nation's domestic and foreign policy (Fernea 1996; Goldstein 1998).

National Geographic's photographic gaze has continued to change over the years. But the concept of the gaze, central to visual anthropology, provides an important tool for thinking about how the form and content of media are shaped by those "behind the camera." As you engage with media throughout your day—through television shows, news broadcasts, websites, tweets, YouTube channels, movies, Facebook pages—can you use the concept of the photographic gaze as a tool to analyze the intentionally and unintentionally expressed worldviews of the owners, editors, designers, videographers, and others behind the scenes?

Ethnographic Films and the Global Mediascape

Ethnographic filmmaking, with a long history in anthropology, has emerged in recent decades as the dominant force in visual anthropology. Classic ethnographic films like Robert Flaherty's silent film *Nanook of the North* (1922) shot among the indigenous Inuit of Canada, John Marshall's many films about the Ju/'hoansi of Namibia, Napoleon Chagnon and Tim Asch's *The Ax Fight* (1975) about the Yanomami in southern Venezuela, and Robert Gardner's *Dead Birds* (1963) set in New Guinea broke significant ground in promoting the use of images for the description, analysis, and interpretation of human behavior, often focusing on individuals and communities in rural, tribal and seemingly isolated settings. More contemporary ethnographic films, like *Exit Zero* and *Leviathan* discussed below, strive to show local communities in their rapidly shifting, friction-filled global contexts, including the complex and changing web of relationships between humans, diverse species, and their environments (Grimshaw and Ravetz 2009; MacDougall 2005; Young 1995).

***Exit Zero*: Families and Global Economic Restructuring** *Exit Zero: Families and Class in Postindustrial Chicago* (2013) by filmmakers Chris Boebel and Christine Walley explores the impact of deindustrialization and globalization on families in Southeast Chicago devastated by steel mill closings in the 1980s and 1990s. Corporate decisions to relocate production offshore eliminated

How can documentary film reveal the human stories of economic globalization? Here Chuck Walley, father of anthropologist and filmmaker Christine Walley, and former steel worker, at the time of Wisconsin Steel's mill closure in 1980, captured in the documentary *Exit Zero*.

the jobs of more than 90,000 white working-class residents in this area along Lake Michigan that had been one of the largest steel-producing regions in the world. Interweaving home movies, found footage and first-person narrative, *Exit Zero* traces the journey of anthropologist Walley's family. Her father, a life-long steelworker before the mill closings, lost his pension and final paychecks and never found work again. Walley walks with her father through vacant lots of former steel mills, now polluted with environmental toxins from industrial waste that may have made her a cancer victim in her twenties. She coaxes out his stories in the family room, living room, and kitchen as he tries to make sense of the economic change and dislocation he has experienced.

The interstate exit ramp near Walley's family home is numbered Zero. Is the story of Chicago's steel mill workers and their families so carefully forgotten that their community is an afterthought on the map? By weaving together the personal, political, institutional, and international, Boebel and Walley's film places the ongoing stories of these workers, their families, and the entire region in sharp relief against the backdrop of a community devastated by the forces of globalization and reveals the power of ethnographic filmmaking to recapture local stories and offer insight into the broader working-class experience in the United States.

Leviathan: Sensory Ethnography on a Fishing Trawler

What is the place of the ocean in the global food chain? Lucien Castaing-Taylor and Verena Paravel's ethnographic film *Leviathan* (2012) follows the weeks-long fishing expedition of a commercial trawler out of New Bedford, Massachusetts—the largest U.S. fishing port, launching 500 ships a month. But this is not a romantic film about an ancient and embattled way of life, with heroic characters like George Clooney in the Hollywood blockbuster *The Perfect Storm*. Instead, *Leviathan* is a 90-minute multisensory exploration into the sights, sounds, rhythms, and colors of the modern commercial fishing industry. There is no dialogue, no monologue, no explicit narrative. Instead, using a dozen GoPro extreme sports cameras, passed between the film crew and the ship crew and deployed above and below water, Paravel and Castaing-Taylor (director of Harvard's Sensory Ethnography Lab) immerse the viewer in an intense sensory experience: the swaying and jerking motions of the boat; the sounds of wind, water, grinding pulleys and engines; the brutality of the mutilated fish flesh—eyes popping and mouths agape; the slosh of seawater onto the boat and draining of fish blood and parts off the boat. In the eerie nighttime light of the trawler, at times it is hard to distinguish the natural from the mechanical, the flesh and blood from the metal and steel of the boat. What is it like to be the fish—netted,

The multispecies and multisensory documentary film *Leviathan* explores the sights, sounds, rhythms, colors, and brutality of the modern commercial fishing industry. Here blood and fish guts mix with seawater pouring off the deck of the fishing trawler after a catch.

hauled, dumped, cut, and sorted? For humans, largely oblivious to the paths food takes to our tables, *Leviathan* pulls back the curtain, immersively and graphically exposing the realities of life and death and offering a direct encounter with the ecological consequences and economic challenges of commercial fishing. In the process, the film engages in an evocative and provocative multispecies ethnography, exposing the deep and expansive relationships between humans, animals, and the sea that is so frequently obscured in our era of globalization, mass production, and consumption (Landesman 2015; Scott 2013; Westmoreland and Luvaas 2015).

Indigenous Media

As we have seen, ethnographic filmmaking has emerged as one form of visual art with tremendous potential to open new windows on a world undergoing dramatic political, economic, and environmental upheaval. But in today's interconnected global age, digital video filmmaking has taken on a key role in giving voice to the concerns of local communities through what visual anthropologists refer to as **indigenous media**. The power of media to overcome boundaries of time and space is increasingly used by people who have experienced massive economic, political and geographic disruption to mediate rapid change and build alternative strategies for communication, survival and empowerment.

indigenous media: The use of media by people who have experienced massive economic, political and geographic disruption to build alternative strategies for communication, survival and empowerment.

Chinese Villagers Stay Connected through Festival Videos
For new immigrants far from home, for instance, the creation and circulation of new media forms like digital video has tremendous potential to unify immigrants, resist dominant narratives of otherness, and reinforce their solidarity with their native communities. My own experience bears out this observation.

In early 2007 I attended a temple festival in a small village on China's southeast coast. I had visited the village previously, but the opportunity to participate in a full two weeks of festivities at the invitation of the temple master was a unique privilege. Vivid rituals, raucous processions, solemn prayers, and bountiful banquets filled the days. But the constant presence of a small film crew documenting every element of temple life surprised me. One afternoon the temple master asked if I would be willing to be interviewed on camera to say a few words about the festival. As a grateful guest—and an oddity as the only non-Chinese at the festival—I readily agreed, gave an interview at the foot of a beautiful new pagoda overlooking the harbor, and thought little more about the matter.

Back in New York a few weeks later, I placed a call to a young woman from the village now living in Flushing, Queens. Her mother, still living in China, had entrusted me to deliver some baby clothes for her new granddaughter. We agreed to meet the next day on a corner of Main Street in Flushing—a meeting that, despite her assurances, I doubted would go smoothly on one of the busiest intersections in New York City.

I patiently waited the next day on the appointed corner. Much to my surprise, at the agreed-upon time a car pulled up, a window rolled down, and a young woman said in Chinese, "Professor Guest, get in!" Over dumplings and tea she explained, "Everyone from the village knows you! You're in the video!" It turns out that in order to keep immigrant villagers connected to the home temple and engaged in its spiritual and financial life, the master regularly produces and circulates festival videos to his devotees now living in the New York metropolitan area. Video of the festival I attended had traversed the globe from a rural Chinese village to the streets of New York City, serving to build solidarity among immigrant villagers now in the United States and to strengthen connections with their kinfolk, fellow townspeople, and religious co-adherents in China.

The forces of globalization move people, money, things—and images. A Chinese village festival had now entered the global mediascape.

Can you also imagine some of the power dynamics that may be revealed by such a video production? Consider all of the players involved: funders, filmmakers, editors, an anthropologist, distributors, and recipients. How might the global exchange of media intersect and affect existing relationships of power?

Today media is reshaping human life in every part of the world as it increasingly permeates the routines of daily life. As you think about the expanding global mediascape, can you see how your everyday actions—friendships, education, love life, job, entertainment, religion, political engagements, communications, and more—are mediated by new technologies in ways unimaginable even two decades ago? The anthropology of media will continue to develop as this global mediascape expands and deepens. What will the next two decades bring? How will anthropologists utilize the tools of our discipline to understand the impact of these changes on people and their communities across the globe?

Thinking Like an Anthropologist: The Landscape of World Art

Art is everywhere in our lives. From the games we play and the songs we sing to the way we dress and the food we eat, we humans express ourselves creatively and interact with one another through creative expression. As we have seen throughout this chapter, communication between artist and audience through art objects, performances, events, and experiences is not limited to elite actors or venues but is present throughout human cultures and deeply rooted in the activities of everyday life. This chapter's opening story described the creative ways in which young people in a Brazilian favela have built community, challenged the political and economic assumptions of the state, and projected their concerns into a national and international dialogue. When do games take on a life of their own? How do they become political action or efforts at community building? How do they become art? What is the relationship among creative expression, play, performance, and art?

Through Morrinho, imaginative young people engage in an evolving drama that performs, imitates, and examines life, constructing artificial scenarios and relationships through which the players explore their own emotional and social worlds. By telling an untold story or history, speaking the truth of a community back to its members and the surrounding culture and political structures, the virtual world of Morrinho explores those boundaries among real life, play, and the creative expressions and engagements that anthropologists call art.

In this chapter we have begun to consider the vast landscape of world art. Where can you find these dynamics in your own life? In what ways are you an artist? How do you use new forms of media technology to express your creativity and communicate with others through the global mediascape?

As you think more about the world of art, remember the opening questions that framed this chapter's inquiries:

- What is art?
- What is unique about how anthropologists study art?
- What is the relationship between art and power?
- How do art and media intersect?

After reading this chapter, you should be able to apply these questions to situations in which you encounter art and media and the intersections of real life, play, politics, and creative expression. Thinking like an anthropologist about the world of art can give you a more complete set of tools for comprehending this complex part of human culture, understanding your own creativity, and engaging the world around you.

Key Terms

For Further Exploration

Cave of Forgotten Dreams. 2010. Directed by Werner Herzog. IFC Films. For this documentary, award-winning filmmaker Werner Hertzog gained exclusive access to the Chauvet caves in southern France.

The Double Dutch Divas! (or the original full-length version *I Was Made to Love Her*). 2001. Directed by Nicole Franklin. Filmmakers Library. The art and play of double dutch.

In and Out of Africa. 1993. Produced by Ilisa Barbash and Lucien Taylor, based on research by Christopher Steiner. Berkeley Media LLC. Documentary film that explores the transnational trade in African art by following the journey of a remarkable art dealer, Gabai Baaré, from Niger in rural West Africa to East Hampton, Long Island.

McAlister, Elizabeth. 2002. *Rara!: Vodou, Power, and Performance in Haiti and Its Diaspora*. Berkeley: University of California Press. Comes with a CD of *rara* band music developed to accompany the book. URL for listening: http://www.ucpress.edu/book.php?isbn=9780520228238.

The Other Side of the Water: The Journey of a Haitian Rara Band in Brooklyn. 2011. Third World Newsreel.

The Exit Zero Project. www.exitzero.org. Interactive website about the *Exit Zero* film and Christine Walley's book *Exit Zero: Family and Class in Postindustrial Chicago* (University of Chicago Press, 2013).

National Public Radio interview with Filmmakers Lucien Castaing-Taylor and Verena Paravel about their ethnographic documentary, *Leviathan*. http://www.npr.org/2013/03/16/174404938/leviathan-the-fishing-life-from-360-degrees.

References

Abu-Lughod, Janet L. 1989. *Before European Hegemony: The World System A.D. 1250–1350*. New York: Oxford University Press.

———. 2000. *Veiled Sentiments: Honor and Poetry in a Bedouin Society*. Berkeley: University of California Press.

———. 2005. *Dramas of Nationhood: The Politics of Television in Egypt*. Chicago: University of Chicago Press.

Agrama, Hussein Ali. 2010. "Ethics, Tradition, Authority: Toward an Anthropology of the Fatwa." *American Ethnologist* 37(1): 2–18.

———. 2012. *Questioning Secularism: Islam, Sovereignty and the Rule of Law in Modern Egypt*. Chicago: Chicago University Press.

Ahearn, Laura M. 2012. *Living Language: An Introduction to Linguistic Anthropology*. Malden, MA: Wiley-Blackwell.

Aiyer, Ananthakrishnan. 2007. "The Allure of the Transnational: Notes on Some Aspects of the Political Economy of Water in India." *Cultural Anthropology* 22(4): 640–58.

Alexander, Edward P. 1996. "What Is a Museum?" In *Museums in Motion: An Introduction to the History and Functions of Museums*, edited by Edward P. Alexander and Mary Alexander. Walnut Creek, CA: AltaMira. Published in cooperation with the American Association for State and Local History.

Alexander, J. 2001. "Islam, Archaeology, and Slavery in Africa." *World Archaeology*, 33(1): 44–60.

Alexander, Michelle. 2012. *The New Jim Crow: Mass Incarceration in the Age of Colorblindness* (rev. ed.). New York: The New Press.

Allison, Anne. 1994. *Nightwork: Sexuality, Pleasure, and Corporate Masculinity in a Tokyo Hostess Club*. Chicago: University of Chicago Press.

Allison, Anthony C. 2004. "Two Lessons from the Interface of Genetics and Medicine." *Genetics* 166: 1591–99.

Alpers, Svetlana. 1991. "Museums as a Way of Seeing." In *Exhibiting Cultures: The Poetics and Politics of Museum Display*, edited by Ivan Karp and Steven Lavine, 25–32. Washington, DC: Smithsonian Institution.

American Academy of Pediatrics. 2000. "Evaluation of the Newborn with Developmental Anomalies of the External Genitalia." *Pediatrics* 106(1): 138–42.

———. 2006. "Children, Adolescents, and Advertising." *Pediatrics* 118(6): 2563–69.

———. 2004. "Statement on Marriage and the Family." www .aaanet.org/issues/policy-advocacy/Statement-on-Marriage -and-the-family.cfm.

———. 2015. "What Is Anthropology?" www.americananthro.org /AdvanceYourCareer/Content.aspx?ItemNumber=2150&navIt emNumber=740

Anand, Nikhil. 2011a. "Infrapolitics: The Social Life of Water in Mumbai." Unpublished dissertation, Department of Anthropology, Stanford University.

———. 2011b. PRESSURE: The PoliTechnics of Water Supply in Mumbai. *Cultural Anthropology* 26(4): 542–64.

———. 2012. Municipal Disconnect: On Abject Water and Its Urban Infrastructures. *Ethnography* 12(4): 487–509.

Anderson, Benedict. 1983. *Imagined Communities: Reflections on the Origin and Spread of Nationalism*. London: Verso.

Anderson, E. N. 2005. *Everyone Eats: Understanding Food and Culture*. New York: NYU Press.

Angelini, Alessandro. 2016. "Favela in Replica: Iterations and Itineraries of a Miniature City." *Journal of Latin American and Caribbean Anthropology* 20(3): 39-60.

Anglin, Mary K. 2002. *Women, Power, and Dissent in the Hills of Carolina*. Urbana: University of Illinois.

Antioch College Sexual Offense Prevention Policy, cited in Cameron, Deborah. 1994. "Degrees of Consent: The Antioch College Sexual Offense Policy." In *The Language and Sexuality Reader*, edited by Deborah Cameron and Don Kulick. New York: Routledge, 2006.

Anton, Susan C. 2003. "A Natural History of *Homo erectus*." In "Yearbook of Physical Anthropology," supplement, *American Journal of Physical Anthropology* 122(37): 126–70.

Anton, Susan C., and Carl C. Swisher III. 2004. "Early Dispersals of *Homo* from Africa." *Annual Review of Anthropology* 33: 271–96.

Aparicio, Ana. 2006. *Dominican-Americans and the Politics of Empowerment*. Gainesville: University of Florida.

Appadurai, Arjun, ed. 1986. *The Social Life of Things: Commodities in Cultural Perspective*. Cambridge, UK: Cambridge University Press.

———. 1990. "Disjuncture and Difference in the Global Cultural Economy." *Public Culture* 2(2): 1–24.

Appiah, Kwame Anthony. 2006. *Cosmopolitanism: Ethics in a World of Strangers*. New York: Norton.

Archetti, Eduardo P. 1999. *Masculinities: Football, Polo and the Tango in Argentina*. Oxford, UK: Berg.

Armstrong, Thomas D. 2013. "China's 'Floating' Population." *Southern California International Review*. http://scir .org/2013/10/chinas-floating-population/.

Arobba, Biagio, Robert E. McGrath, Joe Futrelle, and Alan B. Craig. 2010. *A Community-Based Social Media Approach for Preserving Endangered Languages and Culture*. www.ideals .illinois.edu/bitstream/handle/2142/17078/lat-comm-info-2 -sep-2010.pdf?sequence=2.

Asad, Talal, ed. 1973. *Anthropology and the Cultural Encounter*. London: Ithaca Press.

———. 1992. *Anthropology & the Colonial Encounter*. Atlantic Highlands, NJ: Humanity Books.

———. 1993. *Genealogies of Religion: Discipline and Reasons of Power in Christianity and Islam*. Baltimore: Johns Hopkins University Press.

Asch, Timothy, and Napoleon Chagnon. 1975. *The Ax Fight*. Watertown, MA: Documentary Educational Resources.

Askew, Kelly Michelle, and Richard R. Wilk, eds. 2007. *The Anthropology of Media: A Reader*. Malden, MA: Blackwell.

Baer, Hans A., Merrill Singer, and Ida Susser. 2003. *Medical Anthropology and the World System*. Westport, CT: Praeger.

Baker, Lee D. 1995. "Racism in Professional Settings: Forms of Address as Clues to Power Relations." *Journal of Applied Behavioral Science* 31(2): 186–201.

———. 2004. "Franz Boas Out of the Ivory Tower." *Anthropological Theory* 4(1): 29–51.

Bank for International Settlements. "About Derivatives Statistcs." 2016. www.bis.org/statistics/about_derivatives_stats.htm

Barboza, David, and Keith Bradsher. 2010. "In China, Labor Movement Enabled by Technology." *New York Times*, June 17.

Barker, D. J. P. 1998. *Mothers, Babies, and Health in Later Life* (2nd ed.). Edinburgh and New York: Churchill Livingstone.

Barkow, Jerome H., Leda Cosmides, and John Tooby, eds. 1992. *The Adapted Mind: Evolutionary Psychology and the Generation of Culture*. New York: Oxford University Press.

Barth, Fredrik. 1959. *Political Leadership among Swat Pathans*. London: Athlone Press.

———. 1969. "Introduction." In *Ethnic Groups and Boundaries*, edited by Fredrik Barth. Boston: Little, Brown.

Basso, Keith. 1996. *Wisdom Sits in Places: Landscape and Language among the Western Apache*. Albuquerque: University of New Mexico Press.

The Battle of Algiers. 1965. Directed by Gillo Pontecorvo. Allied Artists Corporation.

Baumann, Gerd. 1995. "Managing a Polyethnic Milieu: Kinship and Interaction in a London Suburb." *Journal of the Royal Anthropological Institute* 1(4): 725–41.

Beall, Cynthia. 2001. "Adaptations to Altitude: A Current Assessment." *Annual Review of Anthropology* 30: 423–56.

———. 2006. "Andean, Tibetan, and Ethiopian Patterns of Adaptation to High-Altitude Hypoxia." *Integrative and Comparative Biology* 46: 18–24.

Behar, Ruth. 2003. *Translated Woman: Crossing the Border with Esperanza's Story* (2nd ed.). Boston: Beacon Press.

———. 1996. *The Vulnerable Observer: Anthropology That Breaks Your Heart*. Boston: Beacon Press.

Beidelman, T. O. 1994. "*African Art in Transit* [Review]." *Anthropos* 89(4/6): 653–54.

Bellah, Robert. 1980. *Varieties of Civil Religion*. San Francisco: Harper & Row.

Bellamy, Carla. 2011. *The Powerful Ephemeral: Everyday Healing in an Ambiguously Islamic Place*. Berkeley: University of California Press.

Benedict, Ruth. 1934. *Patterns of Culture*. Boston: Houghton Mifflin.

———. 1946. *The Chrysanthemum and the Sword: Patterns of Japanese Culture*. Boston: Houghton Mifflin.

Bennett, R. L., et al. 2002. "Genetic Counseling and Screening of Consanguineous Couples and Their Offspring: Recommendations of the National Society of Genetic Counselors." *Journal of Genetic Counseling* 11(2): 97–119.

Bennett, Tony. 2010. "Painting Culture: The Making of an Aboriginal Art [Review]." *International Journal of Cultural Policy* 16(1): 11–12.

Berger, Peter, ed. 1999. *The Desecularization of the World: Resurgent Religion and World Politics*. Grand Rapids, MI: Wm. B. Eerdmans.

Bern, Sandra Lipsitz. 1981. "Gender Schema Theory: A Cognitive Account of Sex Typing." *Psychological Review* 88: 354–64.

———. 1983. "Gender Schema Theory and Its Implications for Child Development: Raising Gender-Aschematic Children in a Gender-Schematic Society." *Signs: Journal of Women in Culture and Society* 8: 598–616.

Bernal, Victoria. 2014. *Nation as Network: Diaspora, Cyberspace and Citizenship*. Chicago and London: The University of Chicago Press.

Besteman, Catherine L. ed. 2002. *Violence: A Reader*. New York: New York University Press.

———. 2016. *Making Refuge: Somali Bantu Refugees and Lewiston, Maine*. Durham, NC: Duke University Press.

Besteman, Catherine L., and Lee V. Cassanelli. 1996. *The Struggle for Land in Southern Somalia: The War Behind the War*. Boulder, CO: Westview Press.

Bestor, Theodore C. 2001. "Supply-Side Sushi: Commodity, Market, and the Global City." *American Anthropologist* 102(1): 76–95.

———. 2004. *Tsukiji: The Fish Market at the Center of the World*. Berkeley: University of California Press.

Bickford, Andrew. 2011. *Fallen Elites: The Military Other in Post-unification Germany*. Stanford, CA: Stanford University Press.

Biehl, Joao, and Adriana Petryna. 2013. *When People Come First: Critical Studies in Global Health*. Princeton, NJ: Princeton University Press.

Binder, Frederick M., and David M. Reimers. 1995. *All Nations under Heaven: An Ethnic and Racial History of New York City*. New York: Columbia University Press.

Black Gold: Wake Up and Smell the Coffee. 2006. Directed by Marc Francis and Nick Francis. Speak It/Fulcrum.

Board of Governors of the Federal Reserve System. 2012. "Changes in U.S. Family Finances from 2007 to 2010: Evidence from the Survey of Consumer Finances." www.federalreserve.gov/pubs/bulletin/2012/pdf/scf12.pdf.

———. 2016a. "Consumer Credit-G.19." www.federalreserve.gov/releases/g19/current/.

———. 2016b. "Mortgage Debt Outstanding." www.federalreserve.gov/econresdata/releases/mortoutstand/current.htm.

Boas, Franz. 1912. "Changes in the Bodily Form of Descendants of Immigrants." *American Anthropologist* 14(3).

———. 1927. *Primitive Art.* New York: Dover.

———. 1966. *Kwakiutl Ethnography* (Classics of Anthropology). edited by Helen F. Codere. Chicago: University of Chicago Press.

Boehm, Christopher. 1999. *Hierarchy in the Forest: The Evolution of Egalitarian Behavior.* Cambridge, MA: Harvard University Press.

Boellstorff, Tom. 2007. "Queer Studies in the House of Anthropology." *Annual Review of Anthropology* 36: 17–35.

———. 2008. *Coming of Age in Second Life: An Anthropologist Explores the Virtually Human.* Princeton, NJ: Princeton University Press.

Boellstorff, Tom, and Cymene Howe. 2015. "Queer Futures." http://culanth.org/fieldsights/709-queer-futures.

Bohannan, Laura. 1966. "Shakespeare in the Bush: An American Anthropologist Set Out to Study the Tiv of West Africa and Was Taught the True Meaning of *Hamlet.*" *Natural History* 75: 28–33.

Bolin, Anne. 1992. "Families We Choose: Lesbians, Gays, Kinship [Review]." *American Anthropologist* 94(4): 947–48.

Bonilla, Yarimar, and Jonathan Rosa. 2015. "#Ferguson: Digital Protest, Hashtag Ethnography, and the Racial Politics of Social Media in the United States." *American Ethnologist* 42(1): 4–17.

Bonilla-Silva, Eduardo. 2010. *Racism without Racists: Color-Blind Racism and Racial Inequality in Contemporary America* (3rd ed.). New York: Rowan and Littlefield.

Bonvillain, Nancy. 2007. *Women and Men: Cultural Constructions of Gender* (4th ed.). Upper Saddle River, NJ: Prentice Hall.

Borofsky, R. (2005). *Yanomami: The Fierce Controversy and What We Can Learn from It* (vol. 12). Berkeley: University of California Press.

Bourdieu, Pierre. 1982. *Ce que parler veut dire.* Paris: Fayard.

———. 1984. *Distinction: A Social Critique of the Judgment of Taste.* Translated by R. Nice. Cambridge, MA: Harvard University Press.

Bourdieu, Pierre, with Jean-Claude Passeron. (1970) 1990. *Reproduction in Education, Society and Culture* (2nd ed.) (Theory, Culture, and Society Series vol. 4). Translated by Lois Wacquant. New York: Sage.

Bowie, Fiona. 2006. *The Anthropology of Religion: An Introduction* (2nd ed.). Malden, MA: Blackwell.

Boyd, Robert, and Joan B. Silk. 2015. *How Humans Evolved.* New York: Norton.

Brash, Julian. 2011. *Bloomberg's New York: Class and Governance in the Luxury City.* Athens: University of Georgia.

Braudel, Fernand. (1979) 1992. *Civilization and Capitalism, 15th to 18th Centuries,* vol. 3, *The Perspective of the World.* Translated by Siân Reynolds. Berkeley: University of California Press.

Brennan, Denise. 2004. *What's Love Got to Do with It? Transnational Desires and Sex Tourism in the Dominican Republic.* Durham, NC: Duke University Press.

Brettell, Caroline B., and C. F. Sargent, eds. 2009. *Gender in Cross-Cultural Perspective* (5th ed.). Upper Saddle River, NJ: Pearson/Prentice Hall.

Brewis, Alexandra A. 2000. "Sambia Sexual Culture [Review]." *American Anthropologist* 102(2): 392–93.

Bridges, Khiara M. 2011. *Reproducing Race: An Ethnography of Pregnancy as a Site of Racialization.* Berkeley: University of California Press.

Bridges, Tristan S. 2007. "Dude You're a Fag: Masculinity and Sexuality in High School [Review]." *Gender and Society* 21(5): 776–78.

Brimelow, Peter. 1995. *Alien Nation: Common Sense about America's Immigration Disaster.* New York: Random House.

———. 1995. *Being Muslim the Bosnian Way: Identity and Community in a Central Bosnian Village.* Princeton, NJ: Princeton University Press.

Bringa, Tone, and Peter Loizos. 2002. *Returning Home: Revival of a Bosnian Village.* Sage Film and Video (Sarajevo).

———. 2007. "Foreword." In *The Gender of Globalization: Women Navigating Cultural and Economic Marginalities,* edited by Nandini Gunewardena and Ann Kingsolver. Santa Fe, NM: School for Advanced Research Press.

Brown, Jacqueline Nassy. 2007. "Suriname, Sweet Suriname [Review]." *GLQ: A Journal of Lesbian and Gay Studies* 13(2–3): 406–8.

Brown, Lester R. 2011a. "When the Nile Runs Dry." *New York Times,* June 1.

———. 2011b. *World on the Edge: How to Prevent Environmental and Economic Collapse.* New York: Norton.

Brown, P., et al. 2004. "A New Small-Bodied Hominin from the Late Pleistocene of Flores, Indonesia." *Nature* 431: 1055–61.

Brubaker, Rogers. 2004. *Ethnicity without Groups.* Cambridge, MA: Harvard University Press.

Brumm, Adam. 2004. "Painting Culture: The Making of an Aboriginal Art [Review]." *Australian Journal of Politics and History* 50(1): 123–24.

Brundage, W. Fitzhugh. 1993. *Lynching in the New South: Georgia and Virginia, 1880–1930.* Chicago: University of Illinois Press.

Brunet, M., et al. 2002. "A New Hominid from the Upper Miocene of Chad, Central Africa." *Nature* 418: 145–51.

Buchli, Victor, ed. 2002. *The Material Culture Reader*. Oxford, UK: Berg.

Buck, Pem Davidson. 2001. *Worked to the Bone: Race, Class, Power, and Privilege in Kentucky*. New York: Monthly Review Press.

———. 2009. *In/equality: An Alternative Anthropology*. Redding, CA: CAT Publishing.

Budrys, Grace. 2010. *Unequal Health: How Inequality Contributes to Health or Illness*. Lanham, MD: Rowman & Littlefield.

Buss, David M. 1991. "Evolutionary Personality Psychology." *Annual Review of Psychology* 42: 459–91.

Butler, Judith. 1990. *Gender Trouble: Feminism and the Subversion of Identity*. New York: Routledge.

Cahn, Naomi. 2004. "Beyond Retribution and Impunity: Responding to War Crimes of Sexual Violence." Public Law and Legal Theory Working Paper 104, George Washington University Law School, Washington DC.

Calderwood, Brent. 2008. "Be Butch or Be Bashed." *Gay and Lesbian Review* 155(1): 38–39.

Cameron, Deborah. 1994. "Degrees of Consent: The Antioch College Sexual Offense Policy." In *The Language and Sexuality Reader*, edited by Deborah Cameron and Don Kulick. New York: Routledge, 2006.

———. 2007. *The Myth of Mars and Venus*. Oxford, UK: Oxford University Press.

Cameron, Deborah, and Don Kulick, eds. 2006. *The Language and Sexuality Reader*. New York: Routledge.

Cann, Rebecca L., Mark Stoneking, and Allan C. Wilson. 1987. "Mitochondrial DNA and Human Evolution." *Nature* 325: 31–36.

Cardoso, Fernando Henrique, and Enzo Faletto. 1969. *Dependencia y desarrollo en American Latina: ensayo de interpretación sociologica*. Mexico City, México: Siglo Veintiuno Editores.

Carneiro, Robert. 1978. "Political Expansion as an Expression of the Principle of Competitive Exclusion." In *Origins of the State*, edited by Ronald Cohn and Elman Service. Philadelphia: Institute for the Study of Human Issues.

———. 1981. "The Chiefdom: Precursor of the State." In *The Transition to Statehood in the New World*, edited by Grant Jones and Robert Kautz, 37–79. Cambridge, UK: Cambridge University Press.

Carney, Judith A. 2002. *Black Rice: The African Origins of Rice Cultivation in the Americas*. Cambridge, MA: Harvard University Press.

Carroll, John B., ed. 1956. *Language, Thought, and Reality: Selected Writings of Benjamin Lee Whorf*. Cambridge, MA: MIT Press.

Carsten, Janet. 1997. *The Heat of the Hearth: The Process of Kinship in a Malay Fishing Community*. Oxford, UK: Clarendon Press.

———. 2004. *After Kinship*. Cambridge, UK: Cambridge University Press.

Casanova, Jose. 1994. *Public Religions in the Modern World*. Chicago: University of Chicago Press.

Cavanagh, John, Daphne Wysham, and Marcos Aruda, eds. 2002. *Alternatives to Economic Globalization: A Better World Is Possible*. San Francisco: Berrett-Koehler.

Cawthon Lang, Kristina. 2005. "Primate Factsheets: Gorilla Taxonomy, Morphology, & Ecology." Primate Info Net. http://pin.primate.wisc.edu/factsheets/entry/gorilla/taxon.

Cazenave, Noel A. 2011. *The Urban Racial State: Managing Race Relations in American Cities*. Lanham, MD: Rowan and Littlefield.

Césaire, Aimé Fernand David. 1955. *Discourse on Colonialism*. Paris: PreÏsence africaine.

Chagnon, Napoleon A. 1968. *Y[[aogonek]]nomamö: The Fierce People*. New York: Holt, Rinehart and Winston.

Chan, Selina Ching. 2006. "Love and Jewelry: Patriarchal Control, Conjugal Ties, and Changing Identities." In *Modern Loves: The Anthropology of Romantic Courtship and Companionate Marriage*, edited by Jennifer S. Hirsch and Holly Wardlow, 35–50. Ann Arbor: University of Michigan Press.

Chang, Grace. 1998. "Undocumented Latinas: The New Employable Mothers." In *Race, Class and Gender* (3rd ed.), edited by Margaret L. Anderson and Patricia Hill Collins. Boulder, CO: Wadsworth.

Chang, Leslie T. 2008. *Factory Girls: From Village to City in a Changing China*. New York: Spiegel & Grau.

Chapman, Gary. 2010. *The 5 Love Languages: The Secret to Love That Lasts*. Chicago: Northfield Publishing.

Chapman, Rachel R., and Jean R. Berggren. 2005. "Radical Contextualization: Contributions to an Anthropology of Racial/Ethnic Health Disparities." *Health* 9(2): 145–67.

Chau, Adam Yuet. 2006. *Miraculous Response: Doing Popular Religion in Contemporary China*. Stanford, CA: Stanford University Press.

Checker, Melissa. 2005. *Polluted Promises: Environmental Racism and the Search for Justice in a Southern Town*. New York: New York University Press.

Chio, Jenny. 2014. *A Landscape of Travel: The Work of Tourism in Rural Ethnic China*. Seattle: University of Washington Press.

Chodorow, Nancy. 1974. "Strategies, Cooperation and Conflict among Women in Domestic Groups." In *Woman, Culture and Society*, edited by Michelle Z. Rosaldo and Louise Lamphere, 97–113. Stanford, CA: Stanford University Press.

Chomsky, Noam. 1957. *Syntactic Structures*. The Hague/Paris: Mouton.

Clifford, James, and George E. Marcus. 1986. "Introduction: Partial Truths." In *Writing Culture: The Poetics and Politics of Ethnography*, edited by James Clifford and George E. Marcus, 1–26. Berkeley: University of California Press.

CNN/ORC International. 2015. "Poll: Do you approve or disapprove of the way Barack Obama is handling his job as president?" http://i2.cdn.turner.com/cnn/2015/images/09/12/iranpoll.pdf

Cochrane, J. 2006. "Religion, Public Health and a Church for the 21st Century." *International Review of Mission* 95(376/377): 59–72.

Cohen, Yehudi A. 1974. *Man in Adaptation: The Cultural Present.* Chicago: Aldine.

Coles, Kimberly. 2007. *Democratic Designs: International Intervention and Electoral Practices in Postwar Bosnia-Herzegovina.* Ann Arbor: University of Michigan Press.

Comaroff, John L., and Jean Comaroff. 2009. *Ethnicity, Inc.* Chicago: University of Chicago Press.

Constable, Nicole. 2007. *Maid to Order in Hong Kong: Stories of Migrant Workers.* Ithaca, NY: Cornell University Press.

Consumer Reports. 2010. "Same Products, Different Prices." www .consumerreports.org/cro/magazine-archive/2010/january /shopping/same-products-different-prices/overview/same -products-different-prices-ov.htm

Coontz, Stephanie. 1988. *The Social Origins of Private Life: A History of American Families 1600–1900.* New York: Verso.

———. 1992. *The Way We Never Were: American Families and the Nostalgia Trap.* New York: Basic Books.

Copelon, Rhonda. 1995. "Gendered War Crimes: Reconceptualizing Rape in Time of War." In *Women's Rights, Human Rights: International Feminist Perspectives,* edited by Julie Peters and Andrea Wolper, 197–215. New York: Routledge.

Counihan, Carole, and Penny Van Esterik, eds. 2013. *Food and Culture: A Reader* (3rd ed.). New York: Taylor and Francis.

Cowen, M. P., and R. W. Shenton. 1996. *Doctrines of Development.* London: Routledge.

Crapanzano, Vincent. 1980. *Tuhami: Portrait of a Moroccan.* Chicago: University of Chicago.

Currah, Paisley, Richard M. Juang, and Shannon Price Minter, eds. 2006. *Transgender Rights.* Minneapolis: University of Minnesota Press.

Curtis, Debra A. 1996. "Review of *Nightwork: Sexuality, Pleasure, and Corporate Masculinity in a Tokyo Hostess Club.*" *Gender and Society* 10(2): 215–16.

———. 2009. *Pleasures and Perils: Girls' Sexuality in a Caribbean Consumer Culture.* New Brunswick, NJ: Rutgers University Press.

Dahlberg, Frances, ed. 1981. *Woman the Gatherer.* New Haven, CT: Yale University Press.

Darian-Smith, Eve. 2004. *New Capitalists: Law, Politics and Identity Surrounding Casino Gaming on Native American Land.* Belmont, CA: Wadsworth Publishing.

Darwin, Charles. 1859. *On the Origin of Species.* London: John Murray.

Das, Veena. 1995. "National Honor and Practical Kinship: Unwanted Women and Children." In *Conceiving the New World Order: The Global Politics of Reproduction,* edited by Faye D. Ginsburg and Rayna Rapp. Berkeley: University of California Press.

Davidson, Julia O'Connell. 1997. "Review of *Nightwork: Sexuality, Pleasure, and Corporate Masculinity in a Tokyo Hostess Club.*" *Signs* 22(3): 759–61.

Davies, G. 2005. *A History of Money from the Earliest Times to Present Day* (3rd ed.). Cardiff, UK: University of Wales Press.

Davies, James B., Susanna Sandstrom, Anthony Shorrocks, and Edward N. Wolff. 2007. *Estimating the Level and Distribution of Global Household Wealth.* Helsinki: UNU-WIDER.

Davis, Georgiann. 2015. *Contesting Intersex: The Dubious Diagnosis.* New York: NYU Press.

Davis, Dána-Ain. 2006. *Battered Black Women and Welfare Reform: Between a Rock and a Hard Place.* Albany: State University of New York.

Davis-Floyd, Robbie. 1992. *Birth as an American Rite of Passage.* Berkeley: University of California Press.

Davis-Floyd, Robbie, and Joseph Dumit, eds. 1997. *Cyborg Babies: From Techno-Sex to Techno-Tots.* London: Routledge.

De León, Jason. 2015. *The Land of Open Graves: Living and Dying on the Migrant Trail.* Berkeley: University of California Press.

Deliege, Robert. 2011. "Caste, Class, and Untouchability." In *A Companion to the Anthropology of India,* edited by Isabelle Clark-Decès. Hoboken, NJ: Wiley-Blackwell.

Deloria, Vine, Jr. 1969. *Custer Died for Your Sins: An Indian Manifesto.* New York: Macmillan.

D'Emilio, John, and Estelle B. Freedman. 1998. *Intimate Matters: A History of Sexuality in America* (2nd ed.). Chicago: University of Chicago Press.

De Vos, George. 1987. "Shamans, Housewives, and Other Restless Spirits: Women in Korean Ritual Life [Review]." *American Ethnologist* 14(2): 407–8.

de Waal, Frans. 2002. "Primate Behavior and Human Aggression." In *Must We Fight?: From the Battlefield to the Schoolyard, a New Perspective on Violent Conflict and Its Prevention,* edited by William L. Ury, 13–25. San Francisco: Jossey-Bass.

Diamond, Jared. 1997. "The Animal with the Weirdest Sex Life." In *Constructing Sexualities: Readings in Sexuality, Gender and Culture,* edited by Suzanne LaFont. Upper Saddle River, NJ: Prentice Hall, 2002.

DiGangi, Christine. 2016. "How Many Credit Cards Does the Average American Have?" Credit.com. http://blog.credit.com /2016/01/how-many-credit-cards-does-the-average-american -have-132997/.

Di Leonardo, Micaela. 1991. "Introduction: Gender, Culture, and Political Economy: Feminist Anthropology in Historical Perspective." In *Gender at the Crossroads of Knowledge: Feminist Anthropology in the Post-Modern Era,* edited by Micaela di Leonardo, 1–51. Berkeley: University of California Press.

Dill, Bonnie Thornton. 1983. "Race, Class and Gender: Prospects for an All-Inclusive Sisterhood." *Feminist Studies* 9: 131–50.

Dolan, Kerry A., and Luisa Kroll. 2016. "Forbes 2016 World's Billionaires: Meet the Richest People on the Planet." *Forbes,* March 1.

Domhoff, G. William. 2012. "Power in America: Wealth, Income, and Power." *Who Rules America?* http://sociology.ucsc.edu /whorulesamerica/power/wealth.html.

Douglas, Mary. 1966. *Purity and Danger: An Analysis of the Concepts of Pollution and Taboo.* London: Routledge & Kegan Paul.

Downey, Greg. 2005. *Learning Capoeira: Lessons in Cunning from an Afro-Brazilian Art.* New York: Oxford University Press.

Dudley, Kathryn Marie. 2000. *Debt and Dispossession: Farm Loss in America's Heartland.* Chicago: University of Chicago Press.

Dunham, Katherine. 1969. *Island Possessed.* Garden City, NY: Doubleday.

Durkheim, Émile. (1912) 1965. *The Elementary Forms of Religious Life.* New York: Free Press.

Durrenberger, E. Paul. 2001. "No Shame in My Game: The Working Poor in the Inner City [Review]." *American Anthropologist* 103(4): 1210–11.

Durrenberger, E. Paul, and Suzan Erem. 2010. *Anthropology Unbound: A Field Guide to the 21st Century* (2nd ed.). Boulder, CO: Paradigm.

Edelman, Marc. 1999. *Peasants against Globalization: Rural Social Movements in Costa Rica.* Stanford, CA: Stanford University Press.

———. 2001. "Social Movements: Changing Paradigms and Forms of Politics." *Annual Review of Anthropology* 30: 285–317.

Edelman, Marc, and Angelique Haugerud. 2005. *The Anthropology of Development and Globalization: From Classical Political Economy to Contemporary Neoliberalism.* Malden, MA: Blackwell.

Ehrenreich, Barbara, and Arlie Russell Hochschild, eds. 2004. *Global Woman: Nannies, Maids, and Sex Workers in the New Economy.* New York: Holt Paperbacks.

El Issa, Erin. 2015. "2015 American Household Credit Card Debt Study." NerdWallet.com. www.nerdwallet.com/blog /credit-card-data/average-credit-card-debt-household/.

Eller, Jack David. 1999. *From Culture to Ethnicity to Conflict: An Anthropological Perspective on Ethnic Conflict.* Ann Arbor: University of Michigan Press.

England, Sarah. 2002. "The Production and Consumption of Pink-Collar Identities in the Caribbean." *Current Anthropology* 43(3): 522–23.

Englund, Harri. 1999. "A Different Kind of War Story [Review]." *Journal of the Royal Anthropological Institute* 5(1): 141–42.

Ericksen, Thomas Hylland. 2010. *Ethnicity and Nationalism* (3rd ed.). Boulder, CO: Pluto Press.

Escobar, Arturo. 1991. "Anthropology and the Development Encounter: The Making and Marketing of Development Anthropology." *American Ethnologist* 18(4): 658–82.

———. 1995. *Encountering Development: The Making and Unmaking of the Third World.* Princeton, NJ: Princeton University Press.

Evans-Pritchard, E. E. 1937. *Witchcraft, Oracles and Magic among the Azande.* Oxford, UK: Clarendon Press.

———. 1940. *The Nuer: A Description of the Modes of Livelihood and Political Institutions of a Nilotic People.* Oxford, UK: Clarendon Press.

———. 1951. *Kinship and Marriage among the Nuer.* Oxford, UK: Clarendon Press.

Fadiman, Anne. 1997. *The Spirit Catches You and You Fall Down: A Hmong Child, Her American Doctors, and the Collision of Two Cultures.* New York: Farrar, Straus, and Giroux.

Falk, R. 1993. "The Making of Global Citizenship." In *Global Visions: Beyond the New World Order*, edited by Jeremy Brecher, John B. Childs, and Jill Cutler, 39–50. Boston: South End.

Falls, Susan. 2014. *Clarity, Cut, and Culture: The Many Meanings of Diamonds.* New York: NYU Press.

Fanon, Frantz. 1961. *The Wretched of the Earth.* Paris: F. Maspero.

Farmer, Paul. 1985. "The Anthropologist Within." *Harvard Medical Alumni Bulletin* 59(1): 23–28.

———. 2003. *Pathologies of Power: Health, Human Rights and the New War on the Poor.* Berkeley: University of California Press.

———. 2006. *AIDS and Accusation: Haiti and the Geography of Blame.* Berkeley: University of California Press.

———. 2010. "Landmine Boy and Stupid Deaths." In *Partner to the Poor: A Paul Farmer Reader*, edited by Haun Saussy. Berkeley: University of California Press.

Farquhar, Judith Brooke. 1986. "Knowledge and Practice in Chinese Medicine." PhD dissertation, University of Chicago, Department of Anthropology.

Fausto-Sterling, Anne. 1993. "The Five Sexes: Why Male and Female Are Not Enough." *The Sciences* May/April: 20–24.

Feagin, Joe R., and Clairece Booher Feagin. 2011. *Racial and Ethnic Relations* (9th ed.). New York: Pearson.

Feagin, Joe R., and Melvin P. Sikes. 1994. *Living with Racism: The Black Middle-Class Experience.* Boston: Beacon Press.

Fedigan, Linda. 1982. *Primate Paradigms: Sex Roles and Social Bonds.* Montreal: Eden Press.

———. 1986. "The Changing Role of Women in Models of Human Evolution." *Annual Reviews of Anthropology* 15: 25–66.

Feldman, Jeffrey D. 2001. "Reproducing Jews: A Cultural Account of Assisted Conception in Israel [Review]." *American Ethnologist* 28(4): 924–25.

Ferguson, Brian R.. 1995. *Yanomami Warfare: A History.* Santa Fe, NM: School of American Research Press.

———. 2002. "The History of War: Fact vs. Fiction." In *Must We Fight?: From the Battlefield to the Schoolyard, a New Perspective on Violent Conflict and Its Prevention*, edited by William L. Ury, 26–37. San Francisco: Jossey-Bass.

———. 2011. "Tribal Warfare." In *Encyclopedia of War*, 1–13. Malden, MA: Blackwell.

Ferguson, James. 1997. "Anthropology and Its Evil Twin: 'Development' in the Constitution of a Discipline." In *International Development and the Social Sciences: Essays on the History and Politics of Knowledge*, edited by Frederick Cooper and Randall Packard, 150–75. Berkeley: University of California Press.

Ferguson, James, and Akhil Gupta. 2002. "Spatializing States: Toward an Ethnography of Neoliberal Governmentality." *American Ethnologist* 29(4): 981–1002.

Fernea, Robert. 1996. "Photographic Politics." *Current Anthropology* 37(1): 183–84.

Fields-Black, Edda L. 2008. *Deep Roots: Rice Farmers in West Africa and the African Diaspora*. Bloomington: Indiana University Press.

FinAid. 2016. "Student Loan Debt Clock." www.finaid.org/loans/studentloandebtclock.phtml.

Finnstrom, Sverker. 2005. "Shadows of War: Violence, Power and International Profiteering in the Twenty-First Century [Review]." *Anthropological Quarterly* 78(2): 491–96.

Fisher, Bonnie, Francis T. Cullen, and Michael G. Turner. 2000. *The Sexual Victimization of College Women*. Washington, DC: U.S. Department of Justice, Office of Justice Programs, National Institute of Justice.

Fisher, Bonnie, Leah E. Daigle, and Francis T. Cullen. 2010. *Unsafe in the Ivory Tower: The Sexual Victimization of College Women*. Los Angeles: Sage Publications.

Fisher, Helen. 2004. *Why We Love: The Nature and Chemistry of Romantic Love*. New York: Henry Holt.

Fisher, Roger, William Ury, and Bruce Patton. 2012. *Getting to Yes: Negotiating an Agreement without Giving In*. London: Random House Business.

Floyd, Charlene J. 1996. "A Theology of Insurrection? Religion and Politics in Mexico." *Journal of International Affairs* 50(1): 142–65.

Flueckiger, Joyce. 2006. *In Amma's Healing Room: Gender and Vernacular Islam in South India*. Bloomington: Indiana University Press.

Fluehr-Lobban, Carolyn. 2006. *Race and Racism: An Introduction*. Lanham, MD: Altamira Press.

Foner, Nancy. 2000. *From Ellis Island to JFK: New York's Two Great Waves of Immigration*. New Haven, CT: Yale University Press.

———. 2003. *American Arrivals: Anthropology Engages the New Immigration*. Santa Fe, NM: School of American Research.

Forster, P., R. Harding, A. Torroni, and H. J. Bandelt. 1996. "Origin and Evolution of Native American mtDNA Variation: A Reappraisal." *American Journal of Human Genetics* 59(4): 935–45.

Fortes, Meyer. 1949. "Time and Social Structure: An Ashanti Case Study." In *Social Structure: Studies Presented to A. R. Radcliffe-Brown*, edited by Meyer Fortes. Oxford, UK: Clarendon Press.

Fortes, Meyer, and E. E. Evans-Pritchard. 1940. *African Political Systems*. London: Published for the International Institute of African Languages & Cultures by the Oxford University Press.

Foucault, Michel. (1976) 1990. *The History of Sexuality*, vol. 1: *An Introduction*. New York: Vintage Books.

———. 1977. *Discipline and Punish: The Birth of the Prison*. New York: Pantheon.

———. 1978. *The History of Sexuality*. New York: Pantheon.

Fouts, Roger. 1997. *Next of Kin: What Chimpanzees Have Taught Me about Who We Are*. New York: William Morrow.

Frank, Andre Gunder. 1969. *Latin America: Underdevelopment or Revolution: Essays on the Development of Underdevelopment and the Immediate Enemy*. New York: Monthly Review Press.

———. 1998. *ReORIENT: Global Economy in the Asian Age*. Berkeley: University of California Press.

Franklin, Sarah. 1997. *Embodied Progress: A Cultural Account of Assisted Conception*. London: Routledge.

———. 2007. *Dolly Mixtures: The Remaking of Genealogy*. Durham, NC: Duke University Press.

Frazer, James George. 1890. *The Golden Bough: A Study in Comparative Religion*. New York: Macmillan.

Freeman, Carla. 2000. *High Tech and High Heels in the Global Economy*. Durham, NC: Duke University Press.

Freeman, Dena. 2002. Initiating Change in Highland Ethiopia: Causes and Consequences of Cultural Transformation. Cambridge University Press.

Freeman, Dena, editor. 2012. Pentecostalism and Development: Churches, NGOs and Social Change in Africa. Palgrave Macmillan UK.

Freud, Sigmund. 1952. *Totem and Taboo: Some Points of Agreement between the Mental Lives of Savages and Neurotics*. New York: Norton.

Freyre, Gilberto. (1933) 1944. *The Masters and the Slaves: A Study in the Development of Brazilian Civilization*. New York: Knopf.

Friedman, Jaclyn, and Jessica Valenti. 2008. *Yes Means Yes! Visions of Female Sexual Power and a World without Rape*. Berkeley, CA: Seal Press.

Friedner, Michele. 2015. *Valuing Deaf Worlds in Urban India*. Rutgers, NJ: Rutgers University Press.

Fuentes, Augustin. 2013. "Blurring the Biological and Social in Human Becomings." In *Biosocial Becomings: Integrating Social and Biological Anthropology*, edited by Tim Ingold and Gisli Palsson, 42–58. New York: Cambridge University Press.

Gallup. 2015. "Fewer Americans Identify as Middle Class in Recent Years." www.gallup.com/poll/182918/fewer-americans-identify-middle-class-recent-years.aspx.

Galvez, Alyshia. 2009. *Guadalupe in New York: Devotion and the Struggle for Citizenship Rights among Mexican Immigrants*. New York: New York University Press.

Gardner, R. Allen, Beatrix T. Gardner, and Thomas E. Van Cantfort, eds. 1989. *Teaching Sign Language to Chimpanzees*. Albany: State University of New York Press.

Gaudio, Rudolf. 2009. *Allah Made Us: Sexual Outlaws in an Islamic African City*. Malden, MA: Wiley-Blackwell.

Gaunt, Kyra Danielle. 2006. *The Games Black Girls Play: Learning the Ropes from Double-Dutch to Hip-Hop*. New York: New York University Press.

Geertz, Clifford. 1973a. "Deep Play: Notes on a Balinese Cockfight." In *The Interpretation of Cultures*. New York: Basic Books.

———. 1973b. "Religion as a Cultural System." In *The Interpretation of Cultures*. New York: Basic Books.

———. 1973c. "Thick Description: Toward an Interpretive Theory of Culture." In *The Interpretation of Cultures*. New York: Basic Books.

Gell, A. F. 1995. "*African Art in Transit* [Review]." *Journal of the Royal Anthropological Institute* 1(4): 841–42.

Gellner, Ernest. 1983. *Nations and Nationalism*. Ithaca, NY: Cornell University Press.

Geromel, Ricardo. 2013. "Forbes' Billionaires World Map." *Forbes*, March 22.

Geyer, Michael. 1989. "The Militarization of Europe, 1914–1945." In *The Militarization of the Western World*, edited by John Gillis, 65–102. New Brunswick, NJ: Rutgers University Press.

Gibson, Jane. 1996. "The Social Construction of Whiteness in Shellcracker Haven, Florida." *Human Organization* 55(4): 379–89.

Giddens, Anthony. 1985. *The Nation-State and Violence*. Cambridge, UK: Polity.

Ginsburg, Faye D., Lila Abu-Lughod, and Brian Larkin, eds. 2002. *Media Worlds: Anthropology on New Terrain*. Berkeley: University of California Press.

Ginsburg, Faye and Rayna Rapp. 2013. "Disability Worlds." In *Annual Review of Anthropology* 42: 53-68.

Glazer, Nathan, and Daniel Patrick Moynihan. 1970. *Beyond the Melting Pot* (2nd ed.). Cambridge, MA: MIT Press.

Gledhill, John. 2000. *Power and Its Disguises: Anthropological Perspectives on Politics*. London: Pluto.

Global Footprint Network. 2013. http://footprintnetwork.org.

Global Witness. 2007. *Hot Chocolate: How Cocoa Fuelled the Conflict in Côte D'Ivoire*. www.globalwitness.org/sites/default/files/pdfs/cotedivoire.pdf.

Gluckman, Max. 1954. *Rituals of Rebellion in South-East Africa*. Manchester, UK: Manchester University Press.

Gmelch, George. 1992. "Superstition and Ritual in American Baseball." *Elysian Fields Quarterly* 11(3): 25–36.

Goldstein, Daniel M. 2016. *Owners of the Sidewalk: Security and Survival in the Informal City*. Durham, NC: Duke University Press.

Goldstein, Donna M. 2003. *Laughter out of Place: Race, Class, Violence, and Sexuality in a Rio Shantytown*. Berkeley: University of California Press.

Goldstein, Judith L. 1998. "Reading *National Geographic* [Review]." *American Ethnologist* 25(1): 9–10.

Goode, Judith, and Jeff Maskovsky, eds. 2001. *The New Poverty Studies: The Ethnography of Power, Politics, and Impoverished People in the United States*. New York: New York University Press.

Goodman, Roger. 2004. "Brokered Homeland: Japanese Brazilian Migrants in Japan [Review]." *Journal of Japanese Studies* 30(2): 465–71.

Gordon, Robert J. 1992. *The Bushman Myth: The Making of a Namibian Underclass*. Boulder, CO: Westview Press.

Gough, Kathleen. 1971. "Nuer Kinship: A Reexamination." In *The Translation of Culture: Essays to E. E. Evans-Pritchard*, edited by Thomas O. Beidelman, 79–121. London: Tavistock Publications.

Gould, Stephen Jay. 1987. *Time's Arrow, Time's Cycle: Myth and Metaphor in the Discovery of Geological Time*. Cambridge, MA: Harvard University Press.

Graeber, David. 2002. "The New Anarchists." *New Left Review* 13 (January–February).

———. 2011. *Debt: The First Five Thousand Years*. Brooklyn, NY: Melville House.

Gramsci, Antonio. 1971. *Selections from the Prison Notebooks*. Quintin Hoare and Geoffrey Nowell Smith, translators and editors. New York: International Publishers.

Gray, John. 1993. *Men Are from Mars, Women Are from Venus: The Classic Guide to Understanding the Opposite Sex*. New York: Harper.

Green, Edward C. 1999. *Indigenous Theories of Contagious Disease*. Walnut Creek, CA: AltaMira.

Green, L. J. 2002. *African American English: A Linguistic Introduction*. Cambridge, MA: Cambridge University Press.

Gregg, Jessica L. 2003. *Virtually Virgins: Sexual Strategies and Cervical Cancer in Recife, Brazil*. Stanford, CA: Stanford University Press.

Gregory, Steven. 1998. *Black Corona: Race and the Politics of Place in an Urban Community*. Princeton, NJ: Princeton University Press.

———. 2006. *The Devil behind the Mirror: Globalization and Politics in the Dominican Republic*. Berkeley: University of California Press.

Gregory, Steven, and Roger Sanjek, eds. 1994. *Race*. New Brunswick, NJ: Rutgers University Press.

Grimshaw, Ana, and Amanda Ravetz. 2009. *Observational Cinema: Anthropology, Film, and the Exploration of Social Life*. Bloomington: Indiana University Press.

Gross, Ariela J. 2010. *What Blood Won't Tell: A History of Race on Trial in America*. Cambridge, MA: Harvard University Press.

Gudmundson, Lowell. 2001. "Peasants against Globalization: Rural Social Movement in Costa Rica [Review]." *Agricultural History* 75(4): 504–6.

Guest, Kenneth J. 2003. *God in Chinatown: Religion and Survival in New York's Evolving Immigrant Community*. New York: New York University Press.

———. 2011. "From Mott Street to East Broadway: Fuzhounese Immigrants and the Revitalization of New York's Chinatown." *Journal of Chinese Overseas* 7(1): 24–44.

Guest, Kenneth J., and Peter Kwong. 2000. "Ethnic Enclaves and Cultural Diversity." In *Cultural Diversity in the United States: A Critical Reader*, edited by Ida Susser and Thomas C. Patterson, 39–50. Malden, MA: Blackwell.

Guilmoto, Christophe Z. 2011. "Demography for Anthropologists: Populations, Castes, and Classes." In *A Companion to the Anthropology of India*, edited by Isabelle Clark-Decès. Hoboken, NJ: Wiley-Blackwell.

Gupta, Akhil, and James Ferguson, eds. 1997. *Culture, Power, Place: Explorations in Critical Anthropology*. Durham, NC: Duke University Press.

Gusterson, Hugh. 1996. *Nuclear Rites: A Weapons Laboratory at the End of the Cold War*. Berkeley: University of California Press.

———. 1997. "Studying Up Revisited." *Political and Legal Anthropology Review* 20(1): 114–19.

———. 2004. *People of the Bomb: Portraits of America's Nuclear Complex*. Minneapolis: University of Minnesota Press.

———. 2008. "When Professors Go to War: Why the Ivory Tower and the Pentagon Don't Mix." *Foreign Policy*, July 21.

———. 2016. *Drone: Remote Control Warfare*. Cambridge, MA: The MIT Press.

Gutmann, Matthew C. 2007. *The Meanings of Macho: Being a Man in Mexico City*. Berkeley: University of California Press. Originally published in 1996.

Hannerz, Ulf. 1996. *Transnational Connections: Culture, People, Places*. London: Routledge.

Harding, Jennifer. 1998. "Investigating Sex: Essentialism and Constructionism." In *Sex Acts*, 8–22. London: Sage Publications.

Hargrove, Melissa D. 2009. "Mapping the 'Social Field of Whiteness': White Racism as Habitus in the City Where History Lives." *Transforming Anthropology* 17(2): 93–104.

Harries, Patrick. 2007. "The Battle of Algiers." In *Black and White in Colour: African History on Screen*, edited by Vivian Bickford-Smith and Richard Mendelsohn. Oxford, UK: James Currey.

Harris, Marvin. 1964. *Patterns of Race in the Americas*. New York: Walker.

———. 1970. "Referential Ambiguity in the Calculus of Brazilian Racial Identity." *Southwestern Journal of Anthropology* 21(1): 1–14.

———. 1974. *Cows, Pigs, Wars, & Witches: The Riddles of Culture*. New York: Random House.

Harris, Reginald. 2009. "Allah Made Us [Review]." *Gay and Lesbian Review Worldwide* 16(6): 42.

Harrison, Faye V. 1998. "Introduction: Expanding the Discourse on 'Race.'" *American Anthropologist* 100(3): 609–31.

———. 2002a. "Subverting the Cultural Logics of Marked and Unmarked Racisms in the Global Era." In *Discrimination and Tolerations*, edited by K. Hastrup and G. Ulrich, 97–125. London: Kluwer Law International.

———. 2002b. "Unraveling 'Race' for the 21st Century." In *Exotic No More: Anthropology on the Front Lines*, edited by Jeremy MacClancy. Chicago: University of Chicago Press.

Harrison, K. David. 2007. *When Languages Die: The Extinction of the World's Languages and the Erosion of Human Knowledge*. New York: Oxford University Press.

Hartigan, John Jr. 1999. *Racial Situations: Class Predicaments of Whiteness in Detroit*. Princeton, NJ: Princeton University Press.

———. 2005. *Odd Tribes: Toward a Cultural Analysis of White People*. Durham, NC: Duke University Press.

Harvey, David. 1990. *The Condition of Postmodernity: An Enquiry into the Origins of Cultural Change*. Malden, MA: Blackwell.

———. 1996. *Justice, Nature and the Geography of Difference*. Oxford: Blackwell.

———. 2003. *The New Imperialism*. Oxford: Oxford University Press.

Haugerud, Angelique. 1998. "Purity and Exile: A Book Review." *International Journal of African Historical Studies* 31(1): 214–16.

Haugerud, Angelique, Margaret Priscilla Stone, and Peter D. Little. 2000. *Commodities and Globalization: Anthropological Perspectives*. Lanham, MD: Rowman & Littlefield.

Hayes, Catherine. 1951. *The Ape in Our House*. New York: Harper.

Hearn, Jonathan. 2006. *Rethinking Nationalism: A Critical Introduction*. New York: Palgrave Macmillan.

Helmreich, Stefan. 2009. *Alien Ocean: Anthropological Voyages in Microbial Seas*. Berkeley: University of California Press.

Helweg, Arthur W. 1998. "Contesting Culture: Discourses of Identity in Multi-Ethnic London [Review]." *International Migration Review* 32(1): 252.

Henshilwood, Christopher S., et al. 2011. "A 100,000-Year-Old Ochre-Processing Workshop at Blombos Cave, South Africa." *Science* 334(6053): 219–22.

Herzog, Werner (director). *Cave of Forgotten Dreams*. 2010. IFC Films.

Higgenbotham, Evelyn Brooks. 1992. "African-American Women's History and the Metalanguage of Race." *Signs: Journal of Women in Culture and Society* 17: 251–74.

Hill, Jane H. 2008. *The Everyday Language of White Racism*. Malden, MA: Wiley-Blackwell.

Hirsch, Jennifer. 2007. "'Love Makes a Family': Globalization, Companionate Marriage, and the Modernization of Gender Equality." In *Love and Globalization: Transformations of Intimacy in the Contemporary World*, edited by Mark Padilla, Jennifer Hirsch, Miguel Munoz-Laboy, Richard Sember, and Richard Parker, 93–106. Nashville, TN: Vanderbilt University Press.

Hirschfeld, Lawrence A. 1989. "The Body Silent: A Review." *Contemporary Sociology* 18(2): 276–77.

Hirschkind, Charles. 2012. "Beyond Secular and Religious: An Intellectual Genealogy of Tahrir Square." *American Ethnologist* 39(1): 49–53.

Ho, Karen. 2009. *Liquidated: An Ethnography of Wall Street.* Durham, NC: Duke University Press.

Hobhouse, L. T. 1915. *Morals in Evolution; A Study in Comparative Ethics.* New York: Holt.

Hobsbawm, Eric, and Terence Ranger. 1983. *Invented Traditions.* Cambridge, UK: Cambridge University Press.

Hockings, Paul Edward, ed. 2003. *Principles of Visual Anthropology* (3rd ed.). Berlin: Mouton De Gruyter.

———. 2005. *The Church of Women: Gendered Encounters between Maasai and Missionaries.* Bloomington: Indiana University Press.

———. 2011. *Being Maasai, Becoming Indigenous: Postcolonial Politics in a Neoliberal World.* Bloomington: Indiana University Press.

Holmes, Janet. 1998. "Women's Talk: The Question of Sociolinguistic Universals." In *Language and Gender: A Reader*, edited by Jennifer Coates, 461–83. Oxford, UK: Blackwell.

Holmes, Seth M. 2013. *Fresh Fruit, Broken Bodies: Migrant Farmworkers in the United States.* Berkeley: University of California Press.

Homewood, Katherine. 2012. "*Being Maasai, Becoming Indigenous: Postcolonial Politics in a Neoliberal World* [Review]." *African Affairs* 111(445): 682–84.

Hondagneu-Sotelo, Pierrette. 1994. *Gendered Transitions: Mexican Experiences of Immigration.* Berkeley: University of California.

———. 2001. *Domestica: Immigrant Workers Cleaning and Caring in the Shadows of Affluence.* Berkeley: University of California Press.

Honwana, Alcinda. 1999. "A Different Kind of War Story [Review]." *American Ethnologist* 26(2): 504–5.

Hostetler, John A. 1993. *Amish Society* (4th ed.). Baltimore: Johns Hopkins University Press.

———. 1997. *Hutterite Society* (2nd ed.). Baltimore: Johns Hopkins University Press.

Howard, David. 2001. "Dominican Republic Spurns Haitian Migrants: Rejection of African Heritage Fuels Anti-Haitian Views." *NACLA Report on the Americas* 35(2): 24–28.

Howell, David L. 2004. "Brokered Homeland: Japanese Brazilian Migrants in Japan [Review]." *Pacific Affairs* 77(1): 130–31.

Hubbard, Ruth. 1990. "The Social Construction of Sexuality." In *The Politics of Women's Biology.* New Brunswick, NJ: Rutgers University Press.

———. 2012. "Democratic Republic of Congo." In *World Report 2012*, 104–9. www.hrw.org/world-report-2012.

Hurston, Zora Neale. 1935. *Mules and Men.* Philadelphia: Lippincott.

———. 1938. *Tell My Horse.* Philadelphia: Lippincott.

Hutchinson, Sharon. 1996. *Nuer Dilemmas: Coping with Money, War and the State.* Berkeley: University of California Press.

Ignatiev, Noel. 1995. *How the Irish Became White.* New York: Routledge Press.

Illouz, Eva. 1997. *Consuming the Romantic Utopia: Love and Cultural Contradictions of Capitalism.* Berkeley: University of California Press.

Inda, Jonathan Xavier, and Renato Rosaldo. 2002. *The Anthropology of Globalization: A Reader.* Malden, MA: Blackwell.

India Resource Center. 2015. www.indiaresource.org/index.html.

Ingold, Tim. 2013. "Prospect. P." In *Biosocial Becomings: Integrating Social and Biological Anthropology*, edited by Tim Ingold and Gisli Palsson, 1–21. New York: Cambridge University Press.

Ingraham, Chrys. 2008. *White Weddings: Romancing Heterosexuality in Popular Culture*, (rev. ed.). New York: Routledge. First published in 1999.

Ingstad, Benedicte, and Susan R Whyte, eds. 2007. *Disability in Local and Global Worlds.* Berkeley: University of California Press

Inhorn, Marcia. 1996. *Infertility and Patriarchy: The Cultural Politics of Gender and Family Life in Egypt.* Philadelphia: University of Pennsylvania Press.

Instituto Cervantes. 2015. "El español: un lengua viva." http://eldiae.es/wp-content/uploads/2015/06/espanol_lengua-viva_20151.pdf.

Internal Displacement Monitoring Center. 2012. "Internal Displacement Global Overview 2011: People Internally Displaced by Conflict and Violence." www.internal-displacement.org/publications/global-overview.

International Monetary Fund. 2014. "World Economic Outlook Database." www.imf.org/external/pubs/ft/weo/2014/02/weodata/index.aspx.

———. 2012. "Global Trends." www.iom.int/cms/en/sites/iom/home/about-migration/facts—figures-1.html.

International Telecommunication Union. 2015. "Statistics." www.itu.int/en/ITU-D/Statistics/Pages/stat/default.aspx.

Ishi, Angelo. 2003. "Transnational Strategies by Japanese-Brazilian Migrants in the Age of IT." In *Global Japan: The Experience of Japan's New Immigrant and Overseas Communities*, edited by Roger Goodman, Ceri Peach, Ayumi Takenaka, and Paul White, 209–21. London: RoutledgeCurzon.

Ivana, Greti-Julia. 2015. "Nation as Network: A Book Review." *Information, Communication and Society* 18(12): 1481–83.

Jablonski, Nina G. 2006. *Skin: A Natural History.* Berkeley: University of California Press.

Jablonski, Nina G., and George Chaplin. 2000. "The Evolution of Skin Coloration." *Journal of Human Evolution* 39: 57–106.

Jacobs, A. J. 2005. "Tsukiji: The Fish Market at the Center of the World [Review]." *Contemporary Sociology* 34(4): 373–75.

Jacobs, Sue-Ellen, ed. 1997. *Two-Spirit People: Native American Gender Identity, Sexuality, and Spirituality.* Champaign: University of Illinois Press.

Jamison, Sandra L. 2006. "The Games Black Girls Play [Review]." *Black Issues Book Review*, Vol. 8 Issue 3, 43–44.

Jaynes, Gregory. 1982. "A Louisiana Lawsuit Asks What It Means to Be Black, White, or 'Colored' in America." *Providence Sunday Journal*, October 14, A-19.

Jenkins, Richard. 1996. *Social Identity*. New York: Routledge.

———. 2008. *Rethinking Ethnicity* (2nd ed.). Thousand Oaks, CA: Sage.

Johanson, Donald C., et al. 1987. "New Partial Skeleton of *Homo habilis* from Olduvai Gorge, Tanzania." *Nature* 327: 205–9.

Jones, Camara Phyllis. 2000. "Levels of Racism: A Theoretic Framework and a Gardener's Tale." *American Journal of Public Health* 90(8): 1212–15.

Jordan, Brigitte. 1993. *Birth in Four Cultures: A Crosscultural Investigation of Childbirth in Yucatan, Holland, Sweden, and the United States*. Rev. and expanded by Robbie Davis-Floyd. Prospect Heights, IL: Waveland Press.

Jordan, Miriam. 2010. "Arizona Grades Teachers on Fluency: State Pushes School Districts to Reassign Instructors with Heavy Accents or Other Shortcomings in Their English." *Wall Street Journal*, April 30.

Juris, Jeffrey S. 2008. *Networking Futures: The Movements against Corporate Globalization*. Durham, NC: Duke University Press.

———. 2012. "Reflections on #Occupy Everywhere: Social Media, Public Space, and Emerging Logics of Aggregation." *American Ethnologist* 39(2): 259–79.

Jurmain, Robert, and Harry Nelson. 1994. *Introduction to Physical Anthropology*, (6th ed.). St. Paul, MN: West Publishing.

Kahn, Susan Martha. 2000. *Reproducing Jews: A Cultural Account of Assisted Conception in Israel*. Durham, NC: Duke University Press.

Kanna, Ahmed. 2011. *Dubai: The City as Corporation*. Minneapolis: University of Minnesota Press.

Kant, Immanuel. 1790. *Critique of Judgement*. Translated by J. H. Bernard. London: Collier Macmillan.

Karp, Ivan, and Steven Lavine. 1991. *Exhibiting Cultures: The Poetics and Politics of Museum Display*. Washington, DC: Smithsonian Institution.

Kasinitz, Philip, Mary C. Waters, John H. Mollenkopf, and Jennifer Holdaway. 2008. *Inheriting the City: The Children of Immigrants Come of Age*. New York: Russell Sage Foundation.

Katz, Jonathan Ned. 2007. *The Invention of Heterosexuality*, with a new preface. Chicago: University of Chicago Press. First published in 1995.

Kearney, M. 1995. "The Local and the Global: The Anthropology of Globalization and Transnationalism." *Annual Review of Anthropology* 24: 547–65.

Kelly, Patty. 2008a. "Legalize Prostitution." *Los Angeles Times*, March 13.

———. 2008b. *Lydia's Open Door: Inside Mexico's Most Modern Brothel*. Berkeley: University of California Press.

Kendall, Laurel. 1985. *Shamans, Housewives, and Other Restless Spirits: Women in Korean Ritual Life*. Honolulu: University of Hawaii Press.

———. 1988. *The Life and Hard Times of a Korean Shaman: Of Tales and the Telling of Tales*. Honolulu: University of Hawaii Press.

Kensinger, Kenneth. 1988. "The Body Silent: A Review." *American Ethnologist* 15: 820–21.

Keynes, John Maynard. (1936) 2007. *The General Theory of Employment Interest and Money*. Houndmills, UK: Palgrave Macmillan.

Kidder, Tracy. 2003. *Mountains beyond Mountains: The Quest of Dr. Paul Farmer, A Man Who Would Cure the World*. New York: Random House.

Kim, Eleana. 2007. "Transnational Adoption: A Cultural Economy of Race, Gender, and Kinship [Review]." *Anthropological Quarterly* 80(2): 589.

———. 2010. *Adopted Territory: Transnational Korean Adoptees and the Politics of Belonging*. Durham, NC: Duke University Press.

Kingfisher, Catherine. 2001. "Poverty and Downward Mobility in the Land of Opportunity." *American Anthropologist* 103(3): 824–27.

Kinsey, Alfred C. 1953. *Sexual Behavior in the Human Female*. Philadelphia: W. B. Saunders.

Kinsey, Alfred C., Wardell Baxter Pomeroy, and Clyde E. Martin. 1948. *Sexual Behavior in the Human Male*. Philadelphia: W. B. Saunders.

Kleinman, Arthur. 1988. *The Illness Narratives: Suffering, Healing, and the Human Condition*. New York: Basic Books.

Knauft, Bruce M. 1987. "Ritualized Homosexuality in Melanesia [Review]." *American Ethnologist* 14(2): 401–4.

———. 1991. "Violence and Sociality in Human Evolution." *Current Anthropology* 32(4): 391–408.

Kohrman, Matthew. 2005. *Bodies of Difference: Experiences of Disability and Institutional Advocacy in the Making of Modern China*. Berkeley: University of California Press

Kolbert, Elizabeth. 2014. *The Sixth Extinction: An Unnatural History*. New York: Henry Holt.

Kopytoff, Igor. 1986. "The Cultural Biography of Things: Commoditization as Process." In *The Social Life of Things: Commodities in Cultural Perspective*, edited by Arjun Appadurai, 64–91. Cambridge, UK: Cambridge University Press.

Korten, David C. 2001. *When Corporations Rule the World*. San Francisco: Berrett-Koehler.

———. 2015. *Change the Story, Change the Future*. Oakland, CA: Berrett-Koehler.

Kottak, Conrad P. 2006. *Assault on Paradise: The Globalization of a Little Community in Brazil* (4th ed.). New York: McGraw-Hill.

Krause, Johannes, et al. 2007. "Neanderthals in Central Asia and Siberia." *Nature* 449: 902–4.

Krause, Johannes, et al. 2010. "The Complete Mitochondrial DNA Genome of an Unknown Hominin from Southern Siberia." *Nature* 464: 894–97.

Kromidas, Maria. 2004. "Learning War/Learning Race: Fourth-Grade Students in the Aftermath of September 11th in New York City." *Critique of Anthropology* 24(1).

———. 2015. "Ending Greece's Bleeding." *New York Times*, July 5.

Kulick, Don. 2003. "No." *Language and Communication* 1: 139–51.

Kulick, Don, and Jens Rydstrom. 2015. *Loneliness and Its Opposite: Sex, Disability, and the Ethics of Engagement.* Durham, NC: Duke University Press.

Kuper, Adam. 1983. *Anthropology and Anthropologists: The Modern British School.* London: Routledge & Kegan Paul.

Kurtz, Donald V. 2001. *Political Anthropology: Power and Paradigms.* Boulder, CO: Westview Press.

Kuzawa, Christopher, et al. 2009. "Fatherhood, Pair-Bonding, and Testosterone in the Philippines." *Hormones and Behavior* 56(4): 429–35.

Labov, William. 1972a. *Language in the Inner City: Studies in the Black English Vernacular.* Philadelphia: University of Pennsylvania Press.

———. 1972b. *Sociolinguistic Patterns.* Philadelphia: University of Pennsylvania Press.

Lan, David. 1985. *Guns and Rain: Guerillas and Spirit Mediums in Zimbabwe.* Berkeley: University of California Press.

Lan, Pei-Chia. 2006. *Global Cinderellas: Migrant Domestics and Newly Rich Employers in Taiwan.* Durham, NC: Duke University Press.

Lancaster, Roger N. 1994. *Life Is Hard: Machismo, Danger, and the Intimacy of Power in Nicaragua.* Berkeley: University of California Press.

Landers, Melissa A., and Gary Alan Fine. 1996. "Learning Life's Lessons in Tee Ball: The Reinforcement of Gender and Status in Kindergarten Sport." *Sociology of Sport Journal* 13(1).

Landesman, Ohad. 2015. "Here, There, and Everywhere, Leviathan and the Digital Future of Observational Ethnography." *Visual Anthropology Review* 31(1), 12–19.

Lansing, J. Steven. 1987. *Priests and Programmers: Technology of Power in the Engineered Landscape of Bali.* Princeton, NJ: Princeton University Press.

Larrain, Jorge, 1989. *Theories of Development: Capitalism, Colonialism and Dependency.* London: Polity Press.

Larsen, Clark Spencer. 2011. *Our Origins: Discovering Physical Anthropology* (2nd ed.). New York: Norton.

———. 2014. *Our Origins: Discovering Physical Anthropology* (3rd ed.). New York: Norton.

Leach, Edmund. 1954. *Political Systems of Highland Burma: A Study of Kachin Social Structure.* Cambridge, MA: Harvard University Press.

Leacock, Eleanor Burke. 1971. *The Culture of Poverty: A Critique.* New York: Simon & Schuster.

———. 1981. *Myths of Male Dominance: Collected Articles on Women Cross-Culturally.* New York: Monthly Review Press.

Leap, William L. 2010. "Allah Made Us [Review]." *Journal of the Royal Anthropological Institute* 16: 938–39.

Lee, Richard B. 1984. *The Dobe !Kung.* New York: Holt, Rinehart and Winston.

———. 2003. *The Dobe JuHoansi* (3rd ed.) (Case Studies in Cultural Anthropology). Belmont, CA: Wadsworth Publishing.

Lee, Richard B., and Irven Devore, eds. 1968. *Man the Hunter: The First Intensive Survey of a Single Crucial Stage of Human Development—Man's Once Universal Hunting Way of Life.* New York: The Wenner-Gren Foundation for Anthropological Research.

Lessinger, Johanna. 1995. *From the Ganges to the Hudson: Indian Immigrants in New York City.* Boston: Allyn & Bacon.

Levitt, Peggy. 2001. *The Transnational Villagers.* Berkeley: University of California Press.

———. 2007. *God Needs No Passport: Immigrants and the Changing American Religions Landscape.* New York: The New Press.

Lewellen, Ted C. 2002. *The Anthropology of Globalization: Cultural Anthropology Enters the 21st Century.* Westport, CT: Praeger.

———. 2003. *Political Anthropology: An Introduction.* Westport, CT: Praeger.

Lewin, Ellen. 1992. "Families We Choose: Lesbians, Gays, Kinship [Review]." *American Ethnologist* 19(4): 825–26.

———. 1995. "Life Is Hard [Review]." *American Ethnologist* 22(2): 441–42.

Lewis, M. Paul, ed. 2009. *Ethnologue: Languages of the World* (16th ed.). Dallas: SIL International.

Lewis, M. Paul, Gary F. Simons, and Charles D. Fennig, eds. 2015. *Ethnologue: Languages of the World,* (18th ed.). Dallas: SIL International.

Lewis, Oscar. 1959. *Five Families: Mexican Case Studies in the Culture of Poverty.* New York: Basic Books.

———. 1966. *La Vida: A Puerto Rican Family in the Culture of Poverty—San Juan and New York.* New York: Random House.

Leys, Colin. 1996. *The Rise and Fall of Development Theory.* Oxford, UK: James Currey.

Li, Jun Z., et al. 2008. "Worldwide Human Relationships Inferred from Genome-Wide Patterns of Variation." *Science* 319: 1100–4.

Liang, Zai. 2012. "Recent Migration Trends in China: Geographic and Demographic Aspects of Development Implications." Presentation for UN Expert Group Meeting on New Trends in Migration: Demographic Aspects, New York, December 3. www.un.org/esa/population/meetings/EGM_MigrationTrends /UN_presentation_Dec_2012_FINAL_SH.pdf.

Liang, Zai, Zhen Li, Zhongdang Ma. 2014. Changing Patterns of the Floating Population in China, 2000–2010. *Population and Development Review* 40(4): 695–716.

Lieberman, Leonard, and Rodney C. Kirk. 1996. "The Trial of Darwin Is Over: Religious Voices for Evolution and the 'Fairness' Doctrine." *Creation/Evolution* 16(2): 1–9.

Life and Debt. 2001. Directed by Stephanie Black. Tuff Gong Pictures.

Limon, Jose E. 1997. "The Meanings of Macho: Being a Man in Mexico City [Review]." *American Anthropologist* 99(1): 185.

Lindenbaum, Shirley. 2009. "Cannibalism, Kuru and Anthropology." *Folia Neuropathologica* 47(2): 138–44.

Livingstone, Frank B. 1958. "Anthropological Implications of Sickle Cell Gene Distribution in West Africa." *American Anthropologist* 60: 533–62.

Lock, Margaret M. 1993. *Encounters with Aging: Mythologies of Menopause in Japan and North America.* Berkeley: University of California Press.

———. 2002. *Twice Dead: Organ Transplants and the Reinvention of Death.* Berkeley: University of California Press.

Loe, Meika. 2004. *The Rise of Viagra: How the Little Blue Pill Changed Sex in America.* New York: New York University Press.

Loomis, William F. 1967. "Skin-Pigment Regulation of Vitamin-D Biosynthesis in Man." *Science* 157: 501–6.

Lopez, Ian Haney. 2006. *White by Law: The Legal Construction of Race* (2nd ed.). New York: New York University Press.

Lorber, Judith. 1994. *Paradoxes of Gender.* New Haven, CT: Yale University Press.

Low, Setha. 2004. *Behind the Gates: Life, Security, and the Pursuit of Happiness in Fortress America.* New York: Routledge.

Low, Setha, and Sally Engle Merry. 2010. "Engaged Anthropology: Diversity and Dilemmas: An Introduction to Supplement 2." *Current Anthropology* 51 (S2): 203–26.

Lowie, Robert Harry. 1920. *Primitive Society.* New York: Harper & Brothers.

Lutz, Catherine. 2001. *Homefront: A Military City and the American Twentieth Century.* Boston: Beacon.

———. 2004. "Militarization." In *A Companion to the Anthropology of Politics,* edited by David Nugent and Joan Vincent, 318–31. Malden, MA: Blackwell.

Lutz, Catherine, and Jane L. Collins. 1993. *Reading National Geographic.* Chicago: University of Chicago Press.

Lydon, Ghislaine. 2009. *On Trans-Saharan Trails: Islamic Law, Trade Networks, and Cross-Cultural Exchange in Nineteenth-Century Western Africa.* Cambridge, UK: Cambridge University Press.

MacClancy, Jeremy, ed. 1996. *Sport, Identity and Ethnicity.* Oxford, UK: Berg.

MacDougall, David. 2005. *Film, Ethnography, and the Senses: The Corporeal Image.* Princeton, NJ: Princeton University Press.

MacKinnon, Catharine A. 1993. *Only Words.* Cambridge, MA: Harvard University Press.

Mahler, Sarah, and Patricia Pessar, eds. 2001. "Special Issue: Gendering Transnational Spaces." *Identities: Global Studies in Culture and Power* 7(4).

Malinowski, Bronislaw. (1922) 2002. *Argonauts of the Western Pacific.* Reprint, London: Routledge.

———. 1927. *Sex and Repression in Savage Society.* London: Kegan Paul, Trench, Trübner & Co.

———. 1929. *The Sexual Life of Savages in North Western Melanesia: An Ethnographic Account of Courtship, Marriage and Family Life among the Natives of the Trobriand Islands, British New Guinea.* London: Kegan Paul, Trench, Trübner & Co.

———. 1930. "Parenthood—The Basis of Social Structure." In *The New Generation: The Intimate Problems of Modern Parents and Children,* edited by Victor F. Calverton and Samuel D. Schmalhausen. London: George Allen & Unwin.

Malkki, Liisa. 1995. *Purity and Exile: Violence, Memory, and National Cosmology Among Hutu Refugees in Tanzania.* Chicago: University of Chicago Press.

Mallory, J. P., and D. Q. Adams. 2006. *The Oxford Introduction to Proto-Indo-European and the Proto-Indo-European World.* Oxford, UK: Oxford University Press.

Mamdani, Mahmood. 2002. *When Victims Become Killers: Colonialism, Nativism, and the Genocide in Rwanda.* Princeton, NJ: Princeton University Press.

Mantsios, Gregory. 2003. "Media Magic: Making Class Invisible." In *Race, Class, and Gender in the United States* (6th ed.), edited by Paula Rothenberg. New York: Worth Publishers.

Marable, Manning. 2000. *The Great Wells of Democracy: The Meaning of Race in American Life.* New York: Perseus.

———. 2002. "Whither Whiteness." *Souls: A Critical Journal of Black Politics, Culture and Society* 4(4): 45–73.

Marcus, George E., and Fred R. Myers. 1995. *The Traffic in Culture: Refiguring Art and Anthropology.* Berkeley: University of California Press.

Mardi Gras: Made in China. 2005. Directed by David Redmon. Carnivalesque Films.

Marks, Jonathan. 1995. *Human Biodiversity: Genes, Race, and History.* New York: Aldine de Gruyter.

Marlowe, Frank. 2010. *The Hadza: Hunter-Gatherers of Tanzania.* Berkeley: University of California Press.

Martin, Emily. 1991. "The Egg and the Sperm: How Science Has Constructed a Romance Based on Stereotypical Male-Female Roles." *Signs: Journal of Women in Culture and Society* 16(3): 485–501.

Martin, Joann. 1999. "Women and Social Movements in Latin America: Power from Below [Review]." *American Ethnologist* 26(2): 482–83.

Martinez, Samuel. 1996. *Peripheral Migrants: Haitians and Dominican Republic Sugar Plantations.* Knoxville: University of Tennessee Press.

———. 2003. "Not a Cockfight: Rethinking Haitian-Dominican Relations." *Latin American Perspectives* 3(3): 80–101.

Marx, Karl. 1867. *Capital.* Reprint, London: Penguin, 1986.

Marx, Karl, and Friedrich Engels. 1848. *The Communist Manifesto.* Reprint, London: Penguin, 1967.

———. 1957. *On Religion.* Moscow: Foreign Languages Publishing House.

Mascia-Lees, Frances E. 2009. *Gender and Difference in a Globalizing World: Twenty-First Century Anthropology.* Prospect Heights, IL: Waveland Press.

Mauss, Marcel. 1979. "Body Techniques." In *Sociology and Psychology: Essays by Marcel Mauss.* Translated by Ben Brewster. London: Routledge and Kegan Paul.

Maybury-Lewis, David. 2002. *Indigenous Peoples, Ethnic Groups and the State.* Boston: Allyn and Bacon.

McAdam, Doug, John D. McCarthy, and Mayer N. Zald. 1996. *Comparative Perspectives on Social Movements: Political Opportunities, Mobilizing Structures, and Cultural Framings.* Cambridge, UK: Cambridge University Press.

McAdoo, Harriette Pipes. 2000. "All Our Kin: Strategies for Survival in a Black Community [Review]." *Journal of Marriage and Family* 62(3): 864–65.

McAlister, Elizabeth A. 2002. *Rara! Vodou, Power, and Performance in Haiti and Its Diaspora.* Berkeley: University of California Press.

McBrearty, Sally, and Alison S. Brooks. 2000. "The Revolution That Wasn't: A New Interpretation of the Origin of Modern Human Behaviour." *Journal of Human Evolution* 39(5): 453–563.

McClaurin, Irma. 2007. "Finding Zora." www.research.ufl.edu /publications/explore/v07n1/zora.htm.

McCracken, Grant. 1991. *Culture and Consumption: New Approaches to the Symbolic Character of Consumer Goods and Activities.* Bloomington: Indiana University Press.

———. 2005. *Culture and Consumption II: Markets, Meaning, and Brand Management.* Bloomington: Indiana University Press.

McFate, Montgomery. 2005. "Anthropology and Counterinsurgency: The Strange Story of Their Curious Relationship." *Military Review* (March-April): 24–38.

McGrath, Charles. 2005. "In Fiction, a Long History of Fixation on the Social Gap." *New York Times,* June 8.

McHenry, Henry M., and Katherine Coffing. 2000. "*Australopithecus* to *Homo*: Transformations in Body and Mind." *Annual Review of Anthropology* 29: 125–46.

McIntosh, Peggy. 1989. "White Privilege: Unpacking the Invisible Knapsack." *Peace and Freedom* (July–August): 10–12.

McKay, Deirdre. 2006. "Friction: An Ethnography of Global Connection [Review]." *Women's Studies Quarterly* 34(1–2): 476–80.

McKibben, William. 2010. *Earth: Making a Life on a Tough New Planet.* New York: Henry Holt.

———. 2012. "Global Warming's Terrifying New Math." *Rolling Stone,* July 19.

McKinnon, Susan, and Sydel Silverman, eds. 2005. *Complexities: Beyond Nature and Nurture.* Chicago: University of Chicago Press.

McWhorter, John H. 2001. *The Power of Babel: A Natural History of Language.* New York: HarperCollins.

Mead, Margaret. 1928. *Coming of Age in Samoa: A Psychological Study of Primitive Youth for Western Civilization.* New York: William Morrow.

———. 1935. *Sex and Temperament in Three Primitive Societies.* New York: William Morrow.

———. 1940. "Warfare Is Only an Invention—Not a Biological Necessity." In *Approaches to Peace: A Reader in Peace Studies,* edited by David P. Barash, 19–22. New York: Oxford University Press, 2000.

Medeiros, Melanie A. "The Other End of the Bargain: The Socioeconomics of Marital Dissolution in Rural Northeast Brazil." *Transforming Anthropology* 22(2): 105–20.

Merry, Sally Engle. 2008. *Gender Violence: A Cultural Perspective.* New York: Wiley-Blackwell.

Miles, H. Lyn White. 1993. "Language and the Orangutan: The Old 'Person of the Forest.'" In *The Great Ape Project,* edited by Paola Cavalieri and Peter Singer, 45–50. New York: St. Martin's Press.

Milkie, Melissa A. 2000. "White Weddings [Review]." *Gender and Society* 14(6): 824–26.

Miller, Daniel, and Sophie Woodward, eds. 2011. *Global Denim.* New York: Berg.

Miller, Raegen, and Diana Epstein. 2011. "There Still Be Dragons: Racial Disparity in School Funding Is No Myth." Center for American Progress. www.americanprogress .org/issues/education/report/2011/07/05/9943/there -still-be-dragons/.

Mills, C. Wright. 1956. *The Power Elite.* New York: Oxford University Press.

Mills, Mary Beth. 2003. "Gender and Inequality in the Global Labor Force." *Annual Review of Anthropology* 32: 41–62.

Miner, Horace. 1956. "Body Ritual among the Nacirema." *American Anthropologist* 58(3): 503–7.

Mintz, Sidney W. 1985. *Sweetness and Power: The Place of Sugar in Modern History.* New York: Viking Penguin.

Molyneux, Maxine. 1999. "Women and Social Movements in Latin America: Power from Below [Review]." *Journal of Latin American Studies* 31(2): 535–37.

Monnier, Oliver. 2013. "Agribusiness: Smoothing Out the Bumps in Côte d'Ivoire." *The Africa Report.* July 25. www.theafricareport .com/West-Africa/agribusiness-smoothing-out-the-bumps-in -Cote-divoire.html.

Moore, Mignon R. 2011. *Invisible Families: Gay Identities, Relationships, and Motherhood among Black Women.* Berkeley: University of California Press.

———. 2012. "Intersectionality and the Study of Black, Sexual Minority Women." *Gender and Society* 26: 33–39.

Morgan, Lewis Henry. (1877) 1964. *Ancient Society.* Cambridge, MA: Belknap Press.

Morrell, Virginia. 2008. "Inside Animal Minds: Birds, Apes, Dolphins and a Dog with a World-Class Vocabulary." *National Geographic*, March.

Mukhopadhyay, Carol C., Rosemary Henze, and Yolanda T. Moses. 2007. *How Real Is Race? A Sourcebook on Race, Culture, and Biology*. Lanham, MD: Rowman & Littlefield.

Muller, Martin N. et al., 2009. "Testosterone and Paternal Care in East African Foragers and Pastoralists." *Proceeding of the Royal Society: Biological Sciences* 276: 347–354.

Mullings, Leith. 2005a. "Interrogating Racism: Toward an Anti-Racist Anthropology." *Annual Review of Anthropology* 34: 667–93.

———. 2005b. "Resistance and Resilience: The Sojourner Syndrome and the Social Context of Reproduction in Central Harlem." *Transforming Anthropology* 13(2): 79–91.

Mullings, Leith, and Alaka Wali. 2001. *Stress and Resilience: The Social Context of Reproduction in Central Harlem*. New York: Kluwer Academic/Plenum Publishers.

Myerhoff, Barbara G. 1974. *Peyote Hunt: The Sacred Journey of the Huichol Indians*. Ithaca, NY: Cornell University Press.

———. 1978. *Number Our Days*. New York: Dutton.

Myers, Daniel L. 1988. "*The Body Silent*: A Review." *American Anthropologist* 90:. 760–1.

Myers, Fred R. 1986. *Pintupi Country, Pintupi Self: Sentiment, Place, and Politics among Western Desert Aborigines*. Washington, DC: Smithsonian Institution.

———. 2002. *Painting Culture: The Making of an Aboriginal High Art*. Durham, NC: Duke University Press.

Nader, Laura. 1972. "Up the Anthropologist: Perspectives Gained from Studying Up." In *Reinventing Anthropology*, edited by Dell H. Hymes, 284–311. New York: Pantheon.

Nahman, Michal Rachel. 2002. "Reproducing Jews: A Cultural Account of Assisted Conception in Israel [Review]." *Canadian Review of Sociology and Anthropology* 39(3): 359–61.

Nakamura, Karen. 2006. *Deaf in Japan: Signing and Politics of Identity*. Ithaca, NY: Cornell University Press.

Nanda, Serena. 1998. *Neither Man nor Woman: The Hijras of India* (2nd ed.). Florence, KY: Wadsworth.

———. 2000. "Hijra and Sadhim: Neither Man nor Woman in India." In *Gender Diversity: Cross-Cultural Variations*. Prospect Heights, IL: Waveland Press.

Nash, June C., ed. 2005. *Social Movements: An Anthropological Reader*. Malden, MA: Blackwell.

National Aeronautics and Space Administration. 2015. "The Consequences of Climate Change." http://climate.nasa.gov /effects/.

Neely, Daniel Tanehill. 2005. "Rara! Vodou, Power, and Performance in Haiti and Its Diaspora [Review]." *Ethnomusicology* 49(1): 126–28.

Nelson, Diane M. 1999. *A Finger in the Wound: Body Politics in Quincentennial Guatemala*. Berkeley: University of California Press.

Nettl, Bruno. 2005. *The Study of Ethnomusicology: Thirty-One Issues and Concepts*. Urbana: University of Illinois Press.

Neubeck, Kenneth J., and Noel A. Cazenave. 2001. *Welfare Racism: Playing the Race Card against America's Poor*. New York: Routledge.

Newman, Andrew. 2015. *Landscape of Discontent: Urban Sustainability in Immigrant Paris*. Minneapolis: University of Minnesota Press.

Newman, Katherine S. (1988) 1999. *Falling from Grace: Downward Mobility in the Age of Affluence*. Berkeley: University of California Press.

———. 1993. *Declining Fortunes: The Withering of the American Dream*. New York: Basic Books.

———. 1999. *No Shame in My Game: The Working Poor in the Inner City*. New York: Vintage.

Nissenbaum, Stephen. 1996. *The Battle for Christmas*. New York: Knopf.

Nordstrom, Carolyn. 1997. *A Different Kind of War Story*. Philadelphia: University of Pennsylvania Press.

———. 2004. *Shadows of War: Violence, Power, and International Profiteering in the Twenty-First Century*. Berkeley: University of California Press.

North, James. 2011. "The Roots of the Côte d'Ivoire Crisis: How the Demand for Chocolate—Yes, Chocolate!—Helped Fuel the Country's Civil War." *The Nation*, April 25, 2011.

Norton, M. I., and D. Ariely. 2011. "Building a Better America— One Wealth Quintile at a Time." *Perspectives on Psychological Science* 6(1): 9–12.

Nugent, David, and Joan Vincent, eds. 2004. *A Companion to the Anthropology of Politics*. Malden, MA: Blackwell.

Number Our Days. 1976. Directed by Lynne Littman. Community Television of Southern California.

Ogasawara, Yuko. 1995. "Review of *Nightwork: Sexuality, Pleasure, and Corporate Masculinity in a Tokyo Hostess Club*." *American Journal of Sociology* 100(4): 1071–73.

Ogden, Cynthia L., Cheryl D. Fryar, Margaret D. Carroll, and Katherine M. Flegal. 2004. "Mean Body Weight, Height, and Body Mass Index, United States 1960–2002." *Advance Data from Vital and Health Statistics* 347(October 27).

Omi, Michael, and Howard Winant. 1994. *Racial Formation in the United States from the 1960s to the 1990s* (2nd ed.). New York: Routledge.

Dennis O'Neil, "Kin Naming Systems: Part 1, The Nature of Kinship." http://anthro.palomar.edu/kinship/kinship_5.htm.

Ong, Aihwa. 1987. *Spirits of Resistance and Capitalist Discipline*. Albany: State University of New York Press.

Ong, Aihwa, and Donald M. Nonini. 1997. *Ungrounded Empires: The Cultural Politics of Modern Chinese Transnationalism*. New York: Routledge.

Ore, Tracy. 2010. *The Social Construction of Difference and Inequality: Race, Class, Gender, and Sexuality*. New York: McGraw-Hill.

Ortner, Sherri. 1974. "Is Female to Male as Nature Is to Culture?" In *Woman, Culture and Society*, edited by Michelle Z. Rosaldo and Louise Lamphere. Stanford, CA: Stanford University Press.

Pacini-Hernandez, Deborah. 1995. *Bachata: A Social History of a Dominican Popular Music*. Philadelphia: Temple University Press.

Palfrey, John, and Urs Gasser. 2008. *Born Digital: Understanding the First Generation of Digital Natives*. New York: Basic Books.

Palsson, Gisli. 2013. "Ensembles of Biosocial Relations." In *Biosocial Becomings: Integrating Social and Biological Anthropology*, edited by Tim Ingold and Gisli Palsson, 23–41. New York: Cambridge University Press.

Parker, Richard. 1999. "The Meanings of Macho [Review]." *American Ethnologist* 26(2): 497–98.

Parsons, Talcott. 1964. *Theory of Social and Economic Organization*. New York: Simon & Schuster.

Pascoe, C. J. 2007. *Dude, You're a Fag: Masculinity and Sexuality in High School*. Berkeley: University of California Press.

Patel, Reena. 2010. *Working the Night Shift: Women in India's Call Center Industry*. Stanford, CA: Stanford University Press.

Patterson, Francine. 1978. "Conversations with a Gorilla." *National Geographic*, October, 438–65.

Payer, Lynn. 1996. *Medicine and Culture: Varieties of Treatment in the United States, England, West Germany, and France*. New York: Henry Holt.

PayScale. 2015. www.payscale.com.

Peletz, Michael G. 1999. "The Heat of the Hearth [Review]." *American Ethnologist* 26(1): 251–52.

Pérez-Alemán, Paola. 1994. "Life Is Hard [Review]." *American Journal of Sociology* 99(5): 1393–95.

Perkins, Morgan, and Howard Morphy, eds. 2006. *The Anthropology of Art: A Reader*. Malden, MA: Blackwell.

Petersen, Glenn. 2009. *Traditional Micronesian Societies: Adaptation, Integration, and Political Organization*. Honolulu: University of Hawaii Press.

———. 2015. "American Anthropology's 'Thailand Controversy': An Object Lesson in Professional Responsibility." *SOJOURN: Journal of Social Issues in Southeast Asia* 30(2): 528–49.

Peterson, Kristin. 2015. *Speculative Markets: Drug Circuits and Derivative Life in Nigeria*. Durham, NC: Duke University Press.

Pew Forum on Religion & Public Life. 2015. "America's Changing Religious Landscape." www.pewforum.org/2015/05/12/americas-changing-religious-landscape.

———. 2013. "Second Generation Americans: A Portrait of the Adult Children of Immigrants." www.pewsocialtrends.org/2013/02/07/second-generation-americans/

Phillips, Sarah. 2011. *Disability and Mobile Citizenship in Postsocialist Ukraine*. Bloomington: Indiana University Press.

Pierce, Ellie. 2008. "Driven by Faith or Customer Service? Muslim Taxi Drivers at the MSP Airport." The Pluralism Project at Harvard University. www.pluralism.org/casestudy/.

Pinker, Steven. 2002. *The Blank Slate: The Modern Denial of Human Nature*. New York: Viking.

Polanco, Mieka Brand. 2014. *Historically Black: Imagining Community in a Black Historic District.* New York: New York University Press.

Polanyi, Karl. (1944) 2001. *The Great Transformation.* Boston: Beacon.

Pordié, Laurent. 2008. *Tibetan Medicine in the Contemporary World: Global Politics of Medical Knowledge and Practice.* London: Routledge.

Portes, Alejandro, Patricia Fernández-Kelly, and William Haller. 2009. "The Adaptation of the Immigrant Second Generation in America: Theoretical Overview and Recent Evidence." *Journal of Ethnic and Migration Studies* 35(7): 1077–1104.

Portes, Alejandro, and Rubén G. Rumbaut. 2001. *Legacies: The Story of the Immigrant Second Generation*. Berkeley: University of California Press.

———. 2006. *Immigrant America: A Portrait*. Berkeley: University of California Press.

Powell, Adam, Stephen Shennan, and Mark G. Thomas. 2009. "Late Pleistocene Demography and the Appearance of Modern Human Behavior." *Science* 324: 1298–1301.

Prashad, Vijay. 2001. *Cataracts of Silence: Race on the Edge of Indian Thought*. Geneva, Switzerland: United Nations Research Institute for Social Development.

Price, David. 2004. *Threatening Anthropology*. Durham, NC: Duke University Press.

———. 2011. *Weaponizing Anthropology: Social Science in Service of the Militarized State*. Oakland, CA: AK Distribution.

Quinn, Naomi. 1977. "Anthropological Studies on Women's Status." *Annual Review of Anthropology* 6: 181–222.

Radcliffe-Brown, A. R. 1950. "Introduction," In *African Systems of Kinship and Marriage*, edited by A. R. Radcliffe-Brown and Daryll Forde. London: Oxford University Press.

Rajakumar, Kumaravel, and Stephen B. Thomas. 2005. "Reemerging Nutritional Rickets." *Archives of Pediatrics & Adolescent Medicine* 159(4): 335–41.

Rapp, Rayna and Faye Ginsburg. 2001. "Enabling Disability: Rewriting Kinship, Reimagining Citizenship." *Public Culture* 13(3): 533–56.

Rathje, William, and Cullen Murphy. 2001. *Rubbish!: The Archaeology of Garbage*. Tucson: University of Arizona Press.

Raymond, Janice G. 1993. *Women as Wombs: Reproductive Technologies and the Battle over Women's Freedom*. San Francisco: Harper San Francisco.

Rebhun, L.A. 1999. *The Heart Is Unknown Country: Love in the Changing Econmy of Northeast Brazil*. Stanford, CA: Stanford University Press.

Redfield, Robert. 1941. *The Folk Culture of the Yucatan*. Chicago: University of Chicago Press.

Redmon, David, 2014. *Beads, Bodies and Trash: Public Sex, Global Labor and the Disposability of Mardi Gras*. New York: Routledge Press.

Reno, Joshua O. 2016. *Waste Away: Working and Living with a North American Landfill*. Berkeley: University of California Press.

Richards, Audrey. 1956. *Chisungu: A Girl's Initiation Ceremony among the Bemba of Northern Rhodesia*. London: Faber.

Richards, Paul. 1999. "A Different Kind of War Story [Review]." *American Anthropologist* 101(1): 214–15.

Richman, Karen. 2001. "High Tech and High Heels in the Global Economy [Review]." *American Ethnologist* 28(4): 954–55.

Rickford, John R., and Russell J. Rickford. 2000. *Spoken Soul: The Story of Black English*. New York: Wiley.

Robbins, Richard H. 2013. *Global Problems and the Culture of Capitalism* (6th ed.). Boston: Pearson.

Roberts, Elizabeth F. S., and Nancy Scheper-Hughes. 2011. "Introduction: Medical Migrations." *Body and Society* 17(2–3): 1–30.

Rodseth, L., R. W. Wrangham, A. M. Harrigan, and B. Smuts. 1991. "The Human Community as a Primate Society." *Current Anthropology* 32: 221–54.

Roediger, David. 1992. *The Wages of Whiteness: Race and the Making of the American Working Class*. New York: Verso.

Root, Robin. 2006. "Mixing as an Ethnoetiology of HIV/AIDS in Malaysia's Multinational Factories." *Medical Anthropology Quarterly* 20(3): 321–44.

———. 2009. "Religious Participation and HIV-Disclosure Rationales among People Living with HIV/AIDS in Rural Swaziland." *African Journal of AIDS Research* 8(3): 295–309.

Rosaldo, Michelle Z. 1974. "Women, Culture and Society: A Theoretical Overview." In *Woman, Culture and Society*, edited by Michelle Z. Rosaldo and Louise Lamphere. Stanford, CA: Stanford University Press.

———. 1980. "The Use and Abuse of Anthropology: Reflections on Feminism and Cross-Cultural Understanding." *Signs: Journal of Women in Culture and Society* 5(3): 389–417.

Roscoe, Will. 1991. *The Zuni Man-Woman*. Albuquerque: University of New Mexico Press.

Roseberry, William. 1997. "Review Essay: On Historical Consciousness." *Current Anthropology*, 38(5): 926–32.

Rosenhouse, Jason. 2012. *Among the Creationists*. New York: Oxford University Press.

Roth-Gordon, Jennifer. 2016. *Race and the Brazilian Body: Blackness, Whiteness and Everyday Life in Rio de Janeiro*. New York: Macmillan.

Roth, Joshua Hotaka. 2002. *Brokered Homeland: Japanese Brazilian Migrants in Japan*. Ithaca, NY: Cornell University Press.

Rouse, Roger. 1994. "Life Is Hard [Review]." *Contemporary Sociology* 23(1): 57–9.

Rubin, Gayle. 1975. "The Traffic in Women: Notes on the 'Political Economy' of Sex." In *Toward an Anthropology of Women*, edited by Rayna Reiter. New York: Monthly Review Press.

Ruby, Jay, and Marcus Banks. 2011. *Made to Be Seen: Historical Perspectives on Visual Anthropology*. Chicago: University of Chicago Press.

Rumbaut, Ruben G., and Alejandro Portes, eds. 2001. *Ethnicities: Children of Immigrants in America*. Berkeley: University of California Press.

Sachs, Jeffrey. 2005. *The End of Poverty: Economic Possibilities for Our Time*. New York: Penguin.

Sacks, Karen Brodkin. 1989. "Toward a Unified Theory of Class, Race, and Gender." *American Ethnologist* 16(3): 534–50.

Sahlins, Marshall D. 1971. *Social Stratification in Polynesia*. Seattle: University of Washington Press.

———. (1974) 2004. *Stone Age Economics*. New York: Routledge.

Saillant, Francine, and Serge Genest, eds. 2007. *Medical Anthropology: Regional Perspectives and Shared Concerns*. Malden, MA: Blackwell.

Sanday, Peggy. 1990. *Fraternity Gang Rape: Sex, Brotherhood, and Privilege on Campus*. New York: New York University Press.

Sanders, Stephanie A., and June Machover Reinisch. 2006. "Would You Say You 'Had Sex' If . . . ?" In *The Language and Sexuality Reader*, edited by Deborah Cameron and Don Kulick. New York: Routledge.

Sanjek, Roger. 1994. "The Enduring Inequalities of Race." In *Race*, edited by Steven Gregory and Roger Sanjek, 1–17. New Brunswick, NJ: Rutgers University Press.

Sapir, Edward, and Morris Swadesh. 1946. "Word 2." In *American Indian Grammatical Categories*, 103–12. Reedited for Dell Hymes in *Language in Culture and Society*, 100–7. New York: Harper & Row, 1964.

Sarroub, Loukia K. 2005. *All American Yemeni Girls: Being Muslim in a Public School*. Philadelphia: University of Pennsylvania Press.

Sassen, Saskia. 1998. *Globalization and Its Discontents*. New York: New Press.

———. 2012. *Cities in a World Economy* (4th ed.). New York: SAGE Publications.

Savage, Michael. 2003. *The Savage Nation: Saving America from the Liberal Assault on Our Borders, Language, and Culture*. Washington, DC: WND Books.

Savage, Michael, and Karel Williams, eds. 2008. *Remembering Elites*. Malden, MA: Blackwell.

Scheid, Volker. 2002. *Chinese Medicine in Contemporary China: Plurality and Synthesis*. Durham, NC: Duke University Press.

Scheld, Suzanne. 2003. "The City in a Shoe: Redefining Urban Africa Through Sebago Footwear Consumption." *City and Society* 15(1): 109–30.

Scheper-Hughes, Nancy. 1989. "Death without Weeping: Has Poverty Ravaged Mother Love in the Shantytowns of Brazil?" *Natural History* 98(10): 8–16.

———. 1992. *Death without Weeping: The Violence of Everyday Life in Brazil*. Berkeley: University of California Press.

———. 1995. "The Primacy of the Ethical: Propositions for a Militant Anthropology." *Current Anthropology* 36(3): 409–20.

———. 2002. "Min(d)ing the Body: On the Trail of Organ-Stealing Rumors." In *Exotic No More: Anthropology on the Front Lines*, edited by Jeremy MacClancy, 33–63. Chicago: University of Chicago Press.

———. 2013. "No More Angel Babies on the Alto do Cruzeiro: A Dispatch from Brazil's Revolution in Child Survival." *Natural History*. www.naturalhistorymag.com/features/282558/no-more-angel-babies-on-the-alto-do-cruzeiro.

Scheper-Hughes, Nancy, and Margaret M. Lock. 1987. "The Mindful Body: A Prolegomenon to Future Work in Medical Anthropology." *Medical Anthropology Quarterly* 1(1): 6–41.

Scheper-Hughes, Nancy, and Philippe Bourgois. 2004. *Violence in War and Peace: An Anthology*. New York: Wiley.

Schneider, Arnd, and Christopher Wright. 2006. *Contemporary Art and Anthropology*. Oxford, UK: Berg.

Schneider, David M. 1980. *American Kinship: A Cultural Account* (2nd ed.). Chicago: University of Chicago Press.

Schneider, Jane. 1977. "Was There a Pre-Capitalist World System?" *Peasant Studies* 6(1): 20–29.

Schoendorf, Kenneth C., Carol J. R. Hogue, and Joel C. Kleinman. 1992. "Mortality among Infants of Blacks as Compared to White College-Educated Parents." *New England Journal of Medicine* 326(23): 1522–26.

Schulz, Amy J., and Leith Mullings. 2006. *Gender, Race, Class, and Health: Intersectional Approaches*. San Francisco: Jossey-Bass.

Scott, A. O. 2013. "Or Would You Rather Be a Fish?" *New York Times,* February 28.

Scott, Eugenie C. 2009. *Evolution vs. Creationism: An Introduction* (2nd ed.). Berkeley: University of California Press.

Scott, James C. 1985. *Weapons of the Weak: Everyday Forms of Peasant Resistance*. New Haven, CT: Yale University Press.

Sebeok, Thomas A., and Donna J. Umiker-Sebeok, eds. 1980. *Speaking of Apes: A Critical Anthology of Two-Way Communication with Man*. New York: Plenum Press.

Service, Elman R. 1962. *Primitive Social Organization; An Evolutionary Perspective*. New York: Random House.

———. 1966. *The Hunters*. Englewood Cliffs, NJ: Prentice Hall.

Severson, Kim. 2011. "Race-Based Names Dot the Landscape." *New York Times,* October 6.

Shakespeare, Tom. 1998. *The Disability Reader: Social Science Perspectives*. London: Cassell.

Shanklin, Eugenia. 1998. "The Profession of the Color Blind: Sociocultural Anthropology and Racism in the 21st Century." *American Anthropologist* 100(3): 669–79.

Shannon, Jonathan Holt. 2006. *Among the Jasmine Trees: Music and Modernity in Contemporary Syria*. Middletown, CT: Wesleyan University Press.

Shapiro, Harry L. 1974. *Peking Man: The Discovery, Disappearance, and Mystery of a Priceless Scientific Treasure*. New York: Simon & Schuster.

Sharma, Aradhana, and Akhil Gupta, eds. 2006. *The Anthropology of the State: A Reader*. Malden, MA: Blackwell.

Shaw, Alison. 1998. "Contesting Culture: Discourses of Identity in Multi-Ethnic London [Review]." *Journal of the Royal Anthropological Institute* 4(1): 174–75.

Shaw, Stephanie. 1996. *What a Woman Ought to Be and to Do: Black Professional Women Workers during the Jim Crow Era*. Chicago: University of Chicago Press.

Shiva, Vandana. 2006. "Building Water Democracy: People's Victory against Coca-Cola in Plachimada." In *Beyond Borders: Thinking Critically about Global Issues*, edited by Paula S. Rothenberg, 580–83. New York: Worth Publishers.

Shweder, Richard A. 2003. "The Moral Challenge in Cultural Migration." In *American Arrivals: Anthropology Engages the New Immigration*, edited by Nancy Foner. Santa Fe, NM: School of American Research.

Siebel, Catherine. 2000. "White Weddings [Review]." *Teaching Sociology* 28(2): 175–76.

Simmons, David. 2012. *Modernizing Medicine in Zimbabwe: HIV/AIDS and Traditional Healers*. Nashville: Vanderbilt University Press.

Simmons, Kimberly Eison. 2011, *Reconstructing Racial Identity and the African Past in the Dominican Republic*. Gainesville: University of Florida Press.

Singer, Merrill, and Hans A. Baer. 2007. *Introducing Medical Anthropology: A Discipline in Action*. Lanham, MD: AltaMira.

Small, Cathy. 1997. *Voyages: From Tongan Villages to American Suburbs*. Ithaca, NY: Cornell University Press.

Smedley, Audrey. 1993. *Race in North America: Origins and Evolution of a Worldview*. Boulder, CO: Westview Press.

Smith, Adam. 1776. *Wealth of Nations*. Reprint, New York: Simon & Brown, 2010.

Smith, Christen. 2016. *Afro-Paradise: Blackness, Violence and Performance in Brazil*. Champaign: University of Illinois Press.

Smith, Neil. 2006. "There's No Such Thing as a Natural Disaster." In *Understanding Katrina: Perspectives from the Social Sciences*. Social Science Research Council. http://understandingkatrina.ssrc.org/Smith.

Smith, Robert C. 2006. *Mexican New York: Transnational Lives of New Immigrants*. Berkeley: University of California Press.

Smith, Roberta. 2014. "In a Mattress, a Lever for Art and Political Protest." *New York Times,* September 21.

Snow, Dean R. 1994. *The Iroquois*. Cambridge, MA: Blackwell.

Solinger, Dorothy J. 1999. *Contesting Citizenship in Urban China: Peasant Migrants, the State, and the Logic of the Market*. Berkeley: University of California Press.

Speed, Shannon. 2006. "At the Crossroads of Human Rights and Anthropology: Toward a Critically Engaged Activist Research." *American Anthropologist* 108(1): 66–76.

———. 2007. *Rights in Rebellion: Indigenous Struggle and Human Rights in Chiapas*. Stanford, CA: Stanford University Press.

Spence, Jonathan D. 2013. *The Search for Modern China* (3rd ed.). New York: Norton.

Spencer, Robert F. 1987. "Shamans, Housewives, and Other Restless Spirits: Women in Korean Ritual Life [Review]." *Man*, new ser., 22(3): 583–84.

Stack, Carol B. 1974. *All Our Kin: Strategies for Survival in a Black Community*. New York: Harper & Row.

Stange, Mary Zeiss. 1997. *Woman the Hunter*. Boston: Beacon Press.

Stark, Rodney, and William Sims Bainbridge. 1985. *The Future of Religion: Secularization, Revival, and Cult Formation*. Berkeley: University of California Press.

Starosielski, Nicole. 2015. *The Undersea Network*. Durham: Duke University Press.

Steele, D. G., and J. F. Powell. 1993. "Paleobiology of the First Americans." *Evolutionary Anthropology* 2: 138–46.

Steiner, Christopher Burghard. 1994. *African Art in Transit*. Cambridge, UK: Cambridge University Press.

———. 1995. "The Art of the Trade: On the Creation of Authenticity in the African Art Market." In *The Traffic in Culture*, edited by George E. Marcus and Fred R. Myers, 151–66. Berkeley: University of California Press.

Stephen, Lynn. 1995. "Women's Rights Are Human Rights: The Merging of Feminine and Feminist Interests among El Salvador's Mothers of the Disappeared (CO-MADRES)." *American Ethnologist* 22(4): 807–27.

Stevens, Carolyn S. 2005. "Tsukiji: The Fish Market at the Center of the World [Review]." *Journal of Asian Studies*, 64(4): 1022–23.

Steward, Julian H. 1956. *The People of Puerto Rico: A Study in Social Anthropology*. Urbana: University of Illinois Press.

Stiglitz, Joseph E. 2008. "Reversal of Fortune." *Vanity Fair*, November, 134–38.

———. 2009. "Capitalist Fools." *Vanity Fair*. January, 48–51.

———. 2010. *Freefall: America, Free Markets, and the Sinking of the World Economy*. New York: Norton.

———. 2012. *The Price of Inequality: How Today's Divided Society Endangers Our Future*. New York: Norton.

Stocking, George W. Jr. 1968. *Race, Culture and Evolution: Essays in the History of Anthropology*. Chicago: University of Chicago Press.

———. 1983. *Observers Observed: Essays on Ethnographic Fieldwork*. Madison: University of Wisconsin Press.

———, ed. 1989. *A Franz Boas Reader: The Shaping of American Anthropology, 1883–1911*. Chicago: University of Chicago Press.

Stoler, Ann Laura. 2010. *Carnal Knowledge and Imperial Power: Race and the Intimate in Colonial Rule* (rev. ed.). Berkeley: University of California Press.

Stoller, Paul. 2002. *Money Has No Smell: The Africanization of New York City*. Chicago: University of Chicago Press.

———. 2003. "Circuits of African Art/Paths of Wood: Exploring an Anthropological Trail." *Anthropological Quarterly* 76(2): 207–34.

Stoller, Paul, and Cheryl Olkes. 1987. *In Sorcery's Shadow: A Memoir of Apprenticeship among the Songhay of Niger*. Chicago: University of Chicago Press.

Stone, Amy L. 2007. "Sexuality and Social Change: Sexual Relations in a Capitalist System." *American Anthropologist* 109(4): 753–55.

Stone, Linda. 2009. *Kinship and Gender: An Introduction* (4th ed.). Boulder, CO: Westview Press.

Straus, Murray, and Richard Gelles. 1990. *Physical Violence in American Families: Risk Factors and Adaptations to Violence in 8,145 Families*. Piscataway, NJ: Transaction Publishers.

Stringer, Chris, and Robin McKie. 1998. *African Exodus: The Origins of Modern Humanity*. New York: Henry Holt.

Suarez-Orosco, Marcelo. 2003. "Right Moves? Immigration, Globalization, Utopia, and Dystopia." In *American Arrivals: Anthropology Engages the New Immigration*, edited by Nancy Foner, 45–74. Santa Fe, NM: School of American Research.

Sue, Derald Wing. 2010. *Microaggressions in Everyday Life: Race, Gender, and Sexual Orientation*. Hoboken, NJ: Wiley.

Sullivan, Daniel Monroe. 2006. "Behind the Gates: Life, Security, and the Pursuit of Happiness in Fortress America [Review]." *Contemporary Sociology* 35(2): 163–64.

Susser, Ida. (1982) 2012. *Norman Street: Poverty and Politics in an Urban Neighborhood*. New York: Oxford University Press.

Swann, Joan. 2007. "Talk Control: An Illustration from the Classroom of Problems in Analysing Male Dominance of Conversation." In *Language and Gender: A Reader*, edited by Jennifer Coates, 185–96. London: Blackwell.

Sweis, Rania. 2012. "Saving Egypt's Village Girls: Humanity, Rights and Gendered Vulnerability in a Global Youth Initiative." *Journal of Middle East Women's Studies* 8(2): 26–50.

Swyngedouw, Erik. 2009. The Political Economy and Political Ecology of the Hydro-Social Cycle. *Journal of Contemporary Water Research and Education* 142: 56–60.

Tannen, Deborah. 2001. *You Just Don't Understand: Women and Men in Conversation* (2nd ed.). New York: Ballantine.

Tattersall, Ian. 2012. *Masters of the Planet: The Search for Our Human Origins*. New York: Palgrave Macmillan.

Tax Policy Center. 2015. "Tax Facts." www.taxpolicycenter.org /taxfacts/displayafact.cfm?Docid=47.

Taylor, Robert Joseph. 2000. "All Our Kin: Strategies for Survival in a Black Community [Review]." *Journal of Marriage and Family* 62(3): 865–67.

Terrace, Herbert S., L. A. Petitto, R. J. Sanders, and T. G. Bever. 1979. "Can an Ape Create a Sentence?" *Science* 206(4421): 891–902.

Tett, Gillian. 2010. *Fool's Gold: The Inside Story of J. P. Morgan and How Wall Street Greed Corrupted Its Bold Dream and Created a Financial Catastrophe*. New York: Free Press.

Thayer, Zeneta M., and Amy L. Non. 2015. "Anthropology Meets Epigenetics: Current and Future Directions." *American Anthropologist* 117(4): 722–35.

Thornton, Sarah. 2009. *Seven Days in the Art World*. New York: Norton.

Tierney, Patrick. 2000. *Darkness in El Dorado: How Scientists and Journalists Devastated the Amazon*. New York: Norton.

Tilly, Charles. "Reflections on the History of European State-Making." In *The Formation of National States in Western Europe*, edited by Charles Tilly. Princeton, NJ: Princeton University Press.

Tooby, Joh, and Leda Cosmides. 1992. "The Psychological Foundations of Culture." In J. Barkow, L. Cosmides, and J. Tooby, eds., *The Adapted Mind: Evolutionary Psychology and the Generation of Culture*, 19–136. New York: Oxford University Press.

Trinkaus, Erik, and Pat Shipman. 1994. *The Neandertals: Of Skeletons, Scientists, and Scandal*. New York: Vintage.

Trouillot, Michel-Rolph. 1994. "Culture, Color, and Politics in Haiti." In *Race*, edited by Steven Gregory and Roger Sanjek, 146–74. New Brunswick, NJ: Rutgers University Press.

———. 2003. *Global Transformations: Anthropology and the Modern World*. New York: Palgrave Macmillan.

Tsing, Anna Lowenhaupt. 2005. *Friction: An Ethnography of Global Connection*. Princeton, NJ: Princeton University Press.

Turnbull, Colin M. (1961) 2010. *The Forest People*. New York: Simon & Schuster.

Turner, Victor. 1957. *Schism and Continuity in an African Society: A Study of Ndembu Village Life*. Manchester, UK: Manchester University Press.

———. 1969. *The Ritual Process: Structure and Anti-Structure*. Chicago: Aldine.

Tylor, Edward. 1920 [1871]. *Primitive Culture*. New York: J. P. Putnam's Sons.

United Nations. 2012. "Millennium Development Goals: End Poverty 2015." www.un.org/millenniumgoals/poverty.shtml.

———. 2015. "The Millennium Development Goals Report 2015." www.un.org/millenniumgoals/2015_MDG_Report/pdf /MDG%202015%20rev%20(July%201).pdf.

United Nations Department of Economic and Social Affairs, Population Division. 2013. "Population Facts." http://esa .un.org/unmigration/documents/The_number_of _international_migrants.pdf.

2015a. *International Migrant Stock 2015*. www.un.org/en /development/desa/population/migration/data/estimates2 /estimates15.shtml.

———. 2015b. "Sustainable Development Goals: 17 Goals to Transform our World." www.un.org/sustainabledevelopment /development-agenda/.

———. 2015c. "World Population Prospects: The 2015 Revision, Key Findings and Advance Tables." Working Paper No. ESA/P/WP.241.

United Nations Development Programme. 2013. "The Millennium Development Goals: Eight Goals for 2015." www.undp.org/mdg/.

United Nations High Commissioner on Refugees. 2015. "UNHCR Global Trends: Forced Displacement in 2014." http://unhcr .org/556725e69.html.

United Nations Human Rights Council. 2015. "Report on the Detailed Findings of the Commission of Inquiry on Human Rights in Eritrea." www.ohchr.org/Documents/HRBodies /HRCouncil/CoIEritrea/A_HRC_29_CRP-1.pdf.

Urciuoli, Bonnie. 1996. *Exposing Prejudice: Puerto Rican Experiences of Language, Race, and Class*. Boulder, CO: Westview Press.

Ury, William, ed. 2002. *Must We Fight? From the Battlefield to the Schoolyard—A New Perspective on Violent Conflict and Its Prevention*. San Francisco: Jossey-Bass.

———. 2007. *The Power of a Positive No: How to Say No and Still Get to Yes*. New York: Bantam.

Useem, Elizabeth. 1992. "Middle Schools and Math Groups: Parents' Involvement in Children's Math Placement." *Sociology of Education* 65: 263–79.

U.S. Census Bureau. 2010. "America's Families and Living Arrangements: 2010," Table FG3. www.census.gov/hhes /families/files/cps2010/tabFG4-all.xls.

———. 2011a. "Income, Poverty, and Health Insurance Coverage in the United States: 2011." www.census.gov/prod/2012pubs/p60 -243.pdf.

———. 2011b. "Native North American Languages Spoken at Home in the United States and Puerto Rico: 2006–2010." www.census.gov/prod/2011pubs/acsbr10-10.pdf.

———. 2012. "The Foreign-Born Population in the United States: 2010." www.census.gov/prod/2012pubs/acs-19.pdf.

———. 2013a. "New Orleans (city), Louisiana." http://quickfacts .census.gov/qfd/states/22/2255000.html.

———. 2013b. "People in Poverty by Selected Characteristics: 2012 and 2013." www.census.gov/hhes/www/poverty/data /incpovhlth/2013/table3.pdf.

———. 2014. "Families and Living Arrangements." www.census .gov/hhes/families/data/families.html.

———. 2015. "Income and Poverty in the United States, 2014." www.census.gov/content/dam/Census/library /publications/2015/demo/p60-252.pdf.

U.S. Centers for Disease Control. 2012. "Births: Final Data for 2010." *National Vital Statistics Reports*, August 28. www.cdc.gov /nchs/data/nvsr/nvsr61/nvsr61_01.pdf#table02.

U.S. Department of Health & Human Services. 2012. "Child Welfare Information Gateway." www.childwelfare.gov.

U.S. Department of Health & Human Services. 2016. "Annual Update of the HHS Poverty Guidelines." www.federalregister .gov/articles/2016/01/25/2016-01450/annual-update-of-the-hhs -poverty-guidelines.

U.S. Department of Justice. Civil Rights Division. 2015. "Investigation of the Ferguson Police Department." March 4.

www.justice.gov/sites/default/files/opa/press-releases /attachments/2015/03/04/ferguson_police_department_report .pdf.

Van Gennep, Arnold. (1908) 1960. *The Rites of Passage*. Chicago: University of Chicago Press.

Venbrux, Eric, Pamela Sheffield Rosi, and Robert L. Welsch. 2006. *Exploring World Art*. Long Grove, IL: Waveland Press.

Vine, David. 2009. *Island of Shame: The Secret History of the US Military Base on Diego Garcia*. Princeton, NJ: Princeton University Press.

Vine, David. 2015. *Base Nation: How US Military Bases Abroad Harm America and the World*. New York: Metropolitan Books/ Henry Holt.

Vitelli, Romeo. 2013. "Television, Commercials, and Your Child." *Psychology Today*, July 22.

Vogel, Susan Mullin. 1991. *Africa Explores: 20th Century African Art*. New York: Center for African Art.

Volkman, Toby Alice. 2005. *Cultures of Transnational Adoption*. Durham, NC: Duke University Press.

Vora, Neha. 2013 *Impossible Citizens: Dubai's Indian Diaspora*. Durham, NC: Duke University Press.

Wacquant, Loic. 2002. "Scrutinizing the Street: Poverty, Morality, and the Pitfalls of Urban Ethnography." *American Journal of Sociology* 107(6): 1468–1532.

Wade, Lisa. 2015. "Five Reasons Why Pointlessly Gendered Products Are a Problem." https://thesocietypages.org /socimages/2015/12/31/five-reasons-why-pointlessly-gendered -products-are-a-problem/

Wade, Lisa, and Myra Marx Ferree. 2015. *Gender: Ideas, Interactions, Institutions*. New York: Norton.

Wakin, Eric. 1992. *Anthropology Goes to War: Professional Ethics & Counterinsurgency in Thailand*. Madison: University of Wisconsin, Center for Southeast Asian Studies.

Walker, Sheila S. 2002. "Africanity vs. Blackness: Race, Class and Culture in Brazil." *NACLA Report on the Americas* 35(6): 16–20.

Walklate, Sandra. 2005. "Behind the Gates: Life, Security, and the Pursuit of Happiness in Fortress America [Review]." *Urban Studies* 42(10): 1882–83.

Wallace, Anthony F. C. 1957. "Political Organization and Land Tenure among the Northwestern Indians, 1600–1830." *Southwest Journal of Anthropology* 13: 301–21.

Wallerstein, Immanuel Maurice. 1974. *World-Systems Analysis: An Introduction*. Durham, NC: Duke University Press.

Walls, Bryan. 2005. "Rara! Vodou, Power and Performance in Haiti and Its Diaspora [Review]." *Latin American Music Review* 26(2): 356–65.

Wardhaugh, Ronald. 2009. *An Introduction to Sociolinguistics* (6th ed.). London: Blackwell.

Wardlow, Holly. 2006. *Wayward Women: Sexuality and Agency in a New Guinea Society*. Berkeley: University of California Press.

Warriner, Christina, and Cecil M. Lewis Jr. 2015. "Microbiome and Health in Past and Present Human Populations." *American Anthropologist* 117(4): 740–41.

Waterston, Alisse. 2009. *An Anthropology of War: Views from War Zones*. New York: Berghahn.

Watson, James L., ed. 1998. *Golden Arches East: McDonald's in East Asia*. Stanford, CA: Stanford University Press.

Watson, James L., and Melissa L. Caldwell, eds. 2004. *The Cultural Politics of Food and Eating: A Reader*. New York: Wiley.

Weber, Eugen. 1976. *Peasants into Frenchmen: The Modernization of Rural France, 1870–1914*. Stanford, CA: Stanford University Press.

Weber, Max. 1905. *The Protestant Ethic and the Spirit of Capitalism*. London: Routledge, 2002.

———. 1919. *Politics as a Vocation*. Philadelphia: Fortress, 1965.

———. (1920) 1946. "Class, Status and Party." In *From Max Weber: Essays in Sociology*, edited and translated by Hans Gerth and C. Wright Mills. New York: Free Press.

———. 1920. *Sociology of Religion*. Boston: Beacon Press, 1993.

Weiner, Annette. 1976. *Women of Value, Men of Renown: New Perspectives in Trobriand Exchange*. Austin: University of Texas Press.

———. 1988. *The Trobrianders of Papua New Guinea*. New York: Holt, Rinehart and Winston.

Weiss, Margot. 2011. "The Epistemology of Ethnography: Method in Queen Anthropology." *GLQ: A Journal of Lesbian and Gay Studies* 17(4): 649–664.

———. 2006. *The Politics of Passion: Women's Sexual Culture in Afro-Surinamese Diaspora*. New York: Columbia University Press.

Welch, Cliff. 2001. "Peasants against Globalization: Rural Social Movement in Costa Rica [Review]." *Latin American Politics and Society* 43(4): 166–68.

Werner, Paul. 2006. *Museum Inc.: Inside the Global Art World*. Chicago: Prickly Paradigm Press.

———. 2008. *An Anthropological Introduction to YouTube*. www .youtube.com/watch?v=TPAO-lZ4_hU&feature=channel.

West, Candace. 1998. "When the Doctor Is a 'Lady': Power, Status and Gender in Physician-Patient Encounters." In *Language and Gender: A Reader*, edited by Jennifer Coates, 396–412. London: Blackwell.

Westmoreland, Mark R., and Brent Luvaas. 2015. "Introduction: *Leviathan* and the Entangled Lives of Species." *Visual Anthropology Review* 31(1), 1–3.

Weston, Kath. 1991. *Families We Choose: Lesbians, Gays, Kinship*. New York: Columbia University Press.

———. 1993. "Lesbian/Gay Studies in the House of Anthropology." *Annual Review of Anthropology* 22: 339–67.

White, Tim D., et al. 2009. "*Ardipithecus ramidus* and the Paleobiology of Early Hominids." *Science* 326: 64, 75–86.

Whitehouse, Bruce. 2012. *Migrants and Strangers in an African City: Exile, Dignity, Belonging*. Bloomington: Indiana University Press.

Whiteside, Alan, Catarina Andrade, Lisa Arrehag, Solomon Dlamini, Themba Ginindza, and Anokhi Parikh. 2006. *The Socio-Economic Impact of HIV/AIDS in Swaziland*. Mbabane, Swaziland: National Emergency Response Council on HIV/AIDS (NERCHA) and Health Economics & HIV/AIDS Research Division (HEARD).

Wiffogel, Karl. 1957. *Oriental Despotism: A Comparative Study of Total Power*. New Haven, CT: Yale University Press.

Wilkins, Amy C. 2008. "Dude You're a Fag: Masculinity and Sexuality in High School [Review]." *Contemporary Sociology* 37(3): 242–43.

Williams, Brackette F. 1995. "The Public I/Eye: Conducting Fieldwork to Do Homework on Homelessness and Begging in Two U.S. Cities." *Current Anthropology* 36(1): 25–51.

Williams, Brett. 2004. *Debt for Sale: A Social History of the Credit Trap*. Philadelphia: University of Pennsylvania Press.

Williams, Walter. 1992. *The Spirit and the Flesh: Sexual Diversity in American Indian Cultures* (2nd ed.). Boston: Beacon Press.

Wilson, William Julius. 1987. *The Truly Disadvantaged: The Inner City, the Underclass, and Public Policy*. Chicago: University of Chicago Press.

Winegar, Jessica. 2006. *Creative Reckonings: The Politics of Art and Culture in Contemporary Egypt*. Stanford, CA: Stanford University Press.

———. 2008. "The Humanity Game: Art, Islam and the War on Terror." *Anthropological Quarterly* 81(3), 651–81.

Wolcott, Victoria W. 2001. *Remaking Respectability: African American Women in Interwar Detroit*. Chapel Hill: University of North Carolina Press.

Wolf, Eric R. 1966. *Peasants*. Englewood Cliffs, NJ: Prentice-Hall.

———. 1982. *Europe and the People without History*. Berkeley: University of California Press.

———. 1990. "Distinguished Lecture: Facing Power—Old Insights, New Questions." *American Anthropologist* 92: 586–96.

———. 1999. *Envisioning Power: Ideologies of Dominance and Crisis*. Berkeley: University of California Press.

———. 2001. "Ethnicity and Nationhood." In *Pathways of Power: Building an Anthropology of the Modern World*. Berkeley: University of California Press.

Wolf, Eric, and Joseph Jorgensen. 1970. "Anthropology on the Warpath in Thailand." *New York Review of Books*, November 19.

Wolf, Margery. 1992. *A Thrice-Told Tale: Feminism, Postmodernism, and Ethnographic Responsibility*. Stanford, CA: Stanford University Press.

Wolf-Meyer, Matthew J. 2012. *The Slumbering Masses: Sleep, Medicine, and Modern American Life*. Minneapolis: University of Minnesota Press.

World Bank, 2015. "Remittances to Developing Countries Edge Up Slightly in 2015." www.worldbank.org/en/news/press-release/2016/04/13/remittances-to-developing-countries-edge-up-slightly-in-2015.

World Health Organization. 2015a. "Drinking-water: Fact sheet no. 391." www.who.int/mediacentre/factsheets/fs391/en/.

———. 2015b. "Life expectancy." http://who.int/gho/mortality_burden_disease/life_tables/en/

Worldwatch Institute. 2015. *State of the World 2015: Confronting Hidden Threats to Sustainability*. Washington, DC: Island Press/Center for Resource Economics.

Worm, Boris, et al. 2006. "Impacts of Biodiversity Loss on Ocean Ecosystem Systems." *Science* 314(5800): 787–90.

Wray, Matt, and Annalee Newitz, eds. 1996. *White Trash: Class, Race and the Construction of American Identity*. London: Routledge.

Yamanaka, Keiko. 2003. "Brokered Homeland: Japanese Brazilian Migrants in Japan [Review]." *International Migration Review* 37(4): 1319–20.

Yan, Yunxiang. 2003. *Private Life under Socialism: Love, Intimacy, and Family Change in a Chinese Village, 1949–1999*. Stanford, CA: Stanford University Press.

———. 2004. "Of Hamburgers and Social Space: Consuming McDonalds in Beijing." In *The Cultural Politics of Food and Eating: A Reader*, edited by James L. Watson and Melissa L. Caldwell. New York: Wiley.

Yang, Guobin. 2009. *The Power of the Internet in China: Citizen Activism Online*. New York: Columbia University Press.

Yngvesson, Barbara. 2003. "Going 'Home': Adoption, Loss of Bearings, and the Mythology of Roots." *Social Text* 74: 7–27.

Young, Colin. 1995. "Observational Cinema." In *Principles of Visual Anthropology*. edited by Paul Hockings, 99–113. Berlin: Mouton de Gruyter.

Younge, Gary. 2010. "What Soccer Says about Us." *The Nation*, July 19.

Zhan, Mei. 2009. *Other-Worldly: Making Chinese Medicine through Transnational Frames*. Durham, NC: Duke University Press.

Zhang, Li. 2001. *Strangers in the City: Reconfigurations of Space, Power, and Social Networks within China's Floating Population*. Stanford, CA: Stanford University Press.

Zhou, Min, and Carl L. Bankston. 1998. *Growing up American: How Vietnamese Children Adapt to Life in the United States*. New York: Russell Sage Foundation.

Zilberg, Jonathan. 1996. "African Art in Transit [Review]." *International Journal of African Historical Studies* 29(1): 147–49.

Zillow. 2014. "Negative Equity Down by Almost Half Since 2012 Peak, But There's Still a Ways to Go." December 16. www.zillow.com/research/negative-equity-2014-q3-8532/.

Zimmer, Carl. 2010. "How Microbes Defend and Define Us." *New York Times*, July 13.

———. 2011. "Bacterial Ecosystems Divide People into 3 Groups, Scientists Say." *New York Times*, April 20.

Zinn, Howard. 2005. *A People's History of the United States: 1492–Present* (rev. ed.). New York: Harper Perennial.

Zirin, David, and Sherry Wolf. 2010. "Let Caster Run!" *The Nation*, April 2.

Credits

Denis Farrell/AP **152 center** Philippe Wojazer/AFP/Getty Images **152 right** © David L. Brill **153 left** John Reader/Science Source **153 right** Emmanuel Laurent/Science Source **154** Tom Stockill/Camera Press/Redux **159** Staff photo Kris Snibbe/Harvard News Office **160** Volker Steger/Science Source **161** Classic Image/Alamy **163 left** AP/Wide World Photos **163 right** AP Photo **165** Breck P. Kent / Animals Animals/ Earth Scenes/National Geographic Creative **170 left** © Institute of Human Origins/Nanci Kahn **170 right** © David Brill **173** Javier Trueba/MSF/Science Source **174** Science VU/NMK/ Visuals Unlimited, Inc. **177** DEA/A. DAGLI ORTI/De Agostini/ Getty Images **178** Photo by Frank Kierman, Yerkes National Primate Research Center **180** Peter Brown **181** Ulrike Welsch/Science Source **182** Joe Robbins/Getty Images **184 top left** Kennan Ward **184 right** William Wallauer/JGI/www.janegoodall.org **184 bottom left** Tom Mchugh/Getty Images **185 bottom left** Dr. Paco Bertolini **185 top left** Clark S. Larsen **185 right** Photo by Etsuko Nogami, provided by Primate Research Institute, Kyoto University. Matsuzawa, T. Humle, T., and Sugiyama, Y. 2011 "The chimpanzees of Bossou and Nimba," Springer **189 left** Tom Grill/Corbis **189 right** Clark Spencer Larsen

Part Opener 2
192-193 Stuart Freedman/Panos Pictures

Chapter 6
Photographs: 194-195 AP Photo/Jeff Roberson **198 left** Inage Source/SuperStock **198 center** Corbis/SuperStock **198 right** Jon Feingersh Photography / SuperStock **199 left** Jon Feingersh Photography/SuperStock **199 center** Image Source/Alamy **199 right** Jorge Rohan/Alamy **202 left** Scott Portelli/Getty Images **202 right** Brand New Images/Getty Images **203** Wikimedia Commons **204 left** The Granger Collection, New York **204-205** The Granger Collection, New York **205** Reinhard Dirscherl/Alamy **207** Benjamin de Menil, iASO Records **211 left** Goh Seng Chong/Bloomberg/ Getty Images **211 top right** Andrew Watson/Getty Images **211 bottom right** John Brown/Alamy **213 left** The Granger Collection, New York **213 right** Bettman/Getty Images **214 left** United States Census Bureau/Wikimedia Commons **214 top** United States Census Bureau/Wikimedia Commons **214 bottom** United States Census **215 both** United States Census Bureau **217** Everett Collection Inc/Alamy **218** Fotosearch/Getty Images **219** Library of Congress **221-222** Reproduced by permission of SAGE Publications Ltd., London, Los Angeles, New Delhi, Singapore and Washington DC, from Maria Kromidas, "Learning War/Learning Race: Fourth-grade Students in the Aftermath of September 11th in New York City," *Critique of Anthropology*, Vol. 2, No. 1, March 2004, pp. 15-33. Copyright © 2004, SAGE Publications. **225** Carl Iwasaki/Time & Life Pictures/Getty Images **227** Jim West/Alamy **228** Courtesy of JB Kwon **233 left** Brenda Ann Kenneally **233 top right** Brenda Ann Kenneally **233 bottom right** Brenda Ann Kenneally

Chapter 7
Photographs: 236-237 Reuters/Kai Pfaffenbach **239** AP Photo/ Desmond Scholtz **241 left** The Granger Collection, New York **241 right** AP Photo/Jeff Christensen **242** David Cupp/The Denver Post via Getty Images **243** Richard Levine/Alamy Stock Photo **247** A. Demotes/Photononstop/Alamy **249** AP Photo/Amel Emric **250 left** Yankee Photography/Alamy **250 right** Mark Peterson/Redux **251 all** Shiho Fukada/The New York Times/ Redux **255** Keystone-France/Gamma-Keystone via Getty Images **259** Courtesy of David Lan **262** Courtesy Haley Duschinski **264** Rodrigo Arangua/AFP/Getty Images **265** Rodrigo Arangua/AFP/ Getty Images **266 top** Paul Popper/Popperfoto/Getty Images **266 bottom** mbbirdy/Getty Images **267 top** Gabe Rogel/Aurora Photos **267 bottom** Brent Stirton / Getty Images

Chapter 8
Photographs: 270-271 U.S. Army photo by Staff Sgt. Scott Brooks **274** Adek Berry/AFP/Getty Images **276** Tanya Constantine/Blend Images/Alamy **277** Toni L. Sandys/The Washington Post/Getty Images **279** Chris Ryan/OJO Images Limited/Alamy **280 top** Cj Gunther/Bloomberg via Getty Images **280 bottom left** Kat Stoeffel/NewYork Magazine **280 bottom right** Lenscap/Alamy Stock Photo **281 top** Patti McConville/Alamy Stock Photo **281 bottom** NY Dept. of Consumer Affairs **282** The Advertising Archives **281** Melanie Stetson Freeman/The Christian Science Monitor via Getty Images **283** Melanie Stetson Freeman/The Christian Science Monitor via Getty Images **285** AP Photo/Anja Niedringhaus **288** Louise Batalla Duran/Alamy **289 left** Anne Medley Missoula Independent **289 right** Kevin Winter/Getty Images for Nederlander **292** Don Pollard, CUNY Graduate Center **294 left** Images & Stories/ Alamy **294 right** Caroline Penn/Alamy **296** Clouds Hill Imaging Ltd./Science Source **298** Hassan Ammar/AFP/Getty Images **300** BOYS DON'T CRY, 1999, TM and ©20th Century Fox Film Corp. All Rights Reserved. **303** COMADRES@Comadres.org **305 top left** John Costello/KRT/Newscom **305 top right** Darcy Padilla **305 bottom right** AP Photo/Stacey Benedict **305 bottom left** David R. Frazier Photolibrary, Inc./Alamy

Chapter 9
Photographs: 310-311 Andrew Burton/Getty Images **313** Richard Levine/Alamy **315 left** Tony Camacho/Science Source **315 right** F. Stuart Westmoreland/Science Source **317 top left** Roberto Herrett / Alamy **317 right** Andrew Harrer/Bloomberg via Getty Images **317 bottom left** Bob Daemmrich/The Image Works **319** Frans Lemmens/Alamy **324** Bettmann/Getty Images **326** AP Photo/Vadim Ghirda **327** Marco Gualazzini/LUZ/Redux **328 left** The Advertising Archives **328 right** mevans/iStock **329 left** Peter Horree/Alamy Stock Photo **329 right** Mary Dougherty/Shutterstock **331** Three Lions/Getty Images **334** Reuters/Jim Young

Xinhua/Lu Zhe/eyevine/Redux **554 top** Reuters /Muhammad Hamed **554 bottom right** Reuters /Paul Hackett **554 bottom left** Roger Hutchings/Alamy **556** Reuters /Navesh Chitrakar **558** Reuters/Juan Carlos Ulate **560** Q. Sakamaki/Redux **562** C. Anne Claus **564** Fatih Pinar/Anzenberger/Redux

Chapter 15

Photographs: 568-569 Stephen Crowley/The New York Times/ Redux **573** Ed Kashi/National Geographic Creative **575** Carla Bellamy **577** Joyce Flueckiger **578** Pictorial Press Ltd/Alamy **579 left** © Pitt Rivers Museum, University of Oxford **579 right** Audrey Richards **581** Ahmad Faizal Yahya/Alamy **583** Glasshouse Images/ Alamy **585** Paul Springett C/Alamy **586** Hulton Archive/Getty Images **589 left** CBW/Alamy **589 right** FRANCES M. ROBERTS/Newscom **591** Images & Stories/Alamy **593 left** AP Photo/ Mary Schwalm **593 right** Keith Torrie/NY Daily News Archive via Getty Images **595** Reuters/Baz Ratner **599** Adam Yuet Chau **600 left** Fedor Selivanov/Shutterstock **600 right** Urs Flueeler/123RF **601 left** Nataliya Hora/123RF **601 right** Universal Images Group/ Getty Images **603** ORIANA ELICABE Agence France Presse/ Newscom **604** Oded Gilad **609 left** Nick Sinclair/Alamy **609 right** AP Photo/Jennifer Szymaszek

Chapter 16

Photographs: 614-615 Jim Rogash/Getty Images **619 left** © Erich Schlegel **619 right** Eye Ubiquitous/Newscom **621** Earl & Nazima Kowall/Corbis Documentary/Getty Images **623** Siewert Falko/ picture-alliance/dpa/AP Images **625** Ian MacNicol/Getty Images **626 left** Courtesy Everett Collection / age photostock **626 right** Fuse/Getty Images **630 left** Ginger Horsburgh/Earthside Birth Photography **630-631** Family Childbirth Center at Swedish/Ballard **631 center** © Alice Proujansky **631 right** Mira / Alamy **634 left** Daniel Wallace/ZUMAPRESS/Newscom **634 center** Wallace, Daniel/ St. Petersburg Times / PSG / Newscom **634 right** AP

Photo/Dieu Nalio Chery **636** Courtesy of David Simmons **643** AP Photo/Eric Gay **644 top** Michael Thornton/Media Bakery **644 bottom right** Andrew Holbrooke/Corbis via Getty Images **644 bottom left** AP Photo/Aijaz Rahi **646 left** Kristoffer Tripplaar / Alamy Stock Photo **646 right** Issouf Sanogo/AFP/Getty Images **647 top right** Ken Weinrich/Shutterstock **647 bottom left** Issouf Sanogo/AFP/Getty Images **651** Manny Crisostomo /MCT/ ZUMAPRESS.com

Chapter 17

Photographs: 654-655 © Alessandro Angelini **656 left** © Alessandro Angelini **656 right** © Alessandro Angelini **658 left** Keith Corcoran/Alamy **658 center** Xinhua/Mohamed Kadri/eyevine/ Redux **658-659** Reuters/Tim Wimborne **659 right** Kevin Schafer/ Alamy **661** Mario Fourmy/Redux **663** John Reader/Science Source **664** JM Labat/Science Source **667** Danita Delimont/Gallo Images/ Getty Images **669 left** Michelle V. Agins/The New York Times/ Redux **669 right** David Kilpatrick/Alamy **670 left** Andrew Crocker/ National Library of Australia **670 top right** Stanislas Fautre/ Figarophoto/Redux **670 bottom right** Stanislas Fautre/Figarophoto/Redux **671 top** Photo by Dan Himbrechts/Newspix **671 bottom** Thomas Samson/AFP/Getty Images **673** © Chantal Regnault **676** Richard B. Levine/Newscom **677 left** Tom Williams/Roll Call/Getty Images **677 right** Ethan Miller/Reuters **678** Courtesy of Aimee Cox **681 right** Mervat Essa, *Saffurya,* © 2000. Courtesy of the Station Museum, Houston, Texas **681 left** © 2015 Museum Associates/LACMA Art Resource, NY **682** Gordon Scammell/ Age Photostock **684 left** David Boyer/Ntaional Geographic/Getty Images **684-685** James P. Blair/National Geographic/Getty Images **685 center** Volkmar K. Wentzel/National Geographic/Getty Images **685 right** Albert Moldvay/National Geographic/Getty Images **686** From *Exit Zero: An Industrial Family Story,* (2016), a film by Chris Boebel and Christine Walley. **687** © Cinema Guild/ courtesy Everett Collection

Glossary/Index

Page numbers in *italics* refer to figures, illustrations, and tables.

agency, 52–53, *53*, 555 The potential power of individuals and groups to contest cultural norms, values, mental maps of reality, symbols, institutions, and structures of power.

aggression among primates, 544–45, *545*

agriculture, 441, 442–45, *444* An intensive farming strategy for food production involving permanently cultivated land.

Ahma, Saeid, *499*
Alabama, *217*
Al Azhar Fatwa Council, 560–61, 564
Algeria, 456–61, *460, 461*
Aliyah Senior Center, 84, *84*
Allah Made Us (Gaudio), 339
All American Yemeni Girls (Sarroub), 518
Allison, Anne, 321
Allison, Anthony, 166
All Our Kin (Stack), 370
Alto do Cruzeiro, 71–75, 88, 94–95, 96, 101
ambilineal descent groups, 350
amchi medicine, 620–23, *621*
American Academy of Pediatrics, 286–87
American Anthropological Association (AAA), 43, 99–100, 380
American dream, 407
American Museum of Natural History, 176
American Revolution, 216
Americas
    early migration to, 161, 168
    gene flow from Europe to, 167
Amish, 390–91, *397*
Amma (healer), 576–77, *577*
Amnesty International, 541
analysis in ethnographic fieldwork, 95
Anand, Nikhil, 426
Anderson, Benedict, 255, 371
Angelini, Alessandro, 655–56
animals
    communication by, *113,* 113–15, *114*
    enculturation in, 36
    See also specific animals
"Animal with the Weirdest Sex Life, The" (Diamond), 314

anonymity (in research), 101 Protecting the identities of the people involved in a study by changing or omitting their names or other identifying characteristics.

Anthropocene, 21, 478 The current historical era in which human activity is reshaping the planet in permanent ways.

anthropologist's toolkit, 88 The tools needed to conduct fieldwork, including information, perspectives, strategies and even equipment.

anthropology, 5–7 The study of the full scope of human diversity, past and present, and the application of that knowledge to help people of different backgrounds better understand one another.
    applied, 9
    archaeology, 14–15
    of art, 657–62, *658, 659, 661*
    and changes in communities, 27
    cultural, 16
    definition of, 7
    engaged, 85–88
    four-field approach of, 12–17
        archaeology in, 12, 14–15, *15*
        cultural anthropology in, 12, 16
        linguistic anthropology in, 12, 15–16
        physical anthropology in, *12,* 12–14, *13*
    globalization and, 17–18, 26–27, 29–31
    history of, 8–9
    linguistic, 15–16
    medical, 616–17
    nineteenth-century, 80
    paleoanthropology, *12,* 13
    physical, 12–14
    political, 528
    research strategies in, 27, 29–31
    unique approach of, 9–12
    visual, 684

anti-apartheid movement, 204
anticolonialism, 258, 455–57, *457*
antimiscegenation laws, 38, 51, 216, 364
Antioch College, 206
Aparicio, Ana, 504
apartheid, 38
apes
    aggressiveness in, 544–45, *545*
    de Waal's study of, 178
    emergence of, 156
    enculturation in, 36
    material culture of, 185
applied anthropology, 9
Arab Americans, 222

archaeology, 14–15 The investigation of the human past by means of excavating and analyzing artifacts.

Archetti, Eduardo, 264
Ardipithecus fossils, 170

Ardipithecus kadabba, 170
Ardipithecus ramidus, 170, *170*
Argentina, *264,* 264–65, 364
Argonauts of the Western Pacific (Malinowski),
   46, 82
Aristotle, 526
Arizona
   homelessness and begging in Tucson, 78–79
   undocumented immigrant law in, 110, 111

arranged marriage, 360 Marriage orchestrated by the families of
the involved parties.

Arruda, Nailza de, 71–72, 90, 96

art, 655–90 All ideas, forms, techniques, and strategies that
humans employ to express themselves creatively and to communicate their creativity and inspiration to others.
   anthropology of, 657–62, *658, 659, 661*
   definition of, 657
   ethnography of, 665–69, *667, 669,* 672, 682
   fieldwork as, 78
   fine vs. popular, 658–59, *658–59*
   in human history, 662–64, *663, 664*
   intersection of media and, 681, 683–89, *684–85, 686, 687*
   as political critique, 672–75, *673*
   power and, 672–77, *673, 676, 677,* 680–81, *681*

artificial insemination, 375–76, 377
Asad, Talal, 595–96, *597*
ascribed status, 424

asexuality, 322 A lack of erotic attraction to others.

Asia
   arranged marriages in, 360
   creation of states in, 258
   early migration from Africa to, 161
   endangered languages in, 142
   European colonization and racial framework in,
      196, 203
   Homo erectus in, 174, 175
   Homo sapiens in, 175, 177
   national independence movements in, 258
   original migration to the Americas from, 168
   World War II and, 456
   See also specific countries
Asian Americans, 222
   adopted, 380–81, 382, *383*
   assimilation of, 254
   poverty rates for, 414, *415*

assimilation, 253–54 The process through which minorities accept
the patterns and norms of the dominant culture and cease to exist
as separate groups.

assisted reproductive technologies
   artificial insemination, 377
   cloning, 378–79
   impact of, 378–79
   Jewish descent and, 375–76
   surrogacy, 378–79
   in vitro fertilization, 377
Auschwitz-Birkenau concentration camp, 612
Australia
   Homo sapiens in, 177
   invention of traditional art forms in, 670–71
Australopithecus, 151–52, *152,* 169–70, 171–73, *172, 173*
   A. aethiopicus, 171, *172*
   A. afarensis, 152, 153, 171, *172*
   A. africanus, 171, *172*
   A. anamensis, 171, *172*
   A. boisei, 171, *172*
   A. garhi, 171–72, *172*
   A. robustus, 171, *172*

authenticity, 666, *667* The perception of an object's antiquity,
uniqueness, and originality within a local culture.

authorizing process, 596 The complex historical and social
developments through which symbols are given power and meaning.

Awash River Valley, *169,* 169–70, *170,* 171
Aymara people, 121, *181*
Azande, 589–91, *590*
Aztec kingdom, 450

Bafokeng, 252–53
Baga, 216
balanced reciprocity, 446, *446*
Bali, 45, 47, *47*
Balinese water temples, 600–601

band, *529,* 529–31, 536 A small kinship-based group of foragers
who hunt and gather for a living over a particular territory.

Bangalore, 19, *423*
Bangladesh, 26, *42, 434, 480, 493,* 524–26
banking, 469
Barbados, *304,* 304–5, *305*
Barker, David, 181
Barker, Holly, 24–25
Barrios, Steven, *287*

barter, 445 The exchange of goods and services one for the other.

Barth, Fredrik, 241
baseball, 592–93, *593*
Basso, Keith, 119–20
Battered Black Women and Welfare Reform (Davis), 368
Battle of Algiers, The (Pontecorvo), 456, 457, *457*
Baumann, Gerd, 370
begging, 78–79
Behind the Gates (Low), 418
Being Maasai (Hodgson), 541
Being Muslim the Bosnia Way (Bringa), 248
Belgium, 246, 364
Bemba people, 8, *579*, 579–80
Benedict, Ruth, 45, *45*
berdache, *See* Two-Spirits
Berlin Conference (1884-85), 455
Bernal, Victoria, 256
Besteman, Catherine, 501
Beyond the Melting Pot (Glazer and Moynihan), 254
Bickford, Andrew, 547
bifurcate collateral kinship patterns, 352–53
bifurcate merging kinship patterns, 352
bilateral descent groups, 350
bilingual educational programs, 148
biological adaptation, 161
biological anthropology, *See* physical anthropology
biology
    gender ideologies and, 295–97
    influences of culture vs., 53–57
    race and, 196–203
    sexuality and, 314–17, *315*
    as tool for discrimination, 45

biomedicine, *623*, 623–24, 627–28 A practice, often associated with Western medicine, that seeks to apply the principles of biology and the natural sciences to the practice of diagnosing disease and promoting healing.

biopower, 287

bipedalism, 170–71 The ability to habitually walk on two legs; one of the key distinguishing characteristics of humans and our immediate ancestors.

birth, *628–29*, 629–32
Birth in Four Cultures (Jordan and Davis-Floyd), 630
bisexuality, 322 Attraction to and sexual relations with members of both sexes.

Black, Stephanie, 467

Black Corona (Gregory), 226
Black Dragon King Temple, 597–98, *599*
Black English, *130*, 130–32, *131*
Black Friday shopping, *60*
BlackLight Project, 679
BlackLivesMatter social movement, 234
Blombos Cave, 662–63, *663*
blue jeans, 64–65
Board of Education, Brown v., 224, *225*
Boas, Franz, 8, 44–45, 80–81, 683
Boateng, Jerome, *236*, 237
Boateng, Kevin-Prince, *236*, 237–38, 242
body
    biomedical conceptions of, 627–29
    childbirth and, across cultures, *628–29*, 629–32
    disability and, 632–33
    See also health; illness
Body Silent, The (Murphy), 632
Boebel, Chris, 686
Boehm, Christopher, 530
Bohannan, Laura, 119
Bolivia, 121, 424–25
Bonilla-Silva, Eduardo, 225
bonobos, 156, 178–79, 315, *315*, 544
Borgoglio, Jorge Mario, *See* Francis, Pope
Born Digital (Palfrey and Gasser), 141
Borneo, 472–73
Bosnia, *248*, 248–49, *249*
Bosnia (documentary film), 249
Boston, Massachusetts
    immigrants in, 66
    speech patterns in, 128–29
Bourdieu, Pierre, 126, 128, 393, 396–99
Bourgeois, Louise, *661*

bourgeoisie, 394–95 Marxist term for the capitalist class that owns the means of production.

Bourgois, Philippe, 101
Boys Don't Cry (film), *300*
Brahmans of Nepal, 362
brain
    of *Homo floresiensis* ("the Hobbit"), 177
    language organization in, 118
    of Neandertals, 175

brain drain, 495, 498 Migration of highly skilled professionals from developing/periphery countries to developed/core countries.
Brazil, 72, 207, 362, *513*
    Alto do Cruzeiro, 71–75, 88, 94–95, 96, 101
    companionate marriage in, 362

favelas in, 208, *654*, 655–56, *656*, 690
human organ harvesting, 104–5, 107
independence of, 456
Japanese Brazilians, 513–14
Morrinho, 655–56, *656*, 690
race, class, and gender in, 207–9
Rio de Janeiro favela, *70*
same-sex marriage in, 364
street children in, 8, *9*
Yanomami people of, 36, 100
Brazzaville, Republic of the Congo, 507, 510, *510*
Brennan, Denise, 338

bridewealth, 364–65 The gift of goods or money from the groom's family to the bride's family as part of the marriage process.

Bridges, Khiara, 640, 642

bridges and barriers, *490–91, 490–92* The factors that enable or inhibit migration.

Bringa, Tone, 248–49
British Petroleum, 26
British structural functionalism, 46
Brodkin, Karen, 220
Brokered Homeland (Roth), 513
Brown, Linda, *225*
Brown, Michael, 195, 196, 234, 420
Brown, Peter, 177
Brown, Terry Lynn, *225*
Brown v. Board of Education, 224, *225*
Brubaker, Rogers, 245–46
Bryan, William Jennings, *163*
Bucharest, wedding industry in, *326*
Buck, Pem Davidson, 216, 405–7, 460
Buddhism, Tibetan, 620–23, *621*

built environment, 92–93 The intentionally designed features of human settlement, including buildings, transportation and public service infrastructure, and public spaces.

Burma, 456
Bush, George H. W., *351*
Bush, George W., *351*
Bush, Jeb, *351*
Bushman Myth, The (Gordon), 441
Butler Act, 164

cable networks, undersea, 146–47
cabs/taxis, African Americans and, 403
Cairo, *53, 192–93, 561, 564, 564–65*

California
   Aliyah Senior Center, 84, *84*
   Chinese immigrants in, *218*, 218–19
   Oakland Unified School District, *131*, 131–32
call system, 113
Cambodia, 456
Canada, 364
Cange, Haiti, *633*, 633–35
cannibalism, disease transmission via, 638–39
capitalism
   consumerism and, *60*, 60–62
   contemporary competition and, 394
   Keynesianism and, 465–66
   in Marx's class theory, 394
   Protestant ethic and, 57, 586
   Weber on, 57, 586
Caribbean
   immigrants from, 498, 499
   indigenous populations' lack of immunity to European diseases, 451, 454
   national independence movements in, 258
Carnal Knowledge and Imperial Power (Stoler), 330

carrying capacity, 444–45 The number of people who can be supported by the resources of the surrounding region.

Carsten, Janet, 366, 371, 638
casinos, 250, *250*
Castaing-Taylor, Lucien, 687–88

caste, 420–24, *421, 422, 556* A closed system of stratification most prominently found in India.

Catalan Atlas, *79*
catequistas, 602, *603*
Catholic Church
   in China, 94
   on evolution, 163
   Gregorian calendar and, 41
   Pope Francis and, *568*, 569–70, 612
   revitalization of, in the U.S., 607–9, *609*
   revolutionary movement in Mexico and, 599, 602, *603*
cattle, 351, 584–85, *585*
cattle ranching, 32–33
Census, U.S., 214–15, 216
Central Africa, confederacies of tribes in, 531
Central America, *See specific countries*
Central Asia, creation of states in, 258
Central Council of American Rabbis, 163
Chad, fossils in, 158–59, *159*
Chagnon, Napolean, 100

definition of, 388
in Dominican Republic, 204–7
inequality and
 caste and, 420–24, *421, 422, 556*
 egalitarian societies and, 390–91, *391*
 global, 424–31
 invisibility of, in the U.S., 417–20
 in ranked societies, 391–93, *392*
intersections of
 colonialism, sexuality, race, nation, and, 330–33, *331*
 race, gender, and, 399–401, 402, 405–7, *407*
 race and, 232–33, *233*
theories of, 393–401, 404
 Bourdieu, 393, 396–99
 Marx, 393–95, *395*
 Mullings, 393, 399–401
 Weber, 395–96
in the United States, 404–17
 consumer culture and, 419–20
 income inequality and, *411,* 411–13, *412, 413*
 media and, 417–18
 middle class and working poor, 407–8
 poor whites in rural Kentucky, 405–7, *407*
 poverty and, 414–17, *415, 416*
 in water contamination crisis in Flint, Michigan, *386,* 387–88, *389,* 404
 wealth, Wall Street, and, 408–10, *410*
 wealth inequality and, 412–14, *413*

Clifford, James, 98

climate change Changes to Earth's climate, including global warming produced primarily by increasing concentrations of greenhouse gases created by the burning of fossil fuels.
 accelerating, 478–79
 definition of, 26
 genetic adaptation and, 188
 globalization and, 21
 historic evidence of, 15
 human activity and, 26
 in Marshall Islands, 24–25
 unequal effects of, 430

cline, 199
Clinton, Bill, 313
cloning, 378–79
Clooney, George, 687
CNN, 63
coal miners, *407*
Coca-Cola Company, *4,* 5–6, 27, 63
Cochabamba, Bolivia, 424, *424*–25, 427

cockfights, 47, *47*
cocoa, *436,* 437–38, 439, 460

code switching, 129–30 Switching back and forth between one linguistic variant and another depending on the cultural context.

cognatic descent groups, 350
Cohen, Yehudi, 440, 441
college, as cross-cultural experience, 6
college campuses
 gender violence on, 300, *310,* 311–12, 344
 sexuality and power on, 332
college students
 consumerism of, 61
 credit industry targeting of, 62
 on sexuality, 314
Collins, Jane, 684–85

colonialism The practice by which a nation-state extends political, economic, and military power beyond its own borders over an extended period of time to secure access to raw materials, cheap labor, and markets in other countries or regions.
 anticolonialism, 258, 455–57, *457*
 bands, tribes, and chiefdoms influenced by, 535–36
 definition of, 203, 451
 Indian caste system and, 422–23
 and intersections of sexuality, race, class, nation, and, 330–33, *331*
 missionaries in South Africa and, *50,* 50–51, *51*
 race and, 196, *203,* 203–12, *204, 205*
 role in forming global economy, 451–62
  Industrial Revolution and, 454–55
  modern world economic system and, 458–62, *460*
  triangle trade and, 451–54, *452, 453*
 in Rwanda, 245–46

color, differences in descriptions and perceptions of, 121
colorblindness (ideology), 225
Columbus, Christopher, 167, 204–5, 448, 450
CO-MADRES, 301–3, *303*
Comaroff, Jean, 50–51, 249–50, 251
Comaroff, John, 50–51, 249–50, 251
Coming of Age in Samoa (Mead), 45, 83
commercials and construction of gender, 279

commodity chains, 472 The hands an item passes through between producer and consumer.
communication
 in the digital age, 141, *144,* 144–45
 gender differences in, 123–25, *124*
 global, undersea cable networks and, 146–47

symbolic, 39

See also language

communication technologies, 6–7

Communist Manifesto (Marx and Engels), 395, 583

communitas, 580 A sense of camaraderie, a common vision of what constitutes a good life, and a commitment to take social action to move toward achieving this vision that is shaped by the common experience of rites of passage.

communities

    gated, 418–19

    globalization and change in, 27

    imagined, 255

companionate marriage, 360–62, *361* Marriage built on love, intimacy, and personal choice rather than social obligation.

Concerned Community Adults (CCA), 226

conflict, ethnicity as source of, 244–49, *247, 249*

conflict resolution

    in Micronesia, 534–35, *535*

    Ury's work on, 58–59

connectedness

    of humans, 11–12, 25

    of natural systems, 25

Connecticut, *250,* 250–51

Constitution, U.S., 216, 268

consumer culture, 419

consumerism

    advertising and, 61–62

    college students and, 61

    culture of, 60

    romance and, 419–20

Consuming the Romantic Utopia (Illouz), 419

consumption, manufacturing desire for, *60,* 60–62

contagious magic, 589 Ritual words or performances that achieve efficacy as certain materials that come into contact with one person carry a magical connection that allows power to be transferred from person to person.

core countries, 459, 460, *460, 461* Industrialized former colonial states that dominate the world economic system.

Corona, Queens (New York City), 226–27

Coronado, Francisco Vásquez de, 112

coronary disease, 181

corporate culture in Japan, 321–22

corporations

    corporate culture of, 408–10, *410*

ethno-corporations, *250,* 250–53, *252*

export-processing zones and, 210–11

flexible accumulation, 204

nation-states and, in global economy, 462–65, *464*

Cortéz, Hernando, 112

cosmonauts, 498–99

cosmopolitanism, 66–69, *67*

Costa Rica, *556,* 556–58, *558*

Côte d'Ivoire, *436, 437,* 437–39, 460

cows, 584–85, *585*

Cows, Pigs, Wars, & Witches (Harris), 584

Cox, Aimee, *678,* 678–79

Crawford, John, III, 234

creationism, 162–64, *163* A belief that God created Earth and all living creatures in their present form as recently as 6,000 years ago.

Creative Reckonings (Winegar), 680

credit card debt, 62, 419–20

critical medical anthropology, 617, 640 An approach to the study of health and illness that analyzes the impact of inequality and stratification within systems of power on individual and group health outcomes.

Croatia, 154

cross-cousins, 363

Crow kinship naming system, *353, 353*

CTE (chronic traumatic encephalopathy), *614,* 615–16

Cuban immigrants, *519, 520*

cultural adaptation, 21, 182, 186, 189 A complex innovation, such as fans, furnaces, and lights, that allows humans to cope with their environment.

cultural anthropology, 16 The study of people's communities, behaviors, beliefs, and institutions, including how people make meaning as they live, work, and play together.

cultural capital, 126, *398,* 398–99 The knowledge, habits, and tastes learned from parents and family that individuals can use to gain access to scarce and valuable resources in society.

cultural construction of gender, 275–79, *277, 279,* 282 The ways humans learn to behave as a man or woman and to recognize behaviors as masculine or feminine within their cultural context.

cultural diffusion, 45

cultural evolution, unilineal, 44, 46

cultural institutions, power of, 48–52

cultural materialism, 584–85 A theory that argues that material conditions, including technology, determine patterns of social organization, including religious principles.

cultural relativism, 43–44, 81 Understanding a group's beliefs and practices within their own cultural context, without making judgments.

cumulative causation, 492–93 An accumulation of factors that create a culture in which migration comes to be expected.

dalits, 421, 421, 422, 422–23, 423, 424, 556 Members of India's "lowest" caste; literally, "broken people." Also called "Untouchables."

deep time, 155–56 A framework for considering the span of human history within the much larger age of the universe and planet Earth.

Denmark, *335*
   redistribution and stratification in, 393
   same-sex marriage in, 364
   sex, disability, and social justice in, 335–37

dependency theory, 459 A critique of modernization theory arguing that despite the end of colonialism, the underlying economic relations of the modern world economic system had not changed.

descent group, 349–57 A kinship group in which primary relationships are traced through consanguineous ("blood") relatives.
   in a Chinese village, 356–57
   definition of, 349
   in Nuer, *351,* 351–52, 354, *355*
   systems for classifying, *352–53,* 352–54, 356
   types of, 350–52, *351*

descriptive linguistics, 16, 115–16 The study of the sounds, symbols, and gestures of a language, and their combination into forms that communicate meaning.

descriptive linguists, 16 Those who analyze languages and their component parts.

development Post–World War II strategy of wealthy nations to spur global economic growth, alleviate poverty, and raise living standards through strategic investment in national economies of former colonies.
   definition of, 458
   modern world economic system and, 461–62
   uneven, 20, 424, 427, 430, *430*

developmental adaptation, 180–81, *181* The way in which human growth and development can be influenced by factors other than genetics, such as nutrition, disease, and stress.

de Waal, Frans, 178–79, 544
Dhaka, Bangladesh, *42, 434, 493,* 525

dialect, 126, 128 A nonstandard variation of a language.

Diamond, Jared, 314–15
diamonds, 328–29

diaspora, 256 A group of people living outside their ancestral homeland yet maintaining emotional and material ties to home.
   Eritreans in, 256–58

Dick, Ramona, *140*

difference model, 124
Different Kind of War Story, A (Nordstrom), 549
diffusion, cultural, 45
digital activism, 141, *144,* 144–45
digital age, 141, *144,* 144–47
digital divide, 145
digital immigrants, 141

digital natives, 141 A generation of people born after 1980 who have been raised in the digital age.

dimorphism, sexual, 273–74
Dinkins, David, 403
disability
   body and, 632–33
   sex, social justice, and, 335–37
Discipline and Punish (Foucault), 50
discrimination, racial
   in employment, 403
   in Ferguson, 195–96
   in housing, 403
   against immigrants to the United States, 218–19
   in individual racism, 223
   resistance to, 226–27
   white privilege and, 230–31

disease A discrete natural entity that can be clinically identified and treated by a health professional.
   definition of, 618
   developmental origins of, 180–81
   illness vs., 618–19
   indigenous populations and, 100, 451, 454
   in Malaysian factory workers, 210, 212
   See also illness

displacement, 114
distribution and exchange, 445–48, *447*
diversity
   human, 6
   language, 137, 143
   theory of evolution on, 161–64
divorce, 377

DNA, 166–67 Deoxyribonucleic acid; the feature of a cell that provides the genetic code for an organism.
   dating by, *160,* 160–61
   definition of, 160
   developmental adaptations and, 180–81
   mutation of, 166–67
   of Neandertal fossil, 154
   racial classifications and, 198

sequencing of, 14
shared among humans, 198, 349
shared by humans and animals, 13

Dobe !Kung, The (Lee), 441
dogs, 113, *113*
dolphins, 315, *315*
Doméstica (Hondagneu-Sotelo), 503
domestic violence, 299–300, 344, 368–69, 503
dominance model, 124–25
Dominican-Americans and the Politics of Empowerment (Aparicio), 504
Dominican Republic, *204, 338*
    race, skin color, and class in, 204–7
    sex tourism in, 338–39, *339*
    U.S. immigrants from, 504
"Do no harm" mandate, *99,* 99–100
Dorow, Sara, 381, 382
Douglas, Mary, 582–83
Dover Area School District, Tammy Kitzmiller v., 164
downward mobility, 407–8

dowry, 364–66 The gift of goods or money from the bride's family to the groom's family as part of the marriage process.

Dramas of Nationhood (Abu-Lughod), 66–68
drones, 550–51
drug dealers, 101
Dubai, 266–67, *499,* 500
Dude, You're a Fag (Pascoe), 278
Durkheim, Émile, 577–79, *578*
Duschinski, Haley, *262,* 262–63

earwax, 202
East Africa, 159, 589 *See also specific countries*
East Asia, 177 *See also specific countries*
Eastern Europe, creation of states in, 258
eating as a cultural practice, 34, *35*
Ebonics, *131,* 131–32
ecological footprint, human, 478–80, *479, 480*
economic strategies, 440–45
    agriculture, 441, 442–45, *444*
    food foraging, 440–41, *441*
    horticulture, 441, 442
    pastoralism, 441, 442

economy A cultural adaptation to the environment that enables a group of humans to use the available land, resources, and labor to satisfy their needs and to thrive.
    culture and, 57, 60
    definition of, 440
    distribution and exchange in, 445–48, *447*

global, *See* global economy
of India, social mobility and, 423
of Kentucky, 405–7, *407*
modern world economic system, 458–62, *460*
purpose of, 440–48
of Trobriand Islands, 291, 294
See also global economy

Edelman, Marc, 556
education
    cultural capital in, 398–99
    debates over language instruction in Arizona, 148
    in France, 255–56
    meritocracy of, 396
    poverty and, 430
    racial segregation in, 223–25, *225*
Education Amendments of 1972, 312
Efe people, 441

egalitarian society, 390–91, *391* A group based on the sharing of resources to ensure success with a relative absence of hierarchy and violence.

egg and sperm, stories about, 295–97, *296*
Egypt
    ancient stele with hieroglyphs from, *117*
    Cairo, *53, 192–93, 561, 564,* 564–65
    cosmopolitanism among rural poor in, 66–69, *67*
    Islamic Fatwa Councils in, 560–61, *564,* 564–65
    marriage among ancient royalty in, 363
    migration of refugees to, 485
    protesters in Tahrir Square, *53*
    television in, 67, *67*
    Village Girl Youth Project in, 645, 648
Ehrenreich, Barbara, 307
Elementary Forms of Religious Life (Durkheim), 578
elites, studies of, 10
El Salvador, *301,* 301–3, *303*
e-mails, 117–18, *118*
Emancipation Proclamation, 216

emic, 95 An approach to gathering data that investigates how local people think and how they understand the world.
    perspective in ethnography, 95

emoticons, 117, *118*

enculturation, 36 The process of learning culture.
    advertising as tool of, 61
    definition of, 36
    as group process, 36–37

Mead's study of, 45
mental maps and, 40

endangered languages, 139–41, *140*

endogamy, 38, 364, 365 Marriage to someone within the kinship group.

energy consumption, *480*

engaged anthropology, 85–88 Applying the research strategies and analytical perspectives of anthropology to address concrete challenges facing local communities and the world at large.

Engels, Friedrich, 395
England
Hertfordshire, 181
immigrants in Southall, 367, 370
London, 367, *367,* 370, *370*
as part of United Kingdom, 238
soccer and, 238
English-only laws, III

entrepreneurial immigrants, 499–501 Persons who move to a new location to conduct trade and establish a business.

environment
genetic adaptation and, 188–89
globalization and, 20–21, *21,* 24–26
human adaptation to, 20–21, 161–62, 180–83, *181, 182,* 186–89, *187, 188*
human impact on, 21, *21,* 24–26, 478–80, *479, 480*
Pope Francis on, 570
See also climate change

epigenetics, 55, 56 An area of study in the field of genetics exploring ways environmental factors directly affect the expression of genes in ways that may be inherited between generations.

epilepsy, 649–50, 651
Eritrea, women in military of, 271
Eritreans in diaspora, *256,* 256–58
Eskimo kinship naming system, *352,* 353
ethical concerns
about cloning, 378–79
about surrogacy, 378–79
in fieldwork, 98–101
Ethiopia
Awash River Valley, *169,* 169–70, *170,* 171
Hadar, 153
Olduvai Gorge, *152,* 153, 172, 173
U.S. adoptions from, 380

ethnic boundary marker, 242 A practice or belief, such as food, clothing, language, shared name, or religion, used to signify who is in a group and who is not.
for Indian Americans, 244

ethnic cleansing, 249, *249* Efforts by representatives of one ethnic or religious group to remove or destroy another group in a particular geographic area.
See also genocide

ethnic groups, 245–46
ethnic identity, 240–41
creating, *241,* 241–44, *243*
of England, 238

ethnicity, 237–69 A sense of historical, cultural, and sometimes ancestral connection to a group of people who are imagined to be distinct from those outside the group.
activating, 244
definition of, 240
as identity, 240–44, *241, 243*
nationalism and, 237–39, 254–65, 268
nations and, 254–61, 264–65
race vs., 240
as source of conflict, 244–49, *247, 249*
as source of opportunity, 249–53, *250, 251*
as term, 240
in the United States, 253–54

Ethnicity, Inc. (Comaroff and Comaroff), 249
Ethnicity without Groups (Brubaker), 245–46
ethnic vs. minority, 240

ethnocentrism, 43–44 The belief that one's own culture or way of life is normal and natural; using one's own culture to evaluate and judge the practices and ideals of others.
counteracting, 43
cultural relativism and, 43–44
definition of, 9

ethno-corporations
Pequot Foxwoods Resort, *250,* 250–51
Royal Bafokeng Nation, 252–53
ethnographic authority, 97

ethnographic fieldwork, 10, 95–98, *98* A primary research strategy in cultural anthropology typically involving living and interacting with a community of people over an extended period to better understand their lives.
in Alto do Cruzeiro, 71–75
definition of, 10, 71, 75
development of idea of, *79,* 79–85, *80, 81, 82, 83, 84,* 88

ethnology and, 17
globalization and changes in, 101, *101*, 104–7
multi-sited, 27, 29–31
participant observation in, 16
techniques in
analysis, 95
mapping, *91*, 91–93
preparation for fieldwork, 88–89
skills and perspectives, 93–95
strategies for gathering data, 89–91
as unique strategy, 75–79

ethnographic films, *686*, 686–88, *687*
ethnography
of art, 665–69, *667*, *669*, 672
multi-sited, 27, 29–31
salvage, 81
skills and perspectives for, 93–95
writing, 95–98, *98*
Ethnologue (SIL), 139

ethnology, 17, 95 The analysis and comparison of ethnographic data across cultures.

ethnomedicine, 619–23, *621* Local systems of health and healing rooted in culturally specific norms and values.

ethnomusicology, 675 The study of music in cultural context.

ethnopharmacology, 620 The documentation and description of the local use of natural substances in healing remedies and practices.

etic, 95 Description of local behavior and beliefs from the anthropologist's perspective in ways that can be compared across cultures.
perspective in ethnography, 95

Europe
Argentinian immigrants from, 264
colonialism by, 203
conceptualizations of sexuality in, 319–20
cultural patterns in, 54
descent groups in, 350
early migration from Africa to, 161
fossils in, 159
gene flow to Americas from, 167
high-tech consumption in, 20
Homo erectus in, 174, 175
Homo sapiens in, 175–76
imagined communities in, 255
migration of refugees to, 485
paleolithic cave paintings in, 663–64, *664*

restrictions on sexuality in colonies of, 330–33, *331*
triangle trade and, 451–54, *452*
U.S. immigrants from, 218, 219, 220
worker-to-CEO pay in, 412
World War II and destruction of economies in, 258
See also specific countries
European Central Bank, 467
Europe and the People without History (Wolf), 84
Evans-Pritchard, E. E., 46, *82*, 82–83, 96, 121, 351, 354, 442, 528, 589–91, 592
evolutionary biology, 315–16
evolutionary psychology, 54–55, 297
exchange of goods, 445–48, *447*
Exit Zero, *686*, 686–87

exogamy, 38 Marriage to someone outside the kinship group.
definition of, 364
gene flow and, 167
in Nuer clans, 351

export-processing zones, 210–11, *211*

Facebook, 6, 130, 541
Fadiman, Anne, 648, 650–51
Fallen Elites (Bickford), 547
Falling from Grace (Newman), 408
Families We Choose (Weston), 378
familles, 347
of choice, 378
nuclear, 348, 373, 376–77, *377*
of same-sex partners, *379*, 379–80
See also descent groups

family of orientation, 376 The family group in which one is born, grows up, and develops life skills.

family of procreation, 376 The family group created when one reproduces and within which one rears children.

family trees, 372–73
Farmer, Paul, 548, 633–35
fast food, *32*, 33–34, 63, *63*
Fatwa Councils, 560–61, *564*, 564–65
Fausto-Sterling, Anne, 286
Feagin, Joe, 232

femininity, 275 The ideas and practices associated with womanhood.

feminism and reflexivity, 84
Ferguson, Missouri, *194*, 195–96, 234, 420
Ferguson, Plessy v., 224

Fertile Crescent, 442
fetal origins hypothesis, 181
fictive kin, 371

field notes, 90 The anthropologist's written observations and reflections on places, practices, events, and interviews.

Fields-Black, Edda, 216
fieldwork, 71–109
  in Alto do Cruzeiro, 71–75
  analysis of data from, 95
  anthropologists transformed by, 76–78
  in engaged anthropology, 86–87
  ethnographic, 75–79; *See also* ethnographic fieldwork
  globalization and changes in, 101, *101*, 104–7
  history of, *79*, 79–85, *80*, *81*, *82*, *83*, *84*, 88
  mapping in, *91*, 91–93
  moral and ethical concerns in, 98–101
  preparation for, 88–89
  strategies for, 89–91
FIFA, 237, 238
films, ethnographic, *686*, 686–88, *687*
financial collapse of 2008, 469
financial services industry, 62

fine art, 658–59, *658–59* Creative expression and communication often associated with cultural elites.

first-cousin marriages, 363
Fisher, Helen, 316

flexible accumulation, 463–64, *464*, 469 The increasingly flexible strategies that corporations use to accumulate profits in an era of globalization, enabled by innovative communication and transportation technologies.
  corporation-worker relationships and, 204
  definition of, 19, 463
  globalization and, 19
  migration experience and, 487

Flint, Michigan, *386*, 387–88, *388*, *389*, 404
Flores, Indonesia, 177
Florida, *232*
  Church of the Lukumi Babulu Ayea v. City of Hialeah, 519–20, *520*
  De Leon Springs, 643–44
  Miami and sea-level rise, 26
  Shellcracker Haven study in, 232–33
Floyd, Charlene, 584, 598

focal vocabulary, 120–21 The words and terminology that develop with particular sophistication to describe the unique cultural realities experienced by a group of people.

food
  culture and, 34, *35*, 54
  power and, 34
  production of, brief survey of, 440–45, *441*, *444*
food, cultural preferences, 54

food foragers, 440–41, *441* Humans who subsist by hunting, fishing, and gathering plants to eat.

food foraging, 297–98, 440–41, *441*, 529
Food for Peace program, 557
Fool's Gold (Tett), 468
football concussions and CTE, *614*, 615–16
Ford, Henry, 463

Fordism, 462–63, *463* The dominant model of industrial production for much of the twentieth century, based on a social compact between labor, corporations, and government.

Forest People, The (Turnbull), 441
Fort Apache Reservation, *119*, 119–20, *120*
Fortes, Meyer, 528
fossilization process, *157*
fossil record, 158–59

fossils The remains of an organism that have been preserved by a natural chemical process that turns them partially or wholly into rock.
  dating of, 159–60
  definition of, 158
  as evidence for human origins, *157*, 158–59, *159*

Foucault, Michael, 50, 287
founder effect, 168

four-field approach, 12–17, 80–81 The use of four interrelated disciplines to study humanity: physical anthropology, archaeology, linguistic anthropology, and cultural anthropology.
  archaeology in, 12, 14–15, *15*
  Boas and, 80–81
  cultural anthropology in, 12, 16
  linguistic anthropology in, 12, 17–18
  physical anthropology in, *12*, 12–14, *13*

Fourteenth Amendment, 216, 268
FOXP$_2$ gene, 115, 154

framing process, 558 The creation of shared meanings and definitions that motivate and justify collective action by social movements.

France, *255*, 664
  Algeria and, 456–61, *461*

sexuality and, 337–41
sex work and, 342–43
the state and, 539–43, *540, 542*
and transition from caste to class, 423
transnational citizenship and, 256–58
uneven development and, 20, 30–31, 145
war and, 549, 552, *552, 553,* 554

global mediascape, 683 Global cultural flows of media and visual images that enable linkages and communication across boundaries in ways unimaginable a century ago.

global warming
genetic adaptation and, 188
sea-level rise and, 26
See also climate change
Glover, Danny, 403
Gluckman, Max, 46
Gmelch, George, 589, 592–93
God in Chinatown (Guest), 96, 487
Golden Arches East (Watson), 63
Golden Bough, The (Frazer), 588
Goldstein, Daniel, 424, 425–26
Goldstein, Donna, 208–9
Goodall, Jane, *13,* 152, 184, *184*
Goode, Judith, 416
Gordon, Robert, 441
gorillas
emergence of, 156
language capacity of, 114, *114*
Gough, Kathleen, 84, 354

grammar, 116 The combined set of observations about the rules governing the formation of morphemes and syntax that guide language use.

Gramsci, Antonio, 50
Gray, Freddie, 234
Gray, Tom, 153
Great Britain
Hong Kong and, 457
Indian caste system and, 422–23
Iraq and, 261
Malaysia and, 209
peppered moths in, *165,* 165–66
Sykes-Picot Agreement and, 261
Zimbabwe and, 259–60
Greece, U.S. immigrants from, 218, 219
greenhouse gases, 479
Gregorian calendar, 41
Gregory, Steven, 226
Griest, Kristen, *270,* 271, 272, 308

Guatemala, U.S. adoptions from, 381
Guest, Kenneth J., 27, 29–31, 487
Chinese popular religion and, 610–11
on migration to Chinatown, New York, 487–88, *489*

guest worker program, 494, 500 A policy that allows labor immigrants to enter a country temporarily to work but denies them long-term rights and privileges.

Guns and Rain (Lan), 259
Gutmann, Matthew, 283

habitus, **396–98** Bourdieu's term to describe the self-perceptions, sensibilities, and tastes developed in response to external influences over a lifetime that shape one's conceptions of the world and where one fits in it.

Hadar, Ethiopia, *152, 153*
Haiti, *204, 633*
independence of, 205, 455–56
migration to Dominican Republic from, 206
public health system in, 633–35, *634*
rara bands in, 672–75, 673
U.S. immigrants from, 519–20, *520*
hajj, 582
Hall, George W., 219
Hanna-Attisha, Mona, 387
Happy Meal, McDonald's, *32,* 33–34, 68
Harlem Birth Right Project, The, 399–401, 402
Harris, Marvin, 73, 89, 584–85
Harrison, David, *142,* 142–43
Harry Potter series (Rowling), *589*
Harsha, Edna, *644*
harvested human organ trafficking, 104–7, *106*
Harvey, David, 463
Haver, Shaye, 271, 272, 308
Hawaiian groups, incest taboos in, 363
Hawaiian kinship naming system, 353, *353*
healing
in India, 620–23, *621*
multiple systems of, 648–53, *651*

health, 615–53 The absence of disease and infirmity, as well as the presence of physical, mental, and social well-being.
Chinese medicine and, *625,* 625–27, *626*
cultural influences on, 618–27
biomedicine, *623,* 623–24, 627–28
childbirth, *628–29,* 629–32
ethnomedicine, 619–23, *621*
illness narratives, 650–53
definition of, 618

imitative magic, 588–89 A ritual performance that achieves efficacy by imitating the desired magical result.

Immigrant and Nationalities Act of 1965, 516
immigrants
    in Argentina, 264
    children of, 148, 504–5
    "cousins" among, 367, 370
    digital, 141
    entrepreneurial, 499–501
    in France, 238
    generations of, 504–5
    health care and, 642–43, *643*
    Indian, *243*, 243–44
    labor, 494–95
    languages spoken by, 112
    from Mali, 506–7, 510, *510*
    professional, 495, 498–99, *499*
    refugees, *17*, 484–86, 501–2, *553*
    in Southall, England, 367, *367*, 370, *370*
    transnational, 512
    types of, 494–95, *495*, 498–502, *499*, *502*
    undocumented, 110, 111, 268, 521
    "whitening" process of, 220
    women, work of, 306–7
    See also migration
immigration
    Arizona's restrictive laws on, 110, 111, 148
    and assimilation vs. multiculturalism, 253–54
    Boas' studies of, 8
    of Chinese to New York, 357
    colonial restrictions on European women immigrating to Asia, 331
    race and, 214–15, *218*, 218–22
    religion and, *609*, 609–11
    United States and, 514–21, *515*, *517*, *518*
    women and, 503, *504*
    See also migration
Immorality Act, 38
Impossible Citizens (Vora), 500
Inca, 363

incest taboo, 362–64 Cultural rules that forbid sexual relations with certain close relatives.

income What people earn from work, plus dividends and interest on investments, along with rents and royalties.
    class and, 388; *See also* class: inequality and
    consumer culture and, 419
    definition of, 411
    inequality, 6, *411*, 411–13, *412*, *413*

    voluntary isolation and, 418–19
    world distribution of, 427

increasing migration, 19 The accelerated movement of people within and between countries.

India, *243*, *432*
    abducted women from Western Punjab, 374–75
    Bangalore, 19, *423*
    caste in, 420–24, *421*, *422*
    consumerism in, 60
    dowries in, 365–66
    endangered languages in, 142
    Husain Tekri shrine in, *575*, 575–76
    immigrant entrepreneurs in Dubai, 500
    incest taboos in, 363
    Kashmiri ethnic community and, 262–63
    Malaysian immigrants from, 209–11
    marriage in, 362
    Mumbai, *426*, 426–27
    partition of Pakistan and, 374, *374*
    sacred cows in, 584–85, *585*
    Tibetan medicine in, 620–23, *621*
    water access in, 5–6, 27, 426–27
Indian immigrants, *243*, 243–44, 498, *499*

indigenous media, 688–89 The use of media by people who have experienced massive economic, political, and geographic disruption to build alternative strategies for communication, survival, and empowerment.

indigenous people
    colonial eradication of, 203
    disease and, 100, 451, 454
    endangered languages of, 142–43
    See also specific peoples

individual racism, 223 Personal prejudiced beliefs and discriminatory actions based on race.

Indonesia
    Aceh province, *13*
    Dutch colonists in, *331*
    Homo floresiensis ("Hobbits") in Flores, 177, *180*
    immigrant workers from, 306, *495*
    Japan and, 456
    Java, *331*, 333
    Kalimantan, 472–73

industrial agriculture, 443–45, 444 Intensive farming practices involving mechanization and mass production of foodstuffs.

Industrial Revolution, 165, 394, 454–55, 577 The eighteenth- and nineteenth-century shift from agriculture and artisanal skill craft to machine-based manufacturing.

inequality
    in Brazilian life, 208–9
    class and, 387–432
        egalitarian societies and, 390–91, *391*
        invisibility of, in the U.S., 417–20
        in ranked societies, 391–93, *392*
        theories of class and, 393–401, 404
    global, 424–31
    in health care, 642–43, *643*
    race and patterns of, 197, 234, 390–93, *392*; *See also* racism
    in school funding, 224–25
    in Swaziland, 606
    in the United States, 404–17
        consumer culture and, 419–20
        in income distribution, 6, *411*, 411–13, *412, 413*
        media and, 417–18
        middle class and working poor and, 407–8
        poor whites in rural Kentucky and, 405–7, *407*
        poverty and, 414–17, *415, 416*
        in water contamination crisis in Flint, Michigan, *386*, 387–88, *389*, 404
        wealth, Wall Street, and, 408–10, *410*
        in wealth distribution, 412–14, *413*
    wedding industry and, 326–27, 330
infant mortality, 399–401
informatics industry, women in, 304–5, *305*

informed consent, 100–101 A key strategy for protecting those being studied by ensuring that they are fully informed of the goals of the project and have clearly indicated their consent to participate.

Ingraham, Chrys, 324–26
Inside Job, The, 410
In Sorcery's Shadow (Stoller and Olkes), 591

institutional racism, 223–25, *225* Patterns by which racial inequality is structured through key cultural institutions, policies, and systems.

intelligent design An updated version of creationism that claims to propose an evidence-based argument to contradict the theory of evolution.
    definition of, 163
    evolution vs., 162–64, *163*
interdependence, increasing levels of, 6

internally displaced persons, 501 Persons who have been forced to move within their country of origin because of persecution, armed conflict, or disasters.

internal migration, 510–12 The movement of people within their own national borders.

International Association of Athletics Federations (IAAF), 284–86
International Cocoa Federation, 439
International Covenant on Civil and Political Rights, 43
International Covenant on Social, Economic, and Cultural Rights, 43
International Criminal Court, 439
international migration, *505*, 505–7, *506*, 510, *510*
International Monetary Fund (IMF), 438, 466, 467, 555, 557
international nonstate actors, *539*, 539–40
Internet
    digital age and, 141, *144*, 144–45
    language related to, 15
    time-space compression and, 18

interpretivist approach, 46–47 A conceptual framework that sees culture primarily as a symbolic system of deep meaning.

interracial marriage, 364
    antimiscegenation laws, 38, 51, 216, 364
    in Brazil, 208–9
    Loving v. Virginia, 38, *365*
    in the United States, 38, *51*, 51–52, *365*

intersectionality An analytic framework for assessing how factors such as race, gender, and class interact to shape individual life chances and societal patterns of stratification.
    of art and media, 681, 683–89, *684–85, 686, 687*
    colonialism and, of sexuality, race, class, nation, and, 330–33, *331*
    definition of, 232, 399
    of race, gender, and class
        Harlem Birth Right Project, 399–401, 402
        poor whites in rural Kentucky, 405–7, *407*
    of race and gender, 403
    of race and sexuality for black gay women, 333–35, 334
    of sex, disability, and social justice, 335–37
    of whiteness and class, 232–33, *233*

intersex, 286–87 The state of being born with a combination of male and female genitalia, gonads, and/or chromosomes.

Intersex Society of North America, 287
interviews in fieldwork, 90
Inuit, *80*, 441, *529*

invented traditions, 255–56, 264

Invisible Families (Moore), 333

in vitro fertilization, 377

iPhone, *461*

Iraq, *260*

    anthropologists as cross-cultural experts in, 100

    refugees from, 484–86

    sense of nationhood in, 260–61

Irish immigrants, 218, 219, 220, 516

Iroquois kinship naming system, 353, *353*

ISIL (the Islamic State in Iraq and the Levant), 260

ISIS, *See* ISIL (the Islamic State in Iraq and the Levant)

Islam

    local expressions and creative adaptations of, 574–77, *575, 577*

    pilgrimage and, *581,* 581–82

    See also Muslims

Islamic Fatwa Councils, 560–61, *564,* 564–65

Israel, *375*

    artificial insemination in, 375–76

    women in military of, 271

Italy

    Homo erectus in, 175

    U.S. immigrants from, 218, 219, 220

Jamaica, 467, *467*

Japan, *513*

    alternate constructions of sexuality in, 321–22

    colonial efforts of, 456

    return migration to, 513–14

    Tokyo, 321, *321,* 474–75

Java, Indonesia, *331,* 333

jeans, blue, 64–65

Jenner, Caitlyn, *287*

Jewish dietary laws, 582–83

Jews, beliefs about Jewish descent, 375–76

Jim Crow, 216–17, 405–6 Laws implemented after the U.S. Civil War to legally enforce segregation, particularly in the South, after the end of slavery.

Johanson, Donald, 153

Johnson, Virginia, 324

John XXIII, 602

Jordan, 485

Jordan, Brigitte, 630, 631

Judge, 219

Juris, Jeffrey, 559–60

Kahn, Susan, 375

Kalimantan, Indonesia, 472–73

Kant, Immanuel, 659–60

Karaim community, 142

Kasanaj, Trobriand Islands, *81*

Kash, MC, 262

Kashmiris, 262–63

Katrina, Hurricane, 431

Katz, Jonathan, 323

Kayakctivists, *540*

Kealing Junior High School, *317*

Kelly, Patty, 339, *342,* 342–43

Kendall, Laurel, 588

Kennedy, John F., *351*

Kennedy, Joseph, Sr., 350, *351*

Kennedy, Robert, *351*

Kennewick Man, *153,* 154

Kentucky, *405*

    economy of, 405–7, *407*

    poor whites in, 405–7, *407*

Kenya

    female marriage among Nandi in, 364

    Nariokotome (Turkana) Boy in, 174, *174*

    sickle-cell anemia in, 166

key informant, 90 A community member who advises the anthropologist on community issues, provides feedback, and warns against cultural miscues. Also called *cultural consultant.*

Keynes, John Maynard, 465

Keynesianism, 465–66, 472

kindred exogamy, 364

kinesics, 116–17, 118 The study of the relationship between body movements and communication.

kinetic orality, 675–77, 676, 677 A musical genre combining body movement and voice.

Kinsey, Alfred C., 324, *324*

kinship, 347–48 The system of meaning and power that cultures create to determine who is related to whom and to define their mutual expectations, rights, and responsibilities.

    in China, 356–59, *378*

    definition of, 348

    by descent, 349–54, 356–57

        in a Chinese village, 356–57

        systems for classifying, *352–53,* 352–54, 356

        types of, 350–52, *351,* 354, *355*

    ethnicity and, 240

    fictive, 371

    in Langkawi, Malaysia, *366,* 366–67

    mapping, 372–73

    as a means to survive poverty, 370–71

    nation-state and, 371, *374,* 374–76, *376*

non-biological/non-marriage, *366, 366–71, 370*
Nuer, *351,* 351–52, 354, *355*
in Southhall, London, 367, 370, *370*
through choice, 378, *378*
through marriage, 360–66
tracing family trees, 372–73
in the United States, 376–83, *377, 379, 383*
in the U.S
impact of assisted reproductive technologies on, 378–79
nuclear family, 376–77, *377*
through choice, 378

kinship analysis, 90 A fieldwork strategy of examining interlocking relationships of power built on marriage and family ties.

Kleinman, Arthur, 651
Koko (gorilla), 114, *114*
Korea, 456, 588
Krafft-Ebing, Richard von, 323
Kromidas, Maria, 220–22
Ku Klux Klan, 217
Kula Ring, 291, 446
Kulick, Don, 125, 335, 336, 337
!Kung san, 441, *441*
Kurds, 260, 261
kuru, 635, 638–39
Kwakiutl indigenous people, 45, 80, 391–92
Kwon, JB, *228,* 228–29

labor immigrants, 494–95 Persons who move in search of a low-skill and low-wage job, often filling an economic niche that native-born workers will not fill.

labor in Marx's class theory, 394
Labov, William, 128–29
Ladakh, India, 620–23, *621*
Laetoli, Tanzania, 153, *153*
Lakoff, Robin, 121
Lakota language, 139–41
Lan, David, 259, 260
Lan, Pei-chia, 306
Lancaster, Roger, 320–21
landfills, 428–29
Langkawi, *366,* 366–67

language, 111–48 A system of communication organized by rules that uses symbols such as words, sounds, and gestures to convey information.
of Arizona's undocumented immigrant law, 110, 111
culture and, 112
dialect and, 126, 128
historical linguistics, 134–35, *135*

"N-word," 16, 122–23, *123*
variation in the United States, 128–33, *130*
definition of, 113
descriptive linguistics, 16, 115–16
in the digital age, 141, *144,* 144–47
focal vocabulary, 120–21
gender and, 123–26, 124
globalization and, *136,* 137–41, 143
diminishing language diversity, 137
hastening language loss, 137–41, *138, 140*
kinesics and, 116–17, 118
in migration, 490
origins of, 113–15
paralanguage, 117–18, *118*
sexuality and, 339, 341
sociolinguistics, 121–36
symbols of, 39
thought and culture shaped by, 118–20
world languages by country, *136*

language continuum, 134–35 The idea that variation in languages appears gradually over distance so that groups of people who live near one another speak in a way that is mutually intelligible.

language diversity, 137, 143

language loss, 137–41, *138, 140* The extinction of languages that have very few speakers.

Laos, 456, *649*
Lascaux Cave, 152, *152,* 153, 663–64, *664*
Latin America
national independence movements in, 258
See also specific countries
Latinos, *See* Hispanics
Laughter Out of Place (Goldstein), 208
Lawrence, John, *365*
Lawrence v. Texas, 365
Leacock, Eleanor Burke, 415
League of Nations, 261
Leakey, Louis, 172
Leakey, Mary, 153, 172
Lebanon, 485, *552*
Lee, Lia, 648–52
Lee, Richard, 293, 441
legal structures, alternative, 560–61, *564,* 564–65
lesbians, *See* gays and lesbians
Lessinger, Johanna, 243

leveling mechanism, 447–48 Practices and organizations that reallocate resources among a group to maximize the collective good.
Leviathan, 687, 687–88

Levi's, 63
Levi-Strauss, Claude, 118
Lewinsky, Monica, 313
Lewis, Oscar, 415
Lewiston, Maine, *501, 501–2, 502*

lexicon, 121 All the words for names, ideas, and events that make up a language's dictionary.

Life and Debt (Black), 467

life chances, 396 An individual's opportunities to improve quality of life and realize life goals.

life expectancy, 639–40, *641*

life history, 90 A form of interview that traces the biography of a person over time, examining changes in the person's life and illuminating the interlocking network of relationships in the community.

Life Is Hard (Lancaster), 320

liminality, 580 One stage in a rite of passage during which a ritual participant experiences a period of outsiderhood, set apart from normal society, that is key to achieving a new perspective on the past, future, and current community.

Lincoln, Abraham, 216
Lindenbaum, Shirley, 635, 638–39

lineage, 350 A type of descent group that traces genealogical connection through generations by linking persons to a founding ancestor.

linguistic anthropology, 15–16 The study of human language in the past and the present.
    See also language

linguistic relativity, 143
linguistics
    descriptive, 16, 115–16
    historical, 16, 134–35, *135*
Linnaeus, Carolus, 41
Liquidated (Ho), 408
literature review, 88
LiveAndTell, 140
Livingstone, Frank B., 166
Living with Racism (Feagin and Sikes), 232
loban, 576
Lock, Margaret, 627–28
London, 367, *367,* 370, *370*
Loneliness and Its Opposite (Kulick and Rydstrom), 335

Loomis, William, 183
Lord of the Rings trilogy (Tolkien), *589*
Louisiana, 217, 431
love, 328–29, 360–62, *361,* 419–20
Loving, Mildred, *365*
Loving, Richard, *365*
Loving v. Virginia, 38, *365*
Low, Setha, 418
Lowe, Bill, *38*
Lowe, Jeanne, *38*
Lucy (Australopithecine), *152,* 153, 158, 170
Lutz, Catherine, 546, 547, 684–85
Lydia's Open Door (Kelly), 342
lynchings, 217
Lynn, Terry, *225*

Maasai, 541–43, *543,* 555
Macau, 457
machismo
    in Mexico, 282–83, *283*
    in Nicaragua, 320–21
Madoff, Bernard, *447*

magic, 588–93, *589, 591, 593* The use of spells, incantations, words, and actions in an attempt to compel supernatural forces to act in certain ways, whether for good or for evil.

Maine, 501–2, *502*
Makah Nation, *392*
Making Refuge (Besteman), 501
Malaysia, *209*
    export-processing zones of, 210–11, *211*
    farmers' slowdown protest in, *53*
    Japan and, 456
    kinship in Langkawi, *366,* 366–67
    Minah Karan, 210–11
    race, gender, and globalization in, 209–12, *212*
    racial framework in, 210
    Scott's agency studies in, 52, *52*
male dominance, early research on, 290–91, 294–95
Mali, *507*
    King of (in 1375), *11*
    migrants from, 506–7, 510, *510*
Malinowski, Bronislaw, 44, 46, *81,* 81–82, 88, 291, 294, 312, 351, 363
Malkki, Liisa, 247–48
Maman (Bourgeois), *661*
Manchuria, Japan's invasion of, 456
Manila, 19, *63,* 490
Mantsios, Gregory, 417

mapping, *91,* 91–93, 372–73 The analysis of the physical and/or geographic space where fieldwork is being conducted.

mental maps of reality Cultural classifications of what kinds of people and things exist, and the assignment of meaning to those classifications.

> cultural differences in, 37, 40–42
> definition of, 40

Merced Community Medical Center (MCMC), 649–50
meritocracy, 396, 418
Metropolitan Museum of Art, *398*
Mexican New York (Smith), 66
Mexico
> childbirth in, 629, *629*, 630, 631
> companionate marriage in, 361, *361*
> factory workers in, *305*
> immigrants from, 496–97
> machismo in, 282–83, *283*
> religion and revolution in, 598–99, *599*, 602, *603*
> Seri people, 140
> sex work in, 342–43
> transnational immigrants from, 512
> Zona Galactica, 342–43

Mexico City, 282–83, *283*
Miami, sea-level rise and, 26
Michigan, *386*, 387–88, *389*, 404

microaggressions, 223 Common, everyday verbal or behavioral indignities and slights that communicate hostile, derogatory and negative messages about someone's race, gender, sexual orientation or religion.

Micronesia, *533*, 533–35, *535*, 543
Middle Awash River Valley, *169*, 169–70, *170*, 172, 175
middle class
> African Americans in, 232
> Americans' perception of, 404
> in Brazil, 209–10
> in Harlem, 400
> Indian entrepreneurs in Dubai, 500
> Marx's class theory and, 394–95
> social mobility in, 407–8
> U.S. media's portrayal of, 427

Middle East
> arranged marriages in, 360
> consumerism in, 60
> creation of states in, 258
> early migration from Africa to, 161
> immigrants from, 220–22, 518–19
> incest taboos in, 363
> national independence movements in, 258
> refugees from, 484–86

Sykes-Picot Agreement and, 261
> *See also specific countries*

migrant farmworkers, 9, 520–21
Migrants and Strangers in an African City (Whitehouse), 506–7
migration, 485–523
> descent groups and, 357
> gendered patterns of, 306–7
> gene flow and, 167
> global, 306–7, 505
> globalization and, 19, 66
> of Haitians, 206
> of *Homo erectus*, 174–75
> of *Homo sapiens*, 175–77, 180
> immigrant generations, 504–5
> internal, 510–12
> international, *505*, 505–7, *506*, 510, *510*
> in Malaysia, 209–10
> Malian migrants, 506–7, 510, *510*
> medical, 643–45, *644*
> reasons for, 486–93
>> bridges and barriers in, *490–91*, 490–92
>> pushes and pulls shaping, 489–90
>> remittances and cumulative causation, 492–93, *493*
> of refugees, 484–86
> return, 513–14
> skin color changes and, 183, 186
> and transference of culture, 66
> transnational, 512
> types of immigrants, 494–95, *495*, 498–502, *499*, *502*
> to the United States, 514–21, *515*, *517*, *518*
> women and immigration, 503, *504*
> *See also* immigration

Miles, Lyn, 114

militarization, 546–47 The contested social process through which a civil society organizes for the production of military violence.

military, women in, *270*, 271–72, *274*, 308
Mills, C. Wright, 546
Minah Karan, 210–12
Miner, Horace, 77
miners, *407*
minority vs. ethnic, 240
Mintz, Sydney, 83, 477
Minutemen, *515*

miscegenation A demeaning historical term for interracial marriage.

> antimiscegenation laws, 38, 51, 216, 364

in Brazil, 208
definition of, 207

missionaries in South Africa, *50*, 50–51, *51*
Missouri, *194*, 195–96, 234, 420
Missouri University, *234*
mitochondrial DNA, 13, 160–61
mobility
downward, 407–8
social, *See* social mobility
Mock Spanish, 132–33, *133*

modernization theories, 458 Post–World War II economic theories that predicted that with the end of colonialism, less-developed countries would follow the same trajectory toward modernization as the industrialized countries.

modern world systems analysis, 459–61, *460, 461*
money, as a symbolic representation of value, 40, *40*
monkeys
emergence of, 156
enculturation in, 36
tool use by, 185

monogamy, 362 A relationship between only two partners.

Moore, Mignon, 333–34, *335*
Mopti, Mali (port of), *7*
Morgan, Lewis Henry, 44, 80

morphemes, 116 The smallest units of sound that carry meaning on their own.

morphology, 116 The study of patterns and rules of how sounds combine to make morphemes.

Morrinho, 655–56, *656*, 690
mortality
infant, 399–401
poverty and, 431
mortal selective neglect, 73
mortgage foreclosures, protest against, *227*
Mothers of "The Disappeared" (in El Salvador), 301–3, *303*
Mountains beyond Mountains (Farmer), 633
Moynihan Report, 370–71
Mozambique, 549, *549*, 552, 554
Muhammad (Prophet), 575
Mullings, Leith, 232, 393, 399–401, *402*, 402–3

multiculturalism, 253–54 A pattern of ethnic relations in which new immigrants and their children enculturate into the dominant national culture and yet retain an ethnic culture.

multi-sited ethnography, 27, 29–31
Mumbai, India, *426*, 426–27
Murphy, Robert, 632–33
music
gender identity through kinetic orality, 675–77, *676, 677*
rara bands, 672–75, *673*
Muslims
in Bosnia, 248–49, *249*
in France, *49*, 49–50, 456–57
in Iraq, 260, *261*
local practices and creative adaptations of, 574–77, *575, 577*
in Nigeria, 340
pilgrimages of, *581*, 581–82
in the United States, 268
See also Islam

mutagen, 167 Any agent that increases the frequency or extent of mutations.

mutation, 166–67 A deviation from the standard DNA code.

mutual transformation, 94–95 The potential for both the anthropologist and the members of the community being studied to be transformed by the interactions of fieldwork.

Myerhoff, Barbara, 84–85

Nacirema, 77, *77*
Nala, 216
Nanda, Serena, 288
Nandi, 364
Narayanan, K. R., 423
Nariokotome Boy, 174, *174*

nation A term once used to describe a group of people who shared a place of origin; now used interchangeably with nation-state.
definition of, 254
as imagined communities, 255
intersections of, colonialism, sexuality, race, class, and, 330–33, *331*
invented traditions of, 255–56
relationship of ethnicity to, 254–65
as term, 240
National Football League, 616
National Geographic magazine, 448, *684–85*, 684–86
National Guard deployment to Flint, Michigan, 387

nationalism The desire of an ethnic community to create and/or maintain a nation-state.
anticolonialism and, 258
definition of, 254

and developing sense of nationhood, 258–61, 264–65
ethnicity and, 237–39, 254–65, 268
imagined communities, 255
invented traditions, 255–56
as term, 240
in Zimbabwe, 259–60

National Liberation Front (NLF), 456
National Origins Act, 219, 516
Nation as Network (Bernal), 256
nationhood
developing sense of, 258–61, 264–65
of England, 238
in Iraq, 260–61

nation-state, 254 A political entity, located within a geographic territory with enforced borders, where the population shares a sense of culture, ancestry, and destiny as a people.
corporations and, in global economy, 462–65
definition of, 254
development of, 258–59
kinship and, 371, *374, 374–76, 376*
as term, 240

Native Americans
Boas' studies of, 80–81
dispossession from lands, 405
ethno-corporations and, *250, 250–51*
founder effect in, 168
fur trade and, *453, 453–54*
genetic structure of, 161
genocide of, 85, 516
kinship naming systems of, *353, 353*
language loss among, 138, 139–41, *140*
Morgan's fieldwork among, 80
in North American colonies, 213
potlatch among, 391–92
Two-Spirits, 288–89, *289*
Western Apache worldview and language, 119–20, *120*
See also individual tribes or people

nativism, 218, 219–20 The favoring of certain long-term inhabitants, namely whites, over new immigrants.
natural selection, 165–66 The evolutionary process by which some organisms, with features that enable them to adapt to the environment, preferentially survive and reproduce, thereby increasing the frequency of those features in the population.

natural world
adapting to, 20–21
humans' shaping of, 21, 26

nature vs. nurture, 12, 53–55, 56
Nazi Germany, 38, 612

Neandertal, 115, *150*, 154, *160*, 175–77, *177*, 180 A late variety of archaic *Homo sapien* prevalent in Europe.

Neel, James, 100
negative reciprocity, 446, *446*
negotiation, Ury's work on, 58–59
Neither Man nor Woman (Nanda), 288
Nelly, 677, *677*

neocolonialism, 459 A continued pattern of unequal economic relations despite the formal end of colonial political and military control.

neoliberalism, 466–68, 472 An economic and political worldview that sees the free market as the main mechanism for ensuring economic growth, with a severely restricted role for government.

Nepal, 362
Netherlands
Malaysia and, 209
mati work in, 319
same-sex marriage in, 364
Newman, Katherine S., 408
New Orleans, 102, 431
New York Chinese School, *37*
New York City, *10, 243*
Chinese immigrants in, 357, 476, 487–88, *489*
Chinese religious rituals in, 610
creation of racial categories study in, 220–22
East Broadway maps, *91*
Harlem Birth Right Project in, 399–401, 402
homelessness and begging in, 78–79
India Day Parade in, *243*, 243–44
Labov's language study in, 128–29
Little India in, 243–44
Mexican Catholicism in, 608–9, *609*
Mexicans in, 66
Mock Spanish in, 132
multi-sited ethnography and, 27, 29–31
political activism of community in, 226–27
public school funding in, 224–25
racial discrimination in, 226, 227
Thanksgiving Day Parade in, 241
women's health care in, 640, 642–43, *643*
New York Climate Change March, *479*
New Zealand, same-sex marriage in, 364
NGOs (nongovernmental organizations), 438, 540–43, 555, 645
Nicaragua, *320*, 320–21, 322

Niçard, *135*
Nice, France, *135*
Niehaus, Isak, 105
Niger, *591,* 591–92
Nigeria, *121, 340*
    Bohannan's fieldwork in, 119
    pharmaceutical drugs in, 646–47
    sexuality, language, and globalization in, 339–41, *341*
    'yan daudu dancing in, 340–41, *341*
Nightwork (Allison), 321
NLF (National Liberation Front), 456
nongovernmental organizations (NGOs), 438, 540–43, 555, 645
Nordstrom, Carolyn, 546, 549, 552, 553
Norman Street (Susser), 292

norms, 37–39 Ideas or rules about how people should behave in particular situations or toward certain other people.

North African refugees, 485
North America
    cultural patterns in, 54
    descent groups in, 350
    European colonization and racial framework in, 196, 203
    Homo sapiens in, 180
    See also specific countries
North Atlantic Biocultural Organisation, 15
Norway
    redistribution and stratification in, 393
    same-sex marriage in, 364
No Shame in My Game (Newman), 420

nuclear family The kinship unit of mother, father, and children.
    definition of, 348
    kinship chart for, 373
    in the United States, 376–77, *377*

nuclear testing, in Marshall Islands, 24–25
Nuer, The (Evans-Pritchard), 46, 82–83
Nuer of Sudan, *355*
    economic strategy of, 442
    Evans-Pritchard's study of, 46, *82,* 82–83, 121, 351, 354
    focal vocabulary of, 121
    Kathleen Gough's study of, 354
    kinship among, *351,* 351–52, 354, *355*
    marriage and, *355,* 364
    polygyny in, 362
Number Our Days (Myerhoff), *84,* 84–85
nurture, nature vs., 12, 53–55, 56
"N-word," 16, 122–23, *123*
Nyar of India, 362
Nyimba of Tibet, 362

Oakland Unified School District, *131,* 131–32
Obama, Barack, 218, 268
Obergefell, "Jim," *317*
occupations, prestigious, 396, *397*
Occupy Boston, 559
Occupy Wall Street (OWS) movement, 405, 420, 558–60, *560*
oceans, pollution of, *21,* 26
offshoring, 19, 463
oil spill by British Petroleum in 2010, 26

Oldowan tools, 172–73, *173* Stone tools shaped for chopping and cutting found in the Olduvai Gorge and associated with *Australopithecus garhi.*

Olduvai Gorge, *152,* 153, 172, 173
Oliveto, Karen, 379
Olkes, Cherl, 591
Omaha kinship naming system, 353, *353*
Omalu, Bennet, 615
"one drop of blood rule," 217–18
1.5-generation immigrant, 504–5
On the Origin of Species (Darwin), 162
Opium War, 450
Orang Asli, 210
orangutans
    emergence of, 156
    language capacity of, 114
    tool use by, 185
Organs Watch, 107
organ trafficking, human, 104–7, *106*

origin myth, 242, 514–16, *515, 517* A story told about the founding and history of a particular group to reinforce a sense of common identity.

Ortiz, David, *593*
Ortner, Sherri, 291
Other-Worldly (Zhan), 635
Ouattara, Alessane, 437–39, *438*
Our Lady of Guadalupe, 608, *609*
Our Lady of Lourdes, *644*

"out of Africa" theory, 176 The theory that modern *Homo sapiens* evolved first in Africa, migrated outward, and eventually replaced the archaic *Homo sapiens.* Also called *replacement theory.*

outsourcing, 19, 463, *464,* 464–65
OWS (Occupy Wall Street) movement, 405, 420, 558–60, *560*
Oxford English Dictionary Supplement, 323

Pääbo, Svante, *154,* 154–55
Pacific Islands
    arranged marriages in, 360
    European colonization and racial framework in, 196, 203
    Homo sapiens in, 177
    Mead's work in, 312
Pacific Ocean, plastic floating in, 26
Pacini-Hernandez, Deborah, 206, 207
Pakistan
    abducted women from Western Punjab, 374–75
    Kashmiri ethnic community and, 262–63
    partition of India and, 374, *374*

paleoanthropology, 12, 13 The study of the history of human evolution through the fossil record.

paleogeneticists, 160
Palfrey, John, 141
Panameno de Garcia, Alicia, 302
Papua New Guinea
    Mead's studies in, 45, 83
    South Fore people, 635, 638–39

paralanguage, 117–18, *118* An extensive set of noises (such as laughs, cries, sighs, and yells) and tones of voice that convey significant information about the speaker.

parallel cousins, 363
Paramaribo, Suriname, 318–20, *319*
Paravel, Verena, 687–88
Paris, headscarf protest in, *49*

participant observation A key anthropological research strategy involving both participation in and observation of the daily life of the people being studied.
    Bronislaw Malinowski and, 82
    as cornerstone of fieldwork, 82
    definition of, 16, 82
    engaged anthropology and, 87
    informed consent and, 100
Partners in Health, 634–35
Pascoe, C. J., 278–79

pastoralism, 441, 442 A strategy for food production involving the domestication of animals.

patrilineal descent groups, 350–52, *351*
Patterns of Culture (Benedict), 45
Patterson, Francine, *114*
Peasants against Globalization (Edelman), 556

Pediatrics, 287
Peking Man, 151
Pell, Claiborne, 24
penguins, genetic variation within, 203
Pennsylvania, 164
People of Puerto Rico, The (Steward, Mintz, and Wolf), 83
People's History of the United States, A (Zinn), 242
People v. Hall, 219
peppered moths *(Biiston betularia), 165,* 165–66
Pequot Foxwoods Resort, *250,* 250–51
Pequot Indians, 250–51

periphery countries, 459, 460, *460, 461* The least-developed and least-powerful nations; often exploited by the core countries as sources of raw materials, cheap labor, and markets.

Personal Responsibility and Work Opportunity Reconciliation Act (PRWORA), 368
Personal Status courts (Egypt), 560, 561
Peru, 19
Petersen, Glenn, 533, 534
Pew Forum on Religion in Public Life, 162
Peyote Hunt (Myerhoff), 84
Phelps, Michael, *625*

phenotype The way genes are expressed in an organism's physical form as a result of genotype interaction with environmental factors.
    definition of, 200
    genetic drift and, 168
    linking genotype and, 200–201

Philippines, *306*
    call centers in, *464,* 465
    immigrant workers from, 306
    Japan and, 456
    Manila, 19, *63,* 490
    U.S. immigrants from, 498, 499
Phipps, Susie, 217

phonemes, 116 The smallest units of sound that can make a difference in meaning.

phonology, 116 The study of what sounds exist and which ones are important in a particular language.

photographic gaze The presumed neutral viewpoint of the camera that in fact projects the perspective of the person behind the camera onto human nature, the natural world, and history.
    of *National Geographic, 684–85,* 684–86

physical anthropology, 12–14 The study of humans from a biological perspective, particularly how they have evolved over time and adapted to their environments.

    definition of, 12
    diversity of human physical forms, 13–14
    paleoanthropology, 14
    primatology, 14

physical attributes
    classification races based on, 197–203
    diversity of, 13–14
    genetic makeup and, 199, 200
physiological adaptation
    current, 186–88
    to UV light, 186
Picasso, Pablo, 661

pilgrimage, *581*, 581–82 A religious journey to a sacred place as a sign of devotion and in search of transformation and enlightenment.

Plachimada, 5–6, *6*, 27
Plessy v. Ferguson, 224
police, African Americans' encounters with, *194*, 195–96, 234
political activism, 141, 144
politics and power, 525–67
    alternative legal systems and, 560–61, *564*, 564–65
    globalization and the state, 539–43, *540, 542*
    origins of history of, 528–36
        bands and, *529*, 529–31, 536
        chiefdoms, 532–35, *535*, 536
        tribes and, 531–32, 536
    of social movements, 555–60, *556, 558, 560*
    the state and, 536–39, 546–48
    violence and, 543–45, 548–49, 552, *552, 553*, 554
Politics of Passion (Wekker), 318
pollution
    genetic adaptation and, 188
    during Industrial Revolution, 165
    water, 6, 21, *21*, 26
Polo, Marco, 79, 449–50, 486

polyandry, 362 Marriage between one woman and two or more men.
polygyny, 362 Marriage between one man and two or more women.

polyvocality, 96 The practice of using many different voices in ethnographic writing and research question development, allowing the reader to hear more directly from the people in the study.

Pondai, Enos, *259*
Pontecorvo, Gillo, 456, 457
poor in the United states, 405–7, *407*

popular art, 658–59, *658–59* Creative expression and communication often associated with the general population.

population, world, 478
Pordié, Laurent, 620, 621–22
Port Authority of New York and New Jersey, 226–27
Porter, Cole, 314
Portugal
    Brazil as colony of, 207, 456
    Indian caste system and, 422
    Malaysia and, 209
    same-sex marriage in, 364
    slavery and, 451–52

potlatch, 391–92 Elaborate redistribution ceremony practiced among the Kwakiutl of the Pacific Northwest.

poverty
    among whites in the U.S., 233, 405–7
    in Brazil, 208–9
    culture of, theory, 415
    in Flint, Michigan, 388
    global, 424–27, 430–31
    global economy and, 20
    human organ harvesting and, 104–7, *106*
    kinship as a means to survive, 370–71
    passive infanticide and, 73–74
    as pathology, 414–15
    by race, 414, *415*
    as structural economic problem, 415–17, *416*
    in the United States, 414–17, *415, 416*
    urban, 408
    working poor and social mobility, 407–8
    of world's population, 20
Powell, John W., 85

power, 48–53 The ability or potential to bring about change through action or influence.
    art and, 672–77, *673, 676, 677*, 680–81, *681*
    balance of, in human relationships, 557
    bands, tribes, and chiefdoms influenced by, 536
    blurring of boundaries between meaning and, 597–99, *599*, 602–3, *603*, 606–7
    class as system of, 388; *See also* class: inequality and
    cultural institutions and, 48–52
    cultural relationships of, 43

international construction of, 203–12

intersections of

colonialism, sexuality, class, nation, and, 330–33, *331*

gender, class, and, 399–401, 402, 405–7, *407*

gender and, 403

intersections of class and, 232–33, *233*

in Malaysia, 209–12, *212*

as system of thinking, 197

in the United States, 212–22

history of racial categories, 213, *213*, 216–17, *217*

immigration and, 214–15, *218*, 218–22

poverty and, 414, *415*

rule of hypodescent and, 217–18

whiteness and, 216–17, 219–20, 230–33, *233*, 406–7

See also African Americans; racism

racial ideology, 225–26 A set of popular ideas about race that allows the discriminatory behaviors of individuals and institutions to seem reasonable, rational, and normal.

racialization, 222 The process of categorizing, differentiating, and attributing a particular racial character to a person or group of people.

racism, 222–27, 230–33 Individuals' thoughts and actions and institutional patterns and policies that create or reproduce unequal access to power, privilege, resources, and opportunities based on imagined differences among groups.

in Brazil, 208

colonialism and, 203–4

definition of, 197, 223

destructive use of, 197

against immigrants, 218–19

individual, 223

institutional, 223–25, *225*

"N-word" and, 16, 122–23, *123*

post–World War II shift in, 204

racial ideology and, 225–26

resisting, 226–27

types of, 223–26

whiteness and, 230–33

white supremacy and, 216–17, *217*

See also African Americans; race

Racism without Racists (Bonilla-Silva), 225

radiocarbon dating, 160

radiopotassium dating, 160

Rand Corporation, 308

Ranger, Terence, 255

ranked society, 391–93, *392* A group in which wealth is not stratified but prestige and status are.

rape

of college women, 300, *310*, 311–12, 332, 344

in El Salvador, 301, 302, 303

in the U.S military, 272

in Western Punjab, 374–75

rap music, 122, *123*

rapport

definition of, 89–90

informed consent and, 100

Rara! (McAlister), 673

rara bands (Haiti), 672–75, *673*

RBN (Royal Bafokeng Nation), 252–53

Reader's Guide to Periodic Literature, 417

Reading National Geographic (Lutz and Collins), 684

reciprocity, 390–91, *391*, 392, 445–46, *446* The exchange of resources, goods, and services among people of relatively equal status; meant to create and reinforce social ties.

redistribution, 391, 446–48 A form of exchange in which accumulated wealth is collected from the members of the group and reallocated in a different pattern.

Redmon, David, 102, 103

reflexivity A critical self-examination of the role the anthropologist plays and an awareness that one's identity affects one's fieldwork and theoretical analyses.

definition of, 84

feminism and, 84

in fieldwork, 84

in writing ethnography, 96–97

refugees, *17*, 484–86, 501–2, *553* Persons who have been forced to move beyond their national borders because of political or religious persecution, armed conflict, or disasters.

relationships, power in, 48, 557

relative dating, 159–60

religion, 569–613 A set of beliefs and rituals based on a unique vision of how the world ought to be, often focused on a supernatural power and lived out in community.

artificial insemination and, 375–76

blurring of boundaries between meaning and power, 597–99, *599*, 602–3, *603*, 606–7

cultural materialism and, 584–85

definition of, 572–73

distribution of adherents to major world religions, *574*

Durkheim on, 577–79, *578*

evolution and, 162–64, *163*

globalization and, 607–11, *609*
Indian caste system and, *421*, 421–22
local expressions and creative adaptations of, 574–77,
    575, 577
magic and, 588–93, *589, 591, 593*
Marx on, 583–85
ritual and, 572, *579*, 579–83, *581*
sexuality and, 341
shamanism and, 587–88
symbols and, 573, 594
as system of meaning, 594–95, *595*
as system of power, *595*, 595–96
in the United States, 570–71, *571*
Weber on, 585–87
See also specific religions

remittances, 492, *493* Resources transferred from migrants working abroad to individuals, families, and institutions in their country of origin.

replacement theory, 176
Reproducing Jews (Kahn), 375
Reproducing Race (Bridges), 640, 642
reproductive technologies, 348
Republic of the Congo
    Brazzaville, 507, 510, *510*
    Homo sapiens in, 176
research strategies, 89–91
    in anthropology, 27, 29–31
    of cultural relativism, 43
    globalization and change in, 27, 29–31
Returning Home (documentary film), 249
return migration, 513–14
Rhodesia, Pondal's imprisonment by, *259*
Rice, Tamir, 234
Richards, Audrey, 8, *579*, 579–80
Riff Raff Immigration (cartoon), *219*

rite of passage, *579*, 579–81 A category of ritual that enacts a change of status from one life stage to another, either for an individual or for a group.

ritual An act or series of acts regularly repeated over years or generations that embody the beliefs of a group of people and create a sense of continuity and belonging.
    in baseball, 592–93, *593*
    definition of, 578
    immigrants' relocating of, from home countries, 609–11
    religion and, 572, *579*, 579–83, *581*
Rockefeller, John D., 350
Rolling Stone, 569

Romania, wedding industry in, *326*
romantic love, 419–20
Roosevelt, Franklin Delano, 465
Root, Robin, 212, 583–84
Rosaldo, Michelle, 291
Roth, Joshua Hotaka, 513, 514
Rowling, J. K., *589*
Royal Bafokeng Nation (RBN), 252–53
Ruiz García, Samuel, 599, 602, *603*
rural social movements, 556–58, *558*
Russia
    consumerism in, 60
    time zones in, 41
Rwanda, *245*, 245–47, *247*
Rydstrom, Jens, 335, 336, 337

Sabin, Ashley, 102, 103

sacred, 578 Anything that is considered holy.

Sadker, David, 127
Sadker, Myra, 127
SAE (Standard American English), 128, 131–32
Sahelanthropus fossils, 170
Sahelanthropus tchadensis, 158–59, *159*, 170
Said, Edward, 263

saint, *575*, 575–76 An individual considered exceptionally close to God and who is then exalted after death.

Sajad, Malik, 262
SALGA (South Asian Lesbian and Gay Alliance), 244

salvage ethnography, 81 Fieldwork strategy developed by Franz Boas to collect cultural, material, linguistic, and biological information about Native American populations being devastated by the westward expansion of European settlers.

same-sex families
    in China, *380*
    in the United States, *379*, 379–80
same-sex marriage, *317*, 364, *379*, 379–80
Samoa, 45, 83
Santería, 519–20, *520*
Sapir, Edward, 118

Sapir-Whorf hypothesis, 118–19 The idea that different languages create different ways of thinking.

Sarroub, Loukia K., 518, 519
Saudi Arabia, *495*

guest workers in, 495, *495*
Hael petroglyphs, *298*
Saussure, Ferdinand de, 118
Savage, Michael, 111
Scheper-Hughes, Nancy, 85, 627–28
    Alto do Cruzeiro fieldwork of, 71–75, 88, 89, 90, 94, 96–97, 101
    human organ harvesting and, 104–5, 107
Schwartz, Barbara, *379*
Scopes, John, *163*, 164
Scopes Trial, *163*, 164
Scott, James, 52, 565
Seau, Junior, *614*
Sebago shoes, 22, 22–23
second-generation immigrants, 504–5, 521
security, balance of privacy and, 39
segregation, 223–25
    Brown v. Board of Education, 224, 225
    Jim Crow laws, 216–17
    Plessy v. Ferguson, 224
self-affirmation, art as, 672–75, *673*
Semenya, Caster, 284–86, *285*

semiperiphery countries, 459, *460, 461* Nations ranking in between core and periphery countries, with some attributes of the core countries but with less of a central role in the global economy.

Senegal, *22*, 22–23, *23*
September 11, 2001, attacks
    controversy in France on headscarves after, 49, *49*
    racialization of Middle Easterners after, 220–22
serial monogamy, 362
Seri people, 140
Service, Elman, 532

sex The observable physical differences between male and female, especially biological differences related to human reproduction.
    alternate, 287–89, *288, 289*
    definition of, 273
    gender vs., 273–75
    intersex, 286–87
sexes, number of, 284–89, *288, 289*
sexology, 324

sex tourism, 338 Travel, usually organized through the tourism sector, to facilitate commercial sexual relations between tourists and local residents in destinations around the world.

sexual activity
    antimiscegenation laws on, 38

gender and meanings of "no" about, 125–26
sexual assaults
    of college women, 300, 311–12, 332, 344
    in military, 272
    See also rape
sexual conduct, code of, 332

sexual dimorphism, 273–74 The phenotypic differences between males and females of the same species.

sexual harassment, 332, 350

sexuality, 311–45 The complex range of desires, beliefs, and behaviors that are related to erotic physical contact and the cultural arena within which people debate about what kinds of physical desires and behaviors are right, appropriate, and natural.
    in advertising, *313*
    alternate constructions of, 287–89, *288, 289*
        in Japan, 321–22
        in Nicaragua, 320–21, 322
        in Suriname, *318*, 318–20, *319*, 322
    biology and, intersection of, 314–17, *315*
    culture and, *317*, 317–18
    definition of, 314
    globalization and, 337–41
    global perspective on, 318–22
    heterosexuality, 322–27
    Malaysian ideas of, 210–12
    power and, relations of, 330–37
    sexology, 324
    in the United States, 312, 322–27, 330
    weddings and, 324–27, *326, 327*, 330

sex work, 338–39, 342–43 Labor through which one provides sexual services for money.

Shaanbei, China, *597*, 597–98
Shadows of War (Nordstrom), 553
"Shakespeare in the Bush" (Bohannan), 119
Shakti, *288*
shamanism, 587–88

shamans, 587–88 Part-time religious practitioners with special abilities to connect individuals with supernatural powers or beings.

Shamans, Housewives, and Other Restless Spirits (Kendall), 588
shared culture, 36–37
sharia law, 561
Shenzhen, China, *461*, 511, *511*
Shia, 260, 261
sickle-cell anemia, 166

sickness, 618–19 An individual's public expression of illness and disease, including social expectations about how one should behave and how others will respond.

Sierra Leone, 19
sign language, primates' use of, 114
Sikes, Melvin, 232
SIL (Summer Institute of Linguistics), 139
Simmons, David, *636,* 636–37

situational negotiation of identity, 242–43 An individual's self-identification with a particular group that can shift according to social location.

skin color
 in Dominican Republic, 204–7
 variations in, 182–83, 186, *187,* 201; *See also* race
slash and burn agriculture, 442
slaves and slavery
 in Brazil, 207, 208–9
 in Dominican Republic, 205
 insight into lives of slaves, 15
 Sojourner Truth's abolition work, 401
 as source of Black English, 131
 triangle trade and, 451–54, *452, 453*
 in the United States, 213, *213,* 216, 405
slave ships, *203, 213,* 216
slave trade, 213, *213,* 216
 as involuntary migration, 516
 justification for, 203
Smith, Adam, 465, 466
Smith, Neil, 431
Smith, Robert, 66, 311, 512
Snyder, Rick, 386
soccer, *236,* 237–39, *239*

social capital, 498 Assets and skills such as language, education, and social networks that can be mobilized in lieu of or as complementary to financial capital.
social class, *See* class

social media, 6 New forms of communication based on computer- and Internet-based technologies that facilitate social engagement, work, and pleasure.
 Black Lives Matter movement and, 234
 definition of, 683
 digital natives and, 141
 language preservation through, 140

social mobility The movement of one's class position, upward or downward, in stratified societies.

in Bourdieu's class theory, 396
definition of, 396
in early United States, 405
in India, 423
policies and programs providing, 416
in the United States, 407–8

social movement, 555–60, *556, 558, 560* Collective group actions that seek to build institutional networks to transform cultural patterns and government policies.

social network analysis, 90 A method for examining relationships in a community, often conducted by identifying whom people turn to in times of need.

social reproduction, 396 The phenomenon whereby social and class relations of prestige or lack of prestige are passed from one generation to the next.

social science, fieldwork as, 78

society, 46 The focus of early British anthropological research whose structure and function could be isolated and studied scientifically.

sociolinguistics, 121–36 The study of the ways culture shapes language and language shapes culture, particularly the intersection of language with cultural categories and systems of power such as age, race, ethnicity, sexuality, gender, and class.
 definition of, 122
 dialect, 126, 128
 dialect and language, 126, 128
 gender and language, 123–26, *124*
 historical linguistics, 134–35, *135*
 language variation in the U.S., 128–33, *130*
 "N-word," 16, 122–23, *123*
 See also language

sociolinguists, 16 Those who study language in its social and cultural contexts.

Sociology of Religion (Weber), 586
Sojourner syndrome, 401
Soloway, Jill, 347
Somali refugees, 501–2, *502*
Sousa, Dominican Republic, 338–39
South Africa, 50–51, *51, 252, 282*
 anti-apartheid movement in, 204
 Bafokeng, 252–53
 Blombos Cave, 662–63, *663*
 blood- and organ-stealing in, 105
 colonialism in, *50,* 50–51, *51*

gay rights in, 341
HIV/AIDS in, 293
Homo erectus in, 174
marriage laws in, 38
same-sex marriage in, 364
Taung, 151, 153
war and violence in, 553
women in military of, 271
Southall, Lodon, Asian "cousins" in, 367, 370, *370*
South America
developmental adaptation in, 181, *181*
European colonization and racial framework in, 196, 203
Homo sapiens in, 180
independence of, 456
indigenous populations' lack of immunity to European diseases, 451, 454
See also specific countries
South-Asian Americans, 222
South Asian Lesbian and Gay Alliance (SALGA), 244
Southeast Asia, export-processing zones in, 210–11, *211*
South Fore people, 635, 638–39
South Korea, 380–81, 588
Spain, 456, *664*
Dominican Republic slaves and, 205
Homo erectus in, 175
paleolithic cave paintings in, 663–64
same-sex marriage in, 364
slavery and, 451–52
U.S. settlement by, 516

species, 170, 186–87 A group of related organisms that can inter-breed and produce fertile, viable offspring.

Speed, Shannon, *86,* 86–87
Spirit Catches You and You Fall Down, The (Fadiman), 648
spirit mediums in Zimbabwe, *259,* 259–60
sports
female athletes and gender stereotypes, 284–86
football concussions and CTE, *614,* 615–16
gender teaching through, 275–78, *277*
Gmelch's study of baseball, 592–93, *593*
identity creation and, 264–65
World Cup soccer tournament, *236,* 237–39, *239*
Sri Lanka, war and violence in, 553
Stack, Carol, 370, 371
Standard American English (SAE), 128, 131–32

state, 254, 536–39 An autonomous regional structure of politi-cal, economic, and military rule with a central government autho-rized to make laws and use force to maintain order and defend its territory.

challenge to sovereignty of, by international nonstate actors, *539,* 539–40
definition of, 254, 536
globalization and, 539–43, *540, 542*
modern western-style, 537–38
power mobilization outside control of, 554–61, *556, 558, 560, 564,* 564–65
war and, 546–48

status
achieved, 424
ascribed, 424
class and, 395; *See also* class: inequality and
in ranked societies, 391–92
Steiner, Christopher, 665–66, 667, 669
Stephen, Lynn, 302
stereotypes
about prostitution, 343
gender, 295
of gender roles, 274–75
of poor whites, 232
Sterk, Claire, 101
Steward, Julian, 83
stock market, 413, 445, 448
Stoler, Ann, 330–31, 333
Stoller, Paul, 589, 591–92, 668, 669
Stone, Linda, 380

stratification The uneven distribution of resources and privileges among participants in a group or culture.
class, *See* class
culture, 34
definition of, 48
gender, 295, 301–3
power reflected in, 48
of power through wealth, 409, 412
as recent development, 393
in Weber's class theory, 395, 396
of whiteness, 232
See also race; racism

stratigraphy, 160

structural functionalism, 46 A conceptual framework positing that each element of society serves a particular function to keep the entire system in equilibrium.

structural gender violence, 300–301 Gendered societal pat-terns of unequal access to wealth, power, and basic resources such as food, shelter, and health care that differentially affect women in particular.

structural racism, 223

student loan debt, 419

Sudan, *352*

    Evans-Pritchard's studies in, 46, *82,* 82–83

    magic in, 589–90

    Nuer of, *See* Nuer of Sudan

Sudanese kinship naming system, 353, *353*

sugar during colonialism, 451

Sulkowicz, Emma, *310,* 311

Summer Institute of Linguistics (SIL), 139

Sundarbans campaign, 525–27, 564

Sunni, 260, 261

Supreme Court, U.S.

    on *Brown v. Board of Education,* 224

    on hypodescent rules, 217

    on interracial marriage, 216, *365*

    Lawrence v. Texas, 365

    on *Plessy v. Ferguson,* 224

    on same-sex marriage, *317*

    on Santería church in Florida, 519–20

Suriname, *318,* 318–20, *319,* 322

survey, 90 An information-gathering tool for quantitative data analysis.

Susser, Ida, *292,* 292–93

sustainability of global economy, 478–81, *479, 480, 481*

Swarthmore College, 526

Swaziland, 603, *603,* 606–7

Sweden, *335*

    childbirth in, 628–29, 631

    redistribution and stratification in, 393

    rune stone on Adelso Island, *117*

    same-sex marriage in, 364

    sex, disability, and social justice in, 335–37

Sweetness and Power (Mintz), 83–84, 477

Sweis, Rania, 645

swidden farming, 442

Sykes-Picot Agreement, 261

symbol Anything that represents something else.

    changes in meaning of, 40

    cultural, 37, 39–40, *40*

    definition of, 39, –598

    interpretivist approach and, 46

    language as system of, 115

    religion and, 573, 594

synchronic approach, 82

syntax, 116 The specific patterns and rules for combining morphemes to construct phrases and sentences.

Syrian refugees, *17,* 484–86, *553*

Tabula Rogeriana, *449*

Taiwan, 98, 306, *306,* 456

Tammy Kitzmiller v. Dover Area School District, 164

Tannen, Deborah, 124

Tanzania, *247, 541*

    Goodall's study of chimpanzees in Gombe, 152

    Hutu refugees in, 247–48

    Laetoli footprints in, 153, *153*

    Maasai demands in, 541–43, *543*

    Olduvai Gorge, *152,* 153, 172, 173

Tarazona, Elas, *504*

Taung, South Africa, 151, 153

Taung Child, 151, *152,* 153, 158, 169

taxes, U.S., 412, 448

taxis/cabs, African Americans and, 403

technocratic birth, 629

technologies

    in the digital age, 141, *144,* 144–45

    for DNA dating, 161

    in eighteenth and nineteenth centuries, 8

    flexible accumulation and, 19

    globalization and, 6

    for mapping, 93

    time-space compression and, 18

    uneven high-tech consumption and, 20

Teena, Brandon, *300*

teeth, adaptation of, 188, *189*

television

    cosmopolitanism and, 66–69, *67*

    invisibility of class in, 417–18

Tennessee, Scopes Trial in, *163,* 164

terrorism, cultural institutions' responses to, 49

Tett, Gillian, 468, *470,* 470–71

Texas, *317*

Texas, Lawrence v., 365

text messages, 117–18, *118*

theory of evolution, 164–69, 186–90 The theory that biological adaptations in organisms occur in response to changes in the natural environment and develop in populations over generations.

    creationism vs., 162–64, *163*

    of culture, 44

    gene flow and, 167

    genetic drift and, 168–69

    mutation and, 166–67

natural selection and, 165–66
nature vs. nurture and, 54–55, 56
sexuality and, 315–16
split of humans from apes, 12–13
Tammy Katzmiller v. Dover Area School District, 164
teaching of, *163*, 164
theory of, 161–64

thick description, 47 A research strategy that combines detailed description of cultural activity with an analysis of the layers of deep cultural meaning in which those activities are embedded.

Thind, Bhagat Singh, 219–20
thought
    race as system of, 197
    as shaped by language, 118–20
Thrice Told Tale, A (Wolf), 98
Tibet, 362
Tibetan Buddhism, 620–23, *621*
Tierney, Patrick, 100
Tilley, Charles, 536
time
    categories of, 41
    deep, 155–56
    language as shaping idea of, 143
Time magazine, 569

time-space compression, 18 The rapid innovation of communication and transportation technologies associated with globalization that transforms the way people think about space (distances) and time.

time zones, 41
Timo, Don, 283
Tiv language, 119
Tokyo, 321, *321*, 474–75
Tolkien, J. R. R., *589*
toolkit, anthropologist's, 88
tools
    Acheulian stone, 174
    chimpanzees making and using, 184, *184*
    Oldowan, 172–73, *173*
Torah, 594, *595*
trade routes, 448–50, *449*
Traditional Micronesian Societies (Petersen), 533
traditions, invented, 255–56

transgender, 288–89, *289*, 300, *346*, *347* A gender identity or performance that does not fit with cultural norms related to one's assigned sex at birth.

transhumance, 442
Transnational Adoption (Dorow), 381
transnational adoptions, 380–83, *383*

transnationalism, 512 The practice of maintaining active participation in social, economic, religious, and political spheres across national borders.

transnational migration, 512
Transparent, 346, 347

triangle trade, 451–54, *452*, *453* The extensive exchange of slaves, sugar, cotton, and furs between Europe, Africa, and the Americas that transformed economic, political, and social life on both sides of the Atlantic.

tribe, 531–32, 536 Originally viewed as a culturally distinct, multiband population that imagined itself as one people descended from a common ancestor; currently used to describe an indigenous group with its own set of loyalties and leaders living to some extent outside the control of a centralized authoritative state.

Trobriand Islands, *291*
    economic system of, 291, 294
    Kula Ring, 291, 446
    Malinowski's studies in, 46, *46*, *81*, 82
    Weiner's study of, 84
    women's economic activity in, 294, *294*
Troxler, Julia, *379*
Truth, Sojourner, 401
Tsing, Anna, 472–73
Tsukiji Fish Market, 474–75
Tswana-speaking people, 50–51
Tucson, homelessness and begging in, 78–79
tuna, 474–75
Turkana Boy, 174, *174*
Turkey, 485, *552*
Turkic languages, 142
Turnbull, Colin, 441
Turner, Victor, 46, 85, 580, 582
Tutsi, 245–47, *247*
Twa, 246
Twitter, 541
Two-Spirits, 288–89, *289*
Tylor, Edward Burnett, 44, *44*, 80

UN, *See* United Nations (UN)
U.N. Development Program's Human Development
    Index, 461

underdevelopment, 459 The term used to suggest that poor countries are poor as a result of their relationship to an unbalanced global economic system.

undersea cable networks, 146–47
undocumented immigrants, 110, 111, 268, 521

uneven development The unequal distribution of the benefits of globalization.
    definition of, 20
    global inequality and, 424, 427, 430, *430*
    globalization and, 20, 30–31, 145
    global migration and, 489

UNICEF, 645

unilineal cultural evolution, 44, 46 The theory proposed by nineteenth-century anthropologists that all cultures naturally evolve through the same sequence of stages from simple to complex.

unilineal descent groups, 350
United Arab Emirates, 500
United Kingdom
    England in, 238
    same-sex marriage in, 364
    See also Great Britain
United Nations (UN)
    on access to safe drinking water, 388
    climate change conference of 2015, 525
    Côte d'Ivoire and, 438–39
    on global poverty, 427
    High Commissioner for Refugees, *553*
    human rights documents of, 43
    on migration, 487
    on refugees, 501
    on world population, 478
United States
    adoptions in, 380–83, *383*
    antimiscegenation laws in, 38, 51
    arranged marriages in, 360
    assimilation vs. multiculturalism in, 253–54
    balance of security and privacy in, 39
    Black English in, *130*, 130–32, *131*
    black gay women in, 333–35, *334*
    childbirth in, *629*, 630
    class and inequality in, 404–17
        consumer culture and, 419–20
        income distribution and, *411*, 411–13, *412, 413*
        invisibility of, 417–20
        media and, 417–18

        middle class and working poor, 407–8
        poor whites in rural Kentucky, 405–7, *407*
        poverty and, 414–17, *415, 416*
        and water contamination crisis in Flint, Michigan, *386*, 387–88, *389*, 404
        wealth, Wall Street, and, 408–10, *410*
        wealth distribution and, 412–14, *413*
    consumerism in, 60, *60*
    credit card debt in, 62
    cultural patterns in, 54
    English-only laws in, 111
    ethnic interaction in, 253–54
    financial collapse of 2008, 469
    fortified milk in, 186
    gender in, 83, 275–78, *277*
    household income in, *413*, 414
    households by type, *377*
    immigration and, 514–21, *515, 517, 518*
    incest taboos in, 363
    interracial marriage in, 38, *51*, 51–52
    kinship in, 376–83, *377, 379, 383*
        impact of assisted reproductive technologies on, 378–79
        nuclear family, 376–77, *377*
        through choice, 378
    language variation in, 112, 128–33, *130*
    marriage in, 360, 363, 364
    median income and wealth by race in, *413*
    migrants from India to, *243*, 243–44, 498, *499*
    military, *99, 270*, 271–72, *274*, 308
    "N-word" in, 122–23, *123*
    origin myths in, 242, 514–16, *515, 517*
    orthodontics industry in, 189
    professional immigrants to, 498
    race in, 212–22; *See also* African Americans; racism
        history of racial categories, 213, *213*, 216–17, *217*
        immigration and, 214–15, *218*, 218–22
        rule of hypodescent and, 217–18
    redistribution and stratification in, 393
    religion in, 570–71, *571*
    revitalism of Catholic Church in, 607–9, *609*
    same-sex marriage in, 364
    sexuality in, 312, 322–27, 330
    slave plantation excavations in, 15
    slavery in, 213, *213*, 216, 405
    teaching of evolution in, *163*, 164
    time zones in, 41
    top occupations by prestige, *397*
    whiteness in, 216–17, 219–20, 230–33, *233*, 406–7
    women's movement in, 313
Universal Declaration of Human Rights, 43

universal gaze, 659–60 An intrinsic way of perceiving art—thought by many in the Western art world to be found across cultures—that informs what people consider to be art or not art.

University of California, 312, 526
Untouchables *(dalits)*, 421, *421, 422,* 422–23, *423,* 424
UPANIACIONAL, 557
urban poverty, 408
Urciuoli, Bonnie, 132
Uruguay, same-sex marriage in, 364
Ury, William, 58–59
U.S. Census, 214–15, 216
U.S. Child Citizen Act, 382
U.S. Department of Agriculture, 33
U.S. Department of Justice
    on Ferguson Police Department, 195–96
    on gender violence on campus, 300
UV light, adaptations to, 182–83, 186, *187,* 189

values, 37, 39, 410 Fundamental beliefs about what is important, what makes a good life, and what is true, right, and beautiful.

van Gennep, Arnold, 579, 580
Vanity Fair, 569
variation (species), 161–62, 203
Vatican II, 602
VGYP (Village Girl Youth Project), 645, 648
Viagra, 282, *282*
Vietnam, 456
Vietnam War, *99, 99*–100
Viki (chimpanzee), 114
Village Girl Youth Project (VGYP), 645, 648
Vine, David, *562,* 562–63
violence
    battered women and kinship in shelters, 368–69
    gender roles enforced through, 299–301, *300*
    human nature and, 543–45, *545*
    kinship-state relationships and, 374–75
    in Micronesia, 534–35, *535*
    war and, 548–49, 552, *552, 553,* 554
Virchow, Rudolf, 639
Virginia
    anti-miscegenation laws in, 38, *365*
    construction of "whiteness" in, 216
Virginia, Loving v., 38, *365*
Virgin of Guadalupe, 602, 608–9

visual anthropology, 684 A field of anthropology that explores the production, circulation, and consumption of visual images, focusing on the power of visual representation to influence culture and cultural identity.

vitamin D, 183, 186
Vora, Neha, 500

Waheed, Mirza, 262
Wallerstein, Immanuel, 459–60
Walley, Christine, 686–87
Walley, Chuck, *686*
Wall Street, 408–10, *410,* 445
Walmart, 19
war
    "dangerous things" and, 548–49, *552*
    drones and, 550–51
    globalization and, 549, 552, *552, 553,* 554
    militarization and, 546–47
    nationalism and, 258
    state and, 546–48
Washoe (chimpanzee), 114
Washoe tribe, *140*
waste, 428–29
water pollution, 6, 21, *21,* 26
water resources
    access to, 34, 388, 426–27
    buying of rights to, 21
    Coca-Cola Company's use of, *4,* 5–6
    water contamination crisis in Flint, Michigan, *386,* 387–88, *389,* 404
Watson, James, 63

wealth The total value of what someone owns, minus any debt.
    in Brazil, 208
    consumer culture and, 419–20
    corporate cultures and, 408–10
    cultural capital and, *398,* 398–99
    definition of, 412
    inequality in the United States, 412–14, *413*
    in Marx's class theory, 394
    transfer of, in the U.S., 413
    voluntary isolation and, 418–19

Wealth of Nations, The (Smith), 465
Weapons of the Weak (Scott), 52
Weber, Max, 57, 393, 395–96, 577, 585–87, *586,* 594
Webster, Mike, 616
weddings, 324–27, *326, 327,* 330 *See also* marriage
Weiner, Annette, 84, 291, 294
Weinreich, Max, 126
Wekker, Gloria, 318–20
West Africa
    art of, 665–69, *667, 669,* 672
    Côte d'Ivoire, *436, 437,* 437–39
    King of Mali (in 1375), *11*
    sickle-cell anemia in, 166

slave market in, 453

See also specific countries

Western Apache, Basso's study of, 119–20

Weston, Kath, 378

whales, enculturation in, 36

What's Love Got to Do with It? (Brennan), 338

White, Luise, 105

Whitehouse, Bruce, 506–7

whiteness, 230–33, *233* A culturally constructed concept originating in 1691 Virginia designed to establish clear boundaries of who is white and who is not, a process central to the formation of U.S. racial stratification.

    construction of, 216–17

    in Kentucky, 405–7

    race, racism, and, 230–33

    U.S. legal definition of, 216–17, 219–20

white privilege, 230–31

"White Privilege" (McIntosh), 230

whites, poverty among, 233, 405–7, 414, *415*

white supremacy, 216–17, *217* The belief that whites are biologically different from and superior to people of other races.

White Weddings (Ingraham), 324–25, 326

WHO (World Health Organization), 388, 645

Whorf, Benjamin Lee, 118–19

Why We Love (Fisher), 316

Williams, Brackette, 78–79

Wilson, Darren, 195

Winegar, Jessica, 680–81

Wiradyana, Ketut, *13*

Wisdom Sits in Places (Basso), 119

witchcraft, *589,* 589–90

Witchcraft, Oracles and Magic among the Azande (Evans-Pritchard), 589

within-group variation, 14

Wolf, Eric, 48, 83, 84, 344

Wolf, Margery, 98

wolves, enculturation in, 36

women

    black gay, 333–35, *334*

    globalization's impact on, 303–7, *305*

    health care and, 642–43, *643*

    HIV/AIDS and, 293

    immigration and, 503, *504*

    mati work in Suriname and, 318–20, *319*

    in the military, 270, 271–72, *274,* 308

    Mothers of "The Disappeared" (in El Salvador), 301–3, *303*

    See also gender; rape

Women of Value, Men of Renown (Weiner), 291

women's movement, U.S., 313

Wonderwerk Cave, 174

Worked to the Bone (Buck), 216, 405, 460

workers

    corporate success and, 408–10

    flexible accumulation corporation-worker relationships, 204

    in Harlem, 400

    in Marx's class theory, 394–95

    Minah Karan, 210–12

    pay of CEOs vs., 412, *412*

    sex, 338–39

    temporary guest workers, 494

    women, globalization's impact on, 303–7, *305*

work ethic

    Protestant, 57

    urban poverty and, 408

working poor, social mobility and, 407–8

World Bank, 427, 466, 467, 555, 557

World Cup soccer tournament, *236,* 237–39, *239*

World Food Programme, 430

World Health Organization (WHO), 388, 645

World Social Forum, 467

world systems analysis, 459–61, *460,* *461*

World Trade Organization (WTO), 466, 555

World War II, colonialism and, 258, 456

WTO (World Trade Organization), 466, 555

'yan daudu, 340–41, *341*

Yang, Foua, *651*

Yanomami tribe, 36, 100

Yemen, U.S. immigrants from, 518–19

You Just Don't Understand (Tannen), 123, 124

Young Earth creationism, 162–63

youth sports, 275–78, *277*

YouTube, 6, 140, 541

Yucatán, childbirth in, 629, *629,* 630, 631

Yugoslavia, ethnic conflict in, 248–49

Zambia, 8, *579,* 579–80, *580*

Zanmi Lasante, 634–35

Zapata, Emiliano, 599

Zapatistas, 599, 602

zeros, 94 Elements of a story or a picture that are not told or seen and yet offer key insights into issues that might be too sensitive to discuss or display publicly.

Zhan, Mei, 625–27

Zheng He, 79, 450

Zhoukoudian, 151, 174

Zimbabwe, *259,* 259–60, 457

Zinn, Howard, 242

Zona Galactica, 342–43